for John Wilton-Ely
with greetings, goodwishes and gratitu
from the AUTHOR

[illegible signature]

December 2001

CHARLES BRIDGEMAN
AND THE ENGLISH LANDSCAPE
GARDEN

Attributed to Jacques Rigaud 1681–1754

Stowe. View of the Queen's Theatre from the Rotunda

Private collection

Christie's Images, London, UK / Bridgeman Art Library

Charles Bridgeman
and the English Landscape Garden

Peter Willis

Reprinted with supplementary plates
and a catalogue of additional documents, drawings
and attributions

Elysium Press Publishers

NEWCASTLE UPON TYNE
2002

Published by Elysium Press Publishers
5 Fenwick Close · Jesmond · Newcastle upon Tyne NE2 2LE
United Kingdom
www.elysiumpress.mac.com

ISBN 0 904712 04 4

First printing 2001

Design of Zwemmer edition by Graham Johnson/Lund Humphries
Design of additional material in Elysium Press edition by Dalrymple

Printed in England by The Cromwell Press Ltd
Trowbridge, Wiltshire

British Library Cataloguing in Publication Data

Willis, Peter, 1933–

Charles Bridgeman and the English landscape garden. – New ed., reprinted
with supplementary plates and a catalogue of additional documents,
drawings and attributions

1. Bridgeman, Charles
2. Landscape gardening – England – History – 18th century
3. Gardeners – England – Biography

I. Title
712.6'092

ISBN 0 904712 04 4

IN MEMORIAM

Robert Willis 1902–1967

and

Mary Ormston Willis 1903–1983

Contents

A Note to the Reader

Access to material in the Elysium Press edition is by means of two indices – the Index to the Zwemmer edition on pp.217–233, and the Index to the Catalogue of Additional Documents, Drawings and Attributions on pp.439–441. Both indices include references to the plates, set in bold figures.

Preface to Elysium Press Edition

Recent years have witnessed a burgeoning of scholarship in English landscape and garden history and a reappraisal of the work of such eighteenth-century figures as Bridgeman, Kent, Brown and Repton. Books, articles and exhibitions have expanded our knowledge and understanding of their contribution to the establishment and promotion of *le jardin anglais*. Since the publication in 1977 of *Charles Bridgeman and the English Landscape Garden* further discoveries have been made which add to our knowledge of Bridgeman's connection with various estates and enable us to ascribe additional layouts to him. The conservation of the buildings and landscape at Stowe, and the restoration of Claremont, are but two instances of ways in which Bridgeman's work has been more widely recognised. Public affirmation came on Friday 18 May 1984 when the Mayor of Westminster unveiled a blue plaque placed by the Greater London Council on Bridgeman's former house, 19 Broad Street (now 54 Broadwick Street) in Westminster, bearing the inscription 'CHARLES BRIDGEMAN/Landscape Gardener/lived here/1723–38'.

The publication of the original edition of *Bridgeman* owed much to the imagination and enterprise of Desmond Zwemmer, of A. Zwemmer Ltd, and it is a cause of great regret that his death late in 2000 meant that he never saw this version published by Elysium Press. Desmond's widow Ann, however, has generously given it her complete support.

Elysium Press here reprints the Zwemmer edition of 1977, with no corrections or revisions, but with a Catalogue of Additional Documents, Drawings and Attributions which aims to give an up-to-date picture of Bridgeman research; lastly, at the end of the book, there is a collection of plates of Bridgemanic drawings, many of them never previously published. Prominent among these are the Bridgemanic plans in the Gough Collection in the Bodleian Library, Oxford. The catalogue is arranged alphabetically by place, and contains cumulative cross-references to material in both the Zwemmer and Elysium Press editions. The plates in the Elysium Press edition cover all drawings currently attributable to the Royal Gardener. In addition, seven diagrams showing formal elements in Bridgeman's signed plans are reproduced here for the first time as *Plates 246* and *247*.

Further gardens or landscapes which now may be suggested as new attributions to Bridgeman are Dallington (Northamptonshire) or The Rolls House (London), Esher (Surrey), Lumley Castle (County Durham), Lodge Park at Sherborne (Gloucestershire), and Wroxall or Wroxhall Manor (Warwickshire). More speculative possibilities are Coopersale (Essex), Hartwell (Buckinghamshire), and Welford (Berkshire).

No new signed drawings by Bridgeman have come to light in recent years, and those which may be ascribed to him generally support already-documented landscapes such as Wimpole rather than provide additional attributions. Other drawings offer visual evidence where little or none existed previously: two Bridgemanic plans of Marble Hill, Middlesex, for instance (*Plates 213a-214b*) link together the Royal Gardener, Roger Morris, the Countess of

Suffolk, and Pope's circle at Twickenham, and show the details of the Thameside garden formerly known only through written descriptions and Heckell and Mason's engraving of 1749 (*Plate 71*). Most striking visually, however, are the two Bridgemanic drawings of Lumley (*Plates 210–212*) which point to the possible partnership there of Bridgeman and Vanbrugh, and which stylistically look to such dramatic set pieces as Amesbury and Stowe.

Again, additional comments by eighteenth-century observers tend to reinforce existing assessments: thus Horace Walpole in a little-known manuscript describes Kingsmill Eyre as 'One of the first Improvers of Gardens in the Style of Bridgman [*sic*] before Kent perfected the new & quite natural Taste', an opinion familiar from Walpole's *The History of the Modern Taste in Gardening* (1780). 'Mr Eyre planted for Sr Rob. Walpole the Garden at Houghton', Horace Walpole continues, 'which was in a much greater manner than the ancient formal Gardens in the Dutch Style'.[1] Elsewhere specific features of Bridgeman's landscapes are endorsed: on 2 October 1723 Lord Orkney writes that 'Bridgeman mackes difficultyes of nothing' in his construction of the amphitheatre at Cliveden,[2] and Joseph Spence, on his grand tour, finds that the fortifications at Geneva 'look extremely neat and the earthworks are like Bridgeman's slopes', and that at Mount Vesuvius the 'sides sloped off for about four mile [*sic*] each way, as prettily as Bridgeman's slopes do in a garden'.[3] More expansively, on 11 March 1733/34 the Duchess of Beaufort exclaims that Bridgeman's 'draught' for Badminton 'is one of the Grandest things' she has seen.[4]

The Duchess of Beaufort's letters also confirm Bridgeman's collaboration at Badminton with Wootton, William Kent, and the architect and master-builder Francis Smith of Warwick. Evidence elsewhere strengthens the links between Bridgeman and Archer, Gibbs, John James, Leoni, and Sir John Vanbrugh: Vanbrugh's treatment by Sarah, Duchess of Marlborough, is called to mind by a group of eight letters written by Bridgeman's widow, Sarah, to the Duchess, pathetically claiming unpaid debts.[5] Little new light has been cast on the royal gardens, but speculation continues that Charles Bridgeman's father (or Bridgeman 'Senior' as he was sometimes called) was a gardener active in the later seventeenth and into the eighteenth century. Other documentation remains elusive: no Bridgeman bank account has been found, nor has a copy of the catalogue for the sales of his possessions (including 'Pictures, Drawings, and Prints') held by Aaron Lambe in London on Tuesday 9 December 1741 onwards. The search for such Bridgemanalia has not lost its fascination.

Much of the supplementary material in the present edition was first published in my essay 'Charles Bridgeman and the English Landscape Garden: New Documents and Attributions', in *English Architecture, Public and Private. Essays for Kerry Downes*, edited by John Bold and Edward Chaney (London and Rio Grande, Ohio: Hambledon Press, 1993), pages 247–264. Financial support for this came from Newcastle University. Among those who shared the results of their researches during the preparation of this article were the late Gervase Jackson-Stops, and Sir Howard Colvin and Andor Gomme, both of whom generously assisted with revisions for the Elysium Press edition. To Sir Howard I am especially indebted for his advice on the Bridgemanic drawings in the Bodleian Library.

Photographs and drawings are reproduced by courtesy of the owners and other sources indicated in the captions to the plates. The Duke of Beaufort permitted me to use and cite material at Badminton, the Duke of Buccleuch to reproduce drawings of Boughton, the Earl of Scarbrough to publish the Bridgemanic drawing of Lumley, and the Trustees of Sir John Soane's Museum those of Buckingham House, St James's Park, and Windsor Castle. Permission to quote from manuscripts was granted, among others, by the British Library, the Lewis Walpole Record Office at Yale, the National Library of Scotland, and Nottingham University Library.

The financing of the Elysium Press edition has benefitted from the generous response of many individuals and institutions to the renewal of permissions for the publication of the plates. Mrs Olive Smith most kindly allowed me free use of the oustanding photographs of her late husband, Edwin Smith, many of which were taken especially for the Zwemmer edition of the book, and the Bodleian Library, Oxford, has made readily available the major collection of Bridgemanic drawings in the Gough Collection. At the Bodleian I was given every assistance by Bruce Barker-Benfield and Colin Harris of the Department of Special Collections and Western Manuscripts.

I have incurred many debts in my research on specific landscapes, notably at Badminton (Margaret Richards), Briggens (Andrew C. Skelton), Chiswick (Richard Hewlings), Cliveden (Christopher Wall), Dawley (B.T. White), Gobions (Paul Evans, Michael Jonas, David Lambert and Nigel Lutt), Spring Wood, Hackwood (Sally Hocking and Michael Wood), Hartwell (Eric Throssell), Kedleston (T.E. Alasdair Barclay and the late Leslie Harris), Lillington (Mark Booth), Lodge Park, Sherborne (Katie Fretwell, Nicholas Kingsley and David Smith), Lumley (Peter Goodchild), Marble Hill (John Alban, Jonathan Draper, Jan Hodges, Jean Kennedy, Paul Rutledge and Andrew Wimble), The Bell Inn, Stilton (Lain McGivern), Stowe (Michael Bevington, George Clarke and Kate Felus), Tring (Alan Fletcher and Ann Mallinson), Warwick (Geoffrey Smith), Wimpole (David Adshead), and Wroxall (Christine Hodgetts). At Hoares Bank in London I was helped by Victoria Hutchings and Maurice Lloyd, and for Goslings material at the Barclays Bank archive, Wythenshawe, by Victoria Wilkinson. Details of the sale in 1983 of the painting 'Stowe. View of the Queen's Theatre from the Rotunda', ascribed to Jacques Rigaud and used as a frontispiece to this book, were provided by Edward Elphick of Christie's.

Others whose assistance I gladly acknowledge are Mavis Batey, Geoffrey Beard, Alan Bell, Camilla Beresford, Briony Blackwell, Michael Bott, Iain Gordon Brown, Terry Burchell, Ian Campbell, David R. Coffin, Lottie Clarke, Judith Colton, Christopher Dingwall, Kerry Downes, Pierre Du Prey, Patrick Eyre, Terry Friedman, Keith Goodway, Maggie Grieve, Frances Harris, John Harris, Richard Hewlings, Charles Wheelton Hind, Alison Hodges, Sally Jeffery, Dorothy B. Johnston, Frank Kelsall, John Lord, Arline Meyer, David Neave, Margaret O'Sullivan, Susan Palmer, Richard Quaintance, Margaret Richardson, John Riely, Malcolm Rogers, Ann Rowe, Kathryn M. Thompson, Michael Tooley, Deborah Turnbull, Jan van der Wateren, Rachel Watson, Elisabeth Whittle, Tom Williamson, Margaret Wills, and Magnus Willis. Advice on the identification of Bridgeman landscapes was freely given by David Jacques, John Phibbs, and Hugh Prince. For permission to quote from their reviews of the original edition I am indebted to Geoffrey Beard, Morris Brownell, Margaret Drabble, and David Irwin.

Documentation on Bridgeman and the English landscape garden has been deposited in the Willis Papers in Durham University Library. I must thank Elizabeth M. Rainey, Sub-Librarian in charge of Special Collections at Durham, for her meticulous organisation of this material and for enabling me to use it fully.

The Elysium Press edition was designed by Robert Dalrymple of the Edinburgh firm of Dalrymple, and I am grateful to him for his commitment to the project. The acknowledgements made in the Preface to the 1977 edition still stand. Research on Bridgeman was first suggested to me in 1955 by Jack Napper, subsequently Professor of Architecture at Newcastle University, and on reflection I owe him far more than I recognised a quarter of a century ago. Similarly I must acknowledge more extensively Professor Carl D. Sheppard, who made possible my initial work on the Stowe Papers at the Huntington Library in California in 1960–61. To Professor Rudolf Wittkower I remain indebted for his faith in the book, personally and tangibly expressed. To my late parents, dedicated support over many years. And to my wife Jenny, and our son Magnus, constancy at all hours and in all weathers.

PETER WILLIS

Summer 2001

[1] This is taken from four pages of manuscript notes in Horace Walpole's hand, pasted into volume II of Daniel Lysons, *The Environs of London …* (1795), now at Yale University in the Lewis Walpole Library, Farmington, Connecticut.

[2] National Library of Scotland, Edinburgh, Fraser Collection, MS 1033, fo.157. Letter from Orkney to one of his brothers, 2 October 1723.

[3] Slava Klima, ed., *Joseph Spence. Letters from the Grand Tour* (Montreal and London, 1975), pp.70, 373–74. On p.420 one 'Bridgeman' is listed by Spence as among those whom he met in Paris in 1733.

[4] Letters at Badminton received by Lord Noel Somerset, later 3rd Duke of Beaufort.

[5] BL, Add MS 61478, fos 9–12, 17–18, 31–34, 43–44, 47–48, and 51–52.

STUDIES IN ARCHITECTURE

Edited by Anthony Blunt, John Harris and Howard Hibbard

Volume XVII

Charles Bridgeman

Peter Willis

Charles Bridgeman
and the
English Landscape Garden

Peter Willis

A. Zwemmer Ltd
London

Published by A. Zwemmer Ltd, 76–80 Charing Cross Road, London, WC1
ISBN 302 02777 7
Designed by Graham Johnson/Lund Humphries
Printed in Great Britain by Lund Humphries, London and Bradford

To the memory of Mrs Robert Woods Bliss 1879–1969

Other books by Peter Willis

Editor
Furor Hortensis. Essays on the History of the English Landscape Garden in Memory of H. F. Clark
Edinburgh: Elysium Press Ltd, 1974

Editor
(with John Dixon Hunt)
The Genius of the Place. The English Landscape Garden, 1620–1820
London: Paul Elek Ltd, 1975

New Architecture in Scotland
London: Lund Humphries Publishers Ltd, 1977

‘To the *gentle Reader*’

I humbly submit my whole worke, unto the correction of the learned . . . And although some perchaunce shall thinke, thei could have doen the same muche better then I have doen, I will not muche contende, in the confessyng and grauntyng thereof. But yet seyng I am one of the first, that attempted the collectyng of the same Arte into a volume, to the publication thereof, for the benefite of the common wealthe . . . alwaies remembryng, that although moste men, can perhappes amende a devise once begun, yet that every first devise, in every thyng, is moste harde, & troublesome.

Valentyne Leigh
The Moste Profitable and Commendable Science, of Surveying of Landes, Tenementes, and Hereditamentes . . .
London, 1577

Contents

List of Plates

Names of photographers are given in brackets; if no photographer is credited, illustrations were provided by the institutions or private owners concerned.

76 Pope's Villa, Twickenham. View from Thames. Engraving by Heckell and Mason 1749. BL.

77 Pope's Villa, Twickenham. Engraving pub. John Serle of *A Plan of Mr Pope's Garden as it was Left at His Death* (1745). BL.

78a Brampton Bryan. Plan. Drawing by Bridgeman (attrib.). Soane, Box of Misc. Drawings (Wren, etc.). Trustees of Sir John Soane's Museum (A. C. Cooper).

78b Edward Harley, 2nd Earl of Oxford. Artist unknown. Trustees of the National Portrait Gallery, London.

79 King's College, Cambridge. Aerial view. Engraving by James Essex *c.*1744. CUL.

80a Gunton. Plan of Mount. Drawing by Bridgeman (attrib.). MSGD a4 fo.75.

80b Wolterton. Plan. Drawing by Bridgeman (attrib.). MSGD a4 fo.20.

81a Houghton. View of South Front. Drawing by Edmund Prideaux *c.*1730. J. C. Prideaux-Brune, Esq. (RIBA).

81b Houghton. Plan. Drawing by Bridgeman (attrib.). MSGD a4 fo.57.

82 Houghton. Plan. Engraving from Ware, *Plans, Elevations, and Sections . . . of Houghton in Norfolk* (1735). BL (Parkinson).

83 Gubbins. Temple and Dovecote. Drawings by Gibbs. Ashmolean Museum, Oxford, Gibbs Collection, III, fos 87a, 87b.

84 Gubbins. View of Bowling Green. Engraving by Chatelain and Tinney 1748. BL (Fleming).

85 Delville. Drawing by Mary Delaney of 'A view of ye Swift & Swans Island in Delville Garden', 1745. National Gallery of Ireland, Dublin, 2722 (24).

86 Badminton. View of North Front. Drawing attributed to Wootton. Badminton. Duke of Beaufort (Copyright *Country Life*).

87 *The Beaufort Hunt*, by Wootton. Badminton. Duke of Beaufort (Copyright *Country Life*).

88a George II, marble bust by Rysbrack 1738. Windsor Castle. Reproduced by gracious permission of H.M. The Queen (Courtauld Institute of Art).

88b Queen Caroline, marble bust by Rysbrack 1739. Wallace Collection, London.

89 Garden implements. Engraving from Liger, *Le nouveau théâtre d'agriculture et ménage des champs* (1723), pl.7. BL (Parkinson).

90a West Wycombe. Scything and brushing. Detail of engraving by Woollett 1757. BL (Parkinson).

90b Carlton House. Brushing and scything. Detail of engraving by Woollett 1760. BL (Parkinson).

91a Stowe. Rolling the Grecian Valley. Detail of engraving from Bickham, pub., *Views of Stowe* (1753), pl.p. BL (Parkinson).

91b Hall Barn. Rolling the lawns. Detail of engraving by Woollett 1760. BL (Parkinson).

92a Moving trees in wooden tubs. Detail of engraving from Kleiner, *Vera et accurata delineatio omnium templorum et cœnobiorum* (1724 et seq.). BL (Parkinson).

92b Clipping hedges. Detail of engraving from Kleiner, *Vera et accurata delineatio omnium templorum et cœnobiorum* (1724 et seq.). BL (Parkinson).

93a Hampton Court. View of South Front. Engraving by Highmore and Tinney *c.*1745. BL (Fleming).

93b Hampton Court. View of East Front from Canal (Edwin Smith).

94 Hampton Court. Aerial view from north-west 1969 (Aerofilms).

95 Hampton Court. Plan. Drawing by Bridgeman *c.*1735, signed 'C.BRIDGMAN FEC'. Soane, Drawer 36.3.1. Trustees of Sir John Soane's Museum, London (Bell).

96a Kensington Gardens. View of Round Pond (Edwin Smith).

96b Kensington Gardens and Hyde Park. View of Serpentine (Edwin Smith).

97a Kensington Gardens and Hyde Park. Detail from Rocque, *An Exact Survey of the City's of London, Westminster . . . and the Country Near Ten Miles Round* (1746). BL (Fleming).

97b Kensington Gardens and Hyde Park. Aerial view 1954 (Aerofilms).

98 Kensington Gardens and Hyde Park. Plan. Drawing by Bridgeman (attrib.). HEH, ST MAP 147.

99a Kensington Gardens. Plan of Palace, Broad Walk, Round Pond and Great Bow. Drawing by Bridgeman (attrib.). MSGD a3* fo.15.

99b Kensington Gardens. View of south-east corner with Mount and Summer House, and King's Old Road (Lamp Road/Rotten Row) by Bernard Lens, the Younger, 1736. Royal Borough of Kensington and Chelsea Central Library, 712.5 KEN/Oa.GC.2251.

100a Kensington Gardens. View from Round Pond towards Palace. Engraving by Rocque and Vivares 1736. BL (Fleming).

131 Stowe. Rigaud, 'View of the *Great Bason*, from the Entrance of the *Great Walk* to the *House*/Veüe du *Grand Bassin*, prise a l'Entree de la *Grand Alleé* qui monte au *Chateau*'. Ink and wash. 1733–34. MMA (Harris Brisbane Dick Fund, 1942), 42.79 (10).

132 Stowe. Rigaud, 'View at the Entrance between the *Pavillions*/Veüe de *l'Entrée* du *Jardin* prise entre les *deux Pavillons*'. Ink and wash. 1733–34. MMA (Harris Brisbane Dick Fund, 1942), 42.79(3).

133 Stowe. Rigaud, 'View of such parts as are seen from the *Building* at the *Head* of the *Lake*/Veüe de ce qui se voit du *Batiment* à la *Tête* du *Lac*'. Ink and wash. 1733–34. MMA (Harris Brisbane Dick Fund, 1942), 42.79(2).

134 Stowe. Rigaud, 'View from the *Head* of the *Lake*/Veüe prise sur le *Bord*, ou a la *Teste* du *Lac*'. Ink and wash. 1733–34. MMA (Harris Brisbane Dick Fund, 1942), 42.79(11).

135 Stowe. Rigaud, 'View from *Gibbs's Building*/ Veüe prise a coté de *Gibbs's Building*'. Ink and wash. 1733–34. MMA (Harris Brisbane Dick Fund, 1942), 42.79(6).

136 Stowe. Rigaud, 'View from the foot of the *Pyramid*/Veüe prise a coté de la *Piramide*'. Ink and wash. 1733–34. MMA (Harris Brisbane Dick Fund, 1942), 42.79(4).

137 Stowe. Rigaud, 'View from the *Brick Temple*/ Veüe prise du *Temple Rouge*'. Ink and wash. 1733–34. MMA (Harris Brisbane Dick Fund, 1942), 42.79(8).

138 Stowe. Rigaud, 'View at the *Lesser Obelisk*/ Veüe prise du *Pied de la Petite Obelisque*'. Ink and wash. 1733–34. MMA (Harris Brisbane Dick Fund, 1942), 42.79(12).

139 Stowe. Rigaud, 'View of the *Queen's Theatre* from the *Rotunda*/Veüe du *Theatre* de la *Reine* prise a coté de la *Rotonde*'. Ink and wash. 1733–34. MMA (Harris Brisbane Dick Fund, 1942), 42.79(7).

140 Stowe. Rigaud, 'View at the *Queen's Statue*/ Veüe prise du *Piedestal* de la *Statue* de la *Reine*'. Ink and wash. 1733–34. MMA (Harris Brisbane Dick Fund, 1942), 42.79(14).

141 Stowe. Rigaud, 'View from *Nelson's Seat*/ Veüe prise a Coté du *Pavillon* de *Nelson's Seat*'. Ink and wash. 1733–34. MMA (Harris Brisbane Dick Fund, 1942), 42.79(9).

142 Stowe Rigaud, 'View from the *Portico* of the *House* to the *Park*/Veüe prise du *Peron* du *Chateau* du Coté du *Parc*'. Ink and wash. 1733–34. MMA (Harris Brisbane Dick Fund, 1942), 42.79(5).

143 Stowe. Rigaud and Baron, 'View of the *House* from the *Equestrian Statue*/Veüe du *Chateau* prise a coté de la *Figure Equestre*', from Sarah Bridgeman, pub., *Views of Stowe* (1739), pl.6. BL.

144 Stowe. Ha-ha. Detail of engraving by Rigaud and Baron, 'View of the *Queen's Theatre* from the *Rotunda*/Veüe du *Theatre* de la *Reine* prise a cote de la *Rotonde*', from Sarah Bridgeman, pub., *Views of Stowe* (1739), pl.8. BL.

145 Stowe. Ha-ha. Detail of engraving by Rigaud and Baron, 'View of such parts as are seen from the *Building* at the *Head* of the *Lake*/Veüe de ce qui se voit du *Batiment* à la *Tête* du *Lac*', from Sarah Bridgeman, pub., *Views of Stowe* (1739), pl.2. BL.

146 Stowe. General Plan. Engraving by Bickham and Chatelain from Bickham, pub., *Views of Stowe* (1753). BL (Parkinson).

147a Stowe. Cascade, Temple of Venus, Egyptian Pyramid, and Fane of Diana. Engraving from Seeley, *Stowe* (1763), pl.2. Mr and Mrs Peter Willis (Fleming).

147b Stowe. Gateway (near Boycotts), Witch House, Temple of Modern Virtue, Temple of Ancient Virtue, and Shell Bridge. Engraving from Seeley, *Stowe* (1763), pl.5. BL (Parkinson).

148 Stowe. Detail of Elysian Fields from *Plate 123*. BL (Fleming).

149 Stowe. Detail of Elysian Fields from *Plate 146*. BL (Parkinson).

150a Stowe. Bickham and Chatelain, 'A View from the Temple of Diana/Le Point de Vüe du Temple de Diane', from Bickham, pub., *Views of Stowe* (1753), pl.d. BL (Fleming).

150b Stowe. Bickham and Chatelain, 'A View of the Queen's Theatre from the Rotundo/Vüe du Theatre de la Reine prise a Cotè de la Rotonde', from Bickham, pub., *Views of Stowe* (1753), pl.g. BL (Parkinson).

151a Stowe. Bickham and Chatelain, 'A View to the Grotto of the Serpentine River in the Alder Grove/Vüe vers la Riviere Serpentine du Bosquet des Auniers prise de la Grotte', from Bickham, pub., *Views of Stowe* (1753), pl.l. BL (Parkinson).

151b Stowe. Bickham and Chatelain, 'A View in the Elysian Fields, from the Spring of Helicon/ Vüe dans les Champs Elisées, prise de la Fontaine de l'Helicon', from Bickham, pub., *Views of Stowe* (1753), pl.m. BL (Parkinson).

152a Stowe. View of Rotunda (Edwin Smith).

152b Stowe. View of Gothic Temple (Edwin Smith).

153a Stowe. View of Temple of British Worthies from Temple of Ancient Virtue in Elysian Fields (Edwin Smith).

153b Stowe. View of Temple of Ancient Virtue from Temple of British Worthies in Elysian Fields (Edwin Smith).

154a Stowe. View from Palladian Bridge across Octagon Lake to Hawkwell Hill and Field (Edwin Smith).

Acknowledgements for Photographs and Drawings

The portraits of George II and Henry Wise (*Plates 88a, 17a*) are reproduced by gracious permission of H.M. The Queen.

All other illustrations of drawings, engravings, and paintings appear by courtesy of the institutions or private owners concerned who (unless indicated otherwise) also provided the photographs. Special prints and enlargements were made by the University Library at the University of Newcastle.

The photographs of gardens by the late Mr Edwin Smith were taken in the 1960's, and those by the author in the 1970's.

Abbreviations

BL	British Library, London
BM	British Museum, London
Bod. Lib.	Bodleian Library, Oxford
Colvin, *Dictionary*	Colvin, H. M., *A Biographical Dictionary of English Architects, 1660–1840* (London, 1954)
C.Life	*Country Life* (periodical)
CRO	County Record Office (prefixed by name)
CTP	*Calendar of Treasury Papers, 1557–1728,* 6 vols (London, 1868–89)
CTB	*Calendar of Treasury Books, 1660–1718*, 32 vols (London, 1904–58)
CTBP	*Calendar of Treasury Books and Papers, 1729–45*, 5 vols (London, 1898–1903)
CUL	Cambridge University Library
DO	Dumbarton Oaks Research Library and Collection (Trustees for Harvard University), Washington, D.C.
DoE	Department of the Environment, London
GLC	Greater London Council
Harl. Soc.	*Harleian Society* (*Publications*) (London, 1869 et seq.)
HEH	Henry E. Huntington Library, San Marino, California
HMC	*Historical Manuscripts Commission* (*Reports*) (London, 1870 et seq.)
MMA	Metropolitan Museum of Art, New York
MS	Manuscript
MSGD	Bodleian Library, Oxford, MS Gough Drawings
NMR (ENGLAND)	National Monuments Record, London
NMR (SCOTLAND)	National Monuments Record, Edinburgh
N.S.	New Series
Pope Correspondence	Sherburn, George W., ed., *The Correspondence of Alexander Pope*, 5 vols (Oxford, 1956)
PRO	Public Record Office, London
RCHM	*Royal Commissions on Ancient and Historical Monuments and Constructions* (*Inventories*) (London, 1910 et seq.)
RIBA	Royal Institute of British Architects, London
RO	Record Office (prefixed by name)
R.P.	Reprinted
S.	Series
SG	Society of Genealogists, London

Soane	Sir John Soane's Museum, London
SRO, Edinburgh	Scottish Record Office, Edinburgh
V&A	Victoria and Albert Museum, London
Vertue	Walpole Society, ed., *Vertue Note Books*, 7 vols (Oxford, 1930–55) Vols I (XVIII), II (XX), III (XXII), IV (XXIV), V (XXVI), I–V Index (XXIX), VI (XXX) (with Index)
VCH	*The Victoria History of the Counties of England* (London, 1900 et seq.)
Vit. Brit.	Campbell, Colin, *et al.*, *Vitruvius Britannicus, or The British Architect,* 6 vols (London, 1715–71) Vols I, 1715; II, 1717; III, 1725; continued by Thomas Badeslade and John Rocque, IV, 1739; continued by John Woolfe and James Gandon, the Elder, IV, 1767; V, 1771
WC	Water-colour
Wren Soc.	*Wren Society* (*Publications*), 20 vols (London, 1924–43)
Yale Walpole	Lewis, Wilmarth S., *et al.*, eds, *The Yale Edition of Horace Walpole's Correspondence* (London and New Haven, 1937 et seq.)

Each year is taken to begin on 1 January and not 25 March, and the dates of documentary references are changed accordingly.

When an original MS has been consulted at the PRO, the documentary reference is cited specifically (e.g. PRO, Works 5/104, fo.3); when the actual MS has not been examined, a reference to the appropriate *Calendar* only is given (e.g. *CTB*, XXVII, pt. 1 (1713), 225).

In quoting direct from a MS, original spelling and punctuation are retained, and raised letters lowered; if a MS has been published (e.g. *Vertue Note Books*) the style of the printed version is adopted. Square brackets [ ] are inserted for editorial additions or variations.

The names used for county and other British record offices are those which were applicable *before* the reorganization of Local Government in April 1974.

Preface

Charles Bridgeman is the unsung pioneer in the establishment of *le jardin anglais*, that remarkable English invention which was to sweep eighteenth-century Europe. Bridgeman's role in the transition from the geometric layouts of the early 1700's to the freer designs of Capability Brown was a crucial one. His activities as Royal Gardener to George II and Queen Caroline embraced Hampton Court, Kensington Palace, and Richmond, whilst for private patrons he was active at Blenheim, Eastbury, Marble Hill, and a host of other country houses. A collaborator with Vanbrugh, Gibbs and Kent, and a friend of writers and artists, Bridgeman brought his work to a peak in the creation of Stowe in Buckinghamshire, the most celebrated landscape of the day.

The present book is the first monograph to be devoted to Bridgeman, and its aims are twofold: to bring together the widely-scattered documentation of his career, and to place him securely in the context of these changes in taste. Such a task is more ambitious than it may seem, for – despite the encomiums of Horace Walpole – writers as industrious as John Claudius Loudon have been defeated by Bridgeman's elusiveness. Loudon, writing in his *Encyclopaedia of Gardening* of 1822, acknowledged that Bridgeman was one of those 'who established the modern style' in England, but confessed that he had been able 'to procure no information' about him. Those who have undertaken research into landscape history will sympathize with Loudon's difficulties, for few art forms are so transient as a garden, and often as not (particularly after the passage of two centuries or more) our historical evidence is minimal: perhaps an account or two, an unsigned plan, some remarks by a traveller and, if we are lucky, a sketch or an engraved view.

This very lack of material, with its accompanying fascination and frustration, has meant that I have had to cast my net wide. In so doing I have become greatly dependent upon the kindness of others, and it is a pleasure to have the opportunity of expressing my debt to them here. Amongst those who willingly shared the results of their own researches with me I am especially grateful to the late Christopher Hussey, Mr George Clarke, Mr Howard Colvin, Mr David Green, Mr Laurence Whistler, and Mr Kenneth Woodbridge. The late H. F. Clark was a constant source of encouragement, as were Professor Carl P. Barbier, Dr John Dixon Hunt, Professor Samuel Holt Monk, and Professor J. H. Napper. Several scholars with expert knowledge of Bridgeman's fellow-artists gave me the benefit of their expertise, notably Miss Juliet Allan on Flitcroft, Dr William Brogden on Switzer, Dr Kerry Downes on Hawksmoor and Vanbrugh, Dr Terry Friedman and Mr Bryan Little on Gibbs, and Dr Timothy Hudson on Leoni. For advice on Italian matters I am beholden to Professor Elisabeth MacDougall and Professor David Coffin, and on French issues to M. André Parreaux and M. Denis Lambin. Others whose generosity I recall are Professor Marcia Allentuck, Mr Geoffrey Beard, Dr Hugh Bilbrough, the late Professor John Butt, Mr Derrick Chalk, Mr David Chase, Mr John Cornforth, Miss Mary Cosh, Dr J. Mordaunt Crook, Miss Catherine E. Cruft, Mr Michael Downing, Mrs Marie P. G. Draper, Mr R. Q. Drayson, the late Professor W. B. Edwards, Dr Andrew Fairbairn, Mr Desmond

Fitz-Gerald (Knight of Glin), Mr Laurence Fricker, Mr Michael Gibbon, Professor Brian Hackett, Mr Miles Hadfield, Mr John Harvey, Professor F. Hamilton Hazlehurst, Dr Derek Linstrum, Dr James Macaulay, Mr Michael McCrum, Mr Edward Malins, Sir Leslie Martin, Sir Robert Matthew, Mr John Newman, Professor Patrick Nuttgens, Professor Ronald Paulson, Mr Malcolm Pinhorn, Mr Hugh Prince, Mr Simon Pugh, Professor John Roach, Professor Samuel A. Roberson, Professor Maren-Sofie Røstvig, Dr Alistair Rowan, Professor Carl D. Sheppard, Mr Derek Sherborn, Mr William Spink, Dr Howard Stutchbury, Dr Alan Tait, Dr Samuel Taylor, Dr Christopher Thacker, Professor Dora Wiebenson, Mr John Wilton-Ely, and Professor H. Bunker Wright. Mrs Olive Smith made available the superb photographs by her late husband, Edwin Smith, many taken especially for this volume; generous grants to cover these and other expenses were awarded by the Research Committee of the University of Newcastle.

I am similarly indebted to the many owners and archivists who granted me access to their gardens and to material in their care. H.M. The Queen graciously permitted me to use the Royal Archives at Windsor, where I was assisted by Sir Owen Morshead and Sir Robin Mackworth-Young. Generous help was forthcoming at Chatsworth from Mr T. S. Wragg and Mr Peter Day; at the Duchy of Cornwall Office from Sir Patrick Kingsley; at the Henry E. Huntington Library from Miss Haydée Noya, Miss Jean Preston, and Dr Robert R. Wark; at the London Museum from Dr John Hayes; at the Metropolitan Museum of Art from the late John McKendry, Miss Janet S. Byrne, and Mrs Alexandrine St Clair; at the National Portrait Gallery from Mr John Kerslake; at Sir John Soane's Museum from Miss Dorothy Stroud and Sir John Summerson; at the Vancouver Art Gallery from Mr Wylie W. Thom, and at the City Art Gallery in York from Mr John Ingamells. My investigations of the accounts of London banks were eased by Miss R. A. Ashbee (Child's Branch of Williams and Glyn's), Miss K. E. Bryon (Barclays), Mr J. R. Cuthbertson and Mr R. G. Must (Drummonds Branch, Royal Bank of Scotland), Mr A. N. Harrisson (Barclays), Miss M. V. Stokes (Coutts and Co.), and Mr R. M. D. Winder (C. Hoare and Co.). I must also thank the owners or custodians of unpublished manuscript material cited in the notes, particularly Earl Cathcart, Sir John Clerk of Penicuik, Bt, the Duke of Devonshire, the Duke of Hamilton, the Duke of Marlborough, Professor James M. Osborn, the Duke of Portland, Viscount Scarsdale, the late Earl Spencer, and G. H. H. Wheler, Esq.

In Sir Anthony Blunt, Mr John Harris, and Professor Howard Hibbard I have had three congenial Editors, and in Mr Desmond Zwemmer an exemplary publisher, patient and good humoured. Valuable editorial help was given me by Mrs Stephen Harbottle, Miss Jane Heller, Mrs Sylvia Rosen, and Mr Kevin Stower, whilst Mr Graham Johnson of Lund Humphries' coped cheerfully and skilfully with the design problems presented by a complicated manuscript. At proof stage I was spared numerous blunders by the perspicacity of Dr William Brogden, Mr George Clarke, Mr Howard Colvin, Dr Terry Friedman, Dr Andor Gomme, Mr Robert Holden, and Dr John Dixon Hunt. Errors of fact and judgement which remain are my own, and I can only leave it to others to make good the deficiencies they most deplore.

I have left to the end those to whom I owe most. Two academic debts stand out above all others: to Sir Nikolaus Pevsner, under whose rigorous and stimulating guidance I wrote my 1962 Cambridge doctoral dissertation on Bridgeman, and to Professor Rudolf Wittkower, whose legendary kindness took the form of timely encouragement and wise counsel, critical reading of the manuscript, and recommendation for publication in the Studies in Architecture series. My debt to my parents, to my wife Jenny and our son Magnus, I can never adequately record. The opportunity to finish the book was given me by the award of a Fellowship by the Trustees for Harvard University, tenable at Dumbarton Oaks Research Library and Collection, Washington, D.C., in 1964–65. Subsequently Mr John Thacher (formerly Director of Dumbarton Oaks), and the Garden Advisory Committee (under the successive Chairmanships of the late Leon Zach and Mr Robert Patterson) have generously supported my endeavours over several years. In the United States, however, my greatest debt is to the late Mrs Robert Woods Bliss, who ensured that my stay at Dumbarton Oaks was such a happy one, and to whose memory the following pages are affectionately dedicated.

Spring 1976 PW

Synopsis of Bridgeman's Life

Dates given to Bridgeman's work on individual landscapes are only approximate

1709 CB at Blenheim with Vanbrugh, Wise, and Switzer

1716 CB begins work at Stowe, and until 1726 collaborates with Vanbrugh there and at Eastbury and Claremont

1717 CB marries Sarah Mist in Gray's Inn Chapel; subscribes to Vol. II of *Vitruvius Britannicus*

1719 CB's son Charles baptized; CB busy on landscapes with South Sea Company connections at Carshalton, Purley, Tring, Briggens, and Sacombe

1720 CB's daughter Sarah born

1721 CB assists Prior with Down Hall, and is active in Harley's Wimpole circle which includes Gibbs, Thornhill, Wootton, and Pope

1723 CB's son John baptized; CB and his family move to No.19 Broad Street, Westminster, where they stay until 1738

1724 CB's daughter Elizabeth baptized; CB at Marble Hill and, in mid-1720's, with Gibbs at King's College, Cambridge, Houghton, Gubbins, and Kedleston

1725 CB's daughter Charlotte baptized; CB leases No.8 Henrietta Street, Marylebone; subscribes to Vol. III of *Vitruvius Britannicus*, and to Pope's translation of the *Odyssey* (1725–26), and publishes his *Report* on the drainage of the Fens (1725)

1726 CB replaces Carpenter as Wise's partner in the royal gardens, and is joined by Gibbs at Stowe; CB is elected to St Luke's Club of Artists

1727 CB subscribes to Kent's *Designs of Inigo Jones*

1728 CB appointed Royal Gardener to George II, his responsibilities including Hampton Court, Kensington, St James's Park, and Richmond; CB subscribes to Gibbs's *Book of Architecture*

1729 CB's daughters Charlotte and Caroline die; CB nominated by Mercier as Steward of St Luke's Club; CB prepares plan of Cavendish Square and is with Flitcroft at Bower, Chicheley, Woburn, and Amesbury

1730 CB in *An Assembly of Virtuosi* by Hamilton or Hogarth; CB subscribes to Thomson's *Seasons*

1731 CB's daughter Ann baptized

1733 CB invites Rigaud to come from France to draw Stowe; CB and Kent at Kensington, Richmond, and Stowe in 1730's

1734 CB in Hogarth's *The Rake's Progress*

1735 CB in Hamilton's *A Club of Artists*

1738 CB dies in Kensington and is buried in St James's Church, Westminster

1739 CB's widow, Sarah, publishes Rigaud and Baron's *Views of Stowe*

1743 or 1744 Widow Bridgeman dies

Introduction

'Mahomet imagined an Elysium', wrote Horace Walpole, 'but Kent created many.'[1] William Kent was not the only English landscape designer to create an Elysium, nor was Mahomet alone in imagining one. Both were joining that quest for a dream-landscape in which 'real prospects are little less than visions'.[2] To Addison such prospects presented 'innumerable subjects for meditation': after the eye has seen, the imagination is stimulated. 'A Poet', he maintained in the *Spectator* in 1712, 'should take as much Pains in forming his Imagination, as a Philosopher in cultivating his Understanding. He must gain a due Relish of the Works of Nature, and be thoroughly conversant in the various Scenary of a Country Life.'[3] Addison goes on to cite instances of this in the works of Homer, Ovid, and of Virgil, who 'is never better pleas'd, than when he is in his *Elysium,* or copying out an entertaining Picture'.[4] The idea of Elysium or the Elysian Fields – the dwelling place of mortals made immortal through the favour of the gods – was interpreted in two different but equally symbolic ways by eighteenth-century landscapists. Either they conceived it as 'delightful Landskips . . . made out of Fields and Woods, Herds of Cattle, and Swarms of Bees',[5] or else as glades populated by temples, ruins, 'marble trophies, carved pillars, and statues of lawgivers, heroes, statesmen, philosophers and poets'.[6]

When Rousseau in *La Nouvelle Héloïse* of 1759 transports Julie into her private *Elisée,* along with her husband and Saint-Preux, it is into an Elysium of the first kind – an abandoned orchard, with an island, shrubs, trees, a stream, birds, countless scattered flowers, and wandering paths carpeted with fine moss and shaded by garlands of trailing vines.[7] Yet Julie explains that all this is the work of art. '*Il est vrai*', she admits, '*que la nature a tout fait, mais sous ma direction, et il n'y a rien là que je n'ave ordonné.*'[8] Rousseau, after discussing

[1] Horace Walpole, *Anecdotes of Painting in England, with Some Account of the Principal Artists,* ed. Ralph N. Wornum (London, [1888]), III, 57.

[2] *Yale Walpole,* X, 314. Walpole to Montagu, 7 July 1770.

[3] No.417 (28 June 1712), in Donald F. Bond, ed., *The Spectator* (Oxford, 1965), III, 563. The texts of subsequent quotations from the *Spectator* are taken from this edition.

[4] 'Elysium or the Isles of the Blest, situated at the ends of the earth, appears in Homer . . . and Hesiod . . . as the place to which certain favoured heroes, exempted from death, are translated by the gods. Elysium appears to be a survival from Minoan religion; when a later age concerned itself with the fate of the blessed *dead,* Elysium was transferred to the nether regions, in conformity with Greek ideas and the Homeric picture'. N.G.L. Hammond and H. H. Scullard, eds, *The Oxford Classical Dictionary,* 2nd edn (Oxford, 1970), 23. See also A. Bartlett Giamatti, *The Earthly Paradise and the Renaissance Epic* (Princeton, N.J., 1966), pp. 11–33.

[5] Addison in the *Spectator,* No.417 (28 June 1712). Addison's ideas on landscape had been expressed initially in 'An Essay on Virgil's *Georgics*' (1697). See Scott Elledge, ed., *Eighteenth-Century Critical Essays* (Ithaca, N.Y., 1961), I, 1–8, 488–91.

[6] Addison in the *Tatler,* No.123 (21 January 1710).

[7] Jean-Jacques Rousseau, *Œuvres complètes,* Bibliothèque de la Pléiade, II (Paris, 1961), 470–88 (pt. iv, letter 11).
Although Rousseau's description of Elysium in this letter was to receive wide publicity, it was by no means unheralded in France. For instance, Laugier presages it in Chapter 6 of his *Essai sur l'architecture* (Paris, 1753), pp.272–93, entitled '*De l'embellissement des jardins*'. Laugier, in common with many other Frenchmen, favours Chinese rather than English influence as the root cause of the changes in French taste. See Wolfgang Herrmann, *Laugier and Eighteenth-Century French Theory* (London, 1962), pp.140–47.

[8] Rousseau, *Œuvres complètes,* II, 472.

the influence of China and the reaction against the formal garden, next compares Julie's imagined *Elisée* with an actual Elysium of the second type, namely Stowe in Buckinghamshire, from 1697 to 1749 the home of Richard Temple, 1st Viscount Cobham. Stowe, says Rousseau,

> *est un composé de lieux très beaux et très pittoresques dont les aspects ont été choisis en différens pays, et dont tout paroit naturel excepté l'assemblage, comme dans les jardins de la Chine dont je viens de vous parler. Le maitre et le créateur de cette superbe solitude y a même fait construire des ruines, des temples, d'anciens édifices, et les tems ainsi que les lieux y sont rassemblés avec une magnificence plus qu'humaine.*[9]

It is significant that the most imaginative area of Stowe's grounds is known as the Elysian Fields, though Rousseau has no patience with it:[10] no matter how splendid the individual parts of Stowe might be, nothing could atone for the failure of its *assemblage* to be *naturel*.[11]

To other eyes Stowe's interplay between 'art' and 'nature', its use of expressive and emblematic themes, its literary and pictorial overtones, and its complex three-dimensional pun on the Temple family motto of *Templa Quam Delecta,* made it the most admired estate of Augustan England.[12] In 1724 Lord Perceval told Daniel Dering that since 1719 Stowe had 'gained the reputation of being the finest seat in England'.[13] Pope was a regular visitor and often included Stowe in the summer rambles he made round the country houses of his friends. In 1725, for example, he noted that he had been 'above a Month strolling about in *Buckinghamshire* and *Oxfordshire,* from Garden to Garden, but still returning to Lord *Cobham*'s with fresh Satisfaction'.[14] In 1731, the year he made Stowe the climax of his *Epistle to Burlington,* Pope was exclaiming to John Knight that 'if any thing under Paradise could set [him] beyond all Earthly Cogitations; Stowe might do it. It is much more beautiful this year than when [he] saw it before, & much enlarged, & with variety.' Eight years later his enthusiasm was unabated. 'This Garden is beyond all description [in] the New part of it', he told Martha Blount. 'I am every hour in it, but dinner & night, [an]d every hour Envying myself the delight of it.'[15] As the century progressed, Stowe changed; indeed what makes Stowe unique is that it is a palimpsest of eighteenth-century gardening history. Stowe's pre-eminence during Pope's lifetime was due in large measure to Charles Bridgeman. Stowe marks the climax of his career: it was his dream-landscape, its fleeting

[9] Ibid., II, 484. Daniel Mornet's note in his edition of *La Nouvelle Héloïse* (Paris, 1925), III, 241, considers Rousseau's incorrect spelling of Stowe as 'Staw' and other textual matters.

[10] Rousseau's description of Stowe is examined in Peter Willis, 'Rousseau, Stowe and *le jardin anglais*. Speculations on Visual Sources for *La Nouvelle Héloïse*', *Studies on Voltaire and the Eighteenth Century*, XC (1972), 1791–98.

[11] Rousseau is only one of many writers to use the landscape garden as a symbol of the relationship between 'man' and 'nature': nearly fifty years after *La Nouvelle Héloïse*, for instance, Goethe made it a setting for *Die Wahlverwandtschaften* (1809), and later in the nineteenth century it was used by Flaubert in his novel *Bouvard et Pécuchet* (1881) to express the aspirations of his two central figures. See Eva M. Neumeyer, 'The Landscape Garden as a Symbol in Rousseau, Goethe and Flaubert', *Journal of the History of Ideas*, VIII (April 1947), 187–217.

[12] If only to judge by the numerous poems and guides it inspired. The earliest guide-book to Stowe appeared in 1744, to the Leasowes in 1764, to Hagley in 1777, and to Blenheim in 1787.

[13] BL, Add MS 47030 (Egmont Papers), fos 156–59. Perceval to Dering, 14 August 1724.

[14] *Pope Correspondence,* II, 314. Pope to Digby, 12 August [1725 ?].

[15] Ibid., III, 217. Pope to Knight, 23 August [1731]; ibid., IV, 185. Pope to Martha Blount, 4 July [1739]. Pope adds a note (p.186): 'Adieu. I'm going into the Elyzian Fields, where I shall meet your Idæa.'

images caught for us momentarily in the *Views of Stowe* which he commissioned a few years before his death. Here Bridgeman set the seal on his reputation.[16]

We can glimpse something of Bridgeman's personality from Hogarth's portrait of him in the Vancouver Art Gallery (*Plate 1*),[17] consisting of a softly modelled life-size head and shoulders, with the Royal Gardener simply dressed in a brown coat, waistcoat, unostentatious wig, and loosely tied stock. The face itself has a good complexion, strong features, and bright eyes, and suggests a man of warmth and humanity – someone who would readily deserve Sarah, Duchess of Marlborough's accolade that he was 'honest and meant to do justly in every thing'.[18] Gibbs's portrait by Hogarth was engraved by Bernard Baron,[19] and Bridgeman may well have been similarly honoured, especially as Samuel Felton recalls seeing an engraving or etching of the Royal Gardener some time before 1780. It made a strong impression on him, and showed Bridgeman as a 'venerable healthy man' with a 'kind-hearted, hale old countenance'. Unable to trace it, Felton concludes that it may have been a private plate of Bridgeman, 'done at the expence of his generous and noble employer, Lord Cobham'.[20]

Cobham, whose portrait by Van Loo is now at Hagley (*Plate 112a*), was a strong Whig, an ambitious soldier and politician, and dedicated to establishing the Temple dynasty as one of the most distinguished and stable in the land. He had his share of good luck: he became an M.P., rose to be one of Marlborough's generals, was dismissed by Queen Anne in 1713, only to be raised to the peerage as a baron on the accession of George I in the following year when the fortunes of all were reversed. By 1718 he was a viscount, and in 1719 he completed a successful and profitable expedition to Vigo. In due course his seat at Stowe became the centre of activity for the group variously known as Cobham's Cubs or the Boy Patriots – that dissident faction of Whigs who sided with Frederick, Prince of Wales, in his squabbles with George II and Sir Robert Walpole.

Cobham took pains to marshal artists of the highest calibre to help him develop the estate. Apart from Bridgeman, Vanbrugh, Gibbs, and Kent, he called in Leoni and perhaps Flitcroft, the painters Nollekens and Sleter, and the sculptors Andrew Carpenter, Rysbrack, Scheemakers, and the elder John Nost. As an inscription on the Cobham Monument at Stowe insists, Cobham's dual claim to fame lay in that he served his country well

[16] Initial acknowledgement was given him by Thomas Seccombe, 'Charles Bridgman or Bridgeman', *Dictionary of National Biography*, XXII (Supplement) (London, 1909), 268–69, and subsequently by Osvald Sirén, *China and Gardens of Europe of the Eighteenth Century* (New York, 1950), pp.20–34; Laurence Whistler, *The Imagination of Vanbrugh and His Fellow Artists* (London, 1954), *passim*; C. Th. Sørensen, *Europas Havekunst, fra Alhambra til Liselund* (Copenhagen, 1959), pp.201–8; and Christopher Hussey, *English Gardens and Landscapes, 1700–50* (London, 1967), esp. pp.32–39, 89–99.

[17] It measures 49·8 × 57·1 cm. Stylistically it is more typical of Hogarth's later than his earlier work, and it may be that it is one of the posthumous portraits Hogarth is known to have produced. See Peter Willis, 'The Gardener and the Painter. A New Attribution to Hogarth', *Apollo*, XCV (January 1972), 30–33. My investigations into the provenance of this painting were helped by the kindness of the Knight of Glin, Mr John Ingamells, Mr John Kerslake, Mr Wylie W. Thom, Dr Robert R. Wark, and the staffs of Christie, Manson and Woods, and Sotheby and Co.

[18] Letter to Sarah Bridgeman, 25 July 1741. See below Appendix IV (vi), p.159.

[19] The best known version is the frontispiece to Gibbs's *Bibliotheca Radcliviana* . . . (London, 1747). See Arthur Oswald, 'James Gibbs and His Portraits', *Country Life Annual* (1963), p.12.

[20] Samuel Felton, *On the Portraits of English Authors on Gardening, with Biographical Notices,* 2nd edn (London, 1830), pp.135–37. See also Albert Forbes Sieveking's comments in *Notes and Queries*, S.11, III (1911), 188. Felton's use of the word 'healthy' reminds us that there are no signs in the Vancouver painting of the dropsy from which Bridgeman was to die, shown so poignantly in Hamilton's *Club of Artists* (*Plate 19*).

with his 'military and civil talents', and that he 'adorned it by a more elegant system of modern gardening, first illustrated on this spot'.[21] This 'more elegant system' was specifically English and was recognized as such: it had its counterparts in Scotland and Ireland, but it was *le jardin anglais, der englische Garten,* or *il giardino inglese* that came to dominate Europe in much the same way that the French formal garden had done. Bridgeman's part in the establishment of this new style was crucial, through both his private commissions at Stowe and elsewhere, and his official work as Royal Gardener to George II from 1728 to 1738.[22]

English Estates

So quickly did the fashion spread that the *World* on 3 April 1755 (No.118) could only express delight at 'the rapid progress of this happy enthusiasm'.[23] Such enthusiasm was well founded, for the landscape garden was more than just another eighteenth-century indication of widespread *anglomanie*. It offered almost limitless scope. In the layout of his country estate the proprietor of taste could express his understanding and love of poetry and philosophy, painting, and architecture; his need for solace in a rural setting; his knowledge

[21] This is the translation in J. Seeley, pub., *Stowe. A Description of the House and Gardens* . . . (London and Buckingham, 1797), pp.29–30. Seeley gives the date of the Cobham Monument as 1747 instead of 1749. The full Latin text, set in an oval plaque over the door, reads as follows:

Ricardo Vicecomiti de Cobham
Exercituum Britannicorum Marescallo
Qui in Castris, et in negotiis
Rempublicam Sustinuit
Et
Elegantiori Hortorum Cultu
His primum in agris illustrato
Patriam ornavit
MDCCXLIX

[22] The term 'Royal Gardener' is used throughout this book to cover the various appointments of those who served the reigning monarch as 'Chief' or 'Master Gardeners' (to cite the terms found in MSS). See the discussion in H. M. Colvin, J. Mordaunt Crook, Kerry Downes and John Newman, *The History of the King's Works, Vol.V: 1660–1782* (London, 1977), pp.457–58.

Strictly speaking the Royal Gardener did not form part of the establishment of the Office of Works, although expenditure on the gardens had to be sanctioned by the Office. The Office of Works did not exercise the same degree of control over the royal gardens as it did over the fabric of the royal palaces. 'For the superintendence of the gardens was in theory the responsibility of an independent Keeper or Surveyor', the authors write, 'and in practice the master-gardeners who came under his jurisdiction were men of high professional standing who required little direction either from their nominal superior or from the Board of architects'. The first man to become Surveyor of the Royal Gardens was Adrian May, an elder brother of Hugh May, Paymaster and later Comptroller of the Works. After a lapse the office was revived in 1715 in favour of Sir John Vanbrugh. He was succeeded in 1726 by Charles Dartiquenave, who kept the post until his death in 1737. Under Vanbrugh the title was extended to that of Surveyor of Gardens and Waters, and the pay raised to £400 a year, though the job still did not carry with it *ex officio* membership of the Board of Works.

[23] The best analysis of the new style remains H. F. Clark's 'Eighteenth-Century Elysiums. The Role of "Association" in the Landscape Movement', *Journal of the Warburg and Courtauld Institutes*, VI (1943), 165–89; R.P. in *England and the Mediterranean Tradition. Studies in Art, History and Literature,* ed. Warburg and Courtauld Institutes (London, 1945), pp.154–78. See also H. F. Clark, *The English Landscape Garden* (London, 1948), *passim*; R.P. with amendments in *House and Garden,* XIX (August, September 1968), 17–39, 66–75. The same period is covered in Peter Willis, ed., *Furor Hortensis. Essays on the History of the English Landscape Garden in Memory of H. F. Clark* (Edinburgh, 1974). Key sources appear in John Dixon Hunt and Peter Willis, eds, *The Genius of the Place. The English Landscape Garden, 1620–1820* (London, 1975).

of classical mythology; his national pride; his sense of ownership and yearning for social prestige. Above all, it afforded a visible demonstration of the fruits of his Continental Grand Tour, seen particularly in his appreciation of the Italian countryside and the landscape paintings of Claude, Nicolas Poussin, Gaspard Dughet, and Salvator Rosa.[24] Sensitivity to landscape increased. 'I cannot help observing with what new and uncommon Sensations I was filled on my first traversing this beautiful and picturesque Country', wrote the painter Thomas Jones after his first expedition to the Alban Hills in 1776. 'Every scene seemed anticipated in some dream – It appeared Magick Land.'[25] Small wonder that Italy provided inspiration for British improvers. William Mason puts it succinctly in *The English Garden* as he addresses the 'heirs of competence, if not of wealth' whose 'genuine taste' must be preserved. 'Your eyes entranc'd', he writes,

Shall catch those glowing scenes, that taught a CLAUDE
To grace his canvass with Hesperian hues:
And scenes like these, on Memory's tablet drawn,
Bring back to Britain; there give local form
To each Idea; and, if Nature lend
Materials fit of torrent, rock and shade,
Produce new TIVOLIS.[26]

As usual, Walpole has an apt comment. 'An open country', he says, 'is but a canvass on which a landscape might be designed.'[27] The countryside of Britain, with its unique climate and topography, its magnificent turf and woodland, provided a canvas of unequalled beauty.

The success of Britain's response owed much to the fact that in the early 1700's, mainly due to the extension of the practice of enclosure, there were many huge estates awaiting exploitation. As deer hunting (which had made extravagant demands on many a royal pocket) was replaced by fox hunting, so the provision of small coverts in which the fox could breed relatively undisturbed became paramount. The hedges and ditches associated with enclosure, together with rides cut through dense woodland, became part of the idealized landscape for sport.[28] Moreover, economic solvency depended upon taking agriculture and silviculture seriously, and therefore – as well as rare books, prints, furniture, pictures, and sculpture – English landowners often returned from their Grand Tour with a collection of plants, and whilst abroad kept a weather eye open for improvements in

[24] See John T. Hayes, 'British Patrons and Landscape Painting', *Apollo,* LXXXII (July 1965), 38–45; LXXXIII (March, June 1966), 188–97, 444–51; LXXXV (April 1967), 254–59; LXXXVI (November 1967), 358–65; Walter J. Hipple, *The Beautiful, the Sublime, and the Picturesque in Eighteenth-Century British Aesthetic Theory* (Carbondale, Ill., 1957); Christopher Hussey, *The Picturesque. Studies in a Point of View* (London and New York, 1927); Elizabeth W. Manwaring, *Italian Landscape in Eighteenth-Century England. A Study Chiefly of the Influence of Claude Lorrain and Salvator Rosa on English Taste, 1700–1800* (New York, 1925); Henry V. S. and Margaret Ogden, *English Taste in Landscape in the Seventeenth Century* (Ann Arbor, 1955). Cf. Martin Price, 'The Picturesque Moment', in Frederick W. Hilles and Harold Bloom, eds, *From Sensibility to Romanticism. Essays Presented to Frederick A. Pottle* (New York, 1965), pp.259–92.

[25] A. P. Oppé, ed., 'Memoirs of Thomas Jones', *Walpole Society,* XXXII (1951), 55.

[26] York edn, 1783, bk. 1, ll.64–71.

[27] Isabel W. U. Chase, *Horace Walpole: Gardenist. An Edition of Walpole's 'The History of the Modern Taste in Gardening', With an Estimate of Walpole's Contribution to Landscape Architecture* (Princeton, N.J., 1943), p.37.

[28] See John Patten, 'The Chase and the English Landscape', *C.Life,* CL (16, 23 September 1971), 660–62, 736–38.

agricultural technique: Jethro Tull, for one, wrought a revolution in methods of cultivation as a result of observing the tillage operations of French vine-growers. Farming methods were radically improved, and drainage, fertilization, and crop rotation were introduced. Flowers, shrubs, and trees were imported from abroad as, following Evelyn's advice in *Sylva,* owners began to 'adorn their . . . demesnes with trees of venerable shade, and profitable timber'.[29] After the strife of the Civil War, herds needed restocking and woods replanting. Oaks came from the Mediterranean countries and across the Atlantic; pines from Corsica, Canada, Georgia, and New England; firs and spruce from Scandinavia and throughout North America. Limes, sycamores, walnuts, and planes were imported too. Nurseries sprang up specializing in such trees as horse chestnuts, laurels, mulberries, cedars of Lebanon, and cypresses. If, as Shenstone maintained, 'the landskip painter is the gardiner's best designer',[30] then the gardener's palette was becoming more colourful, richer, stronger.[31]

In other words, utility and ornament went together. Pope's famous couplets from his *Epistle to Burlington* come to mind:

> Who then shall grace, or who improve the Soil?
> Who plants like BATHURST, or who builds like BOYLE.
> 'Tis Use alone that sanctifies Expence,
> And Splendor borrows all her rays from Sense. (ll.177–80)

This fusion of 'Use' and 'Splendor' had broader implications for Pope. As Professor Maynard Mack has emphasized, 'utility' and 'naturalness' (in an Augustan sense) are the 'two norms which became central to Pope's thinking about gardening and landscaping (as well as about life) throughout his career'.[32] To Pope, furthermore, planting is as critical as building in the creation of an estate. By the 1730's the country seat had achieved unprecedented popularity, with architects finding it hard to keep pace with their commitments.[33] 'Every Man now', said *Common Sense* in 1739, 'be his fortune what it will, is to be *doing something at his Place,* as the fashionable Phrase is; and you hardly meet with any Body, who, after the first Compliments, does not inform you, that he is *in Mortar* and *moving of Earth*; the modest terms for Building and Gardening'.[34] Eager tourists, guides in hand,

[29] York ed., 1801, II, 303. See Hugh Bilbrough, 'The Use of Tree Plantations as Elements of Landscape Design, With Special Reference to Published Texts of the Eighteenth and Nineteenth Centuries' (Ph.D. thesis, University of Manchester, 1971).

[30] 'Unconnected Thoughts on Gardening', in *The Works in Verse and Prose of William Shenstone, Esq.* (London, 1764), II, 129.

[31] See Allan Stevenson, *Catalogue of Botanical Books in the Collection of Rachel McMasters Miller Hunt. Vol.II: Printed Books, 1701–1800* (Pittsburgh, 1961), *passim*. For the introduction of foreign trees into the U.K. and Ireland see Appendix I in J. H. Wilks, *Trees of the British Isles in History and Legend* (London, 1972), pp.222–29; for plants see the Appendix in Ronald Webber, *The Early Horticulturists* (Newton Abbot, 1968), 185–209.

[32] Maynard Mack, *The Garden and the City. Retirement and Politics in the Later Poetry of Pope, 1731–43* (Toronto, Buffalo, and London, 1969), p.53.

[33] See e.g. John N. Summerson, 'The Classical Country House in Eighteenth-Century England', *Journal of the Royal Society of Arts,* CVII (July 1959), 539–87; idem, *Architecture in Britain, 1530–1830,* 5th edn (Harmondsworth, 1969), pp.157–71, 189–226.

[34] Quoted by Manwaring, *Italian Landscape in Eighteenth-Century England*, p.133.

travelled around looking and comparing.[35] The widespread building boom was reflected too in the proliferation of topographical poems,[36] and in the numerous engravings, paintings, and water-colours which advertised the glories of the British country house.[37]

Italy and France

Although such gardens as Levens in Westmorland showed lingering medieval and Dutch influence, during the early 1700's it was the French style which was predominant in England. Here and on the Continent each major house or palace had to have its own resplendent garden in the French manner, as testified in our own day by Herrenhausen in West Germany, Fredensborg in Denmark, the Haus Petersberg in Holland, Peterhof in Russia, or the Villa Crivelli Sormani-Verri at Castellazzo in Italy. In England there is Hampton Court and, on a much smaller scale, Melbourne in Derbyshire. French books and engravings spread the style abroad, notably as it was epitomized in the schemes of Alexandre Le Nôtre, the most illustrious gardener ever to serve the French monarchy. The basis of his ideas was not new and can be traced back to Renaissance Italy, and beyond that to the writings of classical authors. Thanks to the influence of Du Cerceau and the Mollet family – notably Claude Mollet the Elder's *Théâtre des plans et jardinages* of 1652 – this Italian precedent became firmly rooted in French theory and practice.[38]

The ancient Roman garden was simultaneously a sacred site, an idyllic landscape, and a place dedicated to leisure.[39] During the Renaissance the Italians fused planting and buildings in a new way, recognizing that a garden should be a place for *coveniete gravità* with secluded retreats for poets and philosophers. Evidence of this can be found in the sumptuous engravings of Giovanni Battista Falda, notably in *Li giardini di Roma* of about 1683, which

[35] For travellers see Esther Moir, *The Discovery of Britain. The English Tourists* (London, 1964). For guides see John Harris, 'English Country House Guides, 1740–1840', in John N. Summerson, ed., *Concerning Architecture. Essays on Architectural Writers and Writing Presented to Nikolaus Pevsner* (London, 1968), pp.58–74. This should be consulted along with Mr Harris's booklet *A Country House Index* (Isle of Wight, 1971).

[36] For poems see Robert A. Aubin, *Topographical Poetry in Eighteenth-Century England* (New York, 1936), *passim;* G. R. Hibbard, 'The Country House Poem of the Seventeenth Century', *Journal of the Warburg and Courtauld Institutes,* XIX (1956), 159–74; David Sofield, 'English Building Poems, 1600–1680' (Ph.D. thesis, Stanford University, 1971).

[37] Apart from *Vitruvius Britannicus,* the key sets of engravings were Beeverell's *Les délices de la Grand' Bretagne, et de l'Irlande . . .* (Leiden, 1707), and Kip and Knyff's *Britannia Illustrata,* or *Le nouveau théâtre de la Grande Bretagne . . .* (London, 1707, etc.). For a comparative list of Kip and Knyff's plates see Hugh C. Prince, *Parks in England* (Isle of Wight, 1967), pp.23–28.

[38] For the Italian garden see throughout Luigi Dami, *Il giardino Italiano* (Milan, 1924); Francesco Fariello, *Architettura dei Giardini* (Rome, 1967); Georgina Masson, *Italian Gardens* (London, 1961); J. C. Shepherd and G. A. Jellicoe, *Italian Gardens of the Renaissance,* 3rd edn (London, 1966). I am grateful to Miss Masson for advice on several Italian matters.

[39] The literature on early gardens in Italy and Greece is vast. See e.g. Ernst R. Curtius, *European Literature and the Latin Middle Ages,* trans. Willard R. Trask (London, 1953), pp. 183–202; Giamatti, *Earthly Paradise and the Renaissance Epic,* pp.1–47 and bibliography on pp.87–90; Pierre Grimal, *In Search of Ancient Italy,* trans. P. D. Cummins (London, 1964), pp.110–33; idem, *Les jardins romains,* 2nd edn (Paris, 1969); Louis Hautecœur, *Les jardins des dieux et des hommes* (Paris, 1959), pp.11–57, 77–104; Gilbert Highet, *Poets in a Landscape* (London, 1957).

includes a view of the Cortile del Belvedere and Vatican Gardens based on the layout prepared by Bramante for Julius II from about 1505 (*Plate 2*).[40] This was a *carte blanche* commission from the newly elected Pope to create the first great Roman pleasure garden since classical times, and the result was revolutionary.[41] Bramante moulded his design to the terracing, introduced strong axes to bind the scheme together within bastion-like walls, and linked the layout to the surrounding countryside. Monumental steps, ramps, and fountains were everywhere. 'With this one plan', writes Miss Masson, 'Bramante dictated the basis of European garden design for more than two centuries to come. The Italian gardens that followed, and the French ones that drew their inspiration from them, were really variations on his original theme of the discipline of a propitious site to man-made forms in accordance with the Renaissance ideals of symmetry and proportion.'[42] These Renaissance ideals also acknowledged that Greek and Roman religious buildings had been set in a wilder landscape, a fact which led Bramante to reintroduce the antique use of water and sculpture. Later in the sixteenth century this was taken further at the Villa D'Este at Tivoli,[43] whilst in the Farnese Gardens in Rome the architect Vignola laid out the gardens so that (in Falda's words) they merged into the '*Vestigie e ruine del monte Palatino*' (*Plates 3a, 3b*).

The French, as they traversed the Alps, could not fail to be impressed by the settings of Italian villas and palaces. No one needs reminding that Versailles was the supreme French achievement. Begun about 1652 and described by Louis XIV as one of '*les miracles que fait M. Le Nôtre*',[44] the gardens at Versailles came under Le Nôtre's jurisdiction as Surveyor of the Royal Works, and were a favourite subject for painters and engravers. Three examples of their work demonstrate the essence of Le Nôtre's idiom: a plan published *chez Demortain* in 1714, Patel's painting of 1666, and a view by Jacques Rigaud of about 1730 (*Plates 4, 5a, 5b*). Their most pronounced Italianate characteristic is the commanding position occupied by the palace: it is the pivot of the layout, with yews and other trimmed shrubs placed at intervals to emphasize the site lines and enhance the perspective. Within the axial framework are parterres, canals, bosquets, statuary, and triumphal arches and galleries made from timber or wrought-iron *treillage*. Italian motifs have been taken over but adapted for a flatter country with a more temperate climate: at Versailles, evergreen is used for shade where stone is employed in Italy, whilst canals and pools with *iets d'eau* are preferred to Italian wall-fountains and cascades. All round Versailles the

[40] See Diane K. McGuire, 'Giovanni Battista Falda and the Decorative Plan in Three Italian Gardens', *Connoisseur*, CLIX (May 1965), 59–63; idem, 'Old Garden Prints. A Neglected Art Form', *Landscape Architecture*, LIV (July 1964), 284–89. It must be stressed, as Professor Hibbard has told me, that Falda here shows a Vatican garden which was built up over a period of two hundred years. See Howard Hibbard, *Carlo Maderno and Roman Architecture, 1580–1630* (London, 1971), pp.199–201; pl.80c.

[41] See James S. Ackerman, *The Cortile del Belvedere* (Vatican City, 1954), and Masson, *Italian Gardens*, pp.123–28.

[42] Ibid., p.124.

[43] See David R. Coffin, *The Villa D'Este at Tivoli* (Princeton, N.J., 1960).

[44] Quoted by Louis Hautecœur, *L'histoire de l'architecture classique en France* (Paris, 1943–53), II, 389. For the French garden see esp. Marguerite Charageat, *L'art des jardins. Précis historique sur l'art des jardins* (Paris, 1930); Ernest De Ganay, *Les jardins de France et leur décor* (Paris, 1949). Precursors of Le Nôtre are dealt with in Franklin Hamilton Hazlehurst, *Jacques Boyceau and the French Formal Garden* (Athens, Georgia, 1966), and the master himself in Ernest De Ganay, *André Le Nostre* (Paris, 1962).

wooded country merges into the geometric pattern of the avenues, and provides a backcloth to the firework displays, theatrical performances, and the numerous arts of the *fêtes galantes* which add to the savour and sophistication of courtly life. Instead of medieval intimacy or constriction, we have what Louis XIV called '*la grandeur de l'esprit*'. Le Nôtre's success was complete. His gardens, wrote Saint-Simon after the gardener's death, had 'so surpassed the gardens of Italy, that the most famous masters of that country came [to France] to admire and to learn'.[45] So did Englishmen, whose imagination and curiosity were completely captured by Versailles, and in 1688 the *London Gazette* (No.2315) advertised an exhibition in London of 'the model or representation of the most magnificent and royal palace of Versailles, made in copper, gilt over with silver and gold', and displaying 'all the gardens and water-works'.

Equally crucial in England were French theoretical writings. Although Rapin's *Hortorum Libri Quattuor* – the key garden poem of seventeenth-century France, and an undisguised imitation of Virgil's *Georgics* – had endorsed Le Nôtre's style,[46] it was not until 1709, nine years after the gardener's death, that there emerged a comprehensive statement of his precepts in Antoine Joseph Dézallier D'Argenville's *La théorie et la pratique du jardinage*. Seldom has a book laid down the rules of garden design so explicitly. Its success was remarkable, and its influence must have been as enormous as that of the engravings of French gardens which appeared in abundance. Presently, to the growing number of English translations of French publications on garden design was added John James's version of Dézallier D'Argenville's volume, issued in London as *The Theory and Practice of Gardening* in 1712, and again in 1728 and 1743. Its ideas were closely akin to those of George London and Henry Wise, Bridgeman's immediate mentors.[47]

London and Wise

Bridgeman could trace back his pedigree as Royal Gardener to Le Nôtre himself.[48] Le Nôtre had trained at the Tuileries under Claude Mollet, and three of Mollet's sons (André, Charles, and Gabriel) had worked at St James's Park in London before being succeeded there by John Rose in 1666. Rose also had been a pupil of Le Nôtre, having been sent to

[45] Bayle St John, trans., *The Memoirs of the Duke of Saint-Simon* . . . (London and New York, 1902), I, 22.

[46] Rapin later wrote a treatment in prose of the same subject entitled *Réflexions sur la philosophie ancienne et moderne* . . . (Paris, 1676).

[47] Dézallier D'Argenville's French original appeared in Paris in 1709, 1713, 1722, 1732, 1747, and 1760, and in three pirated editions in The Hague in 1711, 1715, and 1739. In The Hague printings the author was erroneously given as Alexandre Le Blond, as it was in James's version. A German translation by Franz Anton Danreiter came out as *Die Gärtnerey, so wohl in ihrer Theorie oder Betrachtung als Praxie oder Uebung* . . . (Augsburg, 1731). See F. M. G. Cardew, 'L.S.A.I.D.A. A Riddle of Horticultural Authorship', *Journal of the Royal Horticultural Society*, LXXIV (June 1949), 256–61; Miles Hadfield, 'John James and the Formal Garden in England', *Connoisseur*, CXLIII (February 1959), 20–22.

[48] The following section is based on Alicia Amherst [Evelyn Cecil], *A History of Gardening in England*, 3rd edn (London, 1910), pp.156–220; David B. Green, *Gardener to Queen Anne. Henry Wise (1653–1738) and the Formal Garden* (London, 1956), *passim*; Miles Hadfield, *A History of British Gardening* (London, 1969), pp.124–78; George W. Johnson, *A History of English Gardening* . . . (London, 1829), pp.112–13, 158–82; John Claudius Loudon, *An Encyclopaedia of Gardening* . . . , 5th edn (London, 1827), pp.68–83; Stephen Switzer, *Ichnographia Rustica* . . . , 2nd edn (London, 1742), I, 59–60, 75–87.

Versailles by the Earl of Essex, and London and Wise seem to have been amongst Rose's apprentices at St James's Park. Rose died in 1677, and during William and Mary's reign William Bentinck, 1st Earl of Portland, was in charge of the royal gardens, with London as his deputy.[49] On William III's death in 1702 Portland disappeared from the scene, and Queen Anne's government contracted directly (on more favourable terms) with the master gardeners. The first of these was Henry Wise (*Plate 17a*). Wise was reappointed by George I in 1714, and thus remained Royal Gardener from 1702 to 1728. Between 1716 and 1726 Wise's partner was Joseph Carpenter. Carpenter died in 1726, and for the next two years his place as partner to Wise was taken by Charles Bridgeman. In 1728, following the accession of George II and Queen Caroline the previous summer, Bridgeman became sole Royal Gardener. On his death a decade later he was replaced not by one but by several successors.

For a contemporary commentary on these activities we must consult the publications of Stephen Switzer, a man of education who – as a friend of London, Wise and Bridgeman, and a colleague of Vanbrugh – was especially well placed to give such an account. His writing centred on garden design, and his foremost book is *The Nobleman, Gentleman, and Gardener's Recreation* of 1715, expanded in 1718 as the first of the three-volume *Ichnographia Rustica*, of which a second edition appeared in 1742.[50] Although it is as an author that Switzer's name is most familiar to us, his connections with practical gardening were far from inconsequential. He proudly described himself as 'Gardener, Several Years Servant to Mr. *London* and Mr. *Wise*',[51] by whom he was employed at Brompton, Blenheim, and St James's Park, and on his own account he also provided designs for a number of other estates. Switzer himself could provide the trees and plants when required to do so, for he set up as a seedsman and nurseryman with gardens at Millbank and a stand 'at the Seedshop in *Westminster-Hall*'.[52]

[49] Two sets of garden accounts of Portland's date are printed in *Wren Soc.*, IV (1927), 29–38.

[50] Apart from editing the periodical *The Practical Husbandman and Planter* . . . (1733–34), Switzer's other writings (with dates of first editions) include *The Practical Fruit Gardener* . . . (London, 1724), *The Practical Kitchen Gardiner* . . . (London, 1727), *A Compendious Method for the Raising of the Italian Brocoli* . . . (London, 1728), *An Introduction to a General System of Hydrostaticks and Hydraulicks* . . . (London, 1729), *A Dissertation on the True Cythisus of the Ancients* . . . (London, 1731), *The Country Gentlemen's Companion* . . . (London, 1732), and *An Universal System of Water and Water-works* . . . (London, 1734).

For bibliographical data on these publications see e.g. L. W. Hanson, *Contemporary Printed Sources for British and Irish Economic History, 1701–1750* (Cambridge, 1963), Nos 2115, 2356, 3265, 3678, 3817, 4167, 4313, 4478, 4650; Blanche Henrey, *British Botanical and Horticultural Literature Before 1800* . . . (Oxford, 1975), III, 125–26 (Nos 1401–1416).

For Switzer see William A. Brogden, 'Stephen Switzer. "La Grand Manier"', in Willis, ed., *Furor Hortensis*, pp.21–30. This is based on Dr Brogden's 'Stephen Switzer and Garden Design in Britain in the Early Eighteenth Century' (Ph.D. thesis, University of Edinburgh, 1973). I am grateful to Dr Brogden for his advice on Switzer's career.

[51] Switzer, *Ichnographia Rustica* (1718), title-pages.

[52] Ibid. (1742), title-pages.

Gardens associated with Switzer, on varying authority, include those at Audley End (Essex), Baumanor (Leics), Blenheim, Bold Hall (Lancs), Breamore (Hants), Castle Howard, Caversham (Berks), Cirencester (Glos), Ebberston Lodge (Yorks), Eresby (Lincs), Eslington (Northumb), Exton (Rutland), Gateshead Park (Co Durham), Grimsthorpe (Lincs), Hampton Court (Herefs), Kensington, Leeswood (Flints), Marston (Som), Nostell Priory (Yorks), Rhual (Flints), Richings (Bucks), Rokeby (Yorks), Shaw House (Berks), Spye Park (Wilts), Stourhead (Wilts), and Wilton (Wilts).

The work of London and Wise is virtually inseparable. London was a man of considerable energy and, comments Switzer, became 'one of the most Illustrious and most Noble-spirited Genius's of this Age'. His initial apprenticeship under Rose at St James's Park was soon put to good use, and he developed an extensive practice, busily travelling round England in four 'circuits'. In the capital itself, London looked after the gardens of the Bishop of London, Henry Compton. 'It will perhaps be hardly believed in time to come', adds Switzer, 'that this one Person actually saw and gave Directions once or twice a Year in most of the Noblemens and Gentlemens Gardens in *England*.' While London was galloping up and down the country, spending many days and doubtless some nights on horseback, his colleague Wise 'manag'd Matters nearer home with a Dexterity and Care equal to his Character'. Switzer expresses it neatly: 'Mr. *London* and Mr. *Wise* being join'd Partners, and thus, as it were, both possesst of the Royal Favour, and the Purses of the King, Queen, and Nobility, left no Stone unturn'd to carry on their Designs.' The partnership of London and Wise owed much to the sponsorship of John Evelyn, whose Advertisement to his translation of Jean De La Quintinie's *Compleat Gard'ner* (1693) speaks eloquently in their praise. Apart from royal gardens at Greenwich, Hampton Court, Kensington, St James's Park, and Windsor, London and Wise's major designs were at Blenheim, Chatsworth, Longleat, and Melbourne. 'In truth', proclaims Switzer, they 'have deserv'd so much of the World, that 'tis but common Justice to transmit their Memory to Ages to come'.[53]

One of their joint enterprises was Brompton Park Nurseries, founded by George London in 1681 on a plot of over a hundred acres in South Kensington. Initially London had three partners, namely Moses Cook (retired 1689), John Field (*d.*1687), and Roger Looker (*d.*1685). Cook was gardener to the Earl of Essex at Cassiobury, Field to the Earl of Bedford at Bedford House and Woburn, and Looker to the Queen Mother at Somerset House. By 1687 Wise had become a partner. The success of the nurseries depended heavily upon the skill of the foremen engaged by London and Wise, starting with Leonard Meager, who published *The English Gardener* in 1670 and *The New Art of Gardening, with the Gardener's Almanack* in 1697. Meager was perhaps followed in his post by Switzer, and later (maybe in the early 1700's) London and Wise may have employed Charles Bridgeman as an apprentice at Brompton. When London died in 1714, Wise had to find partners to assist him with both the nurseries and the royal gardens, and William Smith and Joseph Carpenter promptly assumed control.[54]

No nursery was more admired than Brompton, and besides enjoying the patronage of the Crown it was often visited by such men as Evelyn. On 24 April 1694 Evelyn and his friend Richard Waller called there, and Waller was duly filled with 'admiration at the store

[53] This and earlier quotations in this paragraph are from *Nobleman's Recreation*, pp.60–61.

[54] In 1716 Bridgeman was still connected with the nurseries, as a note sent from Brompton Park on 16 August that year testifies (HEH, Stowe Repair Box, No.6). The Indenture of December 1714 – whereby Wise let parts of Brompton Park and its buildings to Smith and Carpenter for thirty-eight years – is discussed in Green, *Gardener to Queen Anne*, pp.214–15. Attached to the Indenture is a plan showing Wise's house at Brompton Park.

of rare plants & method he found in that noble nursery, & how well cultivated'.[55] Thousands of lime and hornbeam, box, and juniper, stood tended and graded and ready for dispatch. On display were trees of every kind for both 'humble boscage' and 'taller groves', including elms, planes, black cherries, and Constantinople chestnuts. For the flower garden there were seeds, bulbs, and cuttings, and for the kitchen garden seedlings of culinary herbs, salad vegetables, melons, and runner beans. An ancient wall from Cromwell's palace, more than half a mile long, had a collection of grape-vines trained on it. The value of the stock was enormous. In 1705 Bowack estimated in his *Antiquities of Middlesex* that if it were valued at a penny a plant it would be worth over £40,000.[56] 'The Planting and Raising of all sorts of Trees is so much due to this Undertaking', Switzer argues, 'that 'twill be hard for any of Posterity to lay their hands on a Tree in any of these Kingdoms that have not been a part of [London and Wise's] Care.'[57]

In 1685 London's passion for horticulture spurred him to go to Leiden to meet Paul Hermann, the leading cultivator of Cape plants.[58] Stronger than London's Dutch links, however, were those with France. He went to France twice and is said to have visited Chantilly, Fontainebleau, Vaux-le-Vicomte, and Versailles, and to have been shown the gardens by Le Nôtre himself. By the same token London and Wise's two books on horticulture – *The Compleat Gard'ner* (1699) and *The Retir'd Gard'ner* (1706) – are based on French originals.[59] Moreover the libraries left by the two men bear out their interest in Continental matters, containing as they do Dutch, French, and English gardening books.[60] Wise never visited a foreign country, but he did leave a collection of plates of Versailles as well as a 'Collect. of several Volumes of Draughts of Gardens in France, Italy, &c. curiously engrav'd'. Amongst these are ten plans of gardens abroad – three in France which

[55] E. S. De Beer, ed., *The Diary of John Evelyn* (London, 1955), v,176. Another visit to Brompton is recorded by Evelyn on 8 March 1703.

The naming of plants after nurserymen is common practice, and it is tempting to link Bridgeman and Brompton together when Loudon in his *Arboretum et Fruticetum Britannicum* . . . (London, 1838), II, 506, refers to such 'variegated hollies' as 'Bridgman's yellow'. I owe this to Mr Miles Hadfield. Dr William Brogden tells me that a box of loose papers at the Bedford Office, London, contains a bill of 13 February 1708 for trees from Brompton Park provided for Woburn, including '1 Bridgmans' priced at 5*s*.

In 1795 there was a nurseryman called Charles Bridgeman in Hertford. See John H. Harvey, 'Mid-Georgian Nurseries of the London Region', *Transactions of the London and Middlesex Archaeological Society*, XXVI (1975), 300.

[56] Pt. I (1705), p.21. See also Daniel Lysons, *The Environs of London* . . . (London, 1792–96), III, 171.

[57] Switzer, *Nobleman's Recreation*, p.61 After London's death the nurseries fell into decline: a man named Jeffries was there later in the eighteenth century, and in 1795 Lysons notes that 'the ground belongs at present to Messrs Gray and Wear'. By 1835 this was 'Messrs Gray and Son', and Brompton Park had been reduced to thirty acres. See Hadfield, *History of British Gardening*, pp.178, 269, 285, 347; John H. Harvey, 'The Putney Nursery: an Early Plant Centre', *Surrey Archaeological Collections*, LXIX (1973), 135; idem, *Early Nurserymen* (London and Chichester, 1974), 51–55, 71; idem, 'The Stocks Held by Early Nurseries', *Agricultural History Review*, XXII, pt.I (1974), 18–19; Lysons, *Environs of London*, III, 171.

[58] See James Britten, 'Some Early Cape Botanists and Collectors', *Journal of the Linnean Society (Botany)*, XLV (1920–22), 29–52, esp. pp.32–33; James E. Dandy, ed., *The Sloane Herbarium. An Annotated List* . . . (London, 1958), pp. 157–59.

[59] See Green, *Gardener to Queen Anne*, pp.173–78. Martin Lister, *A Journey to Paris in the Year 1698* (London, 1699), pp.37–39, 203, 210, mentions a catalogue which Lister brought back for George London from France.

[60] See *A Catalogue of the Library of George London, Esq., Late Chief Gardener to Her Majesty* (London, 1714), and 'A Catalogue of ye Books belonging to Mr Henry Wise of Brompton Park Feb. 1710/11', in Warwick CRO, Warwick, CR 341/300.

were designed or improved by Le Nôtre (Clagny, Saint-Cloud, and Saint-Germain-en-Laye), and the remainder in Austria, Denmark, Poland, Prussia, and Sweden.[61]

The impact of these diverse influences can best be gauged from the layout of Chatsworth in Derbyshire. Chatsworth, rebuilt by the 1st Duke of Devonshire between 1686 and 1707 with Talman and Archer as architects, benefited from the advice of George London from 1688. Six years later Wise joined him. Chatsworth gives us the best statement of London and Wise's garden style, a style which Horace Walpole characterized as being dominated by 'giants, animals, monsters, coats of arms and mottoes in yew, box and holly'.[62] There was more to it than that: classical precedent came into it. 'All the ingredients of Pliny's [gardens]', Walpole wrote, 'corresponded exactly with those laid out by London and Wise on Dutch principles.' Most of these 'ingredients' can be seen in Kip and Knyff's engraving of Chatsworth of about 1699, and many remain in Smith and Vivares's view of 1744 (*Plates 6, 7a*). Pliny, Walpole continues, 'talks of slopes, terrasses, a wilderness, shrubs methodically trimmed, a marble bason, pipes spouting water, a cascade falling into the bason, bay-trees, alternately planted with planes, and a straight walk, from whence issued others parted off by hedges of box, and apple-trees, with obelisks planted between every two'.[63]

It needs little imagination to transfer this description to Chatsworth, rightly considered the English Versailles. Charles Cotton in *The Wonders of the Peake* (1681) includes Chatsworth as the seventh and last 'wonder', and Celia Fiennes and Daniel Defoe each devote several pages to describing its beauties. Writing in her disarming, breathless way, Fiennes tells us that Chatsworth has

> a large Parke and severall fine Gardens one without another with gravell walkes and squairs of grass with stone statues in them and in the middle of each Garden is a large fountaine full of images [of] Sea Gods and Dolphins and Sea Horses which are full of pipes which spout out water in the bason and spouts all about the gardens.[64]

Numerous other 'Curiosityes' attract her attention as she wanders along the terraces and up and down the steps, and serve to remind us of just how widespread are the sources of the Chatsworth gardens. Predominantly Italian are the high-cut hedges, the statuary, the terracing, and the use of the *piano nobile;* predominantly French are the long straight avenues and canals stretching almost to infinity, the *jets d'eau*, fanciful parterres, and geometric bosquets, the overall flatness of the site; predominantly Dutch or English are the intimate kitchen or herb-gardens close to the house. Garden buildings are few, and none possesses the *brio* of an Italian or French *pavillon*. Nor has Chatsworth the clarity of a Herrenhausen (*Plate 7b*). Kip and Knyff's bird's eye views in *Britannia Illustrata* show that Chatsworth's layout was similar to many in England during the early 1700's. Not that

[61] Green, *Gardener to Queen Anne*, pp.17, 18 and n.

[62] Chase, *Horace Walpole: Gardenist*, p.24. For London and Wise at Chatsworth see Green, *Gardener to Queen Anne*, pp.33–37; Francis W. Thompson, *A History of Chatsworth. Being a Supplement to the Sixth Duke of Devonshire's Handbook* (London and New York, 1949), pp.61, 67, 85; idem, *Chatsworth. A Short History. With a Tour of the House and Gardens* (London, 1951), pp.108–18.

[63] Chase, *Horace Walpole: Gardenist*, pp.7–8.

[64] Christopher Morris, ed., *The Journeys of Celia Fiennes*, 2nd edn (London, 1949), p.97.

Chatsworth had not a special place. Daniel Defoe reminds us of Marshal Camille Tallard's comment to the Duke of Devonshire, following the Frenchman's stay there, that 'when he should give his master the King of France the history of his seven years captivity in England, he would leave out those three days which he had spent so agreeably with his grace, in seeing the finest palace in the world'.[65]

Bridgeman

The reaction to the rigidity of layouts such as Chatsworth's was bound up in the English rejection of French dominance in the arts and in politics: it was an endorsement of liberty and tolerance against tyranny and oppression. As Pope wrote confidently in his *Essay on Criticism* (1711):

But Critic-learning flourish'd most in France:
The rules a nation, born to serve, obeys;
And Boileau still in right of Horace sways.
But we, brave Britons, foreign laws despis'd,
And kept unconquer'd, and unciviliz'd. (ll.712–16)

Horace Walpole gives Bridgeman a prominent place in these changes and, once having described their style, demonstrates little patience with London and Wise. 'Absurdity could go no farther', he goes on, 'and the tide turned.'[66] And with the turn of the tide came Bridgeman. Walpole warms to his subject:

> Bridgman, the next fashionable designer of gardens, was far more chaste; and whether from good sense, or that the nation had been struck and reformed by [Pope's] admirable paper in the Guardian, No 173, he banished verdant sculpture, and did not even revert to the square precision of the foregoing age. He enlarged his plans, disdained to make every division tally to its opposite, and though he still adhered much to strait walks with high clipped hedges, they were only his great lines; the rest he diversified by wilderness, and with loose groves of oak, though still within surrounding hedges.

Occasionally Bridgeman became bolder, and Walpole remarks that he has observed at Gubbins in Hertfordshire those 'many detached thoughts, that strongly indicate the dawn of modern taste'. As Bridgeman's 'reformation gained footing, he ventured farther, and in the royal garden at Richmond dared to introduce cultivated fields, and even morsels of a forest appearance', although he still retained walks that 'stretched out of one into another without intermission'. By this time Bridgeman had led others to break loose from 'rigid

[65] Daniel Defoe, *A Tour Through the Whole Island of Great Britain*, ed. D. C. Browning and G. D. H. Cole, 2nd edn (London, 1962), II, 177.

Tallard, one of Marlborough's prisoners of war from the battle of Blenheim, spent from 1707 to 1711 in England living at Newdigate House (Notts), where London and Wise laid out the garden. It is illustrated and described at the end of Vol.II of *The Retir'd Gard'ner* (1706). See Green, *Gardener to Queen Anne*, pp. xi, 96, 125–27, 174; pl.39.

[66] This and ensuing quotations from Walpole are in Chase, *Horace Walpole: Gardenist*, pp.24–25.

symmetry': by so doing, we might add, they had also broken loose from the crippling cost of laying out and maintaining their estates in a formal manner, and had satisfied their need for expanses of turf interspersed with coverts for fox hunting. As James Thomson put it in his poem *Liberty*: 'Taste, never idly working, saves expense' (pt. v, l.695).[67]

Walpole continues by crediting Bridgeman with a crucial innovation:

> But the capital stroke, the leading step to all that has followed, was (I believe the first thought was Bridgman's) the destruction of walls for boundaries, and the invention of fossès – an attempt then deemed so astonishing, that the common people called them Ha! Ha's! to express their surprize at finding a sudden and unperceived check to their walk.

Shortly afterwards Walpole explains specifically why he regards the ha-ha as so important:

> I call a sunk fence the leading step, for these reasons. No sooner was this simple enchantment made, than levelling, mowing and rolling, followed. The contiguous ground of the park without the sunk fence was to be harmonized with the lawn within; and the garden in its turn was to be set free from its prim regularity, that it might assort with the wilder country without.

The principle of the ha-ha was to remain constant as designers toyed with different means of achieving the same effect.[68] So as 'nature was taken into the plan . . . every step that was made, pointed out new beauties and inspired new ideas'. The impact of the ha-ha was decisive. 'How rich, how gay, how picturesque the face of the country!' exclaimed Walpole. 'The demolition of walls laying open each improvement, every journey is made through a succession of pictures.'[69]

It is well known that this revolution did not occur overnight. Falda's juxtaposition of *boschetti* and formal planting in the Farnese Gardens was but one indication of the widespread popularity in Renaissance Italy of the enclosure of rustic countryside within the confines of the garden (*Plate 3b*).[70] Elsewhere on the Continent this feature was accepted only gradually. In 1628 we have Joseph Furttenbach the Elder's plates in his *Architectura*

[67] See recently Denis Lambin, 'Pleasure with Profit. Some Aspects of Landscape Gardening', *Garden History*, III, No.2 (Spring 1975), 29–36.
Bridgeman's style is analysed below in the Conclusion, esp. pp.130–133.

[68] Sometimes they were just ditches, sometimes ditches with one or two brick or stone walls (or a fence) in them. Occasionally the ditches were filled with water.
For Bridgeman and the ha-ha see Peter Willis, 'From Desert to Eden: Charles Bridgeman's "Capital Stroke"', *Burlington Magazine*, CXV (March 1973), 150–57. More generally see Miles Hadfield, 'History of the Ha-Ha', *C.Life*, CXXXIII (30 May 1963), 1261–62. There seems to be no connection between Bridgeman and Ha Ha Road, London, S.E.18, nor does Jennifer Dawson's novel *The Ha-Ha* (London, 1961) deal with anything of a Bridgemanic kind.

[69] Chase, *Horace Walpole: Gardenist*, pp.25, 36.

[70] See esp. Elisabeth MacDougall, '*Ars Hortulorum*: Sixteenth-Century Garden Iconography and Literary Theory in Italy', in David R. Coffin, ed., *The Italian Garden* (Washington, D.C., 1972), pp.39–59. Perhaps more important, as Dr John Dixon Hunt points out to me, many Italian sites seem to have a natural ha-ha.

Civilis (*Plate 8*),[71] and later in the seventeenth century French engravers and poets took up the theme. Thus Rapin in *Hortorum Libri Quattuor* indulges in a Horatian vision of life

'Far from all noise, all vain applause', and of delightful hours spent

> upon the grassie bank,
> For which no art, but nature we must thank.[72]

Happy is the man, says Rapin,

> who in a countrey Seat,
> From Storms of Business finds a calm Retreat...
> Where all around delightful Landskips lie,
> And pleasing Prospects entertain the Eye.[73]

Echoing Rapin, Dézallier D'Argenville observes in his *Theory and Practice of Gardening* that the designer should 'make Art give place to Nature', and that parts of a garden 'ought to be so placed, that one might think them to be set there by the Author of Nature'. Each site, he says, 'requires a new Turn of Thought, and a Compliance with Nature, so as carefully to redress what is defective, and improve what is happily placed'.[74]

Dézallier D'Argenville occupies a special place in our discussion because of his description of a ha-ha in 1709, the earliest of its kind. The origins of the ha-ha may lie in medieval fortifications, moats, and canals, or more specifically in the *saut de loup* which surrounded French kitchen-gardens. During the 1600's there were ha-has at the Grand Trianon at Versailles and elsewhere in France, whilst in England the first ha-ha may have been constructed by the French gardener Beaumont at Levens from 1692.[75] Both the French and the English editions of *The Theory and Practice of Gardening* describe and illustrate ha-has: there is a plan with two terraces, one at the top centre and the other at the far left, which (to use James's translation) are 'terminated by an Opening, which the *French* call a *Claire-voïe,* or an Ah, Ah, with a dry Ditch at the Foot of it' (*Plate 9*). Later in the volume ha-has are contrasted with grills:

71 Pl.13. See Senta Dietzel, *Furttenbachs Gartenentwürfe* (Nürnberg, 1928), *passim.* It is no accident that Furttenbach is well-known for his stage designs, and that he studied in Italy at the same time as Inigo Jones. See George R. Kernodle, 'Joseph Furttenbach, the Elder, 1591–1667', in Barnard Hewitt, ed., *The Renaissance Stage: Documents of Serlio, Sabbattini and Furttenbach* (Coral Gables, Florida, 1958), pp.178–251. The acknowledged close connection between Roman gardens and theatrical architecture is endorsed by such statements as Vitruvius' that the recognized setting for satyric plays was 'made up of trees, caves and mountains to imitate a landscape'. See Masson, *Italian Gardens*, p.24.

72 René Rapin, *Of Gardens. Four Books. First Written in Latine Verse by Renatus Rapinus . . .*, trans. John Evelyn (London, 1672), pp.121, 123.

73 René Rapin, *Of Gardens. A Latin Poem. In Four Books,* trans. James Gardiner, 2nd edn (London, ?1718), pp.106–7.

74 Antoine Joseph Dézallier D'Argenville, *The Theory and Practice of Gardening . . .*, trans. John James (London, 1712). Cf. Virgil, *Aeneid*, v, 95.

75 For Sir James Graham, documented in MS letters and accounts at Levens, brought to my attention by Mr and Mrs Robin Bagot. See Annette Bagot, 'Monsieur Beaumont and Colonel Grahme. The Making of a Garden, 1689–1710', *Garden History*, III, No.4 (Autumn 1975), 66–78.

> GRILLS of Iron are very necessary Ornaments in the Lines of Walks, to extend the View, and to shew the Country to Advantage. At present we frequently make Thorough-Views, call'd *Ah, Ah,* which are Openings in the Walls, without Grills, to the very Level of the Walks, with a large and deep Ditch at the Foot of them, lined on both Sides to sustain the Earth, and prevent the getting over, which surprizes the Eye upon coming near it, and makes one cry, *Ah! Ah!* from whence it takes its Name. This Sort of Opening is, on some Occasions, to be preferred, for that it does not shut up the Prospect, as the Bars of a Grill do.[76]

Even so, as is evident from the accompanying plate, Dézallier D'Argenville saw the 'Prospect' as no more than an incident in a geometric layout, and he makes no mention of the idea of introducing wilder scenes into the garden which had already become fashionable.

In England, indeed, as early as 1624 Henry Wotton had deduced that as 'Fabriques should bee *regular,* so Gardens should bee *irregular,* or at least cast into a very wilde *Regularitie*'.[77] Then in 1685 Temple referred in *Upon the Gardens of Epicurus* (1699) to the Chinese delight in gardens with *sharawadgi*, based on 'forms wholly irregular' and 'extraordinary dispositions of nature'.[78] In 1700 – under the influence of Worlidge's *Systema Agriculturae* (1669) and *Systema Horti-culturae* (1677), and Burnet's *Theory of the Earth* (1684–90) – Timothy Nourse brought out his book *Campania Fœlix,* containing an essay 'Of a Country House'[79] in which the author recommends that a seat be set 'not amongst Enclosures, but in a champaign, open Country'. A river in the distance, we are told, 'would much contribute to the Beauty and Prospect of the Seat'.[80] Nourse divides the garden into three sections, and urges that the 'Third Region or Wilderness be Natural-Artificial; that is, let all things be dispos'd with that cunning, as to deceive us into a belief of a real Wilderness or Thicket.' Beyond the garden 'let there be planted Walks of Trees to adorn the Landskip . . . and thus at length the Prospect may terminate on Mountains, Woods, or such Views as the Scituation will admit of'.[81] Therefore when Shaftesbury in *The Moralists* of 1709, and Addison and Pope in articles in the *Tatler*, the *Spectator*, and the *Guardian* of 1710–13, made their oft-quoted pronouncements on art, nature, and the garden, they were popularizing what had frequently been said before.[82]

[76] Dézallier D'Argenville, *Theory and Practice of Gardening,* trans. James, pp.28 (describing pl.3A), 77. Dézallier D'Argenville thought of a ha-ha as being a moat without water, i.e. as revetted on both sides.

[77] Henry Wotton, *The Elements of Architecture* . . . (London, 1624), p.109.

[78] Samuel Holt Monk, ed., *Five Miscellaneous Essays by Sir William Temple* (Ann Arbor, 1963), pp.29–30. See also 'A Note on Sharawaggi' (written in collaboration with S. Lang), in Nikolaus Pevsner, *Studies in Art, Architecture and Design* (London, 1968), I, 102–7; Eleanor Von Erdberg, *Chinese Influence on European Garden Structures,* ed. Bremer Whidden Pond (Cambridge, Mass., 1936), p.37; Sirén, *China and Gardens of Europe,* pp.15–19; Hugh Honour, *Chinoiserie. The Vision of Cathay* (London, 1961), pp.144–45. For Temple's estate at Moor Park in Surrey see recently Ruth Isabel Ross, 'Statesman Into Gardener', *C. Life,* CLV (17 January 1974), 76–77.

[79] Timothy Nourse, *Campania Fœlix. Or, a Discourse of the Benefits and Improvements of Husbandry* . . . (London, 1700), pp.297–344.

[80] Ibid., p.300.

[81] Ibid., p.322.

[82] See Nikolaus Pevsner, 'The Genesis of the Picturesque', in *Studies in Art, Architecture and Design,* I, 78–101.

Switzer

Switzer was the earliest British professional gardener to write about the new style, and his books give an added dimension to the theories of poets and other men of letters. Switzer's thinking follows Nourse in being derived from the creed of *beatus ille*.[83] Much of the enjoyment of country life, he believes, may be attributed to 'the rural dweller's intellectual appreciation of nature as a harmonious scheme contrived by a benevolent creator.'[83] The pleasure given by rural thoughts is virtuous, not to say pious. Effectively Switzer implies that nature stirs the imagination more than art, if only because it leads the mind to ponder the system of Creation and the divine art of God – a system which cannot be truly represented by 'Clipt Plants, Flowers, and other trifling Decorations'.[84] Switzer argues that a happy country life pre-supposes that the house will be placed in an open, rural setting, and divides his layouts into the 'specific garden' (to use Walpole's phrase) near the house where 'a little Regularity is allow'd', and the 'rural and extensive garden' beyond it where the designer 'ought to pursue Nature'.[85] As the owner walks from one to the other 'it will not be unpleasant for him to fall into natural Coppices, Paddocks, Corn Fields, and a little Gravel or Sand Walk looks there as pleasant as any thing'.[86] For, Switzer adds, 'whatever some may think of Magnificence, there is an inexpressible Pleasure in these Natural Twinings, and private Walks to a quiet, thoughtful, studious Mind'.[87] By use of 'Serpentine Meanders' the designer can heighten the effects of variety,[88] and indeed Switzer urges him to use 'as many Twinings and Windings as his *Villa* will allow'.[89] All the while the gardener ought to let 'his Design submit to Nature, and not Nature to his Design'.[90] Taking his cue from Addison, Switzer acknowledges his debt to Homer, Virgil, and Ovid. 'From these three and from some others of our own Time, and Country; the ingenuous Designer as well as Poet, may collect noble Thoughts, and Ideas of things, *from the first what is Great, from the second what is Beautiful, and from the last what is Strange*.'[91] In reality Switzer's ideas were not so advanced as it may seem, as the geometric plates in his publications testify. Two illustrations from *Ichnographia Rustica* indicate how misleading his titles can be – 'The Plan of a Forest or Rural Garden' (*Plate 10*), and the

[83] See Maren-Sofie Røstvig, *The Happy Man. Studies in the Metamorphoses of a Classical Ideal,* II (Oslo and Oxford, 1958), 75–111; 2nd edn, II (Oslo and New York, 1971), 38–47. Broader studies are Peter Dixon, *The World of Pope's Satires. An Introduction to the 'Epistles' and 'Imitations of Horace'* (London, 1968), pp.63–89; A. James Sambrook, 'The English Lord and the Happy Husbandman', *Studies on Voltaire and the Eighteenth Century*, LVII (1967), 1357–75. For the literary context of these and subsequent ideas see Edward G. Malins, *English Landscaping and Literature, 1660–1840* (London, 1966). Professor Røstvig's investigations are taken further by E. M. W. Tillyard, *Some Mythical Elements in English Literature* (London, 1961), pp.72–107.

[84] Switzer, *Nobleman's Recreation,* p. xiii. Cf. *Tatler,* No.218 (31 August 1710), commented on by Richmond P. Bond, *The Tatler. The Making of a Literary Journal* (Cambridge, Mass., 1971), pp.122–23.

[85] Switzer, *Ichnographia Rustica* (1718), III, 5–6. Switzer constantly reminds his readers of the economy of his proposals.

[86] Ibid., III, ix.

[87] Ibid., III, 88.

[88] Ibid., III, 47.

[89] Ibid., III, 6.

[90] Ibid., II, 201.

[91] Ibid., III, 7. Virgil's ideas had a widespread effect on agricultural technique. This 'Virgilian husbandry' was of course supported by Switzer, but attacked by Jethro Tull. See G. E. Fussell, *Jethro Tull. His Influence on Mechanized Agriculture* (Reading, 1973), pp.56–65.

plan of Bathurst's estate at Richings, near Colnbrook in Buckinghamshire, which Switzer claims was laid out 'upon the Plan of the *Ferme Ornée*, and the Villa's of the Ancients' (*Plate 11*).[92]

Implicit in Switzer's comments is the need to use a ha-ha to achieve his effects. He urges as a matter of cardinal importance that 'all the adjacent Country be laid open to View, and that the Eye should not be bounded by high Walls'. Instead he would, wherever practicable, flatten the walls and throw the garden open 'to the unbounded Felicities of distant Prospect, and the expansive Volumes of Nature herself'. By means of an 'unaffected manner of Fencing' it will 'look as if the adjacent Country were all a Garden'.[93] And a cheaper garden you could never find. Neither James nor Dézallier D'Argenville had shown a section through a ha-ha, and it was left to Switzer to take the lead. In his *Ichnographia Rustica* of 1718 he included an engraving which demonstrates how earth excavated for a ditch *outside* the garden wall can be used to build up a terrace *inside* it. The ditch, Switzer adds, 'is by the *French* call'd *la Fossé*, from the *Latin, Fossa*, a Pit'.[94] In spite of his admiration for Bridgeman, Switzer does not give him credit for introducing the ha-ha into England, and instead notes enigmatically that its use 'has not been much practis'd by us in *England*, and was first deliver'd to us by a Gentleman, that is deservedly honour'd with some considerable Posts belonging to the Architectural Province, *&* *c.* in his Majesty's Works'.[95] As Bridgeman did not become Royal Gardener until ten years after the appearance of *Ichnographia Rustica*, and Kent was still an unknown painter in Italy, it is more than likely that Switzer was referring indirectly to Sir John Vanbrugh in his capacity as Surveyor of Greenwich Hospital, Surveyor of Gardens and Waters, and Comptroller of the Works to George I. Vanbrugh must have come across the ha-ha or its equivalent in his military exploits in France, and by 1718 he and Bridgeman had probably used ha-has in their work together at Blenheim, Eastbury, and Stowe.[96]

[92] 1718 and 1742 edns, III, pl.35, described on pp.50–51; and pl.39 of 1742 edn, described on pp.9–11 of the Appendix, where Switzer notes the *fermes ornées* at Dawley and Abb's Court or Abscourt in Surrey, owned by George Montagu Dunk, 2nd Earl of Halifax, and leased to the Brownes. Several members of the Browne family were known to Pope, and Antony Browne contributed to Pope's grotto 'several Humming Birds and their Nests' (*Pope Correspondence*, IV, 451. Pope to Mallet [?1743]). Abb's Court appears in Pope's *Imitations of Horace* (1737), 2nd epistle, bk 2, ll. 232–33. See also James M. Osborn, ed., *Joseph Spence. Observations, Anecdotes, and Characters of Books and Men Collected from Conversation* (Oxford, 1966), I, 401–2 (No.1048).

[93] Switzer, *Nobleman's Recreation*, pp. xiv, xxvi, xxviii. On pp. xxviii–xxix, Switzer traces back his ideas to the Ancients and to the Chinese, as interpreted by Sir William Temple. Switzer finds supporting evidence in the woods at Castle Howard, Cassiobury, and New Park.

[94] Switzer, *Ichnographia Rustica* (1718), II, 163–65, describing pl.26. The 1742 edn of *Ichnographia Rustica* gives this detail the title of 'The Profile of a side Terrass Walk & Fossee'. Here, as elsewhere in English texts, there is confusion between the French words for ditch, i.e. *la fosse* and *le fossé*. Switzer's terrace enables us to 'look either forward or backward, and view with Pleasure the rude and distant Scenes of Nature, as well as the more elaborate Works of Art' (p.163).

After 1718, the next occasion on which Switzer shows a ha-ha (not with a wall, but a 'Pallisade' in a ditch with two sloping sides) is in his *Introduction to a General System of Hydrostaticks and Hydraulicks* (1729), I, pl.3, described on pp.129–33, and entitled 'Profile lines for a Reservoir Canal & c'. In 1742 there followed Switzer's plan of Richings with its ha-ha (indicated by the letter 'N') at the end of the canal, to the left in *Plate 11*.

[95] Switzer, *Ichnographia Rustica* (1718), II, 164.

[96] Switzer invokes Vanbrugh and Marlborough's military experience when he writes, apropos the bastion 'after the ancient *Roman* Manner' at Blenheim: 'I need say little as to the reducing Fortification into Gardening; 'tis what will, I believe, be very pleasing to all the martial Genius's of our Country; and it seems somewhat of Wonder, that it has not been made Use of before now'. See ibid. (1718), II, 174, describing pl.27.

Switzer's classical allusions were taken further by Robert Castell in his *Villas of the Ancients Illustrated* (1728), with its reconstruction of the gardens of Laurentinum and Tuscum based on two letters written by the younger Pliny.[97] Dedicated to Burlington, and perhaps sponsored by him, this book was a logical outcome of Burlington and Kent's experiences in Italy, specifically their familiarity with the canvasses of Claude and Poussin and their School, with the Roman Campagna, and with such gardens as those of the Villa Brenzone at San Vigilio. At Tivoli they may have seen Hadrian's Villa and the Temple of the Sibyl.[98] Engravings of Italian villas, palaces, and gardens were circulated widely. Taking up one of Switzer's themes, Burlington was convinced that the 'Rules of the Ancients' (for whom, adds Castell, 'Your Lordship has on all Occasions manifested the greatest Regard') advocated the landscape style, an interpretation which is endorsed by Castell's plates. The layout of Tuscum, for instance, has two areas of open countryside with loosely-knit walks, temples, waterscape, and clumps of trees (*Plate 12*): at the top left is 'The *Pratulum* or little Meadow', whilst at the top right is 'The Imitation of the natural Face of some Country'. Castell points out that the Romans had three ways of laying out gardens: the first was 'a rough Manner' with irregularly-placed plants and trees, the second 'a Manner of laying out the Ground and Plantations of Gardens by the Rule and Line', and the third 'a close Imitation of Nature' in which 'tho' the Parts are disposed with the greatest Art, the Irregularity is still preserved'. This last, called *Imitatio Ruris,* was the most accomplished style. To Roman authority could be added the Chinese. For, continues Castell, 'the Accounts we have' tell us that *Imitatio Ruris* is 'the present Manner of Designing in China'. Castell explains at length that Pliny's garden was a mixture of all three idioms. Burlington's endorsement of the Chinese was doubtless sparked off by Temple, Addison, and Switzer, and by the rising taste in Italy for *chinoiserie*.[99] It was reflected again in his ownership of such engravings as Father Matteo Ripa's of the Imperial Gardens at Jehol of 1713 (*Plate 13a*),[100] and such books as Du Halde's four-volume *Description . . . de l'empire de la Chine et de la Tartarie chinoise* (1735), and Lange's *Journal de la résidence du Sieur Lange . . . à la cour de la Chine* (1726).[101] The implications, echoed by Thomson in *Liberty*, were that Roman and Chinese gardens were each produced by republics in which freedom flourished. It was a short step to the promotion of temples

[97] The plans of Laurentinum and Tuscum are between pp.16–17 and 126–27 respectively, and the key texts are on pp.116–18. Cf. the modern translation of the two letters which form the basis of Castell's volume in Betty Radice, trans., *The Letters of the Younger Pliny* (London, 1969), pp.75–79 (pt. ii, letter 17), 139–44 (pt. v, letter 6). For a comparison between Castell's interpretation and those of other authors see Helen H. Tanzer, *The Villas of Pliny the Younger* (New York, 1924), pp.54–56. A detailed analysis is in Marianne Fischer, 'Die frühen Rekonstruktionen der Landhäuser Plinius' des Jüngeren' (Ph.D. thesis, Free University of Berlin, 1962), pp.91–121.

Although Walpole believed that the gardens of Pliny corresponded with the formal layouts of London and Wise, he has no qualms about claiming classical authority for the 'modern taste' and thereby supporting Switzer and Castell. See Chase, *Horace Walpole: Gardenist*, esp. pp.8–9, 43–47, 50.

[98] See Masson, *Italian Gardens*, pp.24–26, 60, 125.

[99] See Hugh Honour, 'Capricci Cinesi. The Vogue for Chinoiserie in Italy', *Connoisseur Year Book* (1962), pp.42–49.

[100] See Rudolf Wittkower, 'English Neo-Palladianism, the Landscape Garden, China, and the Enlightenment', in *Palladio and English Palladianism* (London, 1974), pp.175–90. Ripa's views are examined in Basil Gray, 'Lord Burlington and Father Ripa's Chinese Engravings', *British Museum Quarterly*, XXII (February 1960), 40–43. There are thirty-six views in the set, and Burlington owned thirty-four.

[101] Chatsworth, Derbys, Devonshire Collection, MS Catalogue of Burlington's Library at Chiswick, fos 13, 57.

and ruins as part of a landscape garden, as Langley demonstrated in his *New Principles of Gardening* which came out in the same year as Castell's volume (*Plate 13b*).[102]

It is against this background of patronage and experiment that Bridgeman emerged.[103] As he discovered, satisfying the demands of the new style was by no means easy: landscape gardening had its own discipline, and its earliest manifestations were as artificial in their irregularity as the formal layouts had been in their regularity. Or, as Horace Walpole noted in a familiar sentence in the *World*, 'there is not a citizen who does not take more pains to torture his acre and a half into irregularities, than he formerly would have employed to make it as formal as his cravat'.[104] To Burlington and others the authority of antiquity, whether Roman or Chinese, had an inescapable appeal. As Pope exhorted in his *Essay on Criticism*:

> Learn hence from ancient rules a just esteem;
> To copy nature is to copy them. (ll.139–40)

However in order to 'copy nature' the sister arts as well as the 'ancient rules' had to be invoked. Walpole again puts it in a nutshell. 'Poetry, Painting & Gardening, or the science of Landscape', he writes, 'will forever by men of Taste be deemed Three Sisters, or *the Three New Graces* who dress and adorn Nature'.[105] The fascination of the Bridgemanic style rests partly upon its role as one of these '*Three New Graces*', and its relationship with painting and poetry.[106] By mid-century the battle joined in Bridgeman's day had been won. 'It is the peculiar happiness of this age', enthused the *World* in 1755, 'to see . . . regularity banished, prospects opened, the country called in, nature rescued and improved, and art decently concealing herself under her own perfections'.[107]

[102] For Langley see Alistair Rowan, 'Batty Langley's Gothic', in Giles Robertson and George Henderson, eds, *Studies in Memory of David Talbot Rice* (Edinburgh, 1975), pp.197–215. The genealogy of Gothic buildings in the English landscape garden is traced to Dr. J. Mordaunt Crook's Introduction to the reprint of Charles L. Eastlake, *A History of the Gothic Revival* (Leicester, 1970), esp. pp.34–57.

[103] Apart from sources already mentioned, see B. Sprague Allen, *Tides in English Taste (1619–1800). A Background for the Study of Literature* (Cambridge, Mass., 1937); Johannes Dobai, *Die Kunstliteratur des Klassizismus und der Romantik in England* (Berne, 1974 et seq.); and the relevant sections in Joseph Burke, *English Art, 1714–1800*, Oxford History of English Art, Vol.XI (Oxford, 1976).

[104] No.6 (8 February 1753), p.34.

[105] Paget J. Toynbee, ed., *Satirical Poems Published Anonymously by William Mason, with Notes by Horace Walpole, Now First Printed from His Manuscript* (Oxford, 1926), p.43. This eulogy appears in Walpole's notes on William Mason's *An Heroic Epistle to Sir William Chambers . . .* (London, 1773).

For essays on Walpole's 'sister arts' see John Dixon Hunt, *The Figure in the Landscape: Poetry, Painting, and Gardening During the Eighteenth Century* (Baltimore and London, 1977), which appeared too late for me to use.

[106] Throughout this book I use the epithet 'Bridgemanic' in preference to any other on the authority of Pope's allusion to a 'Bridgemannick Theatre' when writing to Edward Harley on 22 March 1726. See *Pope Correspondence*, II, 372.

[107] No.118 (3 April 1755), p.709.

Chapter 1

Biography

The protégés who threaded their way through the ranks of eighteenth-century British nobility, adding professional expertise to amateur taste, were mostly men of humble stock. Landscape designers were no exception and Kent, Capability Brown, and Charles Bridgeman each fell into this category.[1] If lack of noble birth were a limitation, Bridgeman did not acknowledge it, and he made friends of people whose backgrounds and interests were wide-ranging, including Whigs and Tories, Protestants and Catholics. Recognition by fellow-artists, and by Court and nobility alike, indicated the rising importance both of Bridgeman himself and of the role of landscapist.[2] As Bridgeman's prestige increased, and he took to calling himself 'Esquire', he moved to a fine but modest house in fashionable Westminster. This was built in 1722–23 as one of a terrace of six, and the direct contractor was John Mist. Bridgeman must have taken an especial interest in watching building operations, for Mist was his brother-in-law.[3]

Family and Property

Bridgeman's domestic life remains obscure until 2 May 1717 when he married Sarah Mist at Gray's Inn Chapel.[4] Charles and Sarah had at least seven children, of whom four survived infancy.[5] Of those that lived, the eldest was Charles (baptized 12 March 1719), followed by Sarah (baptized 18 February 1720), Elizabeth (baptized 26 November 1724), and Ann (baptized 13 November 1731); of the children that died prematurely, the eldest was John (baptized 28 November 1723), two of whose sisters, Charlotte and Caroline, died in 1729.[6] As for these children's grandparents, the Royal Gardener's father may have preceded his son as Harley's gardener at Wimpole in Cambridgeshire, dying there in 1726,[7] whilst Sarah Bridgeman's father, John Mist, was a paviour of St Anne's Parish in Westminster who died sometime before 1716. Apart from her brother John, Sarah had a sister Elizabeth, who was married to the master plumber George Devall, or Duvall. Although

[1] For discussion of Bridgeman's origins, and a family tree, see below Appendix I, pp.148–50. I am grateful to Mr Malcolm Pinhorn for genealogical advice, and for providing me with the references from the Bernau Index.

[2] See the Introduction to Humphry Repton, *Sketches and Hints on Landscape Gardening* . . . (London, 1794), pp.xiii–xvi.

[3] Legal battles involving the Mists are considered below in Appendix I, pp.149–50.

[4] Bridgeman was of Kensington Parish at the time, Sarah of St Andrew's in Holborn. See SG, Boyd's Marriage Index (Middlesex 1701–25); Joseph Foster, *The Register of Admissions to Gray's Inn, 1521–1889. Together With the Register of Marriages in Gray's Inn Chapel, 1695–1754* (London, 1889), pp. xxi, lxxi. The status of the parties is not given.

[5] Basic information is taken from their wills. See below Appendices VII, VIII, pp.169–71

no such post existed, the younger John Mist was virtually Royal Paviour,[8] and he and Bridgeman met often in connection with various undertakings and, apart from royal works, were together at Wimpole, Down Hall, Briggens, and Carshalton.[9] It is likely also that they collaborated on the layout of St James's Square in London. From 1723 Mist rented a farm on Harley's Marylebone Estate and continued there as a tenant until he died.[10] In contrast with the Bridgemans, the Mists seem to have been wealthy enough. Recording John Mist's death on 15 April 1737, Boyer comments that Mist was reported to be worth £50,000, having worked as 'Paviour to Royal Palaces, Paviour to the Office of Works, Slater, Car-Taker, Thatcher, Scavenger, Foundation-digger, & c.' He was, the writer adds, 'a great Undertaker and a slave to Business'.[11]

[6] The daughter Sarah was still a spinster in 1743, but by 1746 her sister Elizabeth was married to Philip Price; John died before 1738; Charlotte was baptized on 21 November 1725 and buried on 4 March 1729; Caroline was buried on 6 October 1729. In her will of 1743 the elder Sarah makes no mention of her son Charles, though she makes bequests to her daughters Sarah, Elizabeth, and Ann; so he may have been dead by then.

At this time the Parishes of Westminster and Kensington each had only one Parish Church, called St James's and St Mary Abbots respectively.

The registers at St James's Westminster (now St James's Piccadilly) give us the dates of the baptisms of John, Charlotte, and Ann. I am grateful to the one-time Rector, the late Rev. J. S. Brewis, for arranging to have these records examined. See G. E. Adams, 'Extracts from the Parish Registers of St James's, Westminster', *Topographer and Genealogist*, III (1957), 491–503; M. E. C. Walcott, *A Handbook for the Parish of St James, Westminster* (London, 1850), pp.13–17.

The records of St Mary Abbots Kensington include the baptism of Charles, and the burials of Charlotte and Caroline. The one-time Vicar, afterwards Bishop of Gibraltar, the late Rt Rev. S. A. H. Eley, kindly had these registers searched.

The baptism of the daughter Sarah Bridgeman is in the baptism register of St Anne's Church, Soho, kept in Westminster City Library, where her birth on 3 February is recorded. Mr. K. C. Harrison and Dr. Alistair Rowan kindly told me of this.

[7] No relevant entry appears in the burial registers at Wimpole between 1700 and 1750 (Pinhorn).

The distinction between Bridgeman 'Senior' and 'Junior' is discussed in Chase, *Horace Walpole: Gardenist*, p.139. In Harley's and Prior's papers in the BL the identity of each is not clear. See BL, Add MS 18240 (Harley Papers), fos 47–48. In BL, Loan 29/317 (Portland Papers), fos 175v, 184v, there are references to 'Mr: Bridgman, Senior', and on fo.11v to 'Charles Bridgeman, Junior' who (together with Thornhill and Wanley) was noted as absent from Prior's funeral in 1721 but who was given a mourning ring. This must be the Royal Gardener, as his son Charles would then be only between 3 and 4 years old. Mourning rings were also given to Dahl, Gibbs, and Wootton, all of whom were present.

[8] John Mist Junior married Elizabeth Carter of St Albans (Herts) in Gray's Inn Chapel on 2 October 1711. See SG, Boyd's Marriage Index (Middlesex 1701–25); Foster, *Register of Gray's Inn*, p. lxx. In 1738 a John Devall married a Sarah Mist at St Anne's Soho. See SG, Boyd's Marriage Index (Middlesex 1726–51).

[9] Mist's royal work appears in the minutes of the Board of Works from 1715–37, in e.g. PRO, Works 4/1–4/8, *passim*; Works 5/56, *passim*. Payments to him for Kew are in the Duchy of Cornwall Office, London, MS Household Accounts, Frederick, Prince of Wales, and Augusta, Princess of Wales, II–VII (Vouchers 1731–37).

MS Accounts at Drummonds Branch, Royal Bank of Scotland Ltd, London, show transactions by John Mist for 1725–37, including one payment to Sarah Bridgeman in 1725, and ten to Charles between 1725 and 1731. See Ledgers 1724–25, fo.310; 1726–27, fo.62; 1727, fo.189; 1728, fo.290; 1729–30, fos 105, 295; 1731, fo.27.

[10] For this and other matters concerning Mist and Harley see BL, Add MSS 18239, 18240, 18242–7 (Harley Papers), *passim*. Edward Harley became 2nd Earl of Oxford in 1724, succeeding his father Robert Harley. Throughout this book Edward is referred to as Lord Harley to distinguish him from his father, who is termed Lord Oxford.

[11] Abel Boyer, ed., *The Political State of Great Britain . . .* (London, 1711 et seq.), LIII (1737), 432. See also *Gentleman's Magazine*, VII (1737), 253; *London Magazine* (1737), 221.

Mist and his wife were buried in the Church of St John the Baptist at Hillingdon in Middlesex, which to this day has a plaque to their memory. See Daniel Lysons, *An Historical Account of Those Parishes in the County of Middlesex Which Are Not Described in 'The Environs of London'* . . . (London, 1800), p.162.

The Charles Bridgemans' home at No.19 Broad Street, now known as No.54 Broadwick Street, is set in one of several terraces that Mist built.[12] Rocque shows it lying between Soho and Golden Squares (*Plate 14*). It is a street with long-standing artistic connections: Blake was born in Broad Street and lived there as a young man, and other residents have included Vardy, Mulready, and Fuseli. Bridgeman and his family spent the years 1723–38 living there,[13] in a house that consists of a basement and four upper stories, three bays wide, each window having a segmental arch (*Plate 15b*). Originally the terrace was faced entirely with red stock brick, but in the nineteenth century the ground floor was stuccoed, although the curved door-cases with hoods on carved brackets were preserved. Inside each house there are two rooms on every floor, with a 'closet' at the rear, and the main floors still have handsome panelling and the remnants of exquisite plasterwork. It was here that Bridgeman drafted designs, and where he kept two drawing boards, assorted T-squares, rulers, and protractors, and a 'Case of brass Instruments', not to mention a spirit level, a theodolite, and 'a wooden Case for taking Prospects'. Today, in spite of a radical change of character, we can sense how elegant these rooms were when Charles, Sarah, and the children used them.[14]

In October 1728, at the age of ten, Bridgeman's son Charles entered Westminster School. Westminster – where Burlington's new dormitory was just nearing completion – rivalled Eton in reputation and had a distinguished roll of former pupils. From 1711 to 1733 the Headmaster was Dr Robert Freind, an uncompromising Tory, though such were the school's prestige and Freind's own qualities that Whigs continued to send their sons there. Freind became a supporter of George II, as well as a close friend of Swift and other wits. In 1733 Freind was succeeded by Dr John Nicoll, under whose twenty-year headmastership the school produced such figures as Warren Hastings, Edward Gibbon, and William Cowper. The younger Charles Bridgeman was at Westminster under both Freind and Nicoll, and presumably was sent there because of his father's strong connections with the school, notably through Matthew Prior and Edward Harley, both former pupils. More than that. Sir John Vanbrugh's only surviving son Charles Vanbrugh was at Westminster from 1732 to 1736, and thus would be a contemporary of the younger Bridgeman. Switzer's boy Thomas, and Christian Zincke (son of the enameller C. F. Zincke), were at the school from 1735 to 1739. The tradition continued further. Scholar-

[12] For background to this area see e.g. Edwin Beresford Chancellor, *The Romance of Soho . . .* (London, 1931), pp. 193–97; Hugh Phillips, *Mid-Georgian London. A Topographical and Social Survey of Central and Western London about 1750* (London, 1964), pp.217–18.

See [Greater London Council], *Survey of London* (London, 1900 et seq.), XXXI–XXXII (St James's Westminster, pt.2) (1963), pp.214–18, for a description of the building of Broadwick Street, and pls 122, 142 for illustrations.

[13] Bridgeman never owned No.19 Broad Street and it is not referred to in his will, although the contents are detailed in his Inventory of 1738. See below Appendix V, pp.161–67. For Bridgeman's neighbours see George G. Williams, *Guide to Literary London* (London, 1973), pp.205–16.

On 28 September 1724 Bridgeman wrote to Pope from 'Broadstreet' (*Pope Correspondence,* II, 261), and in September 1733 he asked Lord Townshend to send any reply to his house 'in Broad-street near Poland Street S. James's, London' (*HMC 19: Townshend*, 352). See below Appendices IV(i), IV(iii), pp.156, 157.

[14] Bridgeman's house is currently subdivided internally. The first floor is now a self-contained flat, and I have to thank the present occupant, Dr Samuel L. Pelz, for showing it to me. The terrace was the subject of a Building Preservation Order in 1960. The description of Bridgeman's drawing instruments is in his Inventory. See below p.161.

ships to Trinity College, Cambridge, and Christ Church, Oxford, were reserved for Westminster boys, and it was to Christ Church – following the usual Harley pattern of education – that Bridgeman's son went from Westminster in 1736. On 23 June 1735 he had joined Henry Wise's second surviving son Henry as a member of the Inner Temple.[15]

It was to his son Charles that the Royal Gardener bequeathed his two properties, namely The Bell Inn at Stilton in Huntingdonshire and a house in Henrietta Street in London. The Bell stands in the main street of Stilton village – a long, low, stone building with a tiled roof and high chimneys topped in ashlar (*Plate 16a*). The street front, with its two adjacent cottages, has three gables and a single dormer window, stone string- and eaves-courses, bay windows, and a wide archway leading to a courtyard. During the eighteenth century, notably whilst under the aegis of the celebrated landlord Cooper Thornhill, the inn was the scene of many colourful activities. Here it was that Stilton cheese (English Parmesan) was originally sold, and it was from the window above the archway that the highwayman Dick Turpin is said to have leapt in his dash north from London which ended on the gallows at York in 1739. The Bell was owned in the early 1700's by John Brownell of Willingham in Cambridgeshire, and Bridgeman inherited it on Brownell's death sometime before 1736. Bridgeman prepared plans for altering The Bell, but he can hardly have had time to realize them before he died. His son Charles, and the widow Sarah, sold the inn about 1741.[16]

By the early 1720's Bridgeman was closely connected with Harley's circle of virtuosi. At this time Harley was building his prestigious estate in Marylebone on land which had come to him in 1713 upon his marriage to Lady Henrietta Cavendish Holles, daughter of the Duke of Newcastle.[17] We can see from Rocque's plan of the area that Harley's scheme was set around Cavendish Square (*Plate 14*). From the start the estate was conceived as a

[15] I was made aware of the Westminster School connection through the goodwill of the late Mr J. B. Whitmore. Details of the headmasterships are in John D. Carleton, *Westminster School. A History*, 2nd edn (London, 1965), esp. pp.24–30 For evidence of the education of the Royal Gardener's son see SG, Inns of Court Box, Inner Temple Admissions, 1660–1799; G. F. Russell Barker and A. H. Stenning, *The Record of Old Westminsters* ... (London, 1928), I, 120; Joseph Foster, *Alumni Oxoniensis. The Members of the University of Oxford, 1715–1886* ... (Oxford, 1887–88), I, 158; Richard A. Roberts, ed., *A Calendar of the Inner Temple Records* ... (London, 1933), IV, 311.

[16] Turpin's stay at The Bell Inn is vouched for by Derek Barlow, *Dick Turpin and the Gregory Gang* (London and Colchester, 1973), p.309. Edward Harley called at The Bell in 1725. He was not impressed. See *HMC 29: Portland VI*, 82. In August 1727 Harley dined there with George Vertue on a tour into the Midlands. See *Vertue*, VI (XXX), 22. See also *VCH: Huntingdonshire*, III (1936), 222, 224.

The Bell Inn closed in 1964, and in 1965 it was bought by Mr and Mrs Thomas Kirby of London. I am grateful for assistance on The Bell's history to them, to Mr D. P. Crossman, and to Mr Malcolm A. Moyer. For details of ownership see the 'Deed of Covenant/for the Production of Title Deeds/Dated 4th. May 1820' prepared for Mr William Oxley, now in the possession of Mr and Mrs Kirby. Bridgeman references occur here between 1737–41. In 1736 there was a court case when the Royal Gardener and Dingley Askham of Conington, Cambridgeshire (described as 'devisees of John Brownell') were involved in proceedings against Nicholas Harding. See Bernau Index, Chancery Court Proceedings, 1714/58 (C11), Bdl.1045 suit 1. Unsigned Bridgemanic sketches of buildings at Stilton are in MSGD a3 fos 40, 40v; 14 fos 3, 51. There is a map of Stilton in MSGD a3 fo. 26.

[17] For descriptions of the building of the estate see C. H. Collins Baker and Muriel I. Baker, *The Life and Circumstances of James Brydges, 1st Duke of Chandos, Patron of the Liberal Arts* (Oxford, 1949), pp.265–95; Francis H. W. Sheppard, *Local Government in St. Marylebone, 1688–1835. A Study of the Vestry and the Turnpike Trust* (London, 1958), pp.16–19; John N. Summerson, *Georgian London*, 2nd edn (London, 1970), pp.105–12.

I am grateful to Sir John Summerson and Mrs Ann Saunders for their advice on Bridgeman's connections with the Marylebone Estate.

handsome residential unit, with its open space, streets, church, and market: a preliminary layout was drafted in 1718, and the next year an engraved plan was published (*Plate 15a*). This was drawn by John Prince, who apparently acted as agent for the Harleys whilst speculating considerably on his own account. The estate was essentially a Tory enterprise, and Bridgeman and Gibbs were both involved in its design. Prior to his impeachment and ruin in 1717, the 1st Earl of Oxford (Harley's father) had extended valuable patronage to Gibbs, who duly became an acknowledged member of Harley's group of *cognoscenti*. Apart from supervising the design of the buildings, and giving advice to the lessees, Gibbs was architect for the Oxford Market (1724–32, demolished 1880) and the Oxford Chapel, St Peter's Vere Street (1723–24). In 1729, if not earlier, Bridgeman prepared a layout for Cavendish Square, the hub of the scheme, which may well have included a statue of Queen Anne in its centre, for one is shown in Prince's plan of 1719.[18] However the square took shape only gradually and remained incomplete until the north side was closed in during the 1770's.[19]

Early in 1725 Bridgeman was considering moving to Marylebone. On 13 March of that year Lord Harley's Steward for the Estate, William Thomas, told his lordship that 'Mr Bridgman has fixed upon ground for a House for himself'. This was on condition that those of Bridgeman's friends who were going to live there did not decide to 'take a piece together in some other part of my Lds. Ground'; if they did, then Bridgeman 'would joyn with them for so much as will be necessary for his own accommodation'.[20] Ultimately Bridgeman took a ninety-nine year lease from Michaelmas 1725 on No.8 Henrietta Street (later known as No.11 Henrietta Place), a house which was probably intended to serve as a prototype for others on the estate (*Plate 15c*).[21] Gibbs must have assisted in its design: the window dimensions were exactly as prescribed by Gibbs for William Thomas's house nearby, the combination of keystones and sill-corbels was Gibbsian, as was the stone Ionic porch which dominated the exterior. This porch, which may once have been pedimented, consisted of two attached and two free-standing columns supporting an entablature with a modillion cornice and an enriched pulvinated frieze. Inside the house, the prominent features were a fine ornamented ceiling, and a stair with turned balusters and Ionic newels. By the 1720's Bridgeman and Gibbs had worked together on several jobs and were soon to own neighbouring property: Gibbs lived at No.5 Henrietta Street from

[18] BL, Add MS 18240 (Harley Papers), fo.35 (42). See also Edwin Beresford Chancellor, *A History of the Squares of London, Topographical and Historical*... (London, 1907), pp.42–60; Gordon Mackenzie, *Marylebone. Great City North of Oxford Street* (London, 1972), pp.37–50; Phillips, *Mid-Georgian London*, pp.242, 247–50, 302–3.

[19] In 1736 Gibbs erected an additional wing to one of the Duke of Chandos's two houses in Cavendish Square. A house in the square owned by Gibbs was left to Robert Pringle. See Bryan D. G. Little, *The Life and Work of James Gibbs, 1682–1754* (London, 1955), pp.121, 159. For recent landscaping of Cavendish Square by Michael Brown, see Sam Lambert, 'Circling the Square', *Architects' Journal*, CLIV (18 August 1971), 332–33.

[20] BL, Add MS 18239 (Harley Papers), fo.17 (27). Miss Juliet Allan tells me that in William Thomas's account in Child's Branch of Williams and Glyn's Bank Ltd, London, there is a payment from Thomas to Flitcroft in 1725, and four to Charles Bridgeman in 1725–26 totalling £223.13*s*.

[21] See John N. Summerson, 'Henrietta Place, Marylebone, and its Associations with James Gibbs', *London Topographical Record*, XXI (1958), 26–36.

1730 until his death, and he leased Nos 9, 10, and 11.[22] Among Bridgeman's other friends, Flitcroft took building leases on three houses on the Marylebone Estate in 1730,[23] by which time Wootton had taken up residence in Cavendish Square, Rysbrack in Vere Street, and Vanderbank in Holles Street.[24] Bridgeman's house remained in the family until several years after the gardener's death, eventually being demolished, along with adjacent properties, in 1956.

Bridgeman, if not his family, apparently shuttled to and fro between Hampton Court, Kensington, and Westminster.[25] In 1726 an old house at Hampton Court was being repaired and fitted up for him,[26] and on his death Bridgeman left behind what his widow Sarah called 'the Master Gardners Capitall house' at Hampton Court, which had been granted to her husband in succession to Wise and Carpenter.[27] Rocque's plan of Hampton Court in 1736 shows 'the Gardners house', and in the same year Bridgeman was described in a lawsuit as 'of Hampton Court, Middlesex, Esqr.'[28] A house at Hampton Court was a perquisite of Royal Gardeners:[29] Wise had at least one there,[30] and in 1764 when Lancelot Brown was made 'Surveyor of His Majesty's Gardens and Waters at Hampton Court' he moved into Wilderness House within the grounds of the palace.[31] Yet it was not at Hamp-

[22] Rate books in St Marylebone Town Hall cited in Summerson, 'Henrietta Place', p.29. The catalogued leases in the Town Hall contain no reference to Bridgeman.

The lease of Nos 4 and 5 from 23 April 1731 is mentioned in BL, Add MS 18240 (Harley Papers), fo.18 (12). In these accounts Nos 9, 10, and 11 are referred to as Nos 1, 2, and 3: Nos 1 and 2 were let to Gibbs from 1 August and No.3 from 1 September 1727. The interior of a room in No.11 Henrietta Place is preserved in the V&A, and is reproduced in Desmond Fitz-Gerald, *Georgian Furniture*, 3rd edn (London, 1969), Nos 13, 14. The ceiling may have been by Giuseppe Artari. See Geoffrey Beard, *Decorative Plasterwork in Great Britain* (London, 1975), p.202.

Gibbs bequeathed his own house to the Scots painter Cosmo John Alexander, and the other three to Thomas, Lord Erskine (heir to the Earl of Mar). See Little, *Gibbs*, p.159.

[23] Colvin, *Dictionary*, p.208.

[24] For Wootton see George E. Kendall, 'Notes on the Life of John Wootton, with a List of Engravings after his Pictures', *Walpole Society*, XXI (1932–33), 23–42, esp. pp.23–24; Phillips, *Mid-Georgian London*, p.303. Wootton lived at No.23 until his death in 1761.

For Rysbrack and Vanderbank see Mary I. Webb, *Michael Rysbrack, Sculptor* (London, 1954), pp.55–57. Rysbrack was resident in Vere Street from 1725 until he died in 1770.

Other Bridgeman neighbours are given in Williams, *Guide to Literary London*, pp.275–81.

[25] There is a large coloured eighteenth-century drawing inscribed 'Mr. Bridgeman's house' at All Souls College, Oxford, brought to my attention by Mr H. M. Colvin. The house remains unidentified.

[26] PRO, Treasury Books and Papers CCLXIII (7) (T1: 263), fo.231, minute of 2 February 1727, indicating that Charles Dartiquenave had submitted an estimate of £450.18*s*.8*d*. for the alterations.

[27] See e.g. below Appendix VI, pp.168. The contents of this house are listed in Bridgeman's Inventory of 1738. See below Appendix V, pp.162–64.

[28] In the suit about The Bell Inn cited in n.16 above, i.e. Bernau Index, Chancery Court Proceedings, 1714/58 (C11), Bdl.1045 suit 1.

[29] See the letter of 18 June 1713 in *CTB*, XXVII, pt. 2 (1713), 255. See also Green, *Gardener to Queen Anne*, pp.67–68.

[30] Green, *Gardener to Queen Anne*, pp.67–68. Apart from Warwick Priory, and other property, Wise also had houses at Blenheim and Brompton Park. See ibid., pp.104, 162.

On 26 August 1733 Anne Wentworth, Countess of Strafford, wrote to Selina Hastings, Countess of Huntingdon, that the Prince of Wales 'has taken his son from Miss Vane and put him to Mr. Bridgeman's (the gardener's) at Hampton Court'. See *HMC 78: Hastings III*, 16. This refers to Anne Vane, maid of honour to Queen Caroline, mistress of Frederick, Prince of Wales, and the subject of Dr Johnson's line: 'Yet Vane could tell what ills from beauty spring.' Her son (supposedly by Frederick) was christened Fitz Frederick Vane in 1732.

[31] Dorothy Stroud, *Capability Brown*, 3rd edn (London, 1975), pp.108–9, 122–23, 125, 201; pl.26b.

Two drawings of George London's house at Thames Ditton in Surrey are in Worcester College, Oxford, YD 3. See H. M. Colvin, ed., *A Catalogue of Architectural Drawings of the Eighteenth and Nineteenth Centuries in the Library of Worcester College, Oxford* (Oxford, 1964), Nos 287, 288; pls 127, 128; Kerry Downes, ed., 'The Kings Weston Book of Drawings', *Architectural History*, X (1967), No.51; pl.99.

ton Court but at Kensington that Bridgeman was living when he married, and it was in Kensington that he died – perhaps in the Master Gardener's house at Kensington Palace which stood at what is now the corner of Palace Avenue and the Kensington Road, and which is shown on Rocque's plan of Kensington of 1736.[32]

Although Bridgeman considered moving to Marylebone, bought a house there and designed Cavendish Square, he never actually lived on Harley's estate. Cavendish Square is situated north-west of Bridgeman's home in Broad Street, and an equal distance south-west lies St James's Square. Sited just north of Pall Mall, St James's was once the finest of all the West End squares.[33] In 1726 the Trustees for its development employed Thomas Ackres to make a survey of it, and in March 1727 an agreement was concluded with Charles Bridgeman for laying it out. To borrow Pope's phrase, Bridgeman 'floated it with a lake', consisting of

> a circle of 150 feet diameter, surrounded by a gravel walk within an iron railing of octagonal form, at the angles of which stood eight stone obelisks surmounted by lamps. Outside the railing the square was paved in Purbeck stone with 'Square Cubick Stones, commonly called French Paving'. The neatness of the paving, possibly laid by the paviour, Mist, was regarded by 18th-century critics as a great beauty of the square.[34]

It was completed in 1728, and Sutton Nicholls's bird's-eye view of 1754 shows us how fine was the result: there is even a lady in a punt (*Plate 16b*).[35] The square now had a central fountain with a plinth apparently intended for a statue of William III, which was finally erected in 1808, with the monarch in the guise of a Roman general. The square has been altered considerably since Bridgeman knew it, and his circular basin was filled in during 1854.

Bridgeman and Mist's work at St James's Square was admired profusely, enhanced as it was later by such architects as Flitcroft, Robert Adam, William Chambers, and Soane. 'St. *James*'s-*Square* has an appearance of grandeur superior to any other plan in town', wrote Ralph in 1734.[36] 'Beautiful and spacious' were Sir John Fielding's words in 1776. 'Although the Appearance of the Square hath an Air of Grandeur', he went on, 'yet that by no Means resulteth from the Pomp and Greatness of the Structures about it; but rather from a prevailing Regularity throughout, joined to the Neatness of the Pavement. The Basin in the Middle contributes not a little in producing the Effect.'[37] The inhabitants of St James's Square in the early eighteenth century were intensely aristocratic, a fact that cannot but have helped Bridgeman in his career. Apart from eminent statesmen, in 1721 no fewer than six dukes lived there (Chandos, Dorset, Kent, Norfolk, Portland, and South-

[32] Noted in e.g. John T. Hayes, *Kensington Palace. A History and Guide* (London, 1969), p.7.

[33] See Chancellor, *Squares of London*, pp.80–105; Phillips, *Mid-Georgian London*, p.65; *Survey of London*, XXIX (1960), esp. pp.55–76; XXX (1960), pls 128, 129.

[34] Ibid., XXIX, 67.

[35] Cf. ibid., XXX, pl.128, which is Sutton Nicholls's view of St James's Square as it was *c*.1722, i.e. before the execution of Bridgeman's design.

[36] [James Ralph], *A Critical Review of the Publick Buildings, Statues and Ornaments in and about London and Westminster* . . . (London, 1734), p.32.

[37] Quoted in *Survey of London*, XXIX (1960),73.

ampton) as well as seven earls, a countess, a baron, a baronet, a baronet's widow, and the widow of a French marquis. Of the untitled residents one was Spencer Compton, later 1st Earl of Wilmington and Bridgeman's client at Compton Place.[38] Apart from their social desirability, St James's Square and its neighbouring streets appealed to finer senses: or, as Thomson put it in *Liberty*, 'Lo! stately streets, lo! squares that court the breeze' (pt. v, l. 702).

Royal Appointments

Drawings provide us with convincing evidence that Bridgeman and Wise collaborated before Wise's appointment as Royal Gardener in 1714: in 1709, shortly after Wise began his spell at Blenheim, Bridgeman drew a plan of the grounds (*Plate 24*); in 1711 a 'survey and rental' of Wise's own property at Warwick Priory was 'taken' by Bridgeman and James Fish (*Plate 18*);[39] whilst in 1713 we are told that Wise was keeping 'one Man constantly in pay and sometimes more' for the purpose of 'making Severall Surveys and Draughts of Her Majesty's Palaces, Gardens, Parks and Plantations'.[40] One such survey may have been Bridgeman's signed drawing of Windsor Forest which conceivably was executed in Queen Anne's reign (*Plates 104, 105*). However, any collaboration between Bridgeman and Wise was not strong enough to prevent Wise from calling on Smith and Carpenter, not Bridgeman, to help run Brompton Park Nurseries after George London's death.

In 1716 Wise entered into partnership with Carpenter for 'the ordering and keeping of all His Majesty's Gardens'. It was an arrangement which led to nothing but trouble, and within a few months Wise had to answer several complaints of negligence.[41] Two years later that 'favourite of the Germans' William Benson persuaded the ministry of George I to dismiss Wren from the Surveyorship of the King's Works which he had held since

[38] Residents of Cavendish Square are given by Phillips, *Mid-Georgian London*, pp.302–3, and of St James's Square by Arthur I. Dasent, *The History of St. James's Square, and the Foundation of the West End of London . . .* (London and New York, 1895), pp.215–64.

[39] There are three drawings of Warwick Priory, and two of Lillington Manor, which may be in Bridgeman's hand. For Warwick Priory see *VCH: Warwickshire*, VIII (1969), 438–41, and the view by James Fish in *Vit.Brit.*, IV (1739), pls 71–72.

There were two James Fishes of Warwick, the father being an antiquary and the son a surveyor. Numerous references to them occur in William Dugdale, *The Restoration of the Beauchamp Chapel at St Mary's Collegiate Church, Warwick, 1674–1742* (Oxford, 1956). See also Cyril E. and Ruth C. Wright, eds, *The Diary of Humfrey Wanley, 1715–26* (London, 1966), I, 83. Presumably Bridgeman's collaborator was the younger Fish (1673–1740). For surveyors such as the Fishes, see Peter Eden, *Dictionary of Land Surveyors and Local Cartographers of Great Britain and Ireland, 1550–1850* (Folkestone, 1975–76).

My enquiries at Warwick benefited from the kindness of the County Archivist, Mr M. W. Farr.

[40] Quoted from Wise's 'State of the Royal Gardens and Plantations at Ladyday 1713' by Green, *Gardener to Queen Anne*, p.103.

[41] See 'The Memorial of Henry Wise and Joseph Carpenter' (1717) in *HMC 23: Cowper III*, 118–20. This and the ensuing ructions are discussed in Green, *Gardener to Queen Anne*, pp.140–44.

There are frequent references to Carpenter in the minutes of the Board of Works. A Memorial of his widow Ruth Carpenter, claiming payment for work at Kensington, is in *CTBP*, I (1729–30), 164. Apart from the royal gardens, Carpenter provided Bridgeman with plants from Brompton for Kedleston, Briggens, Carshalton, Compton Place, Purley, and Stowe. A drawing inscribed 'Carpenters Garden at Bronton by Kensington' is noted in Mark Girouard, ed., 'The Smythson Collection of the RIBA', *Architectural History*, V (1962), 64 (No. IV/17).

1669. Next, having appropriated the job himself, Benson joined Colin Campbell in an effort to uncover other 'abominable abuses'. One of Benson and Campbell's recommendations was that Wise and Carpenter be replaced by Thomas Ackres, who would manage the royal gardens for 'half what they have hitherto cost'. Ultimately Wise and Carpenter kept their posts whilst Benson was dismissed on 17 July 1719 having, in Hawksmoor's opinion, 'got more in one year (for confusing the King's Works) than Sr. Chris. Wren did in 40 years for his honest endeavours'.[42] Campbell, whom Benson had made Chief Clerk and Deputy Surveyor, shared his disgrace. Benson was replaced as Surveyor of the King's Works by Sir Thomas Hewitt, who in turn was succeeded in 1726 by Richard Arundell. Henry Fox (later 1st Baron Holland) took over from Arundell in 1737, and retained his position until 1743.[43]

Bridgeman's rise to the post of Royal Gardener was the result of a combination of merit and good fortune. In 1726, when he replaced Carpenter as Wise's partner, the Board of Works expressed complete confidence in Bridgeman's 'Experience, skill & Ability'.[44] Bridgeman, Wise and 'the Survivor of them' were appointed George I's 'Cheif Gardiners', which meant that they had to 'order keep and maintain' the royal gardens at Hampton Court, Kensington, Newmarket, Windsor, and St James's Palace. These amounted to 148 acres, 2 roods and 20 poles, the largest being Hampton Court (over 73 acres) and Kensington (over 55 acres). Like Wise and Carpenter, Bridgeman and Wise were paid at the annual rate of £20 an acre for their 'Service, care, pains & Expences' in carrying through an agreed 'Scheme': in other words a total of £2,960 a year. Apart from two pavilions at the east end of the bowling green at Hampton Court (which were to remain with Christopher and Mary Tilson), Bridgeman and Wise were permitted to 'have & enjoy all Garden Houses, Priviledges, Liberties, Emoluments and Advantages' that Wise and Carpenter had. Everything was to be done under the 'Cognizance' of the Surveyor of Gardens and Waters, who was to ensure that there were no expenses added to those agreed. From 1726 this meant Charles Dartiquenave – Whig, epicure, wit, and member of the Kit-Cat Club, described by his friend Swift as 'the man that knows every thing, and that every body knows', and 'the greatest punner of this town next myself' (*Plate 17b*).[45]

When George II succeeded to the throne Bridgeman and Wise submitted a statement entitled 'A State of the Royal Gardens, from the Revolution, to the Year 1727'.[46] It was their

[42] Quoted by Colvin, *Dictionary*, p.73.

[43] These and subsequent dates of the tenure of posts in His Majesty's Office of Works are based on Colvin, *Dictionary*, pp.757–66.

[44] See below Appendix II, pp.151–52.

[45] *Journal to Stella*, ed. Harold H. Williams (Oxford, 1948), I, 221, 36. Dartiquenave was Paymaster of the Works from 1706 to 1726. In 1726 Hugh Howard took over, and he held the job until John Harris succeeded him in 1738. The Secretaries of the Board of Works during Bridgeman's spell as Royal Gardener were Hawksmoor (1726–36) and Ware (1736–66).

[46] Henry Wise Register, cited by Green, *Gardener to Queen Anne*, pp.148–50. An almost illegible copy of part of this is in PRO, Treasury Books and Papers CCLXIII (10) (T1: 263), fos 249–50. Contained in fos 236–44 is 'An Account of the Annual Payments in the Office of Works, in all particulars as they stood at the time of the late Kings Demise'. This shows that the £2,960 granted to Bridgeman and Wise used up more than a quarter of the yearly expenditure of £11,896.10*s*.3*d*. The rate of £2,960 for 148 acres had been established by Queen Anne for Wise, and continued by George I. William III paid the Earl of Portland a basic £4,168.19*s*. for looking after 73 acres (about £57 an acre). These figures are given in the statement of 1727.

last joint report. For in 'A Scheme of his Mats: Several Gardens and Plantations' which they submitted in the same year Wise's name is unceremoniously struck out.[47] He was now in his seventies, and his career was at an end: he retired officially on Lady Day 1728, and Warwick Priory was his to enjoy at last.[48]

On 15 March 1728 Bridgeman's formal appointment as Royal Gardener was issued, effective from Lady Day that year, and it included only a single reference to his predecessor.[49] In essence the agreement differed little from earlier ones. Bridgeman was given all buildings formerly allotted to Royal Gardeners, shared or not, but the two pavilions at Hampton Court still remained with the Tilsons.[50] One notable economy made by the Board of Works was that it reduced annual payment from £20 to £15 an acre, and thus gave Bridgeman £2,220 a year. Dartiquenave's annual salary was £500.[51] The attached 'Scheme of His Majesty's Several Gardens and Plantations' outlined Bridgeman's duties at Hampton Court, St James's, Kensington, Newmarket, and Windsor, all of which were to be 'maintained, Kept & Upheld'. Again it was stressed that Dartiquenave as the 'Surveyor of Our Gardens' was to have full knowledge of the work being done, and that he was to 'take care from time to time that the said Charles Bridgeman do well, truly & effectually comply with, execute & perform the said Scheme'. But this scheme by no means covered all Bridgeman's royal commitments, for it expressly excluded any new work, and therefore Bridgeman's extensive landscaping of the enlarged parks at Kensington and Richmond, for instance, demanded separate contracts. The three signatories to Bridgeman's Royal Appointment were indicative of ample support for him from among the influential: Sir Robert Walpole, then Prime Minister and his client at Houghton; Sir Charles Turner of the Turner family of Warham in Norfolk; and George Bubb Dodington, Bridgeman's patron at Eastbury and cousin of Viscount Cobham of Stowe.[52]

[47] PRO, Treasury Books and Papers CCLXIII (7) (T1: 263), fos 251–52. Ackres' second attempt to displace Bridgeman and Wise is documented on fo.253. See the comments in Green, *Gardener to Queen Anne*, pp.78, 150.

[48] Wise had bought the house in 1709 from Sir Henry Puckering on condition that he did not live in it until after the occupant, Lady Bowyer, had died. Her death in October 1727 conveniently coincided with a change in monarch. Wise retained his residence at Brompton Park and instructed Henry Joynes to collect on his behalf the debts owed him by the executors of Carpenter and Smith. See Green, *Gardener to Queen Anne*, pp.131–32, 151–52, 165–69.

[49] See below Appendix III, pp.153–55. Bridgeman was asked to look after 148 acres and two poles, the 2-rood discrepancy from the 1726 appointment being due to faulty addition.

[50] The Tilsons' right to this property is often cited. See e.g. the entries from 1 November 1726 in PRO, Works 6/15, fo.161.

[51] Regular and irregular payments to Bridgeman as Royal Gardener are tabulated in accounts throughout PRO, Works 5/57; 5/58; 5/59; 5/141. From Midsummer Quarter 1728 until July 1738 Bridgeman receives a basic quarterly payment of £555 almost without break; poundage payments to Bridgeman occur in PRO, Works 5/104, fos 16, 21, 22; 5/105, *passim*. Dartiquenave is paid £125 a quarter.

Payments to Bridgeman and Dartiquenave appear together from 31 March 1729 in *CTBP*, I (1729–30), 252, 264, 278, 293, 348, 573, 592, 606. The last of these is for 28 December 1730, after which there are no further payments to them in *CTBP*.

A memorial for payment from Dartiquenave shortly after he became Surveyor of Gardens and Waters is in PRO, Works 5/150, fos 7–8, and a request for adjustment of his payment in PRO, Works 16/39/1, fos 4–5.

The Royal Gardener, or a namesake, had an account with Hoare's Bank. Between May 1716 and January 1717 a Charles Bridgeman put in and took out a total of £350.10*s*.0*d*., and on 20 May 1726 he paid in £107.19*s*.3*d*. only to withdraw it on 25 May. Switzer had an account at Hoare's from 1723 to 1745. See C. Hoare and Co., Bankers, London, MS Accounts.

[52] These three signed the main document of appointment, the 'Scheme' bearing the signature of Bridgeman himself. Presumably Turner and Dodington signed in their roles as Lords of the Treasury.

Walpole and Turner, moreover, were M.P.s for Lynn-Regis, which meant effectively that Bridgeman's appointment as Royal Gardener was endorsed by three clients, for in 1724 Bridgeman had undertaken a survey of the drainage of the Fens. In 1725, when Thomas Badeslade published *The History of the Ancient and Present State of the Navigation of the Port of King's-Lyn, and of Cambridge*, part of the Appendix consisted of *A Report of the Present State of the Great Level of the Fens, Called Bedford-Level, and of the Port of Lynn; and of the Rivers Ouse and Nean, the Two Great Sewers of that Country*. This *Report* was prepared by Charles Bridgeman, reissued in 1766, and was his only publication. It was promptly opposed by Badeslade and Colonel John Armstrong, who were taking up the challenge on behalf of the Corporation of King's Lynn, whose fears had been aroused by Bridgeman's proposals. The scheme for the Fens demanded that Bridgeman grasp the mechanics of drainage on a large scale, and it is a reflection of his competence that since his day most of his propositions have been carried through in spirit if not in detail.[53] The *Report* was addressed to Henry Clinton, 7th Earl of Lincoln, Lord Lieutenant of Cambridgeshire, a member of the Kit-Cat Club, and brother-in-law of the Duke of Newcastle who employed Bridgeman and Vanbrugh at Claremont.[54]

However the *sine qua non* of Bridgeman's Royal Appointment must have lain not so much with these patrons as with the Crown itself, for while Prince of Wales the new king had employed Bridgeman at Marble Hill. Nor would Bridgeman have been appointed without the endorsement, if not the active support, of Queen Caroline, whose enthusiasm for gardening far exceeded her husband's. And it is not difficult to imagine Sir Robert Walpole dropping a word in her ear on Bridgeman's behalf. Once he was Royal Gardener, Bridgeman's circle of professional friends within the Board of Works and around it became wide and influential. Although Bridgeman may have known Wren in the architect's capacity as Surveyor of the King's Works, he would be more familiar with Wren's successors in that post, namely Benson (1718–19), Sir Thomas Hewitt (1719–26), Richard Arundell (1726–37), and Henry Fox (1737–43). In the minutes, accounts, and memoranda of the Board of Works we find Bridgeman's name cheek by jowl with those of such colleagues as Ripley, Westby Gill, Kent, Flitcroft, Joynes, and Roger Morris. Of these, Ripley succeeded Vanbrugh as Comptroller of the Works in 1726 and lasted until 1758; Gill followed Campbell as Deputy Surveyor in 1719, and continued as such until succeeded in 1735 by William Kent who was on his way up from Master Carpenter. Simultaneously Kent took over as Master Mason from Nicholas Dubois who had held the office since 1719. The remaining three men were all Clerks of Works: Flitcroft at Whitehall, Westminster and St James's Palaces from 1726 to 1746, Joynes at Kensington Palace from 1715

[53] Cf. Sigismund Trafford, *An Essay on Draining, More Particularly with Regard to the North Division of the . . . Bedford Level . . .* (London, 1729), *passim*. The proposals, past and present, were explained to me by Mr K. S. G. Hinde and Mr Christopher Taylor. See Henry C. Darby, *The Draining of the Fens* (Cambridge, 1940), esp. p.127.

Armstrong was 'Chief Engineer of England' from 1714 to 1742, became FRS in 1723, served under the 1st Duke of Marlborough, and assisted at Blenheim Palace.

[54] Lincoln and Cobham were dining together in May 1723, just as Bridgeman embarked on his *Report* and as his designs for Stowe were blossoming. See HEH, Stowe (Temple) Account Book, No.131 (1719–23), 31 May 1723. In 1737 Rocque published a Bridgemanic plan of grounds for a house for Lincoln at Weybridge in Surrey, the mansion designed by Burlington but never built.

to 1754, and Morris at the White Lodge at Richmond from 1727 to 1729. By the late 1720's the name of Henry Wise has vanished from the records of the Board of Works, and we hear no more of Bridgeman's relationship with him. Of all Bridgeman's strenuous activities in subsequent years, writes Mr Green, 'Wise, within his walls at Warwick, seems to have been uncaring and impervious, perhaps deliberately so'.[55]

Portraits and St Luke's Club

As the eighteenth century progressed, London clubs and societies concerned with the arts multiplied. The Kit-Cat Club was started by the bookseller Jacob Tonson in 1688; in 1711 an academy was started in Great Queen Street with Kneller as governor; and in 1720 Chèron and Vanderbank opened theirs in St Martin's Lane, the same street in which Hogarth began his academy for painting and sculpture in 1735. Also in St Martin's Lane was Slaughter's Coffee House, described by Baron Bielfeld in 1741 as 'the rendezvous of all the wits, and the greatest part of the men of letters, in town'.[56] Between 1732 and 1734 the Society of Dilettanti was set up, in 1754 the Society of Arts, and in 1768 the Royal Academy. Founded earlier than any of these was St Luke's Club of Artists, a body which may have originated in Van Dyck's practice of acting as host (particularly on St Luke's Day, 18 October) to the leading artists and connoisseurs of his time.[57] In the early 1700's St Luke's was small as well as exclusive: in 1727 it numbered twenty-eight, and in Vertue's heyday the guests at the annual St Luke's Day dinner averaged only about a dozen.[58] It was, as Vertue says, one of the 'Tip top Clubbs of all, for men of the highest Character in Arts & Gentlemen Lovers of Art'.[59]

Bridgeman therefore must have been held in good repute to be admitted to so august a company. As 'King's Gardiner' he was elected to St Luke's in 1726, the same year as Vertue and ten years after Gibbs. Gibbs in fact may have proposed his election, as the prospective member had to be known to a former Steward, and Gibbs had served in that capacity in 1719. In 1729, as 'Gardner to his Majesty', Bridgeman himself was nominated to the Stewardship by the outgoing Steward, Philip Mercier; in his turn Bridgeman selected Vertue to serve as Steward for 1730.[60] The position of Steward was an honoured one. It was his duty to provide the annual feast at a tavern of his choice, and to pay out of

[55] Green, *Gardener to Queen Anne*, p.156.

[56] Mr Hooper, trans., *Letters of Baron Bielfeld* (London, 1768–70), IV, 87–88. For Slaughter's see Mark Girouard 'English Art and the Rococo', *C.Life*, CXXXIX (13, 27 January, 3 February 1966), 58–61, 188–90, 224–27. Detailed documentation of London clubs and coffee-houses is in Ronald Paulson, *Hogarth. His Life, Art, and Times* (New Haven and London, 1971).

[57] For St Luke's see the minutes entitled 'Virtuosi of St. Luke a Clubb in London', BL, Add MS 39167B, fos 73–86; Robert Raines, *Marcellus Laroon* (London and New York, 1966), pp.52–53; *Vertue*, III (XXII), 51, 73, 120, 140; Webb, *Rysbrack*, pp.61–62; William T. Whitley, *Artists and Their Friends in England, 1700–99* (London and Boston, 1928), I, 69–71, 74–77; II, 241–44.

[58] BL, Add MS 39167B, fos 73r, 74r, 75r, 84r–95v.

[59] *Vertue*, III (XXII), 120.

[60] BL, Add MS 39167B, fos 74, 75v, 82r, 84r. For Mercier see notably *Philip Mercier, 1689–1760* (Exhibition Catalogue, York Art Gallery and Iveagh Bequest, Kenwood, 1969), *passim*; Christopher Neve, 'Minor Painter's Influential Role. Philip Mercier and the Rococo in England', *C.Life*, CXLVI (21 August 1969), 448–49.

his own pocket any cost exceeding the crown subscribed by each member. The St Luke's Day dinner arranged by Bridgeman in 1729 was held on 22 November, and it is worthy of note that Charles Dartiquenave (a 'friend of the Stewards') was among those present.[61] When Thornhill was Steward in 1718 he dined the members at his own house in Covent Garden, but thereafter the precise venue of the dinners is not known. Apart from those of 1727 and 1728, Bridgeman attended these functions unfailingly from his election until his death.[62] St Luke's evidently became less active in the 1730's, partly because of the success of Slaughter's, though its prestige never flagged: Vertue's last reference to St Luke's was in 1744 when he stated that it was held 'still in highest esteem'.[63]

Bridgeman appears in several of the group portraits which were painted of clubs such as St Luke's. The best of these is *A Club of Artists* which hangs in the National Portrait Gallery in London (*Plate 19*),[64] the work of Gawen Hamilton, a Scot little documented apart from a few jottings by Vertue. Hamilton's conversation-pieces, writes Vertue, are 'agreeable' and show 'much variety & correctnes of mode & manner of the time & habits. he may well be esteemd a rival to Hogarth. having as much justness. if not so much fire.'[65] This canvas by Hamilton was commissioned for the artist's benefit, and he was paid four guineas by each of the sitters. On completion it was raffled on 15 April 1735 and won by the water-colourist Joseph Goupy.[66]

Vertue gives us an annotated sketch of the assembly, and his identifications tally exactly with the names beneath or above each of the figures on the actual painting. He says there are ten of these, but proceeds to list thirteen, conceivably because Vertue himself, Goupy, and Hamilton were added later.[67] Where such comparisons can be made, the representations resemble other authenticated portraits of the people concerned. The setting is a *salon* with classical décor. Seated in the centre, apparently head of the assembly, is Matthew Robinson, the distinguished amateur landscape painter, dilettante and father of Mrs Elizabeth 'Blue-stocking' Montagu. Directly to the right behind him is Charles Bridgeman, with

[61] BL, Add MS 39167B, fo.84r.

[62] Ibid., fos 78r, 79, 81v, 82r, 83r, 84r, 85. Bridgeman's death is recorded on fo.85r.

Among others who occupied the post of Steward between 1669 and 1735 (after which date no Stewards are recorded) were Grinling Gibbons (1690); William Talman (1700); Hugh Howard (1707); John Rowley (1720); the enamellers Boit (1715) and Zincke (1731); Rysbrack (1735); and the painters Wootton (1717), Goupy (1727), and Dahl (1699). Dahl was known towards the end of his life as the father of the club (he was a member for about fifty years), and his death is in its records of 1743.

[63] *Vertue*, III (XXII), 120. In May 1745 the Rose and Crown Club held its last meeting at the Half Moon Tavern. See ibid., VI (XXX), 127, 137. Laroon, a member of the Rose and Crown, expressed his jealousy of the superiority of St Luke's in *An Extempore* noted by Vertue and cited by Raines, *Marcellus Laroon*, p.52.

[64] For consideration of this painting see Raines, *Marcellus Laroon*, p.53; Ellis Waterhouse, *Painting in Britain, 1530–1790*, 3rd edn (Harmondsworth, 1969), p.133; Webb, *Rysbrack*, pp.58–61; Whitley, *Artists and Their Friends in England*, I, 68–71; William K. Wimsatt, *The Portraits of Alexander Pope* (New Haven and London, 1965), pp.91, 97. Representations of Bridgeman subsequently discussed are compared in Willis, 'The Gardener and the Painter', pp.30–33.

[65] *Vertue*, III (XXII), 71. See also pp.3–5, 41, 48, 61, 81, and H. L. Finberg, 'Gawen Hamilton. An Unknown Scottish Portrait Painter', *Walpole Society*, VI (1918), 51–58.

[66] Later Goupy may have sold it to the Prince of Wales. See *Vertue*, III (XXII), 71–72; Whitley, *Artists and Their Friends in England*, I, 67–70. On p.69 Whitley proposes that Vertue, careful as he was, may have been mistaken about the sale, for Walpole points out that Goupy's collection of pictures dispersed after his death included 'a piece in oil by Hamilton with portraits of several artists'. In 1808 the painting was in the hands of a descendant of Matthew Robinson, and from the Robinson family it went to the National Portrait Gallery.

[67] *Vertue*, III (XXII), 71.

the words 'Bridgman Gar.' above his head. Around him is a sparkling artistic circle which includes Gibbs, Baron, Kent, and Wootton. Vertue describes this gathering as a 'Conversation of Virtuosis' at the King's Arms in New Bond Street. Most likely it was simply an arbitrary composition made up from Hamilton's acquaintances, using the King's Arms as a setting, rather than a representation of St Luke's, the Rose and Crown Club, or one of the other societies with which Vertue was associated.[68] Immediately to Bridgeman's left is Bernard Baron. Baron is holding a roll of drawings tied with ribbon, and may well be discussing with the Royal Gardener the views of Stowe which he was busy with at that moment.[69] Bridgeman himself is dressed in a grey-green coat, and his elegant right hand rests lightly upon his chest. He lacks the animation evident in the glances of Goupy and Baron, and the puffiness of his face indicates that he was already beginning to suffer from the dropsy from which he died.[70] It would be rash to suggest Bridgeman's age but, for comparison, when the painting was completed Gibbs was fifty-three, Baron thirty-nine, Kent fifty, Rysbrack forty-one, and Dahl in his eighties.

Hamilton or Hogarth may have been responsible for another portrait of Bridgeman in fashionable company, namely *An Assembly of Virtuosi* of *c.*1730 in the Ashmolean Museum (*Plate 20*).[71] Its subject and authorship are both in doubt because of the poor condition of the picture,[72] but again it seems to represent an *ad hoc* group rather than a specific society.[73] The identities of eight of the fifteen figures are suggested (rather than established) by the list of names in the upper-left corner, and these tally with the arabic numerals above the individual heads. The specific identifications however are questionable: to judge by other paintings of him, the Royal Gardener is most likely to be the second figure from the right, standing holding a drawing and pointing to it.[74]

[68] St Luke's Club occasionally subscribed to such painters as Hamilton, and gave advice on the formation of art collections. No fewer than seven of the thirteen figures depicted by Hamilton (including Bridgeman) had acted as Stewards of St Luke's prior to 1735. But Goupy may have left the club in 1727, Hamilton was never a member, and Kent did not join until 1743 – by which time Hamilton was dead. See *Vertue*, III (XXII), 140; V (XXVI), 43.

The Rose and Crown Club had been the subject of a similar portrait by John Smibert in 1724. From a sketch by Vertue of Smibert's composition, and a list of the club's subscribers, we can see that at least six of the men in Hamilton's painting (Baron, Huyssing, Rysbrack, Vertue, Wootton, and Hamilton himself) were members of the Rose and Crown Club at one time. See *Vertue,* III (XXII), 4, 14, 24, 69, 120; VI (XXX), frontispiece, 31–37, 127, 137, 161.

This painting and Smibert's connection with London clubs is discussed in Henry Wilder Foote, Jr, *John Smibert, Painter. With a Descriptive Catalogue of Portraits, and Notes on the Work of Nathaniel Smibert* (Cambridge, Mass., 1950), pp.20–25.

[69] See below pp.113–16.

[70] Bridgeman's health may never have been too good. In about 1725 we have Pope wishing him 'total recovery of [his] health' (*Pope Correspondence*, II, 327), and in 1734 Bridgeman apologizes to Harley because 'an indisposition does not admit [him] at present to pay [his] duty to [His] Lordp in person'. See Appendices IV(ii), IV(iv), pp.156, 157. The large number of stoves mentioned in the Royal Gardener's Inventory is indicative of the cold which Bridgeman must have felt with the dropsy.

[71] See Raines, *Marcellus Laroon,* p.53; Webb, *Rysbrack*, pp.57–58; Wimsatt, *Portraits of Alexander Pope,* p.91. The dating is discussed in Ralph Edwards, 'Conversation Pieces in Search of a Painter', *Apollo*, LXVI (October 1957), 90–94.

[72] The apparent inclusion of Kent (with whom Hogarth had quarrelled bitterly) and the similarities of composition with the National Portrait Gallery group tend to favour Hamilton as the artist. See Finberg, 'Gawen Hamilton', p.57.

[73] Of the names given, Gibbons, Hamilton, Laroon, and Rysbrack were members of the Rose and Crown Club, whilst Bridgeman, Dahl, and Gibbs had been Stewards of St Luke's prior to *c.*1730 (i.e. the date of the painting), and Rysbrack was destined to be in 1735.

[74] In similar vein Mrs Webb, *Rysbrack*, p.58, writes: 'The figure which is said to be Rysbrack bears so little resemblance to the other portraits of him that it can be assumed that whoever added the numbers and identifications was ignorant of the real identities.'

No one questions Hogarth's authorship of The Levee in *The Rake's Progress*, in which the rake is being tempted to waste his substance on prize-fighting, racing, fencing, and other pursuits (*Plate 21*). Bridgeman lurks in the background, standing between the rake and the dancing master and holding in his hand a drawing of a formal parterre with the inscription 'Plan 2' beneath it.[75] The rake's antechamber, writes Austin Dobson, 'is thronged with milliners, wigmakers, tailors and hatters . . . A much be-wigged musician is trying over *The Rape of the Sabines* at a harpsichord: a French horn player preludes noisily upon his instrument. He dabbles in Bridgeman's landscape gardening, and maintains one poet, if not two.'[76] Certainly Bridgeman cuts no fine figure here, and his significance is clear. 'A taste for gardening carried to excess', explains Trusler tartly, describing Bridgeman's role, 'must be acknowledged to have been the ruin of numbers, it being a passion that is seldom, if ever, satisfied, and attended with the greatest expense'.[77] Not that Hogarth himself necessarily regarded Bridgeman unsympathetically.[78] Lichtenberg, in his commentary on Riepenhausen's engraving of The Levee, was sufficiently perspicacious to see that the Royal Gardener may have been 'the most honest person in the whole picture', although suffering from 'a little deafness or paralytic shaking of the head'. 'How honest and genuine he looks!' Lichtenberg exclaimed.[79]

Apart from the head of Bridgeman ascribed to Hogarth already discussed (*Plate 1*), there were at least two other individual portraits which may have been of the Royal Gardener. One was by Sir James Thornhill, Hogarth's father-in-law, the second by Michael Dahl. At one time or another Thornhill painted most of the Harley circle, as well as leaving us a sketch entitled *Group of Artists: Five Men before an Arcade* which contains Dahl, Gibbs, Wanley, Wootton, and Thornhill himself.[80] A small pencil sketch of a seated figure

[75] Ireland regards the formal plan as unworthy of the man who 'attempted to *create landscape, to realize painting, and improve nature*'. John Ireland, *Hogarth Illustrated* (London, 1791–98), I,33.

[76] Henry Austin Dobson, *William Hogarth . . .*, 2nd edn (London, 1907), p.41.

[77] John Trusler, ed., *The Works of William Hogarth . . .* (London, 1833), I, 13.

[78] Professor Paulson has pointed out that Hogarth's *Analysis of Beauty* of 1753 'codified the assumptions expressed by Addison, Pope, Stephen Switzer and others on the garden, and by Hogarth himself in his satiric prints'. See Ronald Paulson, 'Hogarth and the English Garden: Visual and Verbal Structures', in John Dixon Hunt, ed., *Encounters. Essays on Literature and the Visual Arts* (London, 1971), esp. p.90.

[79] Innes and Gustav Herdan, trans., *Lichtenberg's Commentaries on Hogarth's Engravings* (London, 1966), p.207. Lichtenberg's description of Bridgeman reads in part:

> Diesem Kopfe sieht man es, dünkt mich, an, dass er ein Porträt ist. Wie ehrlich und gut! vielleicht der ehrlichste Mann auf dem ganzen Blatte, und daher von der Herrschaft ganz vorzüglich – mit dem Rücken angesehen. Ein solches Gesicht ist fürwahr eine Leibrente, nur freylich in diesen Stadium ihrem Ende nah. Etwas Taubheit oder paralytisches Schütteln würde den Kopf in der Natur nicht schlimmer machen.

See Georg Christoph Lichtenberg, the Elder, *Ausführliche Erklärung der Hogarthischen Kupferstiche . . .* (Göttingen, 1794–1834), pt.3 (1796), pp.85–86. The Levee appears as pl.14 in the separate volume of Riepenhausen plates.

For the iconography of the Levee, and Bridgeman's place in it, see Ronald Paulson, *Hogarth's Graphic Works*, 2nd edn (New Haven and London, 1970), I, 158–60, 162–63; II, pls 140, 245; idem, *Hogarth. His Life, Art, and Times*, esp. I, 332–33, pl.121; Joseph Burke and Colin Caldwell, *Hogarth. The Complete Engravings* (London, 1968), pls 150–51, and Catalogue entry. Pertinent too are David Kunzle, 'Plagiaries-by-Memory of the *Rake's Progress* and the Genesis of Hogarth's Second Picture Story', *Journal of the Warburg and Courtauld Institutes*, XXIX (1966), 311–48, and Hilde Kurz, 'Italian Models of Hogarth's Picture Stories', *Journal of the Warburg and Courtauld Institutes*, XV (1952), 136–68.

[80] See William R. Osmun, 'A Study of the Work of Sir James Thornhill' (Ph.D. thesis, University of London, 1950), pp.353, 457. The drawing is at the Art Institute of Chicago, Leonora Hall Gurley Memorial Collection, 1922.1283.

by Thornhill inscribed 'old Master Charles Bridgeman' is now in the possession of Dr Theodore Besterman (*Plate 22a*).[81] Its titling and its rough and earthy quality (particularly of the hands, which are quite dissimilar from the delicate hand shown by Hamilton) suggest that the subject may be the Royal Gardener's father, whom Thornhill might have known as a member of the Harley set. Regrettably the Dahl portrait is lost. All we can say is that in *A Catalogue of the Collection of . . . Edward Earl of Oxford*, documenting the sale starting on 8 March 1742, there appears an item entitled 'Mr. Charles Bridgeman by Mr. Dahl'. It was bought by the Earl of Essex for £1.5*s*.,[82] conceivably because Bridgeman worked for the earl in his gardens at Cassiobury in Hertfordshire: when Horace Walpole visited Cassiobury in September 1761 he noted that he saw among the contents a 'Head of Bridgman, who laid out the Wood'.[83]

Death, Wills, and Memorials

Charles Bridgeman's death on Wednesday 19 July 1738 was reported by Boyer in his *Political State of Great Britain*, where he says that 'Mr. Bridgman, Gardener of all his Majesty's Royal Gardens' died 'Of a Dropsy, at his House in Kensington'.[84] In the August, Samuel Milward was formally put in charge of the royal gardens at St James's and Kensington, George Lowe at Hampton Court, John Kent at Windsor and Newmarket. Later in the year the Greenings were made responsible for those at Richmond.[85] Milward's

[81] It measures 20×18·7 cm. It was last sold at Sotheby's on 21 May 1970, Lot 67. It was bought by Thomas Agnew and Sons on behalf of Dr Besterman. Its previous owners were Dr Richard Bull (in the eighteenth century), Dr Edward Biggall, Herbert Horne, Sir Edward Marsh, H. C. Green, and L. G. Duke.

Writing in *A General History of the Science and Practice of Music* (London, 1776), v, 93, Sir John Hawkins remarks that Thornhill drew portraits 'in pencil' of all Harley's artistic circle.

[82] 1st Day, Lot 6, No.26. See Wilhelm Nisser, *Michael Dahl and the Contemporary Swedish School of Painting in England* (Uppsala, 1927), Catalogue p.54. Dahl painted portraits of Gibbs, William Thomas, Thornhill, and Harley, and his place in the Harley circle is discussed by Nisser, pp.119–20.

[83] Paget J. Toynbee, ed., 'Horace Walpole's Journals of Visits to Country Seats, Etc.', *Walpole Society*, XVI (1927–28), 37.

Dr Terry Friedman mentioned to me that there may have been a Wedgwood portrait medallion of the Royal Gardener, as a 'William Bridgeman' appears in the Wedgwood catalogues for 1773 and 1778. See Robin Reilly and George Savage, *Wedgwood: the Portrait Medallions* (London, 1973), p.71.

[84] Vol.LVI (1739), 94. Other journals which mention Bridgeman's death in similar terms are *Daily Gazetteer*, No.951 (21 July 1738); *Daily Post*, No.5885 (21 July 1738); *London Evening Post*, Nos 1665, 1667 (20, 22 July 1738); *London Magazine* (July 1738), 361; *Weekly Miscellany*, Nos 291, 292 (21, 28 July 1738).

Boyer, recording Wise's death later in 1738 in his *Political State of Great Britain*, LVI (1739), 570–71, estimates that Wise died worth upwards of £200,000. Wise's will reflects his prosperity. See Green, *Gardener to Queen Anne*, pp. 162–63, 165.

See also the table in Colvin, *et al.*, *History of the King's Works*, *Vol.V*, p.477.

[85] For Milward, Lowe, John Kent, and the Greenings' early royal work see PRO, Works 1/2, minutes of 5 October 1738 onwards; 4/7, minutes of 25 July 1738 onwards; 4/8, *passim*; 5/59, accounts of month of July 1738 onwards; 5/105, accounts of quarter to 30 September 1738 onwards; 5/141, accounts of year to Christmas 1738 onwards; 6/8, letters of 12 August 1738 onwards; 6/16, memorials of 15 August 1738 onwards. See also *CTBP*, III (1735–38), 502; *CTBP*, IV (1739–41), 104, 109, 116, 124, 272, 589.

Other names bandied about in connection with the succession to Bridgeman include Dent in *London Magazine* (July 1738), 361, and in *Read's Weekly Journal*, No.725 (29 July 1738); Swinno or Swinlow in *Daily Gazetteer*, No.951 (21 July 1738), and in Green, *Gardener to Queen Anne*, p.215; Turner and Low in *Gentleman's Magazine*, VIII (1738), 436.

letter of appointment was typical. It explained that the royal gardens at St James's and Kensington,

> which with the rest of Our Royal Gardens were lately under the Conduct Care and Maintenance of Charles Bridgeman deceased, shall for the future be sever'd from the rest of Our said Royal Gardens and be under the Conduct, Care and Maintenance of a Person specially to be appointed for that Service.[86]

Apart from the Greenings, whose appointment was back-dated to midsummer 1738, all these posts were taken up officially on 'the day of the Death of the said Charles Bridgeman'.[87] This division of responsibilities ended the concept of the single Royal Gardener that had begun in England with John Rose under Charles II and lasted almost a century. Within that period the royal gardens had increased considerably in size, and although the new 'Gardiners to His Majesty' were still paid at the annual rate of £15 an acre, it cost George II well over double what he had committed himself to pay Bridgeman a decade earlier.[88]

It was in Kensington on 6 July, only a fortnight before his death, that Bridgeman signed his will and stated that he was of St James's Parish in Westminster.[89] On 22 July he was buried in the Wren church of St James's, overlooking his own St James's Square (*Plate 14*).[90] This church has had a chequered history of demolition and rebuilding, and there is no memorial today either to Bridgeman or to members of his family. As he drew Blenheim in 1709, we may assume that Bridgeman would have been at least nearing fifty when he died. His bequests were considerable, especially when compared with those of his widow Sarah five years later. She sounded poverty-stricken, friendless, one of her few requests being that she should be buried in the Tower of London, where she might have had a grace-and-favour residence.[91]

His widow's penury implies that Bridgeman thought he was going to leave more than he did. She was granted £300 in cash, minor income from property, and the 'residue or surplus' after the bequests and expenses had been met. But as the Royal Gardener left

[86] PRO, Works 6/8, letter of 17 August 1738.

[87] The last official record of payment to Bridgeman during his lifetime was on 13 April 1738. See *CTBP*, III (1735–38), 476.

[88] The total annual payment agreed with the Board of Works in 1738 was £4,932.18*s*.6*d*., consisting of £2,580.0*s*.0*d*. to Milward for 172 acres at St James's and Kensington; £1,107.6*s*.0*d*. to Lowe for 73 acres, 3 roods, 11 poles at Hampton Court; £102.15*s*.0*d*. to John Kent for 6 acres, 3 roods, 16 poles at Windsor and Newmarket; and £1,142.17*s*.6*d*. to the Greenings for 79 acres, 3 roods, 35 poles at Richmond.

[89] See below Appendix VII, pp.169–70. The Royal Gardener's widow, and his cousin Charles Bridgeman of Hertford, proved his will on 12 October 1738. Letters of administration with will annexed were granted to Sarah Bridgeman, the daughter, on 20 November 1746 as both the widow Sarah Bridgeman and the cousin had died without fully administering the estate.

[90] Burial registers at St James's Church, Piccadilly. According to SG, Boyd's Index of London Burials, II, 247, two Charles Bridgemans were interred in St James's in 1738.

[91] See below Appendix VIII, p.171. The will was proved on 21 January 1744. On 16 October 1746 letters of administration with will annexed were granted to Elizabeth Price (*née* Bridgeman, wife of Philip Price), as one of the executors (Captain Clement Lemprière of the Tower of London) had died, and the other executor (William Bradshaw of Soho Square) had renounced his executorship.

Lady Mary Wortley Montagu refers to a 'Mrs. Bridgeman' in one letter of 1739 and two of 1742 when her death is noted. See Robert Halsband, ed., *The Complete Letters of Lady Mary Wortley Montagu* (Oxford, 1965–67), II, 133, 266, 294.

£2,000 to each of his daughters Sarah, Elizabeth, and Ann, it meant that his estate had to amount to £6,300 before his widow received anything other than her bare £300. Presumably Bridgeman had not left enough to cover his bequests, and the legal complications of the will led to delay. Perhaps Bridgeman's failing health had given him delusions of grandeur; or his illness may have meant that the true state of his finances was kept from him. In one of her many pathetic pleas for money, Sarah Bridgeman writes to the Treasury that 'with much sorrow [she] is obliged to Inform [their] Lordships, that her husband has kept no regular Accots. of the Money he has received'.[92] Apart from such hints, we can only speculate. One factor does emerge: although Bridgeman's income from his post as Royal Gardener and his private commissions must have been considerable, his outgoings were correspondingly large, and it would have needed a good business head to keep track of the minutiae stipulated in the 'Scheme' for his Royal Appointment. Furthermore, he owned several properties, had a large family, and would doubtless have enjoyed the life of a *bon vivant* with his literary and artistic friends: Vertue admitted, for instance, that London club life was extremely expensive.[93]

In 1739 Sarah Bridgeman published Rigaud and Baron's *Views of Stowe*, thus recording for posterity the finest achievement of her husband's career. The last years of her life were marred with litigation: suits with the Mists and with her daughter Sarah, angry correspondence over payments with the Lords of the Treasury and with Sarah, Duchess of Marlborough.[94] It is a bitter postscript to Bridgeman's life that within months of his death his widow was approaching George II for 'his Majestys Royal Compassion' as she and her family had been left in 'very narrow Circumstances'.[95] Apart from payments owing from private clients,[96] she was able to exact nearly £5,000 from the Board of Works before the summer of 1743.[97] Would that she had been as successful with Sarah Churchill. Sarah Bridgeman's claims in 1741 from the elderly Duchess over bills for Blenheim involved arguments of the worst sort. Although generous in her dealings with the Royal Gardener, the Duchess had been careful to keep all accounts of his work at the palace. Opinions varied on the widow's circumstances. If Sarah Bridgeman were truthful in her statement that her husband had not 'left effects to pay his Debts' and that this would be 'the ruin of his Family', it did not soften the Duchess's indignation. Lastly, in a mood of exasperation, the Duchess threatened to bring a lawsuit unless her adversary proposed 'something that is reasonable'. Bridgeman's widow seems to have been *in extremis*, almost demented. For her, if for no-one else, Boyer's added description of her husband's post of Royal Gardener as 'a Place of Considerable Profit' must indeed have seemed cold comfort.[98]

[92] Undated petition in PRO, Works 6/16, fo.97.

[93] *Vertue*, III (XXII), 120.

[94] See below Appendices IV(v), IV(vi), IV(vii), VI, pp.157–60, 168.

[95] See below Appendix VI, p.168.

[96] E.g. those for Woburn, cited below, p.53n 44.

[97] The settling of these demands can be traced in PRO, Works 1/2, minutes of 5 October 1738, 1 February 1739, 8 July 1740; Works 4/7, minutes of 25 July, 5 October 1738, 1 February, 6 March, 3 April 1739; Works 4/8, *passim*, particularly minutes of 12 February, 4, 12, 18 March 1740, 15 March 1743; Works 5/141, *passim* 1728–40; Works 6/16, minutes of 18 September, 2 October 1738, *passim* 1739–40. See also PRO, Money Book XL (T53:40), fos 195–96; *CTBP*, III (1735–38), 515, 563; *CTBP*, IV (1739–41), 21, 27, 84 (twice), 156, 218, 254, 379.

[98] Boyer, *Political State of Great Britain*, LVI (1739), 94.

Chapter 2

Friends and Fellow-Artists

The impetus given by the writings of Dézallier D'Argenville, Temple, Nourse, Switzer, and the rest soon led to a surge of landscapes reflecting the new ideas. The English man of property, whether freshly returned from the Grand Tour or not, was in no mood to ape Versailles, and the principles adopted by London and Wise at Chatsworth would no longer do. Bridgeman's involvement in these changes cannot be separated from his collaboration with a wide range of architects: three Scots (William Adam, Gibbs, and Campbell), a Frenchman (Dubois), a Venetian (Leoni), and colleagues from the Board of Works (Flitcroft, Kent, and Roger Morris). And there were the noble amateurs Burlington and Pembroke. Above all, however, stood Sir John Vanbrugh, perhaps the most influential friend Bridgeman ever had (*Plate 22b*). Not merely was Vanbrugh a pioneer in both architecture and landscaping, but through the Kit-Cat Club he had the ear of some of the most prominent Whigs who shared his enthusiasm for 'the beauty of natural gardening',[1] notably Addison, Congreve and Steele, Charles Dartiquenave, and such Bridgeman clients as Cobham, Henry Clinton, Spencer Compton, John Montagu, Thomas Pelham-Holles, and Sir Robert Walpole.[2] As well as Stowe, Bridgeman and Vanbrugh collaborated at Blenheim, Eastbury, and Claremont.

Vanbrugh

'When you first begin to build, and make Gardens', wrote Switzer in *Ichnographia Rustica*, 'the Gardener and Builder ought to go Hand in Hand, and to consult together.'[3] In Vanbrugh gardener and builder were one. His tenure of the post of Surveyor of Gardens and Waters from 1715 to 1726 marked official recognition of his concern with landscaping, a concern which went back to the start of his architectural career at Castle Howard, built for Charles Howard, 3rd Earl of Carlisle and fellow-member of the Kit-Cat.[4] Here

[1] Osborn, ed., *Spence's Anecdotes*, I, 407 (No. 1067).

[2] For the Kit-Cat Club see Kathleen M. Lynch, *Jacob Tonson, Kit-Cat Publisher* (Knoxville, Tenn., 1971), *passim*; David T. Piper, *Catalogue of Seventeenth-Century Portraits in the National Portrait Gallery, 1625–1714* (Cambridge, 1963), pp.398–403. Vanbrugh's relationship with men of letters is considered in Richard C. Boys, 'The Architect Vanbrugh and the Wits', *College Art Journal* (New York), VI (1947), 283–90.

[3] 1718 edn, II, 154. Switzer pours scorn on the 'Closet Paper Ingineer', that is the garden designer who never visits a site but sits at home 'resolving upon some regular Scheme in the Closet'. See, e.g., *Ichnographia Rustica* (1742), III, xii, 79.

[4] See Green, *Gardener to Queen Anne*, pp.37–40; Whistler, *Imagination of Vanbrugh*, pp.26–82; and recently Mr George Howard's *Castle Howard* (Castle Howard, 1972). I am grateful for advice on Vanbrugh to Dr Kerry Downes, whose own book on Vanbrugh appeared too late for me to use.

Vanbrugh suggested the demolition of Henderskelfe Castle, village, and Church in order to give a panoramic view of the countryside. In Wray Wood, originally designed by George London, Carlisle advocated the use of a 'Labyrinth', and so successful was he that Switzer regarded the result as 'incomparable' and marking 'the highest pitch that Natural and Polite Gard'ning can possibly ever arrive to . . . from which the Ingenious may draw the best of their Schemes in Natural and Rural Gardening'.[5] In practice, Wray Wood apparently contained straight walks linking circular open spaces with garden features set in them, much as Castell was to show at Pliny's Tuscum over twenty years later (*Plate 12*).[6] Indeed, Vanbrugh and Hawksmoor may well have been influenced by the younger Pliny.[7] Elsewhere at Castle Howard the two architects planted garden buildings which looked as if they had grown there – the obelisk, Temple of the Four Winds, pyramid, and mausoleum, to name the most memorable. Horace Walpole was overwhelmed: Castle Howard, he asserted, is 'the grandest scene of real magnificence I ever saw'.[8]

It was at Blenheim Palace not Castle Howard, however, that Vanbrugh's concern for the pictorial and associative qualities of landscape reached its zenith.[9] 'The charge at Blenheim', wrote Sir Winston Churchill, 'opened to Britain the gateways of the modern world.'[10] On 13 August 1704 the Duke of Marlborough crushed the forces of Louis XIV at Blenheim, and ten months later Lord Treasurer Godolphin signed a warrant appointing Vanbrugh as architect of a palace at Woodstock, the gift of Queen and country to a national hero (*Plate 23b*). The estate consisted of over 2,000 acres divided by the narrow River Glyme meandering through a deep, curving valley. Not until various alternatives had been rejected were Vanbrugh's proposals for the park accepted, and in April 1705 Henry Wise began preparing a detailed layout; assisting Wise was Stephen Switzer, and by 1709 Charles Bridgeman had joined the team. Like most things at Blenheim, their endeavours were carefully scrutinized by Sarah, the Duchess. She it was who dictated policy, checked accounts, questioned extravagance. She it was who dismissed artists: Thornhill survived without mishap, but in 1716 Sarah discharged both Vanbrugh and Wise, the first being followed by Hawksmoor and the second in turn by Tilleman Bobart and John Hughes. When Hughes parted from Blenheim in disgust in 1728, Bridgeman succeeded him; very likely Bridgeman had left Blenheim several years before, and at this juncture had been persuaded to return. In the interim he had established himself as a highly successful practitioner, had proved his mettle to the Duchess in his work for her at Wimbledon House, and had become (or was about to become) Royal Gardener.

Blenheim provides us with our most familiar evidence of Vanbrugh's interest in landscape in his oft-quoted memorandum of 11 June 1709 on the preservation of Woodstock

[5] Switzer, *Ichnographia Rustica* (1718), I, 87; II, 198. See Whistler, *Imagination of Vanbrugh*, pp.30–31, 62–69.

[6] This can be seen in the early plan in ibid., pl.18. Cf. pls 19–22.

[7] See Kerry Downes, *Hawksmoor* (London, 1959), pp.218–21. Dr Downes surmises that influence may have come from Hawksmoor's possession of Jean François Félibien, *Les plans et les descriptions de deux des plus belles maisons de campagne de Pline le Consul* . . . (Amsterdam, 1706).

[8] Toynbee, ed., 'Walpole's Visits to Country Seats', p.72.

[9] For Blenheim see Green, *Blenheim Palace* (London, 1951); idem, *Gardener to Queen Anne*, pp.96–121; Whistler, *Imagination of Vanbrugh*, pp.111–23.

[10] Quoted by Green, *Gardener to Queen Anne*, p.96.

Manor which, he says, with its 'lively and pleasing Reflections' would make 'One of the Most Agreable Objects that the best of Landskip Painters can invent' (*Plate 23a*). If the manor is removed, Vanbrugh concludes mischievously, the damage could only be rectified at '*Vast Expence*'.[11] The Duchess of Marlborough was unimpressed by his fondness for 'an old Building that Stood awry and Spoiled the view'; far from dismayed, in 1713 Vanbrugh went to live in it, having first built himself a round penthouse in the roof as if (said the Duchess) 'to study the Planets'.[12] Whether or not Uvedale Price was correct in claiming that the architect advised the Duchess to 'send for a Landscape painter',[13] Reynolds in his thirteenth *Discourse* (1786) spoke of Vanbrugh 'in the language of a Painter', as an architect who 'composed like a Painter', and as one who understood perfectly 'the general ruling principles of Architecture and Painting'.[14] What is crucial is that the Woodstock Manor incident contains, in embryo, the seeds of thinking about the Picturesque which later in the century were to grow into an elaborate artistic theory.[15]

The suggestion that the Royal Gardener may have played a leading role in the design of the park stems from the words 'Bridgman Descript.' written on the cartouche of a plan of Blenheim dated 1709 (*Plate 24*).[16] Bridgeman's drawing, similar to the plan of 1725 in *Vitruvius Britannicus III* (*Plate 25*), shows a concept which is as forceful as the architecture of the palace itself, bold in imagination and vast in scale. The scheme is dominated by the great avenue of beeches which still remains, and by the road which strides across the countryside and marches over the Grand Bridge and up to the north front; facing the south front Bridgeman has indicated the kitchen garden with bastion walls, straight walks, and winding paths. To the north of the Grand Bridge – which straddles a mere stream, pending Capability Brown's flooding of the lake in 1764 – Bridgeman has judiciously shown the outline of Woodstock Manor, and we can assume that he was party to the dispute about it. No one can be precise about Bridgeman's contribution to Blenheim – it may have involved the creation of a ha-ha before Dézallier D'Argenville described one in print – but there is no question of his intense activity there during his last years.[17]

The letters of 1741 from the Duchess of Marlborough to Widow Sarah Bridgeman are evidence enough.[18] Bridgeman, in 'Performing his articles', had to remove 'some Earth, not much, a few English Elms, and Hedges, and Gravel fetch'd from [the Duchess's] own

[11] Bonamy Dobrée and Geoffrey F. Webb, eds, *The Complete Works of Sir John Vanbrugh* (London, 1927–28), IV, 29–30.

[12] BL, Add MS 38056, cited in Green, *Blenheim Palace*, p.141, and again in *Gardener to Queen Anne*, pp. ix, 117.

[13] Uvedale Price, *Essays on the Picturesque* . . . (London, 1810), II, 116.

[14] Sir Joshua Reynolds, *Discourses on Art*, ed. Robert R. Wark, 2nd edn (New Haven and London, 1975), pp.243–44. See Richard C. Boys, 'Sir Joshua Reynolds and the Architect Vanbrugh. A Footnote to Boswell', *Papers of the Michigan Academy of Arts, Science and Letters*, XXXIII (1947), 323–36.

[15] Dr Watkin, for instance, takes the memorandum of 1709 as a starting point for his discussion of Hope and the Picturesque. See David J. Watkin, *Thomas Hope (1769–1831) and the Neoclassical Idea* (London, 1968), pp.125–33.

[16] Spence comments enigmatically: 'Vanbrugh? had some idea of the beauty of natural gardening. Query: who? from the oaks left in those at Blenheim. (Was it not Bridgeman did that?).' Osborn, ed., *Spence's Anecdotes*, I, 407 (No.1067).

[17] The 1709 plan and that in *Vitruvius Britannicus* both have ha-has around the kitchen garden. According to Green, *Gardener to Queen Anne*, p.100, there was a ha-ha at Blenheim when Defoe visited the house in 1724 – i.e. within Vanbrugh's lifetime – and in 1709 Vanbrugh was writing about finishing 'the present Wall for the Inclosures'. Dobrée and Webb, eds, *Works of Vanbrugh*, IV, 30.

Mr Green encountered Bridgeman's name nowhere in the Blenheim accounts of 1705–16, but in a letter to me of 11 November 1961 suggested that the Bridgeman 1709 plan is 'as executed, possibly down to even the last tree'.

[18] See below Appendices IV (v), IV (vi), IV (vii), pp.157–60.

Ground, to make the Walks as they should be'. Bridgeman also agreed 'to plant all Fruit-trees, Flowers, and to finish the whole place, [and] the Ground in a handsome Manner and to make good all Trees that dye'. He had similarly promised, the Duchess notes, 'to make all the Wood walks clean with Sand, or Gravel, the Terras-walk handsome, to strip up the Trees in the Vineyard-Walk, and the Wood on the outside [of] the House to [her] liking . . . And to begin and finish the Road with all possible Expedition'. One of her Grace's complaints was that, because of Bridgeman's death, she had been denied the year's upkeep of her finished garden, a task which he usually undertook. Worse than that. As soon as the Royal Gardener died his widow withdrew all his men from Blenheim, and as a result the Duchess herself had to pay £700 out of her own pocket to complete the work. Sarah Bridgeman's demands for an extra £1,084.6*s*.5½*d*. (making a total of £3,439.6*s*.5½*d*.) were hotly disputed in the ensuing verbal battle. Blenheim's grounds would have been completed much sooner, the Duchess maintains, had she not been so tolerant, believing that Bridgeman was 'a very honest Man' and realizing that he had 'a great deal to do for others'.

The 'others' included the Dodington family at Eastbury who, as relatives of the Temples, must have been well aware of Bridgeman and Vanbrugh's involvement at Stowe. During the early 1700's Eastbury was a farm owned by George Dodington, a cousin of Viscount Cobham, and it was Dodington who brought in Vanbrugh.[19] Vanbrugh prepared designs for a house which was second only in size to Blenheim and Castle Howard among his country seats (*Plate 28a*). In about 1718 Dodington began to build, engaging Thornhill on interior decoration, but died within a few years. Work stopped, and it was not restarted by his son George Bubb Dodington, Baron Melcombe, until 1724. After Vanbrugh's death the house was completed by Roger Morris in 1733–38, by which time it had served as the centre for a group of friends including Vanbrugh, Thornhill, Christopher Pitt, Edward Young, and James Thomson.[20] Thomson found the appeal of Eastbury and its landscape irresistible, and penned a description of it in the *Seasons*:

Oh lose me in the green delightful walks
Of, Dodington! thy seat, serene and plain;
Where simple nature reigns; and every view,
Diffusive, spreads the pure Dorsetian downs,
In boundless prospect; yonder shagged with wood,
Here rich with harvest, and there white with flocks!
Meantime the grandeur of thy lofty dome,
Far-splendid, seizes on the ravished eye.
New beauties rise with each revolving day;
New columns swell; and still the fresh Spring finds
New plants to quicken, and new groves to green. (Autumn, ll.654–64)

[19] For Eastbury see Arthur Oswald, *Country Houses of Dorset*, 2nd edn (London, 1959), pp.149–53; *RCHM: Dorset*, IV (1972), 90–93; Whistler, *Imagination of Vanbrugh*, pp.156–77. I am grateful to Mr Desmond S. Bonney and Mr Christopher Taylor for their advice on the history of Eastbury.

[20] See Antony Brackenbury, 'The Happy Eastbury Circle', *C.Life*, CXIX (8 March 1956), 422–23; Lloyd Sanders, *Patron and Place-Hunter. A Study of George Bubb Dodington, Lord Melcombe* (London and New York, 1919), pp.71–95.

The texts of my quotations from Thomson's *Seasons* and *Liberty*, here and elsewhere in this book, are taken from the two-volume Aldine Edition of 1860, edited by Sir Harris Nicolas and Peter Cunningham.

The landscape was to have a longer life than the mansion, for after Earl Temple inherited Eastbury on Melcombe's death in 1762 he proceeded to blow up the house. Our sole reminders of Vanbrugh's buildings are the stables and gateway still standing on the site, and the decorative floor of the great saloon at Stowe, made from marble prudently removed from Eastbury before Earl Temple resorted to gunpowder.[21]

Campbell's five engravings of Eastbury in *Vitruvius Britannicus III* consist of two of the house, two of garden buildings, and one of the layout of the grounds, described by Campbell as 'an exact Plan of the Gardens, designed and finished by the ingenious Mr. *Charles Bridgeman*' (*Plate 26*).[22] Eastbury to this day retains the configuration Bridgeman gave it to a remarkable degree (*Plate 27*). The buildings, Campbell tells us, were 'designed and executed by Sir *John Vanbrugh, Anno 1718*'. The park at Eastbury lacked the splendid sweep of Blenheim, its design being focused on a central rectangular lake, two mounts, parterres, bosquets, and the round pond set in an amphitheatre. Seen from the mansion the garden sloped down to the round pond straight ahead, and then up to Vanbrugh's distant Corinthian temple (*Plate 29a*); his Ionic bagnio was placed in the garden wall to the right (*Plate 29b*).[23] The Corinthian temple commanded a splendid view of the surrounding countryside and of the garden proper, with its changes of level and its precise geometry. Bridgeman's own plans of Eastbury in the Bodleian Library are looser than Campbell's, and indicate winding walks, the integration of the 'extensive' with the 'specific' garden by means of ha-has, and the introduction of a woodland amphitheatre as an approach to the house (*Plate 28b*). Bridgeman has replaced the restriction of the *Vitruvius Britannicus* design by a broader concept which sets Vanbrugh's buildings within groves and parkland. Fourteen tree-covered hillocks to the north, and straight rides reaching out in other directions, heighten the dramatic effect, but even the sight of deer playing sportively in the fields cannot compensate for the essential rigidity of the layout.

Less rigid than Eastbury is Claremont, the Surrey estate which Vanbrugh sold in 1714 to Thomas Pelham-Holles, created 1st Duke of Newcastle the following year.[24] Vanbrugh was responsible for Newcastle's alterations to the house, and for designing the White Cottage and the castellated brick belvedere of 1717 – one of the earliest mock-medieval follies in England. Bridgeman was concerned with the landscaping during the 1720's, but Kent evidently took over around 1729, the year in which he began work for Newcastle's brother, Henry Pelham, at Esher Place next door: here, where he was 'Kentissime',[25] '*Kent* and Nature vye[d] for PELHAM'S Love'.[26] Thomson immortalized the two estates in the *Seasons* when he wrote of

[21] See William James Smith, ed., *The Grenville Papers . . .* (London, 1852–53), IV, 9–10. By 1782, as Dr Downes pointed out to me, Earl Temple had 'dismantled the park'. See C. Bruyn Andrews, ed., *The Torrington Diaries . . .* (London, 1934), I, 105.

[22] The only other reference to Bridgeman in *Vitruvius Britannicus* is as a subscriber to the second and third volumes.

[23] A drawing by Vanbrugh of the bagnio is in H. M. Colvin and M. J. Craig, eds, *Architectural Drawings in the Library of Elton Hall by Sir John Vanbrugh and Sir Edward Lovett Pearce* (Oxford, 1964), No.194; pl.39(b).

[24] For Claremont see Phyllis M. Cooper, *The Story of Claremont*, 6th edn (Claremont, 1975); Whistler, *Imagination of Vanbrugh*, pp.151–54 and, most recently, Dorothy Stroud, 'The Gardens at Claremont', *The National Trust Year Book, 1975–76* (London, 1975), pp.32–37.

[25] *Yale Walpole,* IX, 71. Walpole to Montagu, 11 August 1748.

[26] Alexander Pope, *Epilogue to the Satires, Dialogue II* (London, 1738), l.67.

. . . Clermont's terrassed height, and Esher's groves,
Where is the sweetest solitude, embraced
By the soft windings of the silent Mole,
From courts and senates Pelham finds repose.

(Summer, ll.1429–32)

To the north-west of Claremont's 'terrassed height' lay the belvedere, set in a dense wood and approached by sinuous paths. Campbell gives us a layout of Claremont in *Vitruvius Britannicus III* (*Plate 30*) and describes it as 'a Geometrical Plan of the Gardens and Plantations, with several large Pieces of Water, which his Grace has finished at a very great Expence'. The 'Situation' is 'singularly romantick', he continues, 'and from the high Tower [one] has a most prodigious fine Prospect of the *Thames* and adjacent Villas'. Beyond the belvedere is the round pond which, with the adjacent amphitheatre, forms Bridgeman's major contribution to Claremont.

Switzer in his *Introduction to a General System of Hydrostaticks and Hydraulicks* of 1729 includes a plate of the amphitheatre and ascribes its design to the Royal Gardener (*Plate 32a*). 'The upper Part of the Work', he writes,

> may very easily be seen to be a Sketch of the fine Amphitheatre at *Claremont* . . . the Design of the very ingenious Mr. *Bridgeman*; and the lower Part, where the Water Spouts out, is an Addition of my own, from a Work of that kind I have done for the Right Honourable the Earl of *Orrery*, at *Marston* in *Somersetshire*.

Modesty is not Switzer's forte. 'In this Composition', he goes on, 'which I humbly conceive to be the noblest of any in *Europe*, may be seen a very magnificent Taste and Way of thinking.' Switzer disliked the round pond, though he admits that Bridgeman had severe restraints imposed upon him. 'Had the ingenious Designer had more room at *Claremont*', Switzer adds, 'he would certainly have made his Water much larger than that little Circular Basin, which is seen therein, and which is very much eclips'd by the prodigious Grandeur of that Ampitheatre.' Switzer comments on Bridgeman's scheme 'for the Advantage of those who have more Room for such a Purpose'.[27] The fusion of round pond and amphitheatre forms the basis of what was built, and is illustrated by a Bridgemanic sketch in the Soane Museum (*Plate 32b*).[28] Kent took pains to keep Bridgeman's amphitheatre intact when he built a grotto and an island temple nearby, as is apparent from Rocque and Benazech's view of 1754 (*Plate 31*).[29] Kent also softened the outline of the round pond, so much so that Horace Walpole was to comment on the 'small lake edged by a winding bank with scattered trees' which he found at Claremont, Esher, and other Kent gardens.[30] Claremont was one of the houses drawn by Rigaud when in England in 1733–34, and his sketch of the bowling green, with the belvedere in the background, forms a useful contrast with Kent's looser sketch of the same subject (*Plates 165a, 165b*).

[27] Vol. II, p.405, describing pl.37. The amphitheatre is praised by Langley, *New Principles of Gardening* (1728), p. vii.

[28] Soane, Drawer 62.1.2. There is a plan of Choisy-le-Roi, France, in MSGD a3 fo.13. On the back are the words 'Choisie', and 'A Survey of Clare Mount'.

[29] Cf. Rocque's plan of Claremont (1738) in *Vit. Brit.*, IV (1739), pls 19–23.

[30] Chase, *Horace Walpole: Gardenist*, p.30. See Vertue's comments on Kent at Claremont in *Vertue*, III (XXII), 141.

More drastic revisions were to come, for in 1768 the Duke of Newcastle's widow sold Claremont to Lord Clive of Plassey (Clive of India), who engaged Capability Brown to redesign the park and to provide him with a new house on higher ground. To our eyes, Claremont is more 'singularly romantick' today than when Bridgeman and Vanbrugh were there, with the grotto in decay, the island temple in ruins, and the amphitheatre overgrown and eroded. High on the wooded hill the belvedere, ravaged by time and vandals, stands as a defiant reminder of Vanbrugh's affection for 'Something of the Castle Air'.[31]

Flitcroft

Such enthusiasm for the Picturesque hardly characterizes the designs of Henry Flitcroft (*Plate 33b*), but his friendship with Bridgeman and his patronage by Burlington place him firmly amidst the landscape pioneers. Flitcroft, one of Bridgeman's Marylebone neighbours and a colleague at the Board of Works, was son of a gardener to William III at Hampton Court. By 1720 Flitcroft was assisting the Earl of Burlington, and subsequently made drawings for Chiswick and for the plates published in two volumes by Kent, under the aegis of Burlington, as *The Designs of Inigo Jones* (1727). 'Burlington Harry', as Flitcroft was familiarly known, became Master Carpenter at the Board of Works in 1746, and succeeded Kent as Master Mason and Deputy Surveyor in 1748. A decade later Flitcroft took over from Ripley as Comptroller of the Works, although he designed little of significance in his official capacity. Flitcroft's chief buildings are churches and country houses, but he displays none of Vanbrugh's flair, and most of the estates on which Bridgeman and Flitcroft collaborated are modest enough when set alongside Blenheim, Eastbury, or Claremont. If we except royal work, links between Bridgeman and Flitcroft include Bower House (formerly known as Mounthavering), Chicheley, Woburn, Amesbury, and the Northamptonshire seat of the Montagu family at Boughton. After Bridgeman's death Flitcroft was at Wimpole and perhaps at Stowe.

Bower House is a simple, brick, London box with a central pediment, standing on land in Essex once part of the royal estate of Havering-atte-Bower, and built in 1729 by John Baynes, Sergeant-at-Law. An anonymous painting at Ingatestone Hall shows the north front in Bridgeman's day (*Plate 33a*), that is before the addition of the wings which have dominated the south side since about 1800 (*Plate 34a*). The artists employed at Bower were all friends of Bridgeman: Vanderbank painted portraits of Baynes and his wife in 1727, Thornhill may have decorated the stair well, whilst Flitcroft designed the house itself and set it in a Bridgeman landscape – or so it would seem from the plaque in the entrance hall

[31] Dobrée and Webb, eds, *Works of Vanbrugh*, IV, 14. Vanbrugh to Earl of Manchester, 18 July 1707. Drawings in Cooper, *Claremont*, pp.32–33, illustrate the sequence of changes from the early eighteenth-century to the present-day layout at Claremont. For what might have been see Christopher Tunnard, *Gardens in the Modern Landscape*, 2nd edn (London and New York, 1948), pp.155–58.

at Bower which records that 'H. FLITCROFT. ARCHITECTUS. C. BRIDGMAN. DESIGNAVIT'.[32] Apparently Baynes believed in giving credit where credit was due. Flitcroft, then thirty-two and untried as an independent architect, was embarking upon his first major commission, and both he and Bridgeman would be known to Baynes through the Board of Works. Bower House is placed high on a hillock, and its eighteenth-century landscaping was in the Bridgemanic idiom: a writer in 1771 tells us that the 'pleasure grounds [were] extensive, and [had] several visto's affording pleasing prospects, terminated by agreeable and proper objects'. The distant outlook from Bower was, and is, panoramic, commanding 'most delightful and extensive prospects into Kent, and into different parts of the country'.[33] Bridgeman and Flitcroft's happy integration of villa and landscape reminds us of similar estates being laid out at the same time, such as Well Vale in Lincolnshire, a house not unlike Bower (*Plate 35a*).[34]

Bridgeman and Flitcroft's collaboration at Bower came hard on the heels of work at Chicheley, where their client was Sir John Chester, patron of Kent and friend of Burrell Massingberd. In 1722, some two years after he was taken under Burlington's wing, Flitcroft designed a double-storeyed hall at Chicheley, where Francis Smith of Warwick had been engaged in 1719. It is likely that Bridgeman was simultaneously active in the grounds, for in 1726 Chester was writing to Massingberd in terms which imply that Chicheley was then being laid out under Bridgeman's direction.[35] Part of the Royal Gardener's duties involved work on the U-shaped canal which had been constructed by George London and which still exists today (*Plates 38a, 38b*).[36] Canals, of course, are part of Bridgeman's stock-in-trade, and it is not impossible that the canal at Wrest in Bedfordshire – known as the Long Water and culminating in Archer's garden pavilion – may owe something to Bridgeman's intervention (*Plate 35b*).[37]

[32] The complete text of the plaque reads:

M:S
E.RELIQUIIS.ÆDIS.REGALIS.DE.HAVERING.BOWER.
IN.SUMMITATE.COLLIS.SITÆ.
HOC.FUNDAVIT.DOMICILIUM.IOHANNES.BAYNES.
SERVIENS.AD.LEGEM.
UT.IN.OTIA.TUTA.RECEDERET.
ET.SIBI.ET.AMICIS.SUAVITER.VACARET.
A:D:1729
H.FLITCROFT.ARCHITECTUS.C.BRIDGMAN.DESIGNAVIT.
ARMA.REGIS.EDVARDI.TERTII.SUPER.HOC.SCULPTA.
SAXA.VETUSTATEM.SATIS.EVINCUNT.

[33] Peter Muilman, *A New and Complete History of Essex* . . . (Chelmsford, 1770–72), IV, 313–14.

[34] See Gervase Jackson-Stops, 'Well Vale, Lincolnshire', *C.Life*, CLII (14 December 1972), 1650–54. The left-hand bay shown in *Plate 35a* was added late in the eighteenth century. Cf. *Plate 55a* of Stanmer.

[35] SG, Massingberd Papers, quoted by Joan D. Tanner, 'The Building of Chicheley Hall', *Records of Buckinghamshire*, XVII (1961), 48. For Chicheley generally see James Lees-Milne, *English Country Houses: Baroque, 1685–1715* (London, 1970), pp.227–35, and recently Marcus Binney, 'Chicheley Hall, Buckinghamshire', *C.Life*, CLVII (13, 20, 27 February 1975), 378–81, 434–37, 498–501.

[36] London's work at Chicheley is discussed in Arthur Oswald, 'Chicheley Hall', *C.Life*, LXXIX (16 May 1936), 508–9.

[37] Leoni and Kent, as well as Archer, were connected with Wrest. See T. P. Hudson, 'A Ducal Patron of Architects', *C.Life*, CLV (17 January 1974), 78–81. See also Joyce Godber, *History of Bedfordshire, 1066–1888* (Bedford, 1969), esp. pp.299–302, and pls 46a, 46b, 56a, 56b; idem, 'The Marchioness Grey of Wrest Park', *Bedfordshire Historical Record Society (Publications)*, XLVII (1968), 21–22; idem, *Wrest Park and the Duke of Kent (Henry Grey, 1671–1740)* (Bedford (Elstow Moot Hall), 1963), esp. p.8, where Thomas Ackres' plan of the grounds of 1715 is discussed. For Leoni's design of a new house see ibid., p.9. For Archer see Marcus Whiffen, *Thomas Archer. Architect of the English Baroque*, 2nd edn (Los Angeles, 1973), pp.25–27. See the Bridgemanic plan of 1737 by Rocque in *Vit. Brit.*, IV (1739), pls 30–33.

Also in Bedfordshire is Woburn. When Flitcroft was called there in 1747 by John Russell, 4th Duke of Bedford, he was successor to a landscape in which Bridgeman had been involved. The mansion, built between 1626 and 1630, had been inherited by the Duke on his succession to the title in 1732.[38] The Duchess of Bedford's grandmother Sarah, Duchess of Marlborough, took a great interest in Woburn. 'I am sure if it was my house, I would never pull it down', Sarah commented, 'but I would alter several things in it by degrees and make it a better house than any architect can build now.'[39] Undeterred by her remarks, the Duke turned to the architect John Sanderson, whose proposals of 1733 included a brand new residence, a bridge, and three circular temples. Sanderson envisaged a restrained Palladian villa (*Plate 34b*), set in a Bridgeman landscape containing garden ornaments.[40] By 1733, doubtless endorsed by the Duchess of Marlborough, the Bedfords had sought out Bridgeman's services, and Christian Cole was writing thus to the Duchess of Bedford:

> I hear from the Dutches of Manchester that Mr Bridgman was with the Duke of Bedford, and that by the advice of that Ingenious gardener your Grand Park is to be so disposed as to make it beautifull, magnificent, and the admiration of those who travel that way.

Never let anyone say that this smacks of self-indulgence, for, says Cole, we should be glad when such owners of great estates both please themselves and also provide 'an ornament to the kingdome in general'.[41] Four years later, in about 1737, the Duke of Bedford remarks in a notebook that the 'Stairs down to the Bason, and the Drawbridge into the Bowling Green [are] to be settled with Sanderson', and that orders must be given 'about pulling down the Garden walls, and putting the Pheasant Garden in order according to Mr Bridgeman's directions'. The Duke furthermore reminds himself to 'mark wch trees [he] would have taken down this year and to order those Mr Bridgeman marked to be cut down'.[42] Thereafter matters rested in abeyance until Flitcroft was asked to extend the existing house, and to provide a new west front (which proved to be based on Sanderson's designs) and two quadrangular stable courts. Sanderson himself returned in 1761 to supervise the construction of two reservoirs.[43] Eventually Henry Holland and Humphry

[38] A painting by Randolph Schwabe from a plan of Woburn in 1661 by Sir Jonas Moore is reproduced in Gladys Scott Thomson, 'Woburn Abbey. Its Place in History', *Connoisseur*, CXLI (May 1958), 206; idem, *Life in a Noble Household, 1641–1700* (London, 1937), facing p.150. From 1663 to 1687 the gardener at Woburn was John Field, one of George London's partners at Brompton Park. See ibid., pp.239–61. For Flitcroft at Woburn see Christopher Hussey, 'Woburn Abbey, Bedfordshire', *C.Life* (1, 8 September 1955), 434–37, 488–91.

[39] Gladys Scott Thomson, ed., *Letters of a Grandmother, 1732–35. Being the Correspondence of Sarah, Duchess of Marlborough, with Her Granddaughter Diana, Duchess of Bedford* (London, 1943), p.35. Sarah to Diana, 4 July 1732.

[40] See Bedford Office, London, Woburn MSS, HMC No.151, 'Saunderson's Designs for Woburn Abbey'. Subsequent references to the Bedford Office I owe to Mrs M. P. G. Draper and Mrs Noel Blakiston, and to Dr. Brogden, who alerted me to material there. This material is published by courtesy of the Trustees of the Bedford Estates.

[41] Bedford Office, London, Woburn MSS, HMC No.8, Vol. VIII, Item 52. Christian Cole to Diana, Duchess of Bedford, 20 December 1733.

[42] Bedford Office, London, Woburn MSS, HMC No.62. Memorandum Book of John, 4th Duke of Bedford, fos 4–5.

[43] See Gladys Scott Thomson, *Family Background* (London, 1949), pp.38–40. Sanderson's earlier designs were not carried out.

Repton in turn remodelled the grounds, and in 1806 Repton was commenting that Woburn furnished 'an example of greatness in variety and character in its garden scenery'.[44]

The year after Bridgeman was setting to rights the Pheasant Garden at Woburn he did a plan for the grounds at Amesbury in Wiltshire. Amesbury is no longer the house that Bridgeman and Flitcroft knew: in their day it was the building completed by John Webb in 1661 for the Marquis of Hertford and drawn by Flitcroft for Kent's *Designs of Inigo Jones* of 1727 (*Plate 37a*).[45] In 1724 Amesbury was left to Charles Douglas, 3rd Duke of Queensberry and husband of Catherine Hyde, the whimsical beauty immortalized by Walpole, Prior, and Pope. John Gay, her Grace's particular protégé, is said to have written *The Beggar's Opera* (1728) in the gardens at Amesbury, which still boast Gay's Cave as a reminder of the poet's visits.

It is from the correspondence of Catherine and Gay with Mrs Henrietta Howard (wife of the Hon. George Howard, mistress of George II, and later Countess of Suffolk) that we learn of Bridgeman at Amesbury. Henrietta knew the Royal Gardener from Marble Hill, where Gay was frequently entertained, and in 1730 was recommending Bridgeman to the Duchess of Queensberry but finding the role of go-between by no means easy. 'We wonder we have heard nothing from Mr. Bridgeman', Catherine and Gay wrote to Mrs Howard on 20 August 1730, 'if you chance to see him, pray tell him so.'[46] Two days later Henrietta writes to Gay from Windsor, telling him that Bridgeman is there and that she has 'spoken to him about the gardens'. Bridgeman 'says they are kept as they ought to be, and at a very reasonable expense; but he will very soon bring [her] the account, and a positive agreement, if it be such as the duchess approves'.[47] Over the summer of 1731 Mrs Howard evidently met her Grace (though not Gay) at Highclere in Hampshire, and promised to arrange for Bridgeman to visit Amesbury. 'I was never more peevish in my life than I have been about this journey of Bridgeman's', Henrietta wrote impatiently to Gay from Kensington on 5 September. 'I am sure I took true pains that it should be just as the duchess wished. I find upon strict inquiry, that he did not go so soon as I expected.' Mistakes are mistakes, and Henrietta can only lament that she can do no more, hoping that Bridgeman's current absence from Kensington indicates that he may be at Amesbury. But she cannot be sure. 'I shall be very uneasy', she concludes, 'till I hear how this matter has ended.'[48] It cannot have ended too disastrously, as Bridgeman was employed by the

[44] *An Enquiry Into the Changes of Taste in Landscape Gardening* . . . (London, 1806), p.11.
Bridgeman's widow received payments for her husband's work at Woburn after his death. On 1 October 1739 she was paid £200 and on 14 January 1741 a further £329. See Bedford Office, London, Woburn MSS, 4th Duke of Bedford's Cash Book, 1731–63, fos 24 (1 October 1739), 31 (14 January 1741).

[45] Vol. II, pls 7 and 8, which should be compared with Campbell's plate of Amesbury in *Vit. Brit.*, III, pl.7. Cf. Wyatt Papworth's drawing reproduced in John Harris, Stephen Orgel, and Roy Strong, *The King's Arcadia. Inigo Jones and the Stuart Court* (London, 1973), p.207.

[46] J. W. Croker, ed., *Letters to and from Henrietta, Countess of Suffolk* . . . (London, 1824), I, 382. Gay wrote this part of the letter. See C. F. Burgess, ed., *The Letters of John Gay* (Oxford, 1966), p.96.

[47] Croker, ed., *Suffolk Correspondence*, I, 386–87.

[48] Ibid., II, 20–21. Bridgeman's services earned him £54.18*s*. from the Duke of Queensberry on 25 March 1731. See Drummonds Branch, Royal Bank of Scotland Ltd, London, Ledger 1731, fo.166. Also in 1731 the Duchess of Queensberry wrote animatedly: 'Did you ever see Brussels? The whole country round about it is like the best-natured ground that ever was seen, laid out by a Bridgeman some years ago.' Quoted by Manwaring, *Italian Landscape in Eighteenth-Century England*, p.126.

Duchess of Queensberry until 1738, the date of his plan of Amesbury (*Plates 36, 37b*). Its delicacy and bold modelling make it the finest of Bridgeman's signed drawings.

In 1726 Flitcroft made an estate map of Amesbury (*Plate 164*) showing the disposition of the grounds around the house, itself the apogee of Webb's style.[49] Bridgeman's plan is looser than this. It too uses the Webb design as its core: the River Avon has been made more sinuous and given a tributary, the kitchen-garden has been altered, the woodland has become sparser and opens up to embrace a statue or column at the bottom. Amongst existing features used by Bridgeman is the long approach avenue, which serves as a dramatic re-enactment of Cobham's new entrance to Stowe or of the minor access to Blenheim. The iron-age hill-fort known as Vespasian's Camp – together with the barrow which it encloses – lies on the wooded hill rising steeply from Gay's Cave, set in a faceted diamond of grass (*Plate 37b*).[50] Progressing up the slope beyond the cave we move through a Bridgemanic amphitheatre to a circular cabinet in the midst of woodland. All told Bridgeman's layout is fragmented and lacks a dominant, cohesive idea.[51] Nonetheless Bridgeman and Flitcroft's work at Amesbury, with its archaeological overtones, must have fascinated the Hoare family, although Amesbury had none of the symbolism of nearby Stourhead. Flitcroft was at Stourhead from 1744 onwards, continuing a line of Bridgeman's friends who worked there, beginning with Colin Campbell in 1719 and stretching on to Wootton (from 1725) and John Michael Rysbrack (from 1729).[52]

Further afield Bridgeman and Flitcroft were at Boughton, one of the seats of the Montagu family. The diplomat and rake Ralph, 1st Duke of Montagu, had an official lodging in the Cockpit, Whitehall, but his main London home was Montagu House in Blooms-

[49] Wiltshire CRO, Trowbridge, 944/1 (Flitcroft Atlas), pl.1. See *Plate 164* in the present volume.

See Kenneth Woodbridge, *Landscape and Antiquity. Aspects of English Culture at Stourhead, 1718–1838* (Oxford, 1970), pp.21–22. Eight payments to Flitcroft by the Duke of Queensberry between 1731 and 1740 are noted in Drummonds Branch, Royal Bank of Scotland Ltd, London, Ledgers 1729–30, fo.241; 1732 fo.110; 1733 fo.253; 1734 fo.161; 1735 fo.291; 1736 fo.151; 1737 fo.316; 1739 fo.399.

[50] Described by William Stukeley, *Stonehenge. A Temple Restor'd to the British Druids* (London, 1740), p.37. See Woodbridge, *Landscape and Antiquity*, pp.189–90.

[51] In this respect quite unlike the Queensberrys' park at Drumlanrig in Dumfriesshire. See *Vit. Brit.*, IV (1739), pls 45–46.

[52] The possibility that Bridgeman may have advised on Stourhead cannot be ignored. A MS description of Stourhead by Joseph Spence (partially copied into a letter from Spence to Lord Lincoln, 17 September 1765) refers to the view from the Temple of Apollo of 'The Obelisk, & Turkish Tent, in the old (Bridgman) part of the Gardens'. See Nottingham University Library, Newcastle MSS, NeC 3226 (description), and NeC 2951 (letter), quoted by courtesy of the Duke of Newcastle. In 1720 Stephen Switzer received £15.15*s*. from Henry Hoare I, conceivably for a Stourhead garden plan. See C. Hoare and Co., Bankers, London, MS Account Book of Henry Hoare I.

Three other Wiltshire landscapes which may have Bridgeman connections are Trafalgar, Wilbury, and Wilton.

Trafalgar House (formerly Standlynch) was built by Roger Morris for his brother-in-law Sir Peter Vandeput in 1733. Three Bridgemanic plans of Trafalgar are in MSGD a3 fos 24, 25, 36.

Wilbury was once the home of Celia Fiennes, and Bridgeman's client was either William Benson or Benson's nephew Henry Hoare, the Younger, who bought the property from his uncle in 1734. The mansions at Wilbury and Amesbury have common Palladian origins. Bridgeman would know Benson if only through the Board of Works, and their mutual friends Flitcroft, Wootton, and Rysbrack. See Woodbridge, *Landscape and Antiquity*, pp.18–23.

Wilton has a barrow terminating a vista, as at Amesbury, here used by Roger Morris and another friend of Stukeley, the 9th Earl of Pembroke. See ibid., p.94. Dr Brogden tells me that Pembroke's House Book, 1738–45, at Wilton, has payments to Stephen Switzer in 1738 and 1740–45. Switzer's connection with Wilton is noted in James Lees-Milne, *Earls of Creation. Five Great Patrons of Eighteenth-Century Art* (London, 1962), p.63.

bury, on the present site of the British Museum.[53] The earliest Montagu House was designed by Robert Hooke, but was gutted by fire in 1686 and subsequently rebuilt internally in a Gallic mode. The architect for the restoration, and for Boughton, may have been the Frenchman Pierre Pouget. The plan of Montagu House resembled that of a Parisian hotel *entre cour et jardin,* with a square court to the south on the Great Russell Street side and a formal garden to the north (*Plates 39a, 39b*). Between 1725 and 1731 Charles Bridgeman was retained for 'keeping ye Garden',[54] though this can scarcely have amounted to anything revolutionary.[55]

Bridgeman's client at Montagu and Boughton was 'Planter John', in other words Ralph's son John Montagu, 2nd Duke of Montagu, for whom Flitcroft prepared plans for the Boughton armory.[56] When the 1st Duke died in 1709 he left Boughton with a formal landscape with elaborate waterworks and numerous statues and ornaments. The 2nd Duke did not start to modify and extend the existing layout (designed by the Dutchman Van De Meulen and the Frenchman Gabriel Delahaye) until about 1721.[57] The canals were arranged carefully as a continuous spine between the Grand Etang immediately to the west of the house and the south-west corner of the site. In the late 1720's – doubtless with the approval of the Duke's mother-in-law Sarah, Duchess of Marlborough – Bridgeman was called in.[58] The problems of such waterworks on a relatively flat site must have taxed Bridgeman's skill, and he surely would have consulted Stephen Switzer who, appropriately enough, was about to publish his *Introduction to a General System of Hydrostaticks and Hydraulicks* (1729).[59] Convincing visual evidence of the Royal Gardener's designs is provided by the Bridgemanic bird's-eye perspective of about 1725 which emphasizes the linear character of the layout (*Plates 40, 41a*). Wooded areas, with avenues and bosquets cut into them, contrast with deer grazing in open pasture; in the foreground the mount is clearly visible. Little of Bridgeman's scheme remains intact today (*Plate 41b*), although there is still the square pond as a lonely reminder of the canals and lakes which once dominated Boughton (*Plate 42b*). Doubtless this passion for water was due as much to the Duke's enthusiasm as to Bridgeman's. His lordship was no mere cipher: 'I wish you could get Mr. Bridgeman to go down with you to see . . . the scheme I proposed', he wrote to

[53] For Montagu House see J. Mordaunt Crook, *The British Museum* (London, 1972), pp.54–61.

[54] Boughton House, Northants, Montagu MSS, Andrew Marchant's Account Books, VII (i) – XV (1725–31); Montagu MSS, Ledgers VI–VII (1725–31). The rate was £100 a year. I am grateful to Mr P. I. King, Chief Archivist, Northamptonshire CRO, Northampton, for his assistance at Boughton. This and other Boughton material is cited by courtesy of the Duke of Buccleuch and Queensberry.

[55] In 1720 Strype, in his revised edition of Stow's *Survey of London,* wrote admiringly of the gardens of Montagu House with their 'curious' layout. See John Strype, *A Survey of the Cities of London and Westminster . . . Written at first in . . . 1598 by John Stow* . . . (London, 1720), bk. iv, p.85. A plan of 1729, seen by Miss Thomson, shows a formal scheme. See Gladys Scott Thomson, *The Russells in Bloomsbury, 1669–1771* (London, 1940), p.176.

[56] For Boughton see John Cornforth, 'The Making of the Boughton Landscape', *C.Life,* CXLIX (11 March 1971) 536–39. Boughton and other Northamptonshire parks are considered in Jürgen Hohnholz, *Der englische Park als landschaftliche Erscheinung* (Tübingen, 1964), particularly maps 4, 6.

[57] Plans of Boughton by Delahaye (all dated 1712) are in MSGD a4 fo.84; Bod. Lib., MS Maps Northants a1; PRO, MPHH 24 (Cat. No.2818).

[58] The Duke's steward, Charles Lamotte, was expecting him at Boughton in 1729. Boughton House, Northants, Montagu MSS, Lamotte Correspondence. Lamotte to Montagu, 15 September 1729.

[59] The next year Switzer was paid £5.1*s*.6*d*. for seeds at Boughton. Boughton House, Northants, Montagu MSS, Ledger VI, 16 March 1730.

his agent Booth.[60] Any proposal by the Duke was unlikely to be dull: dullness was not a family trait. John the Planter's chief delight, remarked the Duchess of Marlborough, was to 'get people into his garden and wet them with squirts . . . and such pretty fancies'.[61]

Roger Morris, Pembroke, William Adam

Bridgeman's work with Flitcroft leads us to consider Roger Morris.[62] Morris and Flitcroft were both architects for residences overlooking Bridgeman's St James's Square – Flitcroft built a house there for Sir William Heathcote in 1734, Morris for John Hervey, 1st Earl of Bristol, in 1731.[63] Although he owed his main patronage to Archibald Campbell, Earl of Ilay and 3rd Duke of Argyll, and his brother the 2nd Duke, Morris is most noted for his collaboration with Henry Herbert, 9th Earl of Pembroke and owner of Wilton.[64] Roger Morris and Pembroke publicized their ideas through Robert Morris – an architect close to the Burlingtonians, and a kinsman of Roger – whose exegesis of the Morris-Pembroke formula for the villa goes straight back to Palladio: thus Robert's illustrations of an ideal villa in his *Lectures on Architecture* (1734–36) include one that is remarkably similar to the Morris-Pembroke designs for Marble Hill.[65] The *Lectures* also contain views on landscaping with which Bridgeman and the Pembroke circle must have been in general sympathy.[66] Moreover Morris's *Lectures*, together with his *Essay in Defence of Ancient Architecture* (1728), and *An Essay upon Harmony* (1739), provide us with a useful parallel with Castell's *Villas of the Ancients Illustrated.*

[60] Quoted by Cornforth, 'The Making of the Boughton Landscape', p.539.

[61] William Matthews, ed., *The Diary of Dudley Ryder, 1715–16* (London, 1939), p.101.

[62] For Morris, and other material relevant to this section, see Ian G. Lindsay and Mary Cosh, *Inverary and the Dukes of Argyll* (Edinburgh, 1973). Miss Cosh generously helped me on several points. See also Marie P. G. Draper and W. A. Eden, *Marble Hill House and Its Owners* (London, 1970), pp.17–21.

[63] Colvin, *Dictionary*, pp.208, 396.

[64] Apart from Lees-Milne, *Earls of Creation*, pp.59–100, the Pembroke-Morris relationship is examined in e.g. Tresham Lever, *The Herberts of Wilton* (London, 1967), pp.143–68.

A Bridgeman-Argyll connection can be established. From 1731 to 1738 the occupant of No.41 (later known as No.46) Grosvenor Square was John Campbell, Lord Glenorchy and 3rd Earl of Breadalbane. See Arthur I. Dasent, *A History of Grosvenor Square* (London, 1935), p.227. Miss Mary Cosh informs me that on 17 January 1735 Bridgeman received 15*s*. from Glenorchy 'for work done in my garden in town'. See SRO, Edinburgh, GD 112/21/77 (Breadalbane MSS). Sutton Nicholls's view of Grosvenor Square of *c*.1731 illustrates many of the gardens there. See Phillips, *Mid-Georgian London*, pp.256–58.

[65] 2nd edn (1759), fig. D, illustrating Lecture X. Cf. fig. E.

[66] Lectures X–XII. See William A. Gibson, 'Literary Influences on Robert Morris's First Excursion in Architectural Theory', *Rendezvous*, VI, No.2 (Winter 1971), 1–14; Emil Kaufmann, *Architecture in the Age of Reason. Baroque and Post-Baroque in England, Italy and France* (Cambridge, Mass., 1955), pp.22–28. For the wider context of Morris's ideas see Professor Gibson's 'A Preface to a Study of the Relations of Architecture and English Literature, 1650–1750' (Ph.D. thesis, University of Minnesota, 1964).

As Professor Gibson stresses, Morris's ideas on landscape rely heavily upon those of Addison. Thus in Lecture X (p.161) Morris writes as follows about the siting of fig. D:

'Care should be taken so to lay out and dispose of the several Parts, that the neighbouring Hills, the *Rivulets,* the *Woods* and little *Buildings* interspers'd in various Avenues, &c. to give the more agreeable and entertaining Views, should render the Spot a kind of *agreeable Disorder,* or *artful Confusion*; so that by shifting from Scene to Scene, and by serpentine or winding Paths, one should, as it were, accidentally fall upon some remarkably beautiful Prospect, or other pleasing Object.'

Among those who showed interest in Castell's volume were William Adam and Sir John Clerk of Penicuik. On a trip to London in 1727 Clerk, and possibly Adam, visited Burlington at Chiswick and Pembroke at Wilton.[67] Once back in Scotland, Clerk completed his poem *The Country Seat.* This praises Burlington and Pembroke and has passages which call to mind the English estates Clerk had seen on his travels.[68] Beyond the formal garden near the house, he theorizes, there should be a landscape improved by judicious planting, and provided with avenues and eye-catchers:

That Avenue will most delight the Sight
That on some beauteous object shapes its way
Such is a temple whose high towring Spire
Divides the ho'vring Clouds.[69]

Clerk's ideas on landscape also drew on his travels abroad and in Scotland, and on his admiration for Corby Castle in Cumberland. He put his theories into practice at Penicuik in Midlothian, where he established an estate both efficient and beautiful, erecting a bridge, a circular Roman dovecote, a grotto calling to mind the Cave of the Cuman Sybil, and making a path by the River Eden which is reminiscent of a similar walk at Corby.[70]

Clerk and Adam may have met Bridgeman on their English tour, and in 1731 Adam showed how much he shared Clerk's yearning for avenues terminating in 'beauteous objects' when he designed Chatelherault, the handsome eye-catcher 1½ miles from Hamilton Palace, seat of James, 5th Duke of Hamilton. As *Vitruvius Scoticus* indicates, Chatelherault consisted of four linked pavilions (*Plate 42a*). These closed the south avenue and looked down northwards from the summit of the hill to the palace below, and southwards into the ravine of Cadzow with its derelict castle and herd of wild white cattle. However, when John Loveday visited Hamilton Palace in 1732 he found the gardens 'not yet made up' and consisting only of 'a Vista of considerable length'. 'There is', he noted, 'fine room for Improvements.'[71] Loveday's remarks were taken to heart, and in 1733 the Duke of Hamilton's elderly uncle the Earl of Selkirk was consulting Bridgeman about a gardener on behalf of his nephew. On being shown the scheme for Chatelherault, presumably by Adam, Bridgeman remarked that 'he was really surprised to see it and did not think there was any body in that part of the world could draw so well and likewayes thought the building

[67] See John M. Gray, ed., *Memoirs of the Life of Sir John Clerk of Penicuik, Bt., Baron of the Exchequer, Extracted by Himself from His Own Journals, 1676–1755* (Edinburgh, 1892), pp.123–30. On p.142 a visit to London in 1733 is recorded, when friends Clerk met included the Earls of Burlington and Wilmington. For the context of Clerk's visits see John Fleming, *Robert Adam and His Circle in Edinburgh and Rome* (London, 1962), pp.15–32.

[68] See ibid., pp.28–32; Stuart Piggott, 'Sir John Clerk and "The Country Seat"', in H. M. Colvin and John Harris, eds, *The Country Seat. Studies in the History of the British Country House Presented to Sir John Summerson on His 65th Birthday, Together With a Select Bibliography of His Published Writings* (London, 1970), pp.110–16; A. A. Tait, 'William Adam and Sir John Clerk. Arniston and "The Country Seat"', *Burlington Magazine,* CXI (March 1969), 132–41.

[69] SRO, Edinburgh, GD 184/404/1 (Clerk MSS), fo.26. For permission to quote from the Clerk Papers I am grateful to Sir John Clerk of Penicuik, Bt.

[70] See Alistair Rowan, 'Penicuik House, Midlothian', *C. Life,* CXLIV (15, 22 August 1968), 383–87, 448–51; William W. Spink, 'Sir John Clerk of Penicuik. Landowner as Designer', in Willis, ed., *Furor Hortensis,* pp.31–40. This essay is based on Mr Spink's 'The Planning of an Environment, With Reference to the Penicuik Estates' (M.Sc. thesis, University of Edinburgh, 1969).

[71] John Loveday, *Diary of a Tour in 1732 . . .*, ed. John E. T. Loveday (Edinburgh, 1890), p.114. For Chatelherault see James Macaulay, 'The Dogg Kennell att Hamilton', *Architectural Review,* CXXXX (October 1966), 295–98; A. A. Tait, 'William Adam at Chatelherault', *Burlington Magazine,* CX (April 1968), 316–25. Chatelherault served both as kennels for ducal hounds and as a dining pavilion with a small collection of paintings.

magnificent & what would cost one immence sume of monney'. The Royal Gardener's role seems to have been limited to that of adviser, for it was Adam who was paid by the Duke for 'plans of the Gardens of Hamilton in different shapes'.[72] Regular and irregular were juxtaposed. By the end of the century the layout had matured considerably and, as a tourist discovered in 1794, once you left the 'formal and aukward' area you could 'fling yourself into the sylvan recesses, and all the sweetly wild and varied scenery of Chatelherault'.[73] Despite the disastrous demolition of Hamilton Palace in 1927 the drama of this bleak and rugged landscape remains.

Chatelherault was by no means the only castle with Bridgeman connections. Equally dramatic was the siting of Longford, a triangular castle of 1580 set in the Wiltshire downs. In 1736 Jacob Bouverie, 1st Viscount Folkstone, set about improving Longford: Roger Morris and Theodore Jacobsen were perhaps called in for the house, Bridgeman certainly for the grounds, though we have nothing more than mere verbal glimpses of his proposals.[74] 'I have been a good deal at a loss for want of Bridgeman's Company', Bouverie is moaning in 1737. 'However I have not been idle . . . I have been making interest with my neighbours and have let several pretty views into my garden and the bushes on the other side of ye river are cut down.' Doing so, he adds, 'makes the gardens exceedingly pleasant and ye river look half as broad again'.[75]

Less grand than Longford, and less picturesque, was Wimbledon House, where again Morris was joined by Pembroke.[76] The year after the Duke of Marlborough's death in 1722 his widow bought Wimbledon from Sir Theodore Janssen, Bt, who was forced to sell because of his losses in the South Sea crash.[77] Janssen had started to pull down the original manor, and a new one was called for. In 1731 the Duchess brought in Morris and Pembroke as designers for the house, Charles Bridgeman for the landscape, all fresh from their joint enterprise at Marble Hill. For their pains they had to endure Sarah's constant bickering, though as at Blenheim the relationship between the Duchess and the Royal Gardener was amicable enough. By 1732 Sarah was already expressing the hope that, even if she died before all was completed, 'Mr Bridgeman may finish the ground and gardens in the manner I agreed upon with him'.[78]

[72] This and the Bridgeman references are in Lennoxlove, East Lothian, Hamilton MSS, 104, 127, cited by Tait, 'William Adam at Chatelherault', pp.319–20. I quote them by courtesy of the Duke of Hamilton.

[73] John Lettice, *Letters on a Tour Through Various Parts of Scotland, in the Year 1792* (London, 1794), pp.54–55. Cf. Pococke's description in Daniel William Kemp, ed., *Tours in Scotland (1747, 1750, 1760) by Richard Pococke, Bishop of Meath* (Edinburgh, 1887), p.47.

[74] Colvin, *Dictionary*, p.396, cites papers at Longford indicating that Roger Morris was there.

[75] Longford Castle, Wilts, Longford (Folkestone) MSS, quoted in part by John Cornforth, 'Longford and the Bouveries', *Country Life Annual* (1968), p.37. Jacob Bouverie to Hitch Younge, 7 November 1737. Mr Cornforth generously gave me a transcript of this letter, published by courtesy of the Dowager Countess of Radnor.

[76] For Wimbledon see Marie P. G. Draper, 'When Marlborough's Duchess Built', *C.Life*, CXXXII (2 August 1962), 248–50; C. S. S. Higham, *Wimbledon Manor House Under the Cecils* (London, 1962), esp. pp.23, 33–35; Lees-Milne, *Earls of Creation*, pp.92–94.

[77] For Janssen's accounts see [South Sea Company], *The Particulars and Inventories of the Estates of the Late Sub-Governor, Deputy-Governor and Directors of the South Sea Company* (London, 1721), II, No.4. The Duchess had made a profit of £100,000 on the South Sea Bubble, and subsequently invested it in estates, of which Wimbledon was but one. When she died she owned thirty. Others are listed in David B. Green, *Sarah, Duchess of Marlborough* (London, 1967), p.295, and in *A True Copy of the Last Will and Testament of Her Grace Sarah, Late Duchess Dowager of Marlborough* . . . (London, 1744).

[78] MS Will of 1732, one of the Duchess's twenty-nine wills at Althorp, Northants, kindly brought to my attention by the late Earl Spencer.

The plates in *Vitruvius Britannicus V* (1771) show us that the Morris-Pembroke mansion was H-shaped, with an awkwardly-projecting pedimented Ionic portico in the centre of each of its two main sides (*Plate 43a*). It was a clumsy essay in Palladianism, lacking the grace of Marble Hill or White Lodge at Richmond, and its context can be seen in Rocque's plan of 1746 (*Plate 43b*). The surrounding parkland amounted to about 365 acres, and its layout was governed by the Duchess's demand that she enter the house at first floor level. Two Bridgemanic drawings illustrate how he tackled the problem. The first (*Plate 44a*) indicates by plan and section how he 'dug a saucer' to put the residence in; the second (*Plate 44b*) demonstrates how he proposed to use trees and semicircular grass banking in his treatment of the road on the hill. To Sarah this made the house look as if it were 'making a Curtsie'.[79] She was not amused. 'I have always had the misfortune to suffer very great mischiefs from the assistance of architects', she complains to her granddaughter Diana, Duchess of Bedford. 'The cutting through the terrace is almost as bad as setting the house in a pit.'[80] Nonetheless, despite some misgivings, Sarah is sure that Wimbledon will be a 'delightful habitation', and in 1735 (in a letter in which she tells Diana of Bridgeman's proposals to link Wimbledon House to the Common) she assures her granddaughter that very little is needed to make the mansion 'complete according to [her] own taste'.[81] Her taste was not that of her successors, and in 1765 – twenty years before the Morris-Pembroke building was burnt down – her great-grandson John Spencer, 1st Earl Spencer, asked Capability Brown to redesign the estate.[82]

Gibbs, Campbell, Leoni, Dubois

Sarah, Duchess of Marlborough, was one of a few of Bridgeman's clients who gained from the South Sea affair: adventurous attitudes to finance and to landscaping often went together, and at least five other owners implicated in the South Sea Company's boom and crash engaged Bridgeman before disaster struck.[83] Sir John Fellowes, Sub-Governor of the Company, called him in at Carshalton House in Surrey, and Francis Hawes at Purley in Berkshire. The three others lived in Hertfordshire: William Gore at Tring, Robert Chester at Briggens, and Edward Rolt at Sacombe. Accounts confirm payments to the Royal Gardener before 1721 at Carshalton, Purley, Briggens, and Sacombe, whilst Bridgemanic plans exist of all but Briggens and Carshalton. Furthermore on 17 June 1719

[79] Toynbee, ed., 'Walpole's Visits to Country Seats', p.13.

[80] Thomson, ed., *Letters of a Grandmother*, p.142. Sarah to Diana, 5 August 1734.

[81] Ibid., pp.156, 169. Sarah to Diana, 2 July, 21 August 1735.
PRO, Works 16/2/8, fo.1, consists of a document of 21 August 1736 entitled 'The Manor of Wimbledon' in which the Duchess of Marlborough accedes to Queen Caroline's request for 'Free Liberty and License to make an open Road Way or Walk over East Sheene Common . . . to the New Gate in the Wall of the Park called New Park . . . '

[82] Brown's scheme can be seen in Thomas Richardson's survey of 1768, reproduced and discussed by Higham, *Wimbledon Manor House*, pp.33–35; pls 10–11.

[83] Apart from the two volumes of *Particulars and Inventories* cited above in n.77, published accounts will be found in e.g. [South Sea Company], *The Proceedings of the Directors of the South Sea Company* . . . (London, 1721); idem, *The Several Reports of the Committee of Secrecy* . . . (London, [1721]), pp.54–67. For background see John P. Carswell, *The South Sea Bubble* (London, 1961), esp. the biographies of Bridgeman's clients on pp.273–85.

Samuel Tufnell, described in 1721 as amongst those who 'are qualified to vote at the Ensuing Election' for Governor of the South Sea Company, paid a Charles Bridgeman for 'Works & plants in ye Gardens' at Langleys in Essex, a house which Tufnell had acquired in 1711 and which he subsequently rebuilt (*Plate 51b*).[84]

The architects for the South Sea houses were led by James Gibbs and Colin Campbell. Gibbs's two commissions were Tring and Sacombe, each for a Member of Parliament.[85] A Bridgemanic plan of Gore's Tring (*Plate 45a*) shows the mansion looking out onto an open court, with one axis stretching across the octagonal basin up into the amphitheatre. A traveller in 1724 found Tring 'full of fine Slopes' and of 'easy Hills coverd wth Beach & Oak Trees', not to mention 300 head of deer, and remarked that 'a Canal of 1100 feet long & 110 feet broad is going to be made'.[86] This monumental canal is in the forefront of Rocque's perspective (*Plate 45b*), and leads up grass terracing to the pyramid designed by Gibbs. Unlike Tring, Rolt's Sacombe was to have a Gibbs house but, although a scheme was published in his *Book of Architecture*, it was never executed (*Plate 46a*). The grounds at Sacombe, which may owe something to Vanbrugh, demonstrate Bridgeman's typical axiality, and his use of dense woodland, rectilinear canals, a rectangular kitchen garden, an amphitheatre, and an octagonal basin (*Plate 46b*).[87] By 1728 Sacombe already possessed painterly qualities: it was almost as if a landscape painter had been sent for. 'It's hard to say whether Nature or Art be most admirable here', Salmon wrote in his *History of Hertfordshire*. 'The Artist seems to have attempted shewing Nature to greatest Advantage. At the End of one Walk is a Sort of Theatrical Work, shaded by Oaks at unequal Distances, as they happened to grow, such as one would wish represented in a Landschape.'[88]

Gibbs cut little ice with Colin Campbell, either personally or professionally. Campbell is familiar as a protégé of Burlington and an accomplished, if somewhat trite, architect of the Palladian school, a school which he was instrumental in promoting in England through his three volumes of *Vitruvius Britannicus* and his edition of *Andrea Palladio's Five Orders of Architecture* (1729). After his year under Benson as Chief Clerk and Deputy Surveyor of the King's Works in 1718–19, Campbell emerged as architect to George II when Prince of Wales, and in 1726 as Surveyor to Greenwich Hospital in succession to Vanbrugh. Whether or not Campbell ever visited Italy, he was heir to Burlington's ideas on landscape,

[84] Essex CRO, Chelmsford, D/DTu 276, Samuel Tufnell's Receipt Book, May 1701–March 1722. Payment was £156.*7s.2d.* Tufnell was a man of scholarship and taste, a Member of Parliament, and one of the founders of the State of Georgia. See L. G. G. Ramsey, 'Langleys, Essex', *Connoisseur*, CXL (December 1957), 210–17. Samuel Tufnell, the mason, built and may have designed four houses in Cavendish Square. See Colvin, *Dictionary*, pp.628–29. Nicholas Dubois paid a Samuel Tufnell £80 on 29 December 1722. See Drummonds Branch, Royal Bank of Scotland Ltd, London, Ledger 1721, fo.312. The architect of Langleys may have been Captain Edward Tufnell. See Colvin, *Dictionary*, p.628.

[85] For Gibbs see Terry F. Friedman, 'James Gibbs (1682–1754). The Formation of His Architectural Style' (Ph.D. thesis, University of London, 1971). I am grateful to Dr Friedman for detailed advice on Gibbs.

[86] Anonymous, Diary of a Tour in 1724, Yorkshire Archaeological Society, Leeds, MS 328, unnumbered fos. See Terry F. Friedman and Derek Linstrum, 'Country Houses Through Georgian Eyes', and 'A Tour of Architectural Splendour', *C.Life*, CLIII (1, 8 February 1973), 268–70, 334–36.

[87] Between 1715 and 1717 Bridgeman received £304.*0s.3d.* for Sacombe from Edward Rolt. See C. Hoare and Co., Bankers, London, Ledger 18, 2 July 1715, 16 June 1716; Ledger 20, 4 August 1717. A plan of the house and gardens at Sacombe from the office of Sir John Vanbrugh is in Colvin and Craig, eds, *Drawings at Elton Hall*, No.56; pl.24.

[88] P.255.

and successive volumes of *Vitruvius Britannicus* show his increasing recognition of the intrinsic part played by the layout of the grounds in the design of a country seat.

Bridgeman would have been the last to discourage Campbell from this change of emphasis, although the landscapes on which they collaborated were not the most adventurous in the kingdom. At Purley today Francis Hawes' brick Jacobean manor stands overlooking an overgrown lake with a flint temple at its head (*Plate 47a*). Bridgeman had envisaged a quite different design, with a formal lawn and kitchen garden (*Plate 47b*). To the south was a Palladian villa which – with its four pavilions linked by curved arcades to a central block, on the pattern of the Villa Mocenigo – suggests a prototype for plans of a Holkham kind.[89] Very likely Campbell was at Bridgeman's elbow at Purley, particularly as in 1718 the architect had proposed a similar scheme for Ebberston, one of the many Yorkshire houses with which he was connected through the Aislabie family.[90] John Aislabie – the culpable Chancellor of the Exchequer, confidant of Hawes, and Campbell's client at Hall Barn – also owned Studley Royal in Yorkshire, where Campbell and Morris may have provided the banqueting house.[91] Vanbrugh too knew the Aislabies, and the closeness of Castle Howard underlines the possibility that Bridgeman may have joined Campbell at Ebberston and Studley, and Burlington at Londesborough Hall, the earl's Yorkshire seat. Such speculations are given added weight by the existence of four Bridgemanic plans of Scampston for Sir William St Quintin (*Plate 48a*), and three of Ledston Hall for Lady Elizabeth (Betty) Hastings. The most convincing of these (*Plate 48b*) shows an asymmetrical layout, with a strong central axis, lawns, grass banking, and dense woodland containing walks, open groves, and irregular bosquets. Not merely is the design and draughtsmanship Bridgemanic, there is also a two-page description of the plan which may be in Bridgeman's hand. In 1731 Lady Betty was making payments for 'the designe of Mr. Bridgemans' for the grounds, and a painting by Setterington of 1728 also shows an axial scheme, its lines softened by carefully modelled lawns and banking.[92] At the same moment, at the opposite end of England, Bridgeman and Campbell were at

[89] Bridgeman was paid £122.11*s*. 'for laying out the Gardens at Purley', and Joseph Carpenter received £58.11*s*. See [South Sea Company], *Particulars and Inventories*, II, 71. For Bridgeman at Purley see Christopher Hussey, 'Purley Hall, Berkshire', *C.Life*, CXLVII (5 February 1970), 310–13. Hawes became Cashier of the Navy, and held this office under the Treasurerships of Sir Robert Walpole and John Aislabie.

[90] See Howard E. Stutchbury, *The Architecture of Colen Campbell* (Manchester, 1967), pp.44–47.

[91] See W. T. C. Walker, 'Studley Royal', *Archaeological Journal*, CXXV (1968), 360–61; W. A. Eden, 'South Dalton, Yorkshire', in Colvin and Harris, eds, *The Country Seat*, pp.117–20. Bridgemanic plans exist of Houghton (MSGD a4 fo.57) and Mereworth (MSGD a4 fo.52), both Campbell houses.

[92] Reproduced in Hunt and Willis, eds, *Genius of the Place*, pl.3. Also dated 1728 is Setterington's illustration of Wentworth Woodhouse in *Vit.Brit.*, IV (1739), pls 79–81.

Ledston was built about 1655–65. For its pedigree see Nikolaus Pevsner, *Yorkshire: The West Riding*, The Buildings of England, rev. Enid Radcliffe (Harmondsworth, 1967), pp.304–6. A Ledston-Duncombe relationship is suggested in Christopher Hussey, 'Duncombe Park, Yorkshire', *C. Life*, CXXII (5, 12 December 1957), 1198–1202, 1328–31.

The payments to Bridgeman by Lady Betty are in C. Hoare and Co., Bankers, London, Ledger K, 27 March 1731 (£5.19*s*.6*d*.); Ledger L, 5 April (£21), 23 October 1731 (£7.10*s*.6*d*.). The reference to Bridgeman's proposals is in an undated letter to Lady Betty from T. Coke [?] in the Ledston MSS, Otterden Place, Kent. For background see George Hastings Wheler, ed., *Hastings-Wheler Family Letters, 1693–1739*, I (London, 1929); II (Wakefield, 1935). A visit by William Kent to Ledston is chronicled in ibid., II, 173. Selina, Countess of Huntingdon, to Lady Anne Hastings, 12 August 1739.

For access to Ledston material, and other courtesies, I am indebted to the present owner of the house, G. H. H. Wheler, Esq.

Compton Place in Sussex, where the architect remodelled the house for Spencer Compton, 1st Earl of Wilmington, member of the Kit-Cat Club and neighbour of Burlington at Chiswick.[93] Bridgeman was at Compton from 1728 to 1738, and in 1735 a visitor notes that the house is 'most sweetly situated under the downs; from whence you have a pleasant prospect of the sea . . . There is a pretty garden belonging to it; w[i]th a good deal of underwood'.[94] Whilst in Sussex, he would have combined his duties there with those at Westbury House in Hampshire. Admiral Philip Cavendish bought Westbury in 1722 and subsequently sought Bridgeman's advice on planting.[95] A water-colourist in 1834 found Westbury's setting nothing if not picturesque (*Plate 49*).

Sir John Fellowes' Carshalton House is similar in scale to Compton Place and Westbury. Here the architect (at least for the water pavilion) may have been Henry Joynes, Bridgeman's colleague from Blenheim and Clerk of Works at Kensington since 1715.[96] At Carshalton the lake, grotto, and water pavilion are reminders to this day of Bridgeman's involvement, and stand in a setting remarkably like Watts' engraving (*Plates 50a, 50b*). Bridgeman evidently toyed with parallel ideas at Briggens for Sir Robert Chester.[97] Briggens, wrote Salmon in 1728, 'stands upon a beautiful Hill overlooking the Meadows, the River *Stort*, and part of *Essex*', and its features include 'a graceful Plantation of Trees, with Variety of Slopes, adorned with Statues'.[98] The turfed ramps and terraces forming these 'Slopes' are familiar elements in Bridgeman's designs, and appear on such Bridgemanic drawings as those of Moor Park in Hertfordshire for Benjamin Styles (*Plate 51a*), and Farley Hall in Berkshire for John Walters (*Plate 52*). But none does so as effectively as an anonymous painting of Castle Hill in Devon – creation of Hugh Fortescue, 1st Earl of Clinton, in 1730–40 – which could be confused for a twentieth-century view (*Plates*

93 See G. L. M. Goodfellow, 'Colin Campbell's Last Years', *Burlington Magazine*, CXI (April 1969), 185–91; Stutchbury, *Campbell*, pp.68–69.

94 BL, Add MS 15776 (Tour in England 1735), fo.215. See Compton Place, Sussex, Lord Wilmington's Account Book, 1726–40, for payments to Bridgeman on 27 January 1728 of £40, and £120 a year from 10 April 1728 to 13 May 1738. On 4 October 1727 Carpenter was paid £160 'for keeping my Gardens to Michms. 1727'. For other citations from these accounts see Geoffrey Beard, *Georgian Craftsmen and Their Work* (London, 1966), pp.31–33; Christopher Hussey, *English Country Houses. Early Georgian, 1715–60*, 2nd edn (London, 1965), pp. 87–96.

95 Sussex Archaeological Society, East Sussex CRO, Lewes, Gage MSS, G/Ha/66(2a), 'A Particular of the Estate [of the] Late Adml: Cavendish. in / Hampshire'; G/Ha/42, 'A Plan of / Westbury House & Gardens / Together with the Offices ffarm yard / Barns Stabling and Lands adjacent'. The Inventory says that the avenue and pleasure garden were 'Laid out by Mr Bridgman.' Professor Julian Gwyn kindly told me of this material.

For Bridgeman and Westbury see Frances Collins and John Hurst, *West Meon, Hampshire. Some Chapters of Its History* (Petersfield, 1972), pp.56–62; Julian Gwyn, *The Enterprising Admiral. The Personal Fortune of Admiral Sir Peter Warren* (Montreal and London, 1974), pp.145–47. My researches into Westbury were aided by Miss Collins and Mr K. W. Dickins. Between 1694 and 1722 the house was owned by Richard and Mary Markes.

96 [South Sea Company], *Particulars and Inventories*, I, 10, 11, 14. Joynes was paid £21, Bridgeman £138, Joseph Carpenter £200, and John Mist £110. See Derek Sherborn, 'Carshalton House, Surrey', *C.Life*, CV (4 March 1949), 480–83.

Carshalton House should not be confused with Carshalton Park, where Leoni worked for Thomas Scawen from 1723. A plan of the grounds at Carshalton Park dated 1723 is in Leoni's *The Architecture of Leon Battista Alberti . . .* (London, 1726), III, pl. 3.

97 Ibid., I, 51, 54, 56. Bridgeman was allocated £27.13*s*., Carpenter £41, and John Mist £70. MS Accounts at Briggens, shown to me by Lord and Lady Aldenham, indicate that Bridgeman was given an additional £13 for 'trees'.

98 Salmon, *History of Hertfordshire*, p.253.

99 For the connection between Farley and Castle Hill see Christopher Hussey, 'Farley Hill Place, Berkshire', *C.Life*, XCIII (11 June 1943), 1056–59. Castle Hill as we see it was rebuilt in 1935–38 after the fire of 1934. In the grounds, criss-crossed with beech avenues, there is a triumphal arch, a castellate ruin, a temple, and a menagerie. There is a painting by Wootton of Castle Hill at the house.

54a, 54b).[99] The winding walks and temples set freely in dense woodland seen at Moor Park and Farley recur at such Campbell houses as Wanstead, thus hinting at a possible Bridgeman connection there too (*Plate 53*).[100]

Mention of Moor Park introduces Giacomo Leoni, for although Thornhill designed the house the name of Leoni has sometimes been associated with it.[101] Leoni may have come to England to superintend the publication of an English edition of *Palladio*, which duly appeared as *The Architecture of A. Palladio* between 1716 and 1720. Subsequently he perhaps fell under Burlington's patronage, and Leoni's *The Architecture of Leon Battista Alberti* (1726, 1739, 1755) contains lavish praise of the Earl. Bridgeman and Leoni may have been together at Wrest and Stowe, although it is more than likely that Leoni's work for Cobham only dates from after the Royal Gardener's death.[102] In any event Bridgeman and Leoni seem to have counted Shardeloes amongst their commissions, and Badeslade's perspective indicates Bridgemanic rides and garden structures set around a sixteenth-century house (*Plate 72a*). In 1728 Leoni designed (but did not build) 'four new fronts' for Montagu Garrard Drake there,[103] and a century later John Claudius Loudon firmly asserted that Bridgeman was at Shardeloes. Shardeloes, he wrote, is 'situated on the brow of a hill, overlooking a broad sheet of water, planned by Bridgeman. The park is much varied in surface, and richly clothed with beechwoods'.[104]

The translator of Leoni's *Architecture of A. Palladio* was the Frenchman Nicholas Dubois, with whom Bridgeman and Flitcroft may have collaborated on the Earl of Essex's estate at Cassiobury where, Horace Walpole observed, Bridgeman 'laid out the Wood'.[105] Dubois held the Office of Works' post of Master Mason from 1719 until his death in 1735, and thus would have had official access to the Earl.[106] Moreover Bridgeman and Dubois were at Stanmer in Sussex. In 1722–27 Dubois built Stanmer for the Pelhams – that same family who employed Bridgeman, Vanbrugh, and Kent at Claremont – and made proposals for a canal and pumping-engine there. Stanmer House itself (*Plate 55a*), with its three-bay central pediment and unpretentious fenestration, follows much the same pattern as Bower House (*Plate 33a*) or Well Vale (*Plate 35a*). Bridgeman was brought

[100] See Ian Dunlop and Fiske Kimball, 'The Gardens of Wanstead House, Essex', *C.Life*, CVIII (28 July 1950), 294–98.

[101] See T. P. Hudson, 'Moor Park, Leoni and Sir James Thornhill', *Burlington Magazine*, CXIII (November 1971), 657–61. Two plans in the Bodleian Library (MSGD a4 fos 48, 58) point to a Bridgeman link. See *Plate 51a*. Generally see Geoffrey Beard, 'Leoni's English Houses', *Country Life Annual* (1968), pp. 85–87, and T. P. Hudson, 'A Venetian Architect in England: Giacomo Leoni (*c*.1686–1746)', *C. Life*, CLVII (3 April 1975), 830–33. Dr Hudson kindly shared with me the fruits of his researches on Leoni and Dubois.

[102] I.e. the pair of Doric archways on the north front, and possibly the north portico.

[103] George W. Eland, ed., *Shardeloes Papers of the Seventeenth and Eighteenth Centuries* (London, 1947), p.129. Brief notes on the landscaping are on p.136. See John Harris, 'Shardeloes. A Lasting Tribute to a Remarkable Restoration', *Connoisseur*, CXLVIII (December 1961), 268–75.

[104] Loudon, *Encyclopaedia of Gardening*, 5th edn (1827), p.1071, an opinion reiterated by Felton, *On the Portraits of English Authors on Gardening*, p.136, where he says that Bridgeman 'laid out the gardens'.

[105] Toynbee, ed., 'Walpole's Visits to Country Seats', p.37. See above p.41. Drawings of Cassiobury are in MSGD a3 fos 42–71. For Leoni and Dubois see Rudolf Wittkower, 'English Neoclassicism and the Vicissitudes of Palladio's *Quattro Libri*', in *Palladio and English Palladianism*, pp. 71–92.

[106] Essex counted the Rangership of St James's Park among his posts. He made a private payment of £100 to Flitcroft on 2 October 1739. See Drummonds Branch, Royal Bank of Scotland Ltd, London, Ledger 1739, fo.61.

in at Stanmer in 1726, and must have planted some of the fine trees which today surround the house and the adjacent church of 1838.[107]

Kent

Horace Walpole has nothing to say about Vanbrugh in his *History of the Modern Taste in Gardening*,[108] and concentrates on William Kent (*Plate 55b*).[109] Walpole's advocacy of Kent as the landscapist who developed Bridgeman's ideas highlights the significance of the friendship between Kent and the Royal Gardener which may go back to Kent's return to England in 1719 after his decade spent in Italy. Bridgeman and Kent appear together in two group portraits, and both were employed by royalty and by the Board of Works, where Kent's appointment as Master Carpenter in 1726 was followed by his promotion to Master Mason and Deputy Surveyor in 1735, and Portrait Painter to the King in 1739. Kent's early career had progressed from painting to architecture, interior decoration, and furniture design, and it was not until the late 1720's that he actually seems to have turned his hand to landscaping. William Mason commented that 'it is said that Mr. Kent frequently declared he caught his taste in Gardening from reading the picturesque descriptions of Spenser',[110] though some would say that it stemmed from the influence of Italian gardens, countryside, and painting, and from the impact on Kent of Lord Burlington's patronage. The key layout on which Kent and Burlington collaborated was Chiswick House (or 'Lord Burlington's Bijou', to use the late Mr H. F. Clark's memorable description), and it is not unlikely that Charles Bridgeman was there too.

By the late 1720's Burlington's small domain at Chiswick was attracting admirers from far and wide, all anxious to see the villa of the illustrious Maecenas in its novel setting (*Plate 57b*); by contrast, Burlington's activities at Londesborough were relatively unknown.[111] Both house and garden at Chiswick are seminal in the establishment of English Palladianism, and Rocque's plan of 1736 illustrates how they looked in the mid-1730's

[107] BL, Add MS 33085 (Chichester Papers), fo.235. Dubois to Thomas Pelham, 6 July 1726. I owe this to Dr Hudson. See Christopher Hussey, *English Country Houses. Early Georgian, 1715–60* (London, 1955), pp.56–57.

Simultaneously Bridgeman and Dubois may have been consulted about Audley End in Essex. Two Bridgemanic plans in MSGD a4 fos 60, 67 may be connected with visits paid to Audley End by Dubois in 1726 to see Charles Howard, husband of Henrietta Howard of Marble Hill.

[108] Walpole's antagonism to Vanbrugh is encapsulated in his *Anecdotes of Painting* where the architect is described 'in a light that is by no means advantageous to him'. See Walpole, *Anecdotes of Painting,* ed. Wornum, II, 254–57. James Dallaway is fairer to Vanbrugh in his 'Supplementary Anecdotes of Gardening in England' which appeared in his edition of the *Anecdotes of Painting* (London, 1826–28), IV, 284–319.

[109] See Margaret Jourdain, *The Work of William Kent. Artist, Painter, Designer and Landscape Gardener* (London and New York, 1948).

[110] Mason, *The English Garden* (York, 1783), pp.210–11. This links up with Matthew Prior's gift to Bridgeman of a 'Spenser folio' in 1721, with the interpretation of parts of Stowe as a working out of sections of the *Faerie Queene*, and with the inclusion of scenes from the poem's story of Malbecco painted by Sleter in Kent's Temple of Venus there (see below pp.75–76, 117n.44, 137).

[111] See Lees-Milne, *Earls of Creation*, pp.104, 158, 161–64, 168; Richard Wilton, 'Historic Londesborough', *Transactions of the East Riding (Yorkshire) Antiquarian Society*, III (1895), 1–12. It was Burlington, says Wilton on p.5, 'who planned and planted the far-stretching avenues and the far-seen clumps, and formed the lakes and waterfalls which add such beauty to the park'.

(*Plate 56*).[112] The villa itself was begun about 1725 and completed four or five years later, but Burlington had planned a formal garden at Chiswick much earlier. Gay's epistle *A Journey to Exeter* implies that Burlington (with Pope's help) was laying one out in 1716,[113] the year the Earl returned from his first Italian visit. 'His gardens are delightfull', Pope wrote of Burlington in 1716, prior to a visit to Chiswick, 'his musick ravishing'.[114] Campbell was surveying the grounds in 1717 and 1718, as was Sam Savill in 1724 or 1725. By then the river had been dug (though not serpentined) and most of the temples erected, often having been redrawn by Flitcroft from Burlington's initial sketches.[115] There is little doubt that Burlington played the dominant role, at least at the start. As Macky wrote in 1724:

> The whole Contrivance of [the gardens] is the Effect of his Lordship's own Genius, and singular fine Taste; Every Walk terminates with some little Building, one with a Heathen Temple, for instance the *Pantheon*; another a little Villa, where my Lord often dines instead of his House, and . . . another Walk terminates with a Portico, in imitation of *Covent-Garden* Church.[116]

Rocque's plan – which has these buildings scattered round its perimeter – is a mixture of styles, with straight avenues and *pattes d'oies*, potted trees, high clipped hedges, formal pools, statuary, and aggressively sinuous and zigzag paths. Imaginative, yes, but there is little deviation from the Palladian canons of taste. In the 1730's, once he had set the scene, Burlington called in William Kent, who serpentined the river, developed the site to its west, and opened up distant prospects. Kent, moreover, introduced his typical wit and whimsy in that familiar sketch of the exedra which so closely resembles what we see today, and which (with its Roman statues said to have come from Hadrian's Villa at Tivoli) underscores the Italian inspiration for Chiswick (*Plates 58a, 58b*).[117]

[112] As the north point faces left, east is at the top and west at the bottom of the plan.

I am grateful to Professor Wittkower and M. Jacques Carré for advice on Chiswick. For Chiswick see esp. Jacques Carré, 'Lord Burlington's Garden at Chiswick', *Garden History*, I, No.3 (Summer 1973), 23–30; John Charlton, *A History and Description of Chiswick House and Gardens* (London, 1958), pp.27–32; H. F. Clark, 'Lord Burlington's Bijou, or Sharawaggi at Chiswick', *Architectural Review*, XCV (May 1944), 125–29.

[113] The text of the poem, dedicated to Burlington, is in John Gay, *Poetry and Prose*, ed. Vinton A. Dearing and Charles E. Beckwith (Oxford, 1974), I, 203–7.

[114] *Pope Correspondence*, I, 338. Pope to Martha Blount [March 1716?].

[115] See *Catalogue of the Drawings Collection of the RIBA* (Farnborough, Hants, 1969 et seq.).

[116] Macky, *A Journey Through England*, 4th edn (London, 1724), I, 86-87. This section does not appear in the 1714, 1722 (2nd), and 1723 (3rd) editions, but does so in the 5th of 1732.

[117] At one stage Kent designed the exedra as a semi-circle with a pyramid in its centre, similar to his Temple of British Worthies at Stowe (*Plate 153a*). A Kent sketch for Holkham of a variation on this theme is reproduced in Hussey, *English Gardens and Landscapes*, pl.27. For a comparison with Tivoli see Salvatore Aurigemma, *Villa Adriana* (Rome, 1961), pp.44–47.

Although the statues of Palladio and Inigo Jones are by Rysbrack, Mrs Webb presumes that 'most of the statuary in the gardens of the Chiswick villa was by Guelfi'. Mary I. Webb, 'Giovanni Battista Guelfi. An Italian Sculptor Working in England', *Burlington Magazine*, XCVII (May 1955), 144. See also Webb, *Rysbrack*, pp.44, 101.

For Palladio's ideas on the siting of a villa see e.g. his *Quattro libri dell'architettura* (Venice, 1570), bk.2, chap.xii. Cf. Alberti, *De re aedificatoria* (Florence, 1485), bk.5, chap.xvii. For an exploration of these ideas see the Exhibition Catalogue, *Andrea Palladio, 1508–80. The Portico and the Farmyard* (Arts Council of Great Britain, London, and Centro Internazionale di Studi di Architettura Andrea Palladio, Vicenza, 1975).

The theory that Bridgeman may have helped Burlington at Chiswick can be supported on several counts. Bridgeman was well established as a garden designer years before Kent abandoned painting and, as he would know Burlington through Pope and others, there is no reason why he could not have been at the Earl's side as early as 1715. The 1801 edition of Whately's *Observations on Modern Gardening* adds weight to this view. This has an appendix with 'An Essay on the Different Natural Situations of Gardens'. In the 'Fourth Situation', the author writes,

> the serpentine river, the open planting, the lake and island, the moulding the flat into the gentle unevenesses of Kent, have a rural and chearful aspect: of this last particularly, there is a fine instance in Kent's plantation at the back of the house at Chiswick, compared with the phlegmatic plantation of Bridgeman on the same side of the garden.[118]

Clearly this testimony should be treated with reserve, but surely Bridgeman's 'phlegmatic plantation' could have been the section east of the serpentine river into which Kent inserted the exedra and broad avenue? Furthermore, Bridgeman's stylistic pedigree at Chiswick is strong, for Rocque's plan contains nothing that cannot be found elsewhere in Bridgeman's work before 1725: the wiggly walks, temples, and round pond, for instance, can be seen in Bridgeman's designs for Blenheim, Eastbury, and Claremont respectively, whilst many Chiswick features had already appeared in the Bridgemanic bird's-eye view of Stowe of about 1720 (*Plate 116*). Affinities between Chiswick and Stowe can be observed in Rigaud's sketches of the two estates, made whilst he was visiting England in 1733–34: Rigaud's Chiswick drawing of the oval pond, river pavilion, stone bridge, and serpentine river glimpsed though a colonnade of trees (*Plate 57a*) seems to include the same elegant members of society who populate his Stowe views (*Plates 129–43*). By the fourth decade of the century Chiswick's fame had spread far and wide, and with good reason. 'In a Word', said the writer of the Appendix to the 1742 edition of Defoe's *Tour*, 'there is more Variety in this Garden, than can be found in any other of the same Size in *England*, or perhaps in *Europe*'.[119]

Rousham in Oxfordshire, haven of Gay and Pope, is another landscape with Bridgeman and Kent connections.[120] Pope was enthusiastic about it. 'I lay one night at Rowsham', he told Martha Blount, 'which is the prettiest place for water-falls, jetts, ponds inclosed with beautiful scenes of green and hanging wood, that ever I saw.'[121] Rousham was owned by the Dormer family, relatives of the Tyrrells who employed Kent at nearby

118 Thomas Whately, *Observations on Modern Gardening, and Laying Out Pleasure-Grounds, Parks, Farms, Ridings . . .*, new edn (London, 1801), p.153. Between the 1st edition of 1770 and the 1801 edition, of course, Walpole's *History of the Modern Taste in Gardening* had appeared. Whately had died in 1772, and the 1801 edition of his *Observations* was annotated by Walpole, though not published until three years after his death. We have here, therefore, Horace Walpole's testimony that Bridgeman was at Chiswick.

119 III, 290.

120 For Rousham see John Fleming, 'William Kent at Rousham. An Eighteenth-Century Elysium', *Connoisseur*, CLIII (July 1963), 158–65; Hussey, *English Gardens and Landscapes*, pp.147–53; Simon Pugh, 'Nature as a Garden. A Conceptual Tour of Rousham', *Studio International*, CLXXXVI (October 1973), 121–25; Kenneth Woodbridge, 'William Kent's Gardening: the Rousham Letters', *Apollo*, C (October 1974), 282–91. Mr Woodbridge generously shared with me the results of his research on Rousham.

For access to the grounds and manuscript material I am grateful to Mr T. Cottrell-Dormer.

121 *Pope Correspondence*, II, 513. Pope to Martha Blount, 4 September [1728].

Shotover,[122] and it was Lieutenant-General James Dormer who commissioned Kent to alter the existing Jacobean mansion. Dormer was a connoisseur, and a man of cultivated and literary tastes. What gives Rousham its unique appeal is its exquisite site, perfectly suited to the realization of pictorial qualities in landscape, and the complete opposite of Chiswick. A Bridgemanic plan in the Bodleian Library shows its disposition, with the house facing north over a rectangular bowling green, and the steeply-sloping wooded area bounded to the east by the angular River Cherwell, and to the south by the ha-ha facing the paddock (*Plate 61*). Beyond the river edge to the east are views of the Oxfordshire countryside. Similarities between Rousham and the western area of Stowe, as proposed by Bridgeman and Vanbrugh about 1720, are marked (*Plate 116*): some thought the existence of the Cherwell gave Rousham the palm. 'Charming as Stowe certainly is', wrote George Berkeley to Mrs Henrietta Howard in 1734, 'I own a partiality for Rowsham. One advantage must be allowed it; there is at the bottom of a sloping hill . . . a most delightful stream, which runs from thence directly to Marble Hill'.[123] This stream, and Rousham's landscape adjacent to it, today retains the character established by Bridgeman and Kent to a remarkable degree (*Plates 59a–60*).

Authority for the Royal Gardener's involvement rests primarily upon the Bridgemanic drawing of Rousham whose draughtsmanship and style recall his plans of Farley and Moor Park (*Plates 52, 51a*). What is so important about the Rousham sketch is firstly that it contains no elements which cannot be seen in other Bridgeman designs before the mid-1720's, secondly that it includes most of the features which Kent seems to have carried through later, and thirdly that it is specifically derived from a 1721 survey: Bridgeman is exploiting the *genius loci*.[124] Moreover Bridgeman was following at Rousham the precedent he and Vanbrugh had set at Stowe, where, say, the bucolic view from Gurnet's Walk over Home Park resembles that from Rousham's ha-ha over the paddock. The stroller at both Rousham and Stowe is presented with a kaleidoscopic series of views of statuary, garden buildings, and landscape. Allusions at Rousham to other Bridgeman schemes can be strikingly direct: the amphitheatre, for instance, echoes those at Eastbury, Claremont, and Chiswick, to name but three (*Plate 62a*).[125] Bridgeman also shows the Elm Walk and Venus's Vale, with its sites of the Great and Upper Ponds above the Cascade Basin. Venus's Vale was completed much as Kent sketched it, rather as a stage-set (*Plate 62b*): elsewhere he apparently cut away woods and opened up the area towards Heyford Bridge, placing there the Doric Temple of Echo, otherwise known as Townesend's Building. He added the Temple of the Mill, the eyecatcher, the pyramid, and Praeneste. Essentially however Kent did little to disturb the Bridgemanic concept. In 1741, the year in which

122 For Shotover see *VCH: Oxfordshire*, v (1957), 275–81. Dr W. O. Hassall found no reference to Bridgeman in his extensive research on the history of the house. See also Lees-Milne, *English Country Houses: Baroque*, pp.252–57.

123 Croker, ed., *Suffolk Correspondence*, II, 76. Berkeley is alluding to the fact that the Cherwell is a tributary of the Thames.

124 Cf. the three copies of a survey of Rousham Parish dated 1721 preserved at Rousham. The Bridgemanic drawing should be compared with the plan at Rousham conceivably by Kent and reproduced in Hussey, *English Gardens and Landscapes*, pl.202. The handwritten note on the Bridgemanic plan refers to waterworks at Rousham. On its back are the words 'Colonel Dormer', referring to Colonel Robert Dormer, who owned Rousham until his death in 1737, when it passed to James Dormer, his brother.

125 The amphitheatre, sometimes called the 'theatre', is often associated specifically with Bridgeman's name.

James Dormer died, George Vertue found Rousham 'Grand and Noble' and adorned with statues, arcades, temples, cascades, vistas, 'various views of a fine River . . . and distant prospects of various kinds'.[126] Small wonder that Horace Walpole was entranced. 'The whole is as elegant and antique', he cried, 'as if the emperor Julian had selected the most pleasing solitude about Daphne to enjoy a philosophic retirement.'[127]

The 'pleasing solitude' which Walpole found at Rousham, and which attracted Pope as well, is characteristic of Bridgeman's more progressive landscapes. Rousham came towards the end of Bridgeman's career, one of the last achievements of the transitional phase of the English landscape garden which had been ushered in by the controversy over Woodstock Manor in 1709. So far, our examination of Bridgeman's activities has shown him undertaking a great number of projects for a wide variety of clients, yet always exhibiting a responsible pragmatism towards the limitations and opportunities of each estate. No problem and no solution were the same, and the Royal Gardener moved easily from the formality of Boughton to the wildness of Chatelherault, or from the vastness of Blenheim to the intimacy of the Pheasant Garden at Woburn. Bridgeman's friends and professional colleagues were equally varied. Amongst architects there is no question that Vanbrugh and Kent had the most progressive ideas on landscaping. Together with Gibbs, we shall meet them presently working alongside Bridgeman either in the royal gardens, at Stowe, or assisting the *literati* who surrounded Lord Harley. And it is to this group that we must turn now.

[126] *Vertue*, IV (XXIV), 191.

[127] Chase, *Horace Walpole: Gardenist*, p.29.

Chapter 3

Literati and Harley's Circle

Three of Bridgeman's patrons in particular stand out as men of cultural and intellectual distinction: Cobham, Burlington, and Edward Harley, 2nd Earl of Oxford. Their seats at Stowe, Chiswick, and Wimpole were universally admired, and in their differing ways reflected the ideals and aspirations of their creators. Edward Harley's father, Robert Harley, created 1st Earl of Oxford in 1711, had been Chancellor of the Exchequer, Lord Treasurer, and leader of the Tories during the most critical years of Queen Anne's reign. Edward (*Plate 78b*) inherited his father's political beliefs, and it is hardly surprising therefore to find him opposing the Burlingtonians both architecturally and politically.

More than this. Harley inherited the 1st Earl of Oxford's enthusiasm for books, and much preferred to consort with artists and men of letters than politicians and courtiers.[1] Few of his fellow noblemen were so devoted to learning for learning's sake. Some people would add that he could afford to be, for his marriage to Henrietta Cavendish Holles had taken him from the obscurity of Brampton Bryan, in a remote pocket of Herefordshire, into the midst of one of the richest families in the land. Henrietta had brought huge monetary wealth apart from the Marylebone Estate, Welbeck and Wimpole, and Harley spent much of it on the expansion of his father's library. For this task he employed the diligent, scholarly, and shrewd Humfrey Wanley, himself a legacy from the 1st Earl. Wanley was an antiquarian through and through (he was co-founder with John Talman of the Society of Antiquaries of London), and under his watchful eye the library was allowed to become the be-all and end-all of Harley's existence: Harley's collection of pictures, engravings, coins, and antiquities had to take second place to manuscripts and books. Wanley made crisp notes on the library's numerous visitors. Thornhill, Wootton, Gibbs, and Dahl called on Wanley occasionally, but none so frequently as Charles Bridgeman. Bridgeman went to the library a dozen times between 13 February 1721 and 3 April 1725 and looked at 'Rarities' and 'fine books', and on one occasion, Wanley notes cryptically, 'Mr Bridgeman's man disturbed the books'.[2] Harley's book-collecting was never so obsessive as to exclude other forms of patronage, and not without justification Bishop Warburton of Gloucester called Harley 'the most distinguished patron and friend of letters that this age can boast of',[3] and Vertue, who had ample reason to be thankful, wrote that 'Artists or men of superior skill allways meet with this Good Lords Countenance &

[1] For background to this chapter see Lees-Milne, *Earls of Creation*, pp.173–218. Mr Lees-Milne kindly answered several of my queries.

[2] Bridgeman does not appear later as the diary ended on Wanley's death in 1726. See Wright and Wright, eds, *Diary of Humfrey Wanley*, I, 87, 102, 119, 153, 156, 162, 165, 170, 186, 192; II, 246, 350, 359.

[3] Quoted by Lees-Milne, *Earls of Creation*, p.185.

Encouragement'.[4] Many of these 'Artists or men of superior skill' were Stuart sympathizers and Tories with houses on the Marylebone Estate. Notable amongst them were the poets Prior and Pope, the painters Thornhill and Wootton, the architect James Gibbs, and Charles Bridgeman.

The inter-relationship between Bridgeman and Harley's artistic coterie is graphically illustrated in a poem by Sir James Thornhill. In 1721 Thornhill celebrated an excursion to Wimpole by writing a ballad about it entitled 'A Hue and Cry after Four of the King's Liege Subjects, who were Lately suppos'd to be seen at Roystone in Hartfordshire'. The 'Subjects' were disguised as 'Four things like men, that look'd something Wild', named MONTE SPINOSA (Thornhill himself), GIBBESIUS (Gibbs), BURGINION (Wootton), and PONSHOMO (Bridgeman).[5] Thornhill describes each of these in turn:

1st. The one they call'd MONTE SPINOSA I think
A Brownish Complection, a lover of drink
A drawer of Devils they say was his trade
My Landlord drew worse in his House, I'm afraid.

2d. GIBBESIUS, another, a man of great Fame
Who formerly from Calidonia came
An Ædificator was his Profession
A cursed hard name, what 'tis I can't guess on
Of Bears flesh a lover tho never so tough,
Quite raw he would chuse it, & sooner if Rough.

3d. The third was Outlandish I'm sure by his name
A spinner of Battells, of Fire, & Flame
BURGINION they call'd him; whenever he spoke
The fire came out of his mouth in a Joke.

4th. PONSHOMO, the fourth, from Adam descended,
A maker of Vistas, & much he's commended,
This man can make water for miles altogether
They say he'as made Mountains that reach God knows whither.

After spending a night at a hostelry in Royston, and making the landlord and people 'terribly scar'd', they were found out by the 'Patron of WIMPLE' who sent horses to bring them safely to their destination.

4 *Vertue*, VI (XXX), 64.

5 Francis R. D. Needham, ed., *A Collection of Poems by Several Hands, Never Before Published*, Welbeck Miscellany No. 2 (Bungay, Suffolk, 1934), pp. 53–56; *Wren Society*, XVII (1940), 11–13. The nicknames are readily explained, with the exception of BURGINION for Wootton, which is probably an allusion to Jacques Courtois, called Bourguignon (1621–76), the most famous battle painter of his period. Wootton is said to have trained under Jan Wyck, with whom he seems to have collaborated on battle scenes. Two of Bourguignon's battle-pieces at Welbeck are listed in Richard W. Goulding and C. K. Adams, *Catalogue of the Pictures Belonging to His Grace the Duke of Portland, K.G., at Welbeck Abbey, 17 Hill Street, London, and Langwell House* (Cambridge, 1936), p. 436.

Thornhill's sale catalogue of 1735 lists thirteen paintings by Bourguignon, including nine battle scenes. See the editorial, 'Sir James Thornhill's Collection', *Burlington Magazine*, LXXXII (June 1943), 133–36.

In the 1730's the gardener Peter Bourguignon prepared drawings in the Bridgeman manner for Gisburn (Yorks), Thorndon (Essex), and Worksop (Notts).

Thornhill (*Plate 63a*), the writer of these verses, was uniquely placed to chronicle the boisterous capers of Bridgeman, Wootton, and Gibbs. By 1721, following his success at Greenwich and St Paul's, Thornhill's career was reaching a new peak: the previous year had seen him made Sergeant-Painter in succession to Thomas Highmore, Master of the Painter-Stainers Company, and a Knight. In 1722 he became M.P. for his local borough of Weybridge, and in 1723 an F.R.S. Moreover Thornhill's architectural aspirations were becoming apparent, as Bridgeman must have been aware.[6] Bridgeman had probably become acquainted with Thornhill at Blenheim, and thereafter their paths crossed socially at St Luke's Club, and professionally at Wimpole and elsewhere.[7] The significance of Bridgeman's relationship with Thornhill rests on the painter's concern for landscape and garden design. This concern emerges in murals, topographical sketches, and projects for garden temples and stage sets:[8] compare, let us say, his drawing of a *Lakeside Scene, with Figures, Temple and Ruined Bridge* (*Plate 64b*) with his proposals for a moonlit scene in Thomas Clayton's opera *Arsinoë, Queen of Cyprus,* in which there are statues, urns, and clipped hedges in the foreground, and a classical villa set amidst trees and hills at the rear (*Plate 64a*). True, these are no more advanced than Inigo Jones's similar sketches of the 1630's,[9] but they do show Thornhill's interest in the juxtaposition of buildings and countryside.

Even more influential on Bridgeman was John Wootton (*Plate 63b*). Bridgeman and Wootton had ample opportunity to meet: Wootton was a close neighbour of Bridgeman in Cavendish Square, a royal favourite, Steward of St Luke's Club in 1717, and a prominent figure in Hamilton's *Club of Artists* (*Plate 19*).[10] By 1716 Wootton was being employed by Edward Harley on painting animal and landscape scenes, and Harley remained one of his best patrons. Both Bridgeman and Wootton worked for the Duke of Beaufort at Badminton, and it was under Beaufort's patronage that the painter apparently visited Italy about 1721. The Italian streak in Wootton's work gives his relationship with Bridgeman added interest, for by 1722 Vertue was remarking that Wootton's landscapes were 'very much like the pictures of Gaspar Pousin. both as to Invention design & Colouring. he

[6] See Colvin, *Dictionary*, pp.610–12. In 1719 Thornhill was beaten by Hewitt for the Surveyorship of the King's Works, and in 1720 designs for St Martin in the Fields were submitted by Gibbs, John James, Dubois, George Samson, and Sir James Thornhill. See ibid., p.231.

[7] For Thornhill's interiors at such Bridgeman locations as Amesbury, Blenheim, Eastbury, Kensington, Montagu House, Moor Park, and Wimpole, see Edward Croft-Murray, *Decorative Painting in England, 1537–1837* (London, 1962–70), I, 69–78, 265–74; Whistler, *Imagination of Vanbrugh, passim.*

[8] See Edgar De N. Mayhew, *Sketches by Thornhill in the Victoria and Albert Museum* (London, 1967). Cf. Thornhill's MS Sketchbook in the British Museum (1884–7–26–40). For garden temples by Thornhill see Colvin, ed., *Drawings at Worcester College, Oxford,* Nos 72, 75 and pl.114; Mayhew, *Sketches by Thornhill,* No.40 and pl.40.

The significance of stage design in this context has yet to be explored fully, but see S. Lang, 'The Genesis of the English Landscape Garden', in Nikolaus Pevsner, ed., *The Picturesque Garden and Its Influence Outside the British Isles* (Washington, D.C., 1974), pp.1–29.

[9] See e.g. Harris, Orgel, and Strong, *King's Arcadia*, pls 135, 139, 140, 301, 302, 304, 309, 325, 337, 338.

[10] For Wootton see e.g. Luke Herrmann, *British Landscape Painting of the Eighteenth Century* (London, 1973), pp.17–20; Kendall, 'Notes on the Life of John Wootton', pp.23–42; Oliver Millar, *The Tudor, Stuart and Early Georgian Pictures in the Collection of Her Majesty the Queen* (London, 1963), pp.179–83; Walter Shaw Sparrow, *British Sporting Artists from Barlow to Herring* (London, 1922), pp.89–113; Denys Sutton, 'John Wootton Recognised at Last', *C.Life,* CXXIV (4 December 1958), 1290–96. See also the Exhibition Catalogue of the Arts Council of Great Britain, *British Sporting Painting, 1650–1850* (London, 1974), and Goulding and Adams, *Welbeck Catalogue*, pp.168, 492–94.

haveing studied from several peices of that masters painting. has perfectly enterd into his Manner'.[11] Horace Walpole agreed. Wootton's paintings, he noted, 'approached towards Gaspar Poussin, and sometimes imitated happily the glow of Claud Lorrain'.[12] Wootton's pupil George Lambert took a leaf out of his master's book, and he too was painting classical landscapes in the 1720's. Some of the diverse strands in Wootton's style can be seen in his *Harbour Scene* of 1755, with its conscious amalgam of fashionable motifs (*Plate 65a*), in his *Classical Landscape* (*Plate 65b*), and in *The Beaufort Hunt* (*Plate 87*). Not that everyone admired the results. Constable, for one, found the hunting scenes despicable. 'The absurdity of imitation', he exploded, 'is nowhere so striking as in the landscapes of the English Woo[t]ton, who painted country gentlemen in their wigs and jockey caps, and top-boots, with packs of hounds, and placed them in Italian landscapes resembling those of Gaspar Poussin, except in truth and force'.[13] One of the patrons who bought such Wootton canvases was Henry Hoare II, and indeed it may have been Wootton who aroused the Hoares' interest in Claude and Gaspard: when Horace Walpole visited Stourhead in 1762 he noted eight paintings by Wootton, and not more than two by any other artist.[14] And when Wootton himself died in 1761, his personal collection of paintings included eleven copies after Gaspard.

The fourth member of the quartet in Thornhill's ballad was James Gibbs (*Plate 66b*), who was typical of those eighteenth-century artists engaged pre-eminently by members of that political party to which they owed their advancement and success. Born into a middle-class Scots Catholic family, Gibbs found an early supporter in John Erskine, Earl of Mar, but towards the end of Queen Anne's reign he fell in with Edward Harley and others, who saw to it in 1713 that Gibbs was appointed one of the Surveyors to the Commissioners for Building Fifty New Churches. Subsequently architect and patron were drawn together by the Queen's death, the accession of the Hanoverians, the downfall of Jacobite hopes, and the triumph of the Whigs. Harley's backing, together with the many friends made by Gibbs when he was in Italy between about 1703 and 1709, ensured that he enjoyed a wide range of commissions. Moreover Gibbs's publication of his *Book of Architecture* (1728, 1739), *Rules for Drawing the Several Parts of Architecture* (1732, 1738, 1753), and *Bibliotheca Radcliviana* (1747) did nothing to hinder the dissemination of his style and reputation. His work for Harley himself was appropriately varied: apart from the Oxford Market and the Oxford Chapel, Gibbs designed various monuments, and a new front for Harley's home in Dover Street. Not far away was Bridgeman's house in Henrietta Street, seemingly one of those designed by Gibbs for the Marylebone Estate. To these must be added Gibbs's work for Harley at Wimpole, and for Matthew Prior (and Harley) at Down Hall in Essex.

[11] *Vertue*, I (XVIII), 101.

[12] Walpole, *Anecdotes of Painting*, ed. Wornum, II, 322.

[13] C. R. Leslie, *Memoirs of the Life of John Constable, Composed Chiefly of His Letters*, ed. Jonathan Mayne (London, 1951), p.320.

[14] Toynbee, ed., 'Walpole's Visits to Country Seats', pp.41–42. Woodbridge, *Landscape and Antiquity*, p.22, indicates that twelve paintings by Wootton were at one time at Stourhead. For patronage of Wootton see John Hayes, 'British Patrons and Landscape Painting' (April 1967), 254–56.

Prior

Matthew Prior had been a friend of the 1st Earl of Oxford and enjoyed a dual career as diplomat and poet. The son of a Dorset joiner, he was educated at Westminster and St John's College, Cambridge, and duly became secretary to the ambassador at The Hague. He was instrumental in concluding the peace terms with France in 1711 which led to the Treaty of Utrecht in 1713, popularly known as 'Matt's Peace'. At Versailles he bantered in French with Louis XIV. But it was his poetry rather than his diplomacy which brought him recognition in England. In 1719, when Prior was fifty-five, a number of his admirers sponsored the publication of a large folio volume of his collected verse. The sales made a profit of 4,000 guineas, and Harley (whose father was indebted to Prior for political services) added an equal sum to help Prior purchase Down Hall. In return for this payment the property was to revert to Harley on Prior's death.

To have a house in the country was one of Prior's wildest dreams, and he was delighted. Twenty years before, whilst living in Paris, he had given voice to his hopes:

GREAT MOTHER, let Me Once be able
To have a Garden, House, and Stable;
That I may Read, and Ride, and Plant,
Superior to Desire, or Want;
And as Health fails, and Years increase,
Sit down, and think, and die in Peace.[15]

Now, in high spirits, Prior made his first visit to Down with his financial adviser John Morley, and afterwards recounted the experience in his ballad *Down-Hall*.[16] The two men rode by coach to Essex, staying a night at the Bull Inn, Hoddesdon. Next day, as they approached the old house, Prior was frankly dismayed at what he saw through the trees:

Oh! now a low, ruin'd, white Shed I discern,
Until'd, and unglaz'd, I believe 'tis a Barn.

To which Morley retorts:

A Barn! – Why you rave – 'Tis a House for a Squire,
A Justice of Peace, or a Knight of our Shire. (ll.147–50)

Prior's disappointment is little allayed by Morley's assurances, and the poet regrets that the building is made of timber and plaster rather than stone and brick. Morley loses patience with him:

With your Friend JEMMY GIBBS about Building agree;
My Business is Land, and it matters not Me. (ll.158–59)

[15] Lines 8–13 from *Written at Paris, 1700. In the Beginning of Robe's Geography*, in H. Bunker Wright and Monroe K. Spears, eds, *The Literary Works of Matthew Prior*, 2nd edn (Oxford, 1971), I, 189. I am much indebted to Professor Bunker Wright for help and advice on Bridgeman's connection with Prior.

[16] See ibid., I, 550–57, and the commentary in II, 993–95. See also the letter from Pope to Morley of 11 April 1722 referring to this 'very pretty Ballad' in P. L. Heyworth, 'A New Pope Letter', *Times Literary Supplement*, 3 July 1969, p.731. I am grateful to Professor Heyworth for alerting me to this.

Not that Prior has anything but praise for the site itself. 'It is impossible to tell you how beautiful a situation Down is, and how fine the wood may be made', he wrote to Harley, 'but for the house . . . sooner or later I foresee *destruit domum*.'[17] Ignoring Morley's warning that the erection of a new house would ruin him, Prior was soon seeking advice from the friends who frequented his home in Duke Street, Westminster. For rebuilding Down Hall itself he did indeed call upon Jemmy Gibbs; for re-designing the grounds he engaged Charles Bridgeman, his *virtuoso grand jardinier* and *operator hortorum et sylvarum* as he termed him.[18]

During 1720 Gibbs prepared two schemes for the house, and the one Prior selected consisted of a three-storey classical block with two lower side-wings linked to it by curved arcades.[19] Gibbs illustrated his design in his *Book of Architecture* (*Plate 66a*), along with three classical temples for the bowling green, all with octagonal domes. Two of these are plain and rather dull, with projecting entrance porticoes approached by flights of steps (*Plate 69*), but the third (which resembles Gibbs's Lady's Temple at Stowe) has a rusticated ground floor, Venetian windows, and niches for statuary. It is altogether more mature (*Plate 68*). Bridgeman, for his part, prepared two layouts for the grounds, each having kitchen gardens, a spring, an encircling terrace walk, and a walk leading down to a basin fed by a stream. The more adventurous of Bridgeman's drawings also includes sinuous paths and open spaces cut into the woods (*Plate 67*).[20]

Down was conveniently situated between London and Wimpole, and Prior found it easy enough to tap Bridgeman, Gibbs, Dahl, and Wootton for advice. During 1720 and 1721 Bridgeman and Gibbs were often at Down, though Prior made little headway with his resolution to demolish the old house completely and rebuild it from scratch. The landscaping, on the other hand, progressed steadily under Bridgeman's direction. Prior reports that on a journey from Wimpole to Down in the autumn of 1720 he and Bridgeman talked of 'nothing but canals, parades and vistas'.[21] There was also a fish pond (presumably the Great Basin) that would hold ten carp.[22] 'We have laid out squares, rounds and diagonals, and planted quincunxes at Down', Prior wrote. '*Chacun a sa marotte*.' Still, planting had its taxing moments. 'That farm will turn my brain', Prior added.[23] During spring and summer of 1721 work continued apace and soon it was well advanced. Prior, now living at Down, gave himself to the pleasures of country residence. Obviously he was highly satisfied with Bridgeman's efforts. 'I am glad Bridgeman has begun so well', he confided to Harley after the gardener's visit in March. 'He says he will make it the finest and noblest thing in England. The garden side I find he has a mind to be at; he

[17] *HMC 58: Bath III*, 483. Prior to Edward Harley, 2 July 1720. Drawings of the old house are in BL, Loan 29/357 (Portland Papers), set 2.

[18] Ibid., 488–89. Prior to Edward Harley, 13 and 15 September 1720.

[19] Gibbs's drawings for the rejected design are in Bod. Lib., Gough Maps 46, fos 260–61, 263–64.

[20] See Peter Willis, 'A Poets' Gardener', *Listener*, LXXII (24 December 1964), 1007–9.

[21] *HMC 58: Bath III*, 490. Prior to Edward Harley, 27 September 1720.

[22] Prior to Chesterfield, 14 January 1721, quoted in Whitwell Elwin and W. J. Courthope, eds, *The Works of Alexander Pope* . . . (London, 1871–89), VIII, 193–94.

[23] *HMC 58: Bath III*, 492. Prior to Edward Harley, 29 December 1720.

does not open yet, but I think it is rather enlarging than much altering.'[24] Down, Prior enthused, 'I love more than Tully did his Tusculum, or Horace his Sabine field.'[25] Sadly Prior was never to see either the house or grounds completed, for he died whilst visiting Wimpole in the following September, finally overtaken by the slow consumption that had dogged him for years.[26] Harley was stricken with grief. He was not the only one. 'I pray God deliver me from any such Trials', Swift wrote. 'I am neither old nor Philosopher enough to be indifferent at so great a Loss.'[27]

On Edward Harley and Adrian Drift (Prior's secretary) fell the burden of acting as executors of Prior's will.[28] That the poet held Bridgeman, Gibbs, and Dahl in high esteem is evident from two bequests he made. A letter from Drift to Harley of 6 December 1721 explains that Prior had wished to give Bridgeman and Gibbs each a 'Buste of Flora' copied by Richard Dickinson, the sculptor who provided statuary for Wrest and Knowsley.[29] The original, by François Girardon, stood on a marble pedestal, was willed to Harley by Prior, and seems to have been greatly admired by Prior's colleagues.[30] Drift urges Harley to authorize the purchase of the busts, as Prior had wanted to discharge a debt 'due to Two worthy Men whom he much Esteemed'. Harley apparently gave his consent, for on 22 December 1721 there is an entry in Drift's note-book of a payment of £15 to Dickinson for '3 Copies of the Busto of Flora cast in hard Mettal' for Bridgeman, Gibbs, and Dahl.[31] The letter from Drift to Harley goes on to refer to a second present, this time to Bridgeman alone:

> Having sometime before Mr Prior's Death received his Orders to procure for Dear Charles Bridgeman, a Spenser in Folio, if it was to be got for Love or Money (his own words) I set all my Friends of the Literati to work to get One, and soon after my Dearest Masters Death, a Spenser in very good condition was brought to me, price one pound (found in a private Library to be Sold) which I accordingly Paid and (in your Lordships absence) a few days ago presented to Mr: Bridgman, as the Gift intended him by Mr: Prior, presuming that My Lord Harley would be pleased therewith, and with which, I believe, Mr: Bridgeman will himself acquaint Your Lordship in a few days.[32]

Did Spenser have any significance for Down? Could Bridgeman's folio have been a copy of the *Faerie Queene*? We do not know. What we can say is that the goddess Flora (or

[24] Ibid., 498. Prior to Edward Harley, 16 March 1721.

[25] Ibid., 504. Prior to Edward Harley, 8 June 1721.

[26] See Charles K. Eves, *Matthew Prior. Poet and Diplomatist* (New York, 1939), pp.408–9; L. G. Wickham Legg, *Matthew Prior. A Study of His Public Career and Correspondence* (Cambridge, 1921), p.272.

[27] Harold H. Williams, ed., *The Correspondence of Jonathan Swift* (Oxford, 1963–65), II, 406–7. Swift to Archbishop William King, 28 September 1721.

[28] BL, Loan 29/316, 317 (Portland Papers), which consist of two volumes of Prior documents and accounts.

[29] BL, Loan 29/317 (Portland Papers), fos 161r–162r. For Dickinson see Rupert Gunnis, *Dictionary of British Sculptors, 1660–1851*, 2nd edn (London, 1968), p.130.

[30] See H. Bunker Wright and Henry C. Montgomery, 'The Art Collection of a Virtuoso in Eighteenth-Century England', *Art Bulletin*, XXVII (September 1945), 197, 200. Harley had a fourth bust cast for himself. See also Hubert Landais, 'Some Bronzes from the Girardon Collection', *Connoisseur*, CXLVIII (October 1961), 136–44.

[31] BL, Loan 29/317 (Portland Papers), fos 162, 80v. On fo.161, in a letter to Harley of 16 December 1721, Drift says that Bridgeman wanted the third bust to go to Wootton rather than Dahl.

[32] Ibid., fo. 162.

Ceres) appears both as the subject of Girardon's bust and as a figure in Spenser's poem, and that English eighteenth-century landscapes frequently contained garden temples and statuary named after her. Is it not likely therefore that Prior, aided and abetted by Bridgeman and Gibbs, intended to use Girardon's bust at Down Hall, either standing on a pedestal in the grounds or set in a temple dedicated to Flora?

According to the arrangements made with Prior, Harley became owner of Down on the poet's death, and during 1721 and 1722 Harley and Drift were making payments to Bridgeman for work he had done there. Any halt in the evolution of the landscaping was only temporary, and soon Harley was busy planting, cutting down trees to reveal hidden vistas, laying out a bowling green, and using Gibbs to design garden structures.[33] Bridgeman too must have helped Harley with his improvements, for the gardener and Gibbs were frequently at Down as Harley's guests.[34] Wootton, Dahl, and Pope were others who enjoyed Down's fresh air and tranquillity: late in December 1725 Pope and Bridgeman went there for a short stay. Pope wrote enthusiastically of his visit,[35] though he regretted that Harley was as keen as Prior to replace the rambling old house with a spick-and-span villa by Gibbs. Pope says he is 'utterly against' Gibbs's proposals for demolishing Down and rebuilding it: for one thing, he adds mischievously, the present house is surely large enough 'when both Lady Margaret has room to run about all the morning, in her chamber, & Mr Thomas to sport with Bridgman, in his'.[36] The question of what to do with Down was in fact rhetorical, as Harley had no cash to spare to tackle any major rebuilding, and when faced with financial ruin he was forced to sell Down to William Selwin, a London merchant.[37] Long before this Harley had carried through his last act of devotion to Matthew Prior by erecting Gibbs's monument to him in Poets' Corner in Westminster Abbey. The bust was by Coysevox, the attendant figures by Rysbrack – an extravagance made possible because Prior had made provision of £500 to cover the cost. 'I should have been more pleas'd if it had been erected at any other person's charge, rather than his own', wrote Ralph in his *Critical Review*. ''Tis extending our vanity beyond the grave, and making the envy of mankind eternal.'[38]

[33] See Ashmolean Museum, Oxford, Gibbs Collection, IV, fo.33a, which is a drawing of two sundials. As this has Lord Oxford's name on it, the sundials must form part of Harley's (not Prior's) proposals.

[34] Payments to Charles Bridgeman appear (along with minor ones to Campbell, Gibbs, Mist, and Wootton) in Edward Harley's MS Accounts (Ledger 1688–1732) in Child's Branch of Williams and Glyn's Bank Ltd, London. Bridgeman was paid £221 in 1721, £400 in 1722, £470 in 1723, £1,474.3*s*.3*d*. in 1724, £280 in 1725, £126.3*s*.3*d*. in 1726. Although Harley's account continues until 1729, Bridgeman's name does not recur.

[35] *Pope Correspondence*, II, 355. Pope to Edward Harley, 27 December 1725. Pope was at Down until 6 January or so. See also ibid., II, 327.

[36] Ibid., II, 364. Pope to Edward Harley, 22 January 1726. 'Mr Thomas' was the Rev. Timothy Thomas, Harley's chaplain and brother of William Thomas; 'Lady Margaret' was Lady Margaret Harley, Prior's 'noble, lovely, little Peggy', daughter of Edward and Henrietta Harley. On 26 July 1734 Bridgeman wrote congratulating the Harleys on Lady Margaret's marriage to William Bentinck, 2nd Duke of Portland. See below Appendix IV(iv), p.157. Illness prevented Bridgeman paying his respects in person. A list of those who did so is in *HMC 29: Portland VI*, 56.

[37] See Philip Morant, *The History and Antiquities of the County of Essex* . . . (London, 1768), II, 508. Down is shown in John P. Neale, *Views of the Seats of Noblemen and Gentlemen in England, Wales, Scotland and Ireland*, S.I (London, 1818–23), I, pl.66.

[38] P.79.

Pope

Prior and Swift both enjoyed the friendship of Lady Henrietta Harley as well as that of her husband. Alexander Pope was a different matter: Henrietta disliked him, and found a ready ally in Lady Mary Wortley Montagu. Neither seems to have had much sympathy with the poet's enthusiasm for landscaping, an enthusiasm which formed part of the Twickenham scene dominated by Pope, Swift, and Gay – the 'three Yahoos of Twickenham' as Bolingbroke called them.[39] Here the Thameside villas were providing fashionable retreats from the rigours of city life, and in so doing were merging architectural and landscape invention. Defoe was completely won over. 'The whole country . . . shines with lustre not to be describ'd', he wrote. 'Take them in a remote view, the fine seats shine among the trees as jewels shine in a rich coronet; in a near sight they are meer pictures and paintings; at a distance they are all nature, near hand all art; but both in the extreamest beauty.'[40] A generation later, in 1760, when Mrs Pye wrote her description of the houses and gardens around Twickenham, she was moved to apologize for being carried away. 'I have been obliged to a repetition of the words *view, prospect*, &c. till I was tired of them myself', she declared. The 'chief delight' for Twickenham's inhabitants was architecture, 'in which if any one doubts their excelling, let him sail up the river, and view their lovely villas beautifying its banks'. The laws and customs of 'this earthly elysium' are 'dictated by reason, and regulated by social love'.[41]

Pope's villa at Twickenham was within a stone's throw of several key landscapes, including Richmond Park and Gardens (*Plate 70*): as early as 1713 the grounds of Petersham Lodge were laid out in an advanced manner by Henry Hyde, 4th Earl of Clarendon and father of Catherine Hyde, Duchess of Queensberry;[42] in 1710 James Johnston, the Secretary of State for Scotland, built a villa later called Orleans House (to which Gibbs added his Octagon) to the designs of John James, and the landscaping was sufficiently advanced by 1727 for Johnston to regale Sir John Clerk of Penicuik 'with a sight of all his great improvements in Gardening';[43] not far away the Earl of Ilay employed Gibbs and Roger Morris at Whitton, an estate with several remarkable garden structures. Between 1724 and 1729 Ilay had supervised Morris's building of nearby Marble Hill for Mrs Henrietta Howard, and as Bridgeman was active there the possibility that he may have

39 Williams, ed., *Swift Correspondence*, III, 146. Bolingbroke to 'the three Yahoos of Twickenham', 23 July 1726. For Twickenham see John Cornforth, 'When the Thames was England's Brenta', *Country Life Annual* (1963), pp.73–75; Nicholas Lawrence, ed., *Six Views of Twickenham in the Eighteenth Century* (Richmond upon Thames, 1972); Hugh Phillips, *The Thames About 1750* (London, 1951), pp.176–95; John Walker, 'The Thames Through Eighteenth-Century Eyes. Augustine Heckell and His Imitators', *C.Life*, CXLVI (3 July 1969), 24–27.

40 Defoe, *A Tour Through the Whole Island of Great Britain*, ed. Browning and Cole, I, 167.

41 J. Henrietta Pye, *A Peep into the Principal Seats and Gardens in and about Twickenham* . . . (London, 1775), pp.iv, 52.

42 See A. James Sambrook, 'Pope's Neighbours. An Early Landscape Garden at Richmond', *Journal of the Warburg and Courtauld Institutes*, XXX (1967), 444–46. In 1721 Petersham Lodge was destroyed by fire and Burlington rebuilt it for William Stanhope, later 1st Earl of Harrington and owner of Pope's villa. The gardens at Petersham are mentioned in Summer in Thomson's *Seasons*, ll.1415–19.

43 Gray, ed., *Memoirs of Sir John Clerk of Penicuik*, p.125. For Johnston's villa see Friedman, 'James Gibbs', pp.170–79. James may have assisted with the gardens: his translation of Dézallier D'Argenville's *Theory and Practice of Gardening* was dedicated to Johnston.

advised Ilay at Whitton (and his brother John, 2nd Duke of Argyll, at Gibbs's Sudbrooke) is a real one.[44] Although only two letters exchanged by Bridgeman and Pope have come down to us, they contain direct and indirect references to five layouts on which Bridgeman may have advised: Marble Hill was one, the others being Dawley, Brampton Bryan, Wimpole, and Pope's own villa.[45]

Marble Hill is the Palladian house built for Mrs Howard by Campbell, Morris, and Pembroke, partly at the expense of George II when Prince of Wales.[46] Heckell and Mason's view from across the Thames shows the house's 'undecorated Plainness' (to use Robert Morris's phrase) typical of the Morris-Pembroke school (*Plate 71*).[47] Begun in 1724, it has the compactness of Chiswick without its panache. On 28 September 1724 Bridgeman wrote to Pope explaining that since he last saw the poet and Mrs Howard at Twickenham he had been 'continually abroad on business . . . of great Moment' which would keep him in London for the next fortnight. He had returned to Broad Street the previous Friday, and on Saturday began a 'plann' for Pope, presumably (though not necessarily) of Marble Hill.[48] Roger Morris had been engaged by Ilay the previous June. That autumn Bridgeman, Pope, and Bathurst were laying out the grounds there, and during the subsequent twelve months Bathurst and Pope were continually involved in Mrs Howard's 'works'.[49] Pope spent many hours at Sherborne 'drawing new plans' and 'studying' for Marble Hill's gardens.[50] From Heckell and Mason's view it seems that they consisted partly of a lawn sloping down to the Thames, with rows of trees framing the house when seen from the river.[51] Though she may occasionally have regretted doing so, we have seen that Mrs Howard was sufficiently satisfied with Bridgeman's contribution at Marble Hill to recommend him to the Duchess of Queensberry for Amesbury.[52] In 1734 Henrietta severed her increasingly painful friendship with George II and retired to Twickenham, where her hospitality was so successful that in 1735 Pope could write that there was 'a greater court now at Marble hill than at Kensington'.[53] Until Horace Walpole's death Twickenham was to keep its unique place as an artistic and social resort, as the 'home of the Muses and Graces together'.[54]

[44] See Mary Cosh, 'Two Dukes and Their Houses', *C.Life*, CLII (13, 20 July 1972), 78–81, 142–45. For Whitton see also Lindsay and Cosh, *Inverary*, pp.10, 17, 348–49 n.13; for Sudbrooke see ibid., pp.45, 352–53 n.10. Dr James Macaulay places Whitton in a wider context (emphasising links with Vanbrugh) in *The Gothic Revival* (Glasgow and London, 1975), pp.41, 46–48, 52, 56.

[45] For the context of Pope's villa, and other Twickenham houses referred to, see *VCH: Middlesex*, III (1962), 139–55.

[46] For Marble Hill see *Marble Hill House, Twickenham. A Short Account of Its History and Architecture* (London, 1969); Draper and Eden, *Marble Hill House*, esp. pp.15–16; Eden, 'South Dalton, Yorkshire', 117–20. My work on Marble Hill benefited from the kindness of Mrs Draper, Mr Eden, and Dr Malcolm Airs.

[47] Robert Morris, *Select Architecture* . . . (London, 1759), Introduction.

[48] See below Appendix IV(i), p.156.

[49] *Pope Correspondence*, II, 197, 257, 292, 447; III, 34–35, 474; V, 19.

[50] Ibid., II, 240. Pope to Martha Blount, 22 June [1724?].

[51] What claims to be 'an original layout of the gardens' is reproduced in A. T. Bolton, 'Marble Hill, Middlesex', *C.Life*, XXXIX (25 March 1916), 399.

[52] Croker, ed., *Suffolk Correspondence*, I, 386–87; II, 20–21. Mrs Howard to Gay, 22 August [1730], 5 September [1731].

[53] *Pope Correspondence*, III, 478. Pope to Fortescue, 2 August 1735.

[54] A phrase stolen from Mack, *The Garden and the City*, p.17.

Pope, writing to the Royal Gardener in 1725, hints at possible Bridgeman connections with two if not three other estates. The letter itself was sent from Dawley near Twickenham, the house altered by Gibbs which Bolingbroke first occupied in the summer of that year.[55] In 1723, two years earlier, Bolingbroke had returned from his exile in France and – fresh from laying out La Source, near Orléans – set about improving his newly-acquired property at Dawley. Pope implies that Bridgeman may have advised Bolingbroke on Dawley's layout: 'My Lord Bolingbroke received yours', he writes, 'and shall be glad to see you at your conveniency.' Switzer, it will be recalled, had specifically cited Dawley (along with Abb's Court and Richings) as an example of a *ferme ornée*, and had published a plan of Richings to emphasize what he meant (*Plate 11*).[56] Although Rocque's engraving of Dawley gives us precious little indication of bucolic delights (*Plate 72b*), the closeness to the house of fields and meadows contrasts forcibly with a Bridgemanic landscape such as Shardeloes (*Plate 72a*). Bolingbroke did not regard Dawley merely as a place to entertain his friends, for he actually farmed, and set about making his farming pay. His sister Henrietta Knight, Lady Luxborough, said that there were no two ways about it. 'My brother's calling it a farm', she noted, 'was only meant as it was really one.'[57] To drive home his message, Bolingbroke decorated the interior of Dawley with agricultural implements.[58]

By the mid-1720's, already in harness with James Gibbs on other commissions, Bridgeman would have been well placed to collaborate with him at Dawley. Moreover Gibbs was personally and professionally connected with Pope. Such conjecture notwithstanding, the burden of the poet's letter to Bridgeman is an apology for his inability to go with him to 'Lord Oxford's'. The theory that Pope was alluding here to the Harley estate of Brampton Bryan in Herefordshire is supported by the existence of a Bridgemanic plan of Brampton Bryan in the Soane Museum, dated 1722 and addressed to the 1st Earl of Oxford (*Plate 78a*).[59] On the other hand Pope may have been referring to Wimpole Hall, Edward Harley's country home south-west of Cambridge.

In due course the 'MASTER OF WIMPLE' (as Prior called him) was to make Wimpole his favourite residence, and to him it owes much of its substance and most of its fame.[60] Besides using Wimpole for entertaining his friends, Harley altered the house extensively in the 1710's and 1720's, employing Gibbs as architect and Thornhill as painter: the

[55] See below Appendix IV(ii), p.156. For Dawley see H. T. Dickinson, *Bolingbroke* (London, 1970), esp. pp.180, 212, 247; Walter Sichel, *Bolingbroke and His Times* (London, 1901–2), II, 212–21, 293–94, 337. There is a poem on Dawley in *Gentleman's Magazine*, I (1731), p.262. See also *VCH: Middlesex*, III (1962), 258–75, esp. pp.264–65.

[56] Switzer, *Ichnographia Rustica* (1742), III, Appendix, pp.9–10. See above p.23n92.

[57] *Letters Written by the Late Right Honourable Lady Luxborough to William Shenstone, Esq.* (London, 1775), p.173. In a letter on p.38 she contrasts Shenstone's *ferme ornée* with her own *ferme négligée* at Barrells in Warwickshire.

[58] See e.g. *Pope Correspondence*, II, 503. Pope to Swift, 28 June 1728; ibid., II, 525. Pope to Bathurst, 7 November [1728].

Dawley and Stowe were linked together by an antagonist of Pope in 1738:

Does *Stow*'s pure air, or *Dawl[e]y*'s, in an hour,
Cleanse just like soap; like purgatory scour?

See J. V. Guerinot, *Pamphlet Attacks on Alexander Pope, 1711–44. A Descriptive Bibliography* (London, 1969), p.272.

[59] For the Harleys at Brampton Bryan see Nikolaus Pevsner, *Herefordshire*, The Buildings of England (Harmondsworth, 1963), pp.81–82.

[60] For Wimpole see Christopher Hussey, 'Wimpole Hall, Cambridgeshire', *C.Life*, CXLII (30 November 1967), 1400–4; *RCHM: West Cambridgeshire*, I (1968), 210–29; *VCH: Cambridgeshire*, V (1973), 263–65.

present-day south front is mostly an amalgam of work by Gibbs and Flitcroft (*Plate 73a*). As garden designer Harley called upon Charles Bridgeman, and between 1720 and 1724 Bridgeman frequently visited Wimpole, often as not in the company of Pope, Gibbs, Thornhill, Wootton, or Prior.[61] In 1721 Prior is remarking that presumably Thornhill 'has rather been speculating in the chapel he is to paint, than praying in the neighbouring church, and friend Bridgeman's devotion has consisted chiefly in contriving how the diagonal may take Waddon steeple exactly in the middle'.[62] An excursion to Wimpole by Bridgeman and Pope in 1724 had to be postponed because of the illness of Pope's mother. 'I am heartily disappointed', Pope wrote, 'and so is another man, of the Virtuoso-Class as well as I . . . and in My notions, of the higher kind of class, since Gardening is more Antique & nearer God's own Work, than Poetry.' He explains: 'I mean Bridgman, whom I had tempted to accompany me to you.'[63] Further disappointment was to follow, for a visit the next summer also fell through.[64] Pope's affection for Wimpole remained unabated, and the poet was still prepared to dash there 'at an hours warning, from any other part of the land'. No place delighted him more 'be it winter or summer, or spring, or autumn'.[65] The house itself, as Bridgemanic plans make clear, is set at the meeting point of long, straight rides which stretch into the countryside (*Plates 73b, 74, 75*). Near the mansion were parterres, bosquets, and cabinets decorated with the vases shown in Gibbs's *Book of Architecture*.[66] Pope hints that Edward Harley may have hoped to erect garden temples too. 'I salute the Little Gods & antiquities in my way in the Anti-room,' he wrote of a visit to Wimpole in 1730, 'wishing them joy of the New Temples they are to be Inshrined in.'[67] The most memorable feature then and now, however, is the main avenue of elms (broken by the octagonal basin) which does nothing if not heighten the drama of Wimpole's setting in the flat Cambridgeshire countryside.

Bridgeman and Pope must have discussed gardening matters whilst at Wimpole and on other occasions, and the poet refers to Bridgeman several times in his poems and in his notes on them. Indications are that their relationship was somewhat fragile. In 1731 Pope mentions Bridgeman in his *Epistle to Burlington*, originally issued in the *Daily Post-Boy* of 22 December that year. In an early manuscript of the poem Pope had added a four-line footnote after a slighting reference to Bubb Dodington's activities at Eastbury:

Must bishops, lawyers, statesmen, have the skill
To build, to plant, judge paintings, what you will?

[61] *HMC 58: Bath III*, 490–506.

[62] Ibid., 499. Prior to Edward Harley, 18 March 1721. The chapel was a Gibbs design, and Thornhill's decoration of 1721–24 consisted of feigned coffering on the ceiling, statues and niches on the side walls, and at the east end the *Adoration of the Magi* above the reredos. See Croft-Murray, *Decorative Painting in England*, II, 76–77, 273; pl.137.

[63] *Pope Correspondence*, II, 264. Pope to Edward Harley, 8 October 1724. Cf. Pope to Swift, 25 March 1736, in Williams, ed., *Swift Correspondence*, IV, 472.

[64] *Pope Correspondence*, II, 315. Edward Harley to Pope, 30 August 1725.

[65] Ibid., II, 317. Pope to Edward Harley, 7 September 1725. Pope made a further excursion to Wimpole in 1727. See ibid., II, 441. Pope to Fortescue, 5 August [1727].

[66] Pl.138.

[67] Ibid., III, 114. Pope to Edward Harley [June 1730?].

Then why not Kent as well our treaties draw,
Bridgeman explain the gospel, Gibbs the law?[68]

Later in the poem, in the famous passage in which Pope urges Burlington to 'Consult the Genius of the Place in all', the poet writes:

The vast parterres a thousand hands shall make,
Lo! Bridgman comes, and floats them with a lake:
Or cut wide views thro' mountains to the plain,
You'll wish your hill, or shelter'd seat again. (ll.73–76)

Bridgeman seems to have taken offence at this reference to him, and after the first three editions Pope was persuaded to substitute another name for the gardener's: he chose to replace 'Bridgman' by 'COBHAM', whose gardens at Stowe had been alluded to four lines earlier. Pope wrote a note explaining that this change implied 'a high compliment to the noble person on whom it is bestowed [i.e. Cobham], as making him the substitute of good sense'. In the original plan of the poem, he continues, this office 'was given to another man of taste, Bridgeman; who not having the taste to see a compliment was intended him, it convinced the poet it did not belong to him'.[69] Others might say that Bridgeman's reason for declining the immortality of Pope's verse was more likely to be his unwillingness to be praised in a poem in which Sir Robert Walpole and others were severely censured.

Additional light is shed on Pope's attitude to Bridgeman by the anonymous prose pamphlet (probably written by Pope himself) entitled 'A Master Key to Popery, or a True and Perfect Key to Pope's Epistle to the Earl of Burlington', which contains this comment on the offending section of the epistle:

> Here we have a fling at honest Bridgeman. I don't wonder to see his name at length, for he is his [i.e. Pope's] particular Acquaintance. What a Malicious Representation of one who lives by his profession, as taking pleasure to destroy and overflow Gentlemens fine Gardens! . . . As if he should have the Impudence, when a Gentleman has done a wrong thing at a great Expence, to come & pretend to make it a right one? Is it not his business to please Gentlemen? to execute Gentlemen's will and Pleasure, not his own? is he to set up his own Conceits & Inventions against Gentlemen's fine Taste & Superiour Genius? Yet is this what the Poet suggests, with intent (doubtless) to take the Bread out of his mouth, & ruin his Wife & Family.[70]

Although this satiric outburst must be considered with caution, there is a prophetic ring about it. It may have been the result of a Bridgeman-Pope quarrel: our last evidence of the two being in contact is 1728 (that is three years before the *Epistle to Burlington* came out),

[68] Elwin and Courthope, eds, *Works*, III, 174.

[69] Ibid., III, 177. See also William Warburton, ed., *The Works of Alexander Pope . . .* (London, 1751), III, 188.

[70] This was never published in Pope's lifetime, and was first printed by John E. Butt, 'A Master Key to Popery', in *Pope and His Contemporaries. Essays Presented to George Sherburn*, ed. James L. Clifford and Louis A. Landa (Oxford, 1949), pp.41–57, esp. p.51. See also Alexander Pope, *Epistles to Several Persons* (*Moral Essays*), ed. F. W. Bateson, 2nd edn (London and New Haven, 1961), pp.175–88. I am happy to acknowledge the late Professor Butt's advice on Bridgeman's relationship with Pope.

and unquestionably Pope was annoyed at the unexpected reception of his 'fling at honest Bridgeman'. In a footnote to one version of his *Epistle to Dr. Arbuthnot*, published in the 1730's, Pope implies that it is Bridgeman's success that has made him edgy:

I sighed and cursed in bitterness of woe,
Nay, cursed be Fame with all its noise and show,
The Fame that made one worthy man my foe,
If Bridgeman, while his head contrives a maze,
Knows not, good man, my satire from my praise.[71]

When we consider the poet's obsession with his garden at Twickenham, and the professional pride which must have accompanied Bridgeman's so-called 'Fame', it is a fair guess that it must have been the Royal Gardener's connection with Pope's villa that lay at the root of any quarrel.[72]

Here, as before, Gibbs carried out additions to the house whilst Bridgeman may have assisted with the gardens.[73] Pope's villa was a familiar sight across the Thames, and Heckell and Mason's view of it was one of many (*Plate 76*). Pope leased the villa with its five acres of grounds about the end of 1718, and in 1719 was 'pursuing very innocent pleasures, building, planting and gardening'.[74] In May 1720 he was writing that his 'Trees, like new Acquaintances brought happily together, are stretching their Arms to meet each other'.[75] In July 1722 the grotto was ready for visitors,[76] and on 3 February 1723 Gay wrote to Swift that of late Pope had 'talk'd only as a Gardiner'.[77] Our best guide to the layout of Pope's grounds is the celebrated *Plan of Mr. Pope's Garden as it was Left at His Death, with a Plan and Perspective View of the Grotto*, published by his gardener John Serle in 1745, the year after the poet died (*Plate 77*). The house stands proud above a broad lawn sweeping down to the River Thames, with a niche and two term figures on each flank.

[71] In the Chauncy MSS. See Elwin and Courthope, eds, *Works*, III, 263. An alternative reading is in James Prior, *Life of Edmond Malone, Editor of Shakespeare* . . . (London, 1860), p.368.

[72] Bridgeman and Kent, to name but two, were doubtless embarrassed by Pope's attacks on Sir Robert Walpole. See e.g. Kathleen Mahaffey, 'Timon's Villa: Walpole's Houghton', *Texas Studies in Literature and Language*, IX (1967), 193–222, esp. pp.217–18.

Pope's activities as gardener and landscapist have been analysed extensively. Apart from Professor Mack's studies, see recently Peter E. Martin, 'The Garden and Pope's Vision of Order in the *Epistle to Burlington*', *Durham University Journal*, LXV (June 1973), 248–59; Marjorie Hope Nicolson and George S. Rousseau, '*This Long Disease, My Life*'. *Alexander Pope and the Sciences* (Princeton, N.J., 1968), pp.251–65; James M. Osborn, 'Alexander Pope. Apollo of the Arts', in H. T. Swedenborg, ed., *Papers of the Clark Library Seminars* (Los Angeles, 1971), pp.1–24; A. James Sambrook, 'Pope and the Visual Arts', in Peter Dixon, ed., *Writers and Their Background: Alexander Pope* (London, 1972), pp.143–71; idem, 'Alexander Pope as Landscape Gardener', *Times Literary Supplement*, 22 June 1973, pp.715–16. Pope's pictorial vision of landscape is shown in his description of a visit to Netley Abbey in about 1734. See George S. Rousseau, 'A New Pope Letter', *Philological Quarterly*, XLV (1966), 409–18.

Most recently see John Dixon Hunt, 'Gardening, and Poetry, and Pope', *Art Quarterly*, XXXVII (Spring 1974), 1–28, and the essay on 'The Country House Ideal' in Howard Erskine-Hill, *The Social Milieu of Alexander Pope. Lives, Example, and the Poetic Response* (New Haven and London, 1975), pp.279–317.

[73] Of the two surviving letters from Gibbs to Pope (one *c.*1719, the other *c.*1725), the earlier is about the building either of Pope's villa or the London house Pope projected in 1718. See *Pope Correspondence*, II, 4, 298.

[74] Ibid., II, 3. Pope to Broome, 16 February 1719.

[75] Ibid., II, 44. Pope to Digby, 1 May 1720.

[76] Ibid., II, 125. Pope to Broome, 9 July [1722].

[77] Burgess, ed., *Gay Correspondence*, p.43.

Passing through the grotto and underground passage (beneath the road from Hampton Court to London) we emerge in the garden proper facing Kent's shell temple, set next to the large mount. The axis straight ahead of us, though broad, is studiously kept. Beyond the trees to our left are the stoves, vineyard, and kitchen garden, and to our right the orangery and garden house. Scattered about the grounds are urns and statuary. Passing the groves we progress to the bowling green, and so past two small mounts to the obelisk to Pope's mother set in sorrowing cypresses. This is the climax of the layout, and surely is a later version of the 'little Bridgemannick Theatre' which Pope claimed to have 'turfed' in 1725, and which may have been the subject of the 'plann' referred to in Bridgeman's letter of the previous September. This 'Theatre', Pope continues, 'was done by a detachment of His workmen from the Prince's, all at a stroke, & it is yet unpayd for, but that's nothing with a Poetical Genius'.[78] Probably these 'workmen' were taken away from their duties with Bridgeman and George II (whilst Prince of Wales) at nearby Marble Hill.[79] At any rate the total effect of Pope's estate was of intense variety within a small, confined space. Horace Walpole's verdict was typical of the opinion of many visitors. 'It was a singular effort of art and taste', he averred, 'to impress so much variety and scenery on a spot of five acres.'[80]

The lilliputian scale of Pope's domain at Twickenham became the subject of jest between him and his friends: Bathurst, for instance, offered to cut off 'some little corner' of his vast park at Cirencester for Pope to amuse himself in,[81] whilst Bolingbroke wrote of sauntering with 'the jocose dean of St. Patrick's, among the multiplied scenes of [Pope's] little garden'.[82] Although it was miniature and toy-like, Pope's villa attracted many visitors, and its influence was wide-ranging.[83] Dean Swift's enthusiasm for Twickenham did not stop there, as Mary Delany's view of Delville in Ireland reminds us (*Plate 85*).[84] Nearer home, Kent's sketches of Pope's garden are indicators of an active Pope-Kent-Burlington friendship.[85] Horace Walpole, whilst commending Pope for his advice to

[78] *Pope Correspondence*, II, 372. Pope to Edward Harley, 22 March 1726. The 'Bridgemannick Theatre' may have been the area between the bowling green and the mount, with the grove on each side. According to Spence, Kent designed the mount at Twickenham whilst staying at Stowe. See Osborn, ed., *Spence's Anecdotes*, I, 249–50 (No.602), 405–6 (Nos 1060, 1062). Some inaccuracies in Serle's plan are discussed in A. James Sambrook, 'The Shape and Size of Pope's Garden', *Eighteenth-Century Studies*, V (1972), 450–55. Cf. James Boutwood, 'Poet's Essay in the Picturesque. Alexander Pope's Garden at Twickenham', *C.Life*, CXLIII (7 March 1968), 512–14.

[79] I see no reason to suppose, as some commentators do, that Pope is referring to Carlton House. Marble Hill was much nearer Twickenham, and in any case Carlton House could only be called 'the Prince's' (to use Pope's words) after Frederick, Prince of Wales, acquired it in 1732 from the Earl of Burlington's mother. In 1725, the date of Pope's letter, Carlton House passed to Burlington on the death of his uncle, Henry Boyle, Baron Carlton.

[80] Chase, *Horace Walpole: Gardenist*, p.28.

[81] *Pope Correspondence*, III, 134. Bathurst to Pope, 19 September 1730.

[82] *The Works of Lord Bolingbroke* (Philadelphia, 1841), III, 45.

[83] Pope's use of objects to be seen, and meditated upon, from specific parts of the garden, is touched on by Ronald Paulson, 'The Pictorial Circuit and Related Structures in Eighteenth-Century England', in Peter Hughes and David Williams, eds, *The Varied Pattern. Studies in the Eighteenth Century* (Toronto, 1971), 165–70. Professor Paulson deals with these and related matters in *Emblem and Expression. Meaning in English Art of the Eighteenth Century* (London, 1975), pp.19–34.

[84] For Delville see Edward Malins, 'Mrs Delany and Landscaping in Ireland', *Quarterly Bulletin of the Irish Georgian Society*, XI, Nos 2–3 (April–September 1968), 1–16.

[85] No letters between Kent and Pope have survived, but Professor Sherburn prints fifty-three between Pope and Burlington. For Kent and Pope see Wimsatt, *Portraits of Pope*, pp.107–36.

Kent at Rousham, hints that Venus's Vale may have been 'planned on the model of Mr. Pope's'.[86] But he cannot be sure. He does however say that Carlton House gardens were 'evidently borrowed from the poet's at Twickenham',[87] and there is no doubt that Walpole was enchanted by Pope's villa and its setting. 'The passing through the gloom from the grotto to the opening day,' he enthused, 'the retiring and again assembling shades, the dusky groves, the larger lawn, and the solemnity of the termination of the cypresses that lead up to [Pope's] mother's tomb, are managed with exquisite judgement.'[88]

Gibbs

The possible collaboration between Bridgeman and Gibbs at Pope's villa introduces us to further schemes on which the two men worked together, several of them perhaps through the intervention of Edward Harley. Prominent amongst these were Houghton, Gubbins, Kedleston, and Badminton. And then there was the Fellows' Building at King's College, Cambridge, a job which may have resulted from their connections with Harley and with Matthew Prior, who was a Fellow of St John's.[89]

From 1722 Gibbs had been engaged at Cambridge in designs for the Public Buildings, including the Senate House, and these had set him in high standing with the University. In the early eighteenth century King's was right up-to-date in architectural matters, and had engaged Hawksmoor in 1713. Construction of the Fellows' Building started in 1724, and on 20 December that year the Fellows of King's, meeting in Congregation, resolved that 'Mr Provost do Send down Mr Bridgeman to Lay out the Ground from the West side of the new Building to the Road; and to draw two or three Schemes of different designes for our Consideration'.[90] In other words Bridgeman's 'designes' were to be for an area between the Fellows' Building and the present Queens' Road. But to judge by the description of 1763 in *Cantabrigia Depicta* the Royal Gardener was asked to make more extensive proposals:

> There are several Gardens and Orchards belonging to [King's] College; and, besides the River that runs thro' them, there are some Moats and Canals, with thick shady Groves of Elms, which render the Avenues to the College exceeding pleasant: and no Place is capable of greater Improvement, by cutting Vista's through the Grove, and laying out the waste Ground about it into regular Walks and Canals; all which is

[86] Chase, *Horace Walpole: Gardenist*, p.29.

[87] Ibid., p.28.

[88] Ibid., pp.28–29. By no means all critics of the 1770's agreed with Walpole's encomiums. Joseph Heely remarked of Pope in his *Letters on the Beauties of Hagley, Envil, and The Leasowes*... (London, 1777), I, 43, that 'this celebrated genius, who knew so well the theory of gardening' had betrayed 'a puerility in his practice'. Cf. A. Lynn Altenbernd, 'On Pope's "Horticultural Romanticism"', *Journal of English and Germanic Philology*, LV (October 1955), 470–77.

[89] See T. P. Hudson, 'James Gibbs's Designs for University Buildings at Cambridge', *Burlington Magazine*, CXIV (December 1972), 842–48. For King's see also *VCH: Cambridgeshire*, III (1959), 392.

[90] King's College, Cambridge, Congregation Book, 1722–78, fo.12. See also Marcus Whiffen, 'Academical Elysium. The Landscaping of the Cambridge Backs', *Architectural Review*, CI (January 1947), 13.

> designed to be done (when the remaining Part of the great Square is finished) according to the Plan given by the late ingenious Mr. Bridgman.[91]

The formality implicit in this description is seen in James Essex's bird's-eye view, with the never-completed 'great Square' in the foreground, and a geometrical garden beyond with a circular temple overlooking the canal (*Plate 79*).[92]

Cambridge was the gateway to the East Anglian country houses which were gaining in popularity with tourists as the century progressed. In the summer of 1732 Edward Harley was in Norfolk, in the wake of Lord Hervey and Sir Thomas Robinson, and when he visited Houghton he found evidence that Gibbs had been there;[93] in fact Gibbs, Campbell, and Kent all had a hand in its design. This opulent mansion, built in 1722–30 by Sir Robert Walpole to replace a small country manor, is one of three Norfolk seats for which we have Bridgemanic plans – the other two being Gunton (*Plate 80a*) and Wolterton (*Plate 80b*). A sketch by Edmund Prideaux shows Houghton in Bridgeman's day (*Plate 81a*).[94] Many disapproved of Walpole's extravagance, and it has been suggested that, as Timon's Villa, Houghton was satirized in Pope's *Epistle to Burlington*.[95] Walpole wanted the grounds to be as magnificent as the house:[96] tree-planting began there in 1717, and during the next forty years 337 acres of woods, clumps, and avenues were added. According to Horace Walpole, Houghton was laid out in Bridgeman's 'simple though still formal style'.[97] The key description was written by Sir Thomas Robinson, friend of Burlington and architect of the west wing at Castle Howard. On 19 December 1731 he sent his father-in-law, the Earl of Carlisle, his impressions of his visit to Houghton. 'The enclosure of the Park contains seven hundred acres, very finely planted, and the ground [is] laid out to the greatest advantage,' he noted. 'The gardens are about 40 acres, which are only fenced from the Park by a *fossé*, and I think very prettily disposed.' Robinson, warming to his subject, then brings Bridgeman into the picture:

> Sir Robert [Walpole] and Bridgeman showed me the large design for the plantations in the country, which is the present undertaking; they are to be plumps and avenues to go quite round the Park pale, and to make straight and oblique lines of a mile or two in length, as the situation of the country admits of. This design will be about 12 miles in circumference, and nature has disposed of the country so as these plantations will have a very noble and fine effect; and at every angle there are to be obelisks, or some other building.

[91] *Cantabrigia Depicta* (Cambridge, 1763), p.50.

[92] For Bridgeman and Essex at King's see Robert Willis and J. W. Clark, *The Architectural History of the University of Cambridge* (Cambridge, 1886), I, 571–72. The grounds at King's did not take their present form until early in the nineteenth century.

[93] *HMC 29: Portland VI*, 160. See R. W. Ketton-Cremer, *Norfolk Assembly* (London, 1957), 178–84.

[94] The building of Houghton was in the hands of Ripley, who had also been commissioned to design Wolterton for Horatio Walpole, Sir Robert's younger brother. Gunton would be for Sir William Harbord.

Prideaux's drawing of Houghton is considered in John Harris, ed., 'The Prideaux Collection of Topographical Drawings', *Architectural History*, VII (1964), No.50.

[95] Suggested by Mahaffey, 'Timon's Villa: Walpole's Houghton', pp.193–222.

[96] See J. H. Plumb, *Sir Robert Walpole* (1956–60), I, 359–60; II, 83–84.

[97] Chase, *Horace Walpole: Gardenist*, p.25.

Although impressed, Robinson is tactful enough to emphasize that Carlisle's own Castle Howard has its advantages, and he remarks that Houghton has little full-grown timber and no ornamental water. 'In short', Robinson assures Carlisle, 'the outworks at Houghton will be 200 years hence what those at Castle Howard are now . . . take all together, it is a seat so perfectly magnificent and agreeable, that I think nothing but envy itself can find fault.'[98]

From the Bridgemanic plan of Houghton in the Bodleian Library (*Plate 81b*) we can see how the densely wooded area near the house (enclosed by a ha-ha) carries through the design theme we have already encountered in Bridgeman's layouts of, say, Farley, Moor Park, and Rousham.[99] Ware's large estate map in his *Plans, Elevations, and Sections . . . of Houghton in Norfolk* (*Plate 82*), published four years after Robinson's visit, has *ronds-points* linked by avenues, a free-flowing lake, rectangular stands of trees, and a few scattered houses to remind us of the village which was swept away. The overall layout has the military cast of other Bridgeman schemes, and the 'plantations in the country', beyond the garden proper, seem as vast as anything Bridgeman did elsewhere. No matter how 'magnificent and agreeable' Robinson may have found Bridgeman's 'large design' in 1731, thirty years afterwards Horace Walpole could only bewail Houghton's past glories. 'Those groves, those *allées*, where I have passed so many charming moments', he exclaimed, 'are now stripped up, or overgrown; many fond paths I could not unravel, though with a very exact clue in my memory . . . Houghton, I know not what to call it, a monument of grandeur or ruin!'[100]

Another Bridgeman garden mentioned by Walpole in his *History of the Modern Taste in Gardening* is Gubbins (also known as Gobions or More Hall), the Hertfordshire seat of Sir Jeremy Sambrooke where Sir Thomas More is said to have written *Utopia*. It was at Gubbins that Walpole observed 'many detached thoughts, that strongly indicate the dawn of modern taste'. It was all part of Bridgeman's 'reformation'.[101] Here again Gibbs worked alongside the Royal Gardener, altering the house and designing various structures for the gardens, including a dovecote, and temples overlooking the bowling green (*Plates 83, 84*).[102] Gibbs also may have designed the tall sham-medieval folly arch which is one of the few remaining vestiges of Gubbins. In the mid-eighteenth century it was otherwise. George Bickam, the Younger, writing in his *Beauties of Stow* of 1750, boldly proclaims that 'the famous Garden of Sir *Jeremy Sambrook*, at *Gubbins* . . . deserves a Traveller's Admiration', for he would see there 'a sensible Resemblance in Miniature of *Stow*'. He continues:

[98] *HMC 42: Carlisle*, 85. Cf. Philip Yorke's description of 1750 in Joyce Godber, ed., 'The Travel Journal of Philip Yorke, 1744–63', *Bedfordshire Historical Record Society (Publications)*, XLVII (1968), 144. Walpole (Chase, *Horace Walpole: Gardenist*, p.25) says that Houghton was 'laid out by Mr. Eyre, an imitator of Bridgman'. In Horace Walpole, *Aedes Walpolianae; or, a Description of the Collection of Pictures at Houghton Hall in Norfolk . . .*, 2nd edn (London, 1752), p.40, a portrait in the breakfast room is listed as 'Mr. *Harold*, Gardener to Sir *Robert Walpole*, a Head, by *Ellis*'.

[99] There is another plan with a somewhat Bridgemanic cast kept at Houghton, kindly shown to me by Sybil, Lady Cholmondeley.

[100] *Yale Walpole*, IX, 349. Walpole to Montagu, 25–30 March 1761.

[101] Chase, *Horace Walpole: Gardenist*, p.24.

[102] See Ashmolean Museum, Oxford, Gibbs Collection, III, fos 87a, 87b.

> Imagine to yourself a vast Hill, shaded all over with a Forest of Oaks, through which have been cut an infinite Number of Alleys covered with the finest Gravel. Here you meet a Grotto agreeably adorned . . . There you come to a large Square, embellished with Orange-trees and Statues, and with a beautiful Summer-house, whose Windows present on every Side a most delicious Prospect.

Pyramids, orange trees, statuary. The effect is magnificent. 'In short', Bickham ends,

> the Beauty of the Alleys, . . . the pleasing Variety of the Prospects, the Richness of the Ornaments, the singular Taste that prevails through the whole Distribution . . . form all together almost the only Garden in its Kind.

Only Stowe can compete. 'Notwithstanding all the surprising Greatness of *Gubbins*,' Bickham concludes, 'still it must submit to *Stow*.'[103]

The most northerly project on which Bridgeman and Gibbs are found together is Kedleston. The present house testifies to the combined efforts of Paine, Brettingham, and Robert and James Adam, but the Kedleston which concerns us was built in the early 1720's, evidently to the designs of Francis Smith of Warwick. This was an unpretentious brick building, three storeys high, with dormer windows and a walled garden. In Bridgeman's day Kedleston was owned by Sir John Curzon, Bt, and his accounts indicate that he paid 'Mr: Bridgemans man' a guinea on 14 September 1722, and Bridgeman himself sixty guineas on 14 September 1726.[104] On this second occasion Gibbs received ten pounds, doubtless for designing the temple at Kedleston which appeared in his *Book of Architecture* two years later.[105] The size of Bridgeman's fee implies that he gave important advice, and Gibbs hints at the form such advice might have taken. Two of his pavilions, he writes, were to be built 'opposite to one another, on each side of a Vista proposed to be cut through a Wood, and to be terminated with an Obelisque upon a Hill fronting the House'.[106] Such phrases conjure up a landscape of a Bridgeman kind, but Curzon's death in 1727 put paid to these proposals.[107]

[103] George Bickham, the Younger, *The Beauties of Stow* . . . (London, 1750), pp.66–67. Cf. Hertfordshire CRO, Hertford, 34417 and 34418, which are particulars of the sales of Gubbins in 1834 and 1838.

[104] Kedleston Hall, Sir John Curzon's Day Book, 1718–50. Mr Derek Sherborn directed me to this source. On 21 September 1724 the gardener Joseph Carpenter shared a payment of £1.13*s*.3*d*. with a Mr Gray.

[105] Pl.70.

[106] Gibbs, *Book of Architecture* (1728), pp. xviii-xix.

[107] Bridgeman may have preceded Paine at Brocket Hall in Hertfordshire as he had done at Kedleston. Bridgeman's client at Brocket would have been Thomas Winnington, a supporter of Sir Robert Walpole, Lord of the Admiralty, and like Edward Harley a product of Westminster and Christ Church. Our two Bridgemanic drawings of Brocket are more in the way of surveys than design proposals (MSGD a3 fo.7; a4 fo.40), and other evidence of Bridgeman's contribution is hardly more precise. It rests on a letter and an account. The letter is from Lord Hervey to Stephen Fox, 10 August 1734, referring to the execution of 'my friend Winnington's commissions', including giving 'the plan to Bridgman'; the account is a payment of forty guineas by Winnington to Bridgeman's widow in 1739.

The letter is in BL, Add MS 51345 (Holland House Papers), fos 63r–64v, and appeared in Giles Stephen Harold Fox Strangways (6th Earl of Ilchester), *Lord Hervey and His Friends, 1726–38. Based on Letters from Holland House, Melbury and Ickworth* (London, 1950), pp.200–1. A photograph of the letter is in Robert Halsband, *Lord Hervey. Eighteenth-Century Courtier* (Oxford, 1973), pl.7.

The account is in C. Hoare and Co., Bankers, London, Ledger O, 14 June 1739.

Bridgeman is mentioned in another Hervey letter, written to his mother (Lady Bristol) at Ickworth and dated 28 December 1731, in Suffolk CRO, Bury St Edmunds, Hervey MSS, 941/47/2, fos 193–98. Mrs M. P. Statham kindly provided me with a transcript of the Bridgeman reference, which is on fo.197.

Professor Halsband was most helpful in my enquiries about Lord Hervey.

Speculation on further Bridgeman-Gibbs collaboration is endless, but documentation is rare.[108] It is attractive enough, for instance, to suggest that the Royal Gardener may have helped Gibbs and Kent at Badminton in their work for the Duke of Beaufort, where Gibbs designed the house and also the customary garden pavilions.[109] Moreover there is at Badminton a perspective drawing of the landscape entitled 'Bridgman's Design/for Badminton' (*Plate 86*).[110] Even a quick glance reveals that it is hardly likely to be by Bridgeman, but rather is typical of the work of John Wootton, whose painting of *The Beaufort Hunt* it closely resembles (*Plate 87*). The Beauforts were noted Tories, and the Bridgeman-Gibbs-Wootton triumvirate would have found themselves politically at home in such surroundings. Sometime during the 1730's William Kent was called in at Badminton to alter the house, and to design Worcester Lodge, an eye-catcher, and other conceits. His death in 1748 paved the way for Thomas Wright of Durham, the antiquary, astronomer, and author of engravings of grottoes and follies, whose castellated farm buildings at Badminton still stand.

Gibbs's country seat was doubtless a familiar topic of conversation at Wimpole, where Bridgeman must also have met George Vertue. Vertue often visited Edward Harley there, as well as accompanying him on his tours of England and Scotland. The purpose of these tours was partly to enable Harley to visit his wife's far-flung properties, and partly to allow him to examine country houses, churches, and shrines of antiquarian interest. Occasionally Lady Henrietta accompanied her husband, but usually he was attended by Vertue, Timothy Thomas (who had succeeded Wanley as Harley's librarian), John Morley, and a host of servants. Bridgemanic gardens featured in their itineraries: they found the Duchess of Marlborough's house at Wimbledon 'a delightfull pleasant situation fine walks Terrases Views & c. hardly to be conceivd so beautifull and Extensive, so near London',[111] whilst Longford struck them as a 'triangular built house – seated amongst plenty of waters'.[112] Sometimes Harley revised his opinions: in 1732 he judged Houghton 'neither magnificent nor beautiful' and carried out at 'a very great expense without either judgment or taste'. Six years later he had changed his mind. Now the park and plantations were 'very fine and thriving extremely'. Full credit to the Prime Minister. 'These vast plantations are from what Sir Robert has sowed the seeds', wrote Harley. 'I saw the water which is very fine and holds well. There is a basin before the house, which has a very good effect.'[113] Nor was Bridgeman's sortie into Scotland neglected. Whilst at Hamilton Palace in 1745 Lady Henrietta saw Chatelherault. 'In the park is a very pretty building, one wing being an apartment for the Duke and the other a dog

108 E.g. the Gibbs MS Memoir in the Soane Museum, fo.89, notes that at Hackwood in Hampshire the architect 'built a great Many Temples and Ornamental Building' for Charles Paulet, 3rd Duke of Bolton, and evidence of Gibbs's work remains today in Spring Wood. A concise description of this area appears in Nikolaus Pevsner and David Lloyd, *Hampshire*, The Buildings of England (Harmondsworth, 1967), p.262. A Bridgemanic plan of Hackwood is in MSGD a3 fo.4.

109 See H. M. Colvin, 'Georgian Architects at Badminton', *C. Life*, XCLIII (4 April 1968), 800–4.

110 The drawing is in ink and grey wash, on laid paper, measures 1.463 by 463 cm, and hangs in Lady Geraldine's bedroom. I am grateful to the Duke of Beaufort for showing it to me.

111 *Vertue*, III (XXIII), 103.

112 Ibid., V (XXVI), 127.

113 *HMC 29: Portland VI*, 160, 66, 171.

kennel', she wrote. 'The park is eleven miles round and is finely watered by the river Avon.'[114]

Three years earlier, in 1742, Lady Henrietta had lost her husband. In the spring of 1740 Harley's health had sunk into a rapid decline, his body wrecked with heavy drinking. His world had collapsed. As his library had grown, so had his debts: on his death he owned 50,000 printed books, 8,000 volumes of manuscripts, 41,000 prints, and 350,000 pamphlets. And Harley was ruined. His halcyon days at Wimpole would never return. The house itself, like Down Hall before it, passed into other hands. Harley sold it to Philip Yorke, Lord Chancellor Hardwicke, who asked Flitcroft to remodel it. Change was in the air. Bridgeman's formal layout near the mansion was destroyed in 1752–54, and the grounds were altered in turn by Sanderson Miller (whose Gothic tower was erected about 1772), Capability Brown, and Humphry Repton. In his will Harley directed that he should be buried without pomp and with little expense. At his instigation Gibbs had provided a monument in Westminster Abbey for Harley's father-in-law John, Duke of Newcastle, but Harley himself was to have none. Not that he died unloved. 'I allways thought there was more weakness than dishonesty in his actions', commented Lady Mary Wortley Montagu.[115] 'Poor lord *Oxford* is gone to those regions from whence travellers never return', lamented Orrery to Swift.[116] Vertue was as upset as anyone. 'The death of this great and Noble Lover of Arts and encourager of Arts', he wrote, 'was a great and fatal loss to the publick.'[117] Bridgeman, as much as Vertue, had benefited from Harley's patronage, and Bridgeman's experience at Down Hall and Wimpole in the early 1720's was to prove invaluable when he took over the royal gardens: the patronage extended to him there by George II and Queen Caroline was of a different order.

[114] Ibid., 189.

[115] Halsband, ed., *Letters of Lady Mary Wortley Montagu*, II, 247. Lady Mary to Wortley, 15 August [1741].

[116] Williams, ed., *Swift Correspondence*, V, 205. Orrery to Swift, 7 July 1741.

[117] *Vertue*, I (XVIII), 7.

Chapter 4

At Royal Command

Minutes of the Board of Works describe Bridgeman's appointment in 1728 as 'Master Gardiner to His Majesty', yet most of his royal work was undertaken at the behest not of His Majesty King George II (*Plate 88a*) but of Her Majesty Queen Caroline (*Plate 88b*).[1] When, as Prince and Princess of Wales, George and Caroline came to England in 1714, they left behind them at Herrenhausen one of the finest layouts in the Le Nôtre manner outside France (*Plate 7b*).[2] Herrenhausen had been brought to a pinnacle of perfection in the late seventeenth century by Ernest Augustus, Elector of Hanover, and by his wife, the Electress Sophia. Sophia, active supporter of the arts, made Herrenhausen a fitting setting for her patronage: Leibniz and Handel, to name but two, were among the distinguished guests entertained in the orangery where the Electress had her rooms and kept her collections of porcelain and books. The orangery was just two steps from the garden. Here, with the guidance of the Frenchman Martin Charbonnier, Sophia laid out avenues, parterres, and rows of lime trees. Statuary was everywhere. The elaborate waterworks were said to have been designed by William Benson: bordering the garden on three sides was a canal on which Venetian gondolas glided at appointed intervals. Visitors flocked to enjoy the diversions of the garden theatre, which Caroline could have glimpsed from her apartment in the east wing of the orangery. Two years after Caroline settled in England, Lady Mary Wortley Montagu sent an English friend her impressions of the place. 'I was very sorry the ill Weather did not permit me to see Hern-hausen in all its beauty', she wrote, 'but in spite of the snow I thought the Gardens very fine. I was particularly

[1] For royal buildings dealt with in this chapter see throughout Colvin, ed., *History of the King's Works;* idem, *Royal Buildings*, RIBA Drawings Series (London, 1968); William Henry Pyne, *The History of the Royal Residences of Windsor Castle, St James's Palace, Carlton House, Kensington Palace, Hampton Court, Buckingham House and Frogmore* (London, 1819).

Switzer's *Ichnographia Rustica* is the best early-eighteenth-century printed source for the background to Bridgeman's royal gardens. For later descriptions see throughout Alicia Amherst (Evelyn Cecil), *London Parks and Gardens* (London, 1907); Neville Braybrooke, *London Green. The Story of Kensington Gardens, Hyde Park, Green Park and St James's Park* (London, 1959); Richard Church, *The Royal Parks of London*, 2nd edn (London, 1965); Nathan Cole, *The Royal Parks and Gardens of London . . .* (London, 1877); Jacob Larwood (pseud.), *The Story of the London Parks . . .* (London, 1872); Gladys Taylor, *Old London Gardens* (London, 1953); Cyril Ward, *Royal Gardens* (London, 1912); Peter Willis, 'Charles Bridgeman. The Royal Gardens', in Willis, ed., *Furor Hortensis*, pp.41–47.

Bridgeman's royal work is documented throughout PRO, Works 1/1; 1/2; 3/2; 4/3; 4/4; 4/5; 4/6; 4/7; 4/8; 5/57; 5/58; 5/59; 5/104; 5/105; 5/141; 5/150; 6/8; 6/15; 6/16; 6/114; 16/39/1. For other MS references see the indices to *CTP*, VI (1720–28); *CTBP*, I–IV (1729–41).

Future footnotes will make no further reference to these PRO MSS except to demonstrate a specific point.

[2] For Herrenhausen see Karl H. Meyer, *Königliche Gärten. Dreihundert Jahre Herrenhausen* (Hanover, 1961). Its context is seen in Marie Luise Gothein, *Geschichte der Gartenkunst* (Jena, 1914), II, 206–10; Dieter Hennebo and Alfred Hoffman, *Geschichte der Deutschen Gartenkunst* (Hamburg, 1962–65), II, 162–66.

surpriz'd at the vast Number of Orange Trees, much larger than any I have ever seen in England, tho this climate is certainly colder.'[3]

Magnificent Herrenhausen was replaced by a more modest abode as Prince George and Princess Caroline were forced to squeeze with George I into St James's Palace. When, however, the Prince was banished from St James's in 1718 he felt justified in buying Leicester House, a two-storied brick building with a pleasant Dutch garden at the back and separated from the public square by a courtyard.[4] From 1720 Colin Campbell supervised the restoration of Leicester House, and George and Caroline lived here and at Richmond Lodge until their accession. Subsequently, they divided their time between various royal residences: winter was usually spent at St James's Palace, Kensington was preferred for the spring, whilst summer was passed at Hampton Court, Windsor, and Richmond. Wherever she went Caroline indulged her passion for walking, and on many a day she and the King strolled from St James's to Kensington, or else simply 'walked quite round the Park'.[5]

Much as he may have enjoyed these jaunts, George II preferred stag-hunting, and the royal parks provided ample scope for his love of the chase, whether it was at Hampton Court, in the Upper Paddock at Kensington, in Windsor Forest, or at Richmond. When Sir Robert Walpole was Ranger at Richmond, hunting was keenly organized. On 24 August 1728 *Read's Weekly Journal* noted that the previous Saturday 'His Majesty, the Duke, and the Princess Royal hunted on Horseback; her Majesty and the Princess Amelia hunted in a Four Wheel Chaise, and the Princess Carolina in a Two Wheel Chaise, and the Princess Mary and Louisa were in a Coach'. Sir Robert Walpole attended as Ranger, clothed in green. Courage was required for such enterprises, as Lady Mary Wortley Montagu commented in a letter to the Countess of Mar. 'I pass many hours on Horseback', she wrote, 'which I know you stare to hear of. I have arriv'd to vast courrage and skill that way, and am so well pleas'd with it as with the Acquisition of a new sense. His Royal Highness hunts in Richmond Park, and I make one of the Beau monde in his Train.'[6] Lady Mary was not alone in believing that hunting was risky. 'We hunt with great noise and violence', Mrs Howard plaintively told Gay, 'and have every day a very tolerable chance to have a neck broke.'[7]

The King's frequent absence at the hunt freed Caroline for her favourite ploys, aided and abetted by maids of honour such as Mary Bellenden, Mrs Howard, and Mary Lepell. Taking her cue from the Electress Sophia, she made Leicester House into a brilliant

[3] Halsband, ed., *Letters of Lady Mary Wortley Montagu*, I, 290. Lady Mary to the Countess of Mar, 17 December [1716].

[4] Leicester House is illustrated in Charles Chenevix Trench, *George II* (London, 1973), pl.13; Phillips, *Mid-Georgian London*, p.87. The price paid by the Prince was £6,000. See Lewis Melville (pseud.), *Lady Suffolk and Her Circle* (London, 1924), pp.30–31. A plate opposite p.32 shows the position of Leicester House in Leicester Square.

[5] James Joel Cartwright, ed., *The Wentworth Papers, 1705–39* . . . (London, 1883), p.43.

[6] Halsband, ed., *Letters of Lady Mary Wortley Montagu*, II, 54. Lady Mary to the Countess of Mar [August 1725]. The context of this letter indicates that the reference is to the future George II.

[7] Croker, ed., *Suffolk Correspondence*, I, 376. Mrs Howard to Gay, 31 July [1730]. For hunting see also Ruby L. Arkell, *Caroline of Ansbach. George II's Queen* (London, 1939), p.156; Cyril Leslie Collenette, *A History of Richmond Park. With an Account of Its Birds and Animals* (London, 1937), pp.145–49; Alice Drayton Greenwood, *Lives of the Hanoverian Queens of England* (London, 1909), I, 348.

antithesis of the gloomy Court of George I and a centre for Whig intrigue.[8] Pope, Gay, Tickell, and Swift were frequent visitors to the house, and in 1728 (as a result of his visit to England) Voltaire dedicated his poem *La Henriade* to Caroline.[9] As Queen, Caroline's imaginative concern for the arts compensated somewhat for the philistinism of her humdrum husband. If her discovery of some drawings by Leonardo da Vinci and Holbein in an old bureau at Kensington owed more to chance than connoisseurship, Caroline must be credited with a modicum of enlightenment. She patronized the sculptors Guelfi and Rysbrack, and the painters Jervas, Kneller, Wootton, and Zincke, and sat for a portrait by Vanderbank. William Kent she called upon to paint murals, and to design buildings and furniture. Flitcroft, too, was at hand. Furthermore, the Queen brought in a group of theologians and philosophers to give her the spiritual and intellectual stimulus she had relished with Leibniz at Herrenhausen. Notable amongst these was the Deist Dr Samuel Clarke, Rector of St James's, Westminster, and friend of Sir Isaac Newton.[10]

Caroline's overriding enthusiasm was for laying out the royal gardens, and after Dr Clarke's death she placed a bust of him in the Hermitage at Richmond – a reminder, as Pope wrote, that 'gardening is near a-kin to Philosophy, for Tully says *Agricultura proxima sapientiae*'.[11] Bridgeman's activities as Royal Gardener centred on Queen Caroline. Denied any say in the planting of the royal domains during George I's lifetime, and offered little scope at Leicester House, she eagerly grasped the opportunities offered by her husband's accession. Under her aegis the royal parks became as progressive as they had been during the Restoration.[12] Fortunately several Bridgemanic drawings of them have come down to us, some of which were doubtless part and parcel of his widow's claim of £200 in 1738 for 'Plans Curiously done by the Deceas'd, of all the Royall Gardens.'[13] After much to-ing and fro-ing Sarah Bridgeman made her appearance before the Board of Works on 15 March 1743. Their minute reads:

> The Widow Bridgman having laid before the Board several fair drawings of His Majesty's Palaces & Royal Gardens of Hampton Court; Windsor Castle, Richmond and Kensington, the Board upon Examining them found them to be Correct and they being of great Use to this Office, Agreed to allow the Widow Bridgman the Sum of Sixty pounds in full satisfaction to her for the said Drawings.[14]

Sarah duly received her £60, but this was a mere pittance compared with her total claims of £6,264.2*s*.8½*d*., claims which were remarkably successful.[15]

[8] See Arkell, *Caroline of Ansbach*, pp.105–7, 135–37; Greenwood, *Lives of the Hanoverian Queens of England*, I, 241–57; Peter Quennell, *Caroline of England. An Augustan Portrait* (London, 1939), pp.73–76.

[9] See J. Churton Collins, *Voltaire, Montesquieu and Rousseau in England* (London, 1908), pp.69–93.

[10] See Norman Sykes, *Church and State in England in the Eighteenth Century* (Cambridge, 1934), pp.348, 354, 384–88.

[11] *Pope Correspondence*, IV, 6. Pope to Swift, 25 March 1736.

[12] For the context of the royal gardens see Hugh C. Prince, 'Parks and Parkland', in J. T. Coppock and Hugh C. Prince, eds, *Greater London* (London, 1964), 333–57.

[13] See below Appendix VI, p.168. Detailed claims are made in the petition for expenses at Hampton Court and Kensington. Also mentioned are Hyde Park and Richmond, and roads at Barnes Common, Fulham, Hyde Park (the Lamp Road), Richmond, and St James's.

[14] PRO, Works 4/8, minutes of 15 March 1743.

[15] See above pp.43–44. Three Bridgemanic drawings exist of Greenwich Park, and these may have been included amongst those submitted by Sarah. In spite of this, and Wise's activity at Greenwich, we have no documentary proof that Bridgeman worked there. A Bridgemanic plan of Somerset House is in MSGD a4 fo.65.

Bridgeman's Royal Appointment and Inventory disclose just how practical were his responsibilities as Royal Gardener.[16] Kitchen gardens were to be 'Digged & Cropt with the several Variety's of eatables', trees tied up and nailed, hedges and evergreens pruned and clipped, gravel rolled and weeded, lawns mown and swept, and 'Flower roots . . . well managed & kept in good Order'. Bridgeman had to supply 'Horse Dung & all other sorts of dung', as well as carry 'the Kings Sumer Fruit from the several Gardens, daily by relays of Men on foot to the Court'. A tall order. Moreover, in addition to paying for horses and a labour force, Bridgeman had to find and provide 'his own several Tools, Materials and other things'. These 'Utensils' (as the Inventory terms them) reflect the differing styles of the royal gardens. The engraving from Liger's *Le nouveau théâtre d'agriculture* of 1723 reminds us of the varied implements used by eighteenth-century gardeners (*Plate 89*):[17] everyone needed ladders, wheelbarrows, sickles, scythes, pruning hooks, rakes, and spades for the multifarious activities of general horticulture. But not all gardens needed all implements. Indeed often the tools are indicative of the style. Thus at Hampton Court – a layout largely composed of elaborate parterres, gravel paths, high hedges, and potted trees and shrubs – Bridgeman needed a 'Wooden horse to stand on to clip the Hedges' (*Plate 92b*), and a 'Wooden Engine to remove the orange trees', no doubt used in conjunction with the carts on which the trees were moved to and from the orangery (*Plate 92a*). Such mechanical devices were common currency on the Continent, and Caroline must have been familiar with them at Herrenhausen. In contrast, as befitted their freer layouts, Kensington and Richmond needed 'Utensils' which were appropriately simpler: at Kensington there were numerous 'bundles of brooms' for sweeping the lawns (*Plate 90b*), and at Richmond lots of 'Sythes and Sneaths' for ensuring that the grass was always finely shorn (*Plate 90a*). As for wooden, stone, or iron rollers, they could be either pushed by hand (*Plate 91a*) or drawn by oxen or horses (*Plate 91b*).[18] This and other evidence emphasizes that Bridgeman was nothing if not a practical gardener, and one whose royal work covers a wide range of styles.[19]

The most formal of the royal parks was, and is, Hampton Court, the best surviving example in England of Le Nôtre's style.[20] A recent aerial view, and Bridgeman's signed plan of *c.*1736, show its main features and the remarkable way in which they have survived (*Plates 94, 95*).[21] The palace was given to Henry VIII in 1529 by Cardinal Wolsey, who is said to have encircled it with about 2,000 acres. Most of this vast area now forms Home Park to the east and Bushy Park to the north. Under the direction of John Rose,

[16] See below Appendices III, V, pp.153–55, 161–67. See also Peter Willis, 'Creator of the English Garden. Charles Bridgeman's Tools and Techniques', *C.Life*, CLIII (17 May 1973), 1401–4. Cf. London and Wise, *The Retir'd Gard'ner* (1706), I, 247–63.

[17] For garden implements of different periods see Julia S. Berrall, *The Garden. An Illustrated History from Ancient Egypt to the Present Day* (London, 1966), pp.365–81.

[18] The total value of Bridgeman's implements listed in the Inventory was £230.1*s*.9½d.

[19] For Bridgeman and his contemporary gardeners see below pp.133–40.

[20] For Hampton Court see Green, *Gardener to Queen Anne*, pp.59–72. Hampton Court accounts for 1727–32 are throughout PRO, Works 5/104; 5/105. See also David B. Green, *The Gardens and Parks at Hampton Court and Bushy* (London, 1974).

[21] There is a note on the dating of Bridgeman's drawing, and a reproduction of it, in *Wren Soc.*, IV, 77; pl.1. Seven Bridgemanic plans exist for Hampton Court, more than for any other royal garden.

assisted by Adrian May, Charles II laid out the mile-long canal through Home Park which leads to the east front of Wren's block of 1689–94. It is a majestic statement (*Plate 93b*).[22] The three converging avenues in Home Park were probably made by London and Wise whilst active for William and Mary: 'The Gardens were noble', wrote Switzer, 'and their Majesties Designs yet nobler.'[23] London and Wise also made the chestnut avenue which stretches north-south through Bushy Park, filled in the west end of Charles II's canal in Home Park, and planted the semicircular fountain garden.[24] We catch a glimpse of this in Highmore and Tinney's engraving of *c.*1745 looking north along the Broad Avenue, with the Privy Garden to the left, and the canal to the right (*Plate 93a*). This view shows clearly that Bridgeman left Hampton Court gardens much as he found them: his main responsibility had been for maintenance,[25] and although he drew several plans of Hampton Court (including one outlining his proposals for the Lower Wilderness, begun by Wise) he hardly modified what he inherited from his predecessors. In 1727, when Sir John Clerk of Penicuik visited Hampton Court, he had found 'the parterre . . . crowded with Evergreens' consisting of 'Huge trees . . . handsomely form'd . . . into the Shapes of Obelisks on Square pedestals'.[26] Geometry had won the day, and Bridgeman left well alone. Years later Capability Brown took the same attitude, and when George III invited him to sweep away the formal layout in Home Park, so the story goes, he sensibly demurred 'out of respect to himself and his profession'.[27]

The royal parks in London which came under Bridgeman's jurisdiction are virtually linked together, stretching eastwards from Kensington Gardens and Hyde Park (*Plate 97b*) to Green Park and St James's Park (*Plate 102b*). Of these Kensington remains the most formal, with its front walk leading down to the Serpentine which separates Kensington Gardens from Hyde Park (*Plate 97a*).[28] Kensington Palace (then Nottingham House) was acquired by William III in 1689 and subsequently benefited from the architectural skills of Wren, Vanbrugh, Hawksmoor, Benson, and Kent. In the late 1600's Kensington Gardens amounted to only 26 acres until Queen Anne enclosed 100 acres of Hyde Park, and added another 30 acres towards Oxford (now Bayswater) Road. George I added more. A

22 Other French gardeners who may have worked at Hampton Court include Beaumont, De La Quintinie, the Mollets, and Daniel Marot. For Marot see Arthur Lane, 'Daniel Marot. Designer of Delft Vases and of Gardens at Hampton Court', *Connoisseur*, CXXIII (January 1949), 19–24.

23 Switzer, *Nobleman's Recreation*, p.57.

24 See *Hampton Court and Bushy Parks. Sixth Report of the Advisory Committee on Forestry* (London, 1963), which confirms that the major eighteenth-century work at Hampton Court was finished by the end of Queen Anne's reign. Recent examination of the chestnut avenue in Bushy Park testifies that trees planted in 1699–1700 are still standing.

25 E.g. on 24 October 1732 an order was made to Mr Fort to clean the Canal. See PRO, Works 4/5, minutes of 5 September, 24 October 1732.

26 SRO, Edinburgh, GD 18/2107 (Clerk MSS), entry for 1 April 1727.

27 Quoted from Ernest Law, *The History of Hampton Court Palace* (London, 1885–91), III, 296–97.

28 For Kensington Gardens and Hyde Park see Patrick A. Faulkner, 'A Note on the Gardens of Kensington Palace', *Journal of the British Archaeological Association*, XIV (1951), 8–10; Green, *Gardener to Queen Anne*, esp. pp.73–78, 221; Hayes, *Kensington Palace, passim*; Derek Hudson, *Kensington Palace* (London, 1968), pp.40–43.

Horticultural comments on Kensington Gardens and Hyde Park appear in Miles Hadfield, 'London's "Sublime Sylvan Solitude": Kensington Gardens', *C.Life*, CXXXVIII (18 November 1965), 1318–20; Alan E. Mitchell, 'Some Trees in Hyde Park and Kensington Gardens Measured in 1967', *Journal of the Royal Horticultural Society*, XCIII (May 1968), 214–18.

Bridgemanic plan shows us the layout in the 1720's (*Plate 98*).[29] Immediately north of Vanbrugh and Hawksmoor's orangery of 1704–5 was a section laid out by London and Wise, containing the old gravel pit and the old mount. The area to the east up to and including the Serpentine came to be known as the New or Royal Paddock, and contained deer, antelope, and a menagerie. Its main features were the Broad Walk, Round Pond, Great Bow, Front Walk, and the Serpentine. Within its confines also were the Queen's Temple, and the mount and summer house, whilst to its immediate south was the King's Old Road (more familiar as Rotten Row, or the Lamp Road) and the King's New Road, leading from Kensington to Hyde Park Corner. Four of the five Bridgemanic plans of Kensington (and Rocque's of 1736 and 1746) show a ha-ha between the gardens and Hyde Park, and this still remains.

Charles Bridgeman's connections with Kensington date from 1726 and last until his death, although his major activity there was finished by 1733 or so. This centred round the Royal Paddock. Joynes and Flitcroft, in an account of 1731, clarify for us just what lay behind the royal enthusiasm for this area. They tell us that

> the first Intention of the Paddock at Kensington was, that of having Animals of different kinds, kept to run & feed at Liberty all over the whole, in the several Lawns, Quarters, & Walks, the Wooded Quarters excepted.[30]

From 1726 to 1728 Bridgeman and Wise shared the responsibility for laying out the Royal Paddock. In 1727 they were submitting an estimate for making avenues and planting trees at Kensington 'by His Majesty's own direction', and before long the Great Bow was started and the Broad Walk (measuring 2,800 feet long by 80 feet wide) was well nigh complete. When George I died Bridgeman and Wise had spent £1,668.4*s*.2*d*. of the £3,800.15*s*.1*d*. allocated them.[31] However, George II and Caroline had different ideas for the Royal Paddock, as Joynes and Flitcroft explain:

> Their present Majestys altering that first design, have made the whole into a Garden by increasing the Walking parts thereof by planting Espaliers, & sowing Wood to enclose the several Paddock Quarters, which by the first design was to have laid Wild & Open, And Also by several other Improvements & Alterations by their Majestys Orders over & Above the Contracted Work.[32]

[29] Objectors to this feudal gesture were told that 'they should rather rejoice, seeing that the whole would be laid out after the fashion of the Elector of Hanover's famous gardens at Herrenhausen'. Unspecified source cited by Green, *Gardener to Queen Anne*, p.78.

[30] PRO, Works 6/114, fo.30, which is entitled 'A Bill of Word [*sic*] done beyond the Contract of £5,000' and dated 1731. The keeping of animals involved Bridgeman in numerous bizarre jobs, such as 'feeding the tigers in the Royal Paddock Garden' and 'Keeping the Foreign Hogs at Bays Water' (PRO, Money Book XL (T53: 40), fos 195–96). Scutcheon and Penley, two of Bridgeman's foremen, assured the Board of Works after Bridgeman's death that the Royal Gardener had supplied 'the foreign hogs with Corn'. See e.g. PRO, Works 4/8, minutes of 18 March 1740.

[31] Bridgeman and Wise's estimate of £3,800.15*s*.1*d*. was accepted by the Lords of the Treasury on 21 April 1727. See PRO, Works 6/114, fos 12, 16; Works 16/39/1, *passim*. By George I's death, £2,500 of this had been forwarded to Bridgeman and Wise, of which they had spent £1,668.4*s*.2*d*. Thus they had £831.15*s*.10*d*. still in their hands. See PRO, Works 5/104, fo.3. Payments to Bridgeman are in e.g. PRO, Works 5/141, *passim* 1727–40.

[32] PRO, Works 6/114, fo.30. The bill for work 'Performed to Christmas 1731 by Chas. Bridgeman' came to £389.14*s*. more than the £5,000 contracted for. Bridgeman had to wait for payment. See PRO, Works 1/1, minutes of 5 March 1734.

Once Bridgeman was appointed sole Royal Gardener in 1728 he rose to the task, and these new proposals quickly materialized. Not least of them, it turned out, were the extensive waterworks in Kensington Gardens and Hyde Park.

Bridgeman entrusted day-by-day responsibility for them to Charles Withers, Surveyor General of His Majesty's Woods, and he it was who assisted the Royal Gardener with the Round Pond and the Serpentine. The Round Pond – rectangular with chamfered corners, rather than circular as at Chiswick or Claremont – is set in a lawn next to the Great Bow, a semicircular opening in the woodland from which the Front Walk and two other rides extend towards Hyde Park. A Bridgemanic drawing emphasizes the clarity of the basic design, and draws attention to two symmetrically placed mounts with circular temples at their apices (*Plate 99a*). Withers was busy at the Round Pond in 1726, although it was not finished until after the death of George I.[33] It was first filled with water in 1728, and still keeps the outline Bridgeman gave it (*Plate 96a*). His agreement of that year to make several alterations at Kensington included the completion of the Royal Paddock and Round Pond by Lady Day 1730, and 'Raising & finishing the head of the Lake & the Walks round the Same', 'Replanting about 1195 Standard Elms', making 'Serpentine Walks' in the woods, and opening 'the upper Wilderness . . . as her Majesty shall direct'.[34] The Queen was in control.

Simultaneously work on the Serpentine was progressing (*Plate 96b*).[35] Rocque and Vivares' perspective of 1736 concentrates on the setting of the Round Pond (*Plate 100a*), and for the context of the Serpentine we have to turn to Highmore and Tinney's view of some nine years later, taken further back (*Plate 100b*). When Bridgeman's widow in her Petition to the Lords of the Treasury asks for money for making 'the lake in Hyde Park' she is obviously referring to the Serpentine, formed by joining up the marshy ponds of the River Westbourne (a minor tributary of the Thames) which flowed from Hampstead. On 26 September 1730 the *London Journal* is announcing that 'Next Monday they begin upon the Serpentine River and Royal Mansion in Hyde-Park'. The royal mansion, designed by Kent, was wisely abandoned, but the Serpentine went ahead under Withers' watchful eye. Already by 1 May 1731 the *London Journal* could announce that 'Two Yachts are to be placed in the Serpentine River . . . for the Diversion of the Royal Family'. By 7 May the job was completed, and on 15 June 1732 Withers' account was presented for 'laying the six ponds in Hyde Park into one'. In 1736–37 the Knightsbridge end of the Serpentine had to be secured, the outlet improved, and a receiving lake constructed.[36] During 1735 Queen Caroline had begun to make a road inside the boundary wall at Kensington to provide a haven from the bustle outside, and such was her success that years later a lady visitor to Kensington wrote that her 'whole soul was gladdened at the beauty and peace [she] found there'.[37]

[33] See the petition of 1736 about Kensington, including a plan (fo.41), in PRO, Works 6/16.

[34] PRO, Works 6/114, fos 19–21. By 1734 Bridgeman had made a ditch at the side of the Round Pond. See PRO, Works 1/1, letter of 20 March 1734. Cf. Wise's plan of *c.*1705 in Green, *Gardener to Queen Anne*, pl.25.

[35] See throughout PRO, Works 4/4; 4/5; 4/6. Withers' bill for the Serpentine came to £4,755.

[36] See Hudson, *Kensington Palace*, pp.41–42.

[37] Clare Williams, trans., *Sophie in London, 1786. Being the Diary of Sophie Von La Roche* (London, 1933), p.135.

Between 1733 and 1735 Queen Caroline erected at least two garden buildings at Kensington, and Kent may have been called back to design them in the wake of his interior decoration of the palace and his designs for a mansion in Hyde Park. The first was known as the Queen's Temple (now incorporated into a park-keeper's lodge) and had three arcaded bays with a central bay rising above the others (*Plate 100b*);[38] the second was a summer house placed on top of the mount which was formed in the south-east corner of Kensington Gardens (adjacent to the present Mount Gate) by using the earth excavated from the Serpentine. Approached by a spiral path, the summer house commanded fine views, not least over the nearby Lamp Road. A sketch by Bernard Lens, the Younger, indicates that it really amounted to a Windsor seat, complete with pediment and caryatids, and revolving on a pivot so as to be a screen from the wind (*Plate 99b*).[39] We know the material used for both the summer house and the Queen's Temple, for in September 1734 a minute of the Board of Works records that Their Majesties had 'Signified their pleasure of haveing two New Buildings Erected in their Garden at Kensington of Bath Stone.'[40] Bridgeman and Kent must have been involved in the siting of these buildings, though there is scant evidence that Kent assisted in the layout of the gardens themselves, in spite of Horace Walpole's celebrated claim that Kent planted dead trees at Kensington 'to give a greater air of truth to the scene – but he was soon laughed out of this excess'.[41]

The area beyond the Royal Paddock merged into Hyde Park, and Kensington Gardens and Hyde Park were sufficiently close to be regarded as interdependent in Queen Caroline's reign.[42] Bridgeman's involvement at Hyde Park was twofold: 'making and keeping in fine Order the New Garden in the Paddock',[43] and constructing and looking after the two roads to the south. Hyde Park, named after the ancient manor of Hyde, had been reserved for hunting by Henry VIII. James I opened it to the public, and Charles II restocked part of it with deer. It became extremely popular during the seventeenth century, particularly with the prominence given to the Ring, that circular drive round the enclosure which was so favoured by Society. 'I went to *Hide Park* to take the aire', wrote Evelyn on May Day 1661, 'where was his *Majestie* & an inumerable appearance of Gallantry & rich Coaches

[38] An aquatint of it by Bucher of *c.*1790 is reproduced by Faulkner, 'A Note on the Gardens of Kensington Palace', pl.9a. For a 1973 photograph see Willis, 'Charles Bridgeman. The Royal Gardens', pl.15a.

[39] Described as 'A Seat in Kensington Gardens' it appears in John Vardy, *Some Designs of Mr. Inigo Jones and Mr. William Kent* (London, 1744), pl.38. The *Craftsman* saw the summer house as a political parable against Sir Robert Walpole, in which the seat is George II's chair, turned by 'a certain corpulent man who seemed to be his chief minister'. *Craftsman*, No.305 (6 May 1732).

For contemporary descriptions of Windsor seats see Defoe, *Tour Through the Whole Island of Great Britain*, ed. Browning and Cole, I, 303; Switzer, *Ichnographia Rustica* (1718), III, 125–26.

[40] PRO, Works 4/6, minutes of 24 September 1734. On 22 October 1734 there appears in PRO, Works 6/16, Their Majesties' order for making 'a peice of ground in Kensington Gardens & erecting a Seat of Bath Stone thereon'; the groundwork is estimated to cost £430 and the seat £500. On 14 August 1735 in PRO, Works 5/105, the sum of £681.11*s*.6*d*. is allocated for a 'New Stone seat in Kensigton [*sic*] Garden'. See the *Daily Gazetteer*, No.31 (4 August 1735), for an announcement of the extensions to Kensington including 'a pleasure House so high as to command the Country about'. I owe this to Mr and Mrs Robert Holden.

[41] Chase, *Horace Walpole: Gardenist*, p.30.

[42] All Bridgemanic plans of Hyde Park are considered here under Kensington Gardens, apart from those of Hyde Park Road.

[43] On 5 April 1732 he was paid £1,000 for this (PRO, Works 4/5, minutes of 5, 25 April, 23 May 1732), the first of many such payments until his death.

Payment of £1,030.13*s*.7½*d*. for a 'New bridge in Hyde park' is in PRO, Works 5/105, minutes of 16 September 1735.

& c: it being now a time of universal festivity & joy'.[44] The Ring was situated in the eastern area of the park, and consisted of a railed enclosure with a wide road round it. By Bridgeman's day the Ring had fallen out of fashion. 'The Ring . . . being quite disused by the Quality and Gentry,' announced the *London Spy Revived* on 6 December 1736, 'we hear that the Ground will be taken in for enlarging the Royal Gardens at Kensington.'

Soon after William III purchased Nottingham House he began making a road through Hyde Park known as the *Route du Roi*, now Rotten Row, otherwise called the Lamp Road or the King's Old Road, to distinguish it from the King's New Road which George II built to the south of it. Bridgeman's work on these – which he carried out under Richard Arundell's Surveyorship of the King's Private Roads – was just one of several similar burdens he undertook.[45] In 1726 the Frenchman De Saussure was enraptured by the Lamp Road:

> Nothing is more beautiful than the road from London to Kensington, crossing Hyde Park. It is perfectly straight and so wide that three or four coaches can drive abreast. It is bordered on either side by a wide ditch, and has posts put up at even distances, on the tops of which lanterns are hung and lamps placed in them, which are lighted every evening when the Court is at Kensington. When you look from one end of the road to the other the effect is charming.[46]

Lens shows us the lamps in place (*Plate 99b*). As a safety precaution against robbers they were none too effective, as Walpole found in 1749 when he was stopped and robbed of his gold watch and eight guineas. By this time the condition of the two roads had deteriorated: there are two ways through Hyde Park, Lord Hervey wrote in 1736, 'but the new one is so convex, and the old one is so concave, that by this extreme of faults they agree in the common of being, like the high road, impassable'.[47]

Moving eastwards from Hyde Park we pass through Green Park and so to St James's Park (*Plates 102a, 102b*). Green Park was formerly known as Upper St James's Park and is set in the triangle formed by Piccadilly, Constitution Hill, and Queen's Walk. Queen's Walk was named after Queen Caroline, who made a similar walk nearby in 1730, presumably with Bridgeman's help. In 1660–62 Charles II built a snow-house and ice-house and otherwise improved the park, and his habit of taking his 'constitutional' among his subjects there is said to have given the hill its name. During the eighteenth century Green Park became much favoured for walking: Caroline herself took to it, enjoyed promenading

[44] De Beer, ed., *Evelyn's Diary*, III, 285.

[45] Others were at Fulham, Barnes Common, Hampstead, Richmond, and St James's.

For documentation of royal roads see esp. throughout PRO, Works 1/1; 4/3; 4/4; 4/5; 4/6; 4/7; 5/58; 5/59; 5/104; 5/105; 5/141; 5/150. See also throughout *CTP*, VI (1720–28); *CTBP*, I–IV (1729–41).

A Bridgemanic plan of Fulham Road is in PRO, MPE 482 (Cat. No.339), and another is in PRO, MPD 164 (Cat. No.338) entitled 'Hide Park Road'. In 1743 Rocque was living in 'High Park Road', and reasons for regarding it solely as a rate-book name are given in Hugh Phillips, 'John Rocque's Career', *London Topographical Record*, XX (1952), 12–14.

Mention of Bridgeman making 'a private road across the fields to Hampstead' for Queen Caroline occurs in e.g. PRO, Works 4/8, minutes of 18 March 1740; 6/16, fo.109. See also PRO, Money Book XL (T53: 40), fos 195–96.

The Duchess of Marlborough alludes to Bridgeman's work on a road at Blenheim in her letter to his widow of 26 July 1741. See below Appendix IV (vi), p.158.

[46] [César De Saussure], *A Foreign View of England in the Reigns of George I and George II. The Letters of M. César De Saussure to His Family*, trans. and ed. Mme Van Muyden (London, 1902), p.138.

[47] Quoted by Halsband, *Hervey*, p.204. Hervey to Lady Bristol, 27 November 1736.

there, and in 1737 had William Kent design a library for her in St James's Palace overlooking Green Park. The view from the library windows would be pleasant enough: immediately beneath Constitution Hill, a commentator wrote in 1783, 'appears the beautiful lawn of the Green-park, skirted on one side with buildings, which, though irregular, are chearful and neat; and on another by the trees in St. James's-park, and enriched with a view of the abbey at Westminster . . . The lawn consists of the beautiful convexity of two gently rising hills.'[48]

The layout of St James's Park as we see it today is essentially Nash's of 1828.[49] The area was a swamp in the Middle Ages until Henry VIII took it over in 1532 and had it drained to make the park of St James's Palace. James I improved and controlled the water supply, and added a menagerie, whilst Charles I made minor changes. After the Restoration it was opened to the public and remodelled by Charles II in the French manner, and it was he who built Pall Mall and the canal flanked by four avenues of trees. This was all carried through by André, Charles, and Gabriel Mollet (sons of Claude Mollet, Le Nôtre's mentor at the Tuileries), and subsequently by John Rose. London and Wise, it will be recalled, were apparently among Rose's apprentices at St James's. Under Queen Anne, Wise transported trees to St James's, cut and widened the canal, and transferred deer from Hampton Court. The result was that St James's Park continued to be a landscape of considerable variety. Its formality is emphasized for example by the Bridgemanic plan in the Public Record Office with its precise drawing of Buckingham House, probably a Talman scheme of the early 1700's (*Plate 103*).

We get a quite different impression from the view down the Mall of 1741 (*Plate 101a*), and from Rigaud and St Torres' engraving of the view from Buckingham House, in which the straight lines of the Mall and canal contrast with the adjacent meadows with grazing animals (*Plate 101b*). In 1726 the French traveller De Muralt noted that St James's Park consisted of 'a large Extent of Ground with Walks set with Trees all round, which are very agreeable. There's a Canal in the middle edg'd with Trees, where one may see the Ducks swimming; the rest is Meadow, and Pasture for Deer and Cows. Its great Beauty consists in bringing (as it were) the Country into the City.' De Muralt adds that Charles II brought over 'a skillful Person from Paris' (conceivably Le Nôtre) to advise him on the design of St James's but, on examining the park, the Parisian found 'that its native Beauty, Country Air, and Deserts, had something greater in them, than any thing he could contrive, and persuaded the King to let it alone'. As a result, says De Muralt, 'the park remains in the same State, that is, a fine Country-like Place, and is the more agreeable, in my Opinion, because it has neither Art nor Regularity'.[50] During the whole of the eighteenth century

[48] [John Ralph], *Critical Review*, 1783 edn, pp.183–84. A Bridgemanic plan of Green Park is in PRO, Works 32/7.

[49] For St James's Park see Green, *Gardener to Queen Anne*, esp. pp.85–95; S. Lang, 'St. James's Park. The Rise and Threatened Decline of a Model Landscape', *Architectural Review*, CX (November 1951), 292–98; Larwood, *London Parks*, II, 61–272. For detailed documentation of St James's Park 1721–28 see PRO, Works 3/2, *passim*. Bridgeman's Royal Appointment restricts his work at St James's to 'the garden', just over an acre at St James's Palace.

[50] Béat Louis De Muralt, *Letters Describing the Character and Customs of the English and French Nations . . .*, 2nd edn (London, 1726), p.77. Muralt's visit actually took place earlier, and he met Sir William Temple, whose house at Moor Park in Surrey he found 'the Model of an agreeable Place of Retirement'. See ibid., pp.86–88.

The problem of Le Nôtre's possible visit to England to see Charles II is a knotty one. See Kerry Downes, *English Baroque Architecture* (London, 1966), pp.124–25; Lang, 'St. James's Park', pp.295, 297.

only minor changes were made in St James's: sometime between 1714 and 1721 the Decoy to the south-east of the canal was made into an ordinary pond, although the so-called Dutch Island on which William III built a summer house still survived. It seems that Bridgeman was required to do little more at St James's than maintain the park and the gardens adjacent to the palace.[51] At the palace Bridgeman had a good friend in Flitcroft, whose appointment as Clerk of Works in 1726 embraced St James's as well as Whitehall and Westminster, and who in about 1733 refaced Carlton House in the Mall, the home of Frederick, Prince of Wales.[52]

Newmarket and Windsor are specifically mentioned in Bridgeman's appointment as successor to Carpenter as Henry Wise's partner in 1726, and in Bridgeman's own Royal Appointment in 1728.[53] Although we know little of Bridgeman's activities at Newmarket, we do have a Bridgemanic plan of an enclosed garden near Windsor Castle, and the handsome signed survey of Windsor Forest (with typical Bridgeman green and red washes) as it was in the reign of James I (*Plates 104, 105*).[54] The key to Windsor's layout is the two parks, Home Park and Great Park, linked by the Long Walk. Around Great Park stretches Windsor Forest. Home Park, near the castle, is small in scale; Great Park is vast: whereas Hyde Park has never amounted to more than 700 acres, and Richmond Park about 2,000, Windsor Great Park is no less than 4,800 acres.[55] These were part and parcel of the Royal Gardeners' domain, and Wise's duties consisted of looking after the chaise ridings, laying out the Maestricht Garden, and planting the slopes by the castle (*Plate 106a*). From 1728 Bridgeman took on the responsibility of 'keeping the terraces, Great Court and inclosed slopes' for £140 a year instead of the £160 a year allowed to Wise. 'Less was charged and less expected', comments Mr Green.[56] Maybe so. Windsor lost none of its appeal with the change of Royal Gardener, and within a stone's throw of the castle one of Bridgeman's long-standing patrons often tasted the delights of the Windsor landscape. By the 1730's Sarah, Duchess of Marlborough, who was Ranger of Windsor Park, had become attached to Windsor Lodge, the property of her grandson Charles, 3rd Duke of Marlborough and brother of the Duchess of Bedford.[57] Sarah found the lodge 'of all Places that ever [she]

[51] Could the neighbouring Spring Gardens owe anything to Bridgeman's advice or example? There is a Bridgemanic plan of Spring Gardens in PRO, MPE 555 (Cat. No.344).

[52] The Prince bought Carlton House for £6,000 from the 3rd Earl of Burlington's widowed mother Juliana, having borrowed the money from George Bubb Dodington, whose London garden was next to his. See John Walters, *The Royal Griffin. Frederick Prince of Wales, 1707–51* (London, 1972), pp.78–79. See also *Survey of London*, XX (1940), 74.

[53] At Newmarket, Bridgeman's Royal Appointment of 1728 noted, the 'several little Gardens as now made & Planted [were] to be Upheld & kept in good Order'. Subsequently Bridgeman was paid for work in the 'little Gardens', in fact only two roods. Bridgeman's Inventory makes no reference to Newmarket, and thus implies that his connection was minimal. Newmarket races were a frequent haunt of George II, as Wootton's many paintings of horses and races at Newmarket testify.

For Windsor see Green, *Gardener to Queen Anne*, esp. pp.78–84. Bridgeman's work at Windsor from 1729 is detailed in PRO, Works 5/58, *passim*; 5/59, *passim*. His precise duties are spelt out in PRO, Works 6/15, fos 201–4.

[54] PRO, MR 279 (Cat. No.854). The plan is divided into 'Forest Walks' and the table in the upper-right corner lists the number and kind of deer in each, and the names of the keepers.

[55] In 1789 Windsor Forest was nearly 60,000 acres, according to John Fisher Murray, *A Picturesque Tour of the River Thames . . .* (London, 1853), p.353.

[56] Green, *Gardener to Queen Anne*, p.84.

[57] See *Vit. Brit.*, IV (1739), pls 38–39. The Bridgemanic plan of an enclosed garden at Windsor in the Soane Museum, Box of Misc. Drawings (Wren, etc.), is a detail from this. See Thomson, ed., *Letters of a Grandmother*, *passim*.

There are several Windsor drawings, some with a Bridgemanic cast, in the collection of photostats of Henry Wise plans in BL, Maps 188.g.1. The originals are at Windsor Castle.

was in the most agreeable'.[58] Even Blenheim could not compete. 'I never desire to see Blenheim again', she wrote. 'In a lodge I have every thing convenient & without trouble.'[59]

The bucolic delights of Richmond were somewhat different. During the mid-eighteenth century any visitor to Kew would have found two separate gardens in the area now partly occupied by the Royal Botanic Gardens (*Plate 107*).[60] Crossing the Thames at Kew Bridge, he could have followed Kew Road along the east flank of the garden much as we can today, but where the current main entrance stands he would have come to Love Lane (approximately on the line of the present Holly Walk) dividing Kew Gardens on his left from Richmond Gardens on his right. In Kew Gardens (sited near Kew Palace of 1631) was Kew House, otherwise known as the White House, built by Kent for Frederick, Prince of Wales, from about 1729 to 1736 and demolished by James Wyatt in 1802. It was here at the White House that Frederick established his court: after his marriage to Augusta in 1736 he and the princess lived there until his death in 1751, and she alone until hers in 1772. In Richmond Gardens across the way the principal building was Richmond Lodge (standing near the present Kew Observatory) which was altered in 1694 for William III and leased in 1704 to the Duke of Ormonde. The Duke's estates were forfeited on his exile after the 1715, and eventually in 1722 the lodge was granted by George I to George II when Prince of Wales. Subsequently it became Prince George and Princess Caroline's favourite residence, and in 1727 George gave it to his newly crowned Queen, who doubtless found the town of Richmond – with its elegant villas, river, convivial social life, and closeness to London – eminently attractive.

John Rocque's plan of Richmond and vicinity of 1746 shows Richmond Gardens wedged between Richmond Green on the west and Kew Palace on the east (*Plate 107*): to their north is Little Park, south is Richmond Park. Richmond Park as well as Richmond Gardens came under Bridgeman's surveillance. De Saussure explains that Richmond Park is more than 6 miles in circumference and is surrounded by walls. 'It contains woods and fields and some cultivated land', he continues, 'and in the centre is a large pond abounding with fish. This park is full of game – deer, roe-deer, hares, pheasants, partridges, which are all preserved for the King's pleasure.'[61] The King expressed his pleasure by erecting White Lodge in Richmond Park: the house itself was completed in 1727–29 to the designs of the Earl of Pembroke and Roger Morris, and Bridgeman was involved in its landscaping (*Plate 110b*).[62] It is the most distinguished building put up either by George I or

58 Quoted by Green, *Sarah, Duchess of Marlborough*, p.192.

59 Quoted ibid., p.297.

60 For Richmond see notably John Charlton, *Kew Palace* (London, 1956); John Harris, 'Bicentenary of Kew Gardens – I: Fate of the Royal Buildings', *C.Life*, CXXV (28 May 1959), 1182–84; idem, 'Exoticism at Kew', *Apollo*, LXXVIII (August 1963), 103–8; idem, *Sir William Chambers. Knight of the Polar Star* (London, 1970), esp. pp.77–80, 242–44.

For documentary evidence of Bridgeman at Richmond see esp. PRO, Works 4/7, *passim*; 5/58, *passim*; 5/59, *passim*; 6/16, *passim* 1735–37.

Although Bridgeman's Inventory lists tools left by him there, Richmond was not one of the gardens listed in his Royal Appointment.

61 De Saussure, *England in the Reigns of George I and George II*, pp.143–44 (14 June 1746).

62 In 1727 Bridgeman, Morris, and John Mist went to Richmond Park partly to acquire particulars for 'finishing the Estimate for Building a Lodge in Richmond Parke for His Majesty'. See PRO, Works 4/3, minutes of 14 February 1727; 6/15, minutes of 11 July 1728. In Bridgeman's lifetime expenses for 'Richmond Old Lodge' and 'Richmond New Lodge' appear throughout PRO, Works 5/104; 5/105. Sir Robert Walpole, who was Ranger of Richmond Park, had the use of Old Lodge. In 1724 he spent £14,000 on renovating it and installed Molly Skerrett there. See Plumb, *Walpole*, II, 90, 113.

George II, and is now the home of the Royal Ballet School. To give Caroline easy access to it, the Queen's Private Road was made across East Sheen Common, thereby connecting Richmond Gardens with the Park.[63]

Richmond Gardens were Caroline's delight: she took 'great interest in the gardens', observes De Saussure, and 'greatly embellished' them.[64] This embellishment consisted of laying out the grounds with meadows and woodland, winding walks, and garden buildings (*Plate 107*). Richmond Lodge itself, De Saussure assures us, was 'small, but in good taste',[65] although its higgledy-piggledy massing was unlikely to satisfy a Palladian (*Plate 110a*). In 1724 another visitor generously describes it as a 'perfect Trianon' and praises the 'fine avenue which runs from the front of the house to the town of Richmond one way, and from the other front to the river-side'.[66] Facing the river is a handsome terrace. Above all, he concludes, 'the woods, cut out into walks, with plenty of birds singing, made it a most delicious habitation'.[67] Horace Walpole singles out Bridgeman's work at Richmond for particular praise. 'As [Bridgeman's] reformation gained footing', he wrote, 'he ventured farther, and in the royal garden at Richmond dared to introduce cultivated fields, and even morsels of a forest appearance, by the sides of those endless and tiresome walks, that stretched out of one into another without intermission'.[68] Two of the four Bridgemanic drawings of Richmond bear out the accuracy of these observations: a detail of the dairy, canal, and mount near Richmond Lodge (*Plate 106b*) reminds us of Farley (*Plate 52*) and Moor Park (*Plate 51a*), whilst a Bridgemanic drawing of the eastern area of Richmond Gardens (beneath the word ROYAL on Rocque's 1746 plan) reveals how the Royal Gardener proposed to loosen the outline of the fields and replace clumps by wavy belts of trees (*Plate 108*).[69] Endorsing Walpole, Sir John Clerk of Penicuik noted the 'fields of corn interspersed' when he visited Richmond in 1733, and remarked that they had been introduced chiefly 'for the benefite of the game'.[70]

The best known features of Richmond Gardens were the various buildings by William Kent. Kent's designs for a palace there proved abortive,[71] but he did put up the Queen's Pavilion, menagerie, rotunda, and dairy.[72] Bridgeman was responsible for their landscaping. Lady Burlington made use of her access to Caroline to keep her husband in the

[63] For the Queen's Private Road see e.g. PRO, Works 6/16, *passim* 1735–37, esp. fos 89–90; PRO, King's Warrant Book XXXIII (T52: 40), fos 278–80; PRO, Letter Book XIX (T27: 25), fo.496.

Bridgeman was involved in 'making and planting . . . , and keeping the same' from 1735 to 1737. He planted 'Standard Elms' as well as grass, which he mowed and rolled. According to Bridgeman's widow, on his death he was owed £349.10*s*. by the Crown for his work. See below Appendix VI, p.168.

[64] De Saussure, *England in the Reigns of George I and George II*, p.143 (14 June 1726). De Saussure wrote this before Caroline had become Queen, and indicates that she was improving Richmond before Bridgeman became Royal Gardener.

[65] Ibid., p.143 (14 June 1726).

[66] Quoted by Harris, 'Fate of the Royal Buildings', 1182.

[67] Quoted by Arkell, *Caroline of Ansbach*, p.111.

[68] Chase, *Horace Walpole: Gardenist*, pp.24–25.

[69] At least one plan of Richmond was sold to the Board of Works by Sarah Bridgeman. See below Appendix VI, p.168.

[70] SRO, Edinburgh, GD 18/2110 (Clerk MSS), entry for 15 May 1733.

[71] The pearwood model made of Kent's scheme in 1735 is illustrated in Colvin, *Royal Buildings*, pl.22. For Edward Lovett Pearce's proposals see Colvin and Craig, eds, *Architectural Drawings in the Library of Elton Hall*, xlii; No.103.

[72] Rocque's separate plans have views of many of these. See also Harris, 'Fate of the Royal Buildings', 1182.

picture about Bridgeman and Kent's latest ploys. 'There is a new design going forward at Richmond in ye garden, & a building of Kent's design', she wrote to Burlington in 1735. 'I took ye liberty to differ with Mr. Bridgman & I daresay you wd be of my opinion; I want to have you see it; he said that 3 slopes made it look bigger; I think one wou'd be not only handsomer, but look (in his style) more grande. I think it stands to reason', she concludes, 'yt ye more breaks there are in any prospect ye shorter it looks.'[73] Such remarks may well have been directed towards Bridgeman's amphitheatre (or mount) with Kent's rotunda on top, or perhaps to one of the two most memorable follies at Richmond – the Hermitage and Merlin's Cave.[74] Statuary was prominent in both, a feature they share with the Temple of British Worthies at Stowe, also completed about 1733 or so (*Plate 153a*).[75] The Hermitage was a rustic three-arched temple with a prominent central pedimented bay (*Plate 109*), in composition not unlike Kent's octagonal temple at Euston, or the Queen's Temple at Kensington (*Plate 100b*).[76] As a place for philosophical retirement it was a far cry from Stukeley's hermitage at Stamford, or Pope's grotto at Twickenham. Inside was a little pantheon with busts by Rysbrack of Bacon, Boyle, Locke, Newton, and Wollaston, and by Guelfi of Dr Samuel Clarke. It was sited to the south-east of Richmond Lodge, overlooking a circular lawn. To its west, facing a rectangular canal, was Merlin's Cave, a thatched mock-gothic building which Bridgeman set amidst elms on a mount. Inside were three pairs of wax figures: Merlin with his secretary, Elizabeth (wife of Henry VII) with the goddess Minerva, and Queen Elizabeth I with her nurse. Merlin's Cave also housed the thresher-poet Stephen Duck, later promoted by Queen Caroline to the Chapelry at Kew.[77]

Duck's *Poems on Several Occasions* of 1736 contained a poem *On Richmond Park, and Royal Gardens* which was more polite than many others.[78] Caroline's gardening idiosyncrasies became a political pawn and the subject of widespread derision. Journals such as Bolingbroke's *Craftsman* poured scorn on the Hermitage and Merlin's Cave.[79] Poets too had a field day. 'Every man, and every boy, is writing verses on the Royal Hermitage', wrote

[73] Quoted by Lees-Milne, *Earls of Creation*, p.131.

[74] See Edmund Curll, *The Rarities of Richmond. Being Exact Descriptions of the Royal Hermitage and Merlin's Cave . . .* (London, 1736); Vardy, *Designs of Jones and Kent*, pls 31, 32 (Merlin's Cave), 33 (Hermitage).

[75] For statuary at Richmond see Webb, *Rysbrack*, pp.146–54, and at Stowe see ibid., esp. pp.135–36. Three of Rysbrack's subjects in the Hermitage (Bacon, Locke, and Newton) were among the original British Worthies at Stowe, later moved to the Elysian Fields. See below p.118n45. Cf. Webb, 'Giovanni Battista Guelfi', p.144.

[76] For Bridgeman and the Hermitage see the accounts in PRO, Works 5/58, *passim* from March 1731 to March 1734. Its context is noted in John Dixon Hunt, 'A Silent and Solitary Hermitage', *Annual Report of the York Georgian Society* (1970), 47–61, and its meaning is discussed in Judith Colton, 'Kent's Hermitage for Queen Caroline at Richmond', *Architectura* (Munich), IV, No.2 (1974), 181–91. This article is based on material in Professor Colton's 'Monuments to Men of Genius. A Study of Eighteenth-Century English and French Sculptural Works' (Ph.D. thesis, New York University, 1974). More generally see Edith Sitwell, 'Ancient and Ornamental Hermits', in *English Eccentrics*, 2nd edn (London, 1958), pp.37–67.

[77] For Bridgeman and Merlin's Hill see the accounts of 1735–36 in PRO, Works 6/16, fo.90v; PRO, King's Warrant Book XXXIII (T52: 40), fo.280; PRO, Letter Book XIX (T27: 25), fo.496.

[78] See Allen, *Tides in English Taste*, II, 135–38. For Duck see Rose Mary Davis, *Stephen Duck, the Thresher-Poet* (Orono, Maine, 1926) pp.170–80. Duck's *Poems on Several Occasions* was dedicated to Queen Caroline, and had a prefatory biography of Duck by Joseph Spence. Bridgeman was among the subscribers, as were Flitcroft, Thomas and William Greening, Henry Hoare II, William Kent, John Mist, Pope, Swift, and Thomas Wright.

[79] Notably No.480 (13 September 1735), which contains a satirical interpretation of the meaning of the statuary. The figures in Merlin's Cave were from Spenser's *Faerie Queene*, bk. III.

Pope to Gay on 2 October 1732, encouraging Gay to join the fun. 'You would oblige my Lady Suffolk if you tried your muse on this occasion', he adds mischievously.[80] Poems on Kensington, Richmond, St James's, and Windsor appeared as topographical poetry achieved a new vogue.[81] Swift wrote barbed epigrams, inspired by his envy at the recognition Duck had received. Theatrical entertainments drew humour and parody from the Queen's plight, and even the King did little to encourage her. 'You deserve to be abused for such childish silly stuff', he scoffed.[82] Not that everyone felt that Caroline's efforts deserved abuse: the *Gentleman's Magazine* periodically came to her aid, and in 1733 the Duke of Leeds, after a visit to the Duchess of Orléans's estate at Baquolet near Paris, observed that although the grounds there are 'extremely pretty' they 'did not come up to her Majesty's, at Richmond'.[83]

Foreign visitors, such as Baron Bielfeld, were fascinated not so much by Richmond as by the London parks. In 1741 Bielfeld found that St James's Park presented 'at once a scene of the country, of a retreat, of an army, of the city, and the court'.[84] Increasingly the populace began to regard these royal preserves as their own, and would brook no interference with their right to use them. Horace Walpole, as always, puts his finger on it. When Queen Caroline spoke of 'shutting up St. James's Park, and converting it into a noble garden for the palace of that name', he narrates, 'she asked my father what it might probably cost; who replied "*only three* CROWNS"'.[85] It was too great a price. The corollary of this was that the royal parks became centres for the rough and tumble of London life, though they were never so bizarre as Vauxhall and Ranelagh, the most successful of the ring of pleasure gardens around London and described by a contemporary as 'the two grand seminaries of luxury'.[86] The planting at Ranelagh, focused on the rotunda, was even more formal than at Vauxhall where the long vistas were terminated with painted perspectives of landscapes, ruins, temples, and a Chinese garden. Jostling crowds were everywhere, and their prominence led some foreigners to feel that in London the populace reigned supreme. It is a tradition that has never died. Writing in 1820 – when Bridgeman's scheme for Kensington was still relatively intact – Faulkner could say that the gardens there 'are now open every day, winter and summer . . . the great south walk leading to the palace, is crowded on Sunday mornings in the spring and summer, with a display of all the beauty

[80] *Pope Correspondence*, III, 318.

[81] Poems on the royal gardens from 1732 to 1738 are listed in Aubin, *Topographical Poetry*, pp.318–20.

[82] Romney Sedgwick, ed., *Lord Hervey's Memoirs*, 2nd edn (London, 1963), p.109.

[83] Katherine B. Thomson, ed., *Memoirs of Viscountess Sundon, Mistress of the Robes to Queen Caroline . . .*, 2nd edn (London, 1848), II, 215. Duke of Leeds to Viscountess Sundon, 28 June 1733. For Richmond today see Brian Dunning, 'The Majesty of Richmond Park', *C.Life*, CXLVI (11 December 1969), 1574–75.

Richmond Lodge and Merlin's Cave were demolished in the 1770's, and it was left to Brown and Chambers to bring the gardens to their final glory. The destruction of Merlin's Cave was one of the darts which William Mason hurled at Chambers in his *Heroic Epistle* (1773). In 1759 Princess Augusta had initiated a botanical garden at Richmond, but it was not until 1841 that the two royal domains were united to form Kew Gardens as we know them.

Professor Judith Colton generously shared with me her work on Richmond; too late for me to use was her key article, 'Merlin's Cave and Queen Caroline: Garden Art as Political Propaganda', *Eighteenth-Century Studies*, X (1976), 1–20.

[84] Hooper, trans., *Letters of Baron Bielfeld*, IV, 158.

[85] John Pinkerton, ed., *Walpoliana* (London, 1779), I, 8–9.

[86] Daniel Defoe, *A Tour Thro' the Whole Island of Great Britain . . .*, 7th edn (London, 1769), II, 172.

and fashion of the great metropolis, and affords a most gratifying spectacle, not to be equalled in Europe'.[87]

The grounds at Kensington and Richmond were the chief diversion of the last decade of Queen Caroline's life, and such was her expenditure on them that when she died – despite having enjoyed an income of £50,000 a year – she owed £2,000. In Voltaire's words, Caroline '*est née pour encourager tous les arts*', [88] and gardening was but one artistic pursuit which had claims on her purse. The royal gardens in Caroline's time tended to bear out her rejection of the formal style, and if the Queen was ridiculed by the *Craftsman* she was praised by other journals. Unlike his mother's, Prince Frederick's garden activities at Carlton House met with general approval from the press, and Sir Thomas Robinson was not alone in admiring Kent's 'notion of gardening' there. So successful was it, Robinson remarked, that without being told 'one would imagine art had no part in the finishing, and is, according to what one hears of the Chinese, entirely after their models for work of this nature'.[89] Kensington and Richmond in particular bear the marks of Bridgeman and Kent, and we should never forget that the Serpentine and winding walks in the Royal Paddock were under way before Caroline had taken charge. Moreover, we should not ignore the affinities between the rustic scenes at St James's Park and concurrent designs by Bridgeman at Stowe and elsewhere, and between the temples and follies at Kensington, Richmond, and Stowe's Elysian Fields. Not without reason did James Thomson (who lived at Richmond) observe that the age of Queen Caroline would be renowned in the future as much for its gardening as for its poetry and painting. Uniting all three arts is British freedom: the *furor hortensis* links all sorts and conditions of men. Thus Thomson in *Liberty* brings together a poet (Pope), a silviculturist (Bathurst), a queen (Caroline), a man of taste (Burlington), and a soldier (Cobham) when he writes:

See! sylvan scenes, where art alone pretends
To dress her mistress and disclose her charms –
Such as a Pope in miniature has shown,
A Bathurst o'er the widening forest spreads,
And such as form a Richmond, Chiswick, Stowe. (bk. v, ll.696–700)

Richmond and Chiswick lead us to Stowe, and it was at Stowe that Bridgeman's career reached its climax.

[87] Thomas Faulkner, *History and Antiquities of Kensington* . . . (London, 1820), p.411. Cf. Lysons, *Environs of London*, III (1795), 184. A mid-eighteenth-century pleasure garden at Aston was known as 'Bridgeman's Apollo Garden'. See *VCH: Warwickshire*, VII (1964), 218. Two drawings of Aston Park are in MSGD a3 fos 2, 3.

[88] *Lettres sur les Anglais*, ed. Arthur Wilson-Green (Cambridge, 1931), p.37.

[89] *HMC 42: Carlisle*, 143–44. Robinson to Carlisle, 23 December 1734. Kent was at Carlton House in 1736, following work for Prince Frederick on the Royal State Barge, and on the White House at Richmond. See Geoffrey Beard, 'William Kent's Royal Patrons', *Country Life Annual* (1970), pp.22–24. For a panegyric on the Prince's gardening activities, followed by a devastating attack on Queen Caroline's, see the *Craftsman*, Nos 497, 498 (6, 13 September 1735), and cf. *Daily Gazetteer*, No. 70 (18 September 1735).

Chapter 5

Stowe

According to Fredrik Magnus Piper, the Swedish artist-gardener who visited England in 1779, the layout of Stowe betrays Cobham's desire 'to gain renown and to exceed all others in point of expense and magnitude'.[1] No one could doubt Stowe's expense, magnitude, or renown, nor that such celebrity reflected well on Cobham himself (*Plate 112a*). Charles Bridgeman's work at Stowe, and our evidence for it, falls into four phases – initiation, consolidation, maturity, and expansion. The first phase stretches from 1711 to 1720 and is the period of Bridgeman and Vanbrugh's early co-operation; the second from 1721 to 1730 sees the continuation of the Royal Gardener's activity, the culmination of Vanbrugh's and the start of Gibbs's contribution, demonstrated by Bridgeman's bird's-eye view of about 1720 and Perceval's description of 1724; the third from 1731 to 1740 involves Bridgeman, Kent, and Gibbs and is attested to by West's poem *Stowe* of 1732 and Rigaud and Baron's perspectives published in 1739; the fourth from 1740 onwards witnesses the adaptation of Bridgeman's ideas, as chronicled in numerous guidebooks and in Bickham and Chatelain's engravings of Stowe of 1753.[2] By then Stowe was famous. In fact as early as 1735 an anonymous traveller could write that the gardens there 'are esteemed the *finest* of their *Kind* in *England*; & are indeed most *elegantly disposed*, & *beautifully diversifyed* with *Walks* & *Lawns*, *Canals* & *Grotto*'s, *Waterfalls* & *various Buildings*, such as *Temples*, *Rotundas*, *Pyramids*, *Obelisks* & *Colonnades*: in short you find here *beautifull Nature improved* by *happy Art*'.[3] You also find that the features of Stowe must be 'read' symbolically as classical, moral, and political themes blended together. That this was so must have been due to Cobham's own vision – as befits a relative of Sir William Temple – and to the promptings of such literary friends as Pope and Thomson.[4]

[1] Quoted by Sirén, *China and Gardens of Europe*, p.32. The Piper drawings of Stowe, Stourhead, Painshill, and elsewhere in England are in the Royal Academy, Stockholm, Låda XI, Pi-e6–Pi-e14. For Piper see *Svenskt Konstnärslexikon: tiotusen svenska konstnärers liv och verk* (Malmö, 1952–56), IV, 430. For advice on Piper I am indebted to Dr W. T. Stearn and to Dr Kristin Johansson of the Royal Academy, Stockholm.

[2] The ensuing chapter could not have been written without the generous help of the late Mr Christopher Hussey, Mr Laurence Whistler, Mr George B. Clarke, and Mr Michael J. Gibbon. See especially Hussey, *English Gardens and Landscapes*, pp.89–113; Whistler, *Imagination of Vanbrugh*, *passim*; Laurence Whistler, George B. Clarke, and Michael J. Gibbon, *Stowe. A Guide to the Gardens,* 3rd edn (Buckingham, 1974). The ongoing series of articles by Mr Clarke and Mr Gibbon in the *Stoic* was invaluable.

My work at the Huntington Library in 1960–61 and 1965 benefited from the assistance of Miss Haydée Noya, Miss Jean Preston, and Dr Robert R. Wark, and from the hospitality of Mrs William Charnley.

Since my last period in California in 1965 the Grenville Correspondence has been catalogued, and more precise references to it (kindly given to me by Miss Preston, the Curator of Manuscripts) have been incorporated below in Bibliography A.

[3] BL, Add MS 5842 (Tour in England 1735), fo. 260.

[4] In 1733 Cobham spent 6 guineas on copies of the *Seasons*. See HEH, Stowe (Temple) Account Book, No.7 (1732–79), fo.23. For life at Stowe see e.g. Lewis M. Wiggin, *The Faction of Cousins. A Political Account of the Grenvilles, 1733–63* (New Haven, 1958), pp.51–57. See also Michael Gibbon, 'Grenville Family I', *Stoic*, XXV (July 1972), 109–15; idem, 'Grenville Family II', *Stoic*, XXV (December 1972), 164–69.

It is not Pope's *Epistle to Cobham* (1734) but his *Epistle to Burlington* (1731) which provides us with the poet's most sympathetic lines on Stowe. Stowe's restraint, he implies, contrasts sharply with the ostentation of Timon's Villa. The passage bears repeating. Having urged us to 'Consult the Genius of the Place in all', Pope writes:

Still follow Sense, of ev'ry Art the Soul,
Parts answ'ring parts shall slide into a whole,
Spontaneous beauties all around advance,
Start ev'n from Difficulty, strike from Chance;
Nature shall join you, Time shall make it grow
A Work to wonder at – perhaps a STOW. (ll.65–70)

Not merely is this a reiteration of Pope's frequent fusion of 'use' and 'splendour', it is also an affirmation (borne out so well in his own life) that difficulties cannot be merely conquered, they can be transformed into triumphs. Thus at Twickenham the grotto which began as an awkward and gloomy tunnel became, in Pope's hands, a shrine to 'Great Nature'. He had turned, in Swift's words, 'a blunder into a beauty'.[5] Cobham shared Pope's ability to profit from whatever fate threw in his way. 'That thin, decayed carcase of his', it was remarked of Cobham, 'contains a spirit that is surprizing.'[6] At Stowe he mounted a relentless campaign to convert what could only be regarded as a rather mean estate into one of the most admired landscapes in Europe. Stowe has been a public school since 1923, and although some of its beauties are gone forever, and others changed beyond recognition, many remain as a testimony to the early eighteenth-century design which Pope eulogized.[7] The central block of the house, pedimented on both sides, looks southwards to the lake (*Plate 113*) and northwards to an open court with curved arcaded wings and the Equestrian Statue of George I between them; whilst to the south-east lie the Elysian Fields overlooked by the circular Temple of Ancient Virtue, with Stowe Church nearby (*Plate 111*).

Initiation 1711–20

The mansion itself was begun by Cobham's father Sir Richard Temple, 3rd Bt, soon after his marriage in 1675, and was completed by 1683. It replaced a house which had been lived in for a century by the Temple family before its demolition in the 1670's. The surrounding areas were heavily wooded and rose in a northerly direction, so Sir Richard decided to set the new house on the crest of the hill (just north of where the old building

[5] *Pope Correspondence*, II, 326. Swift to Pope, 29 September 1725.

[6] *The Autobiography and Correspondence of Mary Granville, Mrs Delany . . .*, ed. Lady Llanover, S.1 (London, 1861), II, 43. Mrs Pendarves to Mrs Ann Granville, 3 March 1739.
Cobham's family background is discussed in three articles by Mr Clarke in the *Stoic*: 'Rise of the Temple Family I', XXII (July 1967), 261–69; 'Rise of the Temple Family II', XXIII (December 1967), 5–11; 'Early Life of Richard Temple, Viscount Cobham', XXIII (July 1968), 116–20.

[7] See Nikolaus Pevsner, *Buckinghamshire*, The Buildings of England (Harmondsworth, 1960), pp.251–65.

used to be) so that it commanded a fine prospect over 25 miles of Buckinghamshire countryside; simultaneously he may have aligned its axis southwards with the steeple of Buckingham's medieval church.[8] Celia Fiennes, who visited Stowe in about 1694, found a handsome red-brick building with stone dressings and a hipped roof, slightly smaller than the present centre block. As a contemporary sketch shows, it was a stylistic mixture of Belton, Coleshill, and Clarendon House, Piccadilly (*Plate 112b*).[9] There is, Celia Fiennes reports, 'a visto thro' the whole house', so that from the same spot you view to the south 'the gardens which are one below another with low breast walls and taress walkes' and lead down to orchards and woods beyond, whilst to the north you can see the park planted with 'rowes of trees'.[10] It is evident that the layout of Stowe as Cobham inherited it in 1697 imposed restrictions on the expansion of the estate, and a diagrammatic reconstruction of it reveals how every way was blocked (*Plate 114*).[11] To the north lay the house; to the north-west the enclosure and walled garden; to the south-east was Stowe Church, with the main road from Buckingham (called the Hey Way) bringing visitors over the stream at the bottom of the hill, up the narrow valley and round to the north front of the house; whilst to the south, wrecking all symmetry, the Slant Road stretched westwards to meet the Roman road running south-west. The most intractable of Bridgeman's early problems was how to make virtues of these necessities.

It was immediately following his dismissal from his army command in Flanders in 1713 that Cobham turned his attention to Stowe. Bridgeman and Vanbrugh, who may have been at Eastbury helping Cobham's cousin Bubb Dodington, were called in, Vanbrugh for alterations to the mansion itself and for garden buildings, Bridgeman to design and control the landscape. Lord Perceval explains Bridgeman's role. 'Bridgeman laid out the ground and plann'd the whole', he wrote in 1724, 'which cannot fail of recommending him to business'.[12] In 1735 Vertue confirmed Bridgeman's leadership. At Stowe, he says, there were many temples by Vanbrugh, 'who was most concernd in the direction of Ld Cobhams [Gardens] or rather buildings because Mr Bridgeman Gardiner to the King. had the direction & disposition of the Gardens'.[13] Perceval implies that these were begun in 1713, and we have documentary evidence suggesting that Bridgeman was busy at Stowe

[8] Argued by Clarke, 'Sir Richard Temple's House and Gardens', *Stoic*, XXIII (March 1968), 70. This steeple was blown down in 1699, two years after Sir Richard's death, and never rebuilt. Browne Willis, *The History and Antiquities of . . . Buckingham . . .* (London, 1755), p.277, remarks that Cobham's gardens were thus 'divested of what was esteemed by his Father the most valuable Prospect, *viz*. the View of the Steeple of *Buckingham*'. The siting of Stowe is considered in George Clarke, 'Ancient and Medieval Stowe', *Stoic*, XXII (March 1967), 210–16.

[9] The perspective is in a grangerized copy of vol. I, pt. 2 (*Buckinghamshire*), of Lysons's *Magna Britannia* (1806–22). Now owned by the Hon. R. W. Morgan-Grenville, this volume was originally made up in 1820 for William Wyndham Grenville, Baron Grenville, for the library at Dropmore. See Michael Gibbon, 'Stowe House, 1680–1779', *Apollo*, XCVII (June 1973), 552–53.

[10] Morris, ed., *Journeys of Celia Fiennes*, p.30. Stowe Ridings, mature woodland to the north out of which avenues were cut, are shown prominently in the general plan of 1739. Celia Fiennes was related to the Temples.

[11] My drawing is based on one published by Mr Clarke, who discusses it in the light of several plans at the Huntington Library in 'Sir Richard Temple's House and Gardens', 68–80.

[12] BL, Add MS 47030 (Egmont Papers), fos 156–59. Perceval to Dering, 14 August 1724.

[13] *Vertue*, III (XXII), 133.

in 1714[14] – a couple of years before Vanbrugh, whose arrival was surely directly connected with his banishment from Blenheim in 1716. By this time Cobham was a baron, committed to the Hanoverians, and newly-married to the heiress of a wealthy brewer. Activity at Stowe accelerated.

The next three years saw the culmination of Cobham's initial phase, and by 1719 his achievement was considerable. A reconstructed plan illustrates its extent (*Plate 115*).[15] We can see that near the house there were statues, urns, and a classical garden pavilion. In the surrounding areas large numbers of trees had been planted in Hawkwell Field to the east, whilst on the west a 'new Elm Walk' ran along the line of Nelson's Walk. On the north, in Conduit Field, trees had been cased, an operation which may have been connected with removing the pales to allow the deer to graze right up to the forecourt on the north front. At the end of the Course a 'ditch bank' was dug. Excavated earth had been disposed of by the formation of two mounts which served as focal points for the axis running through the centre of the house. This axis was established by the canal on the north and the Abele Walk of poplars on the south.[16] In 1719 Vanbrugh's Temple of Bacchus, and Nelson's Seat, were under way, as was the digging of 'ye first stockeade ditch' along the line of the Lime Walk.[17] In the same year Vanbrugh reported that he had been to Stowe and found Cobham 'very well, and in very good humour: and much entertain'd with (besides his Wife) the Improvements of his House and Gardens, in which he Spends all he has to Spare'.[18] The twelve months after Vanbrugh's visit were a critical period of decision for Cobham. By now his fortunes had been further advanced, and he was a Privy Councillor, a viscount, and had been greatly enriched by the booty from his Vigo expedition. His new status demanded a more distinctive and unified setting at Stowe. Cobham launched a massive construction programme in the autumn of 1720. Bridgeman was put in charge, and he prepared a brilliant scheme.

14 HEH, Box L9F6: Stowe (Temple) Estate Accounts, 1710–20, '1714' (packet). 'Mr bridgmans man' was paid £1.2*s*.6*d*. The account is undated.

More specifically, we have two notes of 1716: one of 11 August in which Bridgeman acknowledges payment of £188.16*s*.0*d*. from William Jacob (then steward at Stowe), and the other of 16 August in which Bridgeman asks Jacob for a further £20.0*s*.0*d*. The address on the back of this last hints that Bridgeman may have been involved at Upper Winchendon (Bucks), the seat of Thomas, 1st Marquess of Wharton, leading Whig and member of the Kit-Cat Club.

These notes were discovered by Mr Clarke at the Huntington Library in 1975 (HEH, Stowe Repair Box, No.6).

15 Again my drawing follows one published by Mr Clarke, and my subsequent interpretation leans on his article 'Vanbrugh-Bridgeman Gardens', *Stoic*, XXIII (July 1969), 257–64.

16 The suggestion that 'Abele' refers to a white poplar tree (*populus alba*) is not universally accepted. A link between the Biblical Abel and the Elysian Fields at Stowe is mentioned by Neumeyer, 'The Landscape Garden as a Symbol', 189. Cobham bought statues of Cain and Abel for Stowe from the sculptor Andrew Carpenter.

17 Cobham's stewards were successively Claridge, Jacob, and Roberts; his head gardeners were successively Wagesfelt, Bissell, Love, and Capability Brown; his foreman gardeners were Nelson, Gurnet, and Rogers (after whom walks were named), and John Lee. Bridgeman's agent in 1716–17 was probably W. Topham.

18 Dobrée and Webb, eds, *Works of Vanbrugh*, IV, 112. Vanbrugh to Tonson, 1 July 1719. Cobham had no children, and by the terms of his father's will Stowe was to pass to a distant and penniless cousin on his death. However in 1717 Cobham managed to buy out his relative and break the entail.

Consolidation 1721–30

Bridgeman's bird's-eye view, doubtless drawn to enable Lord and Lady Cobham to visualize his proposals three-dimensionally, is now in the Bodleian Library (*Plates 116–120b*). Sensitively drawn in ink and pencil, with brown and grey water-colour washes, it displays the area to the west of the Abele Walk stretching down from Stowe House in the middle distance to the Octagon Lake in the right-hand corner. Immediately to the south of the house is the Parterre flanked by sculptured hedges, with Stowe Church to the east at the end of the Great Cross Walk (*Plate 118*). In the centre at the junction between Rogers' Walk and Gurnet's Walk is the Rotunda (*Plate 119a*), facing outwards to Home Park and inwards to the Queen's Theatre with its rectangular Canal and grass banking (*Plate 119b*). To the far right the Lake Pavilions stand guard over the Octagon Lake with its Guglio Fountain (a 70-foot obelisk, with water cascading from the top) (*Plate 120a*). The Abele Walk stretches from the Parterre down to the Octagon Lake. Sweeping diagonally across the left side is the Course, with the Equestrian Statue of George I on the site of the northern mount. Nelson's Walk (parallel to the Course) joins the Great Cross Walk (parallel to the Slant Road) in the left corner of the sketch. The platform there, which begs for a building, may have been the site of Vanbrugh's Pyramid; further west the Boycott Pavilions were to provide a temporary halt to the Roman road. At the north end of Rogers' Walk, where it meets Nelson's Walk, is Nelson's Seat. South of this is Lady Temple's Spinney, with the Temple of Bacchus set in it and Coucher's Obelisk overlooking it from the south (*Plate 120b*). Between the Abele Walk and Gurnet's Walk, set in woodland with winding walks, are the sites of the Temple of Sleep and Cold Bath, although no buildings are shown. In the foreground is Home Park, separated from the garden proper by a ha-ha, which opens up the countryside to the strollers within.

The bird's-eye view emphasizes how Bridgeman superimposed a pattern of avenues linked by *ronds-points* on the earlier ragged fragments, and so tied together the sprawling limbs of the layout. Placed in the centre of the drawing was the Rotunda, set on a prominent vantage point and providing much the same focus as a medieval mount. Elsewhere Bridgeman exploited the existing features and lie of the land, but he determined the position of the Rotunda geometrically (*Plate 124*). He drew a line from the centre of the Octagon Lake to the junction of Nelson's Walk and the Great Cross Walk, and another from Nelson's Seat to the *rond-point* where it meets the Great Cross Walk. This line was projected southwards. The Rotunda (closely akin to the design of the Ionic temple at Duncombe) was sited where the two lines met, and walks were cut to follow these lines and so to focus on the Rotunda. Thus the whole design was locked together – or rather the western area was, for Bridgeman showed nothing on the east beyond Stowe Church. To the west the next step would be the enlargement of the water-course and the enclosure of Home Park.

Within about four years of Bridgeman's completion of his sketch, Lord Perceval is writing to Dering recapitulating his impressions of his Stowe visit of 1724. No matter how speculative Bridgeman's drawing may have been, Perceval's testimony indicates that many of its features were in existence when he was there.[19] After noting Bridgeman's authorship of its design, Perceval goes on to say that 'what adds to the bewty of this garden is, that it is not bounded by walls, but by a ha-Hah, which leaves you the sight of the bewtiful woody country, and makes you ignorant how far the high planted walks extend'. Within the previous five years, he writes, Stowe

> has gained the reputation of being the finest seat in England . . . The Gardens, by reason of the good contrivance of the walks, seem to be three times as large as they are. They contain but 28 acres, yet took us up two hours. It is entirely new, & tho begun but eleven years ago [i.e. 1713], is now almost finished. From the lower end you ascend a multitude of steps . . . to the Parterre, & from thence several more to the house, which, standing high commands a fine prospect. One way they can see 26 miles.

Then Perceval launches into an enthusiastic description of Stowe's layout. It consists, he says, 'of a great number of walks, terminated by summer houses & heathen temples of different structure, and adorned with statues cast from the Anticks'. The Rotunda in particular catches his eye. 'The garden of Venus is delightfull', he writes. 'You see her standing in her Temple [i.e. in the Rotunda], at the head of a noble bason of water, & opposite to her an Amphitheater, with statues of Gods & Goddesses'. After describing King George's Column, the Lake Pavilions, and the Octagon Lake, Perceval expresses his pleasure at the walks which end in 'Vistos, arches & statues . . . You think twenty times you have no more to see, & of a sudden you find your self in some new garden or walk, as finish'd & adorn'd as that you left'. This brings Cobham into the picture:

> Nothing is more irregular in the whole, nothing more regular in the parts, which totally differ one from the other. This shews my Lords good tast, and his fondness to the place appears by the great expence he has been at. We all know how chargeable it is to make a garden with tast; to make one of a sudden is more so; but to erect so many Summer houses, Temples, Pillars, Piramids and Statues, most of fine hewn stone the rest of guilded lead would drain the richest purse.

That, of course, is where Lady Cobham comes in. 'I doubt not', concludes Perceval, 'but much of his wifes great fortune has been sunk in it.'[20]

In essence Bridgeman's drawing covers the 28 acres or so referred to by Perceval. All seven garden features shown by Bridgeman are either by Vanbrugh or attributable to him:

[19] Documentary references in estate records to Bridgeman at Stowe are rare. The next dated one occurs on 26 November 1720 when John Gurnet was paid 9*s*.4*d*. for having a trench dug 'for Mr Bridgman'. HEH, Bundle L9F9: Stowe (Temple) Estate Accounts, 1718–22, 'Garden Work began october ye 3d 1720' (bundle). On 5 July 1721 Cobham went with Bridgeman to see an iron roller, which he later bought. HEH, Stowe (Temple) Account Book, No.131 (1719–23), 5, 10 July 1721. The 'hog pond' between the Rotunda and the Queen's Theatre was being dug in the autumn of 1721, when John Lee notes that 'My Lord woold not have it donn [until] Mr Bridgman Coms'. HEH, Box L9F7: Stowe (Temple) Estate Accounts, 1720–27, 'Farm and Garden Accounts (1721)' (folder).

From 1721–26 Joseph Carpenter of Brompton Park was paid for garden seeds and trees at Stowe. See HEH, Stowe (Temple) Account Books, No.131 (1719–23), 26 July 1721 (£3.13*s*.6*d*.), 10 March 1721 (£3.10*s*.); No.132 (1723–27), 6 February 1723 (£3.12*s*. 6*d*.), 28 January 1725 (£2.7*s*.), 11 February 1726 (£2.15*s*.).

Cobham makes frequent payment for the delivery of letters from Bridgeman. In 1721 they occur undated in HEH, Bundle L9F9: Stowe (Temple) Estate Accounts, 1718–22, 'Garden Work begun October ye 2 1721', and in HEH, Stowe (Temple) Account Book, No.132 (1723–27), 18 August, 6 November 1723; 1 September 1725. The same volume notes that on 22 February 1725 Cobham paid for the delivery of plate which he had bought from Bridgeman.

[20] BL, Add MS 47030 (Egmont Papers), fos 156–59. Perceval to Dering, 14 August 1724. Cf. the description in the Diary of a Tour in 1724, Yorkshire Archaeological Society, Leeds, MS 328, unnumbered fos.

that is to say Nelson's Seat, the two Lake Pavilions, the Brick Temple (or Temple of Bacchus), the Guglio Fountain, Coucher's Obelisk, and the Rotunda. In addition the Temple of Sleep, the Cold Bath, and the Pyramid were Vanbrugh's, though none is indicated.[21] The Bridgeman-Vanbrugh phase of Stowe's history owes nothing to either Gibbs or Kent, so there is no evidence of their buildings on the bird's-eye. Instead we are presented with a variety of structures by Vanbrugh, their setting more informal than those at, say, Castle Howard or Duncombe Park. Sir John was not alone in feeling amply satisfied with the result. He was at Stowe in the autumn of 1724, and again in the summer of 1725 with his wife and Lord Carlisle. 'The Company were so well pleas'd at Stowe, that they stay'd four days', he reported. 'My Lord Carlisle then went on for Castle Howard, and we Stay'd at Stowe a Fortnight, a Place now, so Agreeable, that I had much ado to leave it at all.'[22] But leave it Vanbrugh must, for ever. The following March he was dead.

That autumn Tory succeeded Whig as James Gibbs was engaged at Stowe as Vanbrugh's replacement, and in September 1726 Gibbs was visiting Stowe in Bridgeman's company.[23] By the time that Stowe temples appeared in Gibbs's *Book of Architecture*, two years later, both Gibbs's Building and the Boycotts were under way, as Home Park was enclosed and its south-western limits defined.[24] The new western approach road was completed in 1731, and ran by the south shore of the Eleven-Acre Lake, up Warden Hill, and along the Course (parallel to Nelson's Walk) to the north front. This provided the visitor with a shaded and tantalizing approach to Stowe (with occasional glimpses of Home Park and neighbouring buildings) which culminated in a dramatic arrival at the Entrance Court, as it were from the wings – not unlike Vanbrugh's proposals for Castle Howard and Blenheim. Cobham found the concept appealing and, Vanbrugh writes, told him that he had seen such a layout for a palace in Germany which had produced 'an Admirable good effect'.[25] Once this road was finished Cobham could close the Hey Way and extend his design outwards: so far there was nothing east of the eastern Lake Pavilion, and Cobham had no intention of stopping there. Without delay he pressed ahead with further ambitious plans for the grounds.[26]

[21] The Pyramid is the only building noted by Perceval which does not appear on Bridgeman's bird's-eye view, perhaps because it was sited beyond the left edge of the drawing. Bridgeman is more comprehensive than Perceval, and shows much that is not mentioned by him – notably Coucher's Obelisk, Lady Temple's Spinney, the Equestrian Statue of George I, Nelson's Seat, and the Brick Temple or Temple of Bacchus. Bridgeman does not indicate, nor does Perceval mention, the Temple of Sleep or the Cold Bath. Doubtless both would have appeared had the drawing been published later. A tantalizing hint by Perceval that 'we shall shortly have a graving' of Stowe suggests that Bridgeman's sketch may have been a preliminary study for an engraving.

Other structures at Stowe sometimes credited to Vanbrugh include King George's Column, and the Witch's House.

[22] Dobrée and Webb, eds, *Works of Vanbrugh*, IV, 167. Vanbrugh to Tonson, 12 August 1725.

[23] Cobham records the following visits in HEH, Stowe (Temple) Account Book, No.132 (1723–27): 15 July 1725 (Pope and Wootton), 25 June 1726 (Swift, Gay, and Pope), 16, 21 September 1726 (Bridgeman and Gibbs).

[24] For the Stowe temples see Gibbs, *Book of Architecture* (1728), pls 75–78. The Boycott Pavilions derived their name from the hamlet of Boycott which formerly existed on their site. In 1764 Gibbs's Building was rebuilt elsewhere as the Fane of Pastoral Poetry.

[25] Dobrée and Webb, eds, *Works of Vanbrugh*, IV, 164. Vanbrugh to Carlisle, 10 December 1724.

[26] See Michael Gibbon, 'Lord Cobham's Garden Buildings I', *Stoic*, XXIV (December 1970), 171–82.

Maturity 1731–40

By the early 1730's several of these ambitious plans had been realized. In July 1732 George Vertue visited Stowe's 'delightfull & magnificent' gardens, and at about the same time made reference in his *Note Books* to 'a Poem. Calld Stowe. by Mr West a nephew of Ld Cobhams'.[27] This was Gilbert West, and the allusion was to his poem *Stowe, the Gardens of the Right Honourable Richard, Lord Viscount Cobham*,[28] brought out anonymously in London by Pope's publisher Lawton Gilliver in 1732, and dedicated to Pope:

To Thee, great Master of the vocal String,
O *Pope*, of *Stowe*'s Elyzian Scenes I sing. (p.1)

Cobham himself must have felt that the grounds at Stowe were sufficiently advanced and successful to bear his nephew's encomiums. In essence West's piece consists of a description of, and meditation upon, the features of the estate. He continues by warning Pope:

Yet let not thy superior Skill disdain
The friendly Gift of this *Poetick Plan*.
The same presiding Muse alike inspires
The *Planter*'s Spirit and the *Poet*'s Fires,
Alike, unless the Muse propitious smile,
Vain is the *Planter*'s, vain the *Poet*'s Toil.
All great, all perfect Works from *Genius* flow,
The *British Iliad* hence, and hence the Groves of *Stowe*. (p.2)

As West sees it, both Cobham and Pope need the inspiration of the 'same presiding Muse', otherwise the efforts of planter and poet alike will be equally vain.

A visual record of Stowe at this time is provided by the *Views of Stowe* published by Bridgeman's widow Sarah in 1739. These consist of fifteen perspectives and a general plan (*Plates 122, 123*), a plan whose basic configuration has persisted through more than two centuries (*Plates 124, 125*). As we know, the artists involved were Jacques Rigaud and Bernard Baron.[29] Baron – one of Bridgeman's immediate neighbours in Hamilton's *Club of Artists* – had left France about 1720 and was destined to make his reputation in England with engravings of frescoes, historical paintings, and portraits. He remained in England until his death, apart from a brief visit to Paris in 1729. Baron may have met Rigaud there and possibly have recommended him to Bridgeman on his return. At all events, by the 1730's Rigaud already had a high reputation, if only through his illustrations of *Les maisons royales de France*, and the perspectives of Stowe bear a clear affinity to Rigaud's French work: they are, for instance, titled in English and French, and when a

27 *Vertue*, v (xxvi), 103.

28 Gilbert West was son of Richard West by his wife Maria, daughter of Sir Richard Temple, 3rd Bt, and sister of the 1st Viscount Cobham. Another of Cobham's nephews, George Lyttelton, 1st Baron Lyttelton, was a rising poet and he too had addressed a poem to Pope by 1732.

29 Subsequent discussion is based on Peter Willis, 'Jacques Rigaud's Drawings of Stowe in the Metropolitan Museum of Art', *Eighteenth-Century Studies*, vi (1972), 85–98.

title-page was added in 1746 – emphasizing the eminence of subject, client, and designer, and giving the precise title of each engraving – it was bilingual too (*Plate 121*).[30] The accompanying plan, however, is annotated only in English. As yet no drawing of it has come to light, but fourteen of Rigaud's unsigned views (with English and French titling) are currently preserved in the Department of Prints and Photographs at the Metropolitan Museum of Art in New York (*Plates 129–142*).[31] Missing from Rigaud's originals is No.6 in the engraved set, the 'View of the *House* from the *Equestrian Statue*' (*Plate 143*). Rigaud's sketches are in ink and grey wash and show great sensitivity in their delicately drawn planting and boldly modelled buildings. The engravings follow the original sketches carefully: the antics of dogs, the grouping of animals and figures, are copied precisely. Their liveliness subdues all around them. Taken as a group, the *Views of Stowe* form the most comprehensive set of drawings of any English landscape garden.[32]

It was Bridgeman himself who lay behind their commissioning and ultimate publication, for Vertue makes clear that it was 'at the request of Mr Bridgman the Kings Gardner' that in about February 1733 Rigaud came to England

> to be employd by him to make designs of Gardens. Views & c. of which at Ld Cobhams he has been some time made many drawings most excellently performd. he being perfect

[30] I say 'added' here solely because I have never come across a 1739 title-page. There seems to have been only one printing, in which the numbers on the engravings and the English and French titles correspond to those given on the 1746 title-page. Minor misspellings occur in the titling of the drawings.

[31] MMA (Harris Brisbane Dick Fund, 1942), 42.79, which is an album, bound in red morocco with gold tooling, bearing the arms of the Rt. Hon. Thomas Grenville and the title 'A GENERAL PLAN / AND PROSPECTS / OF L^D^ VIS. COBHAM'S / GARD^NS^ AT STOWE'. Brief comments on these drawings occur in John Harris, 'Some English Architectural and Decorative Drawings in the Museum's Collection', *Bulletin of the Metropolitan Museum of Art*, N.S., XXI (February 1963), 214–22; idem, *A Catalogue of British Drawings for Architecture, Decoration, Sculpture and Landscape Gardening 1550–1900 in American Collections* (Upper Saddle River, N.J., 1971), pp.182–83.

The engraved plan measures 89·5 × 56·5 cm and is to the approximate scale of 1 in.=462 ft (i.e. 7 chains). The engraved perspectives consist of three large prints (Nos 2–4) and twelve small ones (Nos 5–16). In each case Rigaud's sketches are slightly bigger than the engravings, the large drawings measuring approximately 76·8 × 37·1 cm (the prints 74·2 × 35·2 cm) and the small ones approximately 49·5 × 29·5 cm (the prints 48 × 30·5 cm).

Thomas Grenville would be either Viscount Cobham's nephew of that name, a brother-in-law of William Pitt, or else, as is more likely, Cobham's great-nephew Thomas Grenville, book-collector and donor of the Grenville Library to the British Museum. See the family tree in Gibbon, 'Grenville Family I', 110–11.

As Bridgeman's Inventory fails to list them, Rigaud's drawings must have been in someone else's hands by 1738. In all probability they passed from Cobham to the Grenville side of the family.

In 1827 Loudon acknowledges the existence of some drawings of Stowe when he notes in his *Encyclopaedia of Gardening*, 5th edn (1827), p.1072, that Bridgeman's drawings 'are still in possession of the marquis'. They are noted at the time of the Great Sale at Stowe in 1848 by Henry Rumsey Forster, *The Stowe Catalogue, Priced and Annotated* (London, 1848), p. xiii, and again by Henry Austin Dobson, *At Prior Park, and Other Papers* (London, 1912), p.84.

The Rigaud drawings, as such, first appear in Sotheby's, Sale of Sir Thomas Phillipps, Bt, 27–28 June 1938, Day 2, Lot 448, when they were bought by Edwards for £14. They were purchased by the Metropolitan Museum of Art from a New York dealer in 1942.

I gratefully acknowledge the help given me in the Department of Prints and Photographs at the Metropolitan Museum of Art by the late John J. McKendry, Curator in Charge, and by Miss Janet S. Byrne and Mrs Alexandrine St Clair.

[32] The soft, whimsical quality of Rigaud's sketches is lost in the engravings, handsome though these are (cf. *Plate 143*). The *Views of Stowe* should be compared with other drawings done by Rigaud whilst in England, such as his views of Claremont, Greenwich, Hampton Court, Richmond, St James's Chapel, St James's Park, and Chiswick (*Plates 165b, 57a*). In their turn, these should be put alongside such French perspectives as those of Versailles (*Plate 5b*). See M. Ch. Ginoux, *Jacques Rigaud. Dessinateur et graveur Marseillais, improprement prénommé Jean-Baptiste par quelques écrivains (1681–1754)* (Paris, 1898).

For Baron see John E. Ruch, 'Bernard Baron. Un graveur français en Angleterre au début du XVIIIe siècle', *Nouvelles de l'estampe*, No.12 (November–December 1973), 13–21.

> Master of perspective finely disposes his groups of Trees light. & shade & figures in a masterly manner.[33]

Then, after a stay of between twelve and eighteen months, Rigaud returned to Paris, 'leaving Mr Bridgmans works not intirely finishd'. Some friction between Rigaud and Baron is hinted at as Vertue goes on to point out that Baron 'managed it so as to get [Rigaud] away and got the finishing part to himself but Bridgeman dyd before it was published'. Of the sixteen plates of Stowe which resulted, Vertue continues,

> all the draughts [were] drawn by . . . Rigaud highly finishd – and altho' Baron has in the writing joynd his name to both drawing and Engraving – Baron only gravd – No.3 of the large prints

View from the portico of the house	No.5.	of the small
View of Gibbs building	7.	
View of the lesser obelisk	13.	
View from Nelsons Seat	9.	

Vertue implies that the perspectives and a general plan were completed by 1736. The plan, Vertue adds, was executed by another engraver, but as it is unsigned we do not know who this was.[34] Bridgeman surely must have intended to include a plan in the series, and he may have felt all along that a draughtsman other than Rigaud would tackle it: in other words, when Rigaud came to England 'to draw views' (as Vertue put it), it was precisely this that he intended to do. And this alone.[35]

When Bridgeman died in 1738 the engravings were ready for the press. His Inventory indicates that he was 'Proprietor of the Views of Lord Cobhams Seat and Gardens Engraved on fifteen Copper Plates the Value thereof uncertain', and his widow promises that 'so soon as the same shall be disposed of she will Charge herself therewith'.[36] That Sarah Bridgeman maintained control over publication of the *Views of Stowe* is endorsed by the dedication from Sarah to Cobham set within the plan's cartouche – a gay panel surrounded by weapons and trappings of war, and containing two *putti* holding the Temple arms (*Plate 123*). Further, each of the engraved perspectives bears the inscription '*Publish'd by* S. Bridgeman *May 12.1739*' and '*Rigaud & Baron del. & sculp.*' Vertue confirms that the prints were published in 1739, and adds that the whole set was 'sold & subscribed for *four guineas*'.[37] And that is the amount Cobham himself paid when he bought two sets in

[33] *Vertue*, III (XXII), 69.

[34] *Vertue*, VI (XXX), 194. Vertue's numbering of the four prints by Baron corresponds exactly with that of the 1746 title-page, and so we may assume that the ascription to Baron of the engraving of 'No.3 of the large prints' is correct, i.e. the 'View at the Entrance between the *Pavilions*'. Rigaud had started to engrave the others in 1733. See *Vertue*, III (XXII), 69.

[35] Speculation on the authorship and dating of the general plan is endless, particularly as its eastern extensions are not shown in the perspectives. As the *Views of Stowe* were not published until at least nine months after the Royal Gardener's death, a new plan may have been prepared in the interim. Or the old one may have been altered to include the Elysian Fields. For whatever reason, no plan appears in Bridgeman's Inventory.

[36] See below Appendix V, p.167.

[37] *Vertue*, VI (XXX), 194.

the year of publication.[38] They were advertised in such newspapers as the *London Evening Post* in 1740,[39] and again in 1746.[40] In this year the remainder of the 1739 impression (which originally had cost Bridgeman more than £1,400) was sold off at half price. By then Sarah Bridgeman was dead and the original prints, if not the plates, had passed into other hands.[41]

Seen together, side by side, West's poem and Rigaud and Baron's views provide us with a lively picture of Stowe's grounds as they were in the early 1730's. By 1731–32 the western reaches of Home Park were complete, and so West's walk could take the form of a circuit (*Plate 126*). As he leads us, his comments on the dating, authorship, and meaning of the structures make a compelling counterpoint to the perspectives, almost as if the Frenchmen's overpopulous engravings were intended as a stage set for West's scenario. (*Plate 127*).[42]

[38] HEH, Stowe (Temple) Account Book, No.7 (1732–79), fo.91, where between 9 May and Michaelmas 1739 there is recorded that Cobham paid eight guineas 'for 2 setts of Stowe gardens'. For later purchases of prints (not necessarily Sarah Bridgeman's) see loose folios in the same volume, and fos 189, 210, 219, 236, 245, 267, 289.

[39] The following announcement appears seven times in the *London Evening Post* between Thursday 20 March and Saturday 19 April 1740 (Nos 1928, 1931, 1934, 1936, 1938–40):

This Day is publish'd,

A Curious Set of Prints, containing a general Plan, and fifteen Prospects of the Lord Viscount Cobham's Park and fine Gardens, at Stow in Buckinghamshire, drawn and engrav'd by a curious Hand sent for from Paris, and done by the Direction of the late Charles Bridgeman, Esq; Gardener to his Majesty; the like for their beautiful Performance never executed in England before, Price Four Guineas.

To be had of Mrs. Bridgeman at her House in Broadstreet, Soho; and Mr. Overton, Printseller, against St. Dunstan's Church in Fleet-street.

[40] The following entry occurs ten times in the *London Evening Post* between Saturday 1 March and Tuesday 3 April 1746 (Nos 2859–64, 2866, 2867, 2870, 2872):

There being a few Copies left of the first Impression of the following Work, printed on Grand Eagle Paper, formerly sold at Four Guineas in Sheets, may now be had at Two Guineas, in Sheets:

FIFTEEN Perspective Views, and a large Plan of the Gardens, at Stowe in Buckinghamshire, belonging to the Right Hon. the Lord Viscount Cobham, laid out by

Mr. BRIDGMAN,

Principal Gardener to their Majesties King George I. and II.

Mr. Bridgman *being desirous to exhibit to the Publick these fine Gardens, procur'd (at a very great Expence) that celebrated Artist in Perspective, Mons.* Rigaud, *to come over from Paris, to draw the several Views on the Spot, and employ'd Mons.* Barnard Baron *to engrave the same, which for the Grandeur and Delicacy of the Performance, exceeds any Thing hitherto attempted of the Kind.*

N.B. This Grand Set of Prints cost Mr. Bridgman upward of 1400 l.

Sold by T. Bowles, Printseller, in St. Paul's Church-Yard; J. Bowles, Printseller, in Cornhill; C. Hitch, Bookseller, in Pater-noster-Row, and W. H. Toms, in Union-Court, Holborn.

[41] There was every incentive for Sarah Bridgeman to sell the prints, if only to provide herself with much needed money. Bridgeman's lavish expenditure in employing Rigaud and Baron meant that he would have had to sell at least 334 sets of engravings at four guineas a set simply to recoup his basic costs. Financially the *Views of Stowe* must have been a disaster.

[42] Although occasionally he may be guilty of anticipating the completion of several buildings, West is a reliable guide. Some of the structures he describes have since been demolished, others renamed, rebuilt, or removed, but recent research has endorsed the accuracy of his attributions.

West's route is that taken by a typical visitor to Stowe. In brief, we start from the south front of the house, make a circuit of Home Park, and leave by the Boycott Pavilions.[43] So, having absorbed Rigaud's 'View of the *Perterre* from the *Portico* of the *House*' (*Plate 129*), we quickly proceed down the terrace until we can command a 'View of the *House* from the *Parterre*' (*Plate 130*). Here, in West's words,

In a green Niche's over-arching Shrine,
Each tuneful Goddess shrouds her Form divine.
Beneath, in the wide Area's middle Space,
A jetting Fount its chrystal Flood displays.
In whose clear Face again reflected shine
Pierian Phoebus, and the Virgin Nine.
Here too for ever bloom th'*Aonian* Bays,
Ordain'd the Meed of tuneful Poets Lays.
In seemly Order *They* on either Hand,
Alternate in the verdant Arches stand. (pp.3–4)

Once we have descended past Stowe Church and 'thro' the Windings of the mazy Wood' we emerge to find a 'View of the *Great Bason*, from the Entrance of the *Great Walk* to the *House*' (*Plate 131*). Walking on to the Lake Pavilions we turn to see the south front in the distance, at the top of the Abele Walk, as in the 'View at the Entrance between the *Pavillions*' (*Plate 132*). Here

. . . two *Dorick* Edifices grace
An elevated *Platform*'s utmost Space;
From whence, beyond the Brook that creeps below,
Along yon beauteous Hill's green sloping Brow,
The Garden's destin'd Boundaries extend,
Where *Cobham*'s pleasing Toils, tho' late, shall end. (p.6)

From the Lake Pavilions we move westwards on the south side of the Eleven-Acre Lake, along Pegg's Terrace, until we see that

Fair on the Brow, a spacious Building stands,
Th'applauded Work of *Kent*'s judicious Hands:
The spreading Wings in arched Circles bend,
And rustick Domes each arched Circle end. (p.7)

This is Kent's Temple of Venus, and it is from this spot that Rigaud's 'View of such parts as are seen from the *Building* at the *Head* of the *Lake*' is taken (*Plate 133*). After backtracking in order to glance at Kent's ruinous Hermitage,[44] West takes us past a 'View from the

[43] West's route is charted in Michael Gibbon, 'Gilbert West's Walk Through the Gardens in 1731', *Stoic*, XXIV (March 1970), 57–64. The complete text of the poem is in Hunt and Willis, eds, *Genius of the Place*, pp. 215–27.

[44] Whether or not West saw the Hermitage is a mystery, as he mistakenly says that it (not the Temple of Venus) was decorated by Sleter with illustrations from the *Faerie Queene*. At Stowe the Chinese House, Palladian Bridge, Imperial Closet, Temple of Friendship, Lady's Temple, and various interior rooms were also painted by Sleter, and he worked to good effect at such houses as Canons, Grimsthorpe, Mereworth, and Moor Park. See Croft-Murray, *Decorative Painting in England*, II, 18–20, 30, 277–79. The Temple of Bacchus was decorated by Nollekens, who may have painted the seasons on the walls of the lake house (or Russian farm) at Wanstead. See ibid., II, 249.

Head of the *Lake*' (*Plate 134*) and on to Gibbs's Building with its neighbouring statues of British Worthies, visible on the right of the 'View from *Gibbs's Building*' (*Plate 135*). West dwells at length on the achievements of this 'sacred Band / Of Princes, Patriots, Bards, and Sages',[45] before eventually ensuring that we catch a 'View from the foot of the *Pyramid*' (*Plate 136*). Rigaud's 'View from the *Brick Temple*' (*Plate 137*) is our next stopping-place, and here – emerging unscathed from the woodland's temptations – we look out from Lady Temple's Spinney towards the distant Home Park. The 'View at the *Lesser Obelisk*' (*Plate 138*) emphasizes the spectacular siting of the Obelisk just off the line of the Great Cross Walk. At last we come to the 'View of the *Queen's Theatre* from the *Rotunda*' (*Plate 139*), and its complementary 'View at the *Queen's Statue*' (*Plate 140*). West tellingly stresses the Rotunda's central place in Stowe's varied landscape:

Shift now the closer Scene: and view around,
With various Beauties the wide Landskip crown'd.
Here level Glades extend their length'ning Lines,
There in just Order the deep *Quincunce* shines.
Here chrystal Lakes reflect contiguous Shades,
There distant Hills uplift their azure Heads.
Round the free *Lawn* here gadding Heifers stray,
And frisking Lambs in sportive Gambols play.
There murmur to the Wind Groves ever-green,
And inter-mingled Buildings rise between:
The Sun declin'd with milder Glory burns,
And the fair Piece with various Light adorns.
Lo! in the *Centre* of this beauteous *Scene*,
Glitters beneath her *Dome* the *Cyprian Queen*. (pp.18–19)

West's glittering '*Cyprian Queen*' was of course the gilded statue of Venus de' Medici that briefly gave Vanbrugh's Rotunda the name of the Temple of Venus. Queen Caroline's Monument and King George's Column are next observed, overlooking the Queen's Theatre and Canal. Then past the Temple of Sleep:

Forsaking now the Covert of the Maze,
Along the broader Walk's more open Space,
Pass we to where a sylvan Temple spreads
Around the *Saxon Gods*, its hallow'd Shades.[46] (p.24)

[45] The busts of British Worthies (later moved to the Temple of British Worthies in the Elysian Fields) were of Elizabeth I, Shakespeare, William III, Locke, Hampden, Bacon, Newton, and Milton. The sculptor was Rysbrack or Scheemakers. For these two sculptors see John Physick, *Designs for English Sculpture, 1680–1860* (London, 1969), esp. pp.28–34, 81–109, 110–117; Margaret Whinney, *Sculpture in Britain, 1530–1830* (Harmondsworth, 1964). Cf. Rysbrack's provision of busts of Bacon, Locke, and Newton in the Hermitage at Richmond. See above p.103n75. Scheemaker's bust of Viscount Cobham of *c.*1740 is illustrated in Margaret Whinney, *English Sculpture, 1720–1820* (London, 1971), p.61.

[46] The busts of Saxon Deities were of Sunna, Mona, Tiw, Woden, Thuner, Friga, and Seatern, and in due course were placed around the Gothic Temple on the 'beauteous Hill' where, West prophesied, Cobham's 'pleasing Toils' would end (p.6). Rysbrack was the sculptor.

Rysbrack's work may be seen at several places with Bridgeman connections, such as Badminton, Blenheim, Carshalton, Chiswick, Houghton, Kedleston, Kensington, Longford, Richmond, and Sacombe. Other statuary at Stowe was by John Nost, the Elder, and Andrew Carpenter. Many of Stowe's statues are at Anglesey Abbey in Cambridgeshire. See Michael Gibbon, 'Garden Ornaments', *Stoic*, xxv (March 1972), 62–68.

Next we glimpse a 'View from *Nelson's Seat*' (*Plate 141*), before arriving at a 'View from the *Portico* of the *House* to the *Park*' (*Plate 142*), and finally the 'View of the *House* from the *Equestrian Statue*' (*Plate 143*), which gives us our last sight of the mansion:

Behold the *good old King* in Armour clad,
Triumphant Wreaths his sacred Temples shade.
And in his gracious Aspect shine exprest,
The manly Beauties of his gentle Breast;
His Mind, sincere, benevolent and great,
Nor aw'd by *Danger*, nor with *Pow'r* elate;
For *Valour* much, but more for *Justice* known,
Brave in the Field, and *Good* upon the Throne. (p.29)

From here West escorts us to Gibbs's Boycott Pavilions and thence out of Stowe's 'enchanted ground.'[47]

Few can doubt that the essence of Rigaud and Baron's *Views of Stowe* is 'prospect, animated prospect'. Indeed Stowe seems to be a working-out of the belief propounded by Pope, and noted by Spence, that 'all the rules of gardening are reducible to three heads'.[48] Or, in the words of Pope's familiar couplet in his *Epistle to Burlington*:

He gains all points, who pleasingly confounds,
Surprizes, varies, and conceals the Bounds. (ll.55–56)

As at Hall Barn, so at Stowe it was the concealment of bounds that most impressed Lord Perceval. In fact Cobham, alert as ever to a change in taste, was doing no more than follow Addison's injunction in the *Spectator* to throw his whole estate 'into a kind of Garden by frequent Plantations' and so 'make a pretty Landskip of his own Possessions'.[49] The ha-ha at Stowe – the 'capital stroke' which made such changes possible – appears prominently in Rigaud and Baron's perspectives. It takes two principal forms, roughly corresponding to two phases in the completion of the layout.[50] The first consists of stakes projecting from horizontal slabs of turf, kept in place by hurdles, with a low hedge between the ditch and the terrace walk: this is the pattern of 'ye first stockeade ditch by ye Lime Walk' of 1719, and of the salient which was pushed out into Home Park in *c.*1720, and which can be seen in the 'View of the *Queen's Theatre* from the *Rotunda*' (*Plate 144*).[51] The second type has a

[47] Croker, ed., *Suffolk Correspondence*, II, 76. Berkeley to Mrs Howard [June 1734].

[48] Osborn, ed., *Spence's Anecdotes*, I, 254 (No. 612).

Pope was at Stowe in the summer of 1734 and so may have met Rigaud and Baron there. Bridgemanic gardens remained amongst Pope's favoured havens. 'He is actually rambling from one friends house to another. He is now att Cirencester, he came thither from my Lord Cobhams; he came to my Lord Cobhams from Mr Dormers; to Mr Dormers from London, to London from Chiswick; to Chiswick from my Farm, to my Farm from his own Garden, and he goes soon from Lord Bathursts to Lord Peterborows, after which he returns to my farm again. The Daemon of verse sticks close to him.' Williams, ed., *Swift Correspondence*, III, 242. Bolingbroke to Swift, 27 June–6 July 1734.

[49] No.414 (25 June 1712).

[50] See Clark, 'Military Gardening: Bridgeman and the Ha-Ha', *Stoic*, XXIV (December 1969), 11–15; idem, 'Military Gardening at Stowe', *C.Life*, CLI (18 May 1972), 1254–56.

[51] In 1742 Home Park was being described as a 'Field which is enclosed in a military Way, with a staked Fence'. See Defoe, *A Tour Thro' the Whole Island of Great Britain* . . ., 3rd edn (London, 1742), III, 275. A 2nd edn of Defoe had come out in 3 vols in 1738.

dry trench with a slope on the outer side and a vertical stone wall built up to ground level on the inner side: this design was used for the later perimeter ha-ha (finished about 1734) defining the terrace walks running from Nelson's Seat round to the Lake Pavilions, and evident in the 'View of such parts as are seen from the *Building* at the *Head* of the *Lake*' (*Plate 145*).[52] It was this kind of ha-ha which appeared simultaneously at such Bridgeman-Vanbrugh layouts as Blenheim and Eastbury, and at Bridgeman's own Kensington and Houghton.[53]

Ha-has are equally prominent in the general plan of 1739 accompanying the perspectives (*Plates 122, 123*), in itself a record of both past accomplishments and future aspirations. It displays many advances on Bridgeman's bird's-eye view, its most striking feature being that the gardens, as we understand them, are relegated to a small area at the bottom. Northwards beyond the Equestrian Statue of George I is the huge expanse of woodland, consisting of avenues with *ronds-points*, a lake, winding paths, and open spaces with countryside beyond. Similar to Bathurst's contemporary 'forest garden' at Cirencester, and known at Stowe Ridings, this is now partly covered by the Silverstone motor racing track. The tree-lined Roman road runs diagonally towards the Boycott Pavilions, and then turns sharply south-east to begin its circuit of the garden proper. This is cradled in an irregular bastioned pentagon (reminiscent of a Continental fortified town) with straight avenues and temples facing inwards to Home Park and the Eleven-Acre Lake, and outwards to the country. Home Park is closed to south and west, where Gibbs's Building and the Pyramid have been introduced. Except for minor discrepancies (and the exclusion of the Grecian Valley), the area to the east of the Abele Walk is indicated exactly as it was laid out, with the Elysian Fields providing us with the most radical stylistic break with what has gone before. *In toto*, the Rigaud and Baron perspectives tie in well with the general plan. The chief exception is the 'View at the Entrance between the *Pavillions*' where, to the right of the site of the Elysian Fields, there are startling omissions: no bridge can be seen near the Congreve Monument, nor is there a bastioned Hawkwell Hill and Field, and no Upper or Lower River flows into the Octagon Lake.[54]

[52] This exists today. Part of this ha-ha, along Nelson's Walk, is on the same alignment as the earlier layout depicted on Bridgeman's perspective, and may therefore be dated *c.*1720–23. Warden Hill Walk seems to have had an iron fence in the centre of a semicircular ditch.

[53] Seven years before Robinson had commented on the *fossés* at Houghton and Euston (see above p.85), Perceval had described Hall Barn, where Bridgeman may have worked. Perceval remarks that 'the walks are terminated by Ha-ha's, over which you see a fine country, and variety of prospects, every time you come to the extremity of the close winding walks that shut out the sun'. BL, Add MS 47030 (Egmont Papers), fos 147–49. Perceval to Dering, 9 August 1724.

[54] Other exceptions include the 'View from the *Head* of the *Lake*' (*Plate 134*) in which the observer might have seen the Palladian Bridge and Congreve Monument, and the confines of Hawkwell Hill and Field; the 'View from the *Brick Temple*' (*Plate 137*) in which no Temple of Sleep is evident; the 'View at the *Queen's Statue*' (*Plate 140*) in which the avenues are shown incorrectly in front of Queen Caroline's Monument; and the 'View from the *Portico* of the *House* to the *Park*' (*Plate 142*) in which the canal in front of the north front has been replaced by a circular basin. Cf. the 'View of the *House* from the *Equestrian Statue*' (*Plate 143*).

'Lord Cobham began in the Bridgeman taste', wrote Joseph Spence in his commonplace book, ''tis the Elysian Fields that is the painting part of his gardens'.[55] Whatever Spence may have meant by this statement, the general plan of 1739 indicates that the Elysian Fields were quite unlike any other part of Stowe (*Plate 148*), and this is as true today as it was in the eighteenth century. Seeley's guides give us precise descriptions and illustrations of the structures (*Plates 147a, 147b*). Approaching on foot from the Octagon Lake, we pass the Palladian Bridge and Congreve Monument on our right (*Plates 154a, 154b*), and walk upwards beside the Lower River or Serpentine, the Witch House hidden in the Witch Wood on our left. Once we have passed the Shell Bridge we enter the Elysian Fields proper. All buildings here are by Kent. Nestling in the trees on our right is the Temple of British Worthies (*Plate 153a*): facing it across the river, set on a hillock, is the Temple of Ancient Virtue (*Plate 153b*), with the Temple of Modern Virtue next to it. As we move northwards, catching sight of Stowe Church as we do so, we reach the curving Alder River which culminates in the Grotto and Shell Temples. Beyond the Elysian Fields to the east lies Gibbs's Gothic Temple, standing proud on the crown of the hill (*Plate 152b*).

The Elysian Fields were a continuation of Cobham's scheme of emblematic and expressive landscaping. 'I have no patience at building and planting a satire!' Walpole was to remark on a visit to Stowe in 1753.[56] Cobham, on the other hand, as one of Pope's 'Gardening Lords',[57] decided from the start that Stowe would express his own ideologies. Thus the gilded statue of Venus (or Aphrodite) stands in the Rotunda not only as the mother of Aeneas, the goddess of love and beauty, but also as the patroness of gardens and gardeners. Flowers and birds are sacred to her. Having invoked the goddess's blessing on what was to follow, Cobham complimented royal beauty by placing the monuments to King George and Queen Caroline close by. At Gibbs's Building a royal-political theme was taken up, for the statues of British Worthies placed there were all men and women with whom the Hanoverians would have had sympathy.[58] The Elysian Fields themselves stand firmly for Protestant Whiggery. In contrast to Julie's wild *Elisée* in *La Nouvelle Héloïse* – and consequently the target of Rousseau's criticism – the setting of the garden structures is unashamedly contrived. Cobham here presents us with an allegory of the dream described by Addison in the *Tatler* in which he walks along a straight road (represented at Stowe by the Great Cross Walk), at the end of which are Temples of Virtue

[55] Osborn, ed., *Spence's Anecdotes*, I, 423 (No.1122), quoting Southcote *c*.1752. By 'painting part' surely Spence meant that the Elysian Fields demonstrated the unity between landscape and antiquity which we associate with Claude, Poussin, and Salvator Rosa. It comes as no surprise to find Horace's oft-quoted words *ut pictura poesis* used as an epigraph to *The Triumphs of Nature*, Boyse's topographical poem on Stowe of 1742.

Mr Clarke has elaborated his ideas on the Elysian Fields in three articles in the *Stoic*: 'Moral Gardening', XXIV (July 1970), 113–21; 'Kent and the Eastern Gardens', XXIV (July 1971), 265–72; and 'Lancelot Brown's Work at Stowe', XXV (December 1971), 17–22. See also Mr Clarke's 'Grecian Taste and Gothic Virtue. Lord Cobham's Gardening Programme and Its Iconography', *Apollo*, XCVII (June 1973), 566–71. 'Stowe. Ici est né le jardin anglais', *Connaissance des Arts*, No.241 (March 1972), 66–75; 'William Kent. Heresy in Stowe's Elysium', in Willis, ed., *Furor Hortensis*, pp.48–56.

[56] *Yale Walpole*, XXXV, 76. Walpole to Chute, 4 August 1753. Although he admired the buildings themselves Walpole found the ideology rather absurd as, with Cobham's change in politics, it duly became self-contradictory.

[57] *Pope Correspondence*, IV, 459. Pope to Marchmont [July 1743].

[58] West's interpretation of Stowe's references to the monarchy was anticipated by Addison in the *Tatler*, No.161 (20 April 1710). For background see recently William A. Speck, 'Political Propaganda in Augustan England', *Royal Historical Society* (*Transactions*), S.5, XXII (1972), 17–32.

(Ancient Virtue), Honour (British Worthies), and Vanity (Modern Virtue).[59] Such allusions to antiquity point to the contrast between ancient principles of government and the corruption of Sir Robert Walpole's administration.[60] Consequently the Temple of Ancient Virtue, with its four statues of Greek heroes, is described as 'in a very flourishing condition', whilst the ruins and headless statue close to them (Walpole himself, no less) are 'intended to show us the shattered state of Modern Virtue'.[61] The Lower River is to be seen as the Styx, and the Temple of British Worthies (wilfully placed on the opposite bank to Ancient Virtue) contains the busts of those Britons who were worthy to be compared with the Ancients, with the god Mercury in their centre waiting to lead their souls to Elysium. Across the ha-ha to the east of British Worthies is Hawkwell Hill and Field, its Arcadian simplicity recalling Bridgeman's rustic scenes in Home Park, and Southcote's *ferme ornée* at Woburn.

Who was responsible for the landscaping of the Elysian Fields? Here again Cobham's lively imagination must have been stimulated by the interest of Pope and of such enlightened relatives as Gilbert West, George Lyttelton, William Pitt, and Richard Grenville. Grenville – Cobham's nephew, who succeeded to Stowe on his uncle's death in 1749 and became Earl Temple in 1752 – had returned from the Grand Tour in 1732 full of enthusiasm for architecture and archaeology, and two years later he emerged as a founder-member of the Society of Dilettanti begun by Francis Dashwood, lord of the neighbouring seat of West Wycombe and self-styled Prior of Medmenham Abbey. Descriptions of contemporary visitors,[62] and other evidence, suggests that the 1739 general plan is an authentic record of what was actually carried out on the ground. The Elysian Fields themselves were started only after the whole area east of the Hey Way had been enclosed according to Bridgeman's overall design:[63] in other words they were not begun until after Rigaud and Baron had completed their perspectives, and after Cobham had broken with Walpole over the Excise Bill in 1733. Already Bridgeman and Kent may have toyed with similar ideas at, say, Chiswick and Rousham. Moreover in 1734 Aaron Hill, dramatist and friend of Pope, had proposed his Moral Garden climaxed by a Temple of Happiness.[64] Stylistically

[59] No.123 (21 January 1710), an elaboration of essays in Nos 67, 81. Addison takes his cue for the Vale of Tempe from his *Remarks on Several Parts of Italy, Etc., in the Years 1701, 1702, 1703* (London, 1705), pp.368–73. See Clarke, 'Moral Gardening', 113–21; idem, 'Kent and the Eastern Gardens', 265–71; John Dixon Hunt, 'Emblem and Expressionism in the Eighteenth-Century Landscape Garden', *Eighteenth-Century Studies*, IV (1971), 294–317. Parallels between Stowe and Pope's garden at Twickenham are considered in idem, '"What's Water but the Generated Soul?" The Metaphysics of Water in the Landscape Garden', *Garden History Society Occasional Papers*, No.2 (1970), 3–17.

[60] The chief mouthpiece of the Opposition was Bolingbroke's journal the *Craftsman*, founded with the express purpose of attacking Sir Robert Walpole (the 'man of craft') and promoting Frederick, Prince of Wales, who, it was hoped, would become Frederick I on the death of George II.

[61] The four statues inside the Temple of Ancient Virtue were by Scheemakers and were of Homer, Socrates, Lycurgus, and Epaminondas – chosen respectively as the greatest poet, philosopher, law-giver, and general of the ancient world.

In 'Grecian Taste and Gothic Virtue', 568, Mr Clarke traces the connection between Cobham's iconography and Temple Stanyan, *Grecian History* (London, 1707, 1739).

[62] See the anonymous 'Account of the Journey yt Mr Hardness & I took in July 1735', in BL, Add MS 15776, fos 1–10. An illustrated record of a visit to Stowe by another traveller, journeying from 7 June to 9 July 1742, is in BL, Add MS 22926, fos 65–71. Cf. descriptions of two visits in 1751 and 1756 by Dr Pococke in James Joel Cartwright, ed., *The Travels Through England of Dr. Richard Pococke . . . During 1750, 1751, and Later Years* (London, 1888–89), I, 165–66; II, 240–41.

[63] Conjectured by George B. Clarke, 'The Gardens of Stowe', *Apollo*, XCVII (June 1973), 562.

[64] See Watkin, *Thomas Hope*, pp.148–51.

the siting and design of Kent's buildings in the Elysian Fields must have drawn inspiration from Italian gardens made familiar through prints and paintings and visited by Kent and Burlington whilst in Italy: the siting of Kent's Temple of Ancient Virtue stems from that of the Temple of the Sibyl set above the gorge at Tivoli,[65] his Temple of British Worthies from such settings as that of the Roman Emperors at the Villa Brenzone at San Vigilio on Lake Garda (*Plate 177b*),[66] whilst the Elysian Fields are an obvious reference to those Roman sacred landscapes which drew their significance from the religious buildings set in them.

By the mid-1730's Bridgeman and Kent had probably gone from Stowe. Bridgeman's health was failing, and dropsy incapacitating him for all but the lightest and least demanding work. Both men were now more closely allied to royalty – Bridgeman through the royal gardens, Kent through his appointment as Master Mason and Deputy Surveyor in 1735, and his labours for Queen Caroline – and could hardly remain close to Cobham's Boy Patriots as they increased their antagonism to George II and Sir Robert Walpole. It was never too late in the day for change, and Bridgeman and Kent apparently left.

Expansion 1741–53

At the end of the 1730's the Bridgeman–Vanbrugh areas at Stowe were maturing, the Elysian Fields were all but complete, and plans were afoot for extensions of the layout to the north east. It was here – after Frederick, Prince of Wales, had ostentatiously paid a visit to Stowe in 1737 – that the climax of the Bridgeman–Kent proposals was reached. At the southern end of Hawkwell Field the Temple of Friendship confirmed Cobham's allegiance to Prince Frederick, whilst at the northern end the Lady's Temple confirmed his allegiance to Lady Cobham. Midway between was that last trumpet-call of Liberty, Enlightenment, and the Constitution – the Gothic Temple, Gibbs's most original and spectacular building at Stowe. Gibbs had replaced Kent as Cobham's principal architect, and now entered a second phase of activity,[67] as Cobham laid out the Grecian Valley as a Vale of Tempe, with the Lady's Temple, Cobham Monument, and Grecian Temple (almost certainly designed by Richard Grenville) strategically located in it.[68] Cobham's

[65] The Temple of Ancient Virtue is Ionic, whereas the Temple of the Sibyl is Corinthian. See Clarke, 'Grecian Taste and Gothic Virtue', 567–68; idem, 'Moral Gardening', 116.

[66] See Masson, *Italian Gardens*, pp.25–26, 205–6. In addition Kent seems to have designed the gate between the Boycott Pavilions, the Shell Bridge, Pebble Alcove, Temple of Contemplation, and the Congreve Monument.

[67] With the exception of the Palladian Bridge and the Grecian Temple, all buildings at Stowe completed between 1738 and Borra's arrival in 1752 have been ascribed to Gibbs: the Temple of Friendship, Imperial Closet, Gothic Temple, Stowe Castle and the Keeper's Lodge, Cobham's Pillar, and the Queen's Temple (or Lady's Temple) which echoes one of Gibbs's temples for the bowling green at Down Hall (*Plate 68*). See Michael Gibbon, 'Lord Cobham's Garden Buildings II', *Stoic*, XXIV (March 1971), 209–15.

Cobham may have employed Flitcroft, perhaps for decorating the state gallery. Payment of six guineas 'To Mr Flintcroft a present' is recorded by Cobham in HEH, Stowe (Temple) Account Book, No.130 (1735–41), 17 May 1737. See Desmond Fitz-Gerald, 'A History of the Interior of Stowe', *Apollo*, XCVII (June 1973), 574; Michael Gibbon, 'Lord Cobham's House', *Stoic*, XXIII (December 1968), 62.

[68] Richard Grenville's authorship is argued by Michael Gibbon, 'Earl Temple and Giambattista Borra', *Stoic*, XXV (July 1973), 201–2, and Michael McCarthy, 'Eighteenth-Century Amateur Architects and Their Gardens', in Pevsner, ed., *The Picturesque Garden*, pp.31–55.

right-hand man for the landscaping of the Grecian Valley was Lancelot Brown.[69] Perhaps prompted by Bridgeman's death in 1738, and the realization that a successor would be needed, Brown had left the service of Sir William Lorraine at Kirkharle in Northumberland to seek his fame and fortune in the south of England. Brown had a happy knack of establishing good relationships with his clients, and Cobham was no exception. Brown began as head gardener at Stowe in 1741, and within twelve months or so was clerk of works. We know enough of his activities between 1741 and his departure for Croome Court in 1751 to take seriously Repton's claim that Brown himself designed several of Stowe's buildings.[70] Cobham lent Brown to advise at Newnham Paddox in Warwickshire, and had Cobham lived he surely would have asked Brown to help him develop Stowe Ridings.[71]

Hardly was Brown established before the guides to Stowe started to come out: the year 1742 saw the appearance of both Boyse's poem *The Triumphs of Nature* in the *Gentleman's Magazine*, and the Appendix to the third edition of Defoe's *Tour Thro' the Whole Island of Great Britain*. In 1744 we have the earliest of many versions of Seeley's *Description of the Gardens of Lord Viscount Cobham at, Stow*, rivalled only by Bickham's *Beauties of Stow* of 1750 onwards.[72] By this juncture Gilpin had brought out his *Dialogue Upon the Gardens . . . at Stowe* of 1748, based upon a conversation between the 'enthusiasts' Polypthon and Callophilus who, walking solemnly round the grounds, found a moral in every building and a picture in every view.[73]

The changes wrought or proposed since Rigaud and Baron's day can be seen in Bickham and Chatelain's sixteen perspectives for the *Views of Stowe* of 1753.[74] The value of

[69] See Clarke, 'Lancelot Brown's Work at Stowe', 17–22; Stroud, *Capability Brown*, 3rd edn (1975), pp.47–55. Brown's pay was £25 a year in wages, plus £9 a year for board. In 1744 he was married in Stowe Church.

[70] Humphry Repton, *Observations on the Theory and Practice of Landscape Gardening* . . . (London, 1803), p.168.

[71] When Charles Cathcart, 8th Baron Cathcart, stayed with Cobham in 1730, he visited Stowe Ridings, but in spite of what had already been achieved there he felt that what remained to be done would be '*le plus noble de toute*'. See Earl Cathcart Collection, London, MS Cathcart Diaries, 18–19 August 1730, cited by permission of the present Earl Cathcart. I owe this reference to Dr William Brogden.

[72] For these and later editions see Harris, 'Country House Guides', pp.58–74; Stevenson, *Catalogue of Botanical Books*, pt. 2, 229–31; Wimsatt, *Portraits of Pope*, pp.134–36.

[73] Appropriately enough this was Gilpin's first analysis of landscape according to picturesque principles. See Carl P. Barbier, *William Gilpin. His Drawings, Teaching, and Theory of the Picturesque* (Oxford, 1963), pp.21–23, 26, 108–9, 115; William D. Templeman, *The Life and Work of William Gilpin (1724–1804), Master of the Picturesque and Vicar of Boldre* (Urbana, 1939), pp.34–35, 117–30.

The Gothic Temple, begun in 1741, was completed two years after Gilpin wrote. With its command of a circle of views it fulfilled the same function as Vanbrugh's Rotunda had done twenty-five years before. It was the ideological climax to Cobham's gardening.

[74] They were drawn by Jean Baptiste Claude Chatelain, engraved by George Bickham, the Younger, and published by George Bickham, the Elder. For other eighteenth-century plans of Stowe see Clarke, 'The Gardens of Stowe', 18–25.

Unlike the fifteen Rigaud and Baron perspectives, Bickham and Chatelain's engravings are each of identical size. As before, there is English and French titling, and many of the viewpoints are the same. On 24 June 1735 the Act of Parliament was passed protecting engravers and others against piracy for a period of fourteen years. Could it be that Bickham and Chatelain had waited precisely this length of time (from 1739 to 1753) after the publication of Rigaud and Baron's plates?

A small painting in gouache on vellum of 'A View of the Grotto & two Shell Temples', probably by the French painter and stage designer William Delacour, is discussed and reproduced in *C.Life*, CXLVI (27 November 1969), 1382. See John Fleming, 'Enigma of a Rococo Artist', *C.Life*, CXXXII (24 May 1962), 1224–46.

this series is twofold: it illustrates familiar buildings set in an increasingly free landscape, and it shows us new parts of the layout for the first time. The new general plan (*Plate 146*) retains the overall configuration of the earlier version (*Plate 123*), but with softer lines and contours: several ha-has have vanished, a lawn replaces the Parterre, and the shape of the Eleven-Acre Lake has become almost fluid. The Elysian Fields, now that their eastern ha-ha has vanished, merge almost imperceptibly into Hawkwell Hill and Field, dominated by the Gothic Temple.[75] Such alterations are readily seen in the accompanying perspectives. Thus 'A View from the Temple of Diana', when compared to its earlier counterpart (*Plate 150a*), points to revisions in the temple itself, the levelling of ha-has, the removal of the statuary (to the Temple of British Worthies), and the looser treatment of the Eleven-Acre Lake; a similar comparison can be made in the case of 'A View of the Queen's Theatre from the Rotundo' (*Plate 150b*), where the later perspective emphasizes Borra's amendments to Vanbrugh's Rotunda. Few alterations are so radical as those in the eastern precinct, although here again political embarrassment has led Bickham and Chatelain to exclude the Elysian Fields themselves. We have to be content with two engravings of the upper and lower reaches: 'A View to the Grotto of the Serpentine River in the Alder Grove' (*Plate 151a*), showing the Grotto, Shell Temples, and Cold Bath, all probably designed by Kent in the 1730's; and 'A View in the Elysian Fields, from the Spring of Helicon' (*Plate 151b*), illustrating a gently undulating landscape in which are set the Palladian Bridge, the Temple of Friendship, and the Spring of Helicon surrounded by Apollo and the Nine Muses. Gone completely now is much of what George Lyttelton called 'the stiffness of the old Bridgeman Taste'.[76]

Once Earl Temple succeeded to Stowe in 1749 on his uncle's death, the character of the gardens became even less Bridgemanic. Borra was the first of a group of foreign architects who were called in, and his hand is apparent in alterations to the Boycott Pavilions and the Rotunda.[77] The most far-reaching step was the cutting down of the Abele Walk in 1762. Other alterations followed rapidly: the Octagon Lake was made less formal, the Lake Pavilions resited further apart, and in 1765 Earl Temple's cousin Thomas Pitt designed the Corinthian Arch as a focal point on the southern horizon (*Plate 155a*). Four years previously, in 1761, the Oxford Bridge had been built spanning over the Oxford Water, forming a handsome approach to the house past the Boycott Pavilions (*Plate 155b*). Capability Brown had left Stowe in 1751, and Earl Temple himself must be credited with these and other progressive schemes of the 1750's and 1760's. After all, Temple had been born and bred at Wotton, a house famous for its enterprising landscape. Wootton was built between 1704 and 1714 for Richard Grenville, whose wife Hester (*née*

[75] As Mr Clarke has observed, Bickham represents the buildings and walks as *inside* Hawkwell Hill and Field, with the ha-ha on the *outside* of its eastern limits.

[76] HEH, MS MO.1335. Mrs Lyttelton to Mrs Elizabeth Montagu, 24 September 1765. I owe this to Mr Geoffrey Beard. For a perceptive visual analysis of the grounds at Stowe see Sylvia Crowe, *Garden Design* (London, 1958), pp.55–64.

[77] From 1765 Georges-François Blondel was engaged until succeeded by Vincenzo Valdré. Robert Adam was busy at Stowe in 1770–71. See Gibbon, 'Earl Temple and Giambattista Borra', 201–5.

Temple) was Cobham's sister,[78] and its layout has several features similar to those found at Stowe – twin lakes with a bridge, a Turkish temple, Chinese summer house, grotto, rotunda, and a pair of lake pavilions which still stand. Comings and goings between Stowe and Wotton were frequent, and it is not inconceivable that Bridgeman was involved in the early layout at Wotton.[79]

Bridgeman must have met many of the friends and relatives of the Temple family as they came and drew inspiration from Stowe's '*Poetick Plan*', and indeed Rigaud and Baron may well have included them among the elegant members of society populating their perspectives. Visitors were almost universal in their praise: Thomson was not alone in regarding Stowe as a 'fair majestic paradise'.[80] If other poets' verse was often little better than doggerel, there was no question about its meaning. Listen to the elder Nathaniel Cotton in his poem *On Lord Cobham's Garden*:

It puzzles much the sages' brains,
Where Eden stood of yore;
Some place it in Arabia's plains,
Some say it is no more.

But Cobham can these tales confute,
As all the curious know;
For he hath prov'd, beyond dispute,
That Paradise is Stow.[81]

In a letter to Harley's daughter Margaret, Duchess of Portland, Mrs Elizabeth Montagu wrote in similar vein in 1744. Stowe, she said, is 'beyond description, it gives the best idea of Paradise that can be; even Milton's images and descriptions fall short of it'. In contrast to a stroll in Kensington Gardens or down the Mall, she continued, 'at Stowe you walk amidst Heroes and Deities, powers and persons whom we have been taught to honour, who have embellished the world with arts, or instructed it in Science, defended their country and improved it'.[82] This was Bridgeman's style at its most suggestive. Over a

78 Another of Cobham's sisters, Christian, married Sir Thomas Lyttelton (1688–1751), and their son George, 1st Baron Lyttelton (1709–73), was the moving spirit behind the creation of Hagley from *c.*1743. Here was Sanderson Miller's castle, Stuart's Doric temple, the Prince of Wales's column, an obelisk, Palladian bridge, grotto, cascade, hermitage, statue of Venus, and a rotunda, not to mention urns commemorating Pope and Shenstone, and seats to Milton and Thomson. A passage in the *Seasons* (Spring, ll.904–62) describes Hagley. Henry Hoare II was among the many celebrated visitors to the house: George Lyttelton's niece, Hester Lyttelton, married Richard Colt Hoare in 1783.

Sanderson Miller was related to the Temple family and *persona grata* at Stowe. See Anthony C. Wood and William Hawkes, *Sanderson Miller of Radway* (forthcoming). At Radway, Miller was neighbour to the Temple property of Burton Dassett in Warwickshire.

79 For early years of the estate see Maurice Beresford, *History on the Ground. Six Studies in Maps and Landscapes*, 2nd edn (London, 1971), pp.225–28. The later years at Stowe are considered by Mr Clarke and Mr Gibbon in subsequent issues of the *Stoic*.

80 *Seasons*, Autumn, l.1042. The passage on Stowe (Autumn, ll.1037–81) was introduced in the 1744 edition. See Ralph Cohen, *The Unfolding of 'The Seasons'* (London, 1970), pp.225–26.

81 *The Poetical Works of Nathaniel Cotton*, ed. Thomas Park (London, 1806), p.126.

82 Emily J. Climenson, *Elizabeth Montagu. The Queen of the Blue Stockings. Her Correspondence, 1720–61* (London, 1906), I, 189. Mrs Montagu to the Duchess of Portland, 9 August 1744. Cf. BL, Add MS 22926 (Tour in England, 1742), fos 125–37.

quarter of a century later, when Horace Walpole penned his impressions of Stowe on the occasion of Princess Amelia's visit in 1770, the Elysian Fields came in for lavish praise. Here the new Doric arch dedicated to Amelia framed 'a tall landscape . . . [with] over-bowering trees, and comprehending more beauties of light, shade and buildings, than any picture of Albano'. The total effect was captivating. 'Every acre', Walpole exclaimed, 'brings to one's mind some instance of parts or pedantry, of the taste or want of taste, of the ambition, or love of fame, or greatness, or miscarriages of those that have inhabited, decorated, planned or visited the place.' More than that. 'All these images crowd upon one's memory and add visionary personages to the charming scenes, that are so enriched with fanes and temples, that the real prospects are little less than visions.'[83] Praise indeed.[84]

[83] *Yale Walpole*, x, 314–15. Walpole to Montagu, 7 July 1770. Whately's impressions about the same time are in his *Observations on Modern Gardening* (Dublin, 1770), pp.170–81, 194–96.

[84] Also in Buckinghamshire was Lord Orkney's seat at Cliveden. Recent research by Mr Gervase Jackson-Stops (kindly communicated to me in advance of publication) shows that Bridgeman worked there. See Mr Jackson-Stops' two articles, 'Formal Garden Designs for Cliveden: the Work of Claude Desgots and Others for the 1st Earl of Orkney', *The National Trust Year Book, 1976–77* (London, 1976), pp.100–117, and 'Cliveden, Buckinghamshire', *C.Life*, CLXI (3 March 1977), 498–501.

Conclusion

The character of Stowe, and the limitations of our historical evidence, make it impossible to define the individual contributions of its landscape designers, architects, painters, and sculptors.[1] Nonetheless, Stowe does demonstrate again that Bridgeman was a man of wide-ranging abilities, combining membership of the 'Virtuoso-Class' (to use Pope's words)[2] with a down-to-earth knowledge and experience of practical matters. There seems little doubt that at Stowe and elsewhere Bridgeman's clients often took day-to-day responsibility for laying out their estates, although – as the Royal Gardener's appearance in Hogarth's *Rake's Progress* suggests – improvers must have realized that a reckless passion for landscaping could lead to financial ruin. On the other hand few would have denied that the new style admirably suited the needs of fox hunting, and that turf and woodland were easier and less expensive to maintain than box hedges, parterres, and topiary. Viscount Cobham surely understood this as well as anyone. More than that, he was a man of discrimination and taste, and – to use Switzer's description of the Earl of Carlisle – a 'truly Ingenious Lover of Architecture and Gard'ning'.[3]

Bridgeman's work at Stowe adds immeasurably to our total picture of him as a landscapist. His responsibilities, it seems, varied from simply providing trees at Briggens and other places, to planning 'the whole' and having the 'direction & disposition of the Gardens' at Stowe.[4] Between these two extremes, he might be asked to make a survey (as with Fen drainage), to express his opinion on general proposals (as at Kedleston), or to draw 'two or three Schemes of different designes' (as at King's College, Cambridge).[5] Bridgeman's Royal Appointment required him to provide his own 'Working Tools & Materials', to ensure that the royal gardens were 'maintained, Kept & Upheld', and to tackle such menial tasks as keeping the borders in the Maestricht Garden at Windsor 'clean from Weeds, & Cultivated with Dung as often as is necessary for the Benefit of the several Fruit Trees'.[6] Maintenance of such private gardens as Compton Place and Montagu House must have been less arduous and more pleasant, and perhaps involved no more than the offering of occasional advice to the owners. Not that Bridgeman avoided wider commitments: Lord Perceval implied that once Bridgeman was given his brief, the job would be done speedily, and Henrietta Howard indicated that the gardens at Amesbury

[1] Our understanding of Bridgeman's work is hindered by the absence of a plan of Stowe signed by him. Not that we should put too much store by the drawings which bear Bridgeman's signature, for the words 'Discript.', 'FEC^{t}' and 'Pinxit' on the respective cartouches of his plans of Blenheim, Windsor Forest, and Hampton Court (*Plates 162a, 163a, 163b*) tell us nothing about what the Royal Gardener actually did on the ground.

[2] *Pope Correspondence*, II, 264. Pope to Edward Harley, 8 October 1724.

[3] Switzer, *Ichnographia Rustica* (1718), I, 87.

[4] BL, Add MS 47030 (Egmont Papers), fo.158. Perceval to Dering, 14 August 1724; *Vertue*, III (XXII), 133.

[5] King's College, Cambridge, Congregation Book, 1722–78, fo.12.

[6] See below Appendix III, p.154.

were 'kept as they ought to be, and at a very reasonable expense'.[7] It was Bridgeman's custom, the Duchess of Marlborough reminded Mrs Sarah Bridgeman in 1741, to employ a man to look after a garden for a year after its completion – a practice not dissimilar from that of a twentieth-century landscape contractor. And even though the Duchess found Bridgeman expensive, she had sufficient confidence in his ability and integrity to advance him money. 'I did believe Mr: Bridgman honest and meant to do justly in every thing', she wrote to his widow. 'I had a Kindness for him, and upon his Account would agree to do any thing that was tolerably reasonable.'[8]

Wherever Bridgeman was working, and in whatever capacity, tree-planting was frequently involved. He shared Wise and Switzer's affection for elms, and used them at Richmond for the Queen's Private Road and Merlin's Hill, for the Broad Walk at Kensington, the Elm Walk at Rousham, and the main avenue at Wimpole. At Stowe the 'new Elm Walk' ran alongside Nelson's Walk.[9] Elms notwithstanding, variety was more often the order of the day: aloes and cedars of Lebanon in the royal gardens, beeches for the great avenue at Blenheim, horse-chestnuts at Marble Hill, yews at Tring, and at Eastbury a 'vast Collection of foreign Trees of various Kinds'.[10] However, if we are to believe Gilbert West, Stowe rather than Eastbury possessed the most species: in the 'tufted', 'ever-green' and 'nodding Groves' there were white poplars in the Abele Walk, in the wood around the Temple of Sleep, and in the Queen's Theatre; there were pines here too, firs near Nelson's Seat, and 'high Firs' and 'mournful Yews' near Gibbs's Building. '*British* Oaks' ('loose groves of oak' as Walpole termed them) flanked the Temple of Bacchus, whilst close to the house the Parterre had 'odorous Flowers', and the neighbouring Orangery contained '*Hesperian* Oranges'. The ubiquitous clipped hedges were of 'shining laurel' and, as if to emphasize its special function, the Great Cross Walk was of limes. Not that Rigaud and Baron were over-concerned about the exact species at Stowe: the firs and yew which stood near Gibbs's Building, for example, are not shown as coniferous (*Plate 135*), nor are the poplars and pines in the Queen's Theatre drawn as two distinct species (*Plate 144*). Many of the trees at Stowe must have been mature when transplanted, for only in this way could Cobham have hoped to see his efforts rewarded in his lifetime: by the 1720's and 1730's the technique of transplanting large trees was well understood and much used to provide 'instant' effects. Sometimes thinning rather than planting was needed to produce the required result, such as in parts of Blenheim where Bridgeman removed 'a few English

[7] Croker, ed., *Suffolk Correspondence*, I, 386–87. Mrs Howard to Gay, 22 August [1730].

[8] See below Appendix IV(vi), p.159.

[9] The Swedish naturalist Pehr Kalm, visiting London in 1748, remarked: 'There is scarcely any tree which is so much planted in England as the elm-tree; so that it can, in a certain way, be called the Englishman's *favorite tree*. I saw great numbers of them in London, and just outside the town. Nearly all the squares in London were planted round with it. The *Allees* in *St. James's Park*, outside the Royal Palace, were only and solely of this tree, excepting that by the water there were willows'. Joseph Lucas, trans., *Kalm's Account of His Visit to England on His Way to America in 1748* (London and New York, 1892), p.86.

[10] Defoe, *A Tour Thro' the Whole Island of Great Britain*, 3rd edn (1742), III, 299.

Elms, and Hedges',[11] or at Woburn where he spent time marking the trees 'to be cut down'.[12]

Bridgeman as a Designer

Any assessment of Bridgeman as a designer must begin with Horace Walpole, whose analysis of the Royal Gardener's style, though brief, is the most comprehensive we have and worth restating. It will be recalled that Walpole regarded Bridgeman as 'the next fashionable designer of gardens' after London and Wise, but observed that although Bridgeman was 'far more chaste' than his predecessors he still 'adhered much to strait walks with high clipped hedges' for his 'great lines' stretching 'out of one into another without intermission'.[13] However such characteristics, Walpole went on, are quite secondary to Bridgeman's 'many detached thoughts, that strongly indicate the dawn of modern taste', his introduction of 'cultivated fields, and even morsels of a forest appearance', and his use of the 'simple enchantment' of the ha-ha which 'pointed out new beauties and inspired new ideas'. Walpole's remarks demand careful scrutiny, and any attempt to test their validity must rest on three sources: on letters, guides, gardening books, and travellers' descriptions; on Bridgeman's signed plans and those which may be attributed to him; and on contemporary engravings, paintings, water-colours and drawings of Bridgeman gardens. In its turn such an examination will illuminate the relationship between Bridgeman's ideas and those of Vanbrugh, Switzer, Kent, and their successors.

Two general characteristics of Bridgeman's work – both endorsed by Switzer as well as Walpole – may be singled out: first his concern for the *genius loci*, and second his predisposition for vastness of scale. Although Walpole thought of Bridgeman as a 'reformer' and 'innovator', the most popular description of him is as an 'ingenious designer',[14] and it is ingenuity, arguably, which provides us with a key to Bridgeman's designs. For he was fundamentally a pragmatist, exploring the genius of every place. No two of his schemes were alike. Bridgeman responded to the limitations and opportunities of his brief, whether he were producing a scheme for Amesbury (*Plate 36*) which owed its character to the

[11] See below Appendix IV (vi), p.158.

[12] Bedford Office, London, Woburn MSS, HMC No.62. Memorandum Book of John, 4th Duke of Bedford, fo.5.

Bridgeman, despite his practical turn of mind, seems to have kept his horticultural and botanical contemporaries at bay. He was not a member of the Society of Gardeners founded in the 1720's by Philip Miller, Curator of the Chelsea Physick Garden, nor did he subscribe to Miller's *Gardener's Dictionary* of 1731 onwards. Similarly we have no evidence at present that Bridgeman took any interest in the experiments, discoveries and publications of such plantsmen as Bradley, Fairchild, Lawrence, and Sir Hans Sloane.

Mr Harvey has illuminated the role of nurseries in his chapter 'The Age of Planting' in *Early Gardening Catalogues* (London and Chichester, 1972), pp.24–34.

[13] This and succeeding quotations are from Chase, *Horace Walpole: Gardenist*, pp.24–25.

[14] In 1725, for instance, Campbell in *Vitruvius Britannicus*, III, p.[7], describes Eastbury as 'designed and finished by the ingenious Mr. *Charles Bridgeman*'; in 1729 Switzer in his *Introduction to a General System of Hydrostaticks and Hydraulicks*, II, 405, says that the amphitheatre at Claremont was 'the Design of the very ingenious Mr Bridgeman'; in 1733 Christian Cole, writing about Woburn to Diana, Duchess of Bedford, on 20 December, refers to Bridgeman as 'that Ingenious gardener' (Bedford Office, London, Woburn MSS, HMC No.8, Vol.VIII, Item 52).

topography recorded by Flitcroft in 1726 (*Plate 164*), for Stowe where his 'great lines' gave cohesion to the plan, or for Sacombe where he preserved the painterly qualities of the views. In Switzer's words, it was a matter of 'adapting the whole to the Nature and Uses of the Place'[15] – an intepretation which was always subject to change, such as at Claremont where the bowling green of Bridgeman's day (*Plate 165b*) was replaced later by Kent's freer treatment (*Plate 165a*). The 'Uses of the Place' often demanded that Bridgeman provide appropriate settings for country seats such as Bower House, Down Hall and Marble Hill, which were set firmly in the tradition of the classical villa espoused by the Burlingtonians and promoted by Robert Morris in the spirit of Nourse, Switzer and Castell. From such a villa 'many agreeable Views might be had to distant Objects', wrote Morris. '. . . The ancient *Romans* planted their Plots in this *rural* manner', he went on, 'and their *Temples*, dedicated to their peculiar GODS, were dispersed among the *Groves* and *Woods*, which Art or Nature had made, with *Vistas* to them'.[16]

In his poem 'A Hue and Cry' of 1721 Sir James Thornhill remarks that Bridgeman could make 'water for miles altogether' and 'Mountains that reach God knows whither'.[17] Similarly Pope points to Bridgeman's habit of replacing 'vast parterres' by lakes,[18] though in 'A Master Key to Popery' he is at pains to deny the 'Malicious Representation' that Bridgeman takes pleasure in destroying and overflowing 'Gentlemens fine Gardens'.[19] To Switzer such comments are symptomatic of Bridgeman's belief that 'true Greatness consists in Size and Dimension'. 'This aiming at an incomprehensible Vastness, and attempting at Things beyond the reach of Nature', Switzer goes on,

> is in a great measure owing to a late eminent Designer in Gardening [i.e. Bridgeman], whose Fancy could not be bounded; and this Notion has been in many Places carried so far, that no Parterre or Lawn that was not less than 50 or 60 Acres, some of them 80, 90, or 100, were by him esteemed capacious enough, though it sometimes took up the whole Area of Ground, and made the Building or Mansion-house in the middle look very small, and by no means proportionable to it.

Not merely parterres and lawns, but 'Lakes and Pieces of Water' were subject to 'the same extravagant way of thinking', in that Bridgeman designed them 'without any regard to the Goodness of the Land' to be overflowed, and so large 'as to make a whole Country look like an Ocean'.[20] Switzer cites no specific example in support of his argument,

[15] *Ichnographia Rustica* (1742), I, 12.

[16] *Lectures on Architecture*, 2nd edn (1759), p.183. Cf. William A. Gibson, 'Three Principles of Renaissance Architectural Theory in Pope's *Epistle to Burlington*', *Studies in English Literature, 1500–1900*, XI (1971), 487–505. See generally Sir John Summerson's essay 'The Idea of the Villa' in 'The Classical Country House', pp.570–87.

Included amongst the subscribers to Castell's *Villas of the Ancients* were John Baynes (owner of Bower House), Edward Harley, by then Earl of Oxford (owner of Down Hall), and the Earl of Pembroke (co-designer of Marble Hill).

[17] Needham, ed., *A Collection of Poems by Several Hands*, p.55; *Wren Soc.*, XVII (1940), 12.

[18] *Epistle to Burlington*, ll.73–74.

[19] Butt, 'A Master Key to Popery', p.51; Pope, *Epistle to Several Persons* (*Moral Essays*), ed. Bateson, 2nd edn (1961), p.183.

[20] Switzer, *Ichnographia Rustica* (1742), I, 11–12. Switzer indicates in a footnote that Bridgeman is the subject of his remarks.

although he does claim that at Claremont, given the chance, Bridgeman would 'certainly have made his Water much larger than that little Circular Basin'.[21]

Bridgeman – whether exploring the *genius loci*, or expressing his 'extravagant way of thinking' – produced designs which encompassed the *formal*, the *transitional*, and the *progressive*.

Among Bridgeman's *formal* features we should count parterres, kitchen gardens, lakes, and avenues. Parterres and kitchen gardens appear on many Bridgemanic plans, lakes less frequently so but with greater variety – circular at Claremont or Eastbury, octagonal at Tring or Wimpole, rectangular at Moor Park or Scampston. Avenues, often unifying the design, come into their own at Hampton Court, Moor Park, or Wimpole. Visitors to Bridgeman schemes frequently commented on the avenues they found there, whether they were the 'canals, parades and vistas' at Down Hall,[22] or the 'regular Walks and Canals' at King's College, Cambridge.[23] At nodal points, likely as not, these avenues were 'terminated by agreeable and proper objects',[24] which at Houghton meant placing 'at every angle... obelisks or some other building'.[25] At Wimpole, claimed Prior, 'Bridgeman's devotion... consisted chiefly in contriving how the diagonal may take Waddon steeple exactly in the middle'.[26] This 'devotion' often produced a *transitional* result by using established motifs in a new way. Examples of this are the softly-moulded lawns, with grass banking, at Gubbins or Stowe; the mounts, topped with temples, at Kensington or Pope's villa at Twickenham; the amphitheatres at Claremont, Gunton, or Rousham; and the many-faceted cabinets set in woodland which occur almost everywhere. Most pronounced of all, however, was Bridgeman's use of statues and garden buildings. These structures varied from the classical boxes of Down Hall, Gubbins, or Kedleston, to the Hermitage and Merlin's Cave at Richmond; between the two extremes were the belvedere at Claremont, and Gay's Cave at Amesbury. Often, as we have seen, these buildings were juxtaposed with a rural landscape, or set in it, sometimes with the aid of a ha-ha – Bridgeman's 'capital stroke'.[27] It is here that Bridgeman was his most *progressive*, and his thoughts at their most 'detached': Stowe (as depicted by Rigaud) gives us evidence of this, so does St James's Park, with its deer and cows grazing in the meadows and ducks swimming in the canal. In Richmond Gardens there were the 'cultivated fields' and 'morsels of a forest appearance' which suggest that Queen Caroline had an eye for use as well as beauty in her landscaping. It is not far from here to the *ferme ornée* at Dawley, where Bridgeman may have assisted Lord Bolingbroke, perhaps taking his cue from Switzer's advocacy of a 'Farm-like Way of Gardening'. Despite Pococke's claim that the 'first improvement in the farm kind' was at Woburn Farm in Surrey about 1735,[28] Dawley was begun a decade

[21] *Introduction to a General System of Hydrostaticks and Hydraulicks*, II, 405.

[22] *HMC 58: Bath III*, 490. Prior to Edward Harley, 27 September 1720.

[23] *Cantabrigia Depicta*, p.50.

[24] Muilman, *A New and Complete History of Essex*, IV, 314. This refers to Bower House.

[25] *HMC 42: Carlisle*, 85. Robinson to Carlisle, 19 December 1731.

[26] *HMC 58: Bath III*, 499. Prior to Edward Harley, 18 March 1721.

[27] For Bridgeman and the ha-ha see above pp.19–21.

[28] Cartwright, ed., *Travels Through England of Dr. Richard Pococke*, II, 260.

earlier. Moreover, as an active farm and not just an ornamental one, it satisfied the widespread desire to unite profit and pleasure, and was thus set firmly in the tradition of Pliny's *villa rustica*:[29] Switzer for one had no doubt that the *ferme ornée* was an expression of 'the *Roman* Genius' which was 'making great advances in *Britain*'.[30] Indeed we should not rule out Italian inspiration for much of Bridgeman's work – partly through the foreign travels of such friends as Gibbs, Wootton, and Kent, and partly through a visit Bridgeman himself may have made to the Continent in 1732 or so.[31]

Bridgeman and Contemporaries

Any assessment of Bridgeman's place amongst contemporary landscapists must lead ultimately to William Kent, but initially we must look briefly at Bridgeman's relationship with London and Wise, Vanbrugh, and Stephen Switzer.

London and Wise's layout at Chatsworth (*Plate 6*), and Bridgeman's at Eastbury (*Plates 26, 28b*), illustrate the way in which Bridgeman adopted and adapted the formal style he inherited. We have seen that Chatsworth displays a mixture of Italian, French, and Dutch features: long straight avenues, kitchen or herb gardens, high-cut hedges, rectangular canals, fanciful parterres, bosquets, terracing, and 'gravell walkes and squairs of grass with stone statues in them'.[32] The house itself, accessible from the *piano nobile*, is less dominant than at Eastbury, where Vanbrugh's mansion stands at one end of the main axis leading from the parterres up to the Corinthian temple, with its panoramic views of the countryside. With its central canal, mounts, round pond, and amphitheatre, Eastbury's setting is more cohesive than Chatsworth's. Moreover Bridgeman's use of the ha-ha clearly defines the limits of the garden proper, and enables him to display Vanbrugh's buildings set within rides and parkland.

Such thinking, such designing, owes little to London and Wise. Nor, come to that, does it bear much similarity to Blenheim, Claremont, and Stowe, where Bridgeman and Vanbrugh showed their respect for the character of a site, their love of the grand gesture, fondness for strategically-placed temples, and use of devices which Thomas Whately (following Warton) regarded as 'rather *emblematical* than expressive'.[33] The ruthlessness with which Eastbury is imposed upon the rolling contours of Dorset suggests that it is more likely that Bridgeman, rather than Vanbrugh, was responsible for the layout – if indeed the design was not determined by a dominant client. Before he collaborated with Bridgeman at Blenheim, Vanbrugh had already indicated that he 'had some idea of the

[29] See A. N. Sherwin-White, *The Letters of Pliny. A Historical and Social Commentary* (Oxford, 1966), p.329; K. D. White, *Roman Farming* (London, 1970), pp.406–9, 420.

[30] *Ichnographia Rustica* (1742), III, Appendix, p.9.

[31] Evidence of this possibility was kindly given to me by Mr Robert Holden, who discovered the name 'Bridgeman' among people encountered by Joseph Spence in Paris in 1732, as recorded in BL, Add MS 2235 (Egerton Papers), fo.94.

[32] Morris, ed., *Journeys of Celia Fiennes*, 2nd edn (1949), p.97.

[33] Whately, *Observations on Modern Gardening*, p.120, in a passage echoing Joseph Warton, *The Enthusiast: or, the Lover of Nature* (London, 1744).

beauty of natural gardening'[34] in his concept of Wray Wood at Castle Howard which – with its cabinets and linking walks, its fountains, seats, pedestals, steps, and statues – marked (says Switzer) 'the highest pitch that Natural and Polite Gard'ning can possibly ever arrive to'.[35] Through the Kit-Cat Club, and other friends, Vanbrugh seems to have furthered Bridgeman's interests, and Bridgeman's promotion to be Wise's partner in 1726 may have been due to Vanbrugh's support as Surveyor of Gardens and Waters. Vanbrugh, so far as we know, never went to Italy, but he was familiar with Palladio's writings,[36] and several of his garden buildings have clear Italian precedent.[37] Moreover Seaton Delaval – surely the most picturesquely sited of all Vanbrugh's country houses – can be related, in its architecture if not in its setting, to several Italian villas.[38]

Switzer, too, was indebted to Italy, but although he and Bridgeman were contemporaries at Blenheim, and perhaps at Brompton Park Nurseries, we may only conjecture about their connections elsewhere.[39] Switzer, despite various criticisms, recognized that the Royal Gardener was both 'eminent' and 'ingenious', and it is possible that Bridgeman's eminence and ingenuity was due partly to Switzer's friendship. Stylistic similarities between the work of the two men are not hard to find: Switzer's plans of a 'Forest or Rural Garden' (*Plate 10*) and of Richings (*Plate 11*), for example, show Bridgemanic formal canals, 'Serpentine Meanders', and straight avenues with linking cabinets; likewise Switzer's scheme for the Manor of Paston (*Plate 166*) recalls the bastioned kitchen garden at Blenheim on Bridgeman's 1709 drawing (*Plate 24*), a design which (as Stukeley indicates) was taken up again by Switzer at Grimsthorpe (*Plate 167a*). Bridgeman was as opposed as Switzer to 'those crimping, diminutive and wretched performances' in 'the *Dutch* Taste', and often worked in *la grande manière* promoted by Switzer:[40] for instance the parterre at Grimsthorpe (*Plate 167b*) has affinities with a similar area at Stowe, while Grime's Walk and the Duchesses' Bastion (*Plates 168a, 168b*) recall Stowe's Rotunda and the adjacent terrace walks. Bridgeman's grander rides and avenues must have met with approval, for Switzer had an avowed fondness for an 'Ambit, Circuit, or Tour . . . such as in all large Designs can be only done on Horseback, or in a Chaise or Coach'.[41] More generally, Bridgeman's layouts often seem to be a working-out of Switzer's advocacy of a regular section close to the house, with a 'rural and extensive' garden beyond it, and his enthusi-

[34] Osborn, ed., *Spence's Anecdotes*, I, 407 (No.1067).

[35] Switzer, *Ichnographia Rustica* (1718), II, 198.

[36] In 1703 Vanbrugh wrote to Tonson asking if he would get him a copy of a French edition of *Palladio*, complete with plans, though in 1711 he had mislaid it. See Dobrée and Webb, eds, *Works of Vanbrugh*, IV, 9, 236.

[37] See S. Lang, 'Vanbrugh's Theory and Hawksmoor's Buildings', *Journal of the Society of Architectural Historians*, XXIV (May 1965), 138–39.

[38] See Lang, 'Vanbrugh's Theory and Hawksmoor's Buildings', 138. For Seaton Delaval see Brian Hackett 'Some Northumberland Landscapes of the English School', *Journal of the Institute of Landscape Architects*, No.43 (August 1958), 2–4, 12; No.44 (November 1958), 7–9. Vanbrugh's garden buildings are considered in Downes, *English Baroque Architecture*, pp.124–27.

[39] Definite connections are Switzer's provision of seeds at Boughton in 1730, the overlapping of the younger Charles Bridgeman and Thomas Switzer at Westminster School in 1735–36, and the possibility that both the Royal Gardener and Stephen Switzer banked at Hoares', though at different times.

[40] For exploration of this see Brogden, 'Stephen Switzer. "La Grand Manier"', *passim*.

[41] *Ichnographia Rustica* (1742), I, 'A Prooemial Essay', p.13.

asm for the ha-ha which brings in 'the unbounded Felicities of distant Prospect'.[42] And it is not far from here to Switzer's affection for a 'Farm-like Way of Gardening'[43] with which Bridgeman seems to have had some sympathy.

We have seen that Bridgeman and Kent's connections at the Board of Works and in the royal gardens (notably at Kensington and Richmond) were strengthened by collaboration at Stowe and, in varying degrees of probability, at Badminton, Chiswick, Claremont, Rousham, and Pope's garden at Twickenham. Any examination of the parts played by Bridgeman and Kent in the creation of these layouts must involve a wide discussion of Kent's landscaping. Our sources for this are threefold: written descriptions of Kent's style, his illustrations for literary publications, and his landscape sketches.

Written comments are not hard to find. In 1734 Sir Thomas Robinson was explaining to the Earl of Carlisle about the 'new taste in gardening just arisen . . . after Mr. Kent's notion': the Prince of Wales's garden at Carlton House, he adds, 'is more diversified and of greater variety than anything of that compass I ever saw; and this method of gardening is the more agreeable, as when finished, it has the appearance of beautiful nature'.[44] Time and again Joseph Spence stresses that the 'appearance' of Kent's layouts derived from the interplay between gardening and landscape painting, and quotes Southcote as saying that 'Mr. Pope and Kent were the first that practiced painting in gardening'.[45] Whatever the springs of Kent's genius, by his death in 1748, remarks Vertue, 'no noblemen Gardens were thought to be of Tastes, unless Mr Kent had disposd or planted & c.'[46]

However such remarks are somewhat spasmodic, and we must turn to Horace Walpole's *History of the Modern Taste in Gardening* for a comprehensive eighteenth-century statement on Kent as a landscape designer.[47] Walpole leads on from his description of Bridgeman's succession to London and Wise by emphasizing that Kent then took and expanded Bridgeman's ideas. Kent, says Walpole, was

> painter enough to taste the charms of landscape, bold and opinionative enough to dare and to dictate, and born with a genius to strike out a great system from the twilight of imperfect essays. He leaped the fence, and saw that all nature was a garden. He felt the delicious contrast of hill and valley changing imperceptibly into each other, tasted the beauty of the gentle swell, or concave scoop, and remarked how loose groves crowned an easy eminence with happy ornament.

The 'great principles' on which Kent worked, explains Walpole, were perspective, light, and shade. By

> selecting favourite objects, and veiling deformities by screens of plantation; sometimes allowing the rudest waste to add its foil to the richest theatre, he realised the composi-

42 *Nobleman's Recreation*, p.xxvi.

43 A phrase used, e.g., in *Ichnographia Rustica* (1742), III, Appendix, p.10. See the discussion of Switzer and Castell in Martin Battestin, *The Providence of Wit. Aspects of Form in Augustan Literature and the Arts* (Oxford, 1974), pp.46–48, and Dixon, *World of Pope's Satires*, pp.72–77.

44 *HMC 42: Carlisle*, 143. Robinson to Carlisle, 23 December 1734.

45 Osborn, ed., *Spence's Anecdotes*, I, 250 (No.603).

46 *Vertue*, III (XXII), 140.

47 Walpole's section on Kent, from which subsequent quotations are taken, is in Chase, *Horace Walpole: Gardenist*, pp.25–30. In addition, of course, Walpole's letters contain numerous comments on specific layouts by Kent.

tions of the greatest masters in painting. Where objects were wanting to animate the horizon, his taste as an architect could bestow immediate termination. His buildings, his seats, his temples, were more the works of his pencil than of his compasses.

Of all the 'beauties' added by Kent 'to the face of this beautiful country', Walpole avers,

none surpassed his management of water . . . The gentle stream was taught to serpentize seemingly at its pleasure . . . Its borders were smoothed, but preserved their waving irregularity. A few trees scattered here and there on its edges sprinkled the tame bank that accompanied its mæanders.

Thus, by 'dealing in none but the colours of nature, and catching its most favourable features', a 'new creation' opened before men's eyes. 'The living landscape was chastened or polished, not transformed'. Not that Kent was without fault. 'It is true', admitted Walpole,

. . . that the features in Kent's landscapes were seldom majestic. His clumps were puny, he aimed at immediate effect, and planted not for futurity. One sees no large woods sketched out by his direction. Nor are we yet entirely risen above a too great frequency of small clumps, especially in the elbows of serpentine rivers.

Moreover, Kent's 'ruling principle . . . that *nature abhors a straight line*' (in which he preceded Hogarth) led him into such excesses as the planting of dead trees at Kensington.[48] Nonetheless there was no doubt in Walpole's mind that the encomiums which he 'bestowed on Kent's discoveries' were fully deserved, although at least one commentator has found Walpole's remarks unduly favourable to Kent at the expense of Bridgeman. Dallaway, writing in his 'Supplementary Anecdotes of Gardening in England', commented that Bridgeman's ha-has and vistas, and his creation of the Serpentine for Queen Caroline, 'were efforts of genius, and of a bold emancipation from ancient trammels, which appear to entitle him to more praise than he has received, as an original inventor. Kent greatly improved upon his primary idea, and has engrossed the commendation, as he had the singular good fortune *laudari a laudato viro* '.[49]

Many of Kent's book illustrations precede his practice as a landscapist, namely those for the two quarto volumes of Gay's *Poems on Several Occasions* of 1720, for Pope's edition of

[48] Ibid., p.30. Cf. *World*, VI (8 February 1753), 34. Miss Jourdain, *Kent*, p.76, remarks that Kent's action may have been in response to 'a scene after Salvator', and quotes William Marshall, *A Review of 'The Landscape'* . . . (London, 1795), p.158: 'Who, but a student in painting – one who had been accustomed to see dead stumps sticking out of canvas, could have thought of planting dead trees in a living Landscape?' Kent's proposals to remove a healthy tree at Chiswick led to a petition from Pope and others addressed to Lord Burlington. See *Pope Correspondence*, IV, 323–24.

Kent was not the first to teach a stream 'to serpentize'. Daines Barrington reports that Lord Bathurst claimed this honour when he 'ventured to deviate from strait lines, in a brook which he had widened at Ryskins' (*Plate 11*). See Daines Barrington, 'On the Progress of Gardening . . .', *Archaeologia: or Miscellaneous Tracts Relating to Antiquity*, VII (1785), 127.

On the other hand Loudon notes that Sir Christopher Wren's father wrote as follows in his copy of Wotton's *Elements of Architecture* (1624): 'For disposing the current of a river to a mightie length in a little space, I invented the serpentine'. John Claudius Loudon, ed., *The Gardener's Magazine, and Register of Rural and Domestic Improvement*, III (1828), 480. I owe this reference to Mr Miles Hadfield.

[49] See Walpole, *Anecdotes of Painting*, ed. Wornum, III, 97–98.

his translation of the *Odyssey* of 1725–26, and for the first volume of Gay's *Fables* of 1727.[50] Kent's plates in all three volumes contain evidence of his interest in landscape: we can point to the title-pages of Gay's *Poems* with its classical temple set in a wild terrain, and of the *Odyssey* with Achilles and Homer set against a background of ruined classical buildings (*Plate 169a*); to the tailpiece to Book IX of the *Odyssey* with its entrance to a cave, not unlike Pope's grotto (*Plate 169b*);[51] and to several headpieces for the *Fables* which show Palladian garden features. Kent and John Wootton shared the drawings for the *Fables*, in general Wootton taking the fables about dogs and other animals, and Kent those suggesting interior or landscape scenes.[52] Several of Kent's headpieces paid due homage to Lord Burlington: the illustration for 'Cupid, Hymen, and Plutus' (Fable XII) has a circular Ionic temple to the left, with an Ionic portico in the background (*Plate 170a*), whilst 'The Butterfly and the Snail' (Fable XXIV) is accompanied by a view of a terrace on which stand urns on pedestals, a reclining lion, and herm figures set into an arbour of trelliswork. In the distance is Burlington's bagnio from Chiswick (*Plate 170b*). The villa at Chiswick is glimpsed in Kent's plate for 'Autumn', one of four he designed for the first collected edition of Thomson's *Seasons* of 1730.[53] The most familiar of this set is Kent's interpretation of 'Spring' with its Palladian mansion, distant Italian farm, lake, and wild landscape (*Plate 171a*). An even more direct depiction of a Palladian house occurs in Kent's view of Phaedria's island for Spenser's *Faerie Queene*, published posthumously in 1751 (*Plate 171b*).[54]

Features described in Walpole's *History*, or pictured in these book illustrations, reappear in Kent's sketches of landscapes, most of which seem to have been done in the 1730's. Thus Kent's domed temple at Chatsworth, set against a rough hillside sprinkled

[50] See Jeffrey P. Eichholz, 'William Kent's Career as a Literary Illustrator', *Bulletin of the New York Public Library*, LXX (December 1966), 620–46; H. A. Hammelmann and T. S. R. Boase, *Book Illustration in Eighteenth-Century England* (New Haven and London, 1975), pp.57–58. Burlington took out a subscription for fifty copies of the *Poems*.

[51] Kent designed fifty plates for Pope's *Odyssey*. See *Pope Correspondence*, II, 288, n.1. These are discussed, and several reproduced, in the Twickenham Edition of the *Iliad* and *Odyssey* (ed. Maynard Mack, Norman Callan, Robert Fagles, William Frost and Douglas M. Knight) (London and New Haven, 1967), esp. VII, xlv, ccxxiv; IX, xii–xiv; X, xii–xiv. Apart from '*Mr.* Charles Bridgman', subscribers to the *Odyssey* edition of 1725–26 included Bathurst, Burlington, Cobham, Harley, William Kent, the Duchess of Marlborough, Thornhill, and Wootton. In 1734 Kent provided six head and tailpieces for Gilliver's edition of Pope's *Essay on Man*. See Wimsatt, *Portraits of Pope*, pp.111, 125–27.

[52] Wootton and Kent appear together in Hamilton's *Club of Artists* (*Plate 19*), and a study of their relationship would be fruitful.

[53] See Ralph Cohen, *The Art of Discrimination. Thomson's 'The Seasons' and the Language of Criticism* (Berkeley and Los Angeles, 1964), esp. pp.259–65; Joseph D. Masheck, 'The First Plates for Thomson's *Seasons*' (MA thesis, Columbia University, 1967). For the general context of Kent's plates see Bertrand H. Bronson, *Printing as an Index of Taste in Eighteenth-Century England*, 2nd edn (New York, 1963), and for some useful later plates see H. A. Hammelmann, 'The Poet's Seasons Delineated', *Country Life Annual* (1970), 52–54. Bridgeman subscribed to the 1730 edition of the *Seasons*.

[54] Horace Walpole (*Anecdotes of Painting*, ed. Wornum, III, 59–60) describes Kent's illustrations for *The Faerie Queene* as 'ill executed', and criticizes 'the wretchedness of drawing, the total ignorance of perspective, the want of variety, the disproportion of the buildings, and the awkwardness of the attitudes'. Cf. *Yale Walpole*, IX, 116. Walpole to Montagu, 13 June 1751.

Reference has already been made to William Mason's claim that Kent's views on landscaping came from reading Spenser, to connections between Spenser and Stowe, and to the presentation to Bridgeman by Matthew Prior of a 'Spenser folio' in 1721. See above pp.64n110, 75–76, 117n44.

See also J. Corder, 'Spenser and the Eighteenth-Century Informal Garden', *Notes and Queries*, CCIV (January 1959), 19–21.

with conifers (*Plate 172a*), represents those of his buildings which (to Walpole) bestow 'immediate termination'. Here, and in his smaller drawing of a portico overlooking a round pond (*Plate 172b*), Kent seems fascinated by the reflections made by his structures. Two other sketches (*Plates 173a, 173b*), with their 'waving irregularity' and their 'few trees scattered here and there on [the] edges', emphasize how 'none surpassed [Kent's] management of water'. The waterscape shimmers with light, the trees reflected in its smooth surface, as the eye is led through the trees from the foreground to the background with its 'delicious contrast of hill and valley': there are few better instances of Kent's use of his 'great principles' of perspective, light, and shade. Notice too how the tall, slender trees (perhaps birches, larches, or pines) contrast with the rotund bushes, and form screens which give glimpses of what lies beyond. This favourite Kentian device, perhaps of Italian origin, can be seen in Kent's perspectives of Chiswick (*Plates 174a, 174b*), in which trees separate the round pond and Ionic temple from the exedra. Occasions on which Kent uses 'loose groves [to crown] an easy eminence with happy ornament' often involve the introduction of buildings or statuary to 'decorate [the] horizon'. Kent's drawing of the cascade at Rousham indicates one way in which he did this (*Plate 62b*), his view of a wooded glade with an urn on a pedestal indicates another (*Plate 175b*), and his sketch of the area around the canal at Chatsworth yet another (*Plate 176a*). Here Kent has employed saplings to create a small theatre or amphitheatre, as he did in his sketch of the belvedere at Claremont (*Plate 165a*), and in his superb perspective of two herm figures standing in front of a hillock surrounded by trees, perhaps at Claremont or Rousham (*Plate 175a*). Similar herms, and other statues, are seen in Kent's drawings for the exedra at Chiswick, both in the unexecuted (*Plate 174b*) and executed designs (*Plate 58a*). The 'profusion of richness' at Chiswick (to borrow Walpole's phrase about Stowe) recalls the Claudian scenes which appear among the Kent drawings in the Devonshire Collection at Chatsworth (*Plate 176b*).

These and other sketches by Kent show his whimsy and imagination: as Professor Wittkower observed, 'whenever we find fanciful and witty ideas, disregard of reason and rule, odd escapades, we can be sure we have the real Kent before us'.[55] Underlying the remarks of Spence, Southcote, Pope, and Walpole is the fact that Kent saw all landscapes through a painter's eye: Walpole may have been optimistic in claiming that Kent 'realised the compositions of the greatest masters in painting', but Kent was certainly 'painter enough to taste the charms of landscape'. To put it another way, as Walpole did in his *Anecdotes of Painting*, Kent was 'the inventor of an art that realizes painting, and improves nature'.[56] During Kent's decade in Italy he must have become familiar with the Roman Campagna, as well as with Italian masques, painting, wall decoration, and gardens.[57]

[55] 'Lord Burlington and William Kent', in *Palladio and English Palladianism*, p.130.

[56] *Anecdotes of Painting*, ed. Wornum, III, 57.

[57] Future scholarship will surely prove the significance of theatrical influences on the English landscape garden. For the present see Dr Lang's article 'The Genesis of the English Landscape Garden' already cited. Italian wall decorations, such as those provided by Veronese for the Villa Maser, similarly must have been seminal.

These and others are illustrated and discussed in Eva Börsch-Supan, *Garten-, Landschafts- und Paradies-Motive im Innenraum* (Berlin, 1967), and in A. Richard Turner, *The Vision of Landscape in Renaissance Italy* (Princeton, N.J., 1966), pp.193–212.

Kent's English landscapes seem to have drawn on the layout of, say, the Villa Pratolino, with its views from the terrace to the surrounding countryside, its *boschetti* with regular paths, its grottoes and numerous other structures scattered about the grounds.[58] Kent collected Italian paintings, if not engravings,[59] and it could be that his exedra and cascade at Chiswick were inspired by Falda's seventeenth-century prints of the Villa Mattei and the Villa Aldobrandini, Frascati.[60] Furthermore, it is of no little consequence that there was a copy of Falda's *Li giardini di Roma* in Lord Burlington's library at Chiswick.[61] Actual gardens, too, must have been a source for other specific features: the herms and other statuary at Chiswick, for instance, call to mind the Boboli Gardens in Florence, the Villa Marlia, or the Villa Brenzone (*Plate 177b*),[62] whilst the tall hedges converging on a *rond-point* echo those at Castellazzo depicted by Lucchese (*Plate 177a*). Similarly Venus' Vale at Rousham is reminiscent of the *fontana rustica* at the Villa Barbarigo.[63] All told, it is apparent that the design of landscapes fitted William Kent's background and training precisely, drawing on his talents as painter and architect, his sojourn in Italy, his friendship with Pope and other men of letters, and his connection with Burlington and his circle.

The paths of Bridgeman and Kent so frequently overlap that some collaboration must be assumed; indeed their gifts seem to have been complementary. Bridgeman was the more down-to-earth of the two, whereas the last thing Kent would do was regard landscaping *ut pictura horticultura*.[64] Our evidence of Kent's involvement in practical gardening is spasmodic: we know that he planted flowering trees and shrubs at Rousham,[65] and that he

[58] We know that Kent visited Pratolino, and that he was struck by its 'very fine Situation & very fine Groto's adorn'd with Shells & pietrified Stone with pritty water works [such] as Galatea coming out of her Grotto's drawn by Delphins'. See the MS of Kent's Italian Diary 1714–15 in Bod.Lib., MS Rawl.D.1162, fo.2.

[59] In *A Catalogue of the Genuine Collection of Pictures, Models, Coins, and Drawings Framed and Glazed, of William Kent, Esq; Deceased . . .*, dated 13–14th February 1749, there are listed three landscape drawings by Claude, three landscape paintings by Gaspard and another by Salvator Rosa, 'A Nobleman in Armour, on Horseback' by Rosa, and 'A sleeping *Venus*' by Nicolas Poussin.

I have failed to find evidence that Kent owned any landscape *prints*. Professor Manwaring (*Italian Landscape in Eighteenth-Century England*, p.131) claims that he did collect them, and cites as her source the prints of Arthur Pond. This is repeated by Miss Jourdain (*Kent*, p.76) and Professor Chase (*Horace Walpole: Gardenist*, p.141). In 1738 Pond made a caricature of a head of Sebastiano Resta, after a drawing by Pier Leone Ghezzi owned by Kent. This is the only Kent reference in H. M. Hake, 'Pond's and Knapton's Imitations of Drawings', *Print Collector's Quarterly*, IX (December 1922), 324–49.

On the other hand Kent owned many books which were amply illustrated with architectural and other views. See *A Catalogue of the Library of William Kent, Esq. . . .*, recording the sale on 14th February 1749. Both Kent sales were held in Covent Garden.

[60] See Kenneth Woodbridge, 'William Kent as Landscape Gardener: a Re-appraisal', *Apollo*, C (August 1974), 126–37, esp. pls 9, 10, 5. This pioneer article has been of great help in my speculations on Kent's influences from Italy.

The exedra at Chiswick may have given Lord Petre the idea for an unexecuted design at Worksop. See Marcus Binney, 'Worksop Manor, Nottinghamshire', *C.Life*, CLIII (15 March 1973), 682.

For the Villa Aldobrandini see Howard Hibbard, *Carlo Maderno and Roman Architecture, 1580–1630* (London, 1971), pp.47–50, and Ronald M. Steinberg, 'The Iconography of the Teatro dell'Acqua at the Villa Aldobrandini', *Art Bulletin*, XLVII (December 1965), 453–63.

[61] Chatsworth, Derbys, Devonshire Collection, MS Catalogue of Burlington's Library at Chiswick, fo.1.

[62] For the Boboli Gardens and the Villa Marlia see respectively Derek Clifford, *A History of Garden Design*, 2nd edn (London, 1966), pl.9, and Fariello, *Architettura dei Giardini*, pl.92.

[63] See ibid., pl.95.

[64] See Osborn, ed., *Spence's Anecdotes*, I, 252, 425 (Nos 606, 1129).

[65] See Woodbridge, 'William Kent's Gardening: the Rousham Letters', p.288.

'always used to stake out his grovettes before they [were] planted, and to view the stakes every way, to see that no three of them stand in a line'; 'An excell^{t} Rule of Kent's', Spence adds.[66] Horace Walpole tells us that 'Kent's last designs were in a higher style',[67] hinting that there was a progression in Kent's work from a 'lower style' at Chiswick to his later schemes for Claremont and Esher Place.[68] If we compare Kent's landscape sketches with Rigaud's views of Chiswick and Stowe we can see something of Kent's changes: gone now is the structured quality, with temples and statues held securely in a framework of avenues, parterres, hedges and ha-has. Instead Kent's 'higher style' is envisaged as a series of perspectives and viewpoints (no Kent *plan* of a garden has yet been found) which emphasize the ways in which Kent, as a painter, introduced new spacial experiences into his designs. Kent had progressed, where Bridgeman stopped short.

Bridgeman and Successors

'In general', observed Horace Walpole in his *History of the Modern Taste in Gardening*, 'it is probably true, that the possessor, if he has any taste, must be the best designer of his own improvements'.[69] Increasingly, towards the end of Bridgeman's lifetime, landscapes began to bear personal testimony to the ideas and ideals of their owners: at Woburn Farm in Surrey (*Plate 178a*) Philip Southcote began to lay out his *ferme ornée* from 1735; three years later Charles Hamilton at Painshill (*Plate 178b*) started a scheme (set beside a lake and the River Mole) which had a hermitage, a Temple of Bacchus, a Gothic pavilion and abbey, a grotto, and a cascade; at The Leasowes (*Plate 179a*) William Shenstone, following his mother's death in 1743, dedicated himself to a layout with winding paths, a waterfall, and a ruined priory, and simultaneously helped to design the landscape at Enville, not far away; whilst at Hagley (*Plate 179b*) George, 1st Baron Lyttelton, several years after the loss of his wife in 1747, decorated his estate with the Doric Temple of Theseus by 'Athenian' Stuart, a column to the Prince of Wales, an Ionic rotunda, and a ruined castle by Sanderson Miller – all of which seemed appropriate to Lyttelton as a liberal patron of men of letters, and as a nephew of Viscount Cobham of Stowe. Most intact today is Stourhead, where the literary and classical allusions of Henry Hoare, the Younger, are unmatched, and whose beauties were drawn by Fredrick Magnus Piper in 1779 (*Plate 180*). Stourhead is the example *par excellence* of the 'pictorial circuit' – the perimeter walk or ride with specific viewpoints (frequently provided with seats) from which particular scenes may be enjoyed.[70] Often – as with Mason's Walk at Nuneham Courtenay, Gay's Seat at Amesbury, or Pope's Walk at Hagley – these 'circuits' had literary connotations, and led to or through

[66] Osborn, ed., *Spence's Anecdotes*, II, 649.

[67] Chase, *Horace Walpole: Gardenist*, p.29.

[68] Cf. the two Kent sketches for a seat on a mount at Holkham illustrated by Woodbridge, 'William Kent as Landscape Gardener', pls 22, 23, and discussed on pp.133–34.

[69] Chase, *Horace Walpole: Gardenist*, p.37.

[70] See Paulson, 'The Pictorial Circuit', esp. pp.165–68. Switzer, whose affection for an 'Ambit, Circuit, or Tour' has already been noted, indicates a 'Cart, Coach, or Shaise (*sic*) Road round the whole Plantation' on his plan of Richings (*Plate 11*).

a grotto. And it was the grotto above all which became, as Mr H. F. Clark winningly put it, 'a shrine for great Nature, Pope's metaphysical Goddess'.[71]

It is not difficult to see that these landscapes, and others like them – such as Oatlands, Mount Edgcumbe, Piercefield, Shugborough, and West Wycombe – continued the themes established by Bridgeman and Kent. Not so with those of Capability Brown, whose visual grammar and punctuation (as explained by Hannah More in a familiar passage) are literary in quite a different way from his predecessors'.[72] Stowe marked the turning point in Brown's career, and although, as Miss Stroud says, 'there is no single feature in the grounds which can be ascribed with certainty to Brown alone, the creation of the Grecian Valley must by date and deduction be largely his work'.[73] The design of the Grecian Valley illustrates how Brown's style was as different from Bridgeman and Kent's as theirs had been from London and Wise's.[74] This does not mean that Brown was not indebted to the stylistic advances of his predecessors; far from it. 'While there is thus a good deal in a William Kent garden which is not in a park by Brown', remarks Mr Marcus Whiffen, 'there is very little in a Brown park which does not own its existence to the example of Kent'.[75]

This is less true, of course, with Bridgeman. The contrast between Bridgeman's style and Capability Brown's is best demonstrated by looking at two landscapes, involving Bridgeman at an early stage and then Brown at a later. Brown's plan of Wimpole (*Plate 181*) shows how Bridgeman's formal layout near the house, with long avenues stretching into the countryside (*Plate 75*), has been submerged by Brown's bridge and winding lake, and his open grassland bordered by rides and peripheral belts, and dotted with clumps and trees scattered at random. A similar difference can be observed if we compare the Bridgeman plan of Blenheim (*Plate 24*) with Brown's drawing of over fifty years later (*Plate 182a*). Although the line of the great avenue remains, sweeping across the Grand Bridge, the bastioned kitchen garden is no more, the valley has been flooded, and clumps and sprinkled trees have been introduced. Gone too is much of the dense planting. Although twentieth-century Blenheim (*Plate 182b*) may be regarded justly as 'the epitome of Brown's achievement',[76] its success depends largely upon the fundamental design decisions made during Vanbrugh's lifetime and subsequently adopted by Brown. Here – as in his design of gothic buildings for the grounds – Brown was adopting the premises put forward by Vanbrugh in his memorandum to the Duchess of Marlborough of 1709. Essentially, by emphasizing the morphology of the site – the lines, shapes, and masses of its lawns, waterscape, and trees – Brown was simply interpreting the *genius loci* in a different way from Bridgeman and Kent. Unlike them, he had no truck with classical statues or with

[71] Clark, 'Eighteenth-Century Elysiums', 168. See generally ibid., pp.171–77; Hunt and Willis, eds, *Genius of the Place*, pp.26–30; Sirén, *China and Gardens of Europe*, pp.35–46. Cf. the descriptions quoted in Moir, *Discovery of Britain*, pp.77–90.

[72] See William Roberts, ed., *Memoirs of the Life and Correspondence of Mrs Hannah More* (London, 1834), I, 267. Mrs More to her sister, 31 December 1782.

[73] Stroud, *Capability Brown*, 3rd edn (1975), p.52, first argued by Clarke, 'Lancelot Brown's Work at Stowe', 21–22.

[74] Cf. *Plates 146, 156* in this present book.

[75] Marcus Whiffen, 'Architect, Painter and Landscape Gardener', *Listener*, XXXIX (22 April 1948), 654. This sensitive article, published to mark the 200th anniversary of Kent's death, deserves to be better known.

[76] Stroud, *Capability Brown*, 3rd edn (1975), p.129.

temples dedicated to gods, virtues, or the Muses, and without hesitation Brown swept his swards of grass right up to the very walls of his houses, eliminating terraces and other remains of the 'specific garden'. Brown had his detractors as well as his admirers, however, and many of his contemporaries found his designs austere, if not downright dull. Sir William Chambers promoted Chinese solutions, and Richard Payne Knight and Uvedale Price, who prescribed fidelity to the vision of Salvator Rosa, were at one in their dismay at Brown's work. Even Humphry Repton, who rejected the picturesque notions of Knight and Price, discovered that his deliberate attempt to succeed Brown as the leader of British landscapists required a thorough re-assessment of Brownian principles.[77]

On the whole, however, few would disagree with Horace Walpole (referring to Brown) that 'it was fortunate for the country and Mr. Kent, that he was succeeded by a very able master'.[78] Brown's influence on the face of the English countryside is unquestionable, yet it was the Bridgeman-Kent, not the Brown, landscape which was parodied abroad as *le jardin anglais*. 'Our passion for everything French, is nothing to theirs for everything English', Walpole tells Sir Horace Mann in 1762.[79] In 1771, the year in which his *History of the Modern Taste in Gardening* rolled off the press at Strawberry Hill, Walpole is writing exultantly from Paris that 'English gardening gains ground [there] prodigiously'. 'This new *anglomanie* will literally be *mad English*', he adds.[80] The boom in guidebooks to notable gardens – Richardson's edition of Defoe's *Tour* (with its Appendix describing many examples) came out in 1742, two years later Seeley's guides to Stowe started to appear, as did Bickham's in 1750 – had encouraged visitors from abroad to come and see for themselves.[81] Once in England – helped by these guides, and by the plans published by John Rocque[82] – they jotted down their impressions in diaries and notebooks, often commenting on Bridgeman's work, though perhaps unwittingly. '*Le jardin est assez grand et tr[è]s bien entretenu avec beaucoup de Gazon et quelques figures*', wrote an anonymous French visitor to Wimpole in 1724. '*Il est terminé par un grand boulingrin, avec deux pavillons peints et fort propres*

[77] This is not the place to elaborate on later writers and practitioners, but see generally the Introduction to Hunt and Willis, eds, *Genius of the Place*, pp.1–46, and Further Reading, pp.381–82.

[78] Chase, *Horace Walpole: Gardenist*, p.37.

[79] *Yale Walpole*, XXII, 105. Walpole to Mann, 30 November 1762.

[80] Ibid., XXXV, 125–26. Walpole to Chute, 5 August 1771.

[81] Gilpin stresses an 'Advantage, of a public Nature, derived from these elegant Productions of Art [i.e. Stowe's gardens]; and that is their Tendency to raise us in the Opinion of Foreigners . . . So that for the Credit of the Country, I think, something of this kind ought to be exhibited amongst us'. Gilpin, *Dialogue Upon the Gardens . . . at Stowe*, p.48.

[82] The place of John Rocque in English landscape history is intriguing: his brother Bartholomew was a renowned gardener, and on John Rocque's plan of Richmond Gardens (1734) he describes himself as '*dessinateur des jardins*'. This plan was John's first publication, probably issued not long after he and his family came to England from France. Many of Rocque's engravings are titled in English and French, others only in French. This Anglo-French background reinforces the possibility – tentatively put to me by Dr Bilbrough – that the unsigned 1739 general plan of Stowe may have been executed by Rocque for his fellow-Frenchmen Rigaud and Baron. As Rocque included several Bridgemanic gardens among his subjects (Richmond, Chiswick, Kensington, Claremont, and Windsor) we may assume that he and the Royal Gardener knew each other.

Apart from Hugh Phillips' article 'John Rocque's Career' already cited, see also Arnold Horner, 'Cartouches and Vignettes on the Kildare Estate Maps of John Rocque', *Quarterly Bulletin of the Irish Georgian Society*, XIV (October–December 1971), 57–76, and John Varley, 'John Rocque. Engraver, Surveyor, Cartographer and Mapseller', *Imago Mundi. A Review of Early Cartography*, V (1948), 83–91. Generally see Ida Darlington and James Howgego, *Printed Maps of London, c.1553–1830* (London, 1964).

For Bartholomew Rocque see Henrey, *British Botanical and Horticultural Literature Before 1800*, II, 609–11.

en dedans'.[83] Two years later De Saussure was making his favourable remarks on Richmond and Kensington. Thereafter we have a succession of French commentators on the English scene – the year 1731 saw the publication of Voltaire's *Lettres sur les Anglais*, and Prévost's *Mémoires et aventures d'un homme de qualité* which included (in Part V) fulsome praise of England; in 1745 Le Blanc's *Lettres* appeared with their record of his time in England from 1737 to 1738; and then in 1765 Mme du Boccage's *Lettres sur l'Angleterre* (published in English in 1770) documented her English travels of the 1750's.[84] Richmond Park, says Mme du Bocage, was 'filled with deer and all sorts of game', and divided 'into cultivated lands', though it was hardly as impressive as Stowe: 'I should hardly ever make an end', she writes, 'if I was to describe all the beauties of the gardens of *Stowe*'.[85] Swiss and German travellers came to England too:[86] Pöllnitz between 1710 and 1723, and in 1725 De Muralt, the Swiss, who thought St James's Park 'a fine Country-like Place, and . . . the more agreeable in [his] Opinion, because it has neither Art nor Regularity'.[87] Baron Bielfeld made his English journey's in 1741, and shared similar enthusiasms, as did Moritz in 1782, who much preferred Richmond to London: 'Happy, thrice happy am I, I again and again exclaimed, that I am no longer in your gloomy city, but here in *Elysium*, in Richmond.'[88] In 1787 the Count Torre di Rezzonico was giving an Italian's impression of Stowe, with a lengthy description of passing '*alle campagne dell'Eliso*'.[89] The later 1780's provide us with our most illustrious commentator on Bridgeman's gardens, namely Thomas Jefferson, 3rd President of the United States. His 'Memorandums' on his visits to English gardens in 1786, with Whately's *Observations* in his hand, is a key document: Jefferson notes that at Chiswick 'the garden shews still too much of art', that at Blenheim 'the trees are scattered too thinly over the ground & every here & there [are] small thickets of shrubs', whilst at Stowe he is struck by 'considerable portions separated by inclosures & used for pasture'.[90]

[83] V&A, MS 86.M.24 (MS Diary 1728–30), fo.103. I am grateful to the Knight of Glin for alerting me to the existence of this diary, and to Miss Georgina Fuller for giving me both a copy and a translation of it.

[84] For a useful list of these publications see Francesca M. Wilson, *Strange Island. Britain Through Foreign Eyes, 1395–1940* (London, 1955), pp.268–70.

[85] *Letters Concerning England, Holland and Italy* . . . (London, 1770), I, 49, 66.

[86] Essential here is W. D. Robson-Scott, *German Travellers in England, 1400–1800* (Oxford, 1953), esp. pp.117–60, and the Bibliography, pp.217–30.

[87] De Muralt, *Letters*, p.77. This was translated from *Lettres sur les Anglois et les François et sur les voyages* (Zurich, 1725).

[88] P. E. Matheson, ed., *Travels of Carl Philipp Moritz in England in 1782* (London, 1924), p.106.

[89] Bartolommeo Gamba, ed., *Viaggio in Inghilterra di Carlo Castone della Torre di Rezzonico Comasco* (Venice, 1824), pp.120–36. In 1755 John Shebbeare, using the pseudonym Battista Angeloni, had published his *Letters on the English Nation*, supposedly consisting of letters sent back to Italy by an expatriot living in England.

[90] Cited from the MS in the Tucker-Coleman Papers, Earl Gregg Swem Library, College of William and Mary, Williamsburg, Virginia. A complete transcript of this text of the 'Memorandums' (barring a description and drawing of 'Archimedes' screw for raising water' at Kew) is in Hunt and Willis, eds, *Genius of the Place*, pp.333–6.

From 1784 to 1789 Jefferson was Ambassador to France, and during his spell in Europe bought copies of the 1783 edition of Seeley's *Description of* . . . *Stow*, Heely's *Letters on the Beauties of Hagley, Envil, and The Leasowes*, and Castell's *Villas of the Ancients*. Before he left the United States he owned a copy of a 1770 edition of Whately, purchased a second whilst in Europe, and a third in 1821. See the discussion of Jefferson's architectural books in S. Fiske Kimball, *Thomas Jefferson, Architect* . . . (Cambridge, Mass., 1916), pp.90–101. Kimball suggests that Jefferson's landscape interests had been aroused by the acquisition in 1765 of Shenstone's works. See Kimball, 'Romantic Classicism in Architecture', *Gazette des Beaux Arts*, XXV (1944), 106.

Detailed consideration of Jefferson's gardening books is given in E. Millicent Sowerby, comp., *Catalogue of the Library of Thomas Jefferson* (Washington, D.C., 1952–59), IV, 385–99.

For advice on Jefferson's landscape interests I am indebted to Professor Samuel A. Roberson, who is currently expanding his Ph.D. thesis, 'Thomas Jefferson and the Eighteenth Century Landscape Garden Movement in England' (Yale University, 1966).

Stowe, as a special place of pilgrimage, is the subject of Jefferson's longest description.[91] One of the earliest French publications promoting the English landscape style in France was the poem *Les charmes de Stow* – dated 1748, and similar to Gilpin's *Dialogue* of the same year – which reminds us that to many Frenchmen Stowe was *ne plus ultra*;[92] not for nothing were Rigaud's drawings of Stowe titled in both French and English. The appearance in 1753 of Laugier's *Essai sur l'architecture* – with its criticism of Versailles, and its promotion of Chinese taste – moved beyond description to theory, and seems to have sparked off a series of French books on the principles of landscape design, although it is not until the 1770's that we have the major writings: 1770 saw the publication of Grosley's *Londres* with a section on the art of gardening, 1773 Carmontelle's *Le jardin de Monceau*, 1774 Watelet's *Essai sur les jardins*, 1776 Morel's *Théorie des jardins*, followed in 1782 by De Lille's poem *Les jardins*. De Lille reiterated the claim that the English had based their landscaping on Chinese models – an opinion rejected, of course, by Walpole, who brought out a French translation of his *History* in 1785[93] – and christened the results *les jardins anglo-chinois*. So ingrained did this belief become that when Le Rouge issued his *Détails des nouveaux jardins à la mode* (1776–88) he juxtaposed plates of Stowe and Kew, both as representative of Chinese influence (*Plates 156–58*).[94]

The theories of the English landscape garden were put into practice as far afield as Kismarton in Hungary, Arkadia in Poland,[95] and Haga and Drottningholm in Sweden (*Plate 183a*); in Italy there was Cinisello, the Villa Cusani, the Villa Reale, parts of Caserta, and (in the nineteenth century) the designs of Giuseppe Japelli;[96] in Ireland, Delville at Glasnevin (*Plate 85*) was laid out by Patrick Delany (friend of Swift and others in Pope's circle) under the influence of his visits to Rousham and elsewhere, whilst Swift himself at Naboth's Vineyard created a sort of Irish equivalent of Pope's Twickenham garden.[97] In Scotland, Sir John Clerk's Penicuik was only one of a number of similar

[91] Stowe is given equal prominence in the diary of John Adams (at that time Ambassador to the Court of St James's) who accompanied Jefferson. See the description in L. H. Butterfield, *et al.*, eds, *Diary and Autobiography of John Adams* (Cambridge, Mass., 1961), III, 185–86.

[92] *Les charmes* is written in the form of a letter to a lady from 'J.d.C.', and seems to have been one of the sources used by Bickham in writing his *Beauties of Stow* of 1750. For further comment see Willis, 'Rousseau, Stowe and *le jardin anglais*', 1794–95.

[93] The French version (by the Duc de Nivernois) is printed side-by-side with the English, and bears the title *Essai sur l'art des jardins modernes, par M. Horace Walpole*. A French translation of Whately's *Observations* had come out in 1771.

[94] A major study of the English landscape garden in France is at present being undertaken by Professor Dora Wiebenson, to whom I am indebted for advice on this section.

[95] See the two articles in Pevsner, ed., *The Picturesque Garden*, namely Anna Zádor, 'The English Garden in Hungary', pp.77–98, and Brian Knox, 'The Arrival of the English Garden in Poland and Bohemia', pp.99–116.

[96] For Italy see Fariello, *Architettura dei Giardini*, pp.151–52; Hugh Honour, 'English Gardens in Italy', *C.Life*, CXXX (23 November 1961), 1248–50.

For Japelli see Roberto Carta Mantiglia, 'Giuseppe Japelli Architetto', *L'Architettura* (Milan), I (November–December 1955), 538–51, and two articles by Dr Alistair Rowan: 'Japelli and Cigognara', *Architectural Review*, CXLIII (March 1968), 225–28, and 'Japellianum Miscellany', *Architectural Review*, CXLV (April 1969), 297–98.

[97] For Ireland the forthcoming study by the Knight of Glin and Mr Edward Malins is eagerly awaited. Meanwhile see the Exhibition Catalogue, *Irish Houses and Landscapes* (Ulster Museum, Belfast, and Municipal Gallery of Modern Art, Dublin, 1963), and Desmond Fitz-Gerald, 'Irish Gardens of the Eighteenth Century', *Apollo*, LXXXVIII (September 1968), 185–97, 204–9; J. M. Hunt, 'Houses in the Irish Landscape', *C.Life*, CXXXIV (8 August 1963), 320–21; Edward Malins, 'Unique Features of Certain Irish Landscapes and Gardens, 1718–1968', *Garden History Society: Occasional Papers*, No.1 (1969), pp.19–28; Edward Malins and the Knight of Glin, 'Landscape Gardening by Jonathan Swift and His Friends in Ireland', *Garden History*, II (Autumn 1973), 69–93.

landscapes created in the 1720's and 1730's, most notable amongst them being, perhaps, the elder William Boutcher's work for Lord Stair at Castle Kennedy. In 1723 the Society of Improvers in the Knowledge of Agriculture was formed in Edinburgh, at a moment when gardeners such as James Justice were vigorously promoting the cause of practical horticulture in Scotland.[98] Further afield, in Russia there was Bratsevo, Neskuchnoye, and Tsarsko Selo with buildings by Charles Cameron, and in the United States such estates as Jefferson's Monticello, not without its reminders of the President's Continental travels. In Germany, two of the finest examples were Wörlitz (with its lakes, cascades, grottoes, and serpentine walks) and Hohenheim near Stuttgart, where the exotic garden embellishments included the mandatory circular temple (*Plate 183b*).[99] In France a host of gardens proclaimed the new style – among them the Désert de Retz, the Moulin Joli, Malmaison (*Plate 184*), Méréville, the Parc Monceau, and Bagatelle (*Plate 185a*) – all bearing witness to what Hautecoeur calls '*le jardin pittoresque et sentimental*'.[100]

This brings us full circle and back to Rousseau. In 1777 Rousseau's last patron, the Marquis de Girardin, published one of the most authoritative books on the English landscape style, *De la composition des paysages, ou les moyen d'embellir la nature*. Girardin's estate at Ermenonville, near Paris (*Plate 185b*), was said by its owner to be based on Shenstone's *ferme ornée* at The Leasowes, with parts modelled on Rousseau's *Elisée* from *La Nouvelle Héloïse*.[101] To the north of the *château* is the *Grand Etang* and *Grande Rivière*, set in a wild terrain dotted with rustic buildings and monuments; to the south lies the *Petit Etang*, dominated by Rousseau's tomb, the whole effect calling to mind Switzer's observations some fifty years before that 'to Noble and Ingenuous Natures, a Piece of Ruin is more entertaining than the most beautiful Edifice; and the sorrowful Reflections they draw from the Soul ascend the very Heav'ns'.[102] With its grotto, hermitage, and crumbling Temple of Philosophy (*Plate 186a*), this part of Ermenonville seems France's answer to Stowe, but whereas Stowe is dominated by life, Ermenonville is dominated by death. The spirit of Rousseau's tomb pervades everything (*Plate 186b*). Erected about 1780, and set on a lonely island planted with poplars, it can be glimpsed from the shore as if it were a fragment of antique marble set in a landscape by Hubert Robert. Robert in fact

98 Little has been published on the early landscape movement in Scotland, although Dr Brogden (who is preparing a book on the subject) deals with it in his thesis on Switzer. Apart from the articles by Mr Spink and Dr Tait already cited, see recently the important studies by Miss Priscilla Minay, namely 'Early Improvements in the Eighteenth-Century Lothians: the Efforts of the Inter-Related Foulis, Justice, Kinloch, and Fletcher Families', *Bulletin of the Scottish Georgian Society*, II (1973), 3–46, and 'James Justice (1698–1763): Eighteenth-Century Scots Horticulturist and Botanist', *Garden History*, I, No.2 (Spring 1973), 41–62; II, No.2 (Spring 1974), 51–74; III, No.2 (Spring 1975), 37–67; IV, No.2 (Summer 1976), 53–91.

99 See the discussion of Wörlitz and Hohenheim in W. D. Robson-Scott, *The Literary Background of the Gothic Revival in Germany. A Chapter in the History of Taste* (Oxford, 1965), pp.30–34. More generally see Hennebo and Hoffmann, *Geschichte der Deutschen Gartenkunst*, II, 70–89.

100 See Hautecoeur, *Les jardins des dieux et des hommes*, pp.177–90. See also De Ganay, *Les jardins de France et leur décor*, and Marcel Mayer, *Nicolas Michot, ou l'introduction du jardin anglais en France* (Paris, 1942).

For the cultural context of these landscapes see the Exhibition Catalogue, *Les joies de la nature au XVIIIe siècle* (Bibliothèque Nationale, Paris, 1971).

101 The literature on Rousseau at Ermenonville is enormous, but see recently two articles by Dr Christopher Thacker: 'Voltaire and Rousseau: Eighteenth-Century Gardeners', *Studies on Voltaire and the Eighteenth Century*, XC (1972), 1595–1614, and 'Ermenonville. Landscape and Legend', *Landscape Design*, No.97 (February 1972), 11–13.

102 *Nobleman's Recreation*, p.149.

participated in its design. The tomb's power to stimulate meditation upon the greatness of the man buried beneath it was attested to by the many late eighteenth-century visitors who came to pay homage – among them Benjamin Franklin, Gustav III of Sweden, Napoleon, and the Emperor Joseph II of Austria, not to mention the anonymous Englishman who, overcome by emotion, swam over to the tomb and wept upon it. Such effusion seems far from the Augustan restraint and correctness of Stowe. Ermenonville stands for something quite different: '*Ici*', reads an inscription on Rousseau's tomb, '*repose l'homme de la nature et de la vérité*'. Yet Rousseau confessed that as a young man he gained his ideas on nature from England, from the same Joseph Addison whose articles in the *Spectator* must have been so influential on Bridgeman and his friends. Indeed on one occasion Rousseau admitted that he owed much to the *Spectator*. '"*Le Spectateur*"', he wrote, '*surtout me plut beaucoup, et me fit du bien*'.[103]

[103] *Confessions*, ed. Jacques Voisine (Paris, 1964), p.122.

Appendices

As most of the Appendices consist of transcripts from manuscripts, a few words are warranted about the principles adopted. Although in general original spelling and punctuation are retained, raised letters are lowered, square brackets [ ] are inserted for editorial additions, and the punctuation of tables and financial references are simplified. For clarity, the headings and sub-headings in Bridgeman's Inventory are capitalized and italicized.

Charles Bridgeman and His Family

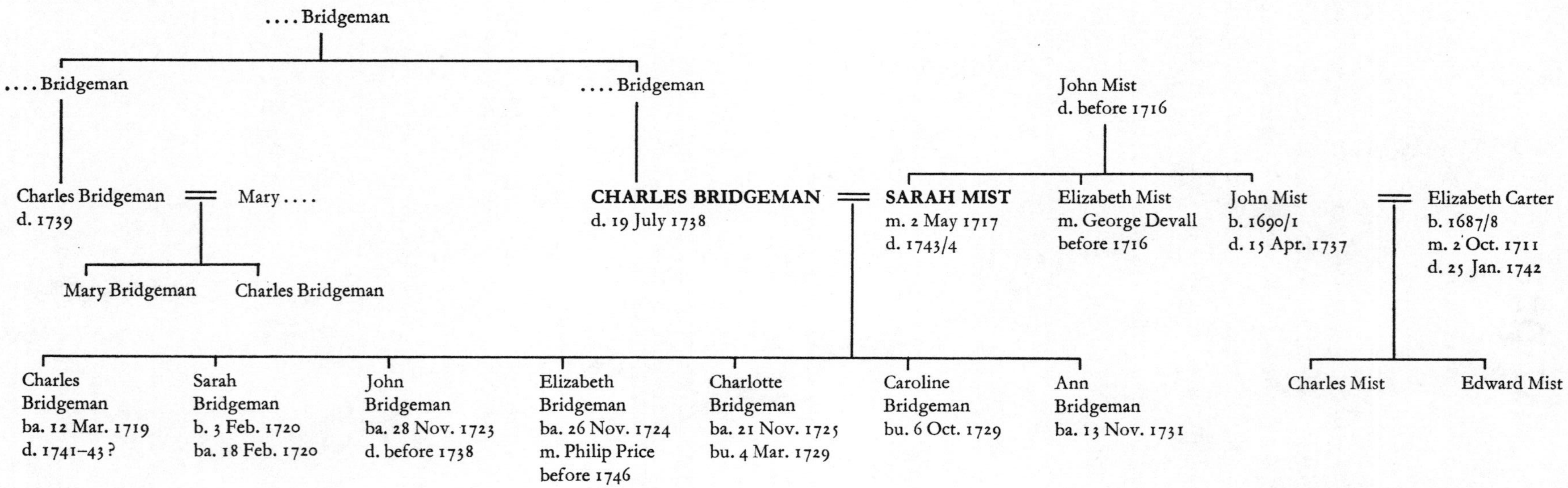

Dates are altered to correspond to the New Calendar beginning on 1 January not 25 March

KEY TO ABBREVIATIONS
b. = born
ba. = baptized
bu. = buried
d. = died
m. = married

Appendix I

Genealogy of Bridgeman's Family

Any attempt to trace Bridgeman's origins is beset with difficulties.[1] The best documented Bridgemans are those of Great Lever, Castle Bromwich, and Weston-under-Lizard,[2] a family which in 1719 was linked to the Earls of Bradford by the marriage of Sir Orlando Bridgeman, 4th Baronet (1695–1764) to Lady Anne Newport (1690–1752), the daughter of the 2nd Earl. It was suggested by J. W. Croker in 1824 that Charles the Royal Gardener was their second son and thus the brother of Sir Henry the 5th Baronet,[3] and this view was subsequently accepted. Yet such a claim is impossible on grounds of date alone, for Sir Henry's brother was not born until 1727 (dying forty years later) and in any case was not called Charles but George.[4] Other alternatives are that Bridgeman's associations with East Anglia imply Suffolk, Norfolk, or Cambridgeshire stock;[5] that his ownership of The Bell Inn at Stilton indicates a Huntingdonshire connection; that he was one of the several Essex gardeners called Bridgeman;[6] that he could be one of the West Country Bridgemans;[7] or that he might be related to the nineteenth-century American horticulturist and writer, Thomas Bridgeman (1786–1850).[8] Such theories are more plausible, but so far remain unsubstantiated. What we can say is that Charles Bridgeman had a cousin of the same name who died in 1739 and who was 'Gent. Alderman and twice Mayor of Hertford.'[9] On 29 September 1733 the Royal Gardener wrote a letter from London, probably to 'Turnip' Townshend, about Nathaniel Brassey's candidacy for Parliament as Member for the Borough of Hertford – a matter in which the Alderman seems to have had some influence. In so doing, the Royal Gardener was satisfying the wishes of a 'good Friend & Patron' at Hampton Court, perhaps George II or Queen Caroline.[10] Whatever their family background, the Bridgemans seem never to have been entirely free from litigation of some sort.[11]

[1] The following attempt will prove this if nothing else. It is intended as a speculative supplement to the biographical material on pp.26–29 above, and no apology is made for documenting somewhat negative results. By so doing it is hoped that in the future blind alleys will be more readily seen.

[2] See W. H. Rylands, ed., 'The Visitation of Warwickshire, 1682–83', *Harl. Soc.*, LXII (1911), 14–15; William Salt Archaeological Society, ed., 'History of the Manor and Parish of Weston-under-Lizard, in the County of Stafford', *Collections for a History of Staffordshire*, N.S., II (1899), facing p.238; H. F. J. Vaughan, 'Oswestry, Ancient and Modern, and Its Local Families', *Archaeologia Cambrensis*, S.5, II (1885), 102.

[3] Croker, ed., *Suffolk Correspondence*, I, 382–83.

[4] Although the Royal Gardener's namesakes occur in the registers of the Bradford Bridgemans, only one Charles Bridgeman (1736–78) does so within his period.

This line is linked to the Vernatti family, but again no affiliation can be established with the Royal Gardener. See W. F. N. Noel, 'Edwards of Welham, County Leicester and of Ketton, County Rutland', *Rutland Magazine*, IV (1909–10), 180; W. D. Sweeting, ed., *Fenland Notes and Queries*, VI (1904–06), 57, 86–87, 134–35, 138, 250, 352.

In 1965 a present-day member of the Bradford Bridgemans, Mr Orlando Bridgeman, completed a *trompe l'œil* of the gardens at Stourhead (believing them to have connections with the Royal Gardener) in the ballroom at Quaglino's Restaurant in London. See 'London Day by Day', *Daily Telegraph*, Wednesday, 29 September 1965, p.16.

[5] The Ashburnham Collection in the Ipswich and East Suffolk CRO, Ipswich, contains many documents about the branch of the Bridgeman family at Combs Hall, but most are too early to be of use here. Mr D. Charman was kind enough to answer my queries.

[6] See the typescript calendar of wills at the Essex CRO, Chelmsford. In particular note the will of Richard Bridgeman of Writtle, gardener, whose will of 29 August 1677 contains a bequest to a son Charles of £30 when he reaches the age of 21 (D/APw W1/74). See Francis W. Steer, ed., *Farm and Cottage Inventories of Mid-Essex, 1635–1749*, 2nd edn (London and Chichester 1969), pp.144–45.

The Stephen Bridgman who worked with the Royal Gardener at Down Hall in Essex may have been the nephew of that name to whom John Bridgeman of Writtle, in a will of 22 September 1720, beqeathes £5 (D/APw R1/75).

For help at the Essex Record Office I am grateful to the former County Archivist, Mr F. G. Emmison, and Miss Nancy R. Briggs.

[7] For the Bridgemans of Nympsfield and Prinknash see W. Bazeley, 'History of Prinknash Park', *Transactions of the Bristol and Gloucestershire Archaeological Society*, VII (1882–83), 306; for those of Gloucester see W. B. Bannerman, ed., *Miscellanea Genealogica et Heraldica*, S.4, V (1914), 285, 291. Note as well Vaughan, 'Oswestry, Ancient and Modern', pp.55, 56–57. Both these families were part of the extensive Bradford strain.

[8] Thomas Bridgeman was born in Abingdon in Berkshire on March 1786, the son of Joseph Bridgeman (1740–99) and the grandson of another Joseph Bridgeman (1707–97),

both of Sutton in Berkshire. Thomas migrated to the United States with his family in 1819–20 and settled in New York City, where he died on 4 April 1850. He is buried in the Eastmond-Bridgeman plot in Green-Wood Cemetery, Brooklyn, Long Island. He had six sons and four daughters and lived at 18th Street and Broadway.

I have been fortunate enough to benefit from the assistance of three of Thomas Bridgeman's descendants in the United States: Miss Anne McIntyre (of Greenwich, Conn.), Miss Iola Moore (of Raleigh, N.C.), and his great-grandson the Rev. Charles Thurley Bridgeman (of Vineyard Haven, Mass.). The evidence they gave me indicates that their ancestor had no connection with the Royal Gardener.

9 John Nichols, *Literary Anecdotes of the Eighteenth Century* . . . (London, 1812–15), IX, 787. The cousin's will is in PRO, PROB. 6/115/RH 36 (HENCHMAN 1739). On 22 February 1739 letters of administration were granted to Mary, the widow and relict. As she died leaving part of the estate unadministered, further letters of administration were granted to her son Charles on 8 April 1745. To this day No.37 West Street, Hertford, is known as Bridgeman House.

10 *HMC 19*: *Townshend*, 352. See below Appendix IV (iii), p.156.

11 As far back as 1716, the year before her marriage to Bridgeman, Sarah Mist was involved in litigation against William Oram, John Mist (her brother), and George Devall and his wife Elizabeth (her brother-in-law and sister). See Bernau Index, Chancery Court Proceedings, 1714/58 (C11), Bdl.852/79. Other Mist suits were in 1720 (ibid., Bdl. 2598/14), 1742 (ibid., Bdl.301/21), 1744 (ibid., Bdl.160/1), 1745 (ibid., Bdl.165/19), 1746 (ibid., Bdl.169/39). I owe these to Mr Malcolm Pinhorn. In her letter of 10 September 1741 to Sarah Bridgeman (*née* Mist), the Duchess of Marlborough mentions Sarah's current suit with the Mists 'for a great Sum'. See below Appendix IV (vii), p.159.

In 1744 the widow Bridgeman and her daughters Elizabeth and Ann (represented by William Bradshaw and Clement Lemprière) were involved in a case against Sarah Bridgeman, the other daughter. See Bernau Index, Chancery Court Proceedings, 1714/58 (C11), Bdl.1596 suit 8.

Mr Pinhorn has also been good enough to tell me of other law suits involving Bridgemans. In Chancery Deponents Before 1714, 108/1, there is a Kent *v.* Bridgeman, whilst a Bridgeman *v.* Bridgeman suit is in Bernau Index, Chancery Court Proceedings, 1703/32 (C11), listed under George I and George II. See also Charles Bridgeman, Thomas Pitt, and Lord Londonderry *v.* Dennis ? Chirac and Abraham Nathan of London, Jewellers, in 1725 (Bernau Index, Chancery Court Proceedings, 1714/58 (C11), Bdl.2282 suit 41); Charles Bridgeman, William Gurnett, Henry Powell, and Martha Gurnett *v.* Lady Elizabeth Diana Mollyneux of Kew, Surrey (widow and relict of Hon. Samuel Mollyneux, Esq., of Kew), in 1730 (ibid., Bdl.83 suit 22). In 1736 there was the suit about The Bell Inn cited above on p.29n16.

Appendix II

Royal Appointment

Bridgeman Replaces Joseph Carpenter as Henry Wise's Partner, 1726
PRO, Works 6/114, fos 7r–10r

George R.

Whereas Our Royal Gardens which have been till the late decease of Joseph Carpenter under the Care & Management of Henry Wise and him the said Joseph Carpenter do according to the last Admeasurement thereof made and certified by the Surveyor of Our Gardens contain 148 Acres two Roods & twenty Perches according to the particulars following Vizt.

	A R P	A R P
AT HAMPTON COURT		
The Melon Ground	2. 3. 0	
Kitchen Garden	8. 1. 24	
Wilderness & Grove	9. 0. 10	
Great Fountain Garden	24. 0. 19	
Privy Garden	4. 2. 8	
Glass case Garden & Pheasant Yard Court	2. 2. 6	
Quadrangle, Princes Court & Tennis Court	0. 3. 18	
Great Terras & Bowling Green	5. 0. 33	
Lower Wilderness	16. 1. 13	
		73. 3. 11
AT KENSINGTON		
The old Gardens from the Green House down to the Road	17. 1. 22	
The new Plantations Kitchen Garden, Coach Court & Peice before the Stoves	38. 0. 0	
		55. 1. 22
AT NEWMARKETT		
The Garden		0. 2. 0
AT WINDSOR		
The several Gardens at Windsor Great Park	10. 1. 0	
Fruit Plantation next the new wall in Mastrick	2. 2. 30	
Little House Garden	3. 0. 33	
Kitchen Garden	0. 0. 33	
		17. 0. 16
AT ST JAMES'S		
The Garden		1. 3. 11
		148. 2. 20

And Whereas We are graciously pleased to allow & approve of a Scheme to which the said Henry Wise & Joseph Carpenter sett their hands to Seals for the order & manner in which Our said Gardens were to be kept up & maintained by them, & that the said Henry Wise & Joseph Carpenter should have & receive in Consideration of their Service, care, pains & Expences in Ordering Keeping up and maintaining all Our Gardens in and according to the Terms and Conditions of the said Scheme & Allowance after the rate of £20 pr Acre which amounted to £2960 pr Ann and the said Allowance hath been accordingly paid to the said Henry Wise & Joseph Carpenter or one of them for the Quarter ended at Michmas last 1726

Now We being minded that the place of the said Joseph Carpenter should be supplyed by another Person, And Confiding much in the Experience, skill & Ability of Charles Bridgeman in and for this service We have thought fit and do hereby Nominate & Appoint the said Charles Bridgeman to be joyned with the said Henry Wise in the Ordering & keeping of Our said Gardens & the said Henry Wise & Charles Bridgeman & the Survivor of them is & are hereby appointd to be our Cheif Gardiners & Gardiner for that purpose accordingly and We do hereby direct & require them the said Henry Wise & Charles Bridgeman to execute under their hand & Seals a Writing containing the like Scheme Which We are hereby graciously pleased to approve as the Scheme by which the said Henry Wise & Charles Bridgeman & the Survivor of them shall order keep and maintain Our said Gardens and that they the said Henry Wise and Charles Bridgeman & the Survivor of them shall have & enjoy all Garden Houses, Priviledges, Liberties, Emoluments and Advantages as were had & enjoyed by the said Henry Wise & Joseph Carpenter (save only & except the two Pavillions at the East End of Our Bowling Green at Hampton Court) & the Out Houses & Buildings belonging thereunto which said two Pavillions & the said Out Houses & Buildings belonging thereunto Our Express will & pleasure is shall be in the sole power possession & keeping of Our Trusty & well beloved Christopher Tilson & Mary his Wife & the Survivor of them without any Molestatn. Hindrance, Interuption or other Obstruction whatever by or from the said Henry Wise & Charles Bridgeman or either of them or any other Our Officers & Ministers whatsoever Our will & pleasure therefore is And We do hereby direct Authorise & Command that you from Michmas 1726 as aforesaid do pay or cause to be paid unto the said Henry Wise & Charles Bridgeman or either of them their or either of their Assignes by the hands of the Paymaster of Our Works for the time being the said Yearly Sum of £2960 by Quarterly or other Paymts, as you in that behalf shall think fitt for & in Consideration of their Service, care, & Expences, in Ordering & keeping up all Our said Gardens according to the Terms & Conditions contained in the said Scheme And Our further pleasure is that this Our Warrant & the Scheme thereby referred to be entered with the Surveyor of Our Gardens to the End he may have Cognizance thereof & take care from time to time that the said Henry Wise & Charles Bridgeman joyntly & severally do fully comply with execute & perform the said Scheme in all things thereby required to be complyed with executed and performed by them or either of them & that We be not burthened with any expences relating to Our said Gardens other than such as by the said Scheme are agreed to be born & defrayed by Us. And the said Warrant & Scheme is also to be entered in the Office of Our Works to the end that the Board of Works may regard this Our Service in all thing appertaining to them and for so doing this shall be your Warrant Given at Our Court at Kensington the 18th. day of October 1726 in the 13th. Year of Our Reign

By His Majestys Command

R. Walpole

Wm. Yonge

G. Dodington

To Commissioners Treasury

Let the Paymaster of His Majesty's Works now & for the time being, take care that His Majesty's Pleasure signified to Us by the aforegoing Warrant under His Majesty's Royal Sign Manual be executed & complyed with from time to time so far as appertains unto him and this with the Acquittances of Henry Wise and Charles Bridgeman or either of them, their or either of their Assignes for the Monies he shall from time to time pay in pursuance thereof, shall be as well to the said Paymaster as to the Auditors & all others concerned in passing & allowing from time to time such Paymts. upon his Accounts a Sufficient Warrant. Whitehall Treary Chambers 20th. Octr. 1726

R.W. W.Y. G.D.

There then follows on fos 8v–10r 'A Scheme of His Majesty's several Gardens & Plantations . . . undertaken to be kept by Henry Wise & Charles Bridgeman'. It was signed by Wise and Bridgeman on 18 October 1726. The text is similar to that adopted for Bridgeman's Royal Appointment in 1728, and the gardens included are Hampton Court, Kensington, Newmarket, and Windsor. To this list, Bridgeman's 'Scheme' of 1728 adds St James's.

NOTE: A slightly different version of the above text, and of Wise and Bridgeman's 'Scheme' of 1726, is in PRO, Works 16/39/1, fos 1r–3v.

Appendix III

Royal Appointment

Bridgeman Becomes Chief Gardener to George II, 1728

PRO, Works 6/114, fos 12v–15v

George R

Whereas Our Royal Gardens according to the last admeasurement thereof made & certifyed in the Reign of Our late Royal Father the King of glorious Memory by the Surveyor of the said Gardens do Contain One hundred forty Eight Acres & Twenty Perches as by the Particulars hereunder mentioned may appear Vizt.

	A	R	P	A	R	P
AT HAMPTON COURT						
The Melon Ground	2.	3.	0			
Kitchen Garden	8.	1.	24			
Wilderness & Grove	9.	0.	10			
Great fountain Garden	24.	0.	19			
Privy Garden	4.	2.	8			
Glass Case Garden & Pheasant Yard Court	2.	2.	6			
Quadrangle, Princes Court & Tennis Court	0.	3.	18			
Great Terras & Bowling Green	5.	0.	33			
Lower Wilderness	16.	1.	13			
				73.	3.	11
AT ST JAMES'S						
The Garden				1.	3.	11
AT KENSINGTON						
The old Garden from the Green House down to the Road	17.	1.	22			
The New Plantation, Kitchen Garden, Coach Court & peice before the Stoves	38.	0.	0			
				55.	1.	22
AT NEWMARKETT						
The Gardens				0.	2.	0
AT WINDSOR						
The several Gardens at Windsor Great Park	10.	1.	0			
Fruit Plantation next the New Wall in Maestrick	2.	3.	30			
Little House Garden	3.	0.	33			
Kitchen Garden	0.	0.	33			
				16.	2.	16
				148.	0.	20

And Whereas We are graciously pleased to Nominate & appoint Charles Bridgeman to be Our Cheif Gardiner And to allow & approve of the Scheme or Contract executed by the said Charles Bridgeman under his hand & Seal which is hereunto annexed, containing the order manner and method in which Our said Gardens are to be maintained kept & upheld by him And We are further Graciously pleased to Grant & allow that the said Charles Bridgeman in consideration thereof Shall have & receive the Yearly Sum of Two Thousand Two hundred & Twenty pounds being after the rate of Fifteen pounds pr Acre for the said One hundred forty Eight Acres of which Our said Gardens by the aforesaid Admeasurement did consist And that the said Allowance shall commence & be accounted payable to him from Lady day next ensuing the date hereof in manner hereunder mentioned And We are also further graciously pleased to Grant & allow that the several Garden Houses Sheds & Places heretofore Used & possessed by Henry Wise Esqr. or other Persons having the Office of Cheif Gardiner to the Crown Seperately or Joyntly shall be had taken & Used & be & remain in the possession of the said Charles Bridgeman for the Use of himself & Servants Save only and except the two Pavillions at the East End of Our Bowling Green at Hampton Court & the Out Houses & Buildings thereunto belonging which said two Pavillions & the said Outhouses & Buildings thereunto belonging Our express will & pleasure is shall be in the Sole Power, Possession & keeping of Our Trusty & Wellbeloved Christopher Tilson Esqr. & Mary his Wife during our pleasure without any Lett hindrance, Molestation or Interruption whatsoever by or from the said Charles Bridgeman or any other Our Officers or Ministers whatsoever wherefore Our Will & pleasure is & We do hereby direct, Authorize & Command You to pay or Cause to be paid unto the said Charles Bridgeman or his Assignes by the Hands of the Paymaster of Our Works for the time being the said Yearly Sum of Two thousand Two hundred & Twenty pounds from Lady day One Thousand Seven hundred Twenty Eight as aforesaid by Quarterly or other Payments as you in that behalf shall think fitt & in Consideration of his service, care, Pains & Expences in Ordering maintaining & keeping up all Our Gardens aforedescribed according to the Terms Conditions & Agreements in the said Scheme contained And Our further pleasure is that this Our Warrant & the Scheme thereby referred to be enter'd with the Surveyor of Our Gardens to the end he may have full Cognizance thereof &

take care from time to time that the said Charles Bridgeman do well, truly & effectually comply with, execute & perform the said Scheme in all things thereby Stipulated to be complyed with Executed & performed by him, And that We be not burthened with any Expences relating to Our said Gardens or any of them, other than such as by the said Scheme are agreed to be born & defrayed by Us. And that the said Warrant & Scheme be also Enterd in the Office of Our Works to the end the Officers of Our Board of Works may strictly regard Our Service in all things Appertaining to them And for so doing this shall be your Warrt. Given at Our Court at St. James's this 15th. day of March 1727 In the first Year of Our Reign

By His Majesty's Command

R. Walpole

C. Turner

G. Dodington

To the Commissioners of Our Treasury now being And to Our High Trea[sur]er or Commissrs. of Our Treasury for the time being

A Scheme of His Majesty's Several Gardens and Plantations as they & each Division therein do require to be maintained, Kept & Upheld, and as the same are undertaken to be maintained, Kept & Upheld by Charles Bridgeman

AT HAMPTON COURT

The Melon Ground Kitchen Garden & Fruit Gardens in Six Divisions	*To be dunged, Digged & Cropt with the several Variety's of eatables most proper for His Majts. Use & the Trees Pruned & Naild*
Wilderness & Grove Great Fountain Garden Privy Garden Glass case Garden & Pheasant Yard Cot. Quadrangle Princes Court & Tennis Court Great Terras & Bowling Green	*The Grass to be mowed Swept & rolled. The Gravell rolled & Weeded. The borders Dunged, Digged, Hoed, Raked & weeded. The several hardy Ever Greens & other Plants to be stak'd Tyed up Pruned & Clipped. And to keep in Good order the several Collections of Housed Greens & Flower Roots*
Lower Wilderness	*The Quarters & Sand Allys to be kept clean from weeds, the Grass mowed, & the hedge Lines Clipped*

AT ST JAMES'S

The Garden	*All which to be kept in good Order by the Grass being Mowed, Rolled & Swept. The Gravell Rolled & Weeded. the Borders Earthed Dunged, digged, Hoed, raked & weeded the Quarters Digged the Hedge Lines Clipped the several hardy ever Greens & other Plants Staked Tyed up Pruned & Clipped the Fruit Trees pruned & naild & the several Collections of Housed Greens & Flower roots to be well managed & kept in good Order*

AT KENSINGTON

The old Gardens from the Green House down to the Road The New Plantation that which was the Coach Court & Peice before the Stoves The several Green Houses & Greens	(as above)
The Kitchen Garden	*To be dunged, digged & Cropt with the sevll. Variety's of Eatables most proper for His Majts. Use & the Trees pruned & Naild*

AT NEWMARKETT

The several little Gardens as now made & Planted to be Upheld & kept in good Order

AT WINDSOR

The several Gardens at Windsor great Park as now made & now kept up to be looked after in all those works as before mentioned finding & providing the several Working Tools & Materials as is Expressed for the several other Gardens Dung only excepted, being allways made at the Stable to the House for it is impossible to have Dung for the Gardens any other way than from what is made at the Stable.

The Fruit Plantation next the Wall in Mastrick—— The Border next the Wall where the Fruit Trees are Planted to the Wall & also the other Border where the Dwarf of Fruit Trees are plantd at about 25 feet distance from the Wall, both which borders are to be kept clean from Weeds, & Cultivated with Dung as often as is necessary for the Benefit of the several Fruit Trees.

Little House Garden with the Green Houses & Kitchen Garden as now made, are to be maintained & kept up in all respects as the like Gardens or Grounds at Hampton Court or Kensington or either of Them are agreed to be maintained & kept.

An Account of the several Tools, Materials & other things that are to be provided by the Undertaker

Brooms
Barrows
Baskets
Bass Matts to Cover the Melon & early Fruits
Carriage of the Kitchen Garden Eatables
Carriage of the Kings Sumer Fruit from the several gardns. daily by relays of Men on foot to the Court
Compost for the Oranges & c.
Dung Forks
Edging Irons
Engine to sprinkle the sevl. Trees & plants
Earthen Pots
Fruit & Sallad Baskets
Flower sticks painted & plain

Fewell for the Hot Houses or Stoves
Gardiners & Labourers wages
Glasses
Grindstones
Grooves
Horses & their keeping for rolling
Horse Dung & all other sorts of dung for the Melon beds & Improvements of the several Gardens
Hoes
Hammers, Nails & list for the Fruit Trees
Handspikes
Jetts
Lines
Melon frames
Orange Tubs
Pruning hooks & knives
Pick Axes
Riding Expences & c. to the Undertaker
Rakes
Reels
Rollers of all Sorts
Skreens
Spades
Sheers
Scyths & Rubbers
Trowells
Wire Seives
Wooden Seives
Water barrows & Straps
Water Tubs
Watering Potts

Also the said Undertaker is at his own proper Costs & charges to make good the several Plantations of Fruit Trees, Forrest Trees, Flowering Shrubs and hardy Evergreens that shall at any time happen to dye by planting others in their Places.

For the Performance of all the aforesaid Works, Finding & providing the several Tools, Materials & other things together with the making good all the several Plantations as aforesaid the said Charles Bridgeman is to have & receive the Sum of Two Thousand Two hundred & Twenty pounds being at the Fifteen Pounds pr Acre for One hundred & forty Eight Acres of which the Gardens hereby meant to be maintained do Consist The same to be paid by Quarterly or other Payments as shall be thought fitt. And to Commence from Lady day One thousand Seven hundred & Twenty Eight & to be had & received out of the Office of Works by the hands of the Paymaster thereof for the same Fees as the same Office pays to the Exchequer.

The said Charles Bridgeman notwithstanding the particulars before enumerated to be provided & maintained by him does declare That it is meant & intended his Majesty shall be at no charge whatsoever in & about the said Gardens or any of them Save only for the Repairs of Green Houses, Stoves, Garden Houses, Sheds, Fences, Doors & Locks, which are to be performed & supply'd by the Officers of His Majestys Works in the Manner & Method they were Used to be Provided nevertheless that in Case his Majesty shall signify his Royal Pleasure to alter the present Disposition of or to new make the Gardens or any of them hereby meant to be maintained & kept up or any part thereof then the Charge & Expence of such Alterations or new making from time to time shall be borne by His Majesty.

That the several Garden Houses, Sheds, or Places heretofore Used by the Kings Gardiners are to be Used & remain in the possession of Charles Bridgeman the Undertaker for the Use of himself & his Servants. Saving & Excepting the two Pavillions at the East end of His Majesty's Bowling Green at Hampton Court & the Outhouses & Buildings thereunto belonging which his Majesty by Warrant under his Royal Sign Manual bearing date this day hath been graciously pleased to put under the Sole power, possession & keeping of Christopher Tilson Esq[r] and Mary his Wife during his Majesty's pleasure
In Confirmation of which agreement the said Charles Bridgeman hath hereunto set his hand & Seal this fifteenth day of March in the first Year of the Reign of Our Sovereign Lord George the Second of Great Britain, France & Ireland King Defender of the Faith & . . . Anno Domini 1727

Witness Charles Bridgeman
Thos. Bowen
Peter Leheup

Intrat in Officio Thomae Foley
Arv Auditoris 9° die Aprilis 1728
Duke Parsons Dep: Aud:
Intrat in Officio honoblis. Edwardi Harley Ari.
Auditoris 17 Die Maÿ 1732
Edwd. Bangham Dep: Aud:

Appendix IV

Letters

This Appendix consists of transcripts of the seven letters so far discovered which passed to or from Charles Bridgeman and his wife Sarah. Four of these (iv–vii) are published here in full for the first time. Bridgeman's letter to the Earl of Oxford is quoted by courtesy of the Duke of Portland, and the three letters from Sarah, Duchess of Marlborough, to Mrs Sarah Bridgeman by courtesy of the Duke of Marlborough.

(i)
From Charles Bridgeman to Alexander Pope, 28 September 1724

BL, Add MS 4809, fo. 141v

Broadstreet Sepr.28th: 1724

Sir / Since I waited on Mrs: Howard & You at Twickenham, I have been continually abroad on business that I then knew not of; but of great Moment, & of which You shall know more when I have the Honr. to see You I came home on Fryday night & had Your kind Letter [O]n Saturday morning I begun on the plann, & have not [lef]t from that time to this so long as I could see, nor shall [I] leave it till 'tis finish'd which I hope will be about tomorrow Noon, but the affair I mention to You above will not let me move from Home this fortnight, so shall be glad if Your affairs call you to Towne on Tuesday or any other day this week that I may a little explain it to you, or if not I will Send it to You by my man on Wednesday morning. I am / Sr Yor. most obliged humb Servt. / Charles Bridgeman

Address: To Mr Pope at / his house in / Twittenham / Middlesex
Postmark: 28 / SE

NOTE: This letter appears in *Pope Correspondence*, II, 261, although my transcript differs in detail from Professor Sherburn's. The subject of Add MS 4809 is part of Pope's translation of Homer's *Odyssey*, and lines from it appear on the back of the letter. Bridgeman's signature on this letter is reproduced as *Plate 160b*.

(ii)
From Alexander Pope to Charles Bridgeman [1725]

Pope Correspondence, II, 327

Dawley, Thursday [1725]

I am sorry it is not possible for me to go to Lord Oxford's with you, so soon: for a hundred objections lye in my way just now. But pray assure my lord faithfully of my truest respects, and earnest desires to see him. I wish you a good journey, and total recovery of your health, being faithfully, dear sir, yours [Alexander Pope].

I hope you will fix that matter with Mrs. Howard. My Lord Bolingbroke received yours, and shall be glad to see you at your conveniency.

NOTE: Professor Sherburn thought that this letter was at one time at Longleat, though he was unable to find it there. See Elwin and Courthope, eds., *Works*, IX, 517.

(iii)
From Charles Bridgeman to Charles Townshend, 2nd Viscount Townshend, 29 September 1733

HMC 19: Townshend, 352

[Dated 29 September 1733 in London but unaddressed]

My Lord, – Just after your Lordp spoke to me at Hamp[ton] Court on Sunday last, my good Friend & Patron orderd me to desire my Cosin Bridgeman not to engage his Vote, & this was the whole of his order at that time: I was since down with my Cosin at Hartford, & he very kindly promis'd me he would not; While I was with him, he told me that Sr Thos Clark & Your Lordp were in the same intention of nominating a second Candidate [for the Borough of Hertford], which I was glad to hear, hoping it was what my Patron meant, but as it was not then certain to me, I could request my Cousin no farther. Yesterday I attended my Patron at Hamp[ton] Cot and acquainted him with what I had done, and likewise that I found your Lordp & Sr Thomas joyn'd in nominating Mr Braccy [Nathaniel Brassey], he was pleased to say that whatever Your Lordp & Sr Thomas Clark did, he should approve; this I was glad to hear, & it occasions this Letter to Your Lordp, not doubting but the great regard my Cousin has for him & You will induce him to declare his other vote, for the Person You recommend...

P.S. I have acquainted him I have wrote to Your Lordp. If there is occasion for a Letter to me please to direct it to my house in Broad-street near Poland Street S. James's, London.

NOTE: The MS of this letter was located at Raynham Hall, Norfolk, when this book was in press.

(iv)
From Charles Bridgeman to Edward Harley, 2nd Earl of Oxford, 26 July 1734

BL, Loan 29/90 (Portland Papers)

My Lord / I hope Your Lordps. goodness will permit me in this manner, 'tho late, to congratulate Your Lordp, and my Lady Oxford, on the mariage of Lady Margaret with His Grace the Duke of Portland; I heartily wishing them a long & a happy Life; and Your Lordp. & my Lady Oxford, all the pleasures & Satisfaction You [c]an hope thereby, humbly beging leave to signify to Your Lordp. that nobody can have a greater honour for Your Lordp, & family than I have, nor feel more sensibly any good enjoy'd, or hop'd for in it.

An indisposition does not admit me at present to pay my duty to Your Lordp in person, which Your Lordp's. goodness will excuse. I am / My Lord / Your Lordps. most obedt. humb Servt. / Charles Bridgeman
Kensington / July 26. 1734.

Address: For / The Right Honourable the Earle / of Oxford / in Dover Street
Mr Charles Bridgman / Kinsington July 26. 1734

NOTE: For a reproduction of this letter see *Plate 161*. Comparison between Bridgeman's signature here and on his will (*Plate 160a*) suggests that the Harley letter is in Bridgeman's hand. If so, it is our best example of his handwriting.

(v)
From Sarah, Duchess of Marlborough, to Mrs Sarah Bridgeman, 6 July 1741

Blenheim Palace, Oxon, Blenheim MSS F1–35

Marlborough house July ye 6th: 1741

Mrs Bridgman, / I writ to you the 20th: of February, which letter I don't doubt but you have, tho' I have not hear'd from you since; for this letter seems to be an Answer to one of your's of the same Date. I need not repeat my letter because you have that. This is only to put you in mind of the Unreasonableness of all your letters to me, and to shew you the Danger you are in by not Complying with Mr: Bridgman's Contracts: Who, I had so much Kindness for, that I would do more a great deal than any Body with reason can propose. I have four Contracts with him Sign'd and Witness'd in the clearest manner that can be in which he promises to Compleat them all for £2542:3:9 without any further Charge on any Account. And I paid him £1150 in five Months: Which he seldom receiv'd of any body at the very beginning of his Work. After that I gave him Mony whenever he ask'd for it, and the whole he receiv'd of me was £2,353 for all which Sums I have his Receipts. And the Contract was a great deal for what he was to do: Which, if he had perform'd, there would be now due to you, or his Executors, £187:3:9. I beleive I might possibly make a Mistake in the last letter by reckoning the Remainder was £287:3:9. but that can admit of no dispute, because I have found all his Acquittances which reduce the Debt to £187:3:9. Now I must repeal your extravagant Proceedings since the Death of Mr: Bridgman. Amongst which you demand £1284:6:5½ more than I have paid, saying only, you will readily allow of any Notes that your Husband has Sign'd to have receiv'd. And then you go on, making a Bill, as if I had no Contract from your Husband for the business to be done, and propose a very ridiculous thing that some Servant of his, who is very honest, shall satisfie me that the Account is very just, as if I had made no Contract, when nothing is more distinct and plain than all the Contracts are. After this, I have several wild Letters of your's, in which you tell me you will send Mr: Bridgman's Creditors to be paid by me, tho' he had received so great a Sum without making his Contracts good. And soon after your Husband dy'd, you stopt the Workmen, and left the finishing the Contracts to me: Which I have done since, and can prove by the Bills paid that I have laid out at least £700 to do what Mr: Bridgman Contracted to do for the above Sum. After this, you seem'd to be ashamed of your Demand, and writ a Letter to me to Wimbledon that you would deduct the Garden affair; which you had Charg'd so wrongly. For Mr: Bridgman is very express in the Articles that the Sum *was to be for all he did*. And in some of your Letters to seem to put it upon my Generosity, and say Mr: Bridgman has not left effects to pay his Debts, and it would be the ruin of his Family, and by these false Arguments you would have me give it, because you cannot contend with me, and 'tis great Charity. When I told you that Mr: Bridgman's agreement with me, which I can prove, was, that his Gardiner he employ'd should be paid for keeping the Garden one year, after all the work was finish'd you Answerd you beleiv'd it; for it was his Way. And, if you should think fit to disown that, besides what I have said, I can prove it by twenty Contracts to other people. But indeed that is not necessary, when so plain a Contract is made, and more Mony paid upon it so long ago, though so great a Sum I have paid to finish what he was to have done. And my Accounts will prove that what I was forc'd to have laid out was done at much more reasonable Rates than what he Contracted with me to pay him for it. If you shew this letter to any friend you have that has Sense they will tell you, how very provoking you have been, and will advise you to make an end of this dispute without law, or more Expence: Since they will see by this letter that Mr: Bridgman has receiv'd many years ago, more than he ought to have had by his own Contracts. And I am willing from the Kindness I had to Mr: Bridgman who, I think, was an honest Man, to Comply with any thing tolerably reasonable and not put his Exors to the Expence of my going to law. There are Bills that I have hear'd of for Cartage, and Sand to Cole, to James Browne, a Smith, and to Mr Hunt for trees, a Nurseryman, which amount to £26:8:0 You know best if these are paid: I have been told you have paid them. All I know, is, that these trees were but a small price in Comparison of what I allowd in ye Contracts And there is a great deal that ought to be deducted by his own agreement for things he had of mine to perform those Contracts. I am very sorry, as you are Mr Bridgman's Wife, I cannot say that I am your Friend, as well as humble Servant, since you have usd me so ill / S Marlborough

Note on back: Copy of a Letter to Mrs: Bridgman Dated the / 6th: of July 1741.

(vi)
From Sarah, Duchess of Marlborough, to Mrs Sarah Bridgeman, 26 July 1741

Blenheim Palace, Oxon, Letter Book No.2, Bills and Estimates . . . , fos 24r–25v

Marlborough House July ye 26th: 1741

I have receiv'd your's in Answer to mine of the 6th: of July. Which was taking a good deal of time; and yet there is nothing in your Letter that is any Answer to mine. You begin with Complaining of many persons who will not pay Mr: Bridgman's just Demands upon them. Which I am not surprised at; beleiving it very possible they may be such Demands you have made upon me. But, supposing it otherwise, that is nothing at all to me: Who have been always ready to pay according to my Contract. And, to prove I did so, I have Acquittances under Mr: Bridgeman's own Hand for the Receipt of £2,355.0.0. And this was a great Sum for removing some Earth, not much, a few English Elms, and Hedges, and Gravel fetch'd from my own Ground, to make the Walks as they should be, with a great deal of my own Gravel there on the place. And the great Sum of Mony above was paid by me, long before he could have expended half of it. My Contracts with Mr: Bridgman were to give him £2,542:3:9 for doing the whole without any further Expence to me of any kind: So that if he had perform'd his Articles, there would be now due to you, or his Exors £187:3:9. Nothing can be more particular than all the Contracts are. He has oblig'd himself to plant all Fruit-trees, Flowers, and to finish the whole place, and Ground in a handsome Manner, and to make good all Trees that dye: and whatever Wood he shall use of mine for Stakes and Poles, to tie the Espaliers, he is to deduct for. He is likewise to make all the Wood walks clean with Sand, or Gravel, the Terrace-walk handsome, to strip up the Trees in the Vineyard-walk, and the Wood on the outside the House, to my liking. And in short, to Compleat everything without any further Charge to me than the Articles. And to begin and finish the Road with all possible Expedition. Chas: Bridgman.

I have said so much upon these Subjects before, that 'tis quite unnecessary to say more of them, than that all his Contracts and Receipts for the Mony, I have to produce. But Mr: Bridgman did not perform the Contracts, as I have told you before in many Instances in former letters, by a very great Sum of Mony I can prove I have paid to finish them. Barely for what he was to do by the Contracts for the above mentioned Sum. You know yourself that soon after your Husband dy'd you put a Stop to these Works, and took away the Servants; for I had none of them, nor any thing to do with it. Tho' Mr: Bridgman had receiv'd so great a Sum before-hand. And yet after that you had the Conscience to send me a Bill of £3,439:6:5½ Allowing that your Husband had receiv'd £2,155. Which is £200 less than I have his Acquittances for. And this Monstrous demand was without performing by many Hundred Pounds what he Articled to do for £2,542:3:9 So that your Demand exceeds all the Contracts by £897:2:8½ And in your last Letter, as well as in former ones, you Complain that I refus'd a Servant of your's to determine what you should have, and invited you to a Law suit. This is as Unreasonable, and ridiculous as if I should desire one of my Servants to be Judge of Mr: Bridgman's Contracts: Which, to be sure, I am oblig'd to pay, tho' they had been vastly more than they ought to have been. But then Contracts are equal, and to be perform'd on both sides. And 'tis lucky for me that I have all his Contracts and Receipts in so exact a Manner. You tell me in your last Letter "you are not in a Condition to do yourself Right in a Course of law; and therefore you must submit yourself to my Mercy and Goodness"; and that you're in "such Misfortunes and difficulties that you cannot keep your Family from the Parish". This, I hope is a Mistake, and writ when you was in a great passion: For I have had an Account from those, who are no Enemies to you, and know your Circumstances, that they are good. But supposing they were not, that would be no reason for me to make you a present of so great a Sum of Mony. You are so very Cautious that you say nothing material in your letter to me. I ask'd you if Mr Bridgman had paid all the Debts for which he receiv'd my Mony? To this you are quite silent: As likewise to every part of my Letter that signifies anything Therefore I write to you now, once for all, to tell you that if you will not write to me something that is reasonable, nor begin the Law-suit, I must give directions to do it myself. And, if I should dye before 'tis ended, put it in my Exors power to recover what may be due from you. And, to be sure, whenever that is brought into Westminster Hall, you will be decreed to pay it with Costs, the whole thing is so demonstrably plain. This is absolutely necessary for me to do, because if the Suit is not begun in Six Years after Mr: Bridgeman's Death, neither side can do any thing from an Act of Parliament. But, as I said before, I did believe Mr: Bridgman honest and meant to do justly in every thing. I had a Kindness for him, and upon his Account would agree to do any thing that was tolerably reasonable, though I have such strong proofs, and you have nothing to say for what you have done in this whole Concern of / Your humble Servant / S: Marlborough

Note on back: To Mrs Bridgman / Copy of a Letter Dated ye 26th: of July 1741.

NOTE: Extracts from this letter appear in Green, *Blenheim Palace*, pp.280–81.

(vii)
From Sarah, Duchess of Marlborough, to Mrs Sarah Bridgeman, 10 September 1741

Blenheim Palace, Oxon, Blenheim MSS F1–35

Wimbledon September the 10th: 1741

I receiv'd your letter of the 3d: of August, which I thought so odd that I was not in Haste to make any Answer. I writ to you in my last what Mony I had paid to Mr: Bridgman. A great part of it, before he had laid out any thing worth naming. And that is very seldom done by others, to pay Mony before 'tis due: Which gave him an Opportunity of making Use of my Mony upon His other Occasions. You say in One of your letters, "that if you have made any Mistake as to the Payments, whatever is short of the Sum he did receive, you will Acknowledge, if he has given the Acquittance for it." That you can't help. And I don't desire to Charge a Penny to Mr Bridgman's Account without producing his own Hand for the Receipt of it. So there is not the least Shadow of a Dispute in that. You make a heavy Complaint of your ill Circumstances, and a Law suit for a great Sum, which you have with the Mists. I hope you are as much mistaken in that, as you certainly have been in your Behaviour to me. But indeed you say in your Letter, "that you have no *Stomach* to go to Law, and are not now in a Condition to engage in another Suit, and therefore choose to submit your self to my pleasure", in Answer to what I desir'd, after I had stated the whole matter between Mr: Bridgman and myself, that for his Sake (whom I thought an honest Man) I would do any thing that was tolerably reasonable, if you would be plain and short in saying upon what Terms you would put an End to all this Matter. I writ you an Account of all the Contracts I had with your Husband, and the Sums I had paid him: Which amounted within a trifle of all the Contracts. And these shew plainly he was to do the whole thing for so much Mony, express'd strongly without puting me to any other Charge than the Contracts oblig'd me to. It happen'd Mr: Bridgman dy'd before he had completed what he agreed to do by a very great Sum: Which I can prove. Though he had receiv'd so near the whole of the Agreement. 'Tis true, you say something in your Letter that seems something of Reason, "that you will submit to my pleasure". But then 'tis so mix'd with other things that I take it to be only a little Cunning (which is very simple in this affair) that you would have me enter into new Debates and Trouble, with you: Which I would not do for a much greater Sum than even you could desire to have. Because I have seen long, that your Passion to have what is not due to you is much stronger than your Reason. I cannot doubt but you have the Copys of all he Sign'd. I told you before, I had all his Contracts Witness'd. But you say nothing to the Point, "but that you are no judge whether He has perform'd his Contracts or not, having not been permitted to have that ffact examined into." And you add, "that what you would have Examin'd is, Extraordinarys, quite out of the Contracts". This I must take the liberty to say is quite Nonsense: For there can be no extraordinarys, beyond what he was to do by the Contracts, without any further Charge to me of any kind. And he was to make a Deduction to me for what he us'd of mine, which would have lessen'd the Sum of the Contracts. I press'd him very often to make an End of his Business: But, having a great deal to do for others, he was too long about mine. And I was not uneasy, because I beleiv'd he was a very honest Man. If you can shew any Contract for the extraordinary Business, I would submit to that, tho' ever so Unreasonable. But if it comes into a Court of Law, no Body can beleive that any thing of your Contriving can succeed: Or, that such a Sum, as you pretend to, could be expended without Contracts, when so exact a Method was taken to have Mr: Bridgman Sign these Contracts in the manner I have describ'd, and to give Receipts for so much Mony. If this Business must come to be decided by Law, I can easily prove the very great Sum I have paid to finish Mr: Bridgman's very express and particular Contracts. I am sure I never gave any Orders, nor Sign'd any Contracts, but those I have in my own Custody. Nor had I anything to do with Mr: Bridgman's Foreman, or any thing in the Works. One Instance of which, is, that I paid Thorney for something I had employ'd him in about selling Wood, and I found he had Cheated me: However, I paid him, but never employ'd him anymore. This shews he was not my Servant. And Mr: Bridgman did, upon finding him a very Ill Man, put another in his place. Now what in the World can be so ridiculous, as for you to give me so much trouble as you have done in this Affair? For I can prove all I have said and that Mr: Bridgman had made an Agreement with me to do all for the Mony stipulated, and desir'd only that his Gardiner might keep my Gardens one year after 'twas all finish'd. This I told you long ago. And you Answer'd "you beleiv'd it, for 'twas his Way". And I know several People that will add to my proof, with whom he made the same Agreement. And indeed 'twas a Natural Way: For he had a great Sum of Mony to make Alterations in the Ground, & c. And no Body but your self can think of making a great Demand, contrary to all Articles and Proofs. You turn'd off Mr: Bridgman's Servants as soon as he Dy'd. And I was forc'd, at a very great Expence, to finish his Contracts. Let me know in short, without any Mixture of what is not worth reading, plainly what you will do to end this Matter. For, unless you do so, which is for your own Advantage, I will never write any more to you, but proceed at Law against Mr: Bridgman's Exors (I don't know who they are) to deduct what the Court will Decree that he has receiv'd more than he should to make good his Contracts. I am / Your humble Servant / S Marlborough

Note on back: Copy of a Letter to Mrs: Bridgman Dated the 10th / Day of September 1741.

Appendix V

Inventory of Charles Bridgeman 1738

PRO, PROB.3/37/95

A true and perfect Inventary of all and singular the Goods Chattells and Credits of Charles Bridgeman late of the Parish of St. James Westminster in the County of Middlesex Esquire deceased which since his death have come to the hands possession or knowledge of Sarah Bridgeman Widow the Relict and one of the Executors named in the last Will and Testament of the said Deceased taken valued and appraized on the twenty fourth twenty eighth twenty ninth and thirty first days of July on the third and fourth days of August and on the seventh and twenty third days of September in the year of our Lord One thousand Seven hundred and thirty eight by Edward Cullen Henry Heasman Thomas Busnett John Wright John Cox and Henry Bristow as follows to wit

AT THE DECEASEDS HOUSE IN BROAD STREET

In the Fore Garrett Back Garrett and Closett
First An old Wainscott broken bedstead a broken field bedstead and some Lumber three old blanketts and an old quilt two old easy Chairs and two small Chairs without bottoms an old bedstead and part of a Linsey furniture an old feather bed two bolsters and one pillow one old blanket and two old quilts and a Childs Chair a blew Cloth Rockello a pair of black Shagg breeches two fine Cloth Suits with gold buttons Two Suits of black and two grey Coats with black Wastcoats and Breeches Two old Cloth Suits Two Ditto Moth eaten Six old Coats Three Cape Coats Two Wastcoats Two pair of Breeches and one pair of leather Ditto Three Banyans and an old Livery Coat Two old dimitty Wastcoats Three Tye Wiggs and four Bobbs . . . pair of Shoes One pair of Spatterdashes . . . pair of Boots [caret with illegible insertion] Three old Hatts and twelve holland Shirts 10.13.6

In the Two pair of Stairs backwards
Also a Bedstead with Scarlet harrateen furniture One pair of Windsor Curtains Ditto Vallens and Rodd a Close Stool and Pewter Pan a feather bolster and one pillow three blankets and one old linnen quilt a Wallnuttree Buroe and a Mahogany Table three old matted bottom Chairs Six Prints and five Print Frames and an old Stove 6.11.0

In the Fore Room Two pairs of Stairs
Also Three pair of old blew Camblet Window curtains and Rodds a Wainscott Library Table Three old Wainscott dressing Tables a drawing board on Trussells a Mahogany Pillar and Claw Table a small Mahogany Dining Table a Wallnuttree Buroe Desk a Wainscott Buroe Ditto a large Wainscott Book Case with glass Doors one ditto smaller a dressing glass and a pair of Globes a small small concave Glass in a black frame a Sword with a Silver hilt and Ebony Gripe a pair of Pistolls and one Pocket Pistoll a pair of small brass barrells Ditto a pair of old brass Candlesticks enammelled a Windsor Chair a Plaster of Pallas bust of Dryden a Venus ditto and brass Bust of Charles the first a Steel Stove and Tin fender a Shot pouch and belt Two joint Stools a Case with two Raizors Six Clasp Garden Knives Five T: Squares two brass Rings for a Gun with a Padlock Five dozen of black lead pencills a Foot Case of brass Instruments Three Protractors and a Penknife a Small Spirit Level in a Case a Theodolate in a Case nine inches over and a wooden Case for taking Prospects 17.10.0

In the Fore Room one pair of Stairs
Also a Bedstead and Green harrateen furniture and one pair of Window Curtains Ditto a feather bed and bolster Two pillows One Check and one white Mattrass one pair of Blankets and a linnen quilt Two old Walnuttree Chest of Drawers Two Windsor Chairs and five matted Chairs a Wainscott dining Table a Pillar and Claw Ditto and Steel Stove compleat Three deal Presses a brass hilt and one Mourning Sword a Cane with an Amber head and two brass Locks 15.5.0

In the Bath Room and Clossett
Also a Wainscott Bedstead and laths Compass Rodd a feather bed and bolster three blanketts and a linnen quilt a Wainscott buroe Desk and Book Case a Matted Chair and Childs Stool a Chimney Glass in the Closett a brass Lock and brass bolt one Iron barr and bolt to the Door and a deal Press 5.10.0

In the Fore Parlour
Also Two pair of Scarlet Window Curtains compleat a Wallnuttree writing Table a Mahogany dining Table a Marble Slabb without a Frame Six Wallnuttree Chairs with lace bottoms A Mahogany Tea Kettle Stand a Canvas Fire Screen Wallnuttree frame and two window Blinds Mahogany frames a Mahogany bottle cistern with brass hoops and handles and Knife Box ditto a Table Clock goes Eight days with an Ebony frame a brass plate Warmer a Steel Stove compleat a pair of Snake brass Arms a pier glass in a black and gold frame Two brass Locks and a small Print 14.8.6

In the Back Parlour and Closset
Also a Harpsicord a Chimney Glass cracked a Table bed a feather bed and bolster Two blankets a Rugg and a linnen quilt a Matted Chair and a deal Desk a Wainscott Press a pair of Pistols and brass barrels a travelling Gun three bells &c and fifteen old Prints in black frames on the Stair Case and Passage 15.16.6

In the Kitchen
Also a Range Cheeks and Iron back a Crane two Pothooks a Stove for Heaters a Fender Fire Shovel Poker and Tongs Two Hangings Spitracks three Trivets a Jack with a Multiplying Wheel Weight Lines and Pullies compleat a pair of bellows a Cleaver Two Trivets for Stoves and two Gridirons a Jack Spit and two Smoothing Irons Two Box Irons and five heaters a tin dripping pan and Iron Stand two Iron Candlesticks and a Flesh Fork Six brass Candlesticks and an Extinguisher a Snuffer Stand and brass drudging box a Ladle ditto Two pair of Iron Snuffers Three Copper boiling pots and Covers Three Stew Pans one large and four small sauce pans do. Two brass sauce pans Three large covers do. a Copper Warming pan a Tea kettle and Chocolate pot a Copper Cullender Tea kettle and Lamp a tin fish kettle Plate and Cover Ten pewter dishes Eight Soop Plates two dozen and Eight other plates a Tureen and Cover a Plate Rack a deal table Two Cupboards and Six Chairs Two washing Tubs a Form and a Tray a Water Pail and Towel Roler a Tin Cake Ring and a Toasting Iron 11.5.6

Linnen and China
Two pair of holland Sheets Six pair and one flaxen Sheets Nine pair and one Coarse Servants Sheets Five pair of old Pillow Cases Four damask and three diaper Table Cloths Eight Huckaback Towells Two dozen and a half of old damask Napkins and five huckaback old Towells A blew and white China dish one dozen of China plates and three China sugar Bowls 8.19.0

Plate
Also one Flaggon one large Cup and Cover one Smaller ditto one large Salver one Smaller ditto Two waiters a Set of Castors Two Standing Candlesticks one pair of Snuffers Stand and Extinguisher one Soop Spoon and Punch Ladle Six Spoons and one Marrow Spoon one half pint Mugg one pepper Castor one Tobacco box Two Shagreen Cases with Twelve Knives twelve forks and twelve Spoons Two ditto Cases with ditto a Case of drawing Instruments a large Silver Watch in a Shagreen case and a small Smooking Candlestick weighing in all Four hundred and thirty eight ounces and one penny weight 118.7.9

Pictures in the Fore Parlour
Also Two small Basso Relievos in gilt frames a Landskip [by] Lambert ditto a History Piece ditto a Mater delarosa ditto a dutch piece ditto The Virgin Mary ditto Two Landskips in black frames a Small history piece in a gilt frame The Virgin Mary with our Saviour and St. John and St. Elizabeth in a gilt frame a Landskip with figures on ditto a Ditto smaller with Cattle in ditto a dutch Conversation ditto Our Saviour in ditto Two small Landskips one in a black frame and the other in a gilt frame An Italian Alter piece ditto An herb Woman on ditto Our Saviour and St. Thomas ditto a Magdalen ditto Two Landskips ditto a Landskip with Ruins and figures ditto a Piece of Ruins ditto an old head in Cryons ditto a Small piece of the Virgin Mary and our Saviour a ditto larger with St. John and Joseph a small Idiot with a Child in a gilt frame and Two Martyrs ditto 18.6.6

In the Back Parlour and Clossett
Pictures
Also The humours of Sr. John Falstaffe a Piece of Sir Peter Paul Rubens a Fruit peice a History piece a Ceiling piece a Mater delarosa no frames a Landskip in an old gilt frame a piece of Judith and Holofernes a History Piece Joseph and Potaphers Wife no frame Our Saviour St. John and the Lamb ditto a small Landskip ditto an old Mathematician in an old gilt frame

In the Dining Room and Closset
Two Family pieces

In the Two pair of Stair forwards
Two Landskips in a black frames [*sic*] and a Battle piece in the back Room 17.15.0

In the Back Room and Cellar
Also a deal Library Table Three Shelves a drawing board a Stove Tongs and fender an Iron Lock and two Rulers an old Machine Wheel and frame One hogshead of Calcabella Wine damaged seventy two bottles of Cyder or seven dozen of prick'd About thirteen dozen of empty bottles of various sorts Four Stellens Two empty Casks and seventeen bottles of Mum 4.5.0

AN ACCOUNT OF THE THINGS THAT CAME FROM KENSINGTON

Also a Wainscott bedstead with Crimson harrateen Furniture compleat Three pair of Crimson Window Curtains ditto a bedstead and old blew printed Stuff Furniture one ditto and old yellow Slop'd harrateen furniture a Marble Slabb for a Side board a few deal Shelves a pair of old yellow harrateen Window Curtains Two Remnants of blew Worsted Damask a Remnant of blew harrateen Moth eaten Eight Virginia Wallnuttree Chairs with matted bottoms a Chimney Glass in a glass frame a Jappan corner Cupboard a Jack compleat and a new Wainscott bedstead 13.6.6

A TRUE AND PERFECT INVENTARY OF ALL AND SINGULAR THE GOODS CHATTELLS AND CREDITS OF THE SAID DECEASED AT HIS HOUSE AT HAMPTON COURT

In the Fore Garrett
Also a half headed Bedstead and sacking bottom a feather bed and bolster three blankets and a Coverlid a suit of old Cloaths a pair of holland sheets a pair of Flaxen Sheets four pillow Cases Four pair of Coarse Servants Sheets Two Table Cloths Four damask Napkins Four huckaback Towells Three Kitchen Table Cloths Three round Towells Three old Chairs and a Lock 5.13.0

In the next Fore Garrett
Also a half headed bedstead and Sacking bottom a feather bed bolster and three blanketts a Coverlid a Lock and five Iron barrs in the Chimney 2.3.6

In the Back Garrett
Also a half headed bedstead and Sacking bottom a feather bed bolster and one pillow three blanketts and a Coverlid three Curtain Rods and a Lock a Boys Livery Suit a Chair a Packing Case and a Bell 2.3.0

In the one pair of Stairs Fore Bed Chamber over the Best Parlour and Back Room
Also a Wainscott Bedstead and blew Stuff damask Furniture a Flanders Tick Bed Bed bolster and pillow Three down Pillows a hair Mattrass and a Flock ditto Two pair of Blankets and a linnen Quilt Two pair of blew damask Window Curtains and Rods Three Iron Locks a Dressing Table five matted bottom Chairs and two Stools covered with Irish Stitch a pair of Doggs Bellows and Brush a Marble Chimney Piece not valued a Wainscott Close Stool and Pewter Pan 22.9.6

In the next Fore Room
Also a Wainscott bedstead and blew stuff damask furniture a flanders tick bed bolster and two pillows Three blankets and a linnen quilt Three pair of blew Stuff damask Window Curtains and Rods a hair Mattrass and flock ditto a Wainscott dressing Table Eight Matted Chairs and a Close Stool Chair a Steel Stove compleat Two Locks and a Bell Line 23.1.6

In the Back Room
Also a Bedstead with blew Camblett Furniture a feather bed and bolster Three blanketts and a quilt a Wainscott dressing Table Six Chamber potts Six Basons a Bell Line and three Locks 3.9.6

In the Back Parlour on the right hand
Also a Bedstead and yellow harrateen furniture a Flanders Tick feather bed bolster and one pillow one down pillow three blanketts and a quilt a Check Mattrass Four matted Chairs Two pair of yellow harrateen window Curtains Two fowling pieces two powder horns and Shott pouch a belt a Rammer and a Screw a Wainscott writing Table with deal Tops and Drawers a Chaise Whip an Ink Glass a Sand box and a Lignum Vitae Stand 15.9.3

In the Back Parlour on the left hand
Also Eight red matted Chairs and an Arm Chair a small Childs Chair a Mahogany oval Table a Wainscott Pillar and Flow [*sic*] Table a small Jappan Tea Table a painted floor Cloth Two pair of blew harrateen window Curtains a Steel Stove compleat bellows and brush a pair of brass Arms two Iron Locks and a ditto Jappaned Twenty Wine glasses Two glass Salts Two Crewetts and one Decanter Eight Water Glasses a burnt China Scollopped Shell and a bowl ditto Sixteen China plates ditto Two large and two smaller ditto Two Sallad dishes six blew and white tea Cups and Saucers six Coffee potts and five Chocolate Cups Three Sugar Cups Tea pott and Spoon boat A two quart Earthen brown Mugg tippt with Silver a broken dressing Glass a Brush and five Cloak pins Two Silver Spoons and tea Spoons a Silver hilted Sword and an Ebony ditto a Chimney Glass on a Pediment frame a carved ovillo round the Chimney Six Water Glasses and Plates Twenty two Jelly Glasses a Crewit and a Silver smoking Candlestick 12.1.6

In the Fore Parlour on the right hand
Also Seven Cane Chairs and two Wainscott Tables a pair of brass Arms and green harrateen Window Curtains Vallens and Rods Three Iron locks a Clock in a Wallnuttree Case by Davis of Windsor 6.6.6

In the best Parlour
Also a Sconce in a gilt frame and brass Arms a small Marble Slabb with Carved and gilt bracketts a small Turkey Carpett Nine India back Chairs with matted bottoms a Stove compleat and brass Fender a Jappan Lock a pair of ordinary double Snake Arms a Jappan Tea board Two pair of green harrateen Window Curtains and rodds The Virgin Mary and our Saviour by Vandyke An old Mans head in Minature a Nuns head Two dutch pieces after Wattean Two pieces of Ruins a Rat Ketcher Two Landskips and a Sea piece by Woodcock The Baths of Diolisian Our Saviour and the Samaritan Woman a Landskip with Figures over the Chimney and a Lyon cutt in Marble 27.11.6

In the Kitchen
Also a large Range Cheeks and Iron Back a Fender two Shovells two pokers and a pair of Tongs a Crane with three hooks a Trivet and a pair of bellows a pair of Racks a Tin dripping pan an Iron Stand two Gridirons and an hanging Iron a large Jack a lead weight and two Spits four Iron Candlesticks a pair of Snuffers ditto an Iron flesh fork a tin Scimmer a pair of Stake Tongs a tinder box pepper box and drudging box a Basket Two Smoothing Irons and a Stand a dutch Iron Two Iron Scewers a Chopping Knife Clever and two Graters an Ironing Cloth a large Copper boiling pot and cover Two small brass boiling pots and Covers a brass dish kettle and Stewpan a tin fish kettle and Cover a Cullender a brass and a Copper Sauce pan a Copper tea kettle two tin Coffee potts and a chocolate pott a Copper Warming pan a Tin Candle box Two hair Sieves a Rowling Pin and a Ladle a Copper pott Nine pewter dishes Three dozen and four plates Eight soop plates and four Spoons Two pails and ten Trenchers a Water bowl dish a bacon rack a fire Screen a Cloaths Screen a Towel Roler Eight Wooden Chairs an old Wainscot Table a Stool a Square deal Table and a brush a Wainscott Table and a Coal box a Knife baskett with four Ivory hafted knives four forks ditto and a Kitchen knife four Earthen dishes and fourteen plates broken and whole 11.10.6

In the Dairy
Also Seven Earthen Milk Pans and Powdering Pans a broken Marble Mortar and Wooden Pestle a Wooden Platter and flower bowl three Churns compleat a quarter measure and pint ditto a Chopping block and board a pair of Wooden Scales a Cloaths baskett and a hair line Three hair Sieves a Plate Rack a Strainer a board for Salting Bacon a soap bowl a Jappan Tea board a tin Funnell and Strainer a Washing Stool and two old Locks 0.16.6

In the first and second Cellar
Also a deal Table a Knife board a brush two long Wicker baskets a Boot Jack a powdering Trough lined with lead a Kilderkin of Cyder turned a hanging Shelf a cupper a Garden box and two Locks

In the Small Beer Cellar
Three half hogsheads with Iron hoops one of ditto full a small Cask of Vinegar a Stillen a Cyder Press a Bench two brass Cocks and a Night Candlestick

In the Wine Cellar
Two hogsheads of beer one of Cyder and Three Kilderkins of Tap tubb three Stillens Two dozen and Six bottles of Shrubb and Rum Five Flasks of Piedmont Water a Stone bottle of Verjuce a Wicker bottle of Tobacco Six Shelves &c 7.15.0

In the Brewhouse
Also Two Coppers compleat and covers a Mash Tubb and Stand a Funnel a Wicker Tap Two lading Troughs a Washing Rake two basketts two Coolers a Cistern lined with lead about Six hundredwts. Two Working Tubbs a Wort Tubb and a Beer Sling a leaden Pail and a Jeft three wash Tubbs three forms and a hogshead a pair of Stepps a Pollard Tubb a Fire Shovel to the Copper a Lock and a Bolt

In the Hen House Bakehouse and Yard
A chicken Coop two Baskets a Wash Tubb a Ladder a Bottle Rack and twenty dozen of bottles a Hamper ditto 8.19.0

In Mr Lows Cellar
Also an Empty Hogshead with Iron hoops a brass Cock a Stillian and three hundred and ten bottles of Beer 2.15.0

In the House on the Green two pair of Stairs
Also Crimson Harrateen Hangings one pair ditto a Curtain ditto

Ground Floor
A Steel Stove compleat a sett Grate and Fender four Iron Box Locks and Five Stock Locks 3.5.0

Also an old Coach and a pair of harness an old Machine Charriot an old four wheel'd Chaise and a pair of Harness an old long shafted Chair and Harness Valued and Appraized at and since sold for 45.10.

Sume Total of the Household Goods &c £2000

AN INVENTARY OF THE UTENSILLS, AT THE SEVERALL ROYAL GARDENS BELONGING TO OR BEING PART OF THE PERSONAL ESTATE OF THE SAID DEC'D AS FOLLOWS TO WIT

AT THE ROYAL GARDENS AT KENSINGTON

Six Wooden hand Rowls	0.	9.	0
One large Iron horse Rowl	12.	0.	0
Two Rowl Carts with Sharps for horses	8.	0.	0
Four Oak and Elm Rowls	6.	10.	0
One large Rope	0.	2.	0
Eighty Bell Glasses	4.	0.	0
One Edging Iron	0.	0.	6
Twenty nine old Matts	0.	3.	7½
Twenty one New ditto	0.	8.	9
Two Two Tyne Forks	0.	1.	0
Two Three Tyne Forks	0.	2.	0
Two Pick Axes	0.	2.	0
Three large Water Tubbs with fourteen Iron hoops	0.	7.	0
Three old Water Tubbs with thirteen Iron hoops	0.	3.	0
Two Asparagus Knives	0.	0.	6
One Dibber shod with Iron	0.	0.	6
Twenty Netts for the Cherrys	1.	0.	0
Two thousand of fourpenny Nails and three hundred of Tenpenny Nails	0.	4.	0
A Reel and Line	0.	0.	9
One Rake with Iron Teeth	0.	0.	6
Two Sythes and Sneaths	0.	3.	0
One Iron Rake	0.	0.	6
One Wooden Rake	0.	0.	2
Two drawing hoes	0.	0.	6
One pair of Sheers	0.	1.	0
A large Cart Copse and Tail ladder with Iron Wheel	5.	10.	0
A Grindstone with Iron Axel tree and two handles	5.	10.	0
Seventeen Wooden Rakes	0.	2.	10
Seven Rakes with Iron Teeth	0.	3.	6
Seven drawing hoes	0.	1.	9
Three dutch hoes	0.	1.	6
Two Turving Irons	0.	2.	0
Two Wooden Scoops	0.	0.	6
Seven long grass Sythes	0.	17.	6
Seven New Sneaths	0.	2.	4
Thirty six pair of Sheers	0.	14.	0
Two grass Edging Irons	0.	1.	0
One Iron Crow	0.	4.	0
One Cutting hay knife	0.	1.	0
Fifteen bundles of new brooms containing about thirty dozen	1.	10.	0
Twenty ditto	0.	2.	0
Twenty three forks	0.	11.	6
One Wooden Rowl unfinished	0.	5.	0
Three Pickaxes	0.	3.	0
Two Mattocks	0.	2.	0
Two Iron Wedges weighing Ten pounds and an half and one Bettle weighing one pound and an half	0.	2.	0
Fifty five Sythes and Sneaths	4.	2.	6
Eight Sneaths without Sythes	0.	2.	8
A Quantity of Dung	4.	0.	0
A Quantity of prepared Earth	1.	0.	0
A large Rick of Hay	21.	0.	0
Four Saddle Horses	41.	4.	0

IN THE STABLES AT THE ROYALL GARDENS AT KENSINGTON

Four Cart Horses Four Setts of harness as Saddles Collars Breechings crupers and all other Necessarys for Equipping a horse for the Rowl Two pair of very good Traces Three pair of old Ditto Two good Ropes and some old pieces Four Combs Three Brushes One old Whip Eight hempen halters Two dutch Collars Four Curb bridles One Snaffle ditto One Martingall Two good Saddles Three indifferent ditto one old Saddle without furniture One Saddle housing One Hare Cloth One Main Comb Two Shovells One Pail with hoops a Byn for Corn a Bench a Cupboard one hard brush and one Oyl brush	10.	0.	0

IN THE ROYAL GARDENS AT ST JAMES'S

A Grass Basket	0.	0.	3
Six Pickaxes	0.	4.	0
One Iron Reel and Line	0.	1.	0
One pair of old Sheers	0.	0.	3
Four Rammers	0.	1.	0
One old Water Pott	0.	0.	6
Two Rakes with Iron Teeth	0.	1.	0
One old Edging Iron	0.	0.	3
One old hoe	0.	0.	3
One old Syth and Sneath	0.	1.	0
One old Ladder	0.	1.	6
Five old Wheel barrows	0.	2.	6

IN THE ROYAL GARDENS AT HAMPTON COURT

One Rake with Iron Teeth One pair of Sheers one dutch hoe and a Grindstone eighteen inches diameter with an Iron handle	0. 3. 0
Two Ricks of Hay one ditto old hay the other new containing about thirty loads	30. 0. 0
One old Syth and Sneath	0. 1. 6
A Bill for cutting of Rods	0. 0. 6
Two Carts with two Setts of Wheels, as Drugg Wheels and Iron Shod Wheels, one of the Carts with Copses Tail Ladder and Wheel Ladder	8. 10. 0
A Rowl Cart	0. 10. 0
Two Harrows	0. 5. 0
A Machine or Horse Scuffle	0. 10. 0
A large Wooden Rowl and Frame about six foot long and eighteen inches in diameter	0. 7. 6
A Grindstone with two Iron handles three foot in diameter and Six inches in thickness	0. 7. 6
Two half Moons for cutting the hedges	0. 0. 6
One dutch hoe	0. 0. 8
A Rake with Iron Teeth	0. 1. 0
Four old Barrow Wheels	0. 1. 6
One pair of Sheers	0. 0. 4
Twenty four Timber Sticks of Ash and Elme be the same more or less	2. 5. 0
Two large Wooden horse Rowls with Sharpes a circular Iron and two Cross Barrs to one them Seven foot in length and two foot in diameter	2. 0. 0
Two Wooden hand Rowls Six foot in length and Eighteen Inches in diameter	0. 10. 0
A Wooden Rowl and frame four foot in length and eighteen inches in diameter	0. 4. 0
A Wheel barrow	0. 1. 0
A Rake with Iron Teeth	0. 0. 2
A Syth and Sneath	0. 1. 6
A Scuffle	0. 0. 2
One hoe	0. 0. 2
Eight Wheel barrows and one old Wheel bound with Iron	0. 12. 0
Two Water barrows	0. 6. 0
One Water Tub	0. 3. 0
One old Syth and Sneath	0. 0. 8
Two Splinter Sieves	0. 0. 8
One hair ditto	0. 0. 6
Four dutch hoes one without a handle	0. 2. 6
Four hoes	0. 1. 4
Three Three Tyne Dung forks	0. 1. 6
Four Asparagus knives	0. 0. 2
A Turfing Iron and Racer	0. 1. 6
Three pair of Garden Sheers	0. 0. 9
Four small hoes	0. 0. 2
One Iron Reel and Line	0. 1. 0
One Dibble Shod with Iron	0. 0. 4
Three Garden Racks with Iron Teeth	0. 1. 6
One Wooden Hay Rake	0. 0. 2
Seven old Watering Potts and three Roses	0. 1. 2
Two One dozen hampers	0. 1. 0
Five Two dozen ditto	0. 3. 9
Seven three dozen ditto	0. 5. 0
Six Four dozen ditto	0. 6. 0
Four new Packing Basketts and one old ditto	0. 5. 0
One small White Hamper	0. 1. 0
Two Tray Basketts	0. 0. 8
One large round Basket	0. 0. 4
One Form	0. 1. 0
A large Number of old Netts	0. 10. 0
One old Water Tubs [*sic*] with four Iron hoops	0. 1. 0
Two loads of Faggotts and one load of round Wood	0. 10. 6
Two Forks	0. 1. 0
Two three Tyne Dung forks	0. 2. 0
One dutch hoe	0. 1. 0
Two hoes	0. 0. 6
Two Rakes with Iron teeth	0. 2. 0
Two hammers	0. 0. 6
Two Dibbers shod with Iron	0. 0. 8
Five old Watering Pots and one Small ditto	0. 0. 10
A Water Jett	0. 0. 6
Three hand barrows	0. 1. 0
Three Water barrows	0. 15. 0
Four Water Tubbs with fourteen Iron hoops	1. 0. 0
One hundred and twenty Matts new and old	1. 10. 0
One old Wire Screen	0. 2. 0
A Garden Reel	0. 1. 0
A Ladder with twenty five rounds	0. 1. 6
Four bundles of Arbour Poles about twenty two in each bundle	0. 4. 0
A Bushel Measure	0. 2. 0
One hundred and fifty six bell glasses	7. 10. 0
Three Stacks and an half of billetting wood	1. 1. 0
Sixteen Pickaxes	0. 16. 0
Five Wheelbarrows	0. 7. 6
Twenty eight old Matts	0. 3. 6
Twelve pair of Garden Sheers	0. 4. 0
A Stepladder with Six rounds	0. 5. 0
A Stand ladder with fourteen Steps	0. 10. 0
A Wooden horse to stand on to clip the Hedges	0. 3. 0
A Trowell	0. 0. 3
A New Garden line	0. 1. 0
A Hammer	0. 0. 2
Twelve Rakes with Iron teeth five new one and Seven old one [*sic*]	0. 9. 0
Three Wooden Rakes	0. 0. 6
Five hoes two large and three small	0. 2. 0
Four Edging Irons	0. 1. 4
Four new Sythes	0. 8. 0
Eight dutch hoes	0. 2. 0
Twelve Sneaths without Sythes but four Rings	0. 1. 0
Twelve new brooms	0. 1. 6
One Iron Crow	0. 3. 0
Five wooden hand Spykes about three foot long	0. 0. 10
Ten ditto about Seven foot Two with Iron hooks	0. 2. 6
An Iron Saw to cut the Weeds in the River	0. 1. 3
Three old hand barrows	0. 0. 6
Twelve Sythes and Tackle compleat	0. 18. 0
A Wooden Engine to remove the Orange trees	0. 10. 6
An old wire Screen	0. 2. 0
Two water barrows	0. 6. 0
One Water Tubb with Six Iron hoops	0. 3. 0

Four pair of Straps	o. 2. o
Two Wheel barrows one very large	o. 2. o
One old harrow	o. o. 6
Two Iron Dragg Rakes	o. 3. o
Four old Barrow Wheels one the Axle tree broke	o. 1. o
Ten old Sythes	o. 1. o
Two large grass Baskets	o. 6. o
One old Water Tubbe with five Iron hoops	o. 1. 3
Two horses	5. o. o
Two Byns for Corn	o. 6. o
Three Cart Saddles	o. 14. o
One pair of Iron Traces	o. 4. o
Two leather halters with Winkers	o. 3. o
Two leather Collars for horses	o. o. 6
A Brush and a Curry Comb	o. o. 6
A Cart Rope	o. 1. o
An Engine to cut Straw with	o. 2. 6
Three Prongs	o. 1. 6
A Short ladder	o. o. 6
Dung and prepared Earth	10. o. o
Twenty one old Sythes	o. 2. o
A Mattock	o. 1. o
Two new dutch hoes	o. 3. 8
A Prong	o. o. 6
A large Iron ladle	o. 1. 6
Eight pair of old Sheers	o. 1. 6
One pair of old Sheers on a long stick	o. o. 2
A Hatchet	o. o. 2
A Pickax with a helve	o. o. 6
A Level about ten foot long	o. 1. o
One old Edging Iron without a handle	o. o. 2
Some old Iron belonging to a Barrow Wheel	o. o. 6
More ditto	o. 1. o
Seven Planks	o. 7. o
Eleven Elm boards and some old boards	o. 7. 6
Two long benches	o. 2. 6
Seventy two Fowls of different sizes	1. 6. 6
A Mattock and Cross Saw	o. 2. o

IN THE ROYAL GARDENS AT WINDSOR

One old Ladder with sixteen rounds	o. 1. 6
Two Water Barrows	o. 6. o
Two Water Tubbs	o. 6. o
Two pair of leather Straps	o. 2. o
Two Close Wheel Barrows	o. 3. o
One long Ladder with twenty three rounds	o. 2. o
Two hand barrows	o. 1. o
Four Sythes and Sneaths	o. 6. o
One Bushel Basket	o. o. 6
Four dutch hoes	o. 2. o
Three pair of old Sheers	o. 2. o
Three Iron Reels and an old line	o. 2. o
Two Turfing Irons	o. 2. o
One Spade	o. 1. 6
Two Grindstones Two foot and Six Inches in diameter Eight and Six inches in thickness	o. 5. o
Four old Rakes with Iron Teeth	o. 2. o
Two Mattocks	o. 2. o
Two Pickaxes	o. 2. o
One Edging Iron	o. o. 4
A Sett of Bourning Staves	o. o. 6
One Ten foot [rod]	o. o. 6
Two pair of hand Spikes	o. 1. o
A Sett of Thill harness	o. 5. o
A Small parcel of old Netts	o. 2. o
Two Pairing Irons	o. 1. o
Three ditto	o. 1. 6
Four old Sythes	o. 1. o
Two old Watering Pots	o. o. 3
A Drugg	o. 1. o
A Wooden Screen	o. 2. 6
One Stand Ladder with twelve rounds	o. 1. o
Three large old Water Tubs with twenty Iron hoops	o. 3. o
One large Stand Ladder with twenty rounds	o. 12. o
One round Fruit basket	o. o. 6
One Wooden Rake	o. o. 3
One Prong	o. o. 6
One small Hoe	o. o. 3
Two Water Tubbs with Roses	o. 2. o
A large Corn Byn	o. 3. o
One old Level ten foot long	o. o. 6
One Load and an half of hay be the same more or less	1. o. o

IN THE ROYAL GARDENS AT RICHMOND

Four wooden hand Rowls	o. 10. o
One wooden horse Rowl	o. 10. o
Six Wheel barrows	o. 9. o
A Level ten foot long	o. 1. 6
Two Water Scoops	o. 1. o
Five dozen of Syth Rubbers	o. 5. o
Two Iron Crows	o. 3. o
A Set of Bourning Staves	o. o. 6
Two Daisy Sythes	o. 1. o
Eight Mattocks	o. 8. o
Eight Pickaxes	o. 8. o
Eighteen old Iron hoops	o. 1. 6
A Ladder about Nine foot long	o. 2. o
Two pair of Sheers	o. 2. o
A large Tubb with Six Iron hoops	o. 3. o
A Stake Dragg	o. 1. o
Two Augers	o. o. 6
One Gouge	o. o. 3
One Spike Bitt	o. o. 2
One Chissell and Mallett	o. o. 6
One drawing knife	o. 1. o
One Shaver	o. o. 6
One Adds	o. o. 6
One hand Saw	o. 1. o
One Wire Sieve	o. 1. o
One Corn Sieve	o. o. 6
One Pottle Measure	o. o. 2
Sixteen Water Tubbs	o. 16. o
A Bushell of Corn	o. 2. o
One Marking Iron	o. o. 3
One pair of hand Sheers	o. o. 6
One Bettle	o. o. 6
Six little hatchetts	o. 3. o
Two Bills	o. 1. o
Six old Iron Rakes	o. 2. o
Six hoes	o. 1. 6
Four dutch hoes	o. 2. o
Two Edging Irons	o. 1. o
One old Turfing Iron and Racer	o. 1. o
Fifteen old Sythes and Sneaths	o. 15. o
Eight pair of Straps and Yokes	o. 8. o
Two Jetts	o. 1. o

One Water Pott	0. 0. 6
Two Ten Foot Rodds	0. 1. 0
A Sett of Harness for the Horse to Rowl	0. 5. 0
One Curry Comb and Brush	0. 0. 6
Two long Barrows	0. 4. 0
Two small Hoes	0. 0. 4
One Garden Line and Reel	0. 1. 0
One Fork	0. 0. 6
Two Stripping Hooks	0. 0. 6
Two Hammers	0. 0. 6
Two Brooms	0. 0. 2
Two large leaf baskets	0. 0. 4
One Grindstone and Iron handle	0. 2. 6
Eleven Rammers	0. 2. 0
One Bushell Basket	0. 0. 6
One half Bushel Basket	0. 0. 3
Six grass Sythes	0. 6. 0
Total of the Implements &c at the Royal Gardens	230. 1. 9½
The Deceaseds Books Maps Plans and Globes Valued at	20. 0. 0

This Exhibitant declares that the said Deced was at the time of his death possessed of an House in Henrietta Street near Cavendish Square lately built on a Lease for the term of Ninety nine years of which there is about Seven years expired and which House was never yet let therefore the Value thereof to be sold is uncertain but this Exhibitant declares that soon as the same shall be disposed of She will charge herself therewith.

This Ex'tant declares that the said Deceased [had] by Lease a House in Broad Street at a full Rack Rent in which Lease there are about Fifteen years yet to come and unexpired therefore believes the same to be of little or no Value.

This Ex'tant declares that the said Deceased was Proprietor of the Views of Lord Cobhams Seat and Gardens Engraved on fifteen Copper Plates the Value thereof uncertain but this Ex'tant declares that so soon as the same shall be disposed of she will Charge herself therewith.

This Ex'tant declares that there are divers Sumes of Money due to the said Deced from the Crown and several of the Nobility and Gentry but how much the same amounts to or the several persons from whom due this Ex'tant cannot at present setforth nor till the Accounts thereof can be made up and adjusted but when the same or any part thereof shall be received by her she will setforth the same and Charge herself therewith or with such part thereof as shall be received by her.

This Exhibitant declares that the said Deceased left behind him at the time of his death one Bank Note for twenty five pounds and in ready money about twenty shillings 26. 0. 0

Lastly this Exhibitant declares that she has not in her Custody Power or Possession any other Goods Chattells and Credits of the said Deceased neither doth she know of any other than what are mentioned and setforth in the foregoing Inventary but if any other should hereafter come to her hands possession or knowledge She will setforth the same and Charge herself therewith when thereto legally Called.

12th. October 1738 Sarah Bridgeman
the said Sarah Bridgeman was
Sworn to the truth of the foregoing
Inventary Before me

Arthr. Collier
Surrogate
present Robt. Bogg Junr NP.

This Inventary was Exhibited on the twelfth day of October in the year of our Lord One thousand Seven hundred and thirty Eight by the said Sarah Bridgeman Widow the Relict and one of the Executors named in the last Will and Testament of the said Charles Bridgeman deceased as and for a true and perfect Inventary of all and singular the Goods Chattells and Credits of the said Deceased which since his death have come to her hands possession or knowledge by virtue of her Corporal Oath Under Protestation nevertheless of adding thereto as occasion shall require.

Note on back: Middx. / Inventory of the Goods of / Charles Bridgeman/Esqr. deceased/Exhibited 12th. Octr. 1738

NOTE: This Inventory was discovered by Mr T E C Walker, and a transcript of it by Mr Hector Carter (with a Note by Peter Willis) was published in *Blackmansbury*, VII, Nos 5–6 (October–December 1970), 88–109. The transcript above contains several amendments and additions to this.

I am grateful to Mr G A Coulson and Mr John Harvey for their help with several doubtful readings.

Appendix VI

Petition from Mrs Sarah Bridgeman to the Lords of the Treasury, 1738

PRO, Treasury Books and Papers CCXCIX (T.1:299), No.10, fos 23–24

To the Right Honble the Lords Commissioners of his Majesty's Treasury

The Memorial of Sarah Bridgman Widow and Executrix of Charles Bridgeman Esqr: his Majesty's Late Gardner Deceased

Most humbly Sheweth

That upon making up the Accounts of your Memorialist's late Husband with ye Crown, to the time of his Death, vizt: to the Nineteenth of July last, there appears to be due to him for keeping the Royall Gardens, pursuant to old and new Contract's; and for Extraordinary Bills at Kensington the Sum of £2125:13*s*:3½*d*. And for keeping the Royall Gardens at Richmond, by Contract, and Extra Bills there, ye Sum of £1847:8*s*:5*d*. And for making the Lamp Road in Hyde Park, Road in St James's Park, and Private Road to Fulham, the sum of £498:1*s*:6*d*. And for making the Severall new Roads in Richmond new Park, Barnes Comon, and the Lake in Hyde Park, ye Sum of £470:9*s*:0*d*. And from his Late Majesty the sum of £600. making together in all the Sum of £5541:12*s*:8½*d*. all which accounts your Memorialist has deliver'd into the proper Offices, That besides the work and Services set forth in these Accounts, your Petitioners late Husband, was at avery [*sic*] great Expence for many years, in providing severall usefull & necessary things for his Majesty's Service, in and about his Majestys Royall Gardens and Plantations at Kensington, and Hampton Court, The Particulars whereof are set forth in the list hereunto Annex't, That your Memorialist and her Family being left in very narrow Circumstances, are become Objects of his Majestys Royal Compassion, and as such,

Your Memorialist most humbly prays your Honours to take the Premisses into your Consideration, And that you will be pleas'd to order the mony's which shall be found due to your Memorialist, on the severall Accounts above mention'd, to be paid, and such Allowance made her for the severall other Particulars in the List Annex't, as your Honour's; in your great Goodness, shall see Reason and your Petitioner as in Duty bound shall ever pray.

Note on back: The Memorial to the / Rt: Honble the Lords of / the Treasury by Sarah / Bridgman 1738. / to be referd to ye proper / officers

AT HAMPTON COURT	£	s.	d.
Paid by Mr: Bridgman for Locks, Bells, Two Marble Chimney Pieces, The one in the one Pair of Stairs Room, and the other in the back Parlour in the Master Gardners Capitall house, And for the Range, Crane and back in the Kitchen, wooden Rack and Stove in the Nursery, and a new strong Lock on the Street door, and never yet allow'd for by the Board of Works, and there now Remaining.	050.	0.	0
Paid by Do: for Painting Whitewashing and severall Repairs done to this house, the Glass house, and house on the Green, and keeping the same in good Repair for Ten years last past	250.	0.	0
For the Nursery of Fruit Trees in the severall Quarters in the Kitchen Garden all Rais'd by the deceas'd at his own Expence	030.	0.	0
To Seventeen Pine Apple Plants	005.	0.	0
Dung and Earth on Beads and Magazines, he having paid for the like to Mr Wise and Mr: Carpenter, when he first Entred on those Grounds	020.	0.	0
Paid Mr: Cook of the ward Robe, for Furniture in the house on the Green and there still Remaining	008.	10.	0
AT KENSINGTON			
A Large Quantity of Fire wood, Two Skreens and Five Large wooden Rools one of which cost Sixty Five Pounds	050.	0.	0
Dung and Earth for the like Reason as before	010.	0.	0
Oaks, Firrs, and Cedars of Lebanon	020.	0.	0
Two Large Stript American Aloes	006.	0.	0
Two Setts of Bowls here, and at Hampton Court	005.	0.	0
The Fish in the severall waters, stock't by the Deceas'd	050.	0.	0
Paid for the Boat there, and Tackle	006.	0.	0
Paid Clark the Bricklayer for Brickwork done in the Gardens	012.	0.	0
NB There are Plans Curiously done by the Deceas'd, of all the Royall Gardens which may be of great Service to the Crown, and for which your Memorialist hopes may be worth	200.	0.	0
Totall	722.	10.	0

Appendix VII

Will of Charles Bridgeman, 1738

Dated 6 July 1738

Proved by Mrs Sarah Bridgeman, after Court Action, 12 October 1738

PRO, PROB. II. 692 (BRODREPP 1738)

Charles Bridgeman Esqr.

In the Name of God Amen

I Charles Bridgeman of St. James's Westminster Esqr. Master Gardener to his Majesty being of sound mind understanding and Memory do make and ordain this my last Will and Testament in the following manner to wit First I desire and Order that my debts and Funerall Charges be paid and then I give to Sarah my well beloved Wife three hundred pounds to be paid her within three Kalender Months after my decease to be solely at and for her use and disposal as also the Interest of Six hundred pounds now in the hands of Thomas Rea Esquire and Mr. George Devall Plumber Executors to the last Will and Testament of Mr. John Mist Paviour deceased my Wife's Brother for and during her natural life I also charge and subject the Bell Inn at Stilton in the County of Huntington and my Leasehold Estate in Henrietta Street Cavendish Square with the payment of Eighty pounds a Year to Sarah my beloved Wife for and during her naturall life to be paid her by equal half yearly payments I give to my beloved Son Charles the Bell Inn at Stilton aforesaid with the Lands thereunto belonging and to the Heirs of his body lawfully begotten and for want of such Heirs to my beloved daughter Sarah and the Heirs of her body lawfully begotten and for want of her heirs to my daughter Elizabeth and her heirs and for want of her heirs to my daughter Ann and her heirs and for want of her heirs to my Cousin Mr. Charles Bridgeman Alderman of Hartford and his heirs and in defect of his heirs to the Crown but Subject to the payment of Eighty pounds a year to my Wife during her natural Life as aforesaid I also give unto my said Son my Copyhold Estate in Henrietta Street aforesaid only Subject jointly with the Bell Inn at Stilton aforesaid to the payment of Eighty pounds a year to my Wife during her natural Life as aforesaid I give to my beloved daughters Sarah Elizabeth and Ann each Two thousand pounds to be paid them as they shall severally arrive at the age of one and twenty years and if my personall Estate Shoud be more than sufficient (as I apprehend it will) for the payment of my Debts Funeral Charges and Legacies aforesaid Then the residue or surplus I give to my beloved Wife during her natural life and at her death to such of her Children as she shall think fitt And in case one or more of my daughters should die before she or they arrive to the age of one and twenty years then such Sum or Sums of Money left to such daughter or daughters aforesaid shall be equally divided among the Surviving of my Children And I do hereby nominate constitute and appoint Sarah my beloved Wife and my beloved Cousin Mr. Charles Bridgeman of Hartford aforesaid Executors of this my last Will and Testament And lastly I do hereby revoke disannull and make void all former Wills and Legacies by me at any time heretofore made or given declaring this and only this to be my last Will and Testament In witness whereof I have hereunto Sett my hand and Seal this Sixth Day of July in the Year of Our Lord One Thousand seven hundred and Thirty eight. The resure in the Fifth Line was made and the word (three) written and in the twentysixth Line the words (two thousand) were written and in these words (or the Children as she shall think fitt) were interlined before the Signing and Sealing hereof. / – Charles Bridgeman.

Signed Sealed Publishd pronounced and declared by the said Charles Bridgeman the Testator as and for his last Will and Testament in the presence of us who have hereunder wrote our names in the presence and at the request of the Testator. /. John Godde Robt: Towell Wm Loughton – Kensington. / .

This Will was proved at London before the Worshipfull William Strahan Doctor of Laws and Surrogate of the Right Worshipfull John Bettesworth Doctor of Laws Master Keeper or Commissary of the Prerogative Court of Canterbury lawfully constituted On the Twelfth day of October in the Year of Our Lord One thousand seven hundred and Thirty eight by the Oath of Sarah Bridgeman Widow the Relict of the deceased And one of the Executors named in the said Will To whom Administration was granted of all and singular the Goods Chattells and Credits of the said deceased She being first Sworn well and duly to administer the same reserving power to make the life Grant to Charles Bridgeman the other Executor named in the said Will when he shall apply for the same. / – Exd:

Note in margin:

On the twentieth day of November in the Year of Our Lord 1746 Admcon (with the Will annexed) of the Goods Chattels and Credits of Charles Bridgeman late of the Parish of St. James Westminster in the County of Middlesex dece'd left unadstred by Sarah Bridgeman Widow the Relict of the said dece'd one of the Extors and the residuary Legatee for life named in the said Will now also dece'd was granted to Sarah Bridgeman Spinster the natural and lawful Daughter and one of the next of kin of the said Charles Bridgeman dece'd (for that Charles Bridgeman the other Extor named in the said Will dyed before he had taken upon him the Execution thereof) being first sworn duly to adster (William Bradshaw the Testamentary Guardian of Ann Bridgeman Spinster a Minor the nat and lawfull Daughter of the said dece'd appointed by the Will of the said Sarah Bridgeman dece'd being first legally cited with usual Intimation and not appearing, and Elizabeth Price (Wife of Philip Price) the other natural and lawfull Daughter of the said dece'd and the said Philip Price her Husband first consenting And the said Philip Price as the Guardian lawfully assigned to the said Ann Bridgeman also consenting. / .

There are two texts of Charles Bridgeman's will in the Public Record Office, the original and a copy; as the copy is the more extensive, it is used as the text for the transcript above. The original (from which Bridgeman's signature reproduced as Plate 160a is taken), has a shorter proof by William Strahan, no marginal note, and is inscribed as follows:

Middx / Will of / Charles Bridgeman / Esqr. / By Decree October 1738. / Inv: exh[ibi]ted same day / Regd / Exd

20th. July 1738 / Sarah Bridgeman the Widow / and one of the Executors / within named was duly sworn / power being reserved to the other / Executors Before Mr. / Will: Strahan / Surrogate.

Prob: dated 12 Oct / Inv: ex[hibi]ted

Appendix VIII

Will of Mrs Sarah Bridgeman, 1743

Dated 17 November 1743
Proved by Clement Lemprière, 21 January 1744
PRO, PROB. II. 731 (ANSTIS 1744)

Sarah Bridgman

In the Name of God Amen

I Sarah Bridgman the Widow and Relict of Charles Bridgman Esqr. his Majesty's late Master Gardner deceased Do by this my last Will and Testament give and bequeath to Sarah my eldest dautr the Sum of Five Pounds And all the rest and residue of my personel Estate I give and bequeath unto my other two dautrs Elizabeth and Ann to be equally divided between them And I do hereby constitute and appoint my loving Friends Mr William Bradshaw of Soho Square Upholsterer and Captain Clement Lempriere of the Tower of London Executors of this my Will and Trustees and Guardians of my said daughter Ann until she shall attain her age of twenty one years And I do hereby give and bequeath to each of my said Executors the sum of Ten pounds for their Care and Trouble in the Execution of this my Will And I do hereby desire and direct to be interred in the Tower of London and that the Charges and Expenses of my Funeral shall not exceed the Sum of Twenty pounds In Witness whereof I have hereunto set my hand and seal this Seventeenth day of November in the Year of our Lord One thousand seven hundred and forty three. Sa. Bridgeman. / .

Signed Sealed published and declared by the said Testative to be her last Will and Testament in the presence of W Plaxton Junr. Am. Smith Servant to Mrs Bridgeman the Testative. Exd.

This Will was proved at London before the Worshipfull William Strahan Doctor of Laws Surrogate of the Right Worshipfull John Bettesworth also Doctor of Laws Master Keeper or Commissary of the Prerogative Court of Canterbury lawfully constituted on the twenty first day of January in the Year of our Lord One thousand seven hundred and forty three By the Oath of Clement Lempriere one of the Executors named in the said Will To whom Administration was granted of all and singlers the Goods Chattels and Credits of the said deceased being first sworn duly to Administer the same (Power reserved of making the like grant to William Bradshaw the other Executor when he shall apply for the same – Exd.

Note in margin:

On the Sixteenth day of October in the Year of Our Lord 1746 Admcon (with the Will annexed) of the Goods Chattels and Credits of Sarah Bridgman late of the Tower of London Widow dece'd left unadministered by Clement Lempriere one of the Extors named in the said Will now also dece'd was granted to Elizabeth Price (Wife of Philip Price) the Daughter and one of the residuary Legatees named in the said Will of the said Sarah Bridgman dece'd (for that William Bradshaw the other Extor named in the said Will formerly renounced the Execution thereof) being first sworn duly to adster. / .

Catalogue of Bridgeman Drawings

Arrangement of Catalogue

This catalogue contains a list of every drawing so far discovered which is either signed by Charles Bridgeman or which may be ascribed to him. All entries refer to plans, unless stated otherwise, and are arranged alphabetically by subject; within each subject, entries are listed according to category of attribution. Attributions – based on style and draughtsmanship – are indicated in the left-hand margin of each entry, and signify the following:

Category A SIGNED by Bridgeman
Category B UNSIGNED but *probably* drawn by Bridgeman
Category C UNSIGNED but *possibly* drawn by Bridgeman

Information about each drawing is given in the following sequence:

Subject and Date (with Plate Number in this book, if any), Location, Title, Inscription on Back, Signature, Medium and Material, Size of Drawing (larger dimension first), Scale (calculated if necessary), Watermark, Notes.

Few drawings, if any, have entries covering every heading, simply because often as not the relevant information is not available: when, for example, no title or scale is given, it should be assumed that the drawing is untitled and that its scale is unknown. Any drawing which has not been examined by the author is marked with an asterisk. Dates which appear in square brackets are purely speculative.

If a drawing in the PRO is listed in *Maps and Plans in the Public Record Office, Vol. I: British Isles c.1410–1860* (London, 1967) a cross-reference is given to the catalogue number in that publication.

Abbreviations in the *Catalogue of Bridgeman Drawings* are those used throughout the book and listed above on p.xx–xxi.

The Gough Collection in the Bodleian Library, Oxford

The main group of Bridgeman drawings is in the Gough Collection in the Bodleian Library, assembled by the antiquarian Richard Gough and bequeathed to the Bodleian on his death in 1809.[1] This bequest consisted of all Gough's 'topographical collections, together with all his books relating to Saxon and Northern Literature . . . his maps and engravings, and all the copper-plates used in the illustrations of various works published

[1] These notes are based upon the entry for Richard Gough by Thompson Cooper in the *Dictionary of National Biography*, VIII, 279–82; W. D. Macray, *Annals of the Bodleian Library, Oxford . . .*, 2nd edn (Oxford, 1890), pp.285–90; Falconer Madan, *A Summary Catalogue of Western Manuscripts in the Bodleian Library, Oxford* (Oxford, 1897), IV, 151–52.

by himself'.[2] Much of this material was probably bought by Gough on his mother's death in 1774, when extensive estates fell to him. He may have acquired the Bridgeman drawings about this time, although it is perhaps more likely that Richard inherited them from his father Harry Gough (1681–1751), a confidant of Sir Robert Walpole.[3] Harry could well have purchased them on Bridgeman's death,[4] though it may be that neither he nor his son realised that others apart from the plan of Amesbury (the only signed drawing at the Bodleian) were the work of the Royal Gardener: Richard Gough's *British Topography* refers to Charles and Sarah Bridgeman, but only briefly.[5]

Watermarks

The watermarks which appear in the *Catalogue of Bridgeman Drawings* show that most of Bridgeman's paper came from France or Holland.[6] Prominent in the watermarks are the symbols IV, IVILLEDARY, and LVG: the first two signify the manufacture of the Frenchman J. Villedary, and the third that of the Dutchman L. Van Gerrevink. Villedary's markings were common in England throughout the eighteenth century, and his simple IV symbol was used by other makers as well. Van Gerrevink's initials LVG were likewise appropriated by others, and even appear below the watermarks of such prominent manufacturers as Whatman, Portal, and Bates. The use of the IHS and cross with the maker's name or initials below was widespread also, especially in combination with the fleur-de-lis. The import of foreign paper into England was quite popular in Bridgeman's time, for although the native industry could meet the home demands for the more ordinary papers it was still unable to compete with the better-grade papers from France, Italy and Holland. French paper in particular was cheap and of high quality, and as part of the trade was controlled from Holland many supposedly Dutch papers were of French manufacture. After 1700 much of what was termed PRO PATRIA paper came from Holland, and the

[2] Macray, *Annals*, p.286.

[3] The Bridgemanic drawings are among those kept in two folio volumes (MS Gough Drawings a3 and a4) which are catalogued in Willis, 'Charles Bridgeman', pp.402–23. See also the entries in Madan, *Summary Catalogue*, IV, 167–68; Bulkeley Bandinel, *A Catalogue of the Books Relating to British Topography, and Saxon and Northern Literature, Bequeathed to the Bodleian Library . . . by Richard Gough, Esq., F.S.A.* (Oxford, 1814), pp.13–14.

[4] So far no sale catalogue for Charles Bridgeman has been encountered. However in 1773 at the sale of the possessions of James West, the politician and antiquary, many items were bought by Richard Gough. West's manuscripts in the British Library include a page entitled 'James West Esq[r] Bot: at Mrs: Bridgeman's Sale' (BL, Add MS 34733 (West Papers), fo.349r), from which we see that West purchased books, medals and prints to the value of £15.10s. Unfortunately this account is undated, but it appears between entries for 21 February 1742 and 15 June 1743 – in other words very close to the date of Bridgeman's widow's death. Alternatively West's purchases may have been made at the sale announced in *A Catalogue of the Entire Library of Mrs Katherine Bridgeman (of Cavendish Square) Deceased*, and held in London on 3–9 February 1743/4.

[5] See Richard Gough, *British Topography . . .*, 2nd edn (London, 1780), I, 188, 197; II, 23. Gough's own copy of *British Topography* in the Bodleian (Gen Top 363–67) helps us not at all: the relevant pages from the first volume are missing, whilst in the second Gough makes no comment.

[6] For Bridgeman watermarks see Edward Heawood, *Watermarks, Mainly of the Seventeenth and Eighteenth Centuries* (Hilversum, 1940), esp. pp.24, 27, 35, 102; A. H. Shorter, *Paper Mills and Paper Makers in England, 1495–1800* (Hilversum, 1957), esp. pp.35, 56–64. The international context is shown in W. A. Churchill, *Watermarks in Paper in Holland, England, France, Etc., in the Seventeenth and Eighteenth Centuries, and Their Interconnection* (Amsterdam, 1935).

Britannia watermark found on it was used in Dutch papers destined for England, more often than not with the name or initials of Van Gerrevink underneath.

Handwriting

Many of the plans in the *Catalogue of Bridgeman Drawings* are the work of more than one draughtsman, and the lettering and handwriting reflect this fact. Our starting point in identifying Charles Bridgeman's hand must be the authentic signature on his will (*Plate 160a*), which should be compared with the signatures on the two letters written by the Royal Gardener which we have in manuscript, one to Pope and one to Harley (*Plates 160b, 161*). All three signatures are alike, but those of the will and the Harley letter especially so. This letter therefore may be said to provide us with the best example of Bridgeman's handwriting.[7]

Attribution of Drawings to Bridgeman

The procedure adopted for analysing Bridgemanic drawings was straightforward. First, Signed Drawings (Category A) were examined, and this led to the establishment of features of Bridgeman's draughtsmanship and design; second, on the basis of these features, we were able to identify Unsigned Drawings which could *probably* (Category B) or *possibly* (Category C) be attributed to Bridgeman. Frequently of course the drawn evidence was buttressed either by documentary or published material, or both.

Bridgeman's design has been considered throughout the text of this book, and only his draughtsmanship is dealt with in subsequent notes.[8]

Category A

Signed Drawings can be limited to five: Windsor Forest, probably drawn in Queen Anne's reign (*Plates 104, 105*), Blenheim of 1709 (*Plate 24*), Warwick Priory of 1711 (*Plate 18*), Hampton Court of about 1735 (*Plate 95*), and Amesbury of 1738 (*Plates 36, 37b*). All are drawn in combinations of ink, pencil and water-colour, and are in either finished or semi-finished state. The basic colouring has close affinities: the hard greens of the trees and the soft greens of the grass, the browns and pink-reds of the buildings, the grey shadows. The trees at Blenheim are round or slightly pointed and have a shaded side and a little shadow beneath; those at Windsor Forest, Hampton Court and Amesbury are more shapely and remind us of the bushes in the Warwick Priory drawing. Compare too the way in which Bridgeman achieves three-dimensional effects in parterres, pools and lawns. There are

[7] The receipt dated 17 June 1719 signed 'Chas Bridgman' for work done at Langleys (Essex CRO, Chelmsford. D/DTu 276, Samuel Tufnell's Receipt Book, May 1701–March 1722) does not seem to be in the Royal Gardener's hand. See above p.60n84.

[8] These only consider selected examples. For more detailed coverage see Willis, 'Charles Bridgeman', pp.226–97.

similarities also in the scales on the plans of Blenheim, Hampton Court and Amesbury, and in the cartouches – Windsor Forest's is the most informative, Blenheim's the grandest, Hampton Court's the simplest, Amesbury's the most refined (*Plates 162a–163b*). Within the cartouches and elsewhere both the upper-case and lower-case lettering is in a variety of hands.

Categories B and C

Unsigned Drawings which may be attributed to Bridgeman are more numerous and more varied. Apart from Bridgeman's characteristic colouring and techniques of drawing trees and other features, similarities can be seen in his cartouches, scales and lettering. Among cartouches, the Blenheim one of 1709 can be found in simpler form in an uncatalogued plan of Windsor Castle in the Henry Wise Collection at Windsor (thus linking Bridgeman's private and royal work), whilst the cartouche on an Eastbury plan (*Plate 28b*) reappears in a drawing of St James's Park (*Plate 103*). None of the scales on the signed drawings is repeated precisely, but comparisons should be made between the scales on plans of Eastbury (*Plate 28b*), Tring (*Plate 45a*), Gunton (*Plate 80a*), and Kensington (*Plates 98, 99a*). As for lettering, the main titles in the signed plans have echoes in those of Eastbury (*Plate 28b*) or Brampton Bryan (*Plate 78a*), and there are parallels between the subsidiary lettering on the survey of Windsor Forest and that on plans of Down Hall (Bod. Lib., Gough Maps 46 fo.262) and Sacombe (MSGD a4 fo.29). Moreover the handwriting on Bridgeman's plan of Rousham (*Plate 61*), Purley (*Plate 47b*), and Tring (*Plate 45a*) should be looked at in the light of his letters to Pope and Harley (*Plates 160b, 161*).

A **AMESBURY Wiltshire 1738**

Plates 36, 37b, 162b
MSGD a3*fo.32
TITLE: 'A/PLAN/of his Grace the/DUKE OF QUEENSBERRY's/Seat at *Ambresbury* in/WILTSHIRE./by *Ch. Bridgeman.*/1738.'
INSCRIPTION ON BACK: 'Duke of Queensburry'
SIGNATURE: '*Ch. Bridgeman.*/1738.'
Ink, pencil and water-colour on laid paper
76·2×52·3 cm
SCALE: 1 inch=100 feet
WATERMARK:
† and coat of arms with 4 beneath
IHS LVG
IVILLEDARY

C **AUDLEY END Essex [c.1726]**

MSGD a4 fo.60
Pencil on laid paper
102·2×75·9 cm
SCALE: 1 inch=160 feet
WATERMARK:
Coat of arms with 4 beneath, and letters IV

C **AUDLEY END Essex [c.1726]**

MSGD a4 fo.67
Ink and water-colour on laid paper
98·4×69·8 cm
SCALE: 1 inch=160 feet
WATERMARK:
Coat of arms with letters 4 beneath
LVG

A **BLENHEIM Oxfordshire 1709**

Plates 24, 162a
Blenheim Palace, Oxfordshire
TITLE: A PLANN/OF/BLENHEIM'
SIGNATURE: '1709/Bridgman Discript.'
Ink and water-colour on paper
129·5×70·2 cm
SCALE: 1 inch=264 feet (4 chains)

C **BLENHEIM Oxfordshire**

Bod. Lib., MS Top Oxon a37* fo.2
TITLE: 'Blenheim'
'Map of the Gardens'
INSCRIPTION ON BACK: 'Maps of Blenheime &/Gardens'
Ink, pencil and wash on laid paper
72×49·9 cm
SCALE: 1 inch=396 feet (6 chains)
WATERMARK:
† and coat of arms with 4 beneath
IHS WR
IVILLEDARY

B **BOUGHTON Northamptonshire [c.1725–31]**

Plates 40, 41a
Boughton House, Northamptonshire
Ink, pencil and water-colour on laid paper on linen
68·9×42·2 cm (inside of frame)
WATERMARK:
Coat of arms with crown and fleur-de-lis
NOTES: Bird's-eye view

C **BOUGHTON Northamptonshire [c.1725–31]**

Boughton House, Northamptonshire
Ink, pencil and wash on laid paper on painted plywood
77·1×61 cm
SCALE: 1 inch=264 feet (4 chains)

C **BOUGHTON Northamptonshire [c.1725–31]**

Boughton House, Northamptonshire
Ink, pencil and water-colour on laid paper on card
50·5×41 cm
SCALE: 1 inch=396 feet (6 chains)

C **BRAMPTON BRYAN Herefordshire 1722**

Plate 78a
Soane, Box of Misc. Drawings (Wren, etc.)
TITLE: 'A / PLAN / OF / BRAMPTON HOUSE, / Castle, Gardens and/lands contiguous:/Belonging/to the Right Honble./ROBERT/EARL OF OXFORD/MDCCXXII
Ink and water-colour on laid paper
56·5×45·1 cm
SCALE: 1 inch=132 feet (2 chains)
WATERMARK: Coat of arms

C **BROCKET Hertfordshire [c.1731–38]**

MSGD a3 fo.7
TITLE: 'BROCKET HALL'
Ink, pencil and water-colour on parchment
54·3×46·3 cm
SCALE: 1 inch=360 feet

C **BROCKET Hertfordshire [c.1731–38]**

MSGD a4 fo.40
Ink and water-colour on laid paper
65·4×48·3 cm

SCALE: 1 inch=360 feet
WATERMARK:
† and coat of arms with 4 beneath
IHS LVG
IVILLEDARY

C **BUCKINGHAM HOUSE London [c.1726–38]**

Soane, Box of Misc. Drawings (Wren, etc.)
Ink and water-colour on laid paper
70·5×55·5 cm
WATERMARK:
† and coat of arms with 4 beneath
IHS LVG
IVILLEDARY

C **CLAREMONT Surrey [c.1724–28]**

Plate 32b
Soane, Drawer 62.1.2
Ink, pencil and wash on laid paper
51·4×37·1 cm
WATERMARK: †
IHS
IVILLEDARY
NOTES: Plan of Amphitheatre and Round Pond

C **DOWN HALL Essex [1720–21]**

Bod. Lib., Gough Maps 46 fo.262
TITLE: 'Down Hall'
INSCRIPTION ON BACK: 'From Wimpole'
Ink and pencil on laid paper
34·6×30·8 cm
NOTES: Version of BL, Loan 29/357 (Portland Papers), set 2

C **DOWN HALL Essex 1720**

Plate 67
BL, Loan 29/357 (Portland Papers), set 2
TITLE: 'Copy of the first Plan/for Down Hall'
INSCRIPTION ON BACK: 'for Mr Prior 1720'
Ink on laid paper
47·6×36·8 cm
WATERMARK: Fleur-de-lis and letters VII
NOTES: Version of Bod. Lib., Gough Maps 46 fo.262

B **EASTBURY Dorset [c.1723]**

Plate 28b
MSGD a3* fo.9
TITLE: 'A PLAN/OF/EASTBURY/the Seat of the R Honble/GEORGE DODINGTON/ESQ^R^.'
Ink and water-colour on laid paper
80×64·8 cm
SCALE: 1 inch=*c.*160 feet
WATERMARK: Pz

B **EASTBURY Dorset [c.1723]**

MSGD a3 fo.10
TITLE: 'A PLAN/OF/EASTBURY/the Seat of the R. Honble/GEORGE DODINGTON/ESQ^R^.'
Ink, pencil and water-colour on laid paper
76·8×63·5 cm
SCALE: 1 inch=160 feet
WATERMARK: Pz

C **EASTBURY Dorset [c.1723]**

MSGD a4 fo.21
Ink and water-colour on laid paper
121·9×73·3 cm
SCALE: 1 inch=40 feet

C **FARLEY Berkshire [c.1730]**

MSGD a4 fo.24
INSCRIPTION ON BACK: 'to be sold'
Ink and pencil on laid paper
41·6×33 cm
SCALE: 1 inch=66 feet (1 chain)
WATERMARK: Coat of arms and letters IONIC

C **FARLEY Berkshire [c.1730]**

Plate 52
MSGD a4 fo.34
Ink, pencil and wash on laid paper
67×50·2 cm
SCALE: 1 inch=132 feet (2 chains)

C **FULHAM ROAD London [c.1715]**

PRO, MPE 482 (Cat. No.339)
TITLE: 'A SURVEY OF HIS MAIESTIE'S/PRIVATE ROADE/FROM LONDON TO FULLHAM'
Ink and water-colour on laid paper on linen
192×50·8 cm
SCALE: 1 inch=528 feet (8 chains)

C **GREENWICH PARK Middlesex [c.1726–38]**

MSGD a4 fo.49
Ink and pencil on laid paper
65·7×48·9 cm
WATERMARK:
Coat of arms with 4 beneath, and letters IV
WR

C **GREENWICH PARK Middlesex [c.1726–38]**

National Maritime Museum, Greenwich, Greenwich Hospital Plans (ART/2), fo.2
Ink and wash on laid paper
74·9×52·1 cm
WATERMARK:
† and coat of arms with 4 beneath
IHS LVG
IVILLEDARY

C **GREENWICH PARK Middlesex [c.1726–38]**

National Maritime Museum, Greenwich, Greenwich Park MSS (ART/6)
TITLE: 'AN EXACT PLAN/OF/GREENWICH PARK . . .'
INSCRIPTION ON BACK: 'Greenwich Park 7'
'x¼'
Ink and water-colour on laid paper on canvas
81·3×57·1 cm
WATERMARK:
† and coat of arms with 4 beneath
IHS LVG
IVILLEDARY

C **GUNTON Norfolk**

Plate 80a
MSGD a4 fo.75
TITLE: '. . . Herbert of Gunton in/[Norfo]lk.'
Ink and water-colour on laid paper
52·7×30·2 cm
SCALE: 1 inch=40 feet
WATERMARK: †
IHS
IVILLEDARY
NOTES: Plan of Mount and Amphitheatre

C **HACKWOOD Hampshire [c.1720–30]**

MSGD a3 fo.4
INSCRIPTION ON BACK: 'Hackwood'
Ink, pencil and water-colour on laid paper on linen
144·1×109 cm
SCALE: 1 inch=130 feet
WATERMARK:
Coat of arms with 4 beneath, and letters IV
WR

A **HAMPTON COURT Middlesex [c.1735]**

Plates, 95, 163b
Soane, Drawer 36.3.1
TITLE: 'A GENERAL PLAN OF/HAMPTON-COURT/PALLACE GARDENS &/PARKS'
INSCRIPTION ON BACK: 'Hampton Court Parks'
'J 2'
SIGNATURE: 'C. BRIDGMAN FEC^{t}'
Ink, pencil and water-colour on paper on linen
53×50·5 cm
SCALE: 1 inch=660 feet (10 chains)

B **HAMPTON COURT Middlesex [c.1736]**

Hovingham Hall Yorkshire, MS vol., Architectural Drawings at Hovingham, fo.39
Ink and grey wash
45·7×31·4 cm
SCALE: 1 inch=198 feet (3 chains)
WATERMARK: Fleur-de-lis
NOTES: Plan of Lower Wilderness. In an eighteenth-century folder of drawings, most if not all of which probably belonged to Thomas Worsley (died 1778), Surveyor-General 1760–78 and builder of Hovingham Hall

C **HAMPTON COURT Middlesex [c.1726–38]**

MSGD a4 fo.62
Ink and water-colour on laid paper
109×93·7 cm
WATERMARK:
† and coat of arms with 4 beneath
IHS LVG
IVILLEDARY

C **HAMPTON COURT Middlesex [c.1726–38]**

MSGD a4 fo.74
Ink and water-colour on laid paper
59·3×23·8 cm
SCALE: 1 inch=110 feet
NOTES: Plan of Islands in River Thames near Hampton Court. Cf. BL, K.XXIX.14u

C **HAMPTON COURT Middlesex [c.1726–38]**

BL, K.XXIX.14u
TITLE: 'Two different designs of Viewing the Thames & Country, from the Great Elms, between/*Hampton Court* Green; & Hampton Town end.'
Ink and water-colour on laid paper
45·4×36·5 cm
SCALE: 1 inch=*c.*165 feet (2½ chains)
WATERMARK: †
IHS
IVILLEDARY
NOTES: Plan of Islands in River Thames near Hampton Court. Cf. MSGD a4 fo.74

C HAMPTON COURT Middlesex [c.1714–27]

PRO, MPD 23 (3) (Cat. No.1343)
TITLE: 'A Survey of the BARGE WAY, & c./in the County of Middlesex,/from Kingston Bridge to a point of Land/opposite to Thames Ditton Church./Belonging to Somerset English, Esq.'
INSCRIPTION ON BACK: '... Way/from Kingston/ to Hampton/Court'
Ink and water-colour on laid paper on linen
104·7×41·5 cm
SCALE: 1 inch=198 feet (3 chains)

C HOUGHTON Norfolk [c.1722–30]

Plate 81b
MSGD a4 fo.57
INSCRIPTION ON BACK: 'Esq[r] Walpole'
Ink and pencil on laid paper
61·6×57·5 cm

C HYDE PARK ROAD London [c.1711]

PRO, MPD 164 (Cat. No.338)
TITLE: 'Hide Park Road'
Ink and pencil on laid paper
50·2×36·8 cm
SCALE: 1 inch=396 feet (6 chains)
WATERMARK:
Coat of arms with 4 WR beneath, and letters IV

B KENSINGTON GARDENS and HYDE PARK London [c.1726–38]

Plate 99a
MSGD a3* fo.15
Ink, pencil and water-colour on laid paper
120×87·6 cm
SCALE: 1 inch=66 feet (1 chain)
WATERMARK:
† IHS IVILLEDARY and coat of arms with 4 LVG beneath
NOTES: Plan of Palace, Broad Walk, Round Pond, and Great Bow

B KENSINGTON GARDENS and HYDE PARK London [c.1729]

Royal Borough of Kensington and Chelsea Central Library, 712.5 KEN/F. Portfolio A33
TITLE: 'A Plan of Kensington Palace, with the Gardens &c. belonging thereto –'
Pen and water-colour
81×58 cm (ruled margin)
SCALE: 1 inch=165 feet (2½ chains)
WATERMARK: J WHATMAN

C KENSINGTON GARDENS and HYDE PARK London [c.1726–38]

BL, K.XXVIII.10.d.1
Ink, pencil and water-colour on laid paper
88·9×53 cm
SCALE: 1 inch=165 feet (2½ chains)
WATERMARK: † IHS IVILLEDARY and coat of arms

C KENSINGTON GARDENS and HYDE PARK London [c.1726–38]

Plate 98
HEH, ST MAP 147
Ink and water-colour on vellum
35·5×24·7 cm
SCALE: 1 inch=420 feet
NOTES: General Plan

C KENSINGTON GARDENS and HYDE PARK London [c.1726–38]*

Nationalmuseum, Stockholm, CC.2753 (Cronstedt Collection)
TITLE: 'KENSINGTON'
Ink and water-colour on vellum
35·1×24·7 cm
SCALE: 1 inch=420 feet
NOTES: General Plan. Exhibition: C. J. Cronstedts Fullerösamling, Nationalmuseum, Stockholm. Exhibition Catalogue 79 (1942), No.371 (Information from Ulf G. Johnsson)

C LEDSTON Yorkshire [c.1731]

MSGD a3 fo.19
Ink, pencil and wash on laid paper
65·7×48·9 cm
SCALE: 1 inch=330 feet (5 chains)
WATERMARK: Coat of arms

C LEDSTON Yorkshire [c.1731]

MSGD a4 fo.85
Ink and wash on laid paper
INSCRIPTION ON BACK: 'Lady Betty Hasting's/ House'
'Lady Hasting'
87·6×68·5 cm
SCALES: 1 inch=40 feet
1 inch=10 feet (Gateway)
WATERMARK: Coat of arms and letters GI

B LEDSTON Yorkshire [c.1731]

Plate 48b
Otterden Place, Kent

TITLE: 'Lady Eliz Hastings at Ledstone Park'
Ink and water-colour on laid paper on linen
57·5 × 46 cm
SCALE: 1 inch=60 feet
WATERMARK:
Coat of arms with fleur-de-lis, and letters IV
NOTES: One of a group of unsigned garden layouts and other drawings at Otterden, apparently of about the same date. A two-page description of the plan is also at Otterden

C **LILLINGTON MANOR Warwickshire 1711**

Warwickshire CRO, Warwick, CR.556/197
TITLE: 'AN EXACT PLAN OF/LILLINGTON MANNOR/ Viz.t the Town Inclosures, Comon/=fields, Meadows, Pastures, and all/other Lands remarkable/taken Anno/MDCCXI
Ink, pencil and wash on laid paper on linen
140·7 × 54 cm
NOTES: Simpler version of Lillington Manor drawing formerly at Lillington Vicarage (see below). Part of the survey of 1711 referred to in the notebook in Warwickshire CRO, CR.26.2.1 (Waller Collection)

C **LILLINGTON MANOR Warwickshire 1711***

Formerly at Lillington Vicarage, now lost
TITLE: 'AN EXACT PLAN OF/LILLINGTON MANNOR/ Viz.t the Town, Inclosures, Common/=fields, Meadows, Pastures, and all/other Lands remarkable/taken Anno/MDCCXI.'
NOTES: Part of the survey of 1711 referred to in the notebook in Warwickshire CRO, CR.26.2.1 (Waller Collection). Reproduced in William Cooper, *The History of Lillington, Leamington Spa* (Long Compton, Shipston-on-Stour, 1940), inside back cover, and discussed on pp.118–26.

C **MEREWORTH Kent [c.1722–25]**

MSGD a4 fo.52
INSCRIPTION ON BACK: 'Lord Westmorelands/but of no use now'
'a small plan without a name' [crossed out]
'Colonell Fanes at Mereworth'
Ink and wash on laid paper
54 × 44·7 cm
SCALE: 1 inch=40 feet
WATERMARK:
Coat of arms with 4 beneath, and letters IV
LVG

C **MOOR PARK Hertfordshire [c.1720–28]**

MSGD a4 fo.48
Pencil on laid paper
64·8 × 48·2 cm
SCALE: 1 inch=110 feet
WATERMARK:
Coat of arms with 4 beneath and letters IV
LVG

C **MOOR PARK Hertfordshire [c.1720–28]**

Plate 51a
MSGD a4 fo.58
INSCRIPTION ON BACK: 'M.r Stiles'
Ink and pencil on laid paper
69·2 × 52·1 cm
WATERMARK:
Coat of arms with 4 beneath and letters IV
WR

C **PURLEY Berkshire [c.1720–21]**

Plate 47b
MSGD a4 fo.54
INSCRIPTION ON BACK: 'Francis Haws Esq.r
Ink, pencil and wash on laid paper
71·4 × 53·7 cm
WATERMARK: Coat of arms with 4 beneath
WR
NOTES: Cf. William Godson's drawing of Purley in MSGD a3 fo.5

B **RICHMOND GARDENS Surrey [c.1726–38]**

Plate 108
PRO, Works 32/96
INSCRIPTION ON BACK: 'OFFICE OF HIS MAJESTY'S WORKS & PUBLIC BUILDINGS' (circular stamp, with central crown)
Ink and wash on laid paper on linen
75 × 51·4 cm
SCALE: 1 inch=132 feet (2 chains)
NOTES: Detailed plan of Richmond Gardens to west of Richmond Lodge

C **RICHMOND GARDENS Surrey [c.1726–38]**

Plate 106b
PRO, Works 32/282
Ink and pencil on laid paper on canvas
165·4 × 64·1 cm
SCALE: 1 inch=198 feet (3 chains)
NOTES: Plan of Richmond Gardens similar to Rocque's of 1734, 1736 (*Vit. Brit.*, IV (1739), pls 9–10), 1748, 1754

C **RICHMOND GARDENS and KEW PALACE Surrey [c.1726–38]**

PRO, MR 528 (Cat. No.1449)
INSCRIPTION ON BACK: 'Richmond–Part of Kew Gardens/and Palace x 51/13'
Ink, pencil and water-colour on laid paper on linen
198·7×44·8 cm
SCALE: 1 inch=66 feet (1 chain)
WATERMARK: † IHS IVILLEDARY and coat of arms

C **RICHMOND GARDENS Surrey [c.1714–27]**

PRO, MR 696 (Cat. No.1437)
TITLE: 'A PLAN/of the Lodge, the Gardens, the Park/and other Grounds at Richmond/belonging to/Their ROYAL HIGHNESSES/the PRINCE and PRINCESS/of/WALES.'
Ink and water-colour on linen
131·8×127·6 cm
SCALE: 1 inch=132 feet (2 chains)
NOTES: A Bridgeman drawing for King George II and Queen Caroline whilst Prince and Princess of Wales?

B **ROUSHAM Oxfordshire [c.1725–37]**

Plates 61, 62a
MSGD a4 fo.63
INSCRIPTION ON BACK: 'Colonel Dormer'
Ink and pencil on laid paper
89·2×62·2 cm
SCALE: 1 inch=*c*.53 feet
WATERMARK:
Coat of arms with 4 beneath, and letters IV

C **SACOMBE Hertfordshire [c.1715–17]**

MSGD a4 fo.29
INSCRIPTION ON BACK: 'Mr Rolt Sacomb'
Ink, pencil and wash on laid paper
68·9×46 cm
WATERMARK:
Coat of arms with 4 WR beneath, and letters IV

C **SACOMBE Hertfordshire [c.1715–17]**

Plate 46b
MSGD a4 fo.64
INSCRIPTION ON BACK 'Mr Rolts Planns'
Ink and water-colour on laid paper
89·8×63·5 cm
WATERMARK:
Coat of arms with 4 beneath, and letters IV

C **ST JAMES'S PARK London [c.1710–25]**

Plate 103
PRO, Works 32/70
INSCRIPTION ON BACK: 'OFFICE OF HIS MAJESTY'S WORKS & PUBLIC BUILDINGS' (two circular stamps, with central crown)
Ink, pencil and water-colour on laid paper on linen
91·1×53·3 cm

C **ST JAMES'S PARK London**

Soane, Drawer 62.1.1
Ink, pencil and water-colour on laid paper
75·5×53·3 cm
WATERMARK:
† IHS IVILLEDARY and coat of arms with 4 LVG beneath

C **SCAMPSTON Yorkshire**

MSGD a4 fo.27
Ink and pencil on laid paper
36·2×34 cm
SCALE: 1 inch=132 feet (2 chains)

C **SCAMPSTON Yorkshire**

MSGD a4 fo.37
INSCRIPTION ON BACK: 'Sr William St Quintin/to be got . . .'
Ink on parchment
62·5×57·1 cm
SCALE: 1 inch=165 feet (2½ chains)

C **SCAMPSTON Yorkshire**

MSGD a4 fo.66
INSCRIPTION ON BACK: 'Sr William St Quintin'
Ink and pencil on laid paper
69·2×52·7 cm
SCALE: 1 inch=*c*.60 feet
WATERMARK:
Coat of arms with 4 WR beneath, and letters IV

C **SCAMPSTON Yorkshire**

Plate 48a
MSGD a4 fo.73
Ink and water-colour on laid paper
64·5×39 cm
SCALE: 1 inch=60 feet
WATERMARK: Coat of arms

C **SPRING GARDENS London 1730**

PRO, MPE 555 (Cat. No.344)
TITLE: 'Map A/A PLAN OF SPRING GARDEN as it was in 1730.'
Ink and wash on laid paper on linen
53 × 44·2 cm
SCALE: 1 inch = 32 feet

C **THE BELL INN STILTON Huntingdonshire [c.1736]**

MSGD a3 fo.40r
Ink on laid paper
33 × 20·6 cm
SCALE: 1 inch = 8 feet
WATERMARK: CAW

C **THE BELL INN STILTON Huntingdonshire [c.1736]**

MSGD a3 fo.40v
TITLE: 'the Stable at Stilton'
Ink on laid paper
33 × 20·6 cm
WATERMARK: CAW

C **THE BELL INN STILTON Huntingdonshire [c.1736]**

MSGD a4 fo.3
INSCRIPTION ON BACK: 'Stilton'
Ink on laid paper
33·3 × 21·3 cm
SCALE: 1 inch = 5 feet
WATERMARK: Britannia and letters PRO PATRIA

C **THE BELL INN STILTON Huntingdonshire [c.1736]**

MSGD a4 fo.51
TITLE: 'Bell Inn at Stilton/29th July 1736'
INSCRIPTION ON BACK: 'Mr. Ransom's Plan of the Bell-Inn at Stilton.'
Ink and pencil on laid paper
67·3 × 48·5 cm
SCALE: 1 inch = 15 feet
WATERMARK:
Coat of arms with 4 beneath, and letters IV

B **STOWE Buckinghamshire [c.1720]**

Plates 116–120b
MSGD a4 fo.46
Ink, pencil and water-colour on laid paper
95·2 × 41·9 cm
WATERMARK: Coat of arms with 4 beneath
WR
NOTES: Bird's-eye view

C **TRAFALGAR Wiltshire [c.1733]**

MSGD a3 fo.24
TITLE: 'A Plan of the Homestead & Parke/at STANDLINCH/belonging to/Sr. Peter Vandeput Barrt.'
Ink, pencil and water-colour on laid paper
144·8 × 54 cm
SCALE: 1 inch = 66 feet (1 chain)
WATERMARK:
† and coat of arms with 4 beneath
IHS LVG
IVILLEDARY

C **TRAFALGAR Wiltshire [c.1733]**

MSGD a3 fo.25
INSCRIPTION ON BACK: 'S. Peter Vandeput's/Seat at Standlynch.'
Ink and pencil on laid paper
39·3 × 31·7 cm
WATERMARK: Britannia, letters PRO PATRIA and CAW, and coat of arms

C **TRAFALGAR Wiltshire [c.1733]**

MSGD a3 fo.36
TITLE: 'Taken From Sr Peter Vandepuet/Plan of his a State'
Ink and pencil on laid paper
31·1 × 21·9 cm
WATERMARK: IVILLEDARY

C **TRING Hertfordshire [c.1720–25]**

MSGD a4 fo.25
Ink and pencil on laid paper
37·8 × 30·2 cm
SCALE: 1 inch = 40 feet
WATERMARK: Cross in lozenge

C **TRING Hertfordshire [c.1720–25]**

MSGD a4 fo.32
INSCRIPTION ON BACK: 'Mr. Gore of Tring'
Ink and pencil on laid paper
69·2 × 52·1 cm
WATERMARK:
Coat of arms with 4 beneath, and letters IV
WR

C **TRING Hertfordshire [c.1720–25]**

Plate 45a
MSGD a4 fo.78
INSCRIPTION ON BACK: 'Mrs Frs Gore'
Ink and pencil on laid paper
51·4×30 cm
SCALE: 1 inch=66 feet (1 chain)
WATERMARK:
Coat of arms with 4 WR beneath, and letters IV

B **WARWICK TOWN and PRIORY [1711]**

Plate 18
Warwickshire CRO, Warwick, CR.26.2.2 (Waller Collection)
TITLE: Three panels, titled respectively 'A DISCRIPTION & ANTIQUITY/OF THE PRIORY', 'ANTIQUITY/OF WOODLOW', and '[GENE]RAL PROSPECT OF THE PRIORY'
Ink and water-colour on paper on linen
216×88·2 cm
NOTES: Described in a notebook in Warwickshire CRO, CR.26.2.1 (Waller Collection), entitled 'An Exact Survey & Rental of ye/Priory at Warwick, the Manors of/Woodlow & Wodcote contiguous to it, & ye/Ldp of Lillington in the said County/ As taken 1711/By/Mr Fish, being assisted &/ Compleated by Cha: Bridgman.'
The bird's-eye view of the priory here was probably drawn by Bridgeman – it is too accomplished for his collaborator James Fish, the Younger – and thus may be a precursor of his bird's eye view of Stowe of *c.*1720 (MSGD a4 fo.46).

C **WARWICK PRIORY Warwick [c.1727]**

Warwickshire CRO, Warwick, CR.56
Ink, pencil and water-colour on paper
109·2×89·8 cm
NOTES: Reproduced in Green, *Gardener to Queen Anne*, pl.40.

C **WARWICK TOWN and PRIORY [1711]**

Warwickshire CRO, Warwick, CR.217, Bundle 1
INSCRIPTION ON BACK: 'THE PRIORY'
Ink and wash on laid paper on linen
140·5×52·7 cm
NOTES: Similar to CR.26.2.2 (Waller Collection), but without drawing of priory. Part of survey of 1711 referred to in the notebook in Warwickshire CRO, CR.26.2.1 (Waller Collection)

B **WIMBLEDON HOUSE Surrey [c.1732–33]**

Plate 44b
MSGD a3 fo.31
INSCRIPTION ON BACK: 'The Plan of the Garden at Wimbledon/belonging to/Her Grace the Dutchess of Marlborough.'
Ink, pencil and water-colour on laid paper
53·6×38·4 cm
SCALE: 1 inch=66 feet (1 chain)

B **WIMBLEDON HOUSE Surrey [c.1732–33]**

Plate 44a
MSGD a4 fo.44
INSCRIPTION ON BACK: 'Wimbledon'
'Sarah Dutchess of Marlborough'
Ink and pencil on laid paper
71·1×54·3 cm
WATERMARK:
Coat of arms with 4 WR beneath, and letters IV

C **WIMPOLE Cambridgeshire [c.1720–24]**

MSGD a4 fo.30
TITLE: 'Wimpole/No.1.'
Ink and pencil on laid paper
71·1×53·6 cm
SCALE: 1 inch=60 feet
WATERMARK:
Coat of arms with 4 WR beneath, and letters IV

C **WIMPOLE Cambridgeshire [c.1720–24]**

MSGD a4 fo.31
TITLE: 'Wimpole No.3.'
INSCRIPTION ON BACK: 'Wimpole'
Ink and pencil on laid paper
214×47 cm
SCALE: 1 inch=165 feet (2½ chains)
WATERMARK: Coat of arms and letters IV
NOTES: Detail of Main Avenue

C **WIMPOLE Cambridgeshire [c.1720–24]**

MSGD a4 fo.35
INSCRIPTION ON BACK: 'Wimple'
Pencil on laid paper
104·1×74·3 cm
SCALE: 1 inch=198 feet (3 chains)
WATERMARK:
† IHS IVILLEDARY and coat of arms with 4 LVG beneath

C **WIMPOLE Cambridgeshire [c.1720–24]**

Plate 75
MSGD a4 fo.69
Ink, pencil and wash on laid paper

64·7×33·3 cm
SCALE: 1 inch=396 feet (6 chains)
WATERMARK:
Coat of arms with 4 beneath, and letters ‡v
LV GERREVINK

C **WIMPOLE Cambridgeshire [c.1720–24]***

Wimpole, Cambridgeshire, Wimpole Album
NOTES: This drawing is referred to in *RCHM: West Cambridgeshire*, I (1968), 215.

C **WINDSOR CASTLE Berkshire [1729–38]**

Soane, Box of Misc. Drawings (Wren, etc.)
Ink and water-colour on laid paper
75·5×46·3 cm
SCALE: 1 in=66 feet (1 chain)
WATERMARK:
Coat of arms with 4 beneath, and letters IV
WR
NOTES: Cf. the 'Plan of the Garden as proposed to be Executed in the Reign of Queen Ann', on Rocque's 1738 engraving of the Duke of Marlborough's estate at Windsor in *Vit. Brit.*, IV (1739), pls 38–39

A **WINDSOR FOREST Berkshire [Queen Anne?]**

Plates 104, 105 163a
PRO, MR 279 (Cat. No.854)
TITLE: 'A GENERAL PLAN OF WINDSOR FOREST . . .'
SIGNATURE: 'Bridgman Pinxit'
Ink and water-colour on laid paper on linen
98×82·7 cm
SCALE: 1 inch=50 chains
NOTES: Plan of Windsor Forest as it was in the reign of James I. Attached to it are layouts of Langley Park and Ditton Park

C **WOLTERTON Norfolk [c.1724–30]**

MSGD a3 fo.33
TITLE: 'A SURVEY of WOOLTERTON HALL & c. belonging to HORATIO WALPOLE Esq.r'
Ink, pencil and wash on paper
45·7×40·6 cm

C **WOLTERTON Norfolk [c.1724–30]**

MSGD a4 fo.10
Ink, pencil and water-colour on laid paper
83·8×52·7 cm
SCALE: 1 inch=99 feet (1½ chains)
WATERMARK: Coat of arms

C **WOLTERTON Norfolk [c.1724–30]**

MSGD a4 fo.18
Ink, pencil and water-colour on laid paper
53·6×42·2 cm
SCALE: 1 inch=99 feet (1½ chains)

C **WOLTERTON Norfolk [c.1724–30]**

Plate 80b
MSGD a4 fo.20
Ink and water-colour on laid paper
85·7×57·8 cm
SCALE: 1 inch=99 feet (1½ chains)

C **WOLTERTON Norfolk [c.1724–30]**

MSGD a4 fo.55
INSCRIPTION ON BACK: 'R.Hon.M.r Walpole'
Ink, pencil and water-colour on laid paper
63·2×47 cm
SCALE: 1 inch=132 feet (2 chains)
WATERMARK: Coat of arms with 4 beneath
WR

C **WOLTERTON Norfolk [c.1724–30]**

MSGD a4 fo.56
INSCRIPTION ON BACK: 'Hon.ble Horatio Walpole Esq.r'
Pencil on parchment
40·3×34·9 cm
SCALE: 1 inch=264 feet (4 chains)

C **WOLTERTON Norfolk [c.1724–30]**

MSGD a4 fo.61
Ink, pencil and water-colour on laid paper
83·2×58·4 cm

C **UNIDENTIFIED**

MSGD a4 fo.22
Ink and water-colour on laid paper
118·8×79·3 cm
SCALE: 1 inch=40 feet

C **UNIDENTIFIED**

MSGD a4 fo.33
Ink, pencil and water-colour on laid paper
69·8=53·3 cm
SCALE: 1 inch=220 feet
WATERMARK:
† and coat of arns with 4 beneath
IHS LVG
IVILLEDARY
NOTES: Cf. MSGD a4 fo.43

C UNIDENTIFIED

MSGD a4 fo.36
Ink and water-colour on laid paper
113 × 52·7 cm
SCALE: 1 inch = 50 feet
WATERMARK:
Coat of arms with 4 beneath, and letters IV

C UNIDENTIFIED

MSGD a4 fo.43
Pencil on laid paper
70·5 × 52·3 cm
SCALE: 1 inch = 220 feet
WATERMARK:
† and coat of arms with 4 beneath
IHS LVG
IVILLEDARY
NOTES: Cf. MSGD a4 fo.33

C UNIDENTIFIED

MSGD a4 fo.81
INSCRIPTION ON BACK: 'Franc[s] Whitaker/
Tyburn Lane'
Ink and wash on laid paper
41 × 32·8 cm
SCALE: 1 inch = 80 feet
WATERMARK: Circular medallion

Bibliography

With minor exceptions (such as the writings of classical authors) the following three bibliographies list all sources cited in the text, footnotes, and appendices.

Several points should, however, be made: drawings have been excluded, although of course detailed information on those by Bridgeman, or attributed to him, appears in the *Catalogue of Bridgeman Drawings* (pp.173–86); with books, only the specific editions referred to are given, dates of reprints are not; and the names used for county and other British record offices are those which were applicable *before* the reorganization of Local Government in April 1974.

Where appropriate, entries follow the citations given in the List of Abbreviations on pp.xx–xxi. Square brackets are used to signify doubtful dates or authors, and for entries listed under subject.

The aim of this Bibliography is to provide a guide to the study of Bridgeman's career and to the early history of the English landscape garden.

Bibliography A
Unpublished manuscripts cited

ALTHORP, Northants.
MS Wills of Sarah, Duchess of Marlborough.

BEDFORD OFFICE, London.
Woburn MSS.

BLENHEIM PALACE, Oxon.
Letters from Sarah, Duchess of Marlborough, to Sarah Bridgeman, in Blenheim MSS, F1–35 (6 July, 10 September 1741); Letter Book No.2, Bills and Estimates . . . (26 July 1741).

BODLEIAN LIBRARY, Oxford (cited as Bod. Lib.)
MS.Rawl.D.1162. William Kent's Italian Diary, 1714–15.

BRITISH LIBRARY, London.

Add MS 2235 (Egerton Papers).
Add MS 5842 (Tour in England 1735).
Add MS 15776 (Tour in England 1735).
Add MSS 18238–48 (Harley Papers).
Add MS 22926 (Tour in England 1742).
Add MS 23076 (Vertue Note Book).
Add MS 33085 (Chichester Papers).
Add MS 34733 (West Papers).
Add MS 38488A (Tour in England 1741).
Add MS 39167B (St Luke's Club).
Add MS 47030 (Egmont Papers).
Add MS 51345 (Holland House Papers).
Loan 29/90, 29/316, 29/317, 29/357 (Portland Papers).

BRITISH MUSEUM, London.
Sir James Thornhill's MS Sketchbook (1884–7–26–40).

CAMBRIDGE, King's College.
Congregation Book, 1722–78.

EARL CATHCART COLLECTION, London.
MS Cathcart Diaries.

CHATSWORTH, Derbys.
Devonshire Collection.
MS Catalogue of Burlington's Library at Chiswick.

CHRISTIE, MANSON AND WOODS LTD, London.
Auction records.

COMPTON PLACE, Sussex.
Lord Wilmington's Account Book, 1726–40.

DUCHY OF CORNWALL OFFICE, London.
MS Household Accounts, Frederick, Prince of Wales, and Augusta, Princess of Wales, II–VII (Vouchers 1731–37).

ESSEX CRO, Chelmsford.
D/DTu 276. Samuel Tufnell's Receipt Book.

C. HOARE AND CO., Bankers, London.
MS Accounts.

HENRY E. HUNTINGTON LIBRARY, San Marino, California (cited as HEH).

Boxes L9F6: Stowe (Temple) Estate Accounts, 1710–20; L9F7: Stowe (Temple) Estate Accounts, 1720–27.

Bundle L9F9: Stowe (Temple) Estate Accounts, 1718–22.

Stowe (Temple) Account Books No.7 (ST164) (1732–79), No.130 (ST161) (1735–41), No.131 (ST162) (1719–23), No.132 (ST163) (1723–27).

MS MO.1335.

IPSWICH AND EAST SUFFOLK CRO, Ipswich.
Ashburnham MSS.

KEDLESTON HALL, Derbys.
Sir John Curzon's Day Book, 1718–50.

KENSINGTON, St Mary Abbots Church.
Baptismal and burial records.

MR AND MRS THOMAS KIRBY COLLECTION, London.
MSS relating to The Bell Inn, Stilton.

LENNOXLOVE, East Lothian.
Hamilton MSS.

LONGFORD CASTLE, Wilts.
Longford (Folkestone) MSS.

NOTTINGHAM UNIVERSITY LIBRARY.
Newcastle MSS.

OTTERDEN PLACE, Kent.
Ledston MSS.

PICCADILLY, St James's Church.
Baptismal and burial records.

PINHORNS, London.
Bernau Index, and other genealogical records.

PUBLIC RECORD OFFICE, London (cited as PRO).

Works 1/1, 1/2, 3/2, 4/1–4/8, 5/56–5/59, 5/104, 5/105, 5/141, 5/150, 6/8, 6/15, 6/16, 6/114, 6/184/4, 16/2/8, 16/3/1, 16/39/1.

PROB. 3/37/95 (Bridgeman's Inventory 1738).

King's Warrant Book XXXIII (T52: 40).
Letter Book XIX (T27:25).
Money Book XL (T53: 40).
Treasury Books and Papers CCLXIII (7) (T1:263), CCXCIII (10) (T1: 293), CCXCIX (10) (T1:299).

WILLS of CHARLES BRIDGEMAN, 1738 (PROB.11.692 (BRODREPP 1738)), and SARAH BRIDGEMAN, 1743 (PROB.11.731 (ANSTIS 1744)).

ROYAL BANK OF SCOTLAND LTD,
Drummonds Branch, London.
MS Accounts.

SCOTTISH RECORD OFFICE, Edinburgh
(cited as SRO, Edinburgh).
GD 18/2107; GD 18/2110; GD 18/4404/1 (Clerk MSS); GD 112/21/77 (Breadalbane MSS).

SIR JOHN SOANE'S MUSEUM, London
(cited as Soane).
MS Memoir of James Gibbs.

SOCIETY OF GENEALOGISTS, London
(cited as Soc. Gen.)
Boyd's Marriage Index (Middlesex 1701–25, 1726–51).
Inner Temple Admissions, 1660–1799.
Boyd's Index of London Burials, 1738.

SOTHEBY AND CO, London.
Auction records.

SUFFOLK CRO, Bury St Edmunds.
Hervey MSS.

SUSSEX ARCHAEOLOGICAL SOCIETY,
East Sussex CRO, Lewes.
Gage MSS.

VICTORIA AND ALBERT MUSEUM, London
(cited as V&A).
MS.86.M.24 (MS Diary 1728–30).

WARWICK CRO, Warwick.
CR 341/300 (Henry Wise MS Catalogue).

WESTMINSTER CITY LIBRARY, London.
Baptismal register of St Ann's Church, Soho.

COLLEGE OF WILLIAM AND MARY,
Williamsburg, Virginia.
Tucker-Coleman Papers.

WILLIAMS AND GLYN'S BANK LTD,
Child's Branch, London.
MS Accounts.

WILTON HOUSE, Wilts.
MS House Book of Henry Herbert, 9th Earl of Pembroke, 1738–45.

WILTSHIRE CRO, Trowbridge.
944/1 (Flitcroft Atlas).

YORKSHIRE ARCHAEOLOGICAL SOCIETY, Leeds.
MS 328. Anonymous. Diary of a Tour in 1724.

Bibliography B
Unpublished theses cited

BILBROUGH, Hugh.
'The Use of Tree Plantations as Elements of Landscape Design, With Special Reference to Published Texts of the Eighteenth and Nineteenth Centuries'.
Ph.D. thesis, University of Manchester, 1971.

BROGDEN, William A.
'Stephen Switzer and Garden Design in Britain in the Early Eighteenth Century'.
Ph.D. thesis, University of Edinburgh, 1973.

COLTON, Judith.
'Monuments to Men of Genius. A Study of Eighteenth-Century English and French Sculptural Works'.
Ph.D. thesis, New York University, 1974.

FISCHER, Marianne.
'Die frühen Rekonstruktionen der Landhäuser Plinius' des Jüngeren'.
Ph.D. thesis, Free University of Berlin, 1962.

FRIEDMAN, Terry F.
'James Gibbs (1682–1754). The Formation of His Architectural Style'.
Ph.D. thesis, University of London, 1971.

GIBSON, William A.
'A Preface to a Study of the Relations of Architecture and English Literature, 1650–1750'.
Ph.D. thesis, University of Minnesota, 1964.

MASHECK, Joseph D.
'The First Plates for Thomson's *Seasons*'.
M.A. thesis, Columbia University, 1967.

OSMUN, William R.
'A Study of the Work of Sir James Thornhill'.
Ph.D. thesis, University of London, 1950.

ROBERSON, Samuel A.
'Thomas Jefferson and the Eighteenth-Century Landscape Garden Movement in England'.
Ph.D. thesis, Yale University, 1966.

SOFIELD, David.
'English Building Poems, 1600–1680'.
Ph.D. thesis, Stanford University, 1971.

SPINK, William W.
'The Planning of an Environment, With Reference to the Penicuik Estates'.
M.Sc. thesis, University of Edinburgh, 1969.

WILLIS, Peter.
'Charles Bridgeman: Royal Gardener'.
Ph.D. thesis, University of Cambridge, 1962.

Bibliography C
Books and articles cited

ACKERMAN, James S.
The Cortile del Belvedere.
Vatican City, 1954.

ADAMS, G. E.
'Extracts from the Parish Registers of St James's, Westminster'.
Topographer and Genealogist, III (1957), 491–503.

ADDISON, Joseph.
Remarks on Several Parts of Italy, Etc., in the Years 1701, 1702, 1703.
London, 1705.

ALBERTI, Leon Battista.
De re aedificatoria.
Florence, 1485.

ALLEN, B. Sprague.
Tides in English Taste (1619–1800). A Background for the Study of Literature.
2 vols.
Cambridge, Mass., 1937.

ALTENBERND, A. Lynn.
'On Pope's "Horticultural Romanticism"'.
Journal of English and Germanic Philology, LV (October 1955), 470–77.

AMHERST, Alicia (Evelyn Cecil).
A History of Gardening in England.
3rd edn.
London, 1910.

AMHERST, Alicia (Evelyn Cecil).
London Parks and Gardens.
London, 1907.

ANDREWS, C. Bruyn, ed.
The Torrington Diaries . . .
4 vols.
London, 1934.

ANGELONI, Battista (i.e. John Shebbeare).
Letters on the English Nation.
2 vols.
London, 1755.

ARKELL, Ruby L.
Caroline of Ansbach. George II's Queen.
London, 1939.

AUBIN, Robert A.
Topographical Poetry in Eighteenth-Century England.
New York, 1936.

AURIGEMMA, Salvatore.
Villa Adriana.
Rome, 1961.

BADESLADE, Thomas.
The History of the Ancient and Present State of the Navigation of the Port of King's-Lyn, and of Cambridge . . .
London, 1725; 2nd edn 1766.

BAGOT, Annette.
'Monsieur Beaumont and Colonel Grahme. The Making of a Garden, 1689–1710'.
Garden History, III, No.4 (Autumn 1975), 66–78.

BAKER, C. H. Collins, and Muriel I.
The Life and Circumstances of James Brydges, 1st Duke of Chandos, Patron of the Liberal Arts.
Oxford, 1949.

BANDINEL, Bulkeley.
A Catalogue of the Books Relating to British Topography, and Saxon and Northern Literature, Bequeathed to the Bodleian Library . . . by Richard Gough, Esq., F.S.A.
Oxford, 1814.

BANNERMAN, W. B., ed.
Miscellanea Genealogica et Heraldica,
S.4, V (1914).

BARBIER, Carl P.
William Gilpin. His Drawings, Teaching, and Theory of the Picturesque.
Oxford, 1963.

BARKER, G. F. Russell, and STENNING, A. H.
The Record of Old Westminsters . . .
2 vols.
London, 1928.

BARLOW, Derek.
Dick Turpin and the Gregory Gang.
London and Chichester, 1973.

BARRINGTON, Daines.
'On the Progress of Gardening . . .'
Archaeologia: or Miscellaneous Tracts Relating to Antiquity, VII (1785), 113–30

BATTESTIN, Martin C.
The Providence of Wit. Aspects of Form in Augustan Literature and the Arts.
Oxford, 1974.

BAZELEY, W.
'History of Prinknash Park'.
Transactions of the Bristol and Gloucestershire Archaeological Society, VII (1882–83), 267–306.

BEARD, Geoffrey.
Decorative Plasterwork in Great Britain.
London, 1975.

BEARD, Geoffrey.
Georgian Craftsmen and Their Work.
London, 1966.

BEARD, Geoffrey.
'Leoni's English Houses'.
Country Life Annual (1968), pp.85–87.

BEARD, Geoffrey.
'William Kent's Royal Patrons'.
Country Life Annual (1970), pp.22–24.

BEEVERELL, James.
Les délices de la Grand' Bretagne, et de l'Irlande . . .
8 vols.
Leiden, 1707; 1727.

BERESFORD, Maurice.
History on the Ground. Six Studies in Maps and Landscapes.
2nd edn.
London, 1971.

BERRALL, Julia S.
The Garden. An Illustrated History from Ancient Egypt to the Present Day.
London, 1966.

BICKHAM, George, the Younger.
The Beauties of Stow . . .
London, 1750; 1753; 1756.

BICKHAM, George, the Elder, pub.
Views of Stowe . . .
London, 1753.

BINNEY, Marcus.
'Chicheley Hall, Buckinghamshire'.
C. Life CLVII (13, 20, 27 February 1975), 378–81, 434–37, 498–501.

BINNEY, Marcus.
'Worksop Manor, Nottinghamshire'.
C.Life, CLIII (15 March 1973), 678–82.

[BOLINGBROKE, Henry St John, 1st Viscount]
The Works of Lord Bolingbroke . . .
4 vols.
Philadelphia, 1841.

BOND, Donald F., ed.
The Spectator.
5 vols.
Oxford, 1965.

BOND, Richmond P.
The Tatler. The Making of a Literary Journal.
Cambridge, Mass., 1971.

BÖRSCH-SUPAN, Eva.
Garten-, Landschafts- und Paradies-Motive im Innenraum.
Berlin, 1967.

BOUTWOOD, James.
'Poet's Essay in the Picturesque. Alexander Pope's Garden at Twickenham'.
C.Life, CXLIII (7 March 1968), 512–14.

BOWACK, John.
The Antiquities of Middlesex . . .
2 pts.
London, 1705–6.

BOYER, Abel, ed.
The Political State of Great Britain . . .
London, 1711 et seq.

BOYS, Richard C.
'The Architect Vanbrugh and the Wits'.
College Art Journal (New York), VI (1947), 283–90.

BOYS, Richard C.
'Sir Joshua Reynolds and the Architect Vanbrugh. A Footnote to Boswell'.
Papers of the Michigan Academy of Arts, Science and Letters, XXXIII (1947), 323–36.

BOYSE, Samuel.
The Triumphs of Nature. A Poem.
Gentleman's Magazine, XII (August 1742), 436.

BRACKENBURY, Antony.
'The Happy Eastbury Circle'.
C.Life, CXIX (8 March 1956), 422–23.

BRAYBROOK, Neville.
London Green. The Story of Kensington Gardens, Hyde Park, Green Park and St James's Park.
London, 1959.

BRIDGEMAN, Charles.
A Report of the Present State of the Great Level of the Fens, Called Bedford-Level, and of the Port of Lynn: and of the Rivers Ouse and Nean, the Two Great Sewers of that Country . . .
London, 1725; 2nd edn 1766.

[BRIDGEMAN, Katherine]
A Catalogue of the Entire Library of Mrs Katherine Bridgeman (of Cavendish Square) Deceased.
London, 1743/4.

BRIDGEMAN, Sarah, pub.
A General Plan of the Woods, Park and Gardens of Stowe . . . with Several Perspective Views in the Gardens.
London, 1739; 2nd edn 1746.

British Sporting Painting, 1650–1850.
Exhibition Catalogue.
Arts Council of Great Britain.
London, 1974.

BRITTEN, James.
'Some Early Cape Botanists and Collectors'.
Journal of the Linnean Society (*Botany*), XLV (1920–22), 29–52.

BROGDEN, William A.
'Stephen Switzer. "La Grand Manier"'.
In Willis, ed., *Furor Hortensis*, pp.21–30.

BRONSON, Bertrand H.
Printing as an Index of Taste in Eighteenth-Century England.
2nd edn.
New York, 1963.

BROWN, Michael.
'Circling the Square'.
Architects' Journal, CLIV (18 August 1971), 332–33.

BURGESS, C. F., ed.
The Letters of John Gay.
Oxford, 1966.

BURKE, Joseph.
English Art, 1714–1800.
Oxford History of English Art, Vol.IX.
Oxford, 1976.

BURKE, Joseph, and CALDWELL, Colin.
Hogarth. The Complete Engravings.
London, 1968.

BURNET, Thomas.
The Theory of the Earth . . .
2 vols.
London, 1684–90.

BUTT, John E.
'A Master Key to Popery'.
In James L. Clifford and Louis A. Landa, eds, *Pope and His Contemporaries. Essays Presented to George Sherburn* (Oxford, 1949), pp.41–57.

BUTTERFIELD, L. H., *et al.*, eds.
Diary and Autobiography of John Adams.
4 vols.
Cambridge, Mass., 1961.

C., J. d.
Les charmes de Stowe: ou description de la belle maison de plaisance de Mylord Cobham.
London, 1748.

Calendar of Treasury Papers, 1557–1728
(cited as *CTP*).
6 vols.
London, 1868–89.

Calendar of Treasury Books, 1660–1718
(cited as *CTB*).
32 vols.
London, 1904–58.

Calendar of Treasury Books and Papers, 1729–45
(cited as *CTBP*).
5 vols.
London, 1898–1903.

CAMPBELL, Colin.
Andrea Palladio's Five Orders of Architecture . . .
London, 1729.

CAMPBELL, Colin, *et al.*
Vitruvius Britannicus, or The British Architect
(cited as *Vit. Brit.*)
6 vols.
London, 1715–71.
Vols I, 1715; II, 1717; III, 1725; continued by Thomas Badeslade and John Rocque, IV, 1739; continued by John Woolfe and James Gandon, the Elder, IV, 1767; V, 1771.

Cantabrigia Depicta. A Concise and Accurate Description of the University and Town of Cambridge . . .
Cambridge, 1763.

CARDEW, F. M. G.
'L.S.A.I.D.A. A Riddle of Horticultural Authorship'.
Journal of the Royal Horticultural Society, LXXIV (June 1949), 256–61.

CARLETON, John D.
Westminster School. A History.
2nd edn.
London, 1965.

CARMONTELLE, Louis Carrogis de.
Le jardin de Monceau.
Paris, 1773.

CARRÉ, Jacques.
'Lord Burlington's Garden at Chiswick'.
Garden History, I, No.3 (Summer 1973), 23–30.

CARSWELL, John P.
The South Sea Bubble.
London, 1961.

CARTER, Hector.
'The Inventory of Charles Bridgeman (d.1738), Master Gardener to George II'.
Blackmansbury, VII, Nos 5–6 (October–December 1970), 88–109.

CARTWRIGHT, James Joel, ed.
The Travels Through England of Dr. Richard Pococke . . . During 1750, 1751, and Later Years.
2 vols.
London, 1888–89.

CARTWRIGHT, James Joel, ed.
The Wentworth Papers, 1705–39 . . .
London, 1883.

CASTELL, Robert.
The Villas of the Ancients Illustrated.
London, 1728.

CHANCELLOR, Edwin Beresford.
A History of the Squares of London, Topographical and Historical . . .
London, 1907.

CHANCELLOR, Edwin Beresford.
The Romance of Soho . . .
London, 1931.

CHARAGEAT, Marguerite.
L'art des jardins. Précis historique sur l'art des jardins.
Paris, 1930.

CHARLTON, John.
A History and Description of Chiswick House and Gardens.
London, 1958.

CHARLTON, John.
Kew Palace.
London, 1956.

CHASE, Isabel W. U.
Horace Walpole: Gardenist. An Edition of Walpole's 'The History of the Modern Taste in Gardening', With an Estimate of Walpole's Contribution to Landscape Architecture.
Princeton, N.J., 1943.

CHENEVIX TRENCH, Charles.
George II.
London, 1973.

CHURCH, Richard.
The Royal Parks of London.
2nd edn.
London, 1965.

CHURCHILL, W. A.
Watermarks in Paper in Holland, England, France, Etc., in the Seventeenth and Eighteenth Centuries, and Their Interconnection.
Amsterdam, 1935.

CLARK, H. F.
'Eighteenth-Century Elysiums. The Role of "Association" in the Landscape Movement'.
Journal of the Warburg and Courtauld Institutes, VI (1943), 165–89; R.P. in Warburg and Courtauld Institutes, ed., *England and the Mediterranean Tradition. Studies in Art, History, and Literature* (London, 1945), pp.154–78.

CLARK, H. F.
The English Landscape Garden.
London, 1948; R.P. with amendments in *House and Garden*, XIX (August, September 1968), 17–39, 66–75.

CLARK, H. F.
'Lord Burlington's Bijou, or Sharawaggi at Chiswick'.
Architectural Review, XCV (May 1944), 125–29.

CLARKE, George B.
'Ancient and Medieval Stowe'.
Stoic, XXII (March 1967), 210–16.

CLARKE, George B.
'Early Life of Richard Temple, Viscount Cobham'.
Stoic, XXIII (July 1968), 116–20.

CLARKE, George B.
'The Gardens of Stowe'.
Apollo, XCVII (June 1973), 558–65.

CLARKE, George B.
'Grecian Taste and Gothic Virtue. Lord Cobham's Gardening Programme and Its Iconography'.
Apollo, XCVII (June 1973), 566–71.

CLARKE, George B.
'Kent and the Eastern Gardens'.
Stoic, XXIV (July 1971), 265–72.

CLARKE, George B.
'Lancelot Brown's Work at Stowe'.
Stoic, XXV (December 1971), 17–22.

CLARKE, George B.
'Military Gardening: Bridgeman and the Ha-Ha'.
Stoic, XXIV (December 1969), 11–15.

CLARKE, George B.
'Military Gardening at Stowe'.
C.Life, CLI (18 May 1972), 1254–56.

CLARKE, George B.
'Moral Gardening'.
Stoic, XXIV (July 1970), 113–21.

CLARKE, George B.
'Rise of the Temple Family I'.
Stoic, XXII (July 1967), 261–69.

CLARKE, George B.
'Rise of the Temple Family II'.
Stoic, XXIII (December 1967), 5–11.

CLARKE, George B.
'Sir Richard Temple's House and Gardens'.
Stoic, XXIII (March 1968), 65–80.

CLARKE, George B.
'Stowe. Ici est né le jardin anglais'.
Connaissance des Arts, No.241 (March 1972), 66–75.

CLARKE, George B.
'Vanbrugh-Bridgeman Gardens'.
Stoic, XXIII (July 1969), 257–64.

CLARKE, George B.
'William Kent. Heresy in Stowe's Elysium'.
In Willis, ed., *Furor Hortensis*, pp.48–56.

CLIFFORD, Derek.
A History of Garden Design.
2nd edn.
London, 1966.

CLIMENSON, Emily J.
Elizabeth Montagu. The Queen of the Blue Stockings. Her Correspondence, 1720–61.
2 vols.
London, 1906.

COFFIN, David R., ed.
The Italian Garden.
Washington, D.C., 1972.

COFFIN, David R.
The Villa D'Este at Tivoli.
Princeton, N.J., 1960.

COHEN, Ralph.
The Art of Discrimination. Thomson's 'The Seasons' and the Language of Criticism.
Berkeley and Los Angeles, 1964.

COHEN, Ralph.
The Unfolding of 'The Seasons'.
London, 1970.

COLE, Nathan.
The Royal Parks and Gardens of London . . .
London, 1877.

COLLENETTE, Cyril Leslie.
A History of Richmond Park. With an Account of Its Birds and Animals.
London, 1937; R.P. with Introduction by Gilbert Turner, 1971.

COLLINS, Frances, and HURST, John.
West Meon, Hampshire. Some Chapters of Its History.
Petersfield, 1972.

COLLINS, J. Churton.
Voltaire, Montesquieu and Rousseau in England.
London, 1908.

COLTON, Judith.
'Kent's Hermitage for Queen Caroline at Richmond'.
Architectura (Munich), IV, No.2 (1974), 181–91.

COLVIN, H. M., and CRAIG, M. J., eds.
Architectural Drawings in the Library of Elton Hall by Sir John Vanbrugh and Sir Edward Lovett Pearce.
Oxford, 1964.

COLVIN, H. M.
A Biographical Dictionary of English Architects, 1660–1840 (cited as Colvin, *Dictionary*).
London, 1954.

COLVIN, H. M., ed.
A Catalogue of Architectural Drawings of the Eighteenth and Nineteenth Centuries in the Library of Worcester College, Oxford.
Oxford, 1964.

COLVIN, H. M., and HARRIS, John, eds.
The Country Seat. Studies in the History of the British Country House Presented to Sir John Summerson on His 65th Birthday, Together With a Select Bibliography of His Published Writings.
London, 1970.

COLVIN, H. M.
'Georgian Architects at Badminton'.
C.Life, CXLIII (4 April 1968), 800–4.

COLVIN, H. M., CROOK, J. Mordaunt, DOWNES, Kerry, and NEWMAN, John.
The History of the King's Works. Vol. V: 1660–1782.
London, 1977.

COLVIN, H. M.
Royal Buildings.
RIBA Drawings Series.
London, 1968.

Common Sense, 1739.

COOPER, Anthony Ashley, 3rd Earl of Shaftesbury.
The Moralists. A Philosophical Rhapsody.
London, 1709.

COOPER, Phyllis M.
The Story of Claremont.
6th edn.
Claremont, 1975.

COOPER, Thompson.
'Richard Gough'.
Dictionary of National Biography, VIII (London, 1908), 279–82.

CORDER, J.
'Spenser and the Eighteenth-Century Informal Garden'.
Notes and Queries, CCIV (January 1959), 19–21.

CORNFORTH, John.
'Longford and the Bouveries'.
Country Life Annual (1968), pp.28–37.

CORNFORTH, John.
'The Making of the Boughton Landscape'.
C.Life, CXLIX (11 March 1971), 536–39.

CORNFORTH, John.
'When the Thames was England's Brenta'.
Country Life Annual (1963), pp.73–75.

COSH, Mary.
'Two Dukes and Their Houses'.
C.Life, CLII (13, 20 July 1972), 78–81, 142–45.

COTTON, Charles.
The Wonders of the Peake.
London, 1681.

Craftsman, 1732, 1735.

CROFT-MURRAY, Edward.
Decorative Painting in England, 1537–1837.
2 vols.
London, 1962–70.

CROKER, J. W., ed.
Letters to and from Henrietta, Countess of Suffolk . . .
2 vols.
London, 1824.

CROOK, J. Mordaunt.
The British Museum.
London, 1972.

CROWE, Sylvia.
Garden Design.
London, 1958.

CURLL, Edmund.
The Rarities of Richmond. Being Exact Descriptions of the Royal Hermitage and Merlin's Cave . . .
London, 1736.

CURTIUS, Ernst R.
European Literature and the Latin Middle Ages.
Trans. Willard R. Trask.
London, 1953.

Daily Gazetteer, 1735, 1738.

Daily Post, 1738.

Daily Telegraph, 1965.

DALLAWAY, James, ed.
Anecdotes of Painting in England . . .
5 vols.
London, 1826–28.

DAMI, Luigi.
Il giardino Italiano.
Milan, 1924.

DANDY, James E., ed.
The Sloane Herbarium. An Annotated List . . .
London, 1958.

DANREITER, Franz Anton.
Die Gärtnerey, so wohl in ihrer Theorie oder Betrachtung als Praxi oder Uebung . . .
Augsburg, 1731.

DARBY, Henry C.
The Draining of the Fens.
Cambridge, 1940.

DARLINGTON, Ida, and HOWGEGO, James.
Printed Maps of London, c.1553–1830.
London, 1964.

DASENT, Arthur I.
A History of Grosvenor Square.
London, 1935.

DASENT, Arthur I.
The History of St. James's Square, and the Foundation of the West End of London . . .
London and New York, 1895.

DAVIS, Rose Mary.
Stephen Duck, the Thresher-Poet.
Orono, Maine, 1926.

DE BEER, E. S., ed.
The Diary of John Evelyn.
6 vols.
Oxford, 1955.

DEFOE, Daniel.
A Tour Thro' the Whole Island of Great Britain . . .
3 vols.
London, 1724–27; 2nd edn, 1738; 3rd edn, 4 vols., 1742.

DEFOE, Daniel.
A Tour Through the Whole Island of Great Britain . . .
Ed. D. C. Browning and G. D. H. Cole.
2 vols.
2nd edn.
London, 1962.

DE GANAY, Ernest.
André Le Nostre, 1613–1700.
Paris, 1962.

DE GANAY, Ernest.
Les jardins de France et leur décor.
Paris, 1949.

DE LA QUINTINIE, Jean.
The Compleat Gard'ner . . .
Trans. John Evelyn.
2 vols.
London, 1693.

DE LILLE, Jacques.
Les jardins, ou l'art d'embellir les paysages.
Paris, 1782.

DÉZALLIER D'ARGENVILLE, Antoine Joseph.
Die Gärtnerey, so wohl in ihrer Theorie oder Batrachtung als Praxie oder Uebung . . .
Trans. Franz Anton Danreiter.
Augsburg, 1731.

DÉZALLIER D'ARGENVILLE, Antoine Joseph.
La théorie et la pratique du jardinage . . .
Paris, 1709, 1713, 1722, 1732, 1747, 1760; The Hague, 1711, 1715, 1739.

DÉZALLIER D'ARGENVILLE, Antoine Joseph.
The Theory and Practice of Gardening . . .
Trans. John James.
London, 1712, 1728, 1743.

DICKINSON, H. T.
Bolingbroke.
London, 1970.

DIETZEL, Senta.
Furttenbachs Gartenentwürfe.
Nürnberg, 1928.

DIXON, Peter.
The World of Pope's Satires. An Introduction to the 'Epistles' and 'Imitations of Horace'.
London, 1968.

DOBAI, Johannes.
Die Kunstliteratur des Klassizismus und der Romantik in England.
3 vols.
Berne, 1974 et seq.

DOBRÉE, Bonamy, and WEBB, Geoffrey F., eds.
The Complete Works of Sir John Vanbrugh.
4 vols.
London, 1927–28.

DOBSON, Henry Austin.
At Prior Park, and Other Papers.
London, 1912.

DOBSON, Henry Austin.
William Hogarth . . .
2nd edn.
London, 1907.

DOWNES, Kerry.
English Baroque Architecture.
London, 1966.

DOWNES, Kerry.
Hawksmoor.
London, 1959.

DOWNES, Kerry.
'The Kings Weston Book of Drawings'.
Architectural History, X (1967), 7–88.

DOWNES, Kerry.
Vanbrugh.
London, 1977.

DU BOCCAGE, Mme (FIQUET DU BOCCAGE, Marie Anne).
Letters Concerning England, Holland and Italy . . .
Trans. from the French.
2 vols.
London, 1770.

DU BOCCAGE, Mme (FIQUET DU BOCCAGE, Marie Anne).
Lettres sur l'Angleterre . . .
2 vols.
Paris, 1765.

DRAPER, Marie P. G.
'When Marlborough's Duchess Built'.
C.Life, CXXXII (2 August 1962), 248–50.

DRAPER, Marie P. G., and EDEN, W. A.
Marble Hill House and Its Owners.
London, 1970.

DUCK, Stephen.
Poems on Several Occasions.
London, 1736.

DUGDALE, William.
The Restoration of the Beauchamp Chapel at St Mary's Collegiate Church, Warwick, 1674–1742.
Oxford, 1956.

DU HALDE, Jean Baptiste.
Description . . . de l'empire de la Chine et de la Tartarie chinoise . . .
4 vols.
Paris, 1735.

DUNLOP, Ian, and KIMBALL, Fiske.
'The Gardens of Wanstead House, Essex'.
C.Life, CVIII (28 July 1950), 294–98.

DUNNING, Brian.
'The Majesty of Richmond Park'.
C.Life, CXLVI (11 December 1969), 1574–75.

EASTLAKE, Charles L.
A History of the Gothic Revival.
Ed. J. Mordaunt Crook.
Leicester, 1971.

EDEN, Peter, ed.
Dictionary of Land Surveyors and Local Cartographers of Great Britain and Ireland, 1550–1850.
3 pts.
Folkestone, 1975–76.

EDEN, W. A.
'South Dalton, Yorkshire'.
In Colvin and Harris, eds, *The Country Seat,* pp.117–20.

EDWARDS, Ralph.
'Conversation Pieces in Search of a Painter'.
Apollo, LXVI (October 1957), 90–94.

EICHHOLZ, Jeffrey P.
'William Kent's Career as Literary Illustrator'.
Bulletin of the New York Public Library, LXX (December 1966), 620–46.

ELAND, George W., ed.
Shardeloes Papers of the Seventeenth and Eighteenth Centuries.
London, 1947.

ELLEDGE, Scott, ed.
Eighteenth-Century Critical Essays.
2 vols.
Ithaca, N.Y., 1961.

ELWIN, Whitwell, and COURTHOPE, W. J., eds.
The Works of Alexander Pope . . .
10 vols.
London, 1871–86.

ERDBERG, Eleanor Von.
Chinese Influence on European Garden Structures.
Ed. Bremer Whidden Pond.
Cambridge, Mass., 1936.

ERSKINE-HILL, Howard.
The Social Milieu of Alexander Pope. Lives, Example, and the Poetic Response.
New Haven and London, 1975.

EVELYN, John.
Sylva, or A Discourse of Forest-Trees, and the Propagation of Timber . . .
3rd edn.
2 vols.
York, 1801.

EVES, Charles K.
Matthew Prior. Poet and Diplomatist.
New York, 1939.

FALDA, Giovanni Battista.
Li giardini di Roma con le loro pianta alzate e vedute in prospettiva.
Rome, *c.*1683.

FARIELLO, Francesco.
Architettura dei Giardini.
Rome, 1967.

FAULKNER, Patrick A.
'A Note on the Gardens of Kensington Palace'.
Journal of the British Archaeological Association, XIV (1951), 8–10.

FAULKNER, Thomas.
History and Antiquities of Kensington . . .
London, 1820.

FÉLIBIEN, Jean François.
Les plans et les descriptions de deux des plus belles maisons de campagne de Pline le Consul . . .
Amsterdam, 1706.

FELTON, Samuel.
On the Portraits of English Authors on Gardening, with Biographical Notices.
2nd edn.
London, 1830.

FINBERG, H. L.
'Gawen Hamilton. An Unknown Scottish Portrait Painter'.
Walpole Society, VI (1918), 51–58.

FITZ-GERALD, Desmond.
Georgian Furniture.
3rd edn.
London, 1969.

FITZ-GERALD, Desmond.
'A History of the Interior of Stowe'.
Apollo, XCVII (June 1973), 572–85.

FITZ-GERALD, Desmond.
'Irish Gardens of the Eighteenth Century'.
Apollo, LXXXVIII (September 1968), 185–97, 204–9.

FLAUBERT, Gustave.
Bouvard et Pécuchet.
Paris, 1881.

FLEMING, John.
'Enigma of a Rococo Artist'.
C.Life, CXXXII (24 May 1962), 1224–26.

FLEMING, John.
Robert Adam and His Circle in Edinburgh and Rome.
London, 1962.

FLEMING, John.
'William Kent at Rousham. An Eighteenth-Century Elysium'.
Connoisseur, CLIII (July 1963), 158–65.

FOOTE, Henry Wilder.
John Smibert, Painter. With a Descriptive Catalogue of Portraits, and Notes on the Work of Nathaniel Smibert.
Cambridge, Mass., 1950.

FORSTER, Henry Rumsey.
The Stowe Catalogue, Priced and Annotated.
London, 1848.

FOSTER, Joseph.
Alumni Oxonienses. The Members of the University of Oxford, 1715–1886 . . .
4 vols.
Oxford, 1887–88.

FOSTER, Joseph.
The Register of Admissions to Gray's Inn, 1521–1889. Together With the Register of Marriages in Gray's Inn Chapel, 1695–1754.
London, 1889.

FRIEDMAN, Terry F., and LINSTRUM, Derek.
'Country Houses Through Georgian Eyes'.
C.Life, CLIII (1 February 1973), 268–70.

FRIEDMAN, Terry F., and LINSTRUM, Derek.
'A Tour of Architectural Splendour'.
C.Life (8 February 1973), 334–36.

FURTTENBACH, Joseph, the Elder.
Architectura Civilis . . .
Ulm, 1628.

FUSSELL, G. E.
Jethro Tull. His Influence on Mechanized Agriculture.
Reading, 1973.

GAMBA, Bartolommeo, ed.
Viaggio in Inghilterra di Carlo Castone della Torre di Rezzonico Comasco.
Venice, 1824.

GAY, John.
The Beggar's Opera.
London, 1728.

GAY, John.
Fables.
2 vols.
London, 1727, 1738.

GAY, John.
An Epistle to the Right Honourable the Earl of Burlington. A Journey to Exeter.
London, [1716].

GAY, John.
Poems on Several Occasions.
2 vols.
London, 1720.

GAY, John.
Poetry and Prose.
Ed. Vinton A. Dearing and Charles E. Beckwith.
2 vols.
Oxford, 1974.

Gentleman's Magazine, 1731, 1737, 1738, 1743.

GIAMATTI, A. Bartlett.
The Earthly Paradise and the Renaissance Epic.
Princeton, N.J., 1966.

GIBBON, Michael J.
'Stowe House, 1680–1779'.
Apollo, XCVII (June 1973), 552–57.

GIBBON, Michael J.
'Earl Temple and Giambattista Borra'.
Stoic, XXV (July 1973), 201–5.

GIBBON, Michael J.
'Garden Ornaments'.
Stoic, XXV (March 1972), 62–68.

GIBBON, Michael J.
'Gilbert West's Walk Through the Gardens in 1731'.
Stoic, XXIV (March 1970), 57–64.

GIBBON, Michael J.
'Grenville Family I'.
Stoic, XXV (July 1972), 109–15.

GIBBON, Michael J.
'Grenville Family II'.
Stoic, XXV (December 1972), 164–69.

GIBBON, Michael J.
'Lord Cobham's Garden Buildings I'.
Stoic, XXIV (December 1970), 171–82.

GIBBON, Michael J.
'Lord Cobham's Garden Buildings II'.
Stoic, XXIV (March 1971), 209–15.

GIBBON, Michael J.
'Lord Cobham's House'.
Stoic, XXIII (December 1968), 158–64.

GIBBS, James.
Bibliotheca Radcliviana ...
London, 1747.

GIBBS, James.
A Book of Architecture, Containing Designs of Buildings and Ornaments.
London, 1728; 2nd edn 1739.

GIBBS, James.
Rules for Drawing the Several Parts of Architecture ...
London, 1732; 1738; 1753.

GIBSON, William A.
'Literary Influences on Robert Morris's First Excursion in Architectural Theory'.
Rendezvous, VI, No.2 (Winter 1971), 1–14.

GIBSON, William A.
'Three Principles of Renaissance Architectural Theory in Pope's *Epistle to Burlington*'. *Studies in English Literature, 1500–1900*, XI (1971), 487–505.

GILPIN, William.
A Dialogue Upon the Gardens of the Right Honourable the Lord Viscount Cobham, at Stowe in Buckinghamshire.
London, 1748; 1749; 1751.

GINOUX, M. Ch.
Jacques Rigaud. Dessinateur et graveur Marseillais, improprement prénommé Jean-Baptiste par quelques écrivains (1681–1754).
Paris, 1898.

GIRARDIN, René-Louis, Marquis de.
De la composition des paysages, ou des moyen d'embellir la nature.
Paris, 1777.

GIROUARD, Mark.
'English Art and the Rococo'.
C.Life, CXXXIX (13, 27 January, 3 February 1966), 58–61, 188–90, 224–27.

GIROUARD, Mark, ed.
'The Smythson Collection of the RIBA'.
Architectural History, V (1962), 21–184.

GODBER, Joyce.
History of Bedfordshire, 1066–1888.
Bedford, 1969.

GODBER, Joyce.
'The Marchioness Grey of Wrest Park'.
Bedfordshire Historical Record Society (Publications), XLVII (1968), 7–123.

GODBER, Joyce, ed.
'The Travel Journal of Philip Yorke, 1744–63'.
Bedfordshire Historical Record Society (*Publications*), XLVII (1968), 125–63.

GODBER, Joyce.
Wrest Park and the Duke of Kent (*Henry Grey, 1671–1740*).
Bedford (Elstow Moot Hall), 1963.

GOETHE, Johann Wolfgang Von.
Die Wahlverwandtshaften.
Tübingen, 1809.

GOODFELLOW, G. L. M.
'Colin Campbell's Last Years'.
Burlington Magazine, CXI (April 1969), 185–91.

GOTHEIN, Marie Luise.
Geschichte der Gartenkunst.
2 vols.
Jena, 1914.

GOUGH, Richard.
British Topography . . .
2nd edn.
2 vols.
London, 1780.

GOULDING, Richard W., and ADAMS, C. K.
Catalogue of the Pictures Belonging to His Grace the Duke of Portland, K. G., at Welbeck Abbey, 17 Hill Street, London, and Langwell House.
Cambridge, 1936.

GRAY, Basil.
'Lord Burlington and Father Ripa's Chinese Engravings'.
British Museum Quarterly, XXII (February 1960), 40–43.

GRAY, John M., ed.
Memoirs of the Life of Sir John Clerk of Penicuik, Bt., Baron of the Exchequer, Extracted by Himself from His Own Journals, 1676–1755.
Edinburgh, 1892.

[Greater London Council]
Survey of London.
London, 1900 et seq.

GREEN, David B.
Blenheim Palace.
London, 1951.

GREEN, David B.
Gardener to Queen Anne. Henry Wise (1653–1738) and the Formal Garden.
London, 1956.

GREEN, David B.
The Gardens and Parks at Hampton Court and Bushy.
London, 1974.

GREEN, David B.
Sarah, Duchess of Marlborough.
London, 1967.

GREENWOOD, Alice Drayton.
Lives of the Hanoverian Queens of England.
2 vols.
London, 1909.

GRIMAL, Pierre.
Les jardins romains.
2nd edn.
Paris, 1969.

GRIMAL, Pierre.
In Search of Ancient Italy.
Trans. P. D. Cummins.
London, 1964.

GROSLEY, Pierre Jean.
Londres . . .
2 vols.
Lausanne, 1770.

Guardian, 1713.

GUERINOT, J. V.
Pamphlet Attacks on Alexander Pope, 1711–44. A Descriptive Bibliography.
London, 1969.

GUNNIS, Rupert.
Dictionary of British Sculptors, 1660–1851.
2nd edn.
London, 1968.

GWYN, Julian.
The Enterprising Admiral. The Personal Fortune of Admiral Sir Peter Warren.
Montreal and London, 1974.

HACKETT, Brian.
'Some Northumberland Landscapes of the English School'.
Journal of the Institute of Landscape Architects, No.43 (August 1958), 2–4, 12; No.44 (November 1958), 7–9.

HADFIELD, Miles.
A History of British Gardening.
London, 1969.

HADFIELD, Miles.
'History of the Ha-Ha'.
C.Life, CXXXIII (30 May 1963), 1261–62.

HADFIELD, Miles.
'John James and the Formal Garden in England'.
Connoisseur, CXLIII (February 1959), 20–22.

HADFIELD, Miles.
'London's "Sublime Sylvan Solitude": Kensington Gardens'.
C.Life, CXXXVIII (18 November 1965), 1318–20.

HAKE, H. M.
'Pond's and Knapton's Imitations of Drawings'.
Print Collector's Quarterly, IX (December 1922), 324–49.

HALSBAND, Robert, ed.
The Complete Letters of Lady Mary Wortley Montagu.
3 vols.
Oxford, 1965–67.

HALSBAND, Robert.
Lord Hervey. Eighteenth-Century Courtier.
Oxford, 1973.

HAMMELMANN, Hanns A., and BOASE, T. S. R.
Book Illustrators in Eighteenth-Century England.
New Haven and London, 1975.

HAMMELMANN, Hanns A.
'The Poet's Seasons Delineated'.
Country Life Annual (1970), 52–54.

HAMMOND, N. G. L., and SCULLARD, H. H., eds.
The Oxford Classical Dictionary.
2nd edn.
Oxford, 1970.

Hampton Court and Bushy Parks. Sixth Report of the Advisory Committee on Forestry.
London, 1963.

HANSON, L. W.
Contemporary Printed Sources for British and Irish Economic History, 1701–1750.
Cambridge, 1963.

Harleian Society (Publications)
(cited as *Harl. Soc.*).
London, 1869 et seq.

HARRIS, John.
'Bicentenary of Kew Gardens – 1: Fate of the Royal Buildings'.
C.Life, CXXV (28 May 1959), 1182–84.

HARRIS, John.
A Catalogue of British Drawings for Architecture, Decoration, Sculpture and Landscape Gardening 1550–1900 in American Collections.
Upper Saddle River, N.J., 1971.

HARRIS, John.
A Country House Index.
Isle of Wight, 1971.

HARRIS, John.
'English Country House Guides, 1740–1840'.
In John N. Summerson, ed., *Concerning Architecture. Essays on Architectural Writers and Writing Presented to Nikolaus Pevsner* (London, 1968), pp.58–74.

HARRIS, John.
Sir William Chambers. Knight of the Polar Star.
London, 1970.

HARRIS, John.
'Exoticism at Kew'.
Apollo, LXXVIII (August 1963), 103–8.

HARRIS, John, ORGEL, Stephen, and STRONG, Roy.
The King's Arcadia. Inigo Jones and the Stuart Court.
London, 1973.

HARRIS, John, ed.
'The Prideaux Collection of Topographical Drawings'.
Architectural History, VII (1964), 17–108.

HARRIS, John.
'Shardeloes. A Lasting Tribute to a Remarkable Restoration'.
Connoisseur, CXLVIII (December 1961), 268–75.

HARRIS, John.
'Some English Architectural and Decorative Drawings in the Museum's Collection'.
Bulletin of the Metropolitan Museum of Art, N.S., XXI (February 1963), 214–22.

HARVEY, John H.
Early Gardening Catalogues.
London and Chichester, 1972.

HARVEY, John H.
Early Nurserymen.
London and Chichester, 1974.

HARVEY, John H.
'Mid-Georgian Nurseries of the London Region'.
Transactions of the London and Middlesex Archaeological Society, XXVI (1975), 293–308.

HARVEY, John H.
'The Putney Nursery: an Early Plant Centre'.
Surrey Archaeological Collections, LXIX (1973), 135–42.

HARVEY, John H.
'The Stocks Held by Early Nurseries'.
Agricultural History Review, XXII, pt.1 (1974), 18–35.

HAUTECOEUR, Louis.
L'histoire de l'architecture classique en France.
7 vols.
Paris, 1943–53.

HAUTECOEUR, Louis.
Les jardins des dieux et des hommes.
Paris, 1959.

HAWKINS, John.
A General History of the Science and Practice of Music.
5 vols.
London, 1776.

HAYES, John T.
'British Patrons and Landscape Painting'.
Apollo, LXXXII (July 1965), 38–45; LXXXIII (March, June 1966), 188–97, 444–51; LXXXV (April 1967), 254–59; LXXXVI (November 1967), 358–65.

HAYES, John T.
Kensington Palace. A History and Guide.
London, 1969.

HAZLEHURST, Franklin Hamilton.
Jacques Boyceau and the French Formal Garden.
Athens, Georgia, 1966.

HEAWOOD, Edward.
Watermarks, Mainly of the Seventeenth and Eighteenth Centuries.
Hilversum, 1940.

HEELY, Joseph.
Letters on the Beauties of Hagley, Envil, and The Leasowes . . .
2 vols.
London, 1777.

HENNEBO, Dieter, and HOFFMANN, Alfred.
Geschichte der Deutschen Gartenkunst.
3 vols.
Hamburg, 1962–65.

HENREY, Blanche.
British Botanical and Horticultural Literature Before 1800 . . .
3 vols.
Oxford, 1975.

HERDAN, Innes and Gustav, trans.
Lichtenberg's Commentaries on Hogarth's Engravings.
London, 1966.

HERRMANN, Luke.
British Landscape Painting of the Eighteenth Century.
London, 1973.

HERRMANN, Wolfgang.
Laugier and Eighteenth-Century French Theory.
London, 1962.

HEYWORTH, P. L.
'A New Pope Letter'.
Times Literary Supplement, 1969.

HIBBARD, G. R.
'The Country House Poem of the Seventeenth Century'.
Journal of the Warburg and Courtauld Institutes, XIX (1956), 159–74.

HIBBARD, Howard.
Carlo Maderno and Roman Architecture, 1580–1630.
London, 1971.

HIGHAM, C. S. S.
Wimbledon Manor House Under the Cecils.
London, 1962.

HIGHET, Gilbert.
Poets in a Landscape.
London, 1957.

HIPPLE, Walter J.
The Beautiful, the Sublime, and the Picturesque in Eighteenth-Century British Aesthetic Theory.
Carbondale, Ill., 1957.

Historical Manuscripts Commission (*Reports*) (cited as *HMC*).
London, 1870 et seq.

HOGARTH, William.
The Analysis of Beauty.
London, 1753.

HOHNHOLZ, Jürgen.
Der englische Park als landschaftliche Erscheinung.
Tübingen, 1964.

HONOUR, Hugh.
'Capricci Cinesi. The Vogue for Chinoiserie in Italy'.
Connoisseur Year Book (1962), 42–49.

HONOUR, Hugh.
Chinoiserie. The Vision of Cathay.
London, 1961.

HOOPER, Mr, trans.
Letters of Baron Bielfeld . . .
4 vols.
London, 1768–70.

HORNER, Arnold.
'Cartouches and Vignettes on the Kildare Estate Maps of John Rocque'.
Quarterly Bulletin of the Irish Georgian Society, XIV (October–December 1971), 57–76.

HOWARD, George.
Castle Howard.
Castle Howard, 1972.

HUDSON, Derek.
Kensington Palace.
London, 1968.

HUDSON, T. P.
'A Ducal Patron of Architects'.
C.Life, CLV (17 January 1974), 78–81.

HUDSON, T. P.
'James Gibbs's Designs for University Buildings at Cambridge'.
Burlington Magazine, CXIV (December 1972), 842–48.

HUDSON, T. P.
'Moor Park, Leoni and Sir James Thornhill'.
Burlington Magazine, CXIII (November 1971), 657–61.

HUDSON, T. P.
'A Venetian Architect in England: Giacomo Leoni (*c.*1686–1746).
C.Life, CLVII (3 April 1975), 830–33.

HUNT, John Dixon.
'Emblem and Expressionism in the Eighteenth-Century Landscape Garden'.
Eighteenth-Century Studies, IV (1971), 294–317.

HUNT, John Dixon.
The Figure in the Landscape: Poetry, Painting, and Gardening During the Eighteenth Century.
Baltimore and London, 1977.

HUNT, John Dixon.
'Gardening, and Poetry, and Pope'.
Art Quarterly, XXXVII (Spring 1974), 1–28.

HUNT, John Dixon, and WILLIS, Peter, eds.
The Genius of the Place. The English Landscape Garden, 1620–1820.
London, 1975.

HUNT, John Dixon.
'A Silent and Solitary Hermitage'.
Annual Report of the York Georgian Society (1970), 47–61.

HUNT, John Dixon.
'"What's Water but the Generated Soul?" The Metaphysics of Water in the Landscape Garden'.
Garden History Society Occasional Papers, No.2 (1970), 3–17.

HUNT, J. M.
'Houses in the Irish Landscape'.
C.Life, CXXXIV (8 August 1963), 320–21.

HUSSEY, Christopher.
'Duncombe Park, Yorkshire'.
C.Life, CXXII (5, 12 December 1957), 1198–1202, 1328–31.

HUSSEY, Christopher.
English Country Houses. Early Georgian, 1715–60.
London, 1955; 2nd edn 1965.

HUSSEY, Christopher.
English Gardens and Landscapes, 1700–50.
London, 1967.

HUSSEY, Christopher.
'Farley Hill Place, Berkshire'.
C.Life, XCIII (11 June 1943), 1056–59.

HUSSEY, Christopher.
The Picturesque. Studies in a Point of View.
London and New York, 1927.

HUSSEY, Christopher.
'Purley Hall, Berkshire'.
C.Life, CXLVII (5 February 1970), 310–13.

HUSSEY, Christopher.
'Wimpole Hall, Cambridgeshire'.
C.Life, CXLII (30 November 1967), 1400–4.

HUSSEY, Christopher.
'Woburn Abbey, Bedfordshire'.
C.Life, CXVIII (1, 8 September 1955), 434–37, 488–91.

IRELAND, John.
Hogarth Illustrated.
3 vols.
London, 1791–98.

Irish Houses and Landscapes.
Exhibition Catalogue, Ulster Museum, Belfast, and Municipal Gallery of Modern Art, Dublin, 1963.

JACKSON-STOPS, Gervase.
'Well Vale, Lincolnshire'.
C.Life, CLII (14 December 1972), 1650–54.

JOHNSON, George W.
A History of English Gardening...
London, 1829.

Les joies de la nature au XVIIIe siècle.
Exhibition Catalogue, Bibliothèque Nationale, Paris, 1971.

JOURDAIN, Margaret.
The Work of William Kent. Artist, Painter, Designer and Landscape Gardener.
London and New York, 1948.

KAUFMANN, Emil.
Architecture in the Age of Reason. Baroque and Post-Baroque in England, Italy and France.
Cambridge, Mass., 1955.

KEMP, Daniel William, ed.
Tours in Scotland (1747, 1750, 1760) by Richard Pococke, Bishop of Meath.
Edinburgh, 1887.

KENDALL, George E.
'Notes on the Life of John Wootton, with a List of Engravings after His Pictures'.
Walpole Society, XXI (1932–33), 23–42.

[KENT, William]
A Catalogue of the Genuine Collection of Pictures, Models, Coins, and Drawings Framed and Glazed, of William Kent, Esq; Deceased... London, 1749.

[KENT, William]
A Catalogue of the Library of William Kent, Esq...
London, 1749

KENT, William.
The Designs of Inigo Jones..., With Some Additional Designs.
2 vols.
London, 1727.

KERNODLE, George R.
'Joseph Furttenbach, the Elder, 1591–1667'.
In Barnard Hewitt, ed., *The Renaissance Stage: Documents of Serlio, Sabbattini and Furttenbach*
(Coral Gables, Florida, 1958), pp.178–251.

KETTON-CREMER, R. W.
Norfolk Assembly.
London, 1957.

KIMBALL, S. Fiske.
'Romantic Classicism in Architecture'.
Gazette des Beaux Arts, XXV (1944), 95–112.

KIMBALL, S. Fiske.
Thomas Jefferson, Architect...
Cambridge, Mass., 1916.

KIP, John, and KNYFF, Leonard.
Britannia Illustrata..., or Le nouveau théâtre de la Grande Bretagne...
London, 1707 et seq.

KNOX, Brian.
'The Arrival of the English Garden in Poland and Bohemia'.
In Pevsner, ed., *The Picturesque Garden*, pp.99–116.

KUNZLE, David.
'Plagiaries-by-memory of the *Rake's Progress* and the Genesis of Hogarth's Second Picture Story'.
Journal of the Warburg and Courtauld Institutes, XXIX (1966), 311–48.

KURZ, Hilde.
'Italian Models of Hogarth's Picture Stories'.
Journal of the Warburg and Courtauld Institutes, XV (1952), 136–68.

LAMBERT, Sam.
'Circling the Square'.
Architects' Journal, CLIV (18 August 1971), 332–33.

LAMBIN, Denis.
'Pleasure with Profit. Some Aspects of Landscape Gardening'.
Garden History, III, No.2 (Spring 1975), 29–36.

LANDAIS, Hubert.
'Some Bronzes from the Girardon Collection'.
Connoisseur, CXLVIII (October 1961), 136–44.

LANE, Arthur.
'Daniel Marot. Designer of Delft Vases and of Gardens at Hampton Court'.
Connoisseur, CXXIII (January 1949), 19–24.

LANG, S.
'The Genesis of the English Landscape Garden'.
In Pevsner, ed., *The Picturesque Garden*, pp.1–29.

LANG, S.
'St James's Park. The Rise and Threatened Decline of a Model Landscape'.
Architectural Review, CX (November 1951), 292–98.

LANG, S.
'Vanbrugh's Theory and Hawksmoor's Buildings'.
Journal of the Society of Architectural Historians, XXIV (May 1965), 127–51.

LANGE, Lorenz.
Journal de la résidence du Sieur Lange... à la cour de la Chine, dans les années 1721 et 1722.
Trans. from the German.
Leiden, 1726.

LANGLEY, Batty.
New Principles of Gardening...
London, 1728.

LARWOOD, Jacob [pseud.].
The Story of the London Parks...
2 vols.
London, 1872.

LATHAM, Robert, and MATTHEWS, William, eds.
The Diary of Samuel Pepys.
London, 1970 et seq.

LAUGIER, Marc-Antoine.
Essai sur l'architecture.
Paris, 1753.

LAW, Ernest.
The History of Hampton Court Palace.
3 vols.
London, 1885–91.

LAWRENCE, Nicholas, ed.
Six Views of Twickenham in the Eighteenth Century.
Richmond upon Thames, 1972.

LE BLANC, Jean-Bernard.
Lettres d'un François.
3 vols.
The Hague, 1745.

LEES-MILNE, James.
Earls of Creation. Five Great Patrons of Eighteenth-Century Art.
London, 1962.

LEES-MILNE, James.
English Country Houses: Baroque, 1685–1715.
London, 1970.

LEONI, Giacomo.
The Architecture of A. Palladio...
Trans. Nicholas Dubois.
4 vols.
London, 1716–20.

LEONI, Giacomo, trans.
The Architecture of Leon Battista Alberti...
3 vols.
London, 1726; 1739; 1755.

LE ROUGE, Georges Louis.
Détails des nouveaux jardins à la mode...
21 cahiers.
Paris, 1776–88.

LESLIE, Charles R.
Memoirs of the Life of John Constable, Composed Chiefly of His Letters.
Ed. Jonathan Mayne.
London, 1951.

LETTICE, John.
Letters on a Tour Through Various Parts of Scotland, in the Year 1792.
London, 1794.

LEVER, Tresham.
The Herberts of Wilton.
London, 1967.

LEWIS, Wilmarth S., *et al.*, eds.
The Yale Edition of Horace Walpole's Correspondence
(cited as *Yale Walpole*).
London and New Haven, 1937 et seq.

LICHTENBERG, Georg Christoph, the Elder.
Ausfürliche Erklärung der Hogarthischen Kupferstiche . . .
14 vols.
Göttingen, 1794–1834.

LIGER, Louis.
Le nouveau théâtre d'agriculture et ménage des champs . . .
Paris, 1723.

LINDSAY, Ian G., and COSH, Mary.
Inverary and the Dukes of Argyll.
Edinburgh, 1973.

LISTER, Martin.
A Journey to Paris in the Year 1698.
London, 1699.

LITTLE, Bryan D. G.
The Life and Work of James Gibbs, 1682–1754.
London, 1955.

LLANOVER, Lady (Augusta Hall), ed.
The Autobiography and Correspondence of Mary Granville, Mrs Delany . . .
S.1, 3 vols.
London, 1861.

[LONDON, George.]
A Catalogue of the Library of George London, Esq., Late Chief Gardener to Her Majesty.
London, 1714.

LONDON, George, and WISE, Henry.
The Compleat Gard'ner . . .
London, 1699.

LONDON, George, and WISE, Henry, trans.
The Retir'd Gard'ner . . .
2 vols.
London, 1706; 1 vol., ed. Joseph Carpenter, 1717.

London Evening Post, 1738, 1740, 1746.

London Gazette, 1688.

London Journal, 1730, 1731.

London Magazine, 1737, 1738.

London Spy Revived, 1736.

LOUDON, John Claudius.
Arboretum et Fruticetum Britannicum . . .
8 vols.
London, 1838.

LOUDON, John Claudius.
An Encyclopaedia of Gardening . . .
5th edn.
London, 1827.

LOUDON, John Claudius, ed.
The Gardeners' Magazine and Register of Rural and Domestic Improvements
19 vols.
London, 1826–43.

LOVEDAY, John.
Diary of a Tour in 1732 . . .
Ed. John E. T. Loveday.
Edinburgh, 1890.

LUCAS, Joseph, trans.
Kalm's Account of His Visit to England on His Way to America in 1748.
London and New York, 1892.

[LUXBOROUGH, Lady (Henrietta Knight)]
Letters Written by the Late Right Honourable Lady Luxborough to William Shenstone, Esq.
London, 1775.

LYNCH, Kathleen M.
Jacob Tonson, Kit-Cat Publisher.
Knoxville, Tenn., 1971.

LYSONS, Daniel.
The Environs of London . . .
4 vols.
London, 1792–96.

LYSONS, Daniel
An Historical Account of Those Parishes in the County of Middlesex Which Are Not Described in 'The Environs of London' . . .
London, 1800.

LYSONS, Daniel.
Magna Britannia. Being a Concise Topographical Account of the Several Counties of Great Britain.
6 vols.
London, 1806–22.

MACAULAY, James.
'The Dogg Kennell att Hamilton'.
Architectural Review, CXXXX (October 1966), 295–98.

MACAULAY, James.
The Gothic Revival.
Glasgow and London, 1975.

MCCARTHY, Michael.
'Eighteenth-Century Amateur Architects and Their Gardens'.
In Pevsner, ed., *The Picturesque Garden*, pp.31–55.

MACDOUGALL, Elisabeth B.
'*Ars Hortulorum:* Sixteenth-Century Garden Iconography and Literary Theory in Italy'.
In Coffin, ed., *The Italian Garden*, pp.37–59.

MACDOUGALL, Elisabeth B., and HAZLEHURST, F. Hamilton, eds.
The French Formal Garden.
Washington, D.C., 1974.

MCGUIRE, Diane K.
'Giovanni Battista Falda and the Decorative Plan in Three Italian Gardens'.
Connoisseur, CLIX (May 1965), 59–63.

MCGUIRE, Diane K.
'Old Garden Prints. A Neglected Art Form'.
Landscape Architecture, LIV (July 1964), 284–89.

MACK, Maynard.
The Garden and the City. Retirement and Politics in the Later Poetry of Pope, 1731–43.
Toronto, Buffalo and London, 1969.

MACKENZIE, Gordon.
Marylebone. Great City North of Oxford Street.
London, 1972.

MACKY, John.
A Journey Through England, in Familiar Letters, from a Gentleman Here to His Friend Abroad.
2 vols.
London, 1714; 2nd edn.1722; 3rd edn.1723; 4th edn. 1724; 5th edn. 1732.

MACRAY, W. D.
Annals of the Bodleian Library, Oxford . . .
2nd edn.
Oxford, 1890.

MADAN, Falconer.
A Summary Catalogue of Western Manuscripts in the Bodleian Library, Oxford.
7 vols.
Oxford, 1897.

MAHAFFEY, Kathleen.
'Timon's Villa: Walpole's Houghton'.
Texas Studies in Literature and Language, IX (1967), 193–222.

MALINS, Edward.
'Mrs Delany and Landscaping in Ireland'.
Quarterly Bulletin of the Irish Georgian Society, XI, Nos 2–3 (April–September 1968), 1–16.

MALINS, Edward.
English Landscaping and Literature, 1660–1840.
London, 1966.

MALINS, Edward, and THE KNIGHT OF GLIN.
'Landscape Gardening by Jonathan Swift and His Friends in Ireland'.
Garden History, II (Autumn 1973), 69–93.

MALINS, Edward.
'Unique Features of Certain Irish Landscapes and Gardens, 1718–1968'.
Garden History Society: Occasional Papers No.1 (1969), 19–28.

MANTIGLIA, Roberto Carta.
'Giuseppe Japelli Architetto'.
L'Architettura (Milan), I (November–December 1955), 538–51.

MANWARING, Elizabeth W.
Italian Landscape in Eighteenth-Century England. A Study Chiefly of the Influence of Claude Lorrain and Salvator Rosa on English Taste, 1700–1800.
New York, 1925.

Marble Hill House, Twickenham. A Short Account of Its History and Architecture.
London, 1969.

[MARLBOROUGH, Sarah, Duchess of]
A True Copy of the Last Will and Testament of Her Grace Sarah, Late Duchess Dowager of Marlborough . . .
London, 1744.

MARSHALL, William.
A Review of 'The Landscape' . . .
London, 1795.

MARTIN, Peter E.
'The Garden and Pope's Vision of Order in the *Epistle to Burlington*.'
Durham University Journal, LXV (June 1973), 248–59.

MASON, William.
The English Garden . . .
New edn.
York, 1783.

MASON, William.
An Heroic Epistle to Sir William Chambers . . .
London, 1773.

MASSON, Georgina.
Italian Gardens.
London, 1961.

MATHESON, P. E. ed.
Travels of Carl Philipp Moritz in England in 1782.
London, 1924.

MATTHEWS, William, ed.
The Diary of Dudley Ryder, 1715–16.
London, 1939.

MAYER, Marcel.
Nicolas Michot, ou l'introduction du jardin anglais en France.
Paris, 1942.

MAYHEW, Edgar De N.
Sketches by Thornhill in the Victoria and Albert Museum.
London, 1967.

MEAGER, Leonard.
The English Gardener . . .
London, 1670.

MEAGER, Leonard.
The New Art of Gardening, with the Gardener's Almanack . . .
London, 1697.

MELVILLE, Lewis (pseud.).
Lady Suffolk and Her Circle.
London, 1924.

[MERCIER, Philip]
Philip Mercier, 1689–1760.
Exhibition Catalogue, York Art Gallery and Iveagh Bequest, Kenwood, 1969.

MEYER, Karl H.
Königliche Gärten. Dreihundert Jahre Herrenhausen.
Hanover, 1961.

MILLAR, Oliver.
The Tudor, Stuart and Early Georgian Pictures in the Collection of Her Majesty the Queen.
2 vols.
London, 1963.

MILLER, Philip.
The Gardener's Dictionary . . .
2 vols.
London, 1731–39.

MINAY, Priscilla.
'Early Improvements in the Eighteenth-Century Lothians: the Efforts of the Inter-Related Foulis, Justice, Kinloch, and Fletcher Families'.
Bulletin of the Scottish Georgian Society, II (1973), 3–46.

MINAY, Priscilla.
'James Justice (1698–1763): Eighteenth-Century Scots Horticulturist and Botanist'. *Garden History,* I, No.2 (Spring 1973), 41–62; II, No.2 (Spring 1974), 51–74; III, No.2 (Spring 1975), 37–67; IV, No.2 (Summer 1976), 53–91.

MITCHELL, Alan F.
'Some Trees in Hyde Park and Kensington Gardens Measured in 1967'.
Journal of the Royal Horticultural Society, XCIII (May 1968), 214–17.

MOIR, Esther.
The Discovery of Britain. The English Tourist.
London, 1964.

MOLLET, Claude, the Elder.
Théâtre des plans et jardinages . . .
Paris, 1652.

MONK, Samuel Holt, ed.
Five Miscellaneous Essays by Sir William Temple.
Ann Arbor, 1963.

MORANT, Philip.
The History and Antiquities of the County of Essex . . .
2 vols.
London, 1768.

MORE, Sir Thomas.
Utopia.
Louvain, 1516.

MOREL, Jean-Marie.
Théorie des jardins . . .
2 vols.
Paris, 1776.

MORRIS, Christopher, ed.
The Journeys of Celia Fiennes.
2nd edn.
London, 1949.

MORRIS, Robert.
An Essay in Defence of Ancient Architecture: or, a Parallel of the Ancient Buildings with the Modern . . .
London, 1728.

[MORRIS, Robert]
An Essay upon Harmony. As It Relates Chiefly to Situation and Building.
London, 1739.

MORRIS, Robert.
Lectures on Architecture. Consisting of Rules Founded Upon Harmonick and Arithmetical Proportions in Building . . .
London, 1734–36, 1759.

MORRIS, Robert.
Select Architecture . . .
London, 1755, [1759].

MUILMAN, Peter.
A New and Complete History of Essex . . .
6 vols.
Chelmsford, 1770–72.

MURALT, Béat Louis De.
Letters Describing the Character and Customs of the English and French Nations . . .
2nd edn.
London, 1726.

MURRAY, John Fisher.
A Picturesque Tour of the River Thames . . .
London, 1853.

NEALE, John P.
Views of the Seats of Noblemen and Gentlemen in England, Wales, Scotland and Ireland.
6 vols.
London, 1818–23.
5 vols.
London, 1824–29.

NEEDHAM, Francis R. D.
A Collection of Poems by Several Hands, Never Before Published.
Welbeck Miscellany No. 2.
Bungay, Suffolk, 1934.

NEUMEYER, Eva M.
'The Landscape Garden as a Symbol in Rousseau, Goethe and Flaubert'.
Journal of the History of Ideas, VIII (April 1947), 187–217.

NEVE, Christopher.
'Minor Painter's Influential Role. Philip Mercier and the Rococo in England'.
C.Life, CXLVI (21 August 1969), 448–49.

NICHOLS, John.
Literary Anecdotes of the Eighteenth Century ...
9 vols.
London, 1812–15.

NICOLSON, Marjorie Hope, and ROUSSEAU, George S.
'This Long Disease, My Life'. Alexander Pope and the Sciences.
Princeton, N.J., 1968.

NISSER, Wilhelm.
Michael Dahl and the Contemporary Swedish School of Painting in England.
Uppsala, 1927.

NIVERNOIS, Jules Henri Barbon Mazarini Mancini, Duc de, trans.
Essai sur l'art des jardins modernes, par M. Horace Walpole.
London, 1785.

NOEL, W. F. N.
'Edwards of Welham, County Leicester and of Ketton, County Rutland'.
Rutland Magazine, IV (1909–10), 177–80.

NOURSE, Timothy.
Campania Fœlix. Or, a Discourse of the Benefits and Improvements of Husbandry ...
London, 1700.

OGDEN, Henry V. S. and Margaret S.
English Taste in Landscape in the Seventeenth Century.
Ann Arbor, 1955.

OPPÉ, A. P., ed.
'Memoirs of Thomas Jones'.
Walpole Society, XXXII (1951).

OSBORN, James M.
'Alexander Pope. Apollo of the Arts'.
In H. T. Swedenborg, ed.
Papers of the Clark Library Seminars (Los Angeles, 1971), pp. 1–24.

OSBORN, James M., ed.
Joseph Spence. Observations, Anecdotes, and Characters of Books and Men Collected from Conversation.
2 vols.
Oxford, 1966.

OSWALD, Arthur.
'Chicheley Hall'.
C.Life, LXXIX (16 May 1936), 508–9

OSWALD, Arthur.
Country Houses of Dorset.
2nd edn.
London, 1959.

OSWALD, Arthur.
'James Gibbs and His Portraits'.
Country Life Annual (1963), pp. 12–13.

[OXFORD, Edward Harley, 2nd Earl of]
A Catalogue of the Collection of ... Edward Earl of Oxford.
London, 1742.

[PALLADIO, Andrea]
Andrea Palladio, 1508–80. The Portico and the Farmyard.
Exhibition Catalogue.
Arts Council of Great Britain, London, and Centro Internazionale di Studi di Architettura Andrea Palladio, Vicenza, 1975.

PALLADIO, Andrea.
Quattro libri dell'archittetura.
Venice, 1570.

PARK, Thomas, ed.
The Poetical Works of Nathaniel Cotton.
London, 1806.

PATTEN, John.
'The Chase and the English Landscape'.
C.Life, CL (16, 23 September 1971), 660–62, 736–38.

PAULSON, Ronald.
Emblem and Expression. Meaning in English Art of the Eighteenth Century.
London, 1975.

PAULSON, Ronald.
'Hogarth and the English Garden: Visual and Verbal Structures'.
In John Dixon Hunt, ed., *Encounters. Essays on Literature and the Visual Arts* (London, 1971), pp. 82–93.

PAULSON, Ronald.
Hogarth. His Life, Art, and Times.
2 vols.
New Haven and London, 1971.

PAULSON, Ronald.
Hogarth's Graphic Works.
2 vols.
2nd edn.
New Haven and London, 1970.

PAULSON, Ronald.
'The Pictorial Circuit and Related Structures in Eighteenth-Century England'.
In Peter Hughes and David Williams, eds, *The Varied Pattern. Studies in the Eighteenth Century* (Toronto, 1971), pp.165–87.

PEVSNER, Nikolaus.
Buckinghamshire.
The Buildings of England.
Harmondsworth, 1960.

PEVSNER, Nikolaus.
'The Genesis of the Picturesque'.
In *Studies in Art, Architecture and Design*, I, 78–101.

PEVSNER, Nikolaus, and LLOYD, David.
Hampshire.
The Buildings of England.
Harmondsworth, 1967.

PEVSNER, Nikolaus.
Herefordshire.
The Buildings of England.
Harmondsworth, 1963.

PEVSNER, Nikolaus, and LANG, S.
'A Note on Sharawaggi'.
In *Studies in Art, Architecture and Design*, I, 102–7.

PEVSNER, Nikolaus, ed.
The Picturesque Garden and Its Influence Outside the British Isles.
Washington, D.C., 1974.

PEVSNER, Nikolaus.
Studies in Art, Architecture and Design.
2 vols.
London, 1968.

PEVSNER, Nikolaus.
Yorkshire: The West Riding.
Rev. Enid Radcliffe.
The Buildings of England.
Harmondsworth, 1967.

PHILLIPS, Hugh.
'John Rocque's Career'.
London Topographical Record, XX (1952), 9–25.

PHILLIPS, Hugh.
Mid-Georgian London. A Topographical and Social Survey of Central and Western London about 1750.
London, 1964.

PHILLIPS, Hugh.
The Thames About 1750.
London, 1951.

PHYSICK, John.
Designs for English Sculpture, 1680–1860.
London, 1969.

PIGGOTT, Stuart.
'Sir John Clerk and "The Country Seat"'.
In Colvin and Harris, eds, *The Country Seat*, pp.110–16.

PINKERTON, John, ed.
Walpoliana.
2 vols.
London, 1779.

PIPER, David T.
Catalogue of Seventeenth-Century Portraits in the National Portrait Gallery, 1625–1714.
Cambridge, 1963.

PLUMB, J. H.
Sir Robert Walpole.
2 vols.
London, 1956–60.

POPE, Alexander.
Epilogue to the Satires, Dialogue II.
London, 1738.

POPE, Alexander.
An Epistle from Mr. Pope to Dr. Arbuthnot.
London, 1735.

POPE, Alexander.
An Epistle to the Right Honourable Richard, Earl of Burlington . . .
London, 1731.

POPE, Alexander.
An Epistle to the Right Honourable Richard, Lord Viscount Cobham.
London, 1734.

POPE, Alexander.
Epistles to Several Persons (Moral Essays).
Ed. F. W. Bateson.
2nd edn.
London and New Haven, 1961.

POPE, Alexander.
An Essay on Criticism.
London, 1711.

POPE, Alexander.
An Essay on Man.
London, 1734.

POPE, Alexander.
The Iliad of Homer.
Ed. Maynard Mack, Norman Callan, Robert Fagles, William Frost, and Douglas M. Knight.
2 vols.
London and New Haven, 1967.

POPE, Alexander.
Imitations of Horace.
London, 1733–37.

POPE, Alexander.
The Odyssey of Homer.
2 vols.
London, 1725–26.

POPE, Alexander.
The Odyssey of Homer.
Ed. Maynard Mack, Norman Callan, Robert Fagles, William Frost, and Douglas M. Knight.
2 vols.
London and New Haven, 1967.

PRÉVOST D'EXILES, Antoine François.
Mémoires et aventures d'un homme de qualité ...
7 pts.
Paris, 1731.

PRICE, Martin.
'The Picturesque Moment'.
In Frederick W. Hilles and Harold Bloom, eds, *From Sensibility to Romanticism. Essays Presented to Frederick A. Pottle* (New York, 1965), pp.259–92.

PRICE, Uvedale.
Essays on the Picturesque ...
3 vols.
London, 1810.

PRINCE, Hugh C.
'Parks and Parkland'.
In J. T. Coppock and Hugh C. Prince, eds, *Greater London* (London, 1964), pp.333–57.

PRINCE, Hugh C.
Parks in England.
Isle of Wight, 1967.

PRIOR, James.
Life of Edmond Malone, Editor of Shakespeare ...
London, 1860.

PRIOR, Matthew.
Down-Hall; A Ballad ...
London, 1721.

[PUBLIC RECORD OFFICE, London]
Maps and Plans in the Public Record Office. Vol. I: British Isles, c.1410–1860.
London, 1967.

PUGH, Simon.
'Nature as a Garden. A Conceptual Tour of Rousham'.
Studio International, CLXXXVI (October 1973), 121–25.

PYE, J. Henrietta.
A Peep into the Principal Seats and Gardens in and about Twickenham ...
London, 1775.

PYNE, William Henry.
The History of the Royal Residences of Windsor Castle, St James's Palace, Carlton House, Kensington Palace, Hampton Court, Buckingham House and Frogmore.
3 vols.
London, 1819.

QUENNELL, Peter.
Caroline of England. An Augustan Portrait.
London, 1939.

RADICE, Betty, trans.
The Letters of the Younger Pliny.
London, 1969.

RAINES, Robert.
Marcellus Laroon.
London and New York, 1966.

[RALPH, James]
A Critical Review of the Publick Buildings, Statues and Ornaments in and about London and Westminster ...
London, 1734.

RAMSEY, L. G. G.
'Langleys, Essex'.
Connoisseur, CXL (December 1957), 210–17.

RAPIN, René.
Hortorum Libri Quattuor ...
Paris, 1665.

RAPIN, René.
Of Gardens. Four Books. First Written in Latine Verse by Renatus Rapinus ...
Trans. John Evelyn.
London, 1672.

RAPIN, René.
Of Gardens. A Latin Poem. In Four Books.
Trans. James Gardiner.
2nd edn.
London, [1718].

RAPIN, René.
Réflexions sur la philosophie ancienne et moderne ...
Paris, 1676.

Read's Weekly Journal
(i.e. *The Weekly Journal: or, The British Gazetteer*), 1728, 1738.

REILLY, Robin, and SAVAGE, George.
Wedgwood: the Portrait Medallions.
London, 1973.

REPTON, Humphry.
An Enquiry into the Changes of Taste in Landscape Gardening ...
London, 1806.

REPTON, Humphry.
Observations on the Theory and Practice of Landscape Gardening ...
London, 1803.

REPTON, Humphry.
Sketches and Hints on Landscape Gardening...
London, 1794.

REYNOLDS, Sir Joshua.
Discourses on Art.
Ed. Robert R Wark.
2nd edn.
New Haven and London, 1975.

RIGAUD, Jacques.
Les maisons royales de France.
Paris, 1730's.

ROBERTS, Richard A., ed.
A Calendar of the Inner Temple Records...
Vol.IV.
London, 1933.

ROBERTS, William, ed.
Memoirs of the Life and Correspondence of Mrs Hannah More.
4 vols.
London, 1834.

ROBSON-SCOTT, W. D.
German Travellers in England, 1400–1800.
Oxford, 1953.

ROBSON-SCOTT, W. D.
The Literary Background of the Gothic Revival in Germany. A Chapter in the History of Taste.
Oxford, 1965.

ROSS, Ruth Isabel.
'Statesman Into Gardener' [Sir William Temple].
C.Life, CLV (17 January 1974), 76–77.

RØSTVIG, Maren-Sofie.
The Happy Man. Studies in the Metamorphoses of a Classical Ideal.
2 vols.
1st edn Oslo and Oxford, 1954–58;
2nd edn Oslo and New York, 1962–71.

ROUSSEAU, George S.
'A New Pope Letter'.
Philological Quarterly, XLV (1966), 409–18.

ROUSSEAU, Jean-Jacques.
Les confessions.
Ed. Jacques Voisine.
Paris, 1964.

ROUSSEAU, Jean-Jacques.
La Nouvelle Héloïse.
Paris, 1759.

ROUSSEAU, Jean-Jacques.
La Nouvelle Héloïse.
Ed. Daniel Mornet.
4 vols.
Paris, 1925.

ROUSSEAU, Jean-Jacques.
La Nouvelle Héloïse.
In *Œuvres complètes*, Bibliothèque de la Pléiade, Vol.II.
Paris, 1961.

ROWAN, Alistair.
'Batty Langley's Gothic'.
In Giles Robertson and George Henderson, eds. *Studies in Memory of David Talbot Rice* (Edinburgh, 1975), pp.197–215.

ROWAN, Alistair.
'Japelli and Cicognara'.
Architectural Review, CXLIII (March 1968), 225–28.

ROWAN, Alistair.
'Japellianum Miscellany'.
Architectural Review, CXLV (April 1969), 297–98.

ROWAN, Alistair.
'Penicuik House, Midlothian'.
C.Life, CXLIV (15, 22 August 1968), 383–7, 448–51.

Royal Commission on Ancient and Historical Monuments and Constructions (Inventories)
(cited as *RCHM*).
London, 1910 et seq.

[ROYAL INSTITUTE OF BRITISH ARCHITECTS, London]
Catalogue of the Drawings Collection of the RIBA.
Farnborough, Hants., 1969 et seq.

RUCH, John E.
'Bernard Baron. Un graveur français en Angleterre au début du XVIIIe siècle'.
Nouvelles de l'estampe, No.12 (November–December 1973), 13–21.

RYLANDS, W. H., ed.
'The Visitation of Warwickshire, 1682–83'.
Harl. Soc., LXII (1911).

ST JOHN, Bayle, trans.
The Memoirs of the Duke of Saint-Simon...
4 vols.
London and New York, 1902.

SALMON, Nathaniel.
The History of Hertfordshire...
London, 1728.

SAMBROOK, A. James.
'Alexander Pope as Landscape Gardener'.
Times Literary Supplement, 22 June 1973.

SAMBROOK, A James.
'The English Lord and the Happy Husbandman'.
Studies on Voltaire and the Eighteenth Century, LVII (1967), 1357–75.

SAMBROOK, A James.
'Pope and the Visual Arts'.
In Peter Dixon, ed., *Writers and Their Background: Alexander Pope* (London, 1972), pp.143–71.

SAMBROOK, A James.
'Pope's Neighbours. An Early Landscape Garden at Richmond'.
Journal of the Warburg and Courtauld Institutes, XXX (1967), 444–46.

SAMBROOK, A. James.
'The Shape and Size of Pope's Garden'.
Eighteenth-Century Studies, V (1972), 450–55.

SANDERS, Lloyd.
Patron and Place-Hunter. A Study of George Bubb Doddington, Lord Melcombe.
London and New York, 1919.

[SAUSSURE, César De]
A Foreign View of England in the Reigns of George I and George II. The Letters of M. César De Saussure to His Family.
Trans. and ed. Mme Van Muyden.
London, 1902.

SECCOMBE, Thomas.
'Charles Bridgman or Bridgeman'.
Dictionary of National Biography, XXII (Supplement) (London, 1909), 268–69.

SEDGWICK, Romney, ed.
Lord Hervey's Memoirs.
2nd edn.
London, 1963.

SEELEY, B., pub.
A Description of the Gardens of Lord Viscount Cobham, at Stow . . .
Northampton, 1744.

SEELEY, J., pub.
Stowe. A Description of the House and Gardens . . .
London and Buckingham, 1797.

SERLE, John.
A Plan of Mr. Pope's Garden as it was Left at His Death, with a Plan and Perspective View of the Grotto . . .
London, 1745.

SHENSTONE, William.
'Unconnected Thoughts on Gardening'.
In *The Works in Verse and Prose of William Shenstone, Esq.* (London, 1764), II, 125–47.

SHEPHERD, J. C., and JELLICOE, G. A.
Italian Gardens of the Renaissance.
3rd edn.
London, 1966.

SHEPPARD, Francis H. W.
Local Government in St Marylebone, 1688–1835. A Study of the Vestry and Turnpike Trust.
London, 1958.

SHERBORN, Derek R.
'Carshalton House, Surrey'.
C.Life, CV (4 March 1949), 480–83.

SHERBURN, George W., ed.
The Correspondence of Alexander Pope
(cited as *Pope Correspondence*).
5 vols.
Oxford, 1956.

SHERWIN-WHITE, A. N.
The Letters of Pliny. A Historical and Social Commentary.
Oxford, 1966.

SHORTER, A. H.
Paper Mills and Paper Makers in England, 1495–1800.
Hilversum, 1957.

SICHEL, Walter.
Bolingbroke and His Times.
2 vols.
London, 1901–2.

SIEVEKING, Albert Forbes.
Notes and Queries, S.11, III (1911), 188.

SIRÉN, Osvald.
China and Gardens of Europe of the Eighteenth Century.
New York, 1950.

SITWELL, Edith.
English Eccentrics.
2nd edn.
London, 1958.

SMITH, William James, ed.
The Grenville Papers . . .
4 vols.
London, 1852–53.

SØRENSEN, C. Th.
Europas Havekunst, fra Alhambra til Liselund.
Copenhagen, 1959.

[SOUTH SEA COMPANY]
The Particulars and Inventories of the Estates of the Late Sub-Governor, Deputy-Governor and Directors of the South Sea Company . . .
2 vols.
London, 1721.

[SOUTH SEA COMPANY]
The Proceedings of the Directors of the South Sea Company . . .
London, 1721.

[SOUTH SEA COMPANY]
The Several Reports of the Committee of Secrecy . . .
London, [1721].

SOWERBY, E. Millicent, comp.
Catalogue of the Library of Thomas Jefferson.
5 vols.
Washington, D.C., 1952–59.

SPARROW, Walter Shaw.
British Sporting Artists from Barlow to Herring.
London, 1922.

SPECK, William A.
'Political Propaganda in Augustan England'.
Royal Historical Society (Transactions), S.5, XXII (1972), 17–32.

Spectator, 1711–12.

SPENSER, Edmund.
The Faerie Queene.
London, 1589–96; 1751.

SPINK, William W.
'Sir John Clerk of Penicuik. Landowner as Designer'.
In Willis, ed., *Furor Hortensis*, pp.31–40.

STANYAN, Temple.
Grecian History.
2 vols.
London, 1707; 1739.

STEER, Francis W., ed.
Farm and Cottage Inventories of Mid-Essex, 1635–1749.
2nd edn.
London and Chichester, 1969.

STEINBERG, Ronald M.
'The Iconography of the Teatro dell'Acqua at the Villa Aldobrandini'.
Art Bulletin, XLVII (1965), 453–63.

STEVENSON, Allan, comp.
Catalogue of Botanical Books in the Collection of Rachel McMasters Miller Hunt. Vol.II: Printed Books, 1701–1800.
2 pts.
Pittsburgh, 1961.

STOW, John.
A Survey of London . . .
6th edn.
2 vols.
London, 1754–55.

STRANDBERG, Runar.
'The French Formal Garden After Le Nostre'.
In MacDougall and Hazlehurst, eds, *The French Formal Garden*, pp.41–67.

STRANGWAYS, Giles Stephen Harold Fox (6th Earl of Ilchester).
Lord Hervey and His Friends, 1726–38. Based on Letters from Holland House, Melbury and Ickworth.
London, 1950.

STROUD, Dorothy.
Capability Brown.
3rd edn.
London, 1975.

STROUD, Dorothy.
'The Gardens at Claremont'.
The National Trust Year Book, 1975–76
(London, 1975), pp. 32–37.

STRYPE, John.
A Survey of the Cities of London and Westminster . . . Written at first in . . . 1598 by John Stow . . .
2 vols.
London, 1720; 6th edn, 1754–55.

STUKELEY, William.
Stonehenge. A Temple Restor'd to the British Druids.
London, 1740.

STUTCHBURY, Howard E.
The Architecture of Colen Campbell.
Manchester, 1967.

SUMMERSON, John N.
Architecture in Britain, 1530–1830.
5th edn.
Harmondsworth, 1969.

SUMMERSON, John N.
'The Classical Country House in Eighteenth-Century England'.
Journal of the Royal Society of Arts, CVII (July 1959), 539–87.

SUMMERSON, John N.
Georgian London.
2nd edn.
London, 1970.

SUMMERSON, John N.
'Henrietta Place, Marylebone, and its Associations with James Gibbs'.
London Topographical Record, XXI (1958), 26–36.

SUTTON, Denys.
'John Wootton Recognised at Last'.
C. Life, CXXIV (4 December 1958), 1290–96.

Svenskt Konstnärslexikon: tiotusen svenska konstnärers liv och verk.
4 vols.
Malmö, 1952–56.

SWEETING, W. D. ed.
Fenland Notes and Queries, VI (1904–6).

SWIFT, Jonathan.
Journal to Stella.
Ed. Harold H. Williams.
2 vols.
Oxford, 1948.

SWITZER, Stephen.
A Compendious Method for the Raising of the Italian Brocoli . . .
London, 1728.

SWITZER, Stephen.
The Country Gentlemen's Companion . . .
London, 1732.

SWITZER, Stephen.
A Dissertation on the True Cythisus of the Ancients . . .
London, 1731.

SWITZER, Stephen.
Ichnographia Rustica . . .
3 vols.
London, 1718; 2nd edn, 1742.

SWITZER, Stephen.
An Introduction to a General System of Hydrostaticks and Hydraulicks . . .
2 vols.
London, 1729.

SWITZER, Stephen.
The Nobleman, Gentleman, and Gardener's Recreation . . .
London, 1715.

SWITZER, Stephen.
The Practical Fruit Gardener . . .
London, 1724.

SWITZER, Stephen, ed.
The Practical Husbandman and Planter . . .
2 vols.
London, 1733–34.

SWITZER, Stephen.
The Practical Kitchen Gardiner . . .
London, 1727.

SWITZER, Stephen.
An Universal System of Water and Waterworks . . .
London, 1734.

SYKES, Norman.
Church and State in England in the Eighteenth Century.
Cambridge, 1934.

TAIT, A. A.
'William Adam at Chatelherault'.
Burlington Magazine, CX (April 1968), 316–25.

TAIT, A. A.
'William Adam and Sir John Clerk. Arniston and "The Country Seat"'.
Burlington Magazine, CXI (March 1969), 132–41.

TANNER, Joan D.
'The Building of Chicheley Hall'.
Records of Buckinghamshire, XVII (1961), 41–48.

TANZER, Helen H.
The Villas of Pliny the Younger.
New York, 1924.

Tatler, 1710.

TAYLOR, Gladys.
Old London Gardens.
London, 1953.

TEMPLE, Sir William.
Upon the Gardens of Epicurus. Or, Of Gardening, in the Year 1685.
London, 1699.

TEMPLEMAN, William D.
The Life and Work of William Gilpin (1724–1804), Master of the Picturesque and Vicar of Boldre.
Urbana, 1939.

THACKER, Christopher.
'Ermenonville. Landscape and Legend'.
Landscape Design, No. 97 (February 1972), 11–13.

THACKER, Christopher.
'Voltaire and Rousseau: Eighteenth-Century Gardeners'.
Studies on Voltaire and the Eighteenth Century, XC (1972), 1595–1614.

THOMPSON, Francis W.
Chatsworth. A Short History. With a Tour of the House and Gardens.
London, 1951.

THOMPSON, Francis W.
A History of Chatsworth. Being a Supplement to the Sixth Duke of Devonshire's Handbook.
London and New York, 1949.

THOMSON, Gladys Scott.
Family Background.
London, 1949.

THOMSON, Gladys Scott, ed.
Letters of a Grandmother, 1732–35. Being the Correspondence of Sarah, Duchess of Marlborough, with Her Granddaughter Diana, Duchess of Bedford.
London, 1943.

THOMSON, Gladys Scott.
Life in a Noble Household, 1641–1700.
London, 1937.

THOMSON, Gladys Scott.
The Russells in Bloomsbury, 1669–1771.
London, 1940.

THOMSON, Gladys Scott.
'Woburn Abbey. Its Place in History'.
Connoisseur, CXLI (May 1958), 204–11.

THOMSON, James.
Liberty. A Poem.
London, 1735–36.

[THOMSON, James]
The Poetical Works of James Thomson.
Ed. Harris Nicolas and Peter Cunningham.
2 vols.
London, 1860.

THOMSON, James.
The Seasons.
London, 1730.

THOMSON, Katherine B. (Mrs A. T. Thomson), ed.
Memoirs of Viscountess Sundon, Mistress of the Robes to Queen Caroline . . .
2 vols.
2nd edn.
London, 1848.

[THORNHILL, Sir James]
'Sir James Thornhill's Collection'.
Burlington Magazine, LXXXII (June 1943), 133–36.

TILLYARD, E. M. W.
Some Mythical Elements in English Literature.
London, 1961.

TOYNBEE, Paget J., ed.
'Horace Walpole's Journals of Visits to Country Seats, Etc.'
Walpole Society, XVI (1927–28), 9–80.

TOYNBEE, Paget J., ed.
Satirical Poems Published Anonymously by William Mason, with Notes by Horace Walpole, Now First Printed from His Manuscript.
Oxford, 1926.

TRAFFORD, Sigismund.
An Essay on Draining, More Particularly with Regard to the North Division of the . . . Bedford Level . . .
London, 1729.

TRUSLER, John, ed.
The Works of William Hogarth . . .
2 vols.
London, 1833.

TUNNARD, Christopher.
Gardens in the Modern Landscape.
2nd edn.
London and New York, 1948.

TURNER, A. Richard.
The Vision of Landscape in Renaissance Italy.
Princeton, N.J., 1966.

VARDY, John.
Some Designs of Mr. Inigo Jones and Mr. William Kent.
London, 1744.

VARLEY, John.
'John Rocque. Engraver, Surveyor, Cartographer and Mapseller'.
Imago Mundi. A Review of Early Cartography, V (1948), 83–91.

VAUGHAN, H. F. J.
'Oswestry, Ancient and Modern, and Its Local Families'.
Archaeologia Cambrensis, S.5, I (1884), 193–224; II (1885), 49–64, 97–119.

The Victoria History of the Counties of England
(cited as *VCH*).
London, 1900 et seq.

Vitruvius Scoticus.
Edinburgh, 1810.

VOLTAIRE, François Arouet De.
La Henriade.
London, 1728.

VOLTAIRE, François Arouet De.
Lettres sur les Anglais.
Ed. Arthur Wilson-Green.
Cambridge, 1931.

WALCOTT, M. E. C.
A Handbook for the Parish of St James's, Westminster.
London, 1850.

WALKER, John.
'The Thames Through Eighteenth-Century Eyes. Augustine Heckell and His Imitators'.
C.Life, CXLVI (3 July 1969), 24–27.

WALKER, W. T. C.
'Studley Royal'.
Archaeological Journal, CXXV (1968), 360–61.

WALPOLE, Horace.
Aedes Walpolianae; or, a Description of the Collection of Pictures at Houghton Hall in Norfolk . . .
2nd edn.
London, 1752.

WALPOLE, Horace.
Anecdotes of Painting in England, with Some Account of the Principal Artists.
Ed. Ralph N. Wornum.
3 vols.
London, [1888].

WALPOLE, Horace.
The History of the Modern Taste in Gardening, or *The Modern Taste in Gardening*, or *Essay on Modern Gardening*, or *On Modern Gardening.*
London, 1780, 1782, 1785, 1786, etc.

WALPOLE SOCIETY, ed.
Vertue Note Books
(cited as *Vertue*).
7 vols.
Oxford, 1930–55.
Vols. I (XVIII), II (XX), III (XXII), IV (XXIV), V (XXVI), I–V Index (XXIX), VI (XXX) (with Index).

WALTERS, John.
The Royal Griffin. Frederick Prince of Wales, 1707–51.
London, 1972.

WARBURTON, William, ed.
The Works of Alexander Pope . . .
9 vols.
London, 1751.

WARD, Cyril.
Royal Gardens.
London, 1912.

WARE, Isaac.
Designs of Inigo Jones and Others.
London, ?1735.

WARE, Isaac.
The Plans, Elevations, and Sections . . . of Houghton in Norfolk . . .
London, 1735.

WARTON, Joseph.
The Enthusiast: or, the Lover of Nature.
London, 1744.

WATELET, Claude-Henri.
Essai sur les jardins . . .
Paris, 1774.

WATERHOUSE, Ellis.
Painting in Britain, 1530–1790.
3rd edn.
Harmondsworth, 1969.

WATKIN, David.
Thomas Hope (1769–1831) and the Neoclassical Idea.
London, 1968.

WEBB, Mary I.
'Giovanni Battista Guelfi. An Italian Sculptor Working in England'.
Burlington Magazine, XCVII (May 1955), 139–45.

WEBB, Mary I.
Michael Rysbrack, Sculptor.
London, 1954.

WEBBER, Ronald.
The Early Horticulturists.
Newton Abbot, 1968.

Weekly Miscellany, 1738.

WEST, Gilbert.
Stowe, the Gardens of the Right Honourable Richard, Lord Viscount Cobham.
London, 1732.

WHATELY, Thomas.
Observations on Modern Gardening, Illustrated by Descriptions.
Dublin, 1770.

WHATELEY, Thomas.
Observations on Modern Gardening, and Laying Out Pleasure-Grounds, Parks, Farms, Ridings . . .
New edn.
London, 1801.

WHELER, George Hastings, ed.
Hastings-Wheler Family Letters, 1693–1739.
2 vols.
London, 1929 (Vol.I); Wakefield, 1935 (Vol.II).

WHIFFEN, Marcus.
'Academical Elysium. The Landscaping of the Cambridge Backs'.
Architectural Review, CI (January 1947), 13–18.

WHIFFEN, Marcus.
'Architect, Painter and Landscape Gardener' [William Kent].
Listener, XXXIX (22 April 1948), 653–54.

WHIFFEN, Marcus.
Thomas Archer. Architect of the English Baroque.
2nd edn.
Los Angeles, 1973.

WHINNEY, Margaret.
English Sculpture, 1720–1830.
London, 1971.

WHINNEY, Margaret.
Sculpture in Britain, 1530–1830.
Harmondsworth, 1964.

WHISTLER, Laurence.
The Imagination of Vanbrugh and His Fellow Artists.
London, 1954.

WHISTLER, Laurence, CLARKE, George B., and GIBBON, Michael J.
Stowe. A Guide to the Gardens.
3rd edn.
Buckingham, 1974.

WHITE, K. D.
Roman Farming.
London, 1970.

WHITLEY, William T.
Artists and Their Friends in England, 1700–99.
2 vols.
London and Boston, 1928.

WICKHAM LEGG, L. G.
Matthew Prior. A Study of His Public Career and Correspondence.
Cambridge, 1921.

WIGGIN, Lewis M.
The Faction of Cousins. A Political Account of the Grenvilles, 1733–63.
New Haven, 1958.

WILKS, J. H.
Trees of the British Isles in History and Legend.
London, 1972.

WILLIAM SALT ARCHAEOLOGICAL SOCIETY, ed.
'History of the Manor and Parish of Western-under-Lizard, in the County of Stafford'.
Collection for a History of Staffordshire, N.S. 2 (1899).

WILLIAMS, Clare, trans.
Sophie in London, 1786. Being the Diary of Sophie Von La Roche.
London, 1933.

WILLIAMS, George G.
Guide to Literary London.
London, 1973.

WILLIAMS, Harold H., ed.
The Correspondence of Jonathan Swift.
5 vols.
Oxford, 1963–65.

WILLIS, Browne.
The History and Antiquities of . . . Buckingham . . .
London, 1755.

WILLIS, Peter.
'Charles Bridgeman. A Problem in Genealogy'.
Blackmansbury, VII (June–August 1970), 55–68.

WILLIS, Peter.
'Charles Bridgeman. The Royal Gardens'.
In Willis, ed., *Furor Hortensis*, pp.41–47.

WILLIS, Peter.
'Creator of the English Garden. Charles Bridgeman's Tools and Techniques'.
C.Life, CLIII (17 May 1973), 1401–4.

WILLIS, Peter.
'From Desert to Eden: Charles Bridgeman's "Capital Stroke"'.
Burlington Magazine, CXV (March 1973), 150–57.

WILLIS, Peter, ed.
Furor Hortensis. Essays on the History of the English Landscape Garden in Memory of H. F. Clark.
Edinburgh, 1974.

WILLIS, Peter.
'The Gardener and the Painter. A New Attribution to Hogarth'.
Apollo, XCV (January 1972), 30–33.

WILLIS, Peter.
'Jacques Rigaud's Drawings of Stowe in the Metropolitan Museum of Art'.
Eighteenth-Century Studies, VI (1972), 85–98.

WILLIS, Peter.
'A Poets' Gardener'.
Listener, LXXII (24 December 1964), 1007–9.

WILLIS, Peter.
'Rousseau, Stowe and *le jardin anglais*. Speculations on Visual Sources for *La Nouvelle Héloïse*'.
Studies on Voltaire and the Eighteenth Century, XC (1972), 1791–98.

WILLIS, Robert, and CLARK, J. W.
The Architectural History of the University of Cambridge . . .
4 vols.
Cambridge, 1886.

WILSON, Francesca M.
Strange Island. Britain Through Foreign Eyes, 1395–1940.
London, 1955.

WILTON, Richard.
'Historic Londesborough'.
Transactions of the East Riding (Yorkshire) Antiquarian Society, CXI (1895), 1–12.

WIMSATT, William K.
The Portraits of Alexander Pope.
New Haven and London, 1965.

WITTKOWER, Rudolf.
'English Neoclassicism and the Vicissitudes of Palladio's *Quattro Libri*'.
In *Palladio and English Palladianism*, pp.71–92.

WITTKOWER, Rudolf.
'English Neo-Palladianism, the Landscape Garden, China, and the Enlightenment'.
In *Palladio and English Palladianism*, pp.175–90.

WITTKOWER, Rudolf.
'Lord Burlington and William Kent'.
In *Palladio and English Palladianism*, 113–32.

WITTKOWER, Rudolf.
Palladio and English Palladianism.
London, 1974.

WOOD, Anthony C., and HAWKES, William.
Sanderson Miller of Radway.
Forthcoming.

WOODBRIDGE, Kenneth.
Landscape and Antiquity. Aspects of English Culture at Stourhead, 1718–1838.
Oxford, 1970.

WOODBRIDGE, Kenneth.
'William Kent as Landscape Gardener: a Re-appraisal'.
Apollo, C (August 1974), 126–37.

WOODBRIDGE, Kenneth.
'William Kent's Gardening: the Rousham Letters'.
Apollo, C (October 1974), 282–91.

World, 1753, 1755.

WORLIDGE, John.
Systema Agriculturae. Being the Mystery of Husbandry Discovered and Laid Open.
London, 1669.

WORLIDGE, John.
Systema Horti-culturae: or, The Art of Gardening.
London, 1677.

WOTTON, Henry.
The Elements of Architecture . . .
London, 1624.

Wren Society (Publications)
(cited as *Wren Soc.*).
20 vols.
London, 1924–43.

WRIGHT, Cyril E. and Ruth C., eds.
The Diary of Humfrey Wanley, 1715–26.
2 vols.
London, 1966.

WRIGHT, H. Bunker, and MONTGOMERY, Henry C.
'The Art Collection of a Virtuoso in Eighteenth-Century England'.
Art Bulletin, XXVII (September 1945), 195–204.

WRIGHT, H. Bunker, and SPEARS, Monroe K., eds.
The Literary Works of Matthew Prior.
2 vols.
2nd edn.
Oxford, 1971.

ZÁDOR, Anna.
'The English Garden in Hungary'.
In Pevsner, ed., *The Picturesque Garden*, pp.77–98.

Index

References in bold figures are to plates.

Plates

1 Charles Bridgeman, attributed to William Hogarth. Vancouver Art Gallery.

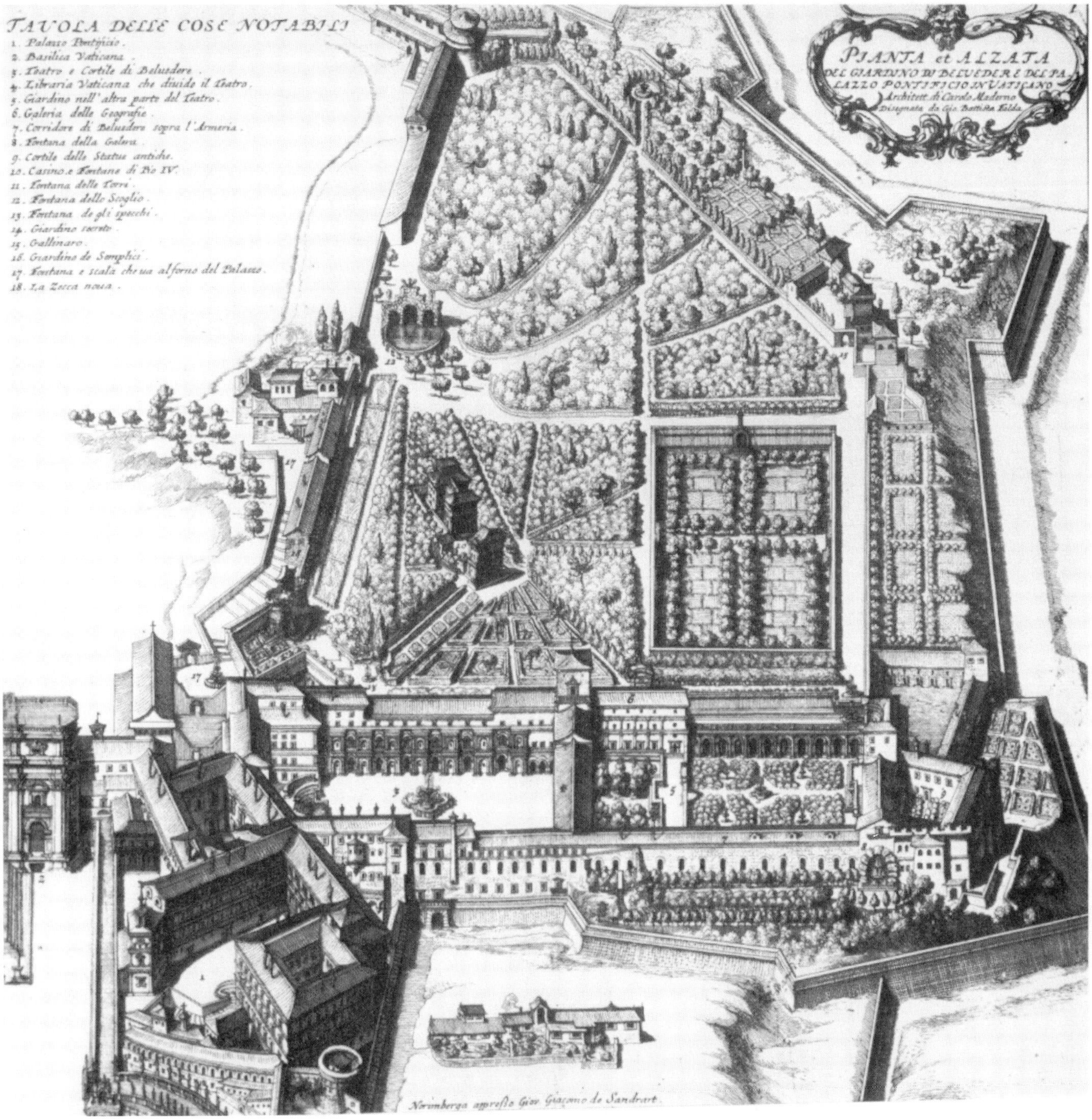

2 Rome. Garden of the Belvedere. Engraving from Falda, *Li Giardini di Roma* (1683), pl.1.

3a Rome. View of Farnese Gardens. Engraving from Falda, *Li Giardini di Roma* (1683), pl.12.

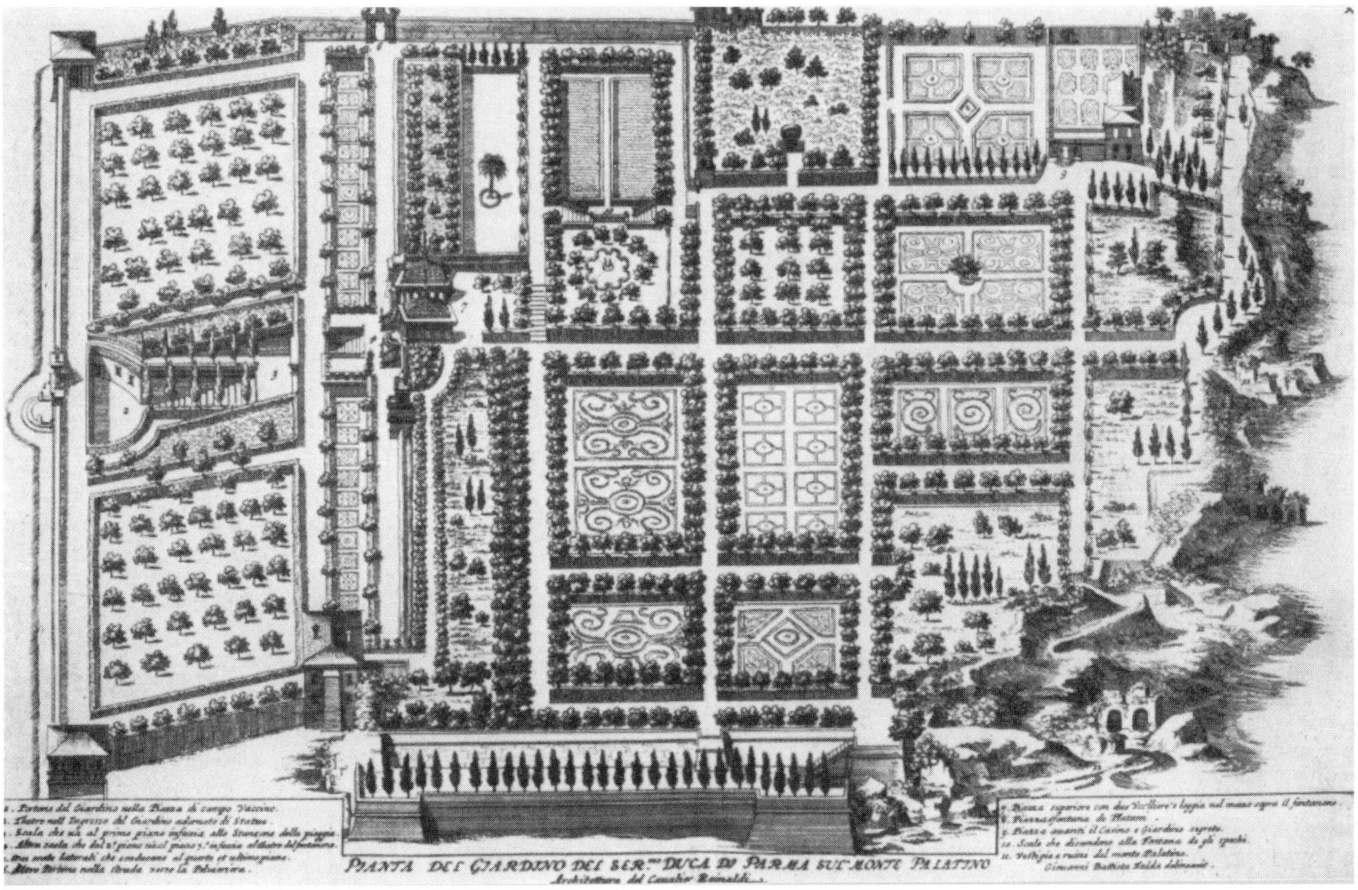

3b Rome. Plan of Farnese Gardens. Engraving from Falda, *Li Giardini di Roma* (1683), pl.11.

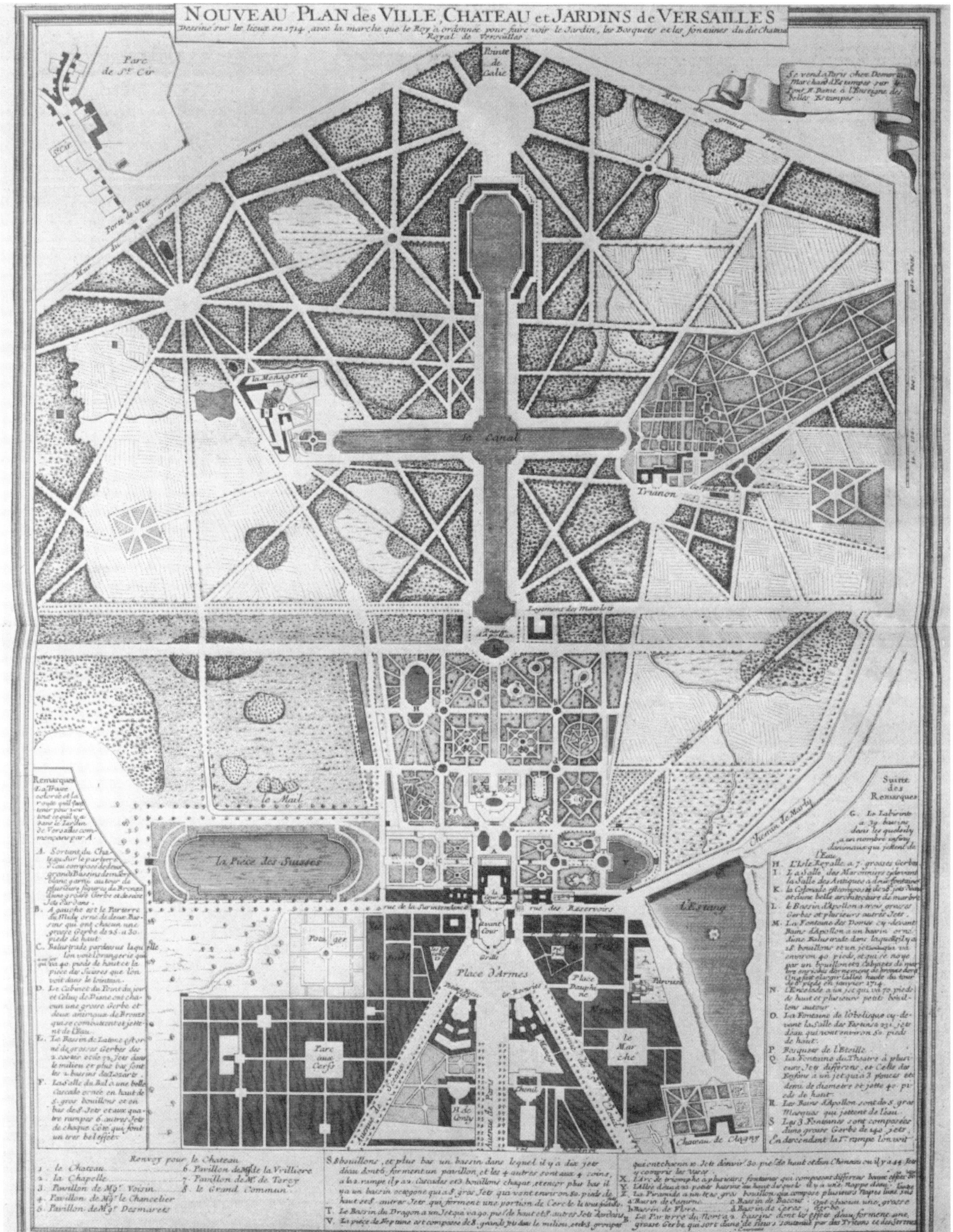

4 Versailles. Plan. Engraving pub. *Chez Demortain* 1714.

5a Versailles. View. Painting by Patel 1668. Musée National du Château de Versailles.

5b Versailles. View from Orangery across La Pièce des Suisses. Engraving by Rigaud *c.*1730.

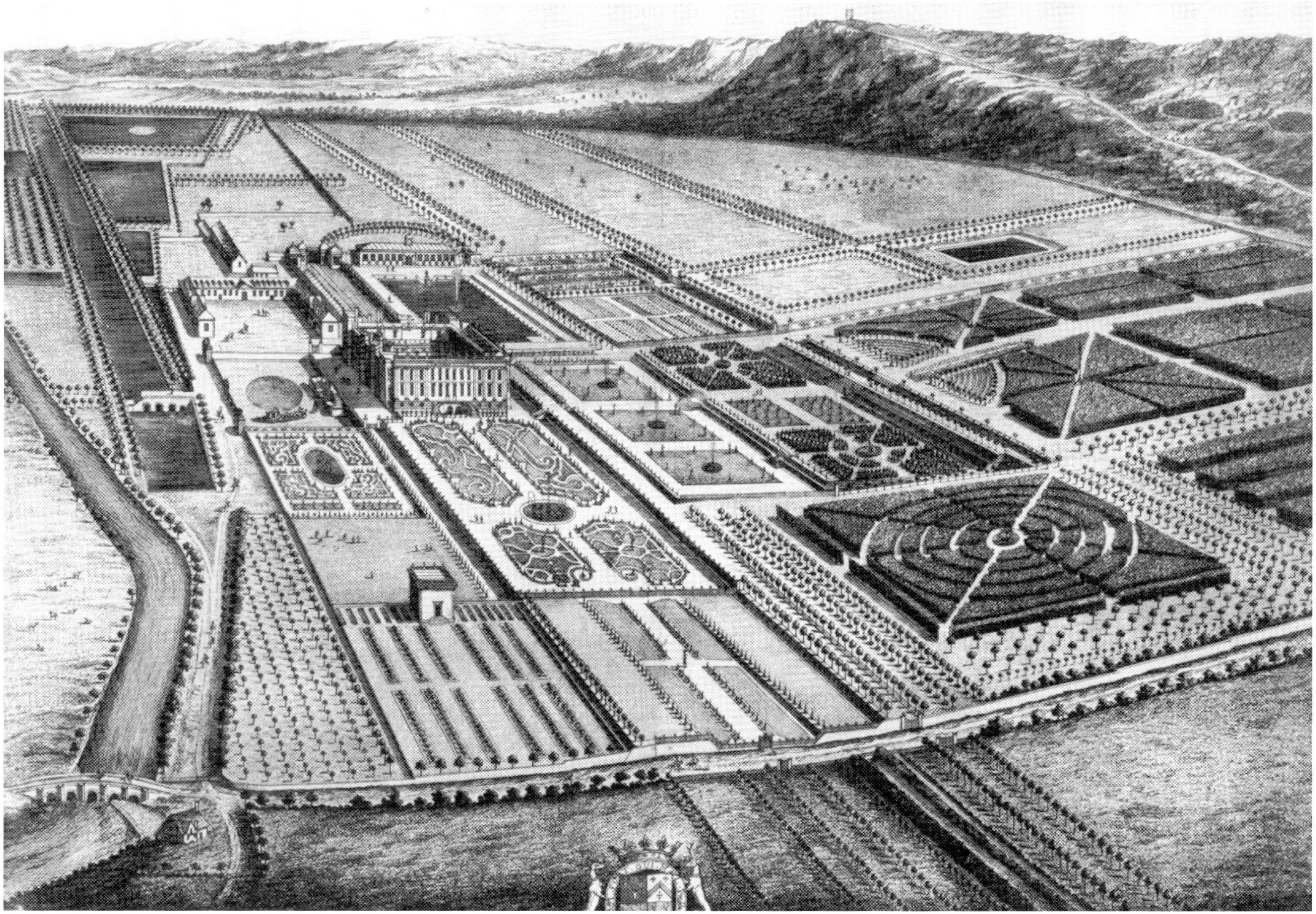

6 Chatsworth. View. Engraving by Kip and Knyff *c.*1699.

7a Chatsworth. View. Engraving by Smith and Vivares 1744.

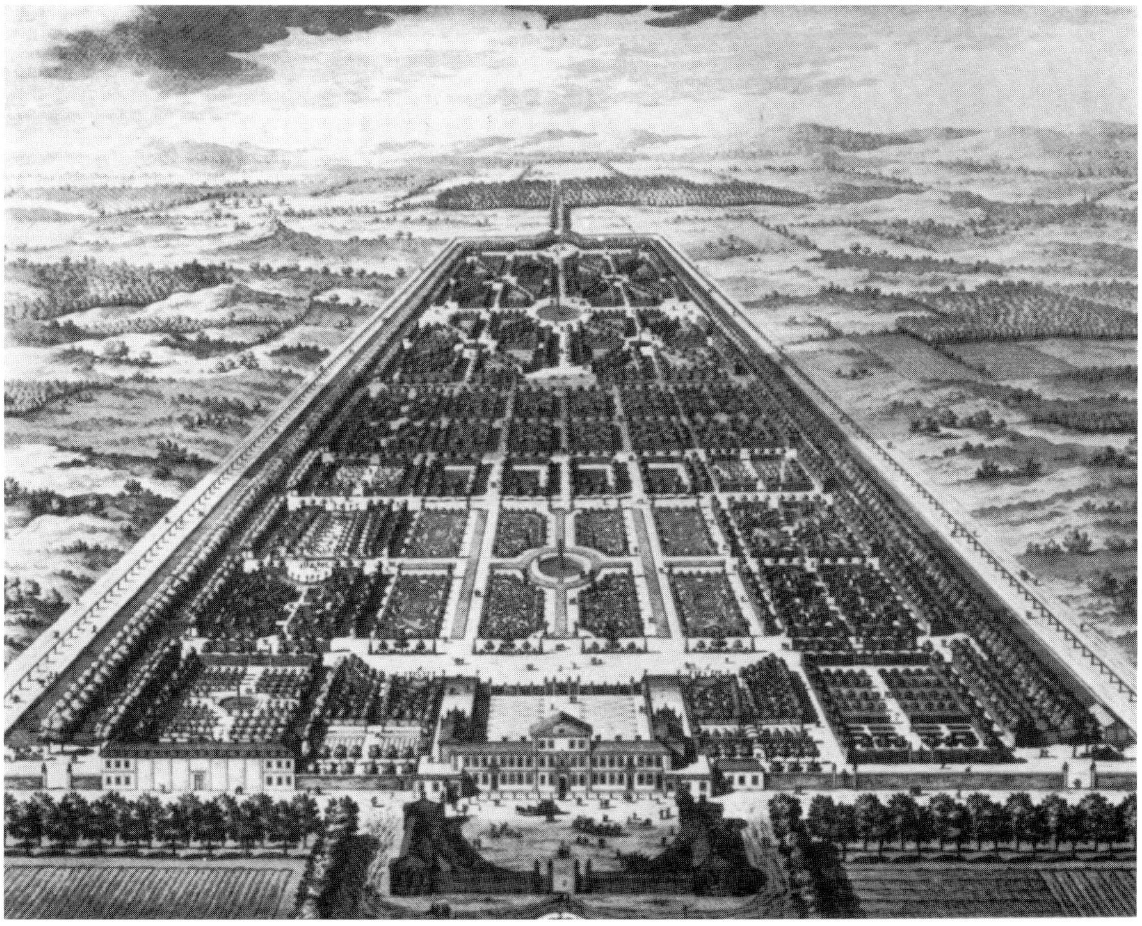

7b Herrenhausen. View. Engraving by J. van Sasse and J. J. Müller 1751.

8 Engraving from Furttenbach, *Architectura Civilis* (1628), pl.13.

9 Engraving from Dézallier D'Argenville, *La théorie et la pratique du jardinage,* trans. James (1712), pl.3dA.

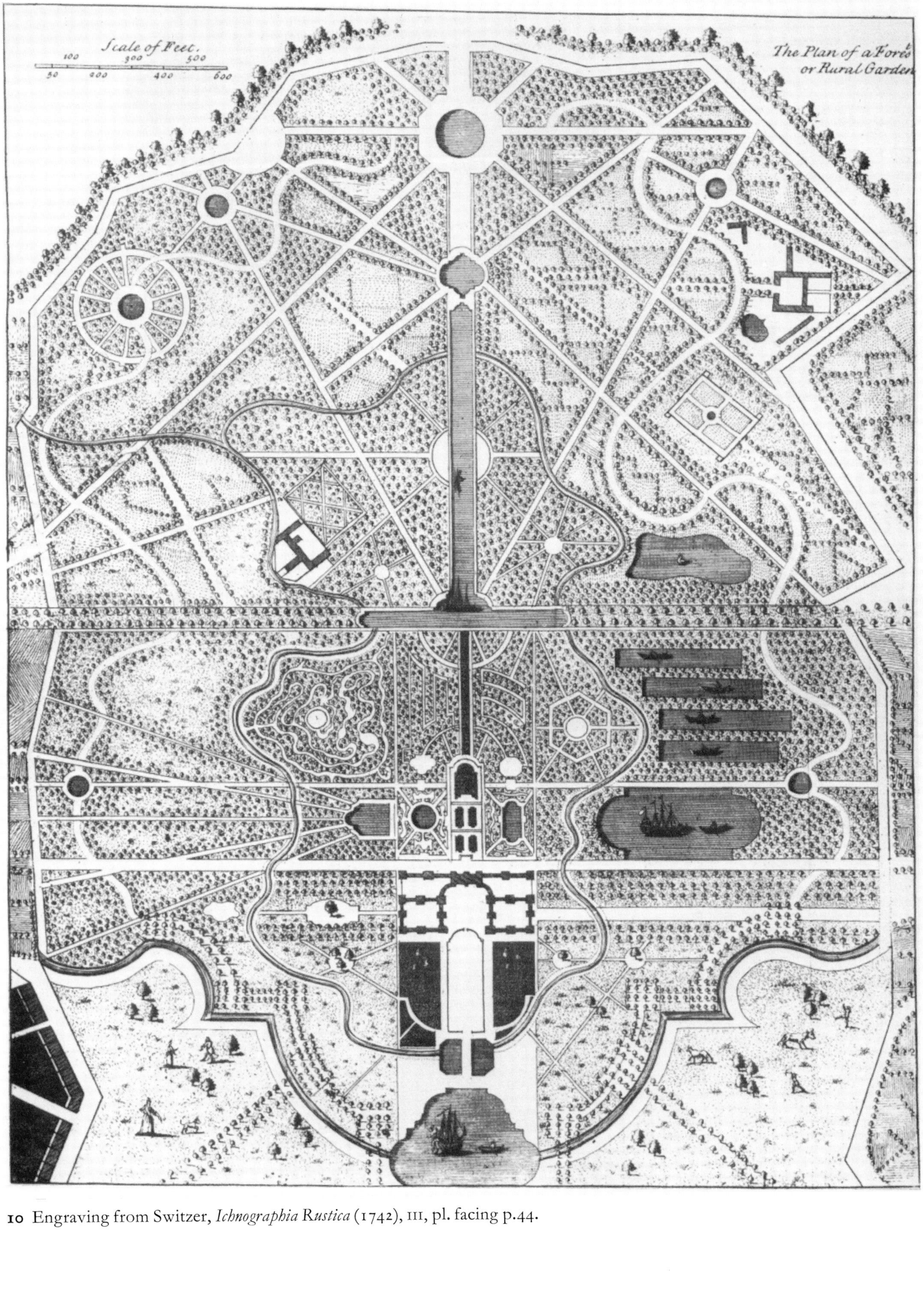

10 Engraving from Switzer, *Ichnographia Rustica* (1742), III, pl. facing p.44.

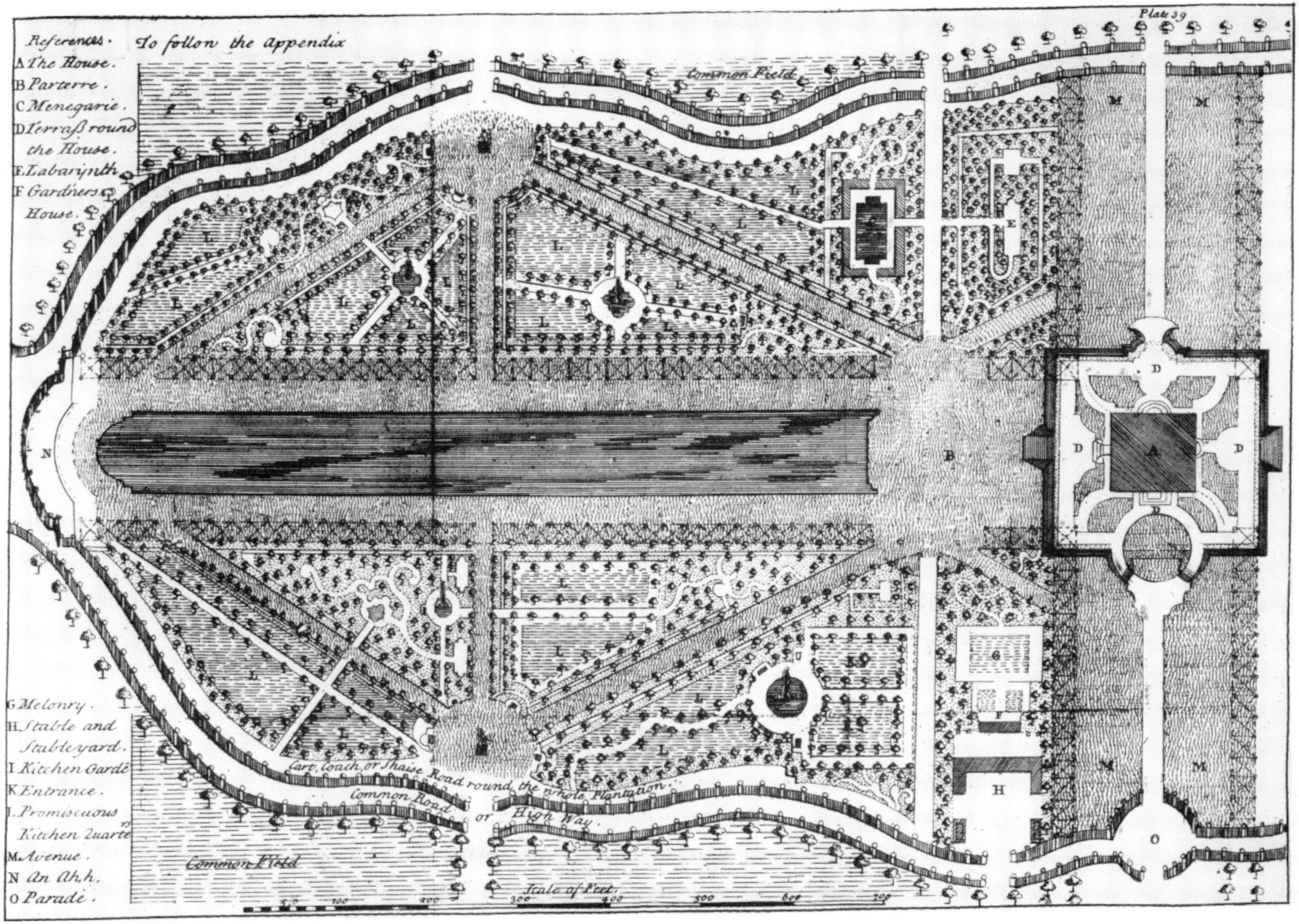

11 Richings. Plan. Engraving from Switzer, *Ichnographia Rustica* (1742), Appendix, pl.39.

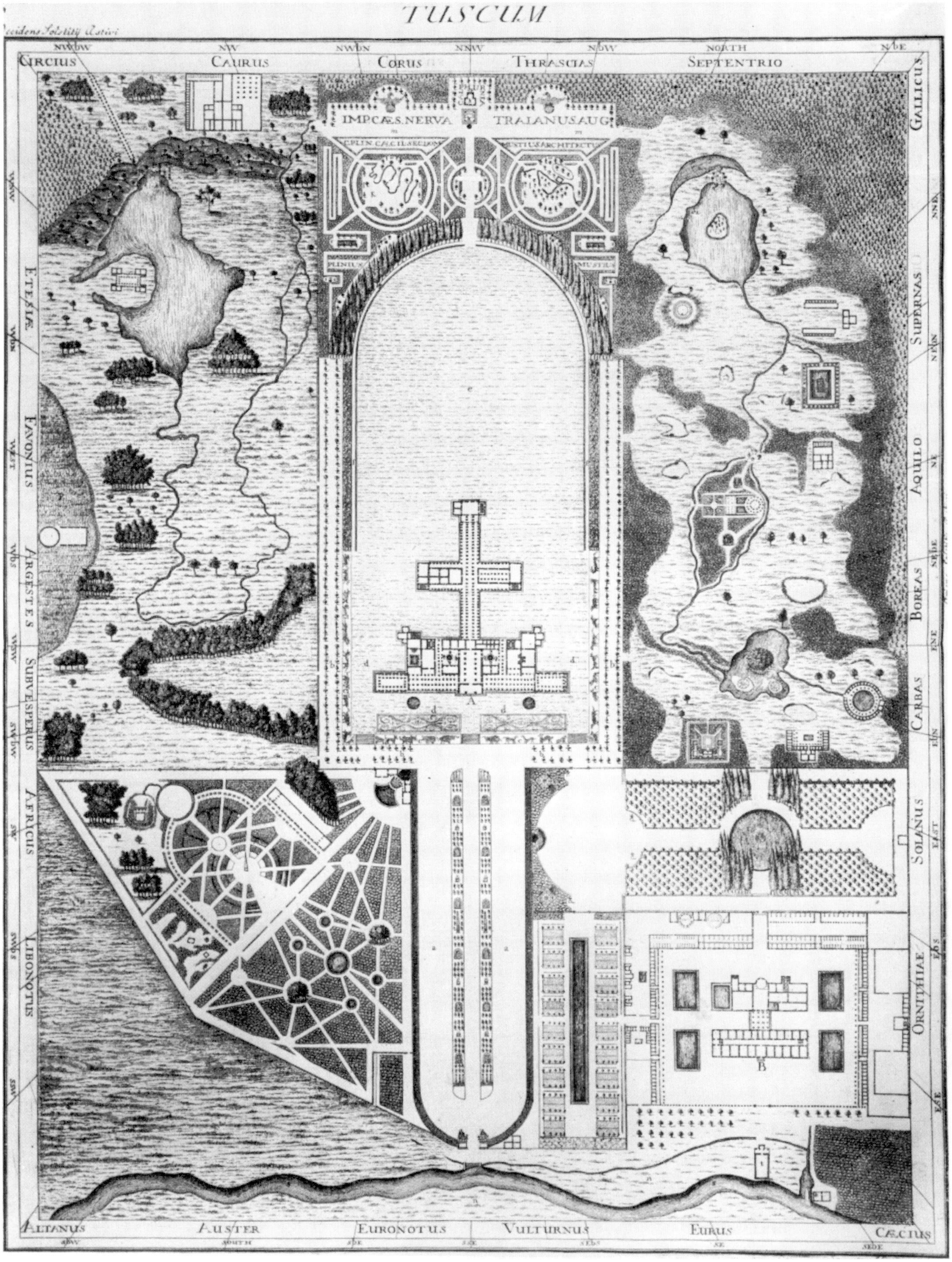

12 Tuscum. Plan. Engraving from Castell, *Villas of the Ancients Illustrated* (1728), pl. between pp. 126–27.

13a Imperial Gardens at Jehol. View. Engraving by F. Matteo Ripa 1713.

13b Engraving from Langley, *New Principles of Gardening* (1728), pl.20.

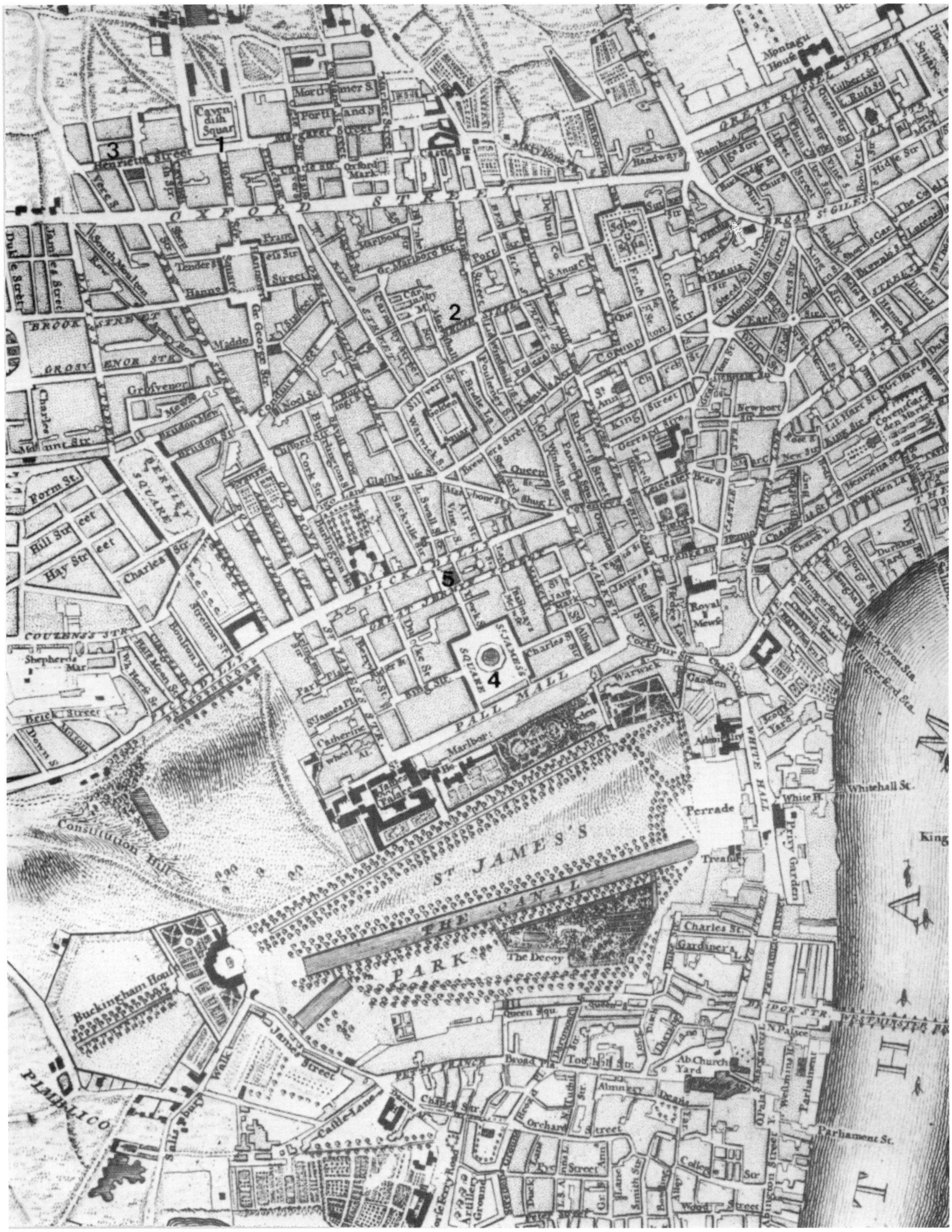

14 Marylebone and area southwards. Detail from Rocque, *An Exact Survey of the City's of London, Westminster . . . and the Country Near Ten Miles Round* (1746).

KEY: **1** Cavendish Square; **2** Bridgeman's House, No.19 Broad Street; **3** Bridgeman's House, No.8 Henrietta Street; **4** St James's Square; **5** St James's Church, Westminster (now Piccadilly)

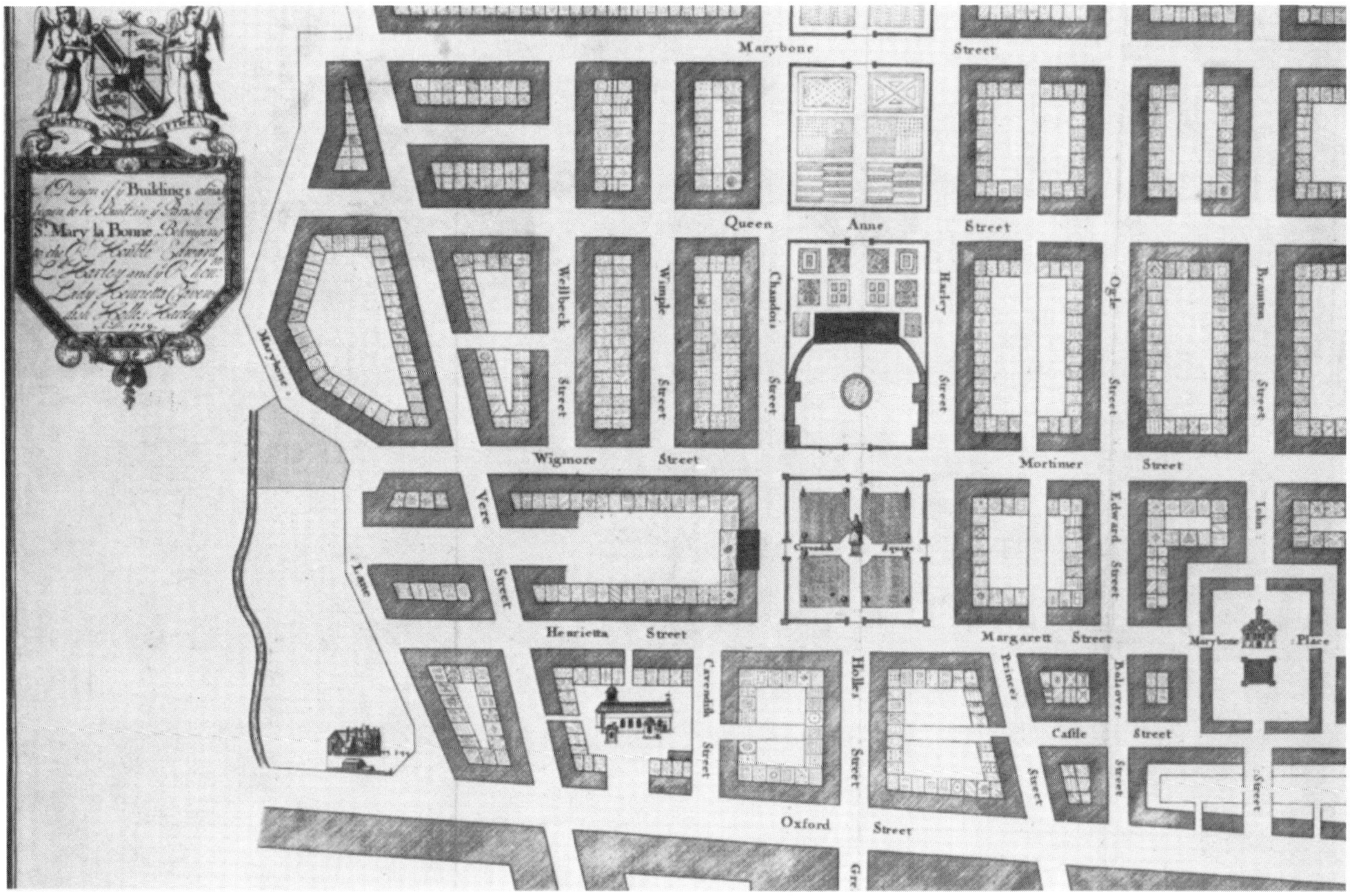

15a Lord Harley's Estate, Marylebone. Plan by John Prince, engraved by Sutton Nicholls 1719.

15b Bridgeman's House, No.54 Broadwick Street (formerly No.19 Broad Street), Westminster.

15c Bridgeman's House, No.11 Henrietta Place (formerly No.8 Henrietta Street), Marylebone (demolished 1956).

16a The Bell Inn, Stilton, before closure in 1964.

16b St James's Square, Westminster. View of Bridgeman's layout of 1727–28. Engraving by Sutton Nicholls 1754.

17a Henry Wise, by Sir Godfrey Kneller. Kensington Palace.

17b Charles Dartiquenave, by Sir Godfrey Kneller. National Portrait Gallery, London.

18 Warwick Priory. Detail of drawing by Bridgeman and Fish (attrib.) 1711. Warwickshire CRO, Warwick, CR. 26.2.2 (Waller Collection).

19 *A Club of Artists,* attributed to Gawen Hamilton *c.*1735. National Portrait Gallery, London.

LEFT TO RIGHT: George Vertue, Hans Huyssing, Michael Dahl, William Thomas, James Gibbs, Joseph Goupy (standing), Matthew Robinson (seated), Charles Bridgeman, Bernard Baron, John Wootton, John Michael Rysbrack, Gawen Hamilton, William Kent

20 *An Assembly of Virtuosi*, attributed to Gawen Hamilton or William Hogarth *c.*1730. Ashmolean Museum, Oxford.

LEFT TO RIGHT: Gawen Hamilton, Michael Dahl (seated), Unknown, Unknown (seated), Gibbons or Gibbs (standing), Marcellus Laroon (standing under left statuette), Unknown (standing), Unknown (seated), John Michael Rysbrack (seated), John Vanderbank (seated), William Kent (standing under right statuette), Unknown (seated), Charles Bridgeman ?, Charles Bridgeman ?, Unknown

21 *The Rake's Progress* (Plate 2: The Levee), by William Hogarth 1734–35. Sir John Soane's Museum, London.

22a 'Old Master Charles Bridgeman'. Pencil sketch by Sir James Thornhill. Collection of the late Theodore Besterman.

22b Sir John Vanbrugh, attributed to Jonathan Richardson. RIBA.

23a Woodstock Manor. View. Water-colour 1714. BL, K.XXXV.28.d.

23b Blenheim. Aerial view of North (Entrance) Front 1969.

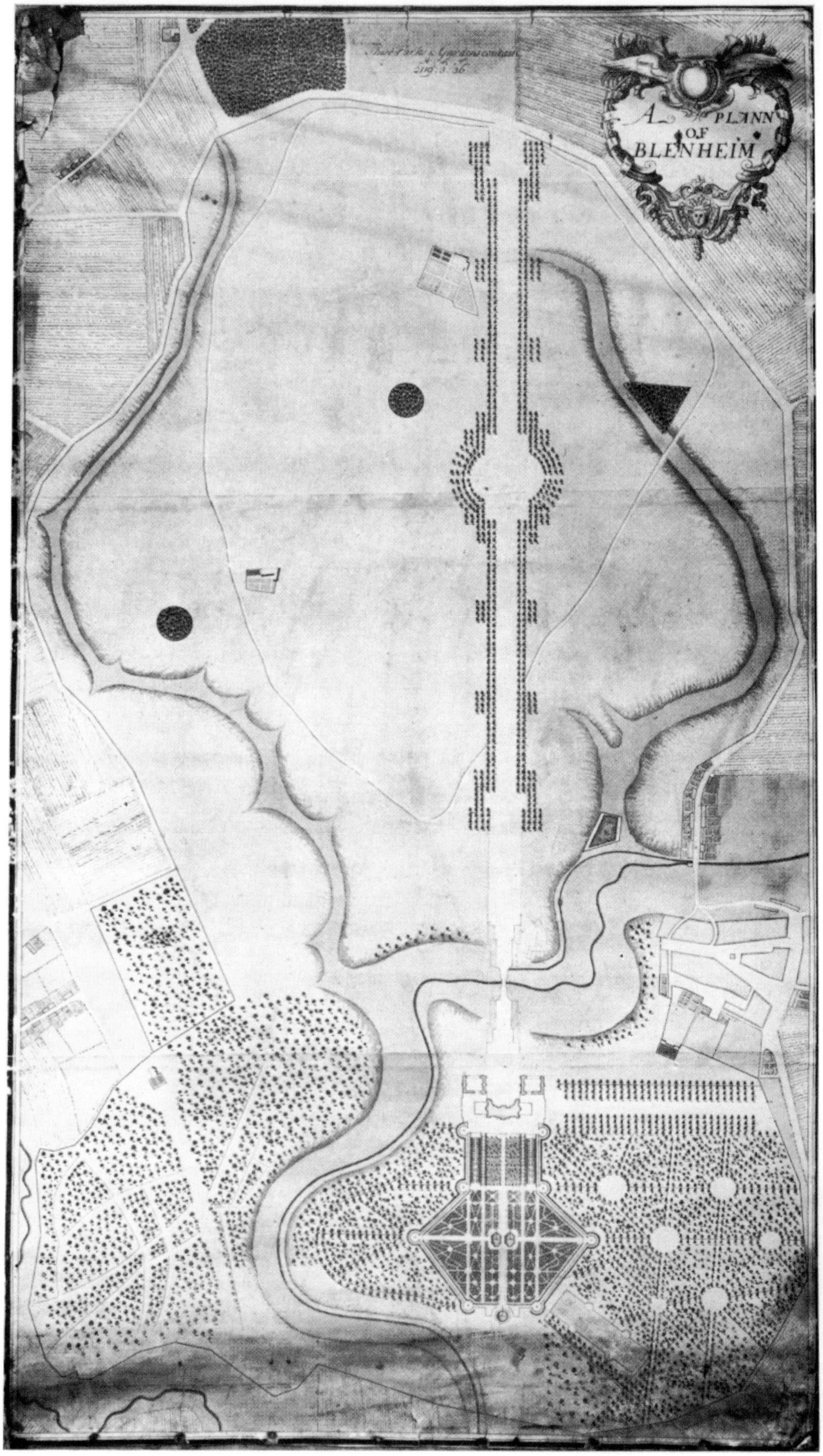

24 Blenheim. Plan. Drawing by Bridgeman signed '1709/Bridgman Discript.' Blenheim.

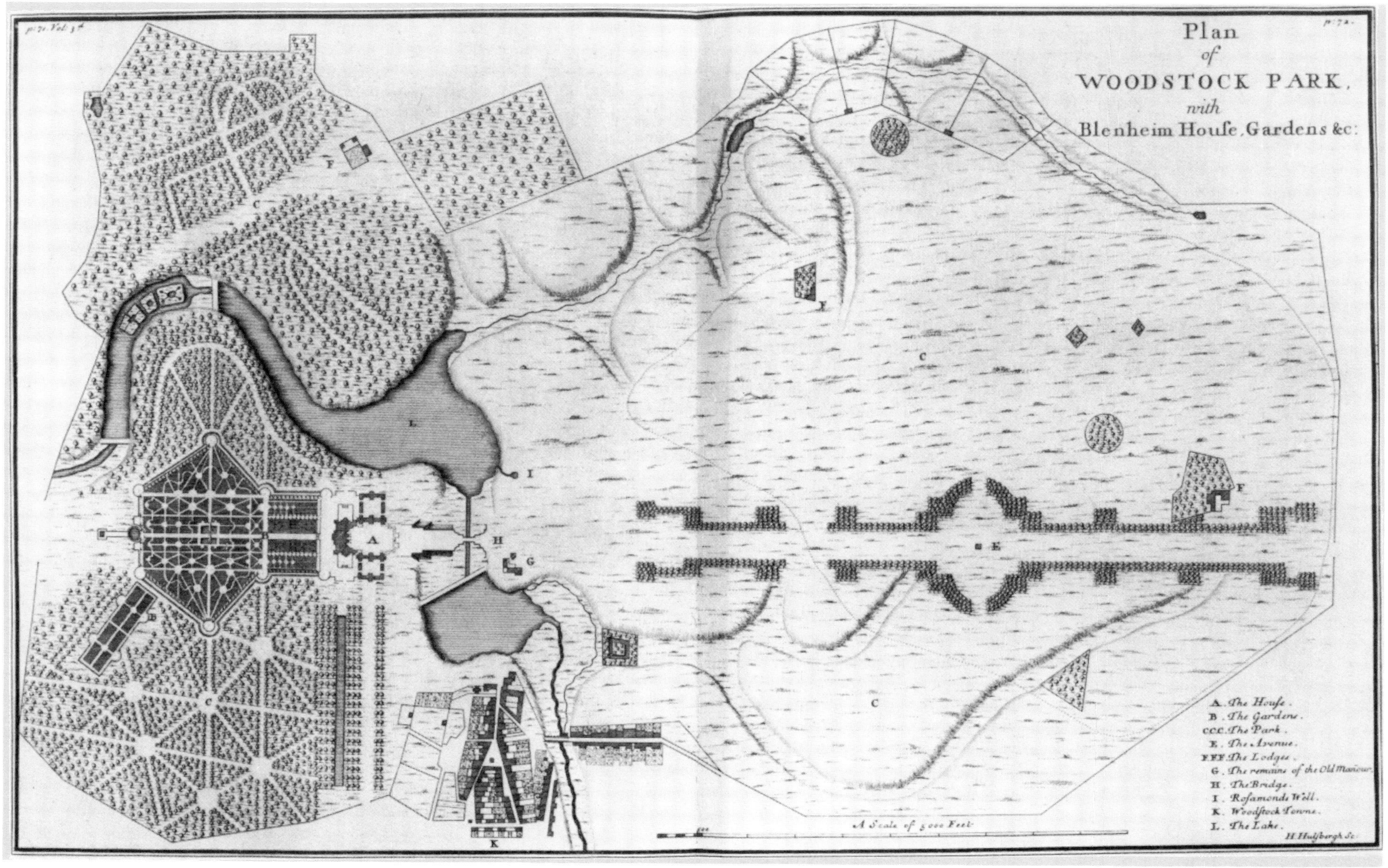

25 Blenheim. Plan. Engraving from *Vitruvius Britannicus III* (1725), pls 72–73.

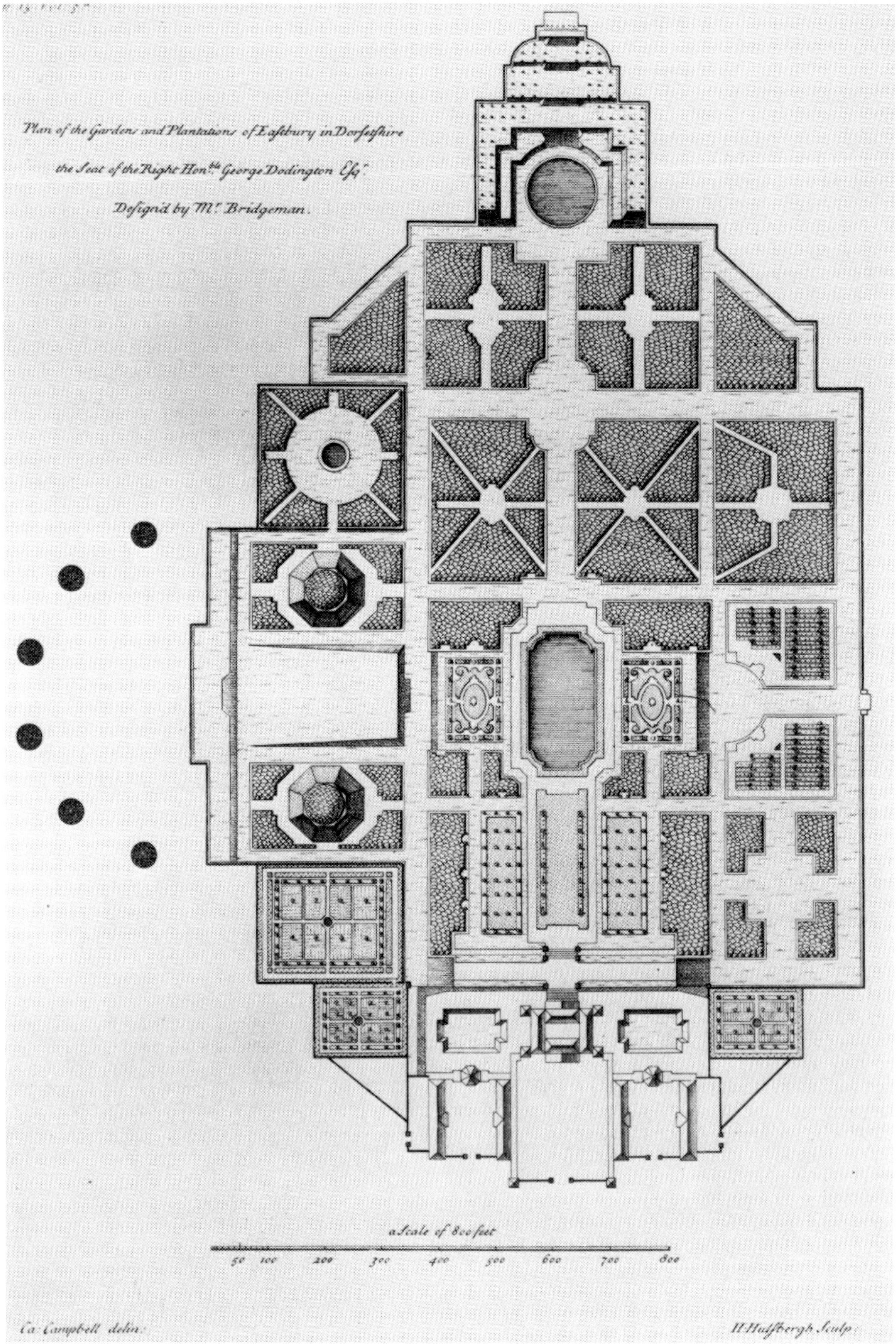

26 Eastbury. Plan. Engraving from *Vitruvius Britannicus III* (1725), pl.15.

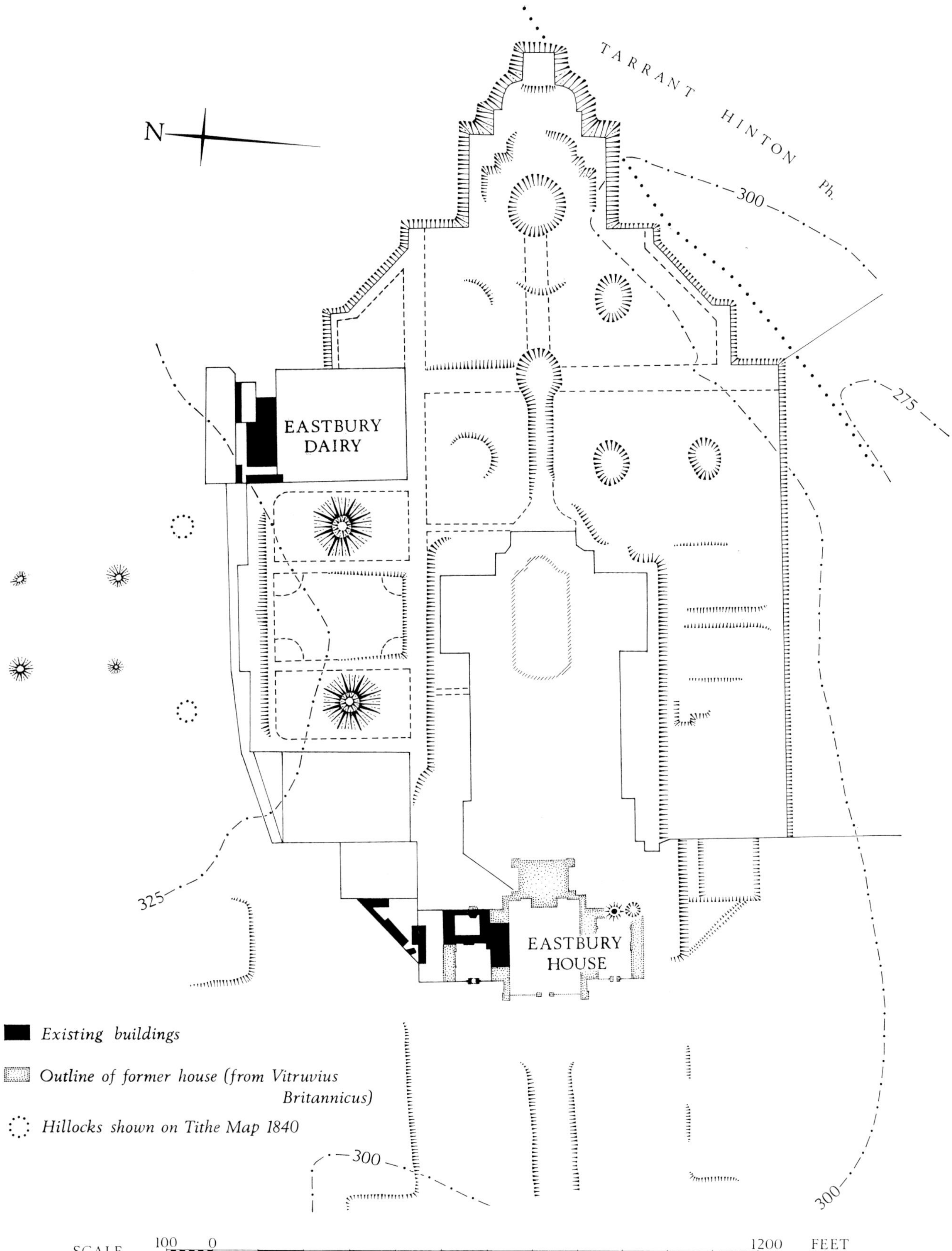

27 Eastbury. Plan. Survey published in *RCHM: Dorset*, IV (1972), p.92.

28a Eastbury. East (Garden) Front. Engraving from *Vitruvius Britannicus III* (1725), pl.17.

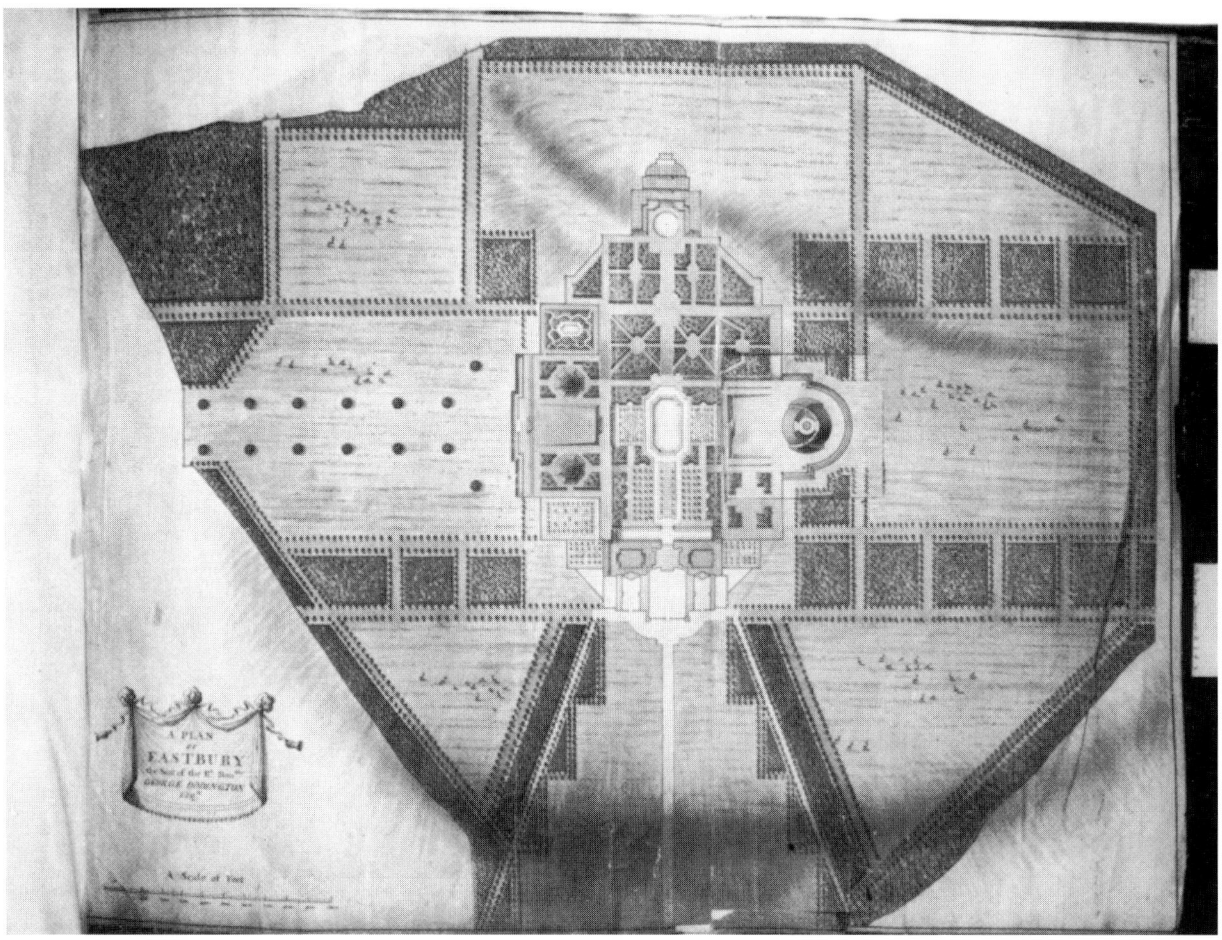

28b Eastbury. Plan. Drawing by Bridgeman (attrib.). MSGD a3*fo.9.

29a Eastbury. Temple. Engraving from *Vitruvius Britannicus III* (1725), pl.18.

29b Eastbury. Bagnio. Engraving from *Vitruvius Britannicus III* (1725), pl.19.

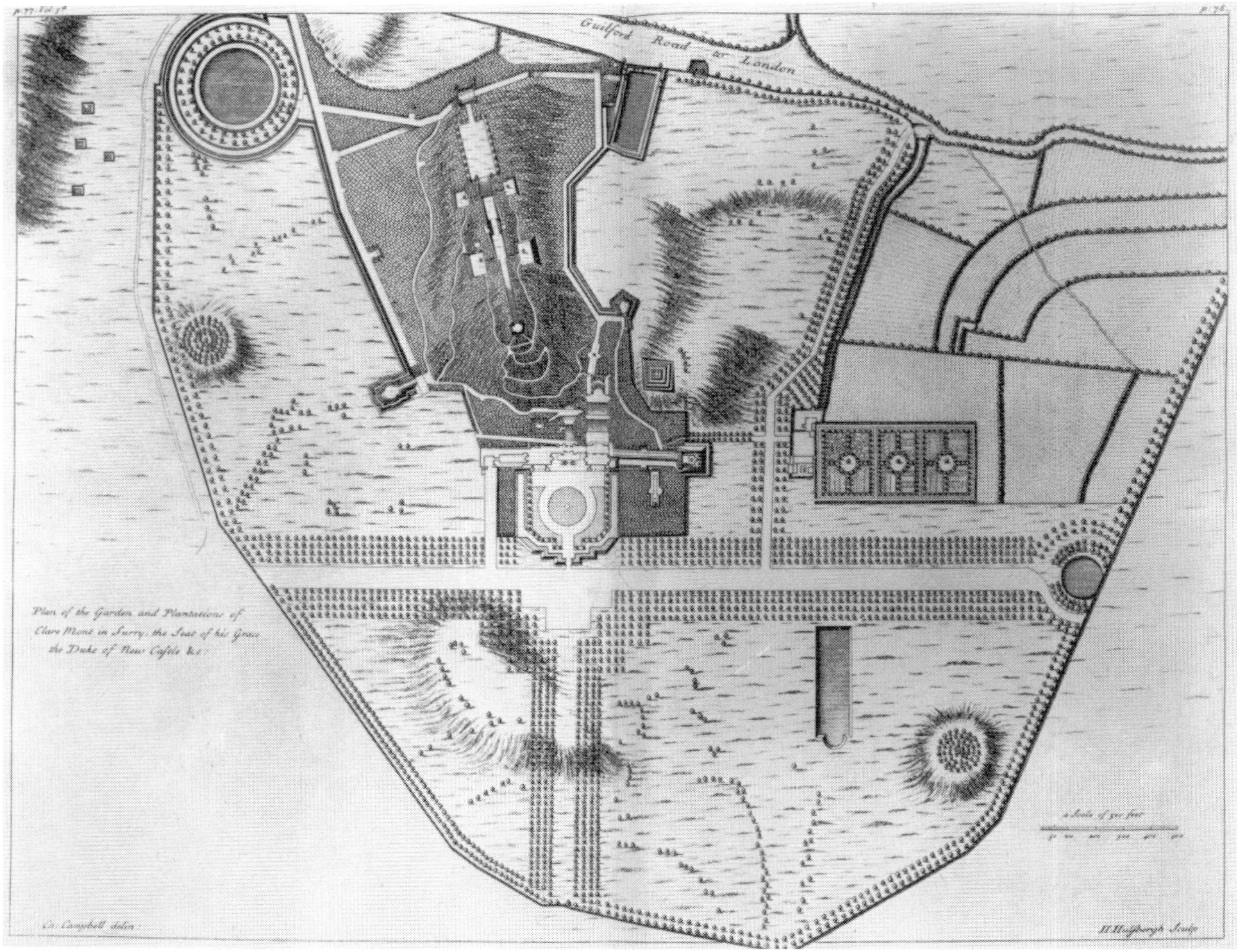

30 Claremont. Plan. Engraving from *Vitruvius Britannicus III* (1725), pls 67–68.

31 Claremont. View of Amphitheatre, Lake, and Island Temple. Engraving by Rocque and Benazech 1754.

32a Claremont. Plan of Amphitheatre. Engraving from Switzer, *An Introduction to a General System of Hydrostaticks and Hydraulicks* (1729), pl.37.

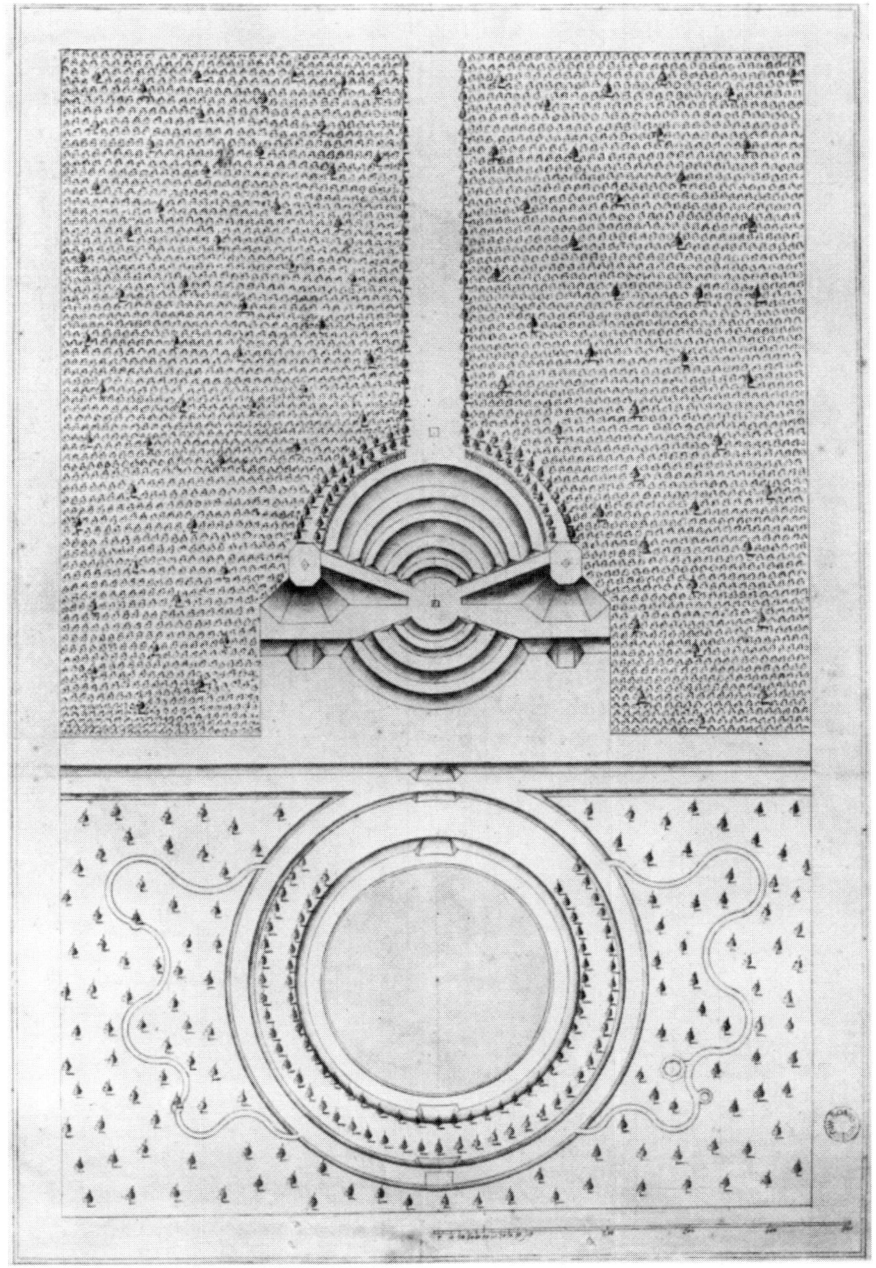

32b Claremont. Plan of Amphitheatre and Round Pond. Drawing by Bridgeman (attrib.). Soane 39, Drawer 62.1.2.

33a Bower House. View of North (Entrance) Front. Detail of anonymous painting. Ingatestone Hall, Essex.

33b Henry Flitcroft, attributed to Bartholomew Dandridge. RIBA.

34a Bower Houes. View of South (Garden) Front.

34b Woburn, Beds. Elevation. Drawing by Sanderson 1733. Bedford Office, London, Woburn MSS, HMC No.151.

35a Well Vale. View from west.

35b Wrest. View of Long Water and Garden Pavilion.

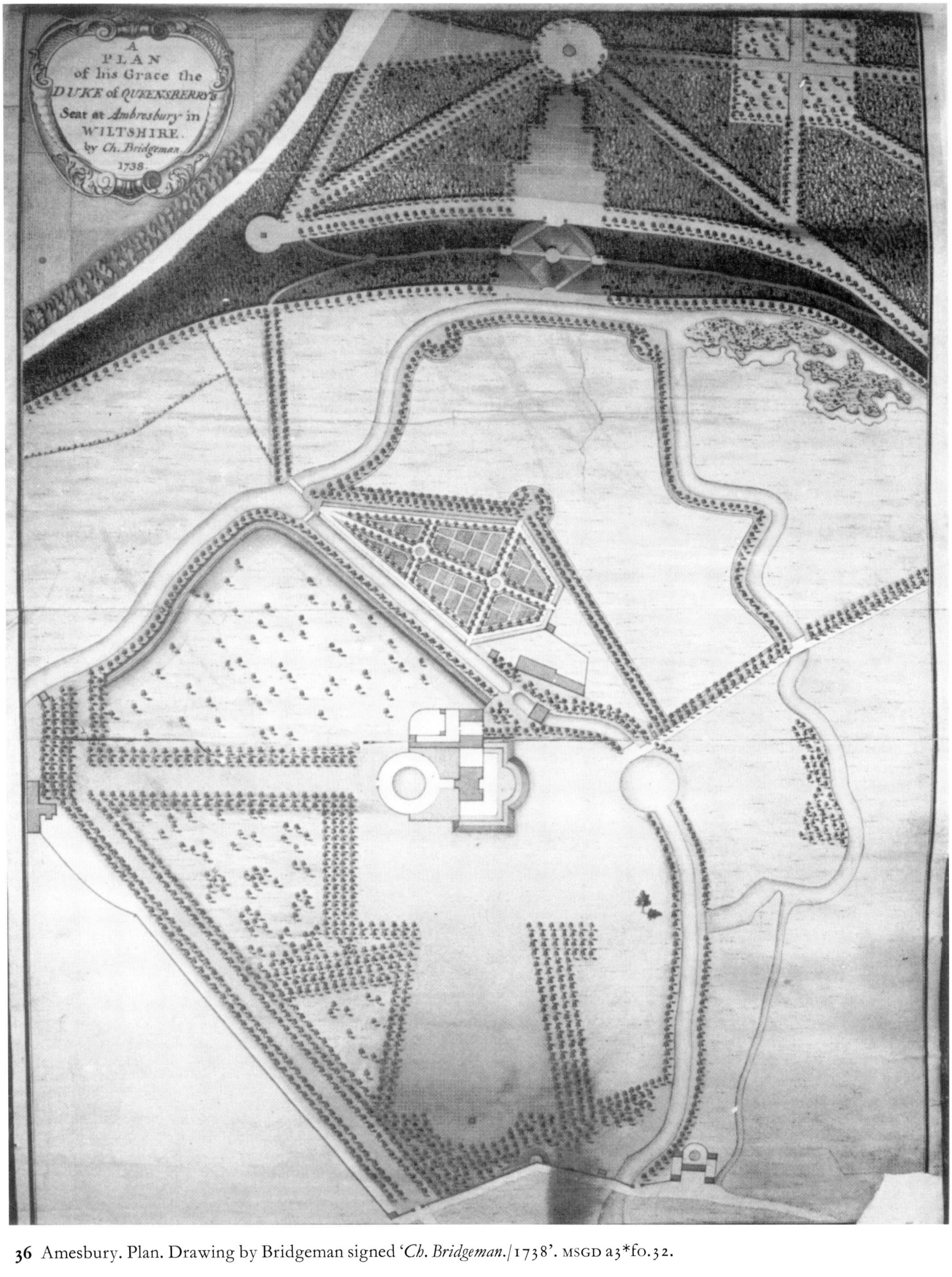

36 Amesbury. Plan. Drawing by Bridgeman signed '*Ch. Bridgeman.*/1738'. MSGD a3*fo.32.

37a Amesbury. South (Entrance) Front. Engraving from Kent, *The Designs of Inigo Jones* (1727), II, pl.7.

37b Amesbury. Plan. Detail from *Plate 36*.

38a Chicheley. Aerial view of South Front.

38b Chicheley. View of Canal.

39a Montagu House. North (Garden) Front. Engraving by James Simon 1715.

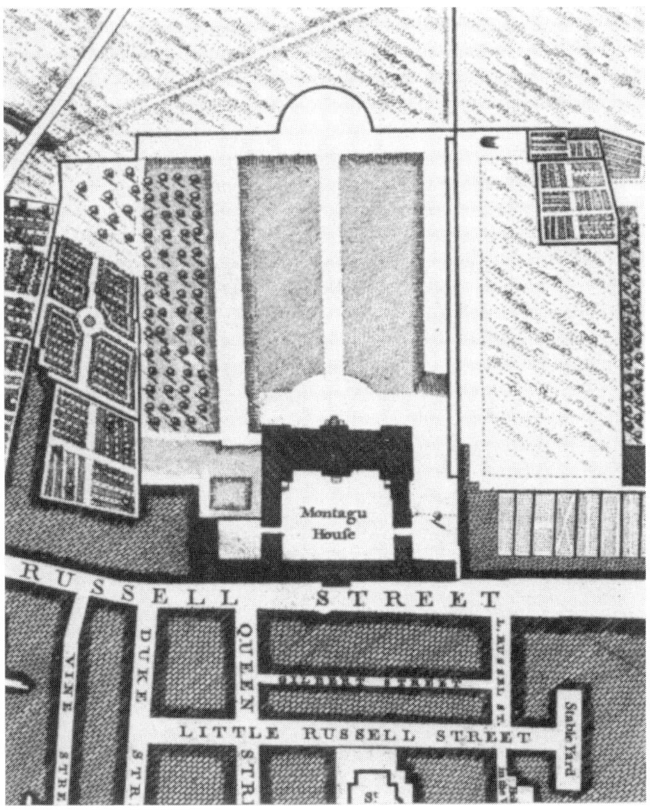

39b Montagu House. Plan. Detail from Rocque, *An Exact Survey of the City's of London, Westminster . . . and the Country Near Ten Miles Round* (1746).

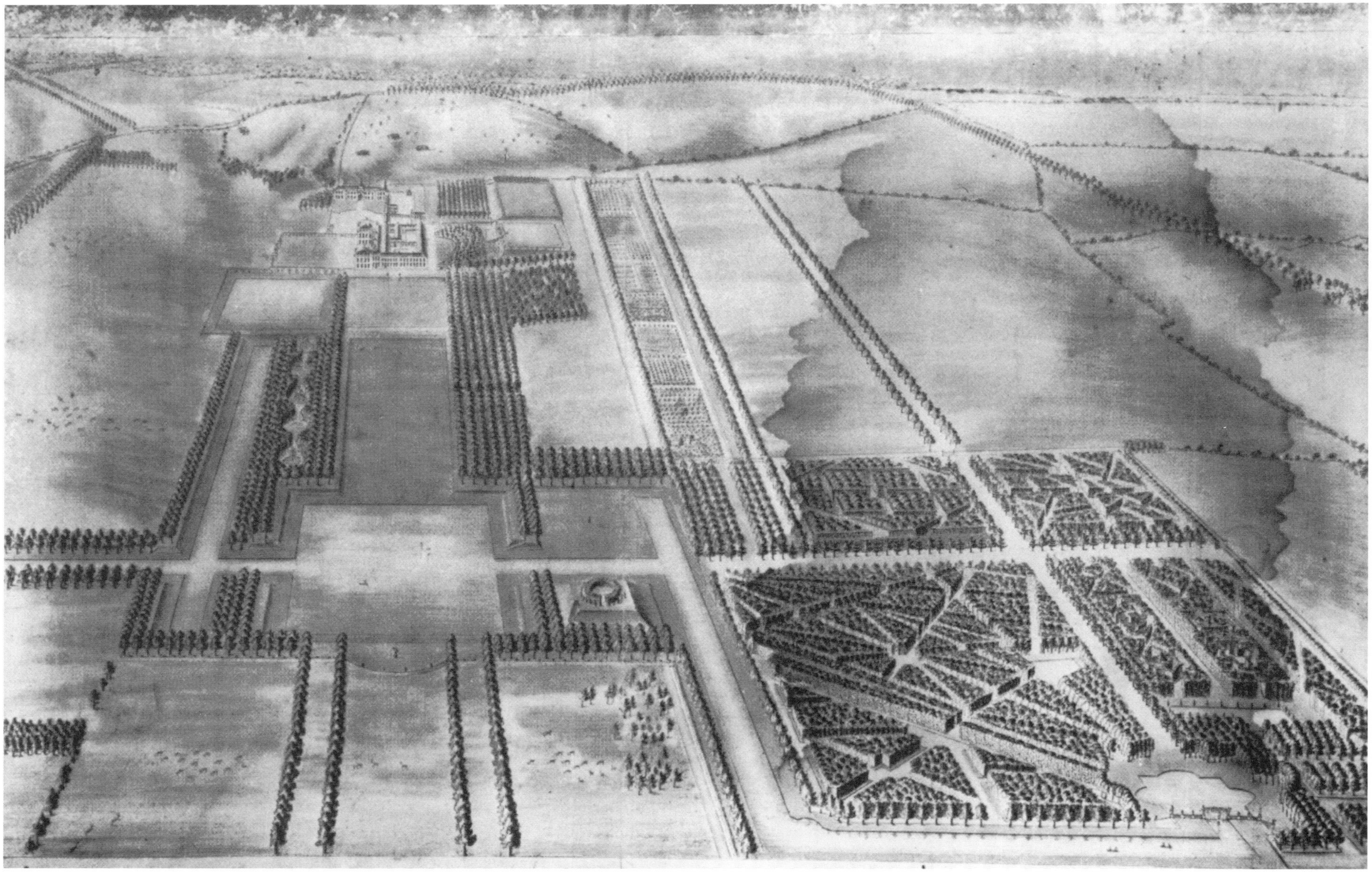

40 Boughton. Bird's-eye view from west *c.*1725. Drawing by Bridgeman (attrib.). Boughton.

41a Boughton. Detail of *Plate 40*.

41b Boughton. Aerial view from south-west 1957.

42a Chatelherault. North Front facing site of Hamilton Palace. Engraving from *Vitruvius Scoticus* (1810), pl.160.

42b Boughton. View of Square Pond to south.

43a Wimbledon. South Front. Engraving from *Vitruvius Britannicus V* (1771), pl.21.

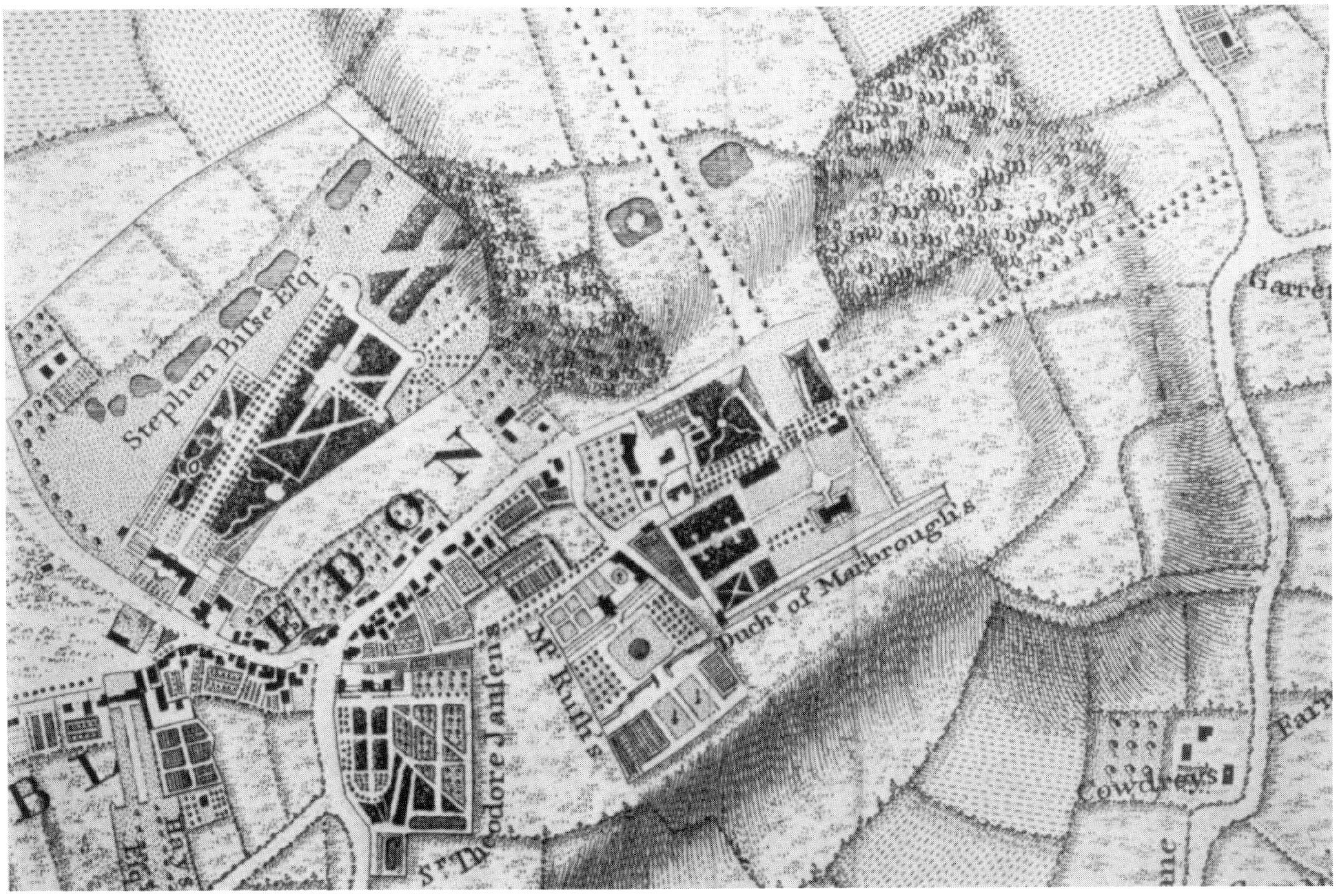

43b Wimbledon. Plan. Detail from Rocque, *An Exact Survey of the City's of London, Westminster . . . and the Country Near Ten Miles Round* (1746).

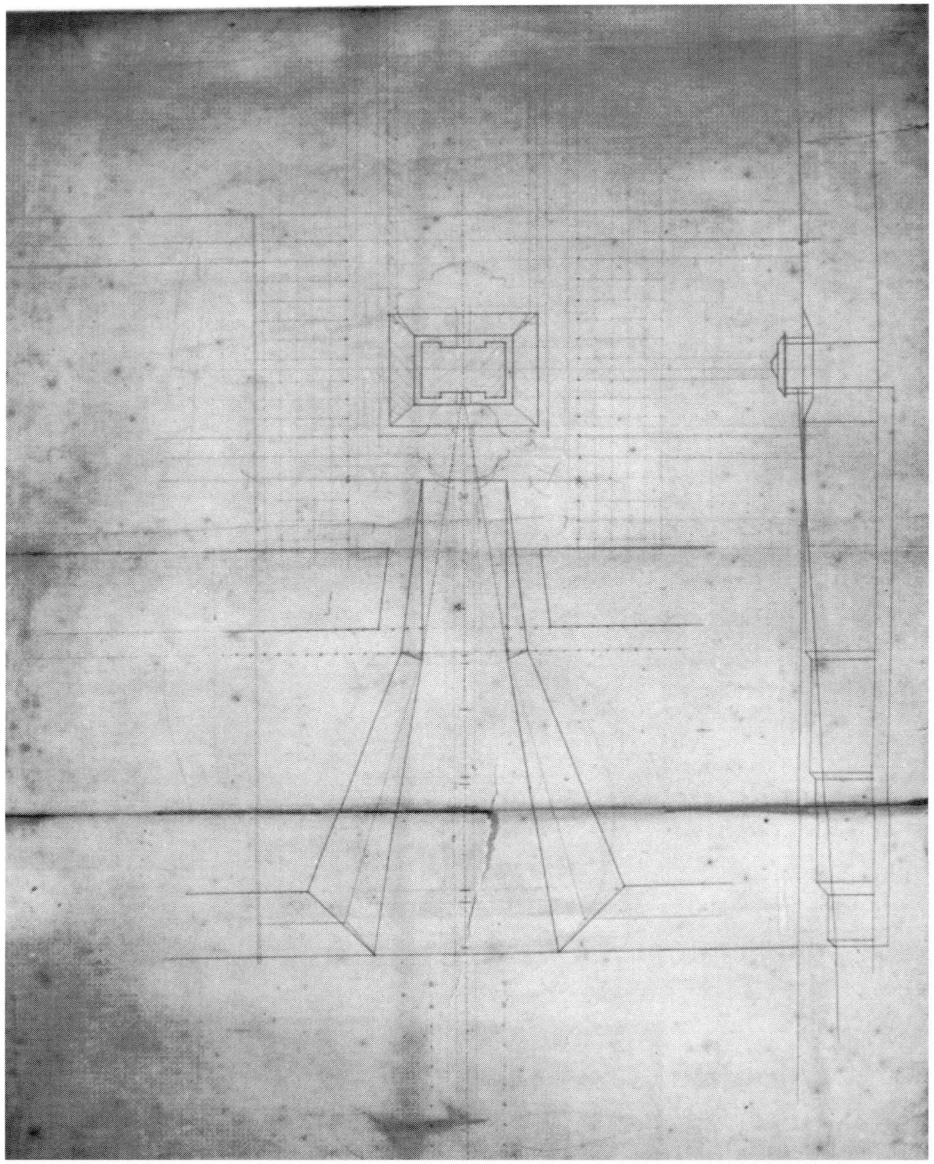

44a Wimbledon. Plan. Drawing by Bridgeman (attrib.). MSGD a4 fo.44.

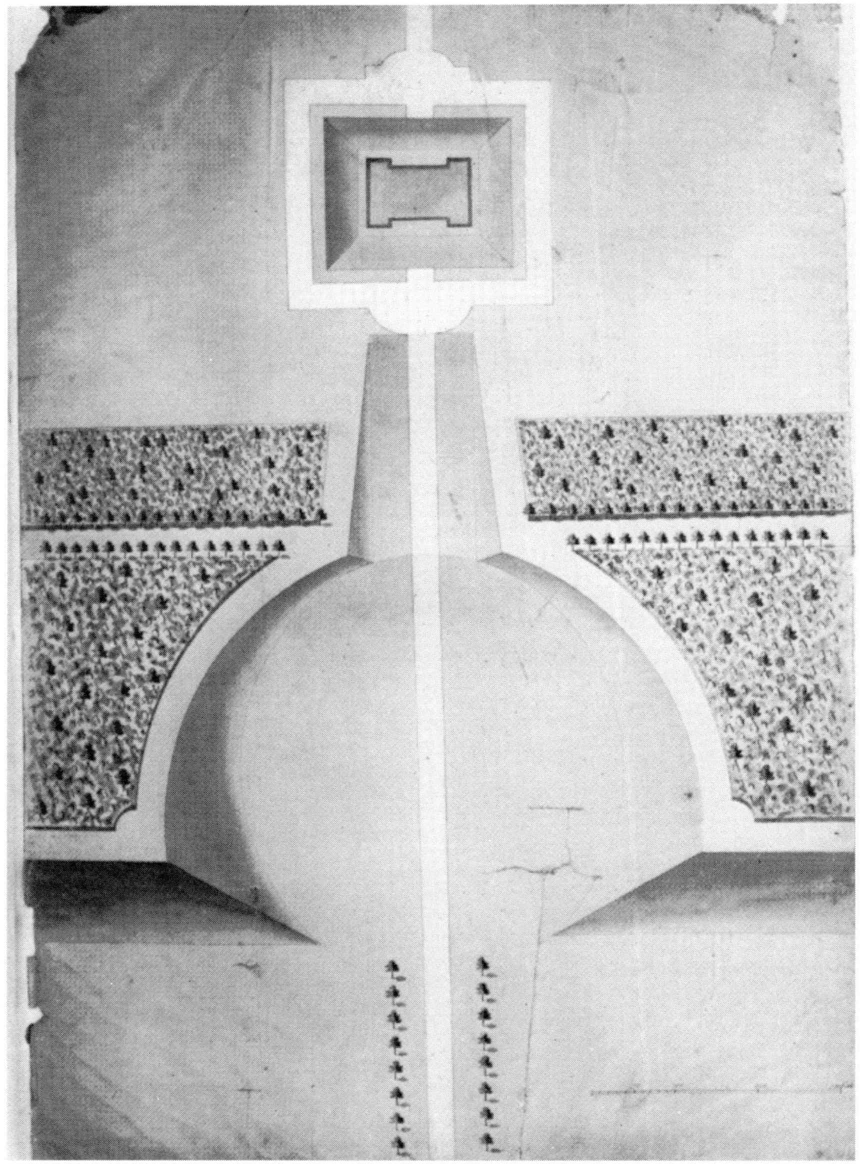

44b Wimbledon. Plan. Drawing by Bridgeman (attrib.). MSGD a3 fo.31.

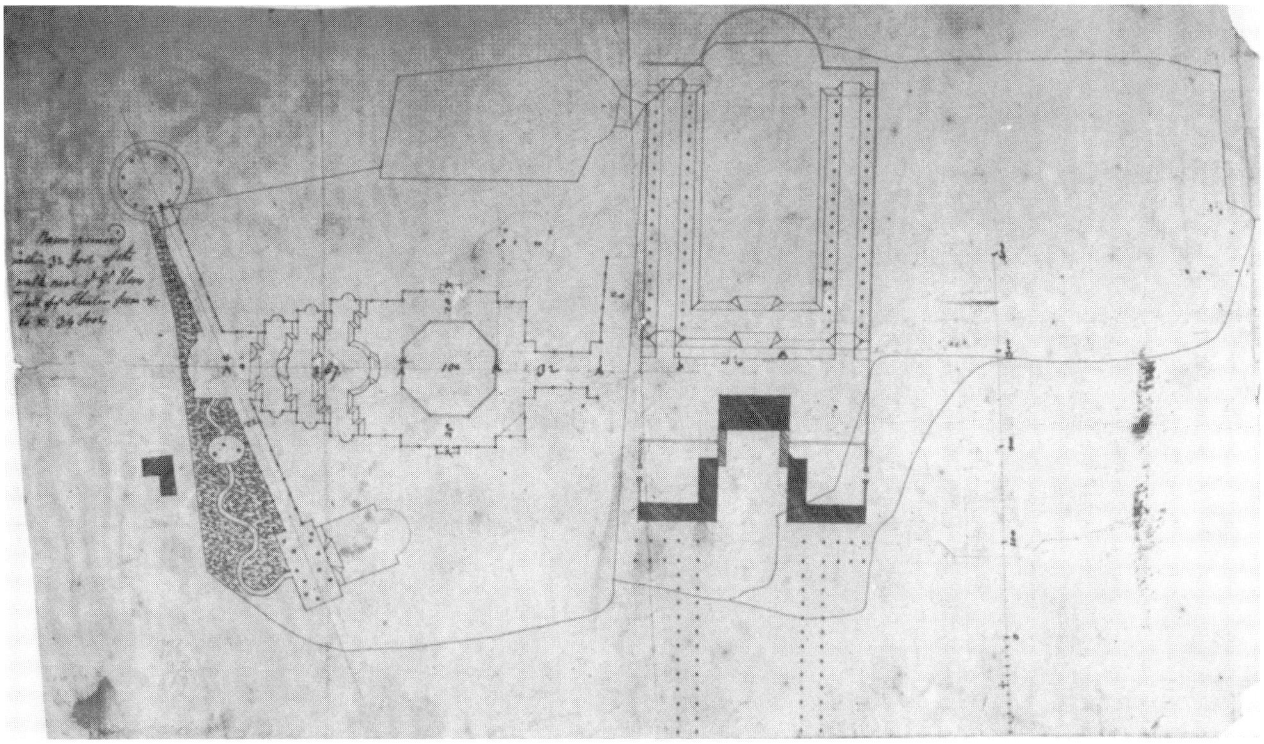

45a Tring. Plan. Drawing by Bridgeman (attrib.). MSGD a4 fo.78.

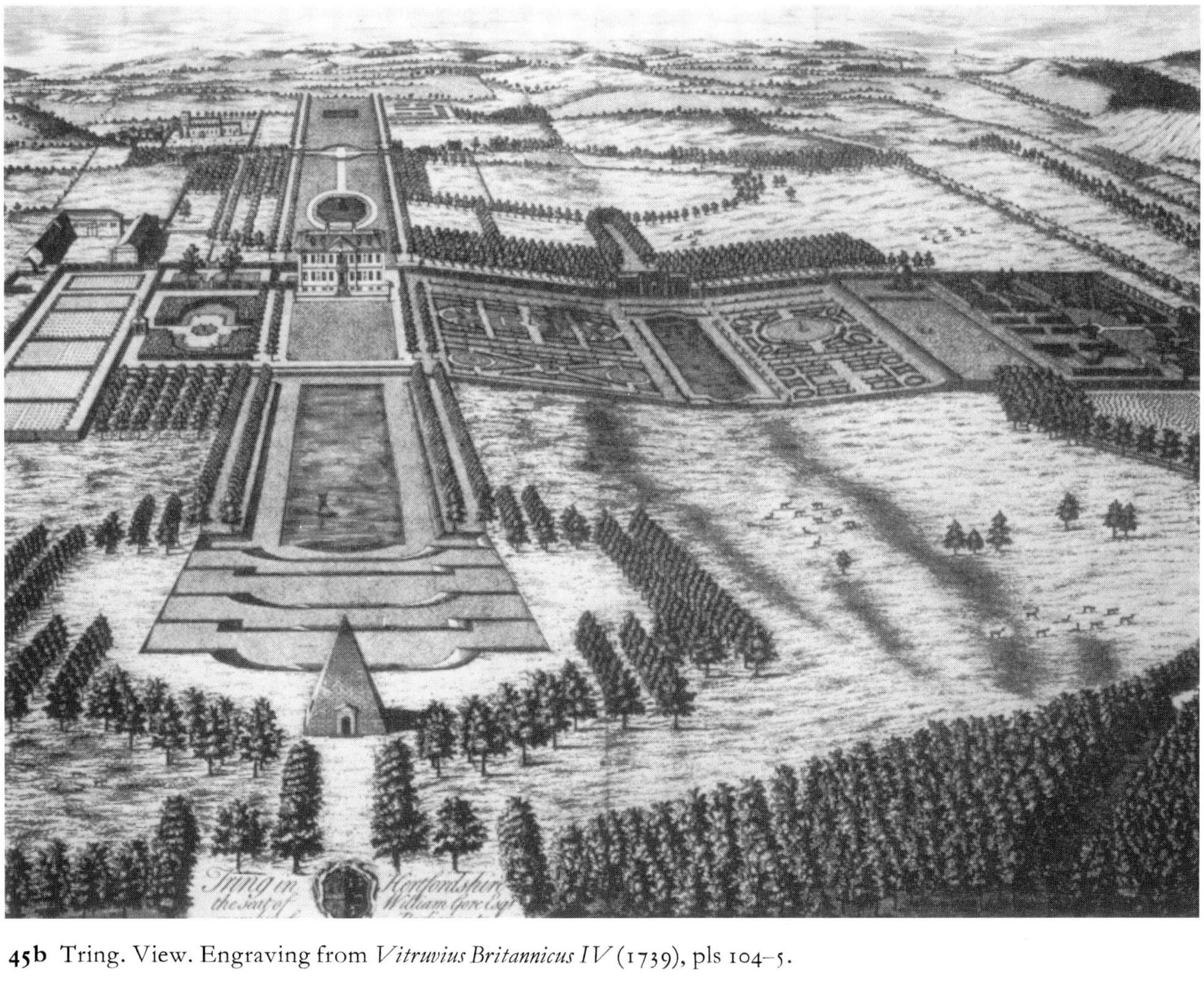

45b Tring. View. Engraving from *Vitruvius Britannicus IV* (1739), pls 104–5.

46a Sacombe. Garden or Entrance Front. Engraving from Gibbs, *A Book of Architecture* (1728), pl.53.

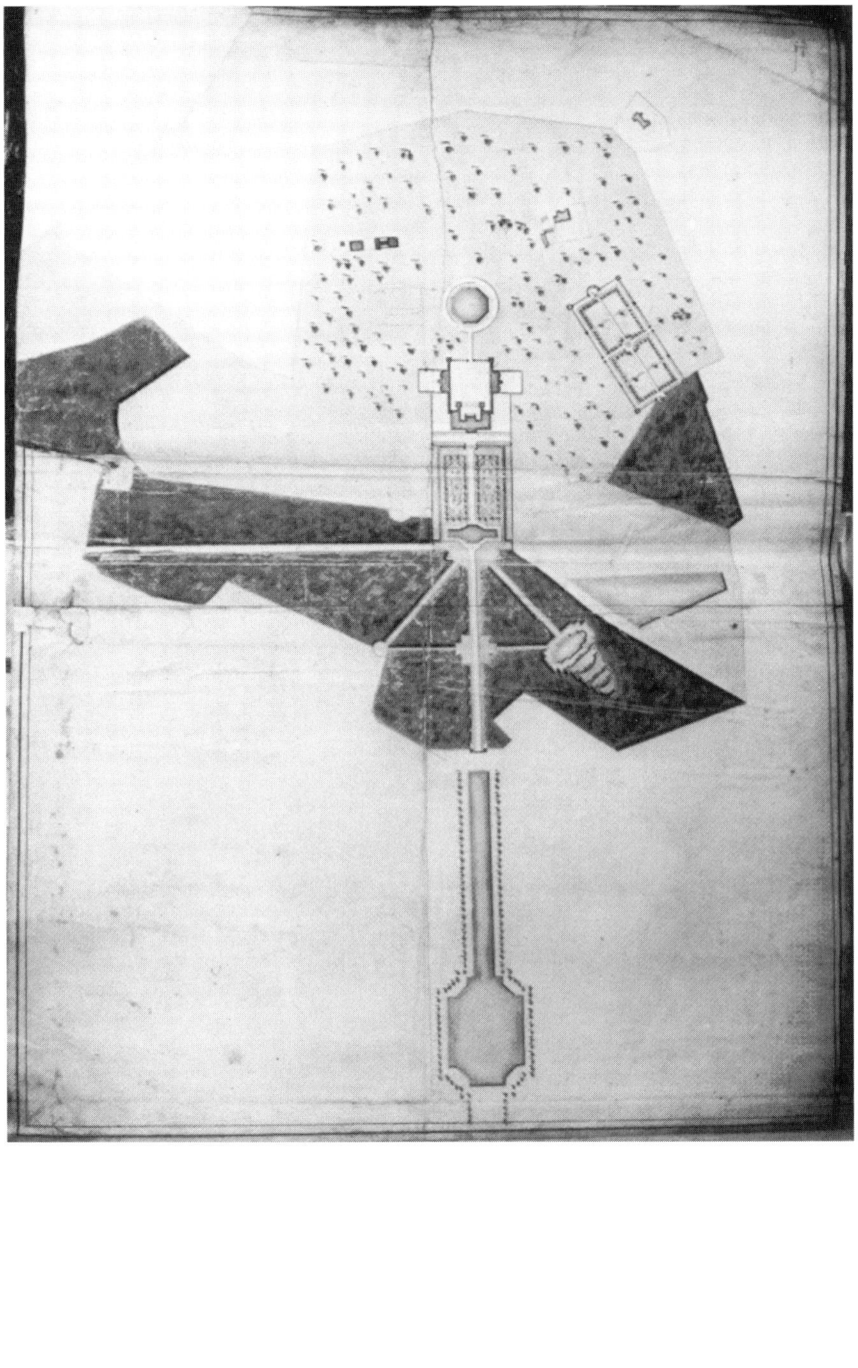

46b Sacombe. Plan. Drawing by Bridgeman (attrib.). MSGD a4 fo.64.

47a Purley. View of Flint Temple.

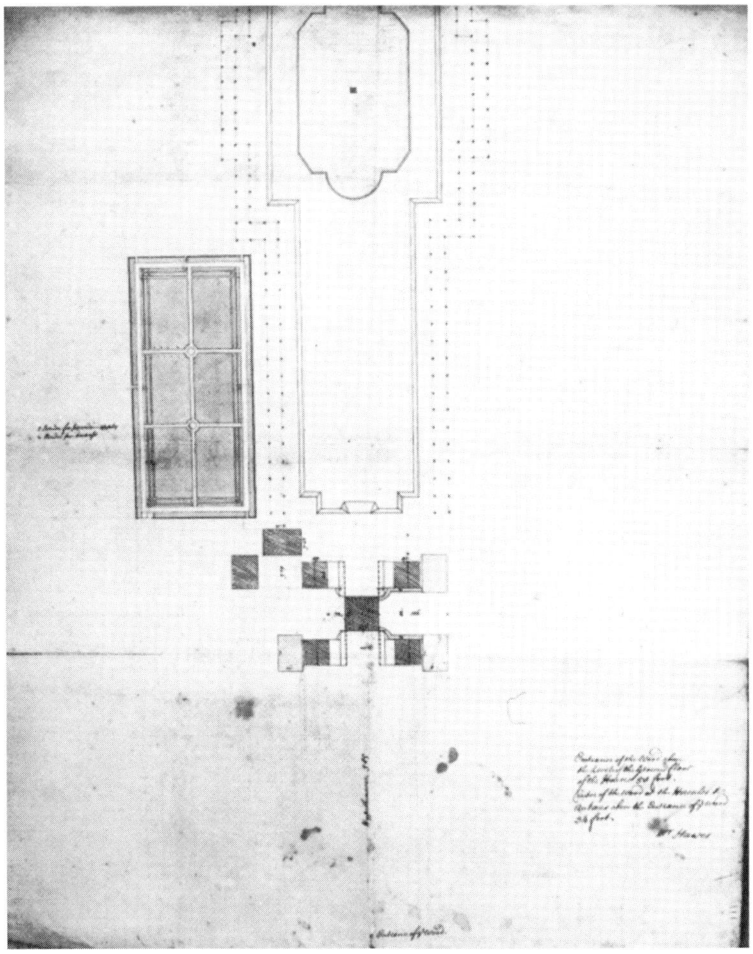

47b Purley. Plan. Drawing by Bridgeman (attrib.). MSGD a4 fo.54.

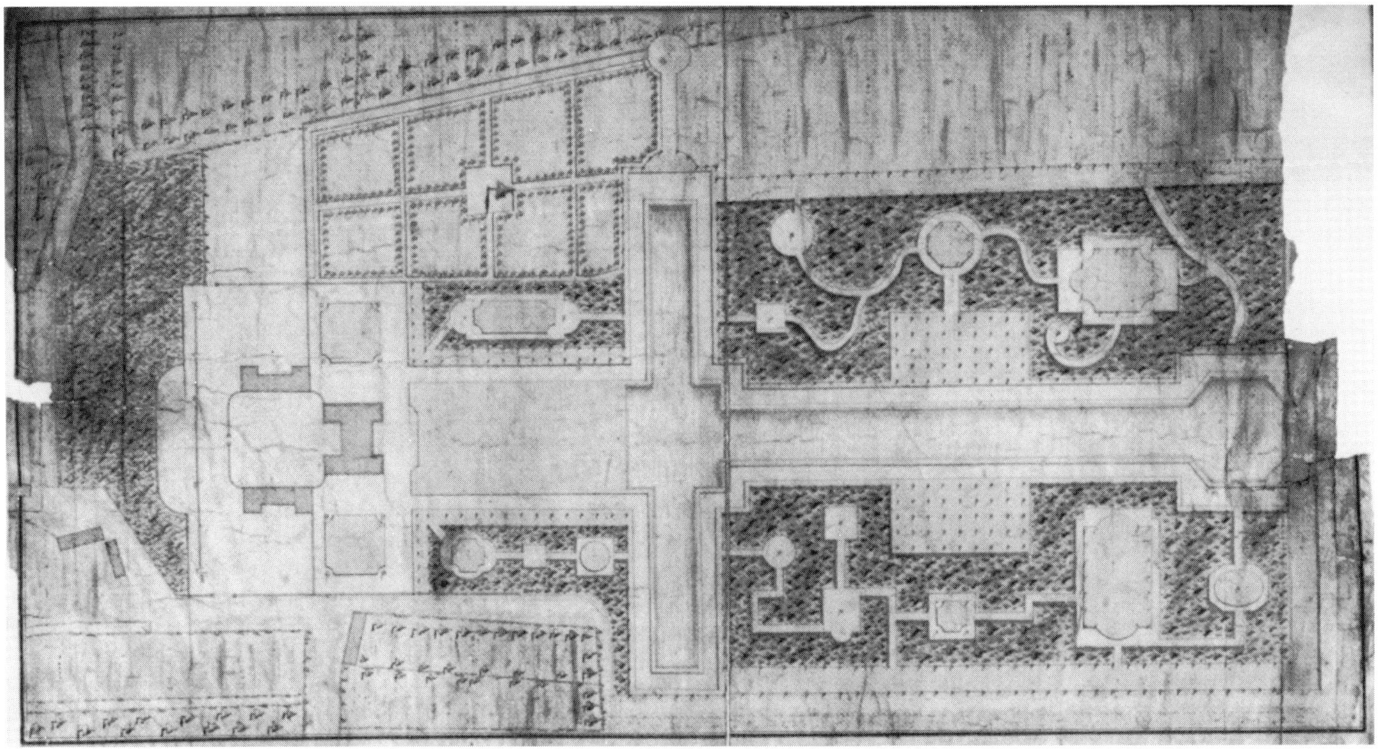

48a Scampston. Plan. Drawing by Bridgeman (attrib.). MSGD a4 fo.73.

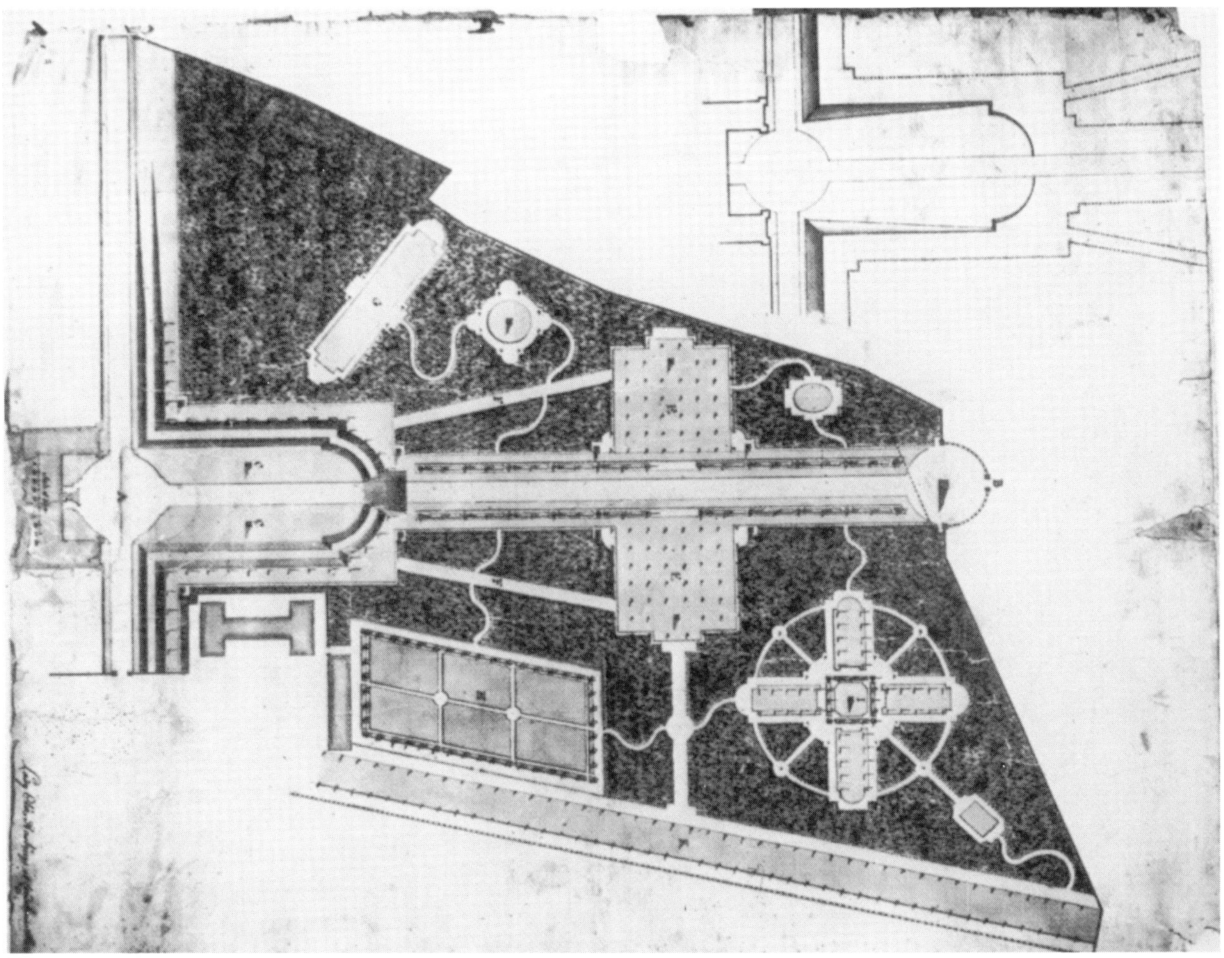

48b Ledston. Plan. Drawing by Bridgeman (attrib.). Otterden Place, Kent.

49 Westbury. View of early 18th-century House. Anonymous water-colour 1834. Firle Place, Sussex.

50a Carshalton House. View of South Front with Lake, Grotto and Water Pavilion. Engraving from Watts, *Seats of the Nobility and Gentry* (1783).

50b Carshalton House. View of South Front with Lake and Water Pavilion.

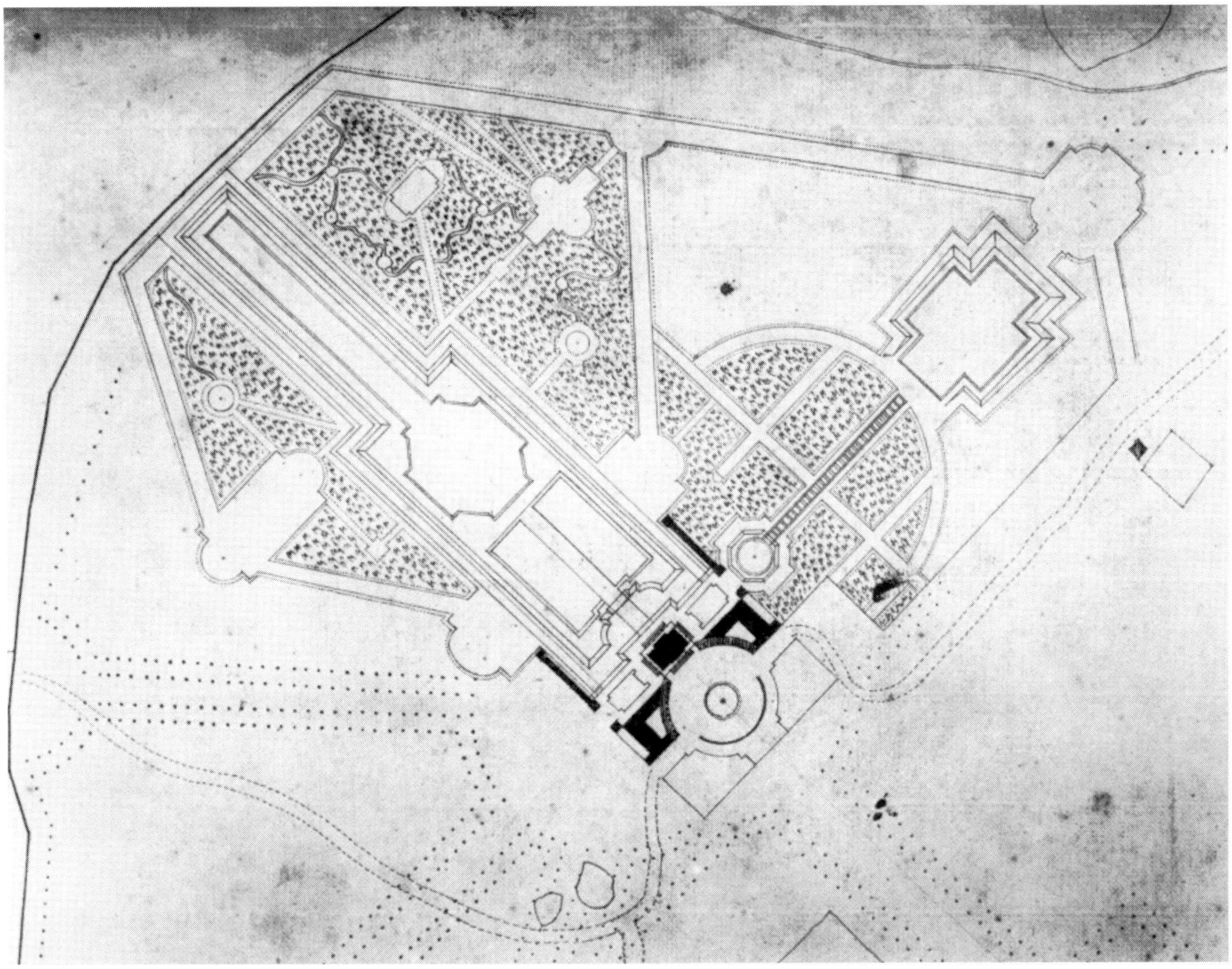

51a Moor Park. Plan. Drawing by Bridgeman (attrib.). MSGD a4 fo.58.

51b Langleys. View of West (Entrance) Front. Engraving from Muilman, *A New and Complete History of Essex* (1770–72), I, pl. facing p.325.

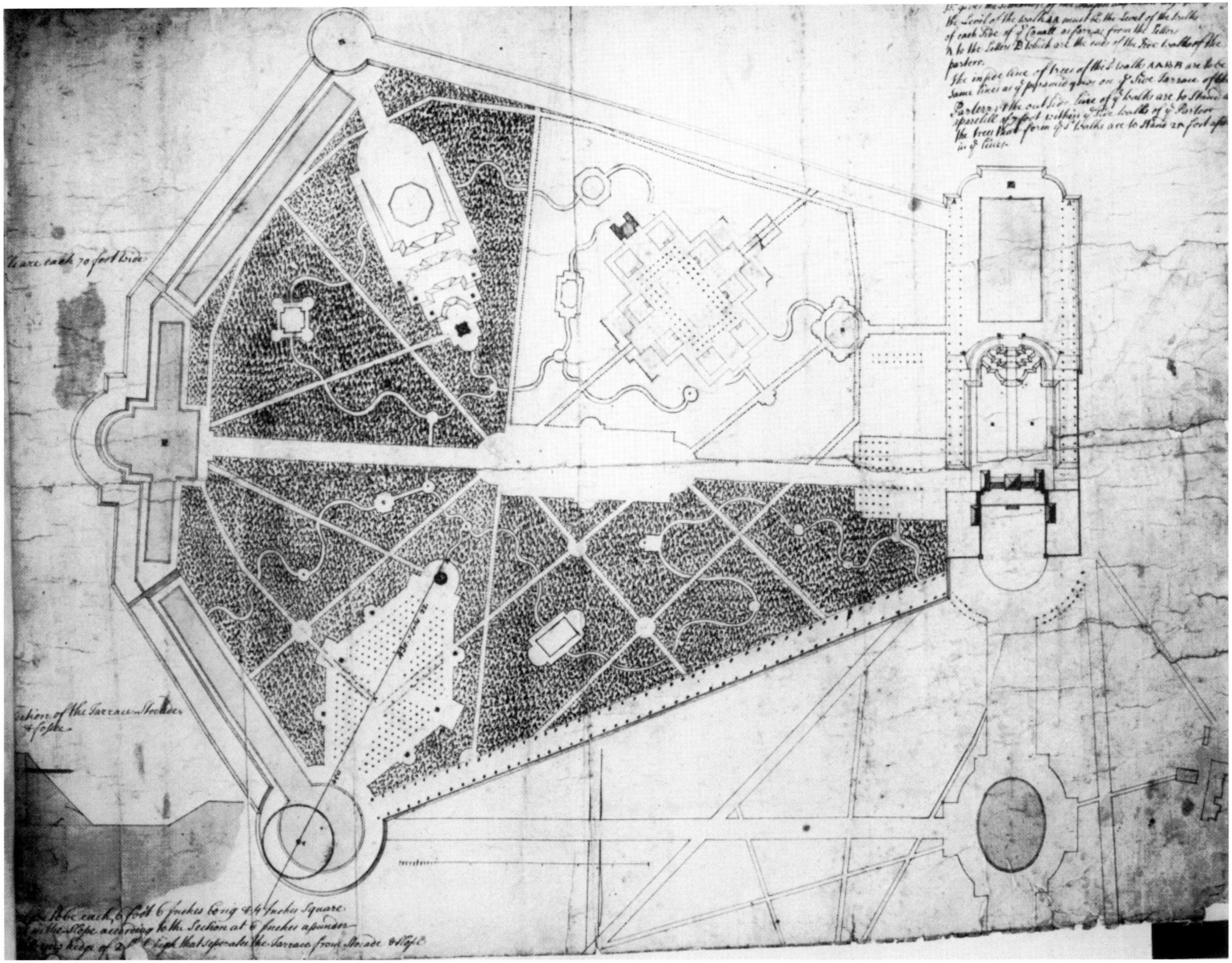

52 Farley. Plan. Drawing by Bridgeman (attrib.). MSGD a4 fo.34.

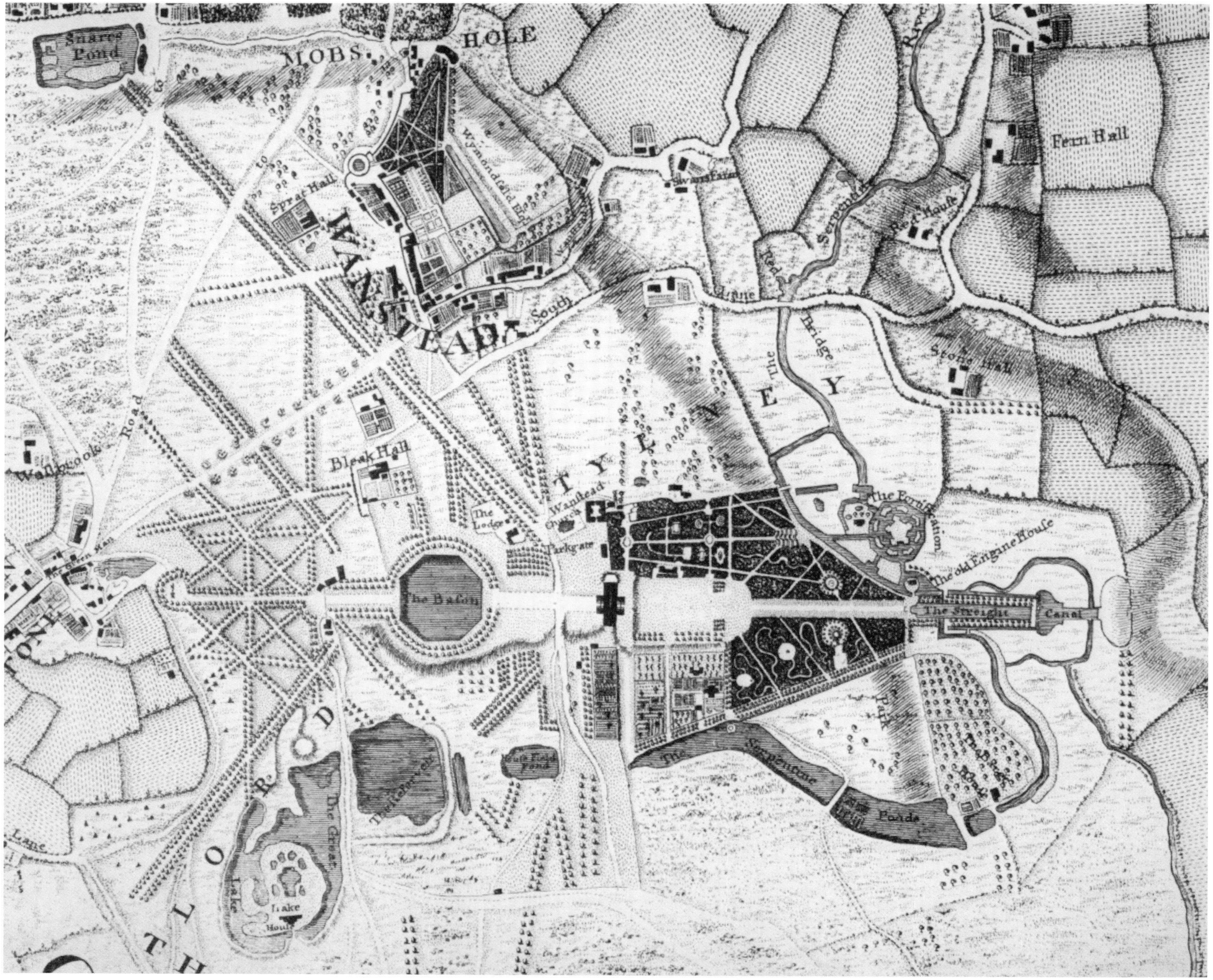

53 Wanstead. Plan. Detail from Rocque, *An Exact Survey of the City's of London, Westminster . . . and the Country Near Ten Miles Round* (1746).

54a Castle Hill. View from south. Anonymous painting *c.* 1730

54b Castle Hill. View from south.

55a Stanmer. View of East (Entrance) Front.

55b William Kent, by Benedetto Luti. Devonshire Collection, Chatsworth.

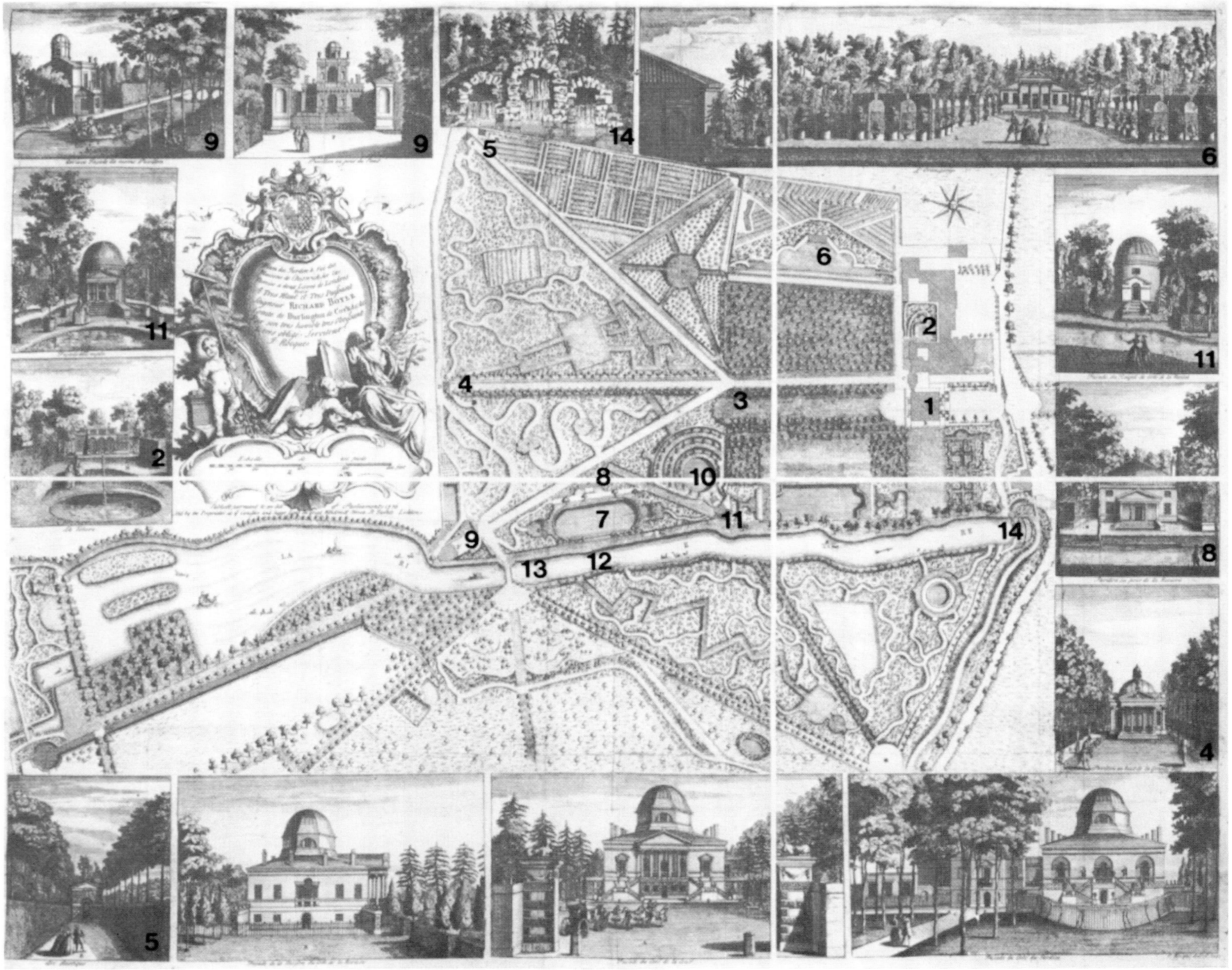

56 Chiswick. Plan. Engraving by Rocque 1736 from *Vitruvius Britannicus IV* (1739), pls 82–83.

KEY: **1** House; **2** Aviary; **3** Exedra; **4** Pavilion; **5** Rustic Arch; **6** Orangery; **7** Oval Pond; **8** River Pavilion; **9** Bagnio; **10** Round Pond; **11** Ionic Temple; **12** Serpentine River; **13** Stone Bridge; **14** Cascade

57a Chiswick. View of Serpentine River, Oval Pond, River Pavilion and Stone Bridge. Drawing by Rigaud 1733–34. Devonshire Collection, Chatsworth.

57b Chiswick. View from west across Serpentine River.

58a Chiswick. View of Exedra. Drawing by Kent. Devonshire Collection, Chatsworth.

58b Chiswick. View of Exedra.

59a Rousham. View of Amphitheatre from banks of River Cherwell.

59b Rousham. View of River Cherwell from Amphitheatre.

60 Rousham. View from Kitchen Garden eastwards to Bowling Green and slope down to River Cherwell.

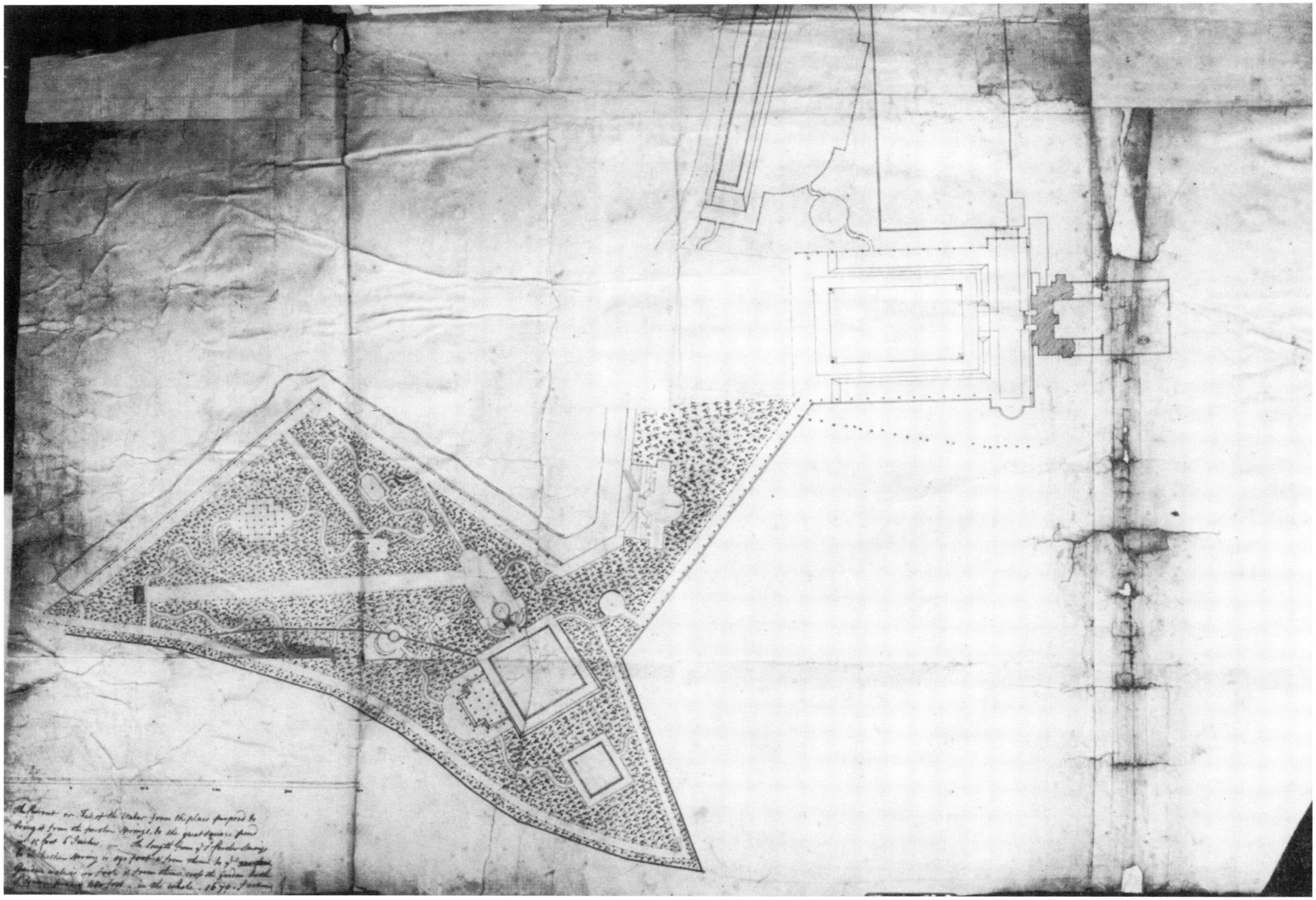

61 Rousham. Plan. Drawing by Bridgeman (attrib.). MSGD a4 fo.63. North is approximately to the left.

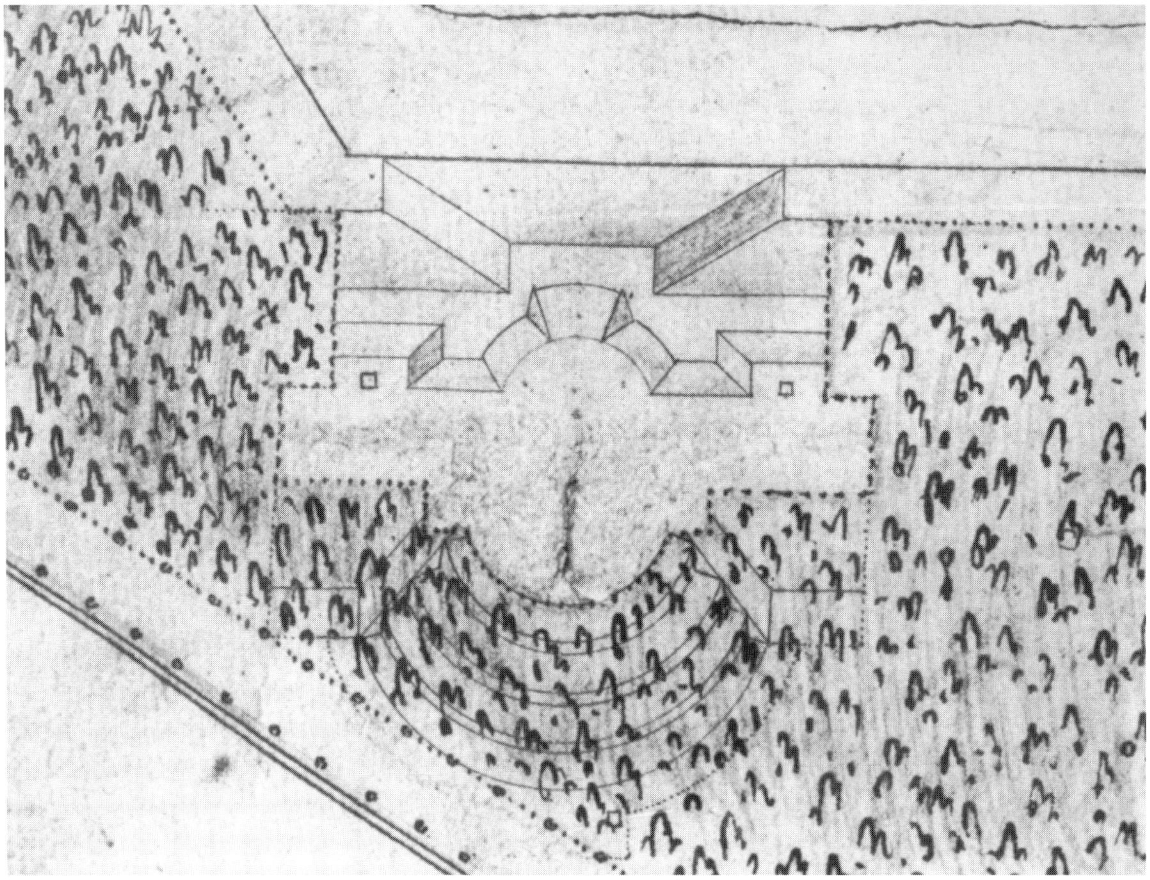

62a Rousham. Plan. Detail of Amphitheatre from *Plate 61*.

62b Rousham. Venus's Vale. Drawing by Kent. Devonshire Collection, Chatsworth.

63a Sir James Thornhill, by Jonathan Richardson. National Portrait Gallery, London.

63b John Wootton. Self-portrait. Private Collection.

64a *Arsinoë, Queen of Cyprus*. Sketch for scenery by Thornhill *c.*1704. V&A, D.26–1891.

64b *Lakeside Scene, with Figures, Temple and Ruined Bridge*. Sketch by Thornhill. V&A, Dyce 622.

65a *Harbour Scene,* by Wootton 1755. Boughton.

65b *Classical Landscape,* by Wootton *c.*1730. Whitworth Art Gallery, University of Manchester.

66a Down. Entrance Front. Engraving from Gibbs, *A Book of Architecture* (1728), pl.55.

66b James Gibbs, by John Michael Williams. National Portrait Gallery, London.

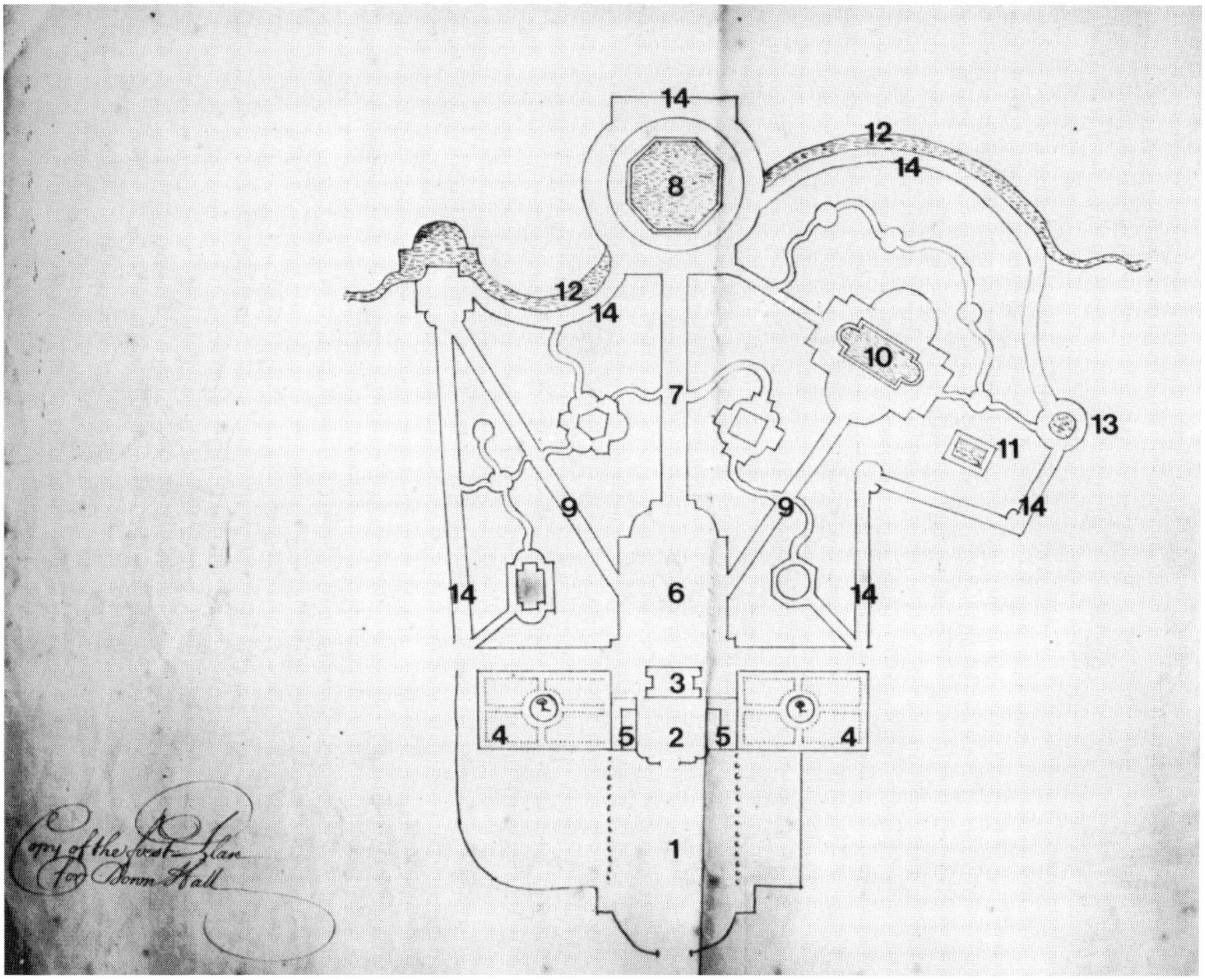

67 Down. Plan. Drawing by Bridgeman (attrib.). BL, Loan 29/357 (Portland Papers), set 2.

*KEY: 1 Parade; 2 Court; 3 Proposed New House; 4 Kitchen Garden; 5 Offices; 6 Lawn; 7 Great Walk; 8 Great Basin; 9 Diagonal Walk; 10 Large Basin and Lawn for Water Fowl; 11 Stew Pond; 12 Brook; 13 Fine Spring; 14 Terrace Walk

*Based on legend to Down plan in Bod. Lib., MS Gough Maps 46 fo.262

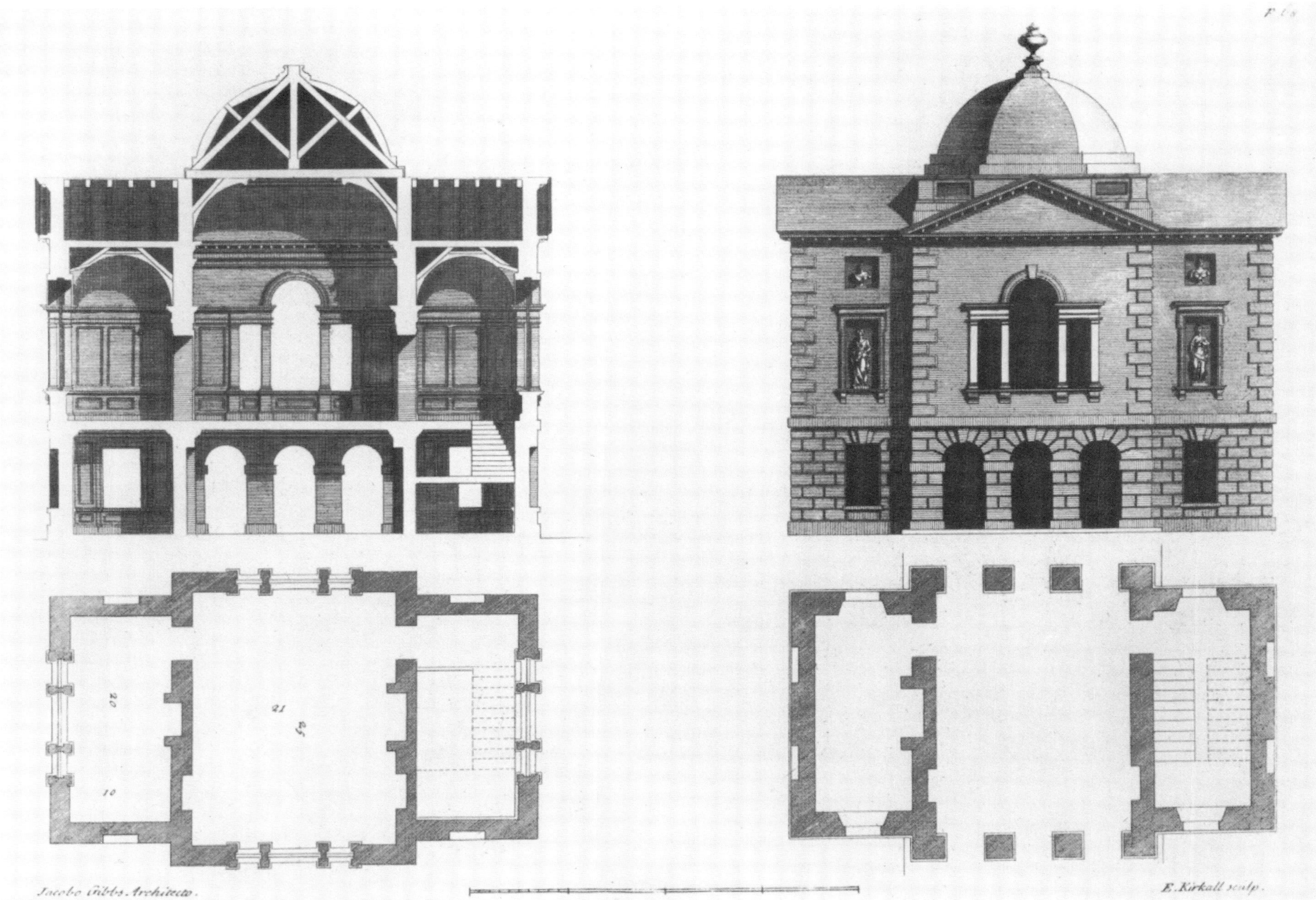

68 Down. Temple for Bowling Green. Engraving from Gibbs, *A Book of Architecture* (1728), pl.68.

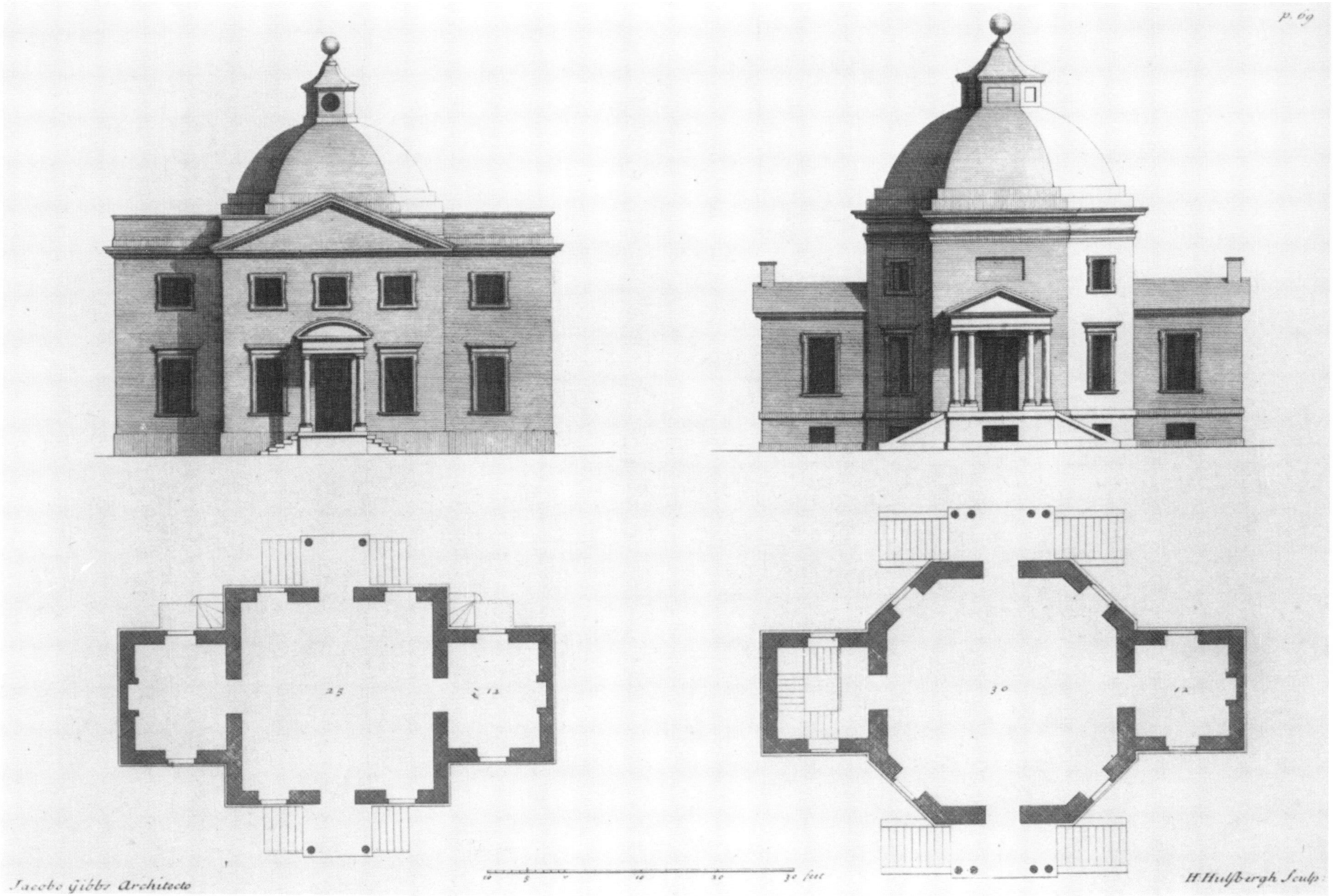

69 Down. Two Pavilions for Bowling Green. Engraving from Gibbs, *A Book of Architecture* (1728), pl.69.

70 Thameside area round Twickenham and Richmond. Plan. Detail from Rocque, *An Exact Survey of the City's of London, Westminster . . . and the Country Near Ten Miles Round* (1746).

KEY: **1** Pope's Villa; **2** Marble Hill; **3** Sudbrooke, Petersham; **4** Ham House; **5** Twickenham Park; **6** Syon House; **7** Richmond Lodge and Gardens (George II and Caroline); **8** Kew House, or the White House (Prince Frederick and Princess Augusta); **9** Richmond Park; **10** Queen's Private Road to Richmond Park

71 Marble Hill. View of South Front from the Thames. Engraving by Heckell and Mason 1749.

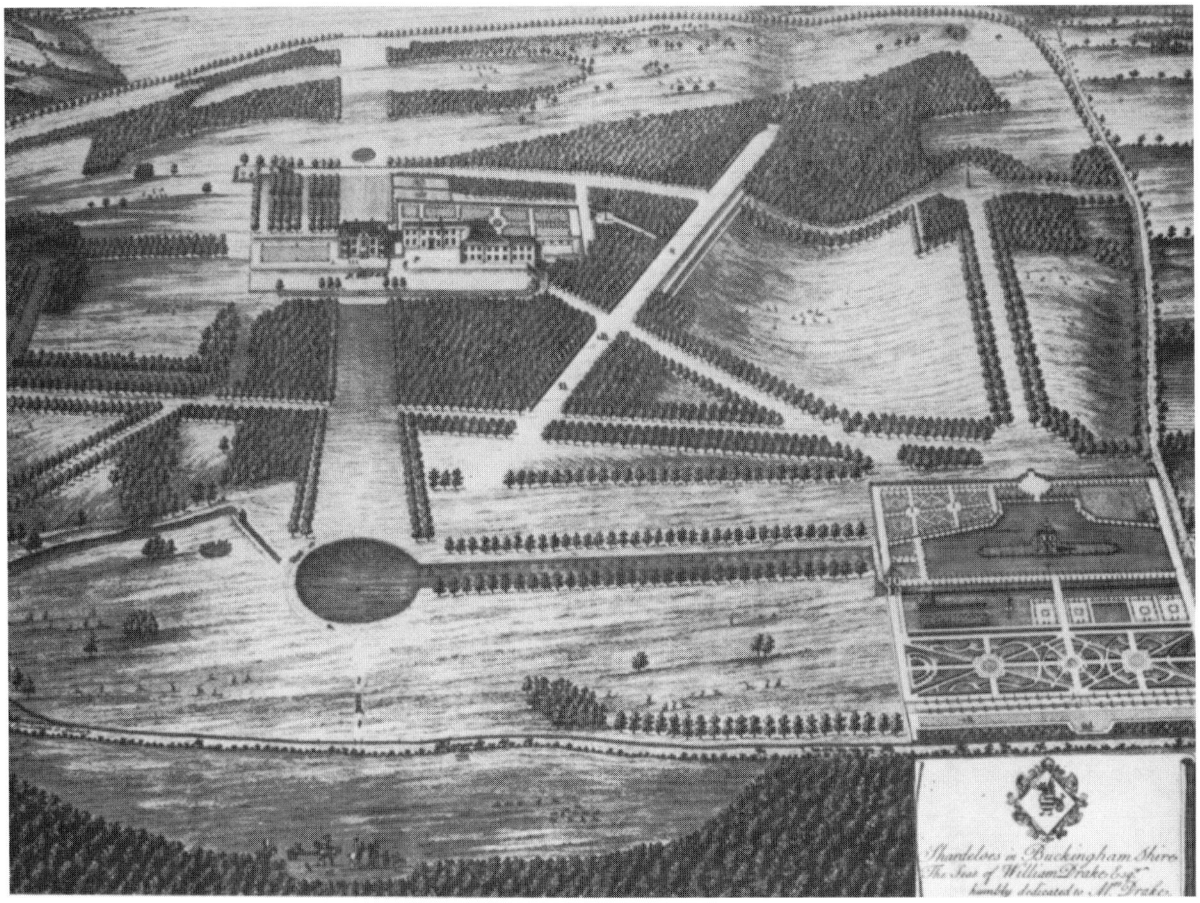

72a Shardeloes. View. Engraving from *Vitruvius Britannicus IV* (1739), pls 100–1.

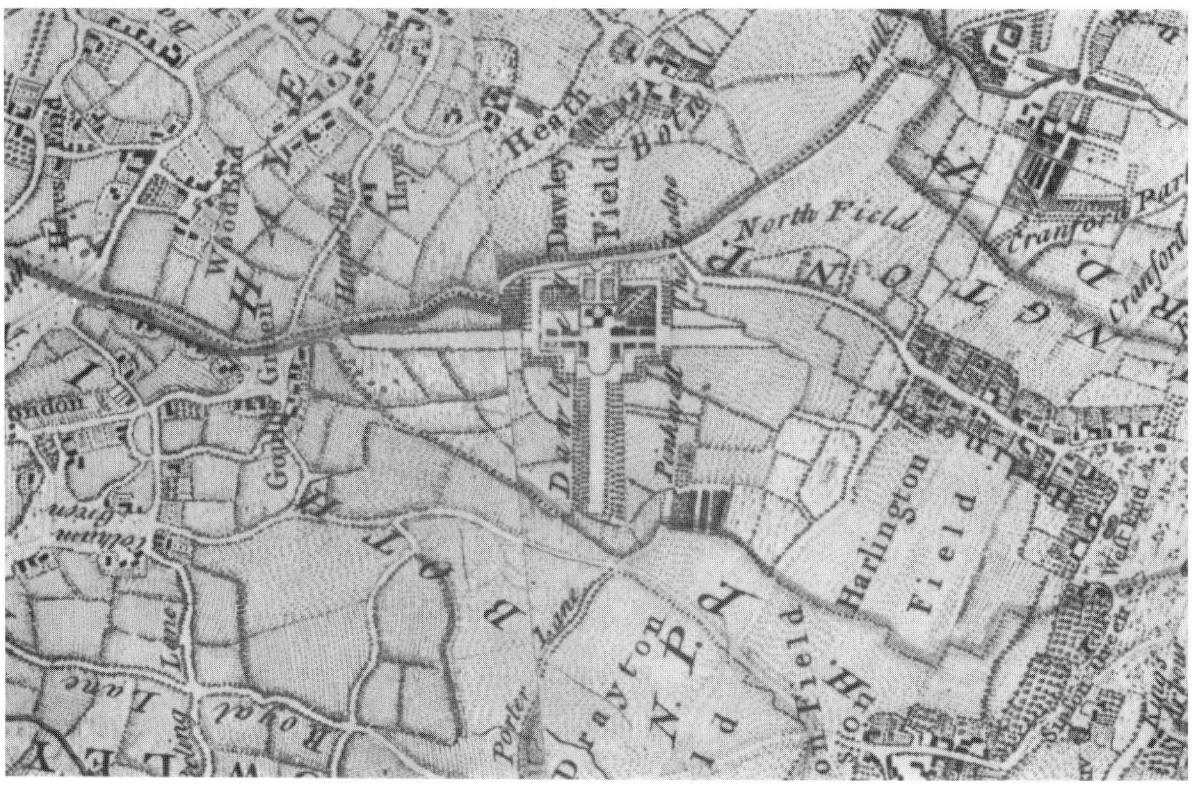

72b Dawley. Plan. Detail from Rocque, *Carte topographique de la comté de Middlesex* (1754).

73a Wimpole. View from south.

73b Wimpole. Main Avenue from Entrance to House.

74 Wimpole. Aerial view southwards down Main Avenue.

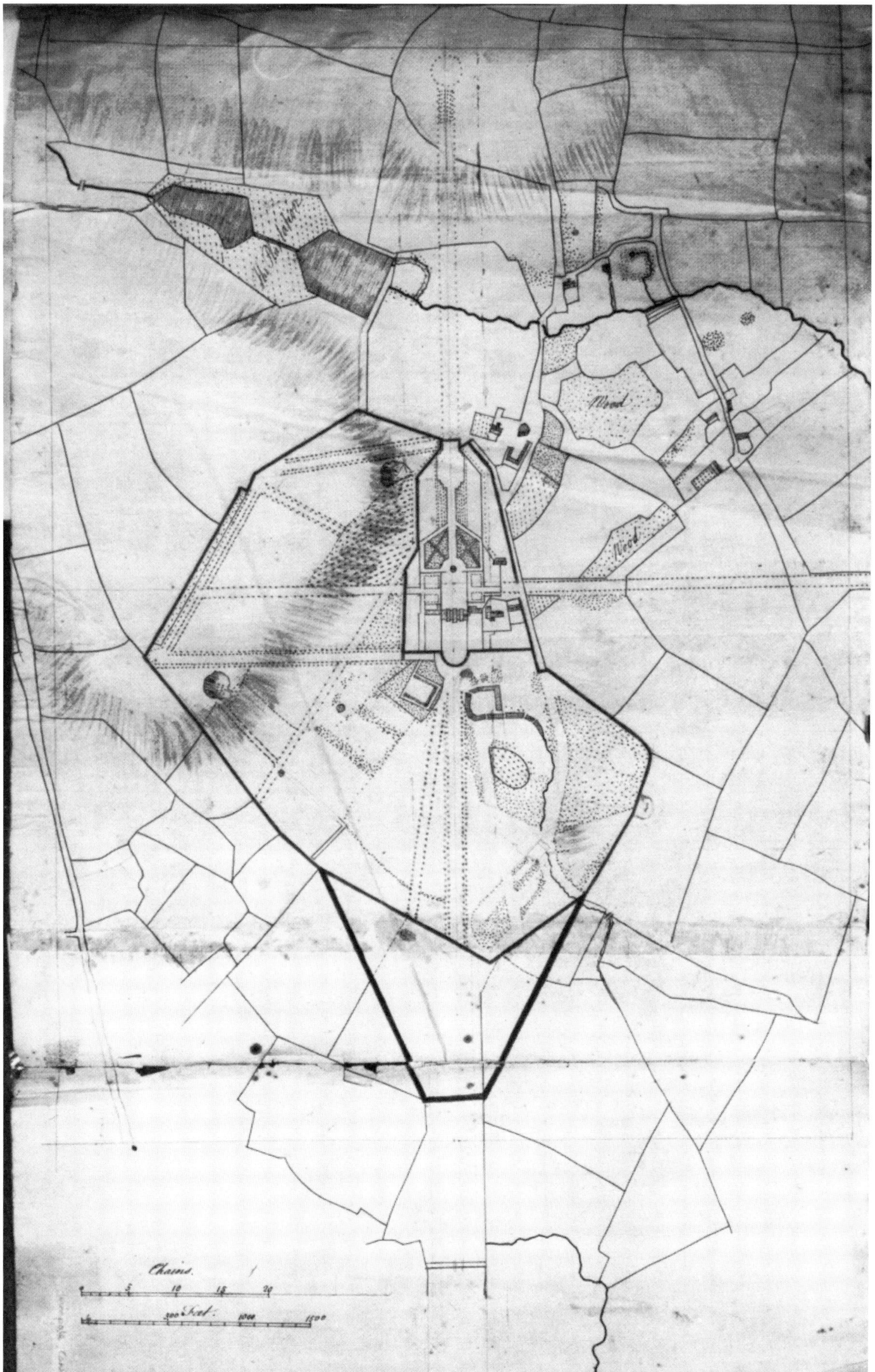

75 Wimpole. Plan. Drawing by Bridgeman (attrib.). MSGD a4 fo.69.

76 Pope's Villa, Twickenham. View from Thames. Engraving by Heckell and Mason 1749.

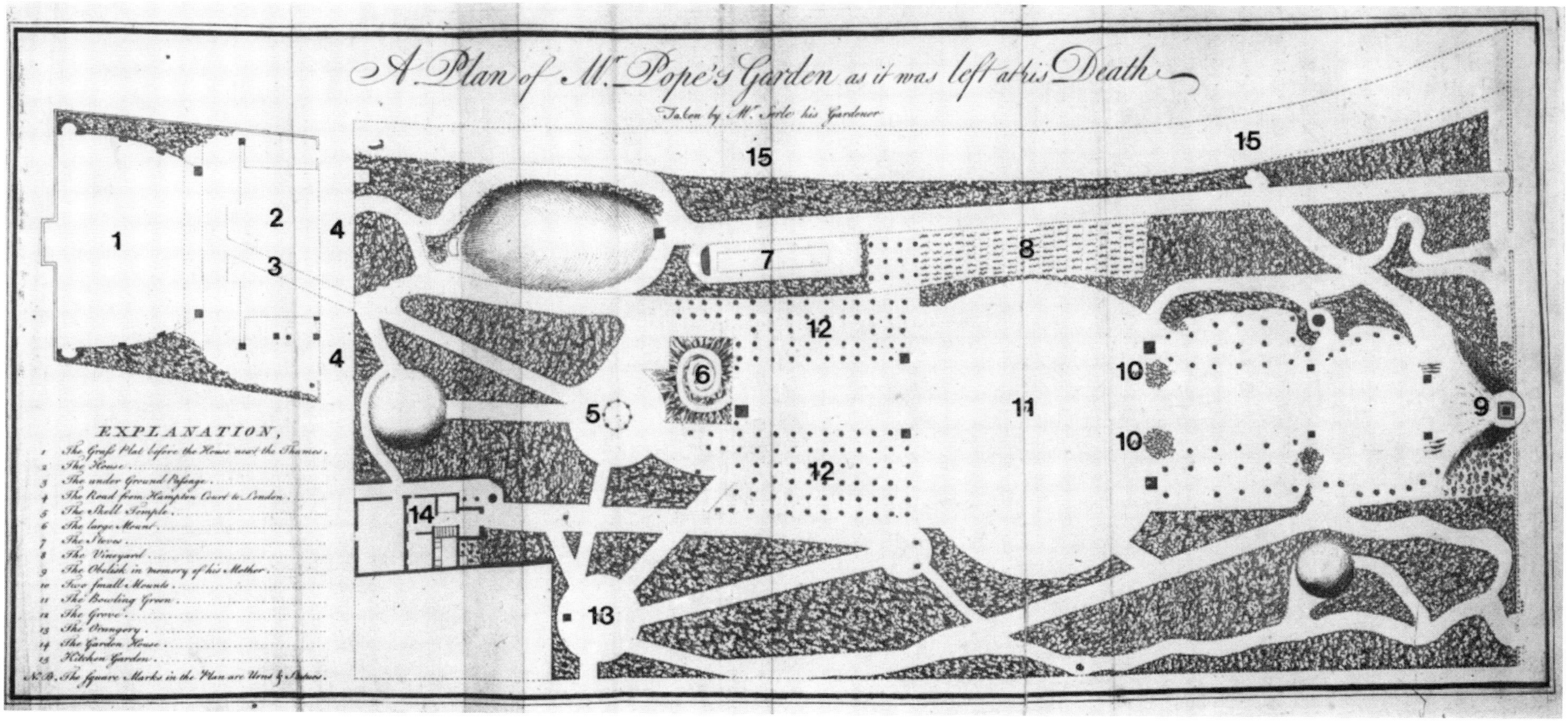

77 Pope's Villa, Twickenham. Engraving pub. John Serle of *A Plan of Mr Pope's Garden as it was Left at His Death* (1745).

*KEY: **1** Grass Plot between House and River Thames; **2** House; **3** Grotto and Underground Passage; **4** Road from Hampton Court to London; **5** Shell Temple; **6** Large Mount; **7** Stoves (i.e. Hothouses); **8** Vineyard; **9** Obelisk in memory of Pope's Mother; **10** Two Small Mounts; **11** Bowling Green; **12** Grove; **13** Orangery; **14** Garden House; **15** Kitchen Garden

Square marks indicate urns and statues

*Based on the inscription on the plan itself

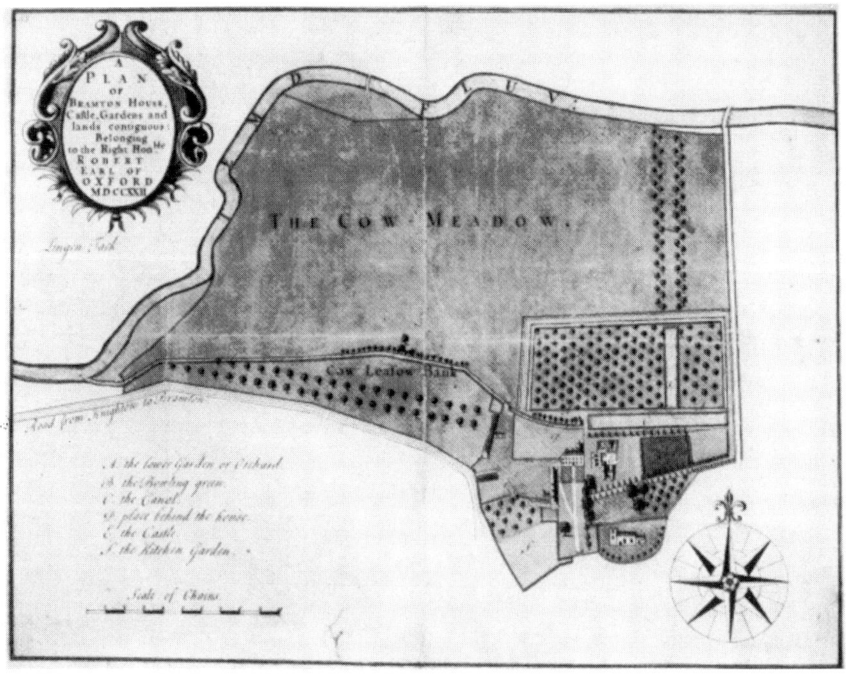

78a Brampton Bryan. Plan. Drawing by Bridgeman (attrib.). Soane, Box of Misc. Drawings (Wren, etc.).

78b Edward Harley, 2nd Earl of Oxford. Artist unknown. National Portrait Gallery, London.

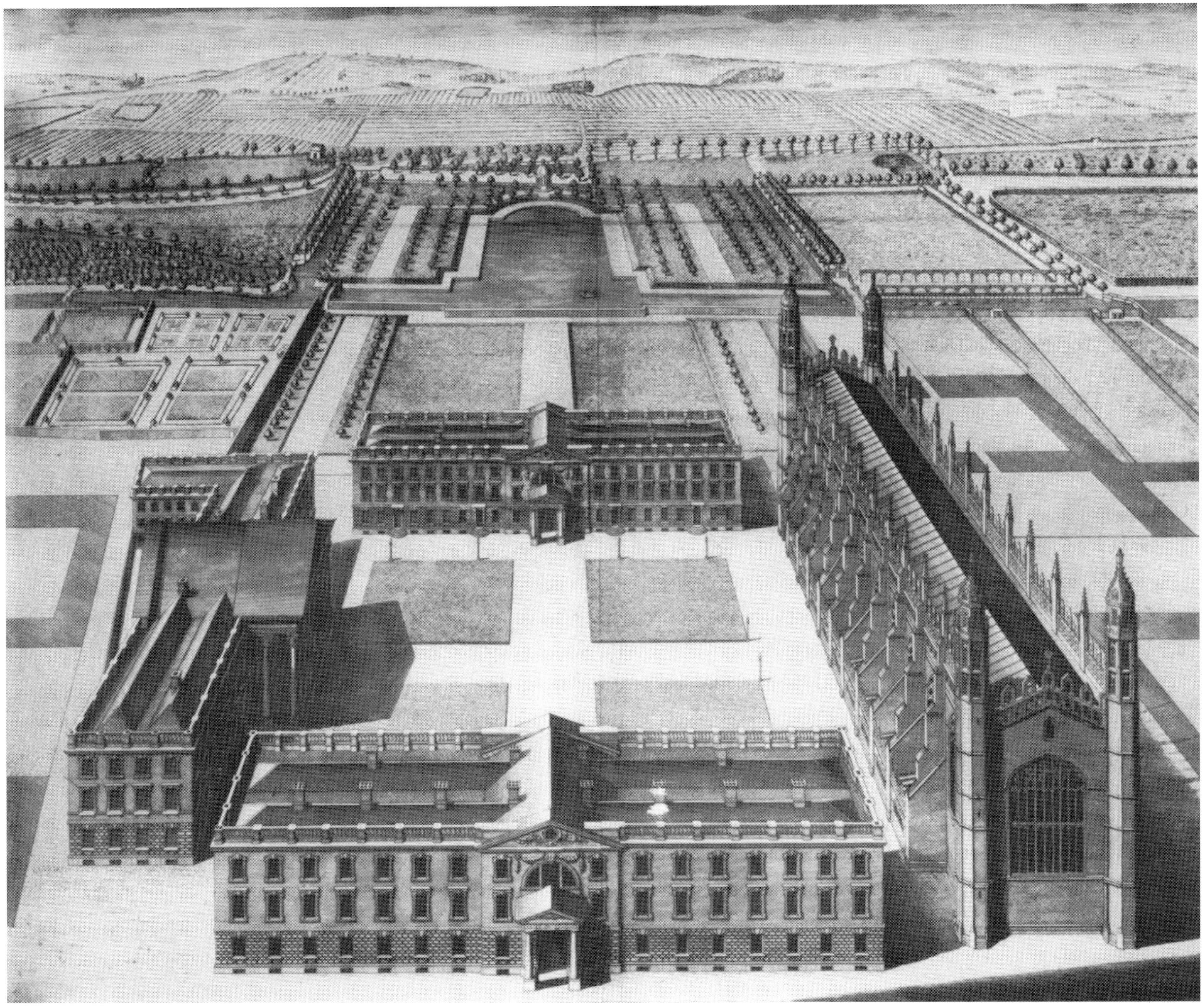

79 King's College, Cambridge. Aerial view. Engraving by James Essex *c*.1744.

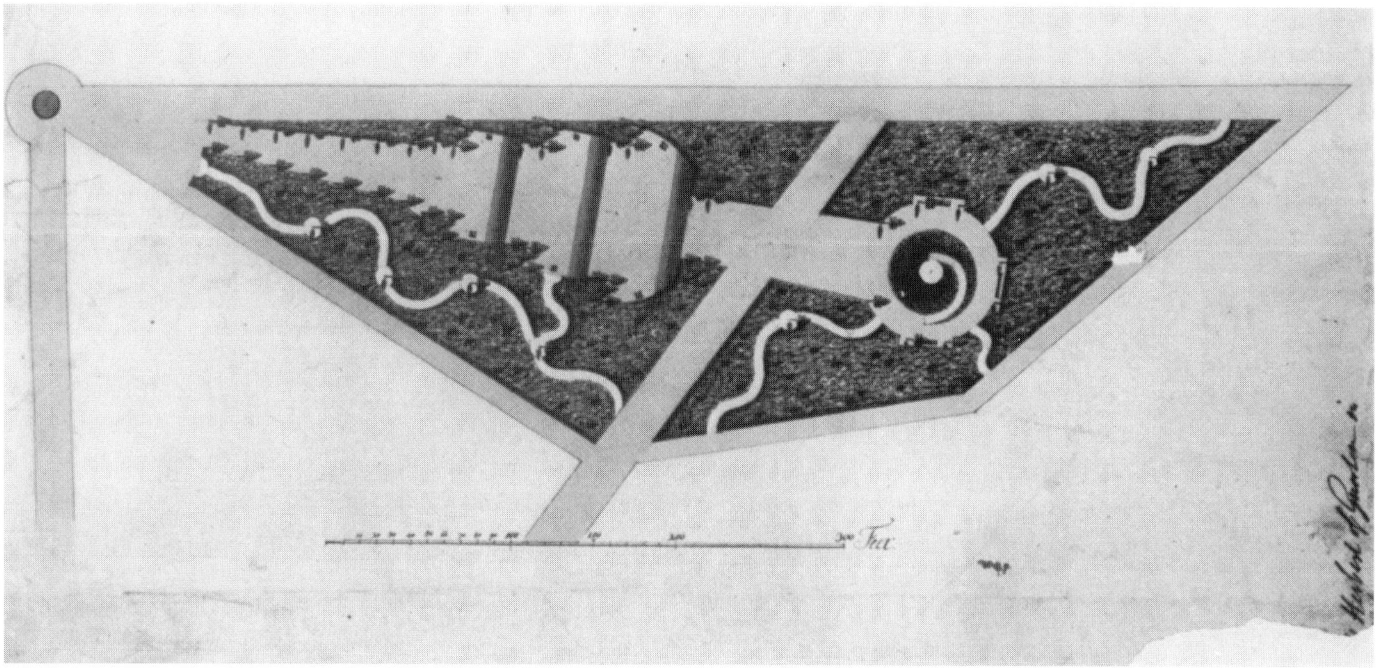

80a Gunton. Plan of Mount. Drawing by Bridgeman (attrib.). MSGD a4 fo.75.

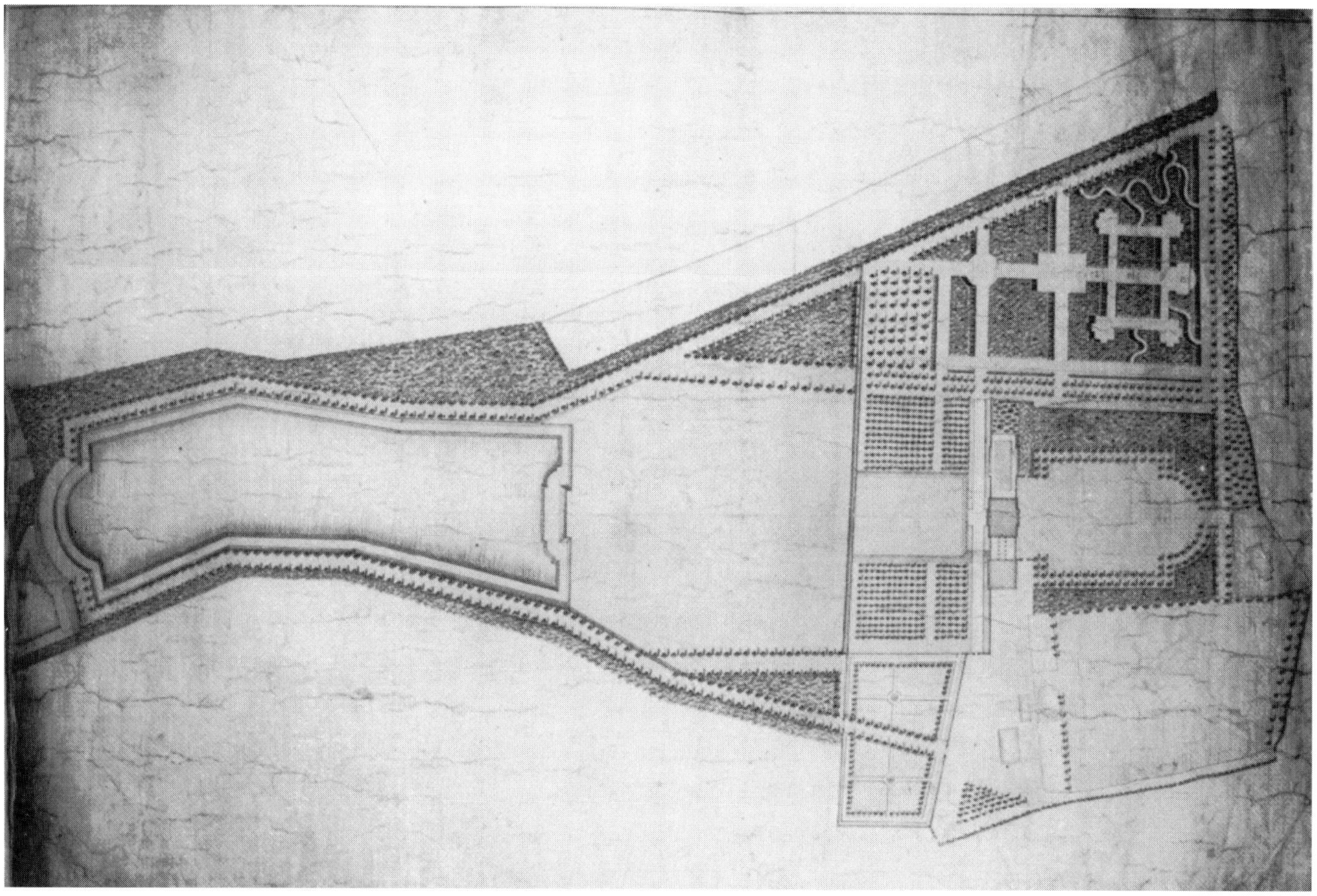

80b Wolterton. Plan. Drawing by Bridgeman (attrib.). MSGD a4 fo.20.

81a Houghton. View of South Front. Drawing by Edmund Prideaux *c.*1730.

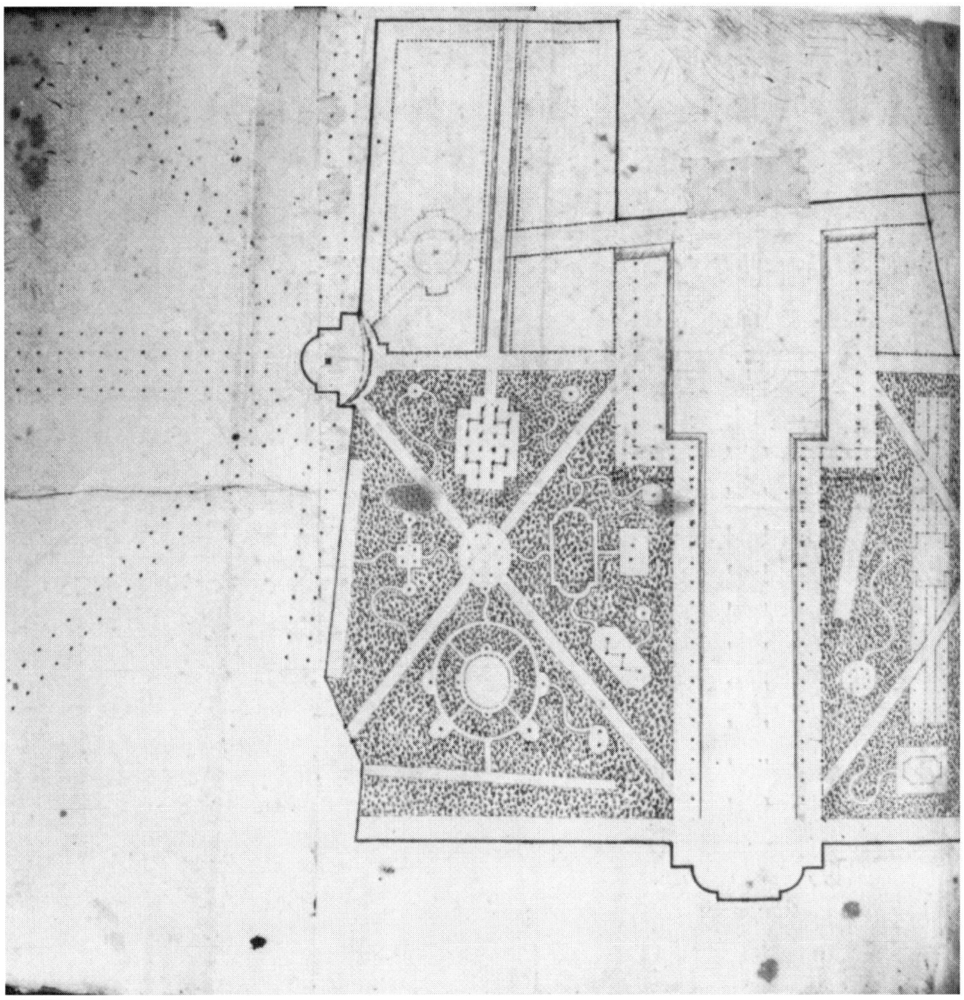

81b Houghton. Plan. Drawing by Bridgeman (attrib.). MSGD a4 fo.57.

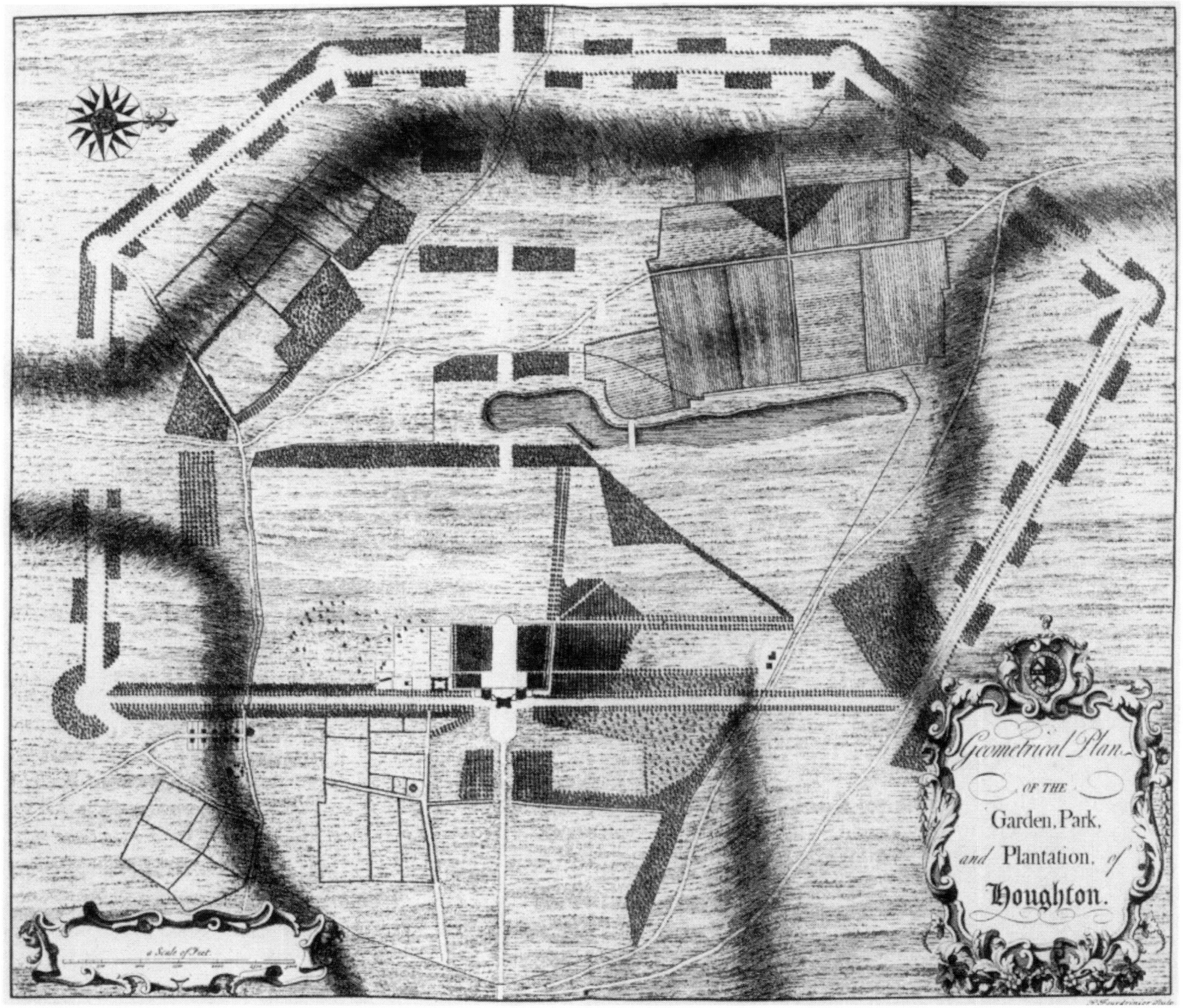

82 Houghton. Plan. Engraving from Ware, *Plans, Elevations, and Sections . . . of Houghton in Norfolk* (1735).

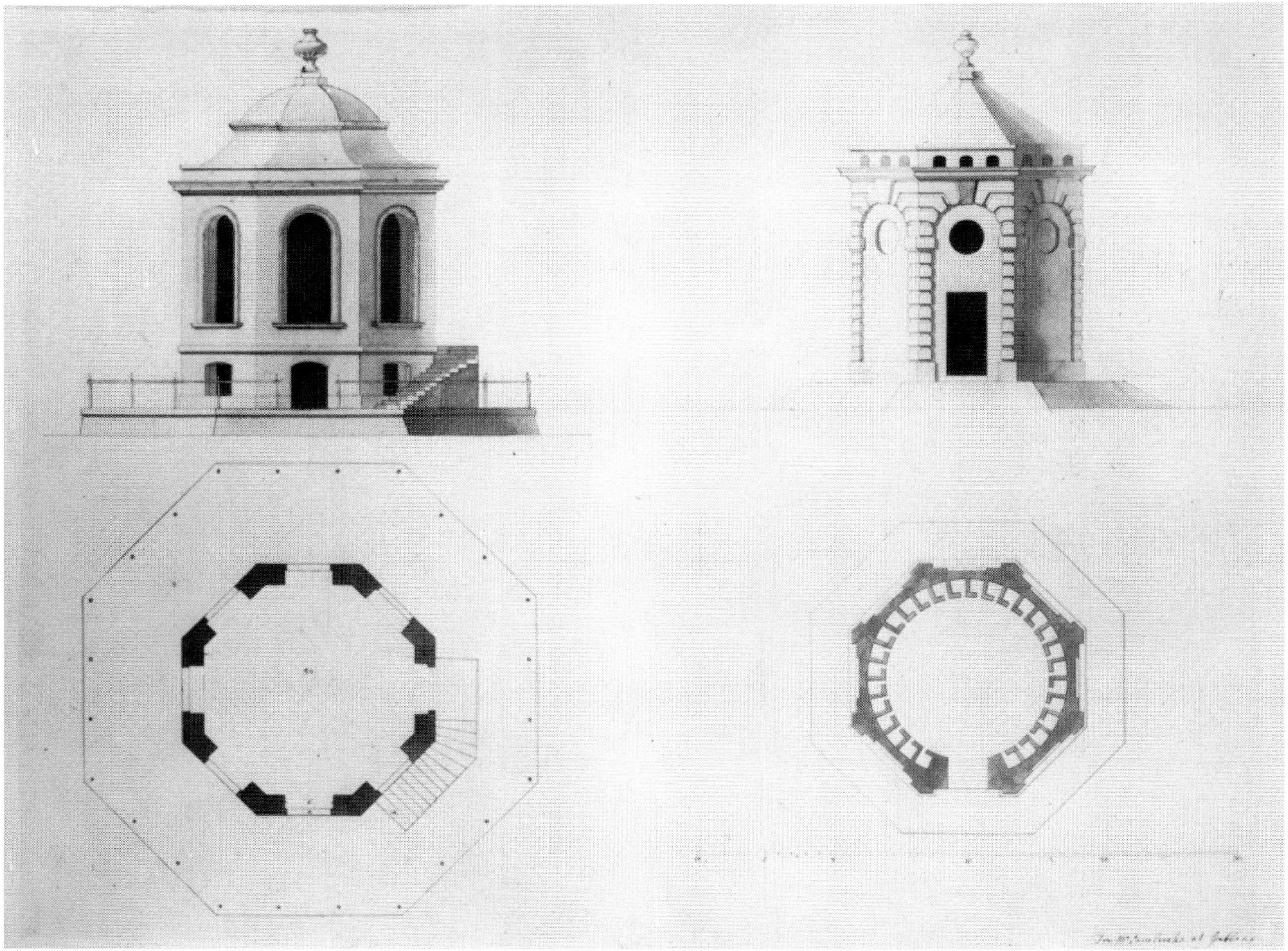

83 Gubbins. Temple and Dovecote. Drawings by Gibbs. Ashmolean Museum, Oxford, Gibbs Collection, III, fos 87a, 87b.

84 Gubbins. View of Bowling Green. Engraving by Chatelain and Tinney 1748.

85 Delville. Drawing by Mary Delany of 'A view of ye Swift & Swans Island in Delville Garden', 1745. National Gallery of Ireland, Dublin, 2722 (24).

86 Badminton. View of North Front. Drawing attributed to Wootton. Badminton.

87 *The Beaufort Hunt,* by Wootton. Badminton.

88a George II, marble bust by Rysbrack 1738. Windsor Castle.

88b Queen Caroline, marble bust by Rysbrack 1739. Wallace Collection, London.

89 Garden implements. Engraving from Liger, *Le nouveau théâtre d'agriculture et ménage des champs* (1723), pl. 7.

KEY: **8** Ladder; **10** Cart drawn by Oxen; **12** Cart for Dung; **15** Wheelbarrow; **18** Clod Breaker; **21** Hatchet; **22** Billhooks; **23** Sickle; **24** Scythe; **25** Pruning Hook; **28** Pickaxes; **29** Hoe; **35** Sieve; **38** Rake; **39** Spade; **45** Saw

90a West Wycombe. Scything and brushing. Detail of engraving by Woollett 1757.

90b Carlton House. Brushing and scything. Detail of engraving by Woollett 1760.

91a Stowe. Rolling the Grecian Valley. Detail of engraving from Bickham, pub., *Views of Stowe* (1753), pl.p.

91b Hall Barn. Rolling the lawns. Detail of engraving by Woollett 1760.

92a Moving trees in wooden tubs. Detail of engraving from Kleiner, *Vera et accurata delineatio omnium templorum et cœnobiorum* (1724 et seq.).

92b Clipping hedges. Detail of engraving from Kleiner, *Vera et accurata delineatio omnium templorum et cœnobiorum* (1724 et seq.).

93a Hampton Court. View of South Front. Engraving by Highmore and Tinney *c.*1745.

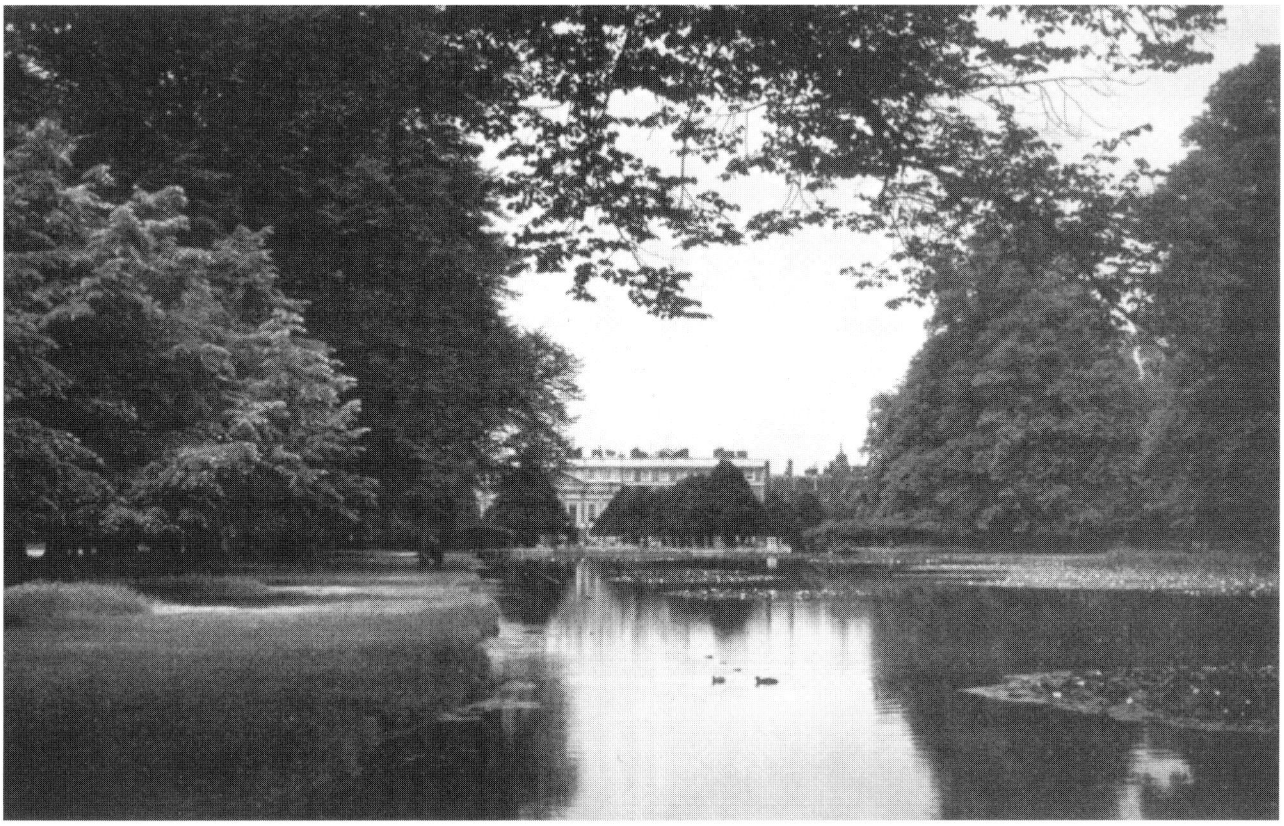

93b Hampton Court. View of East Front from Canal.

94 Hampton Court. Aerial view from north-west 1969.

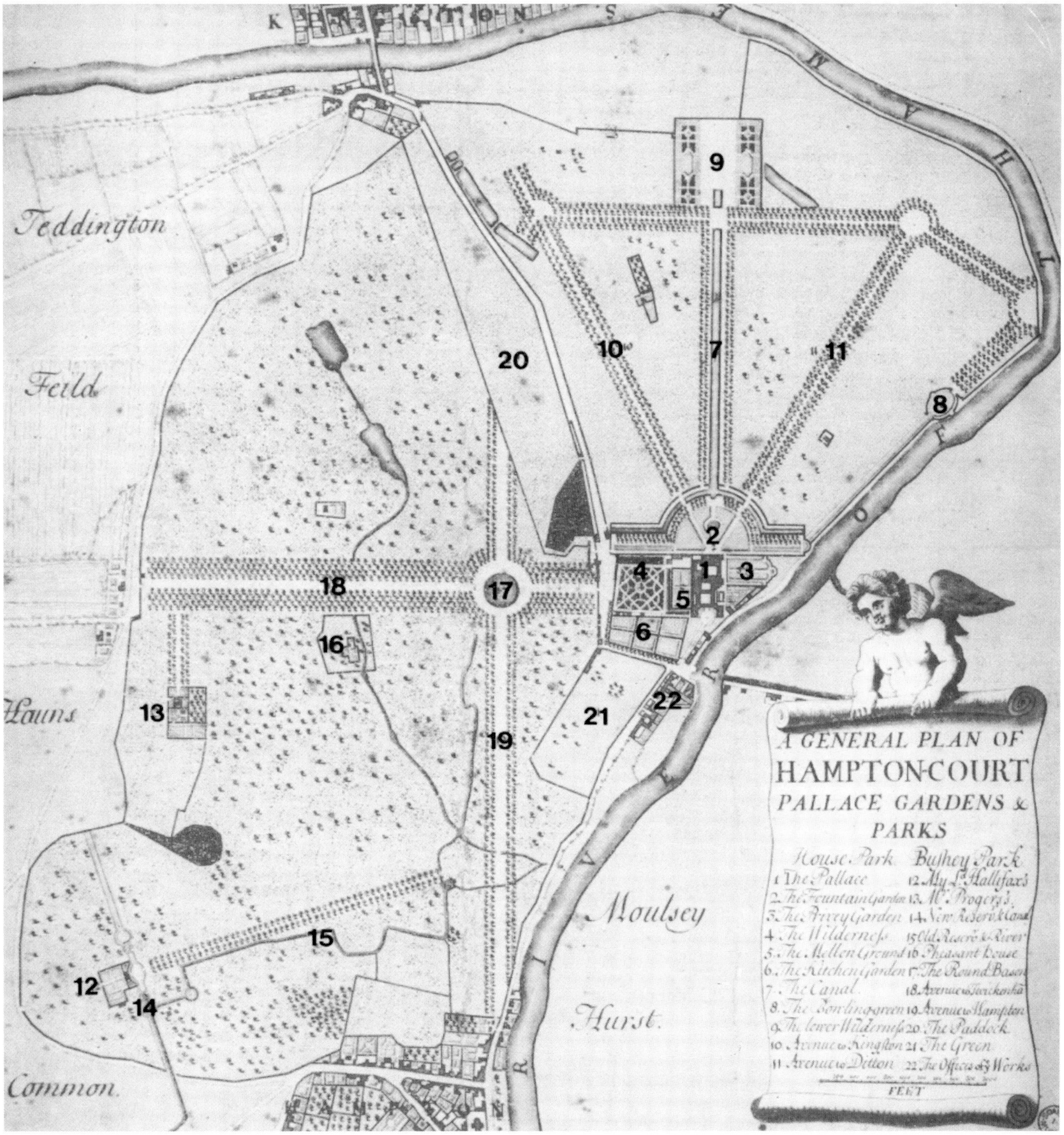

95 Hampton Court. Plan. Drawing by Bridgeman *c.*1735, signed 'C.BRIDGMAN FEC!'. Soane, Drawer 36.3.1.

*KEY: *House Park* **1** Palace; **2** Fountain Garden; **3** Privy Garden; **4** Wilderness; **5** Melon Ground; **6** Kitchen Garden; **7** Canal; **8** Bowling Green; **9** Lower Wilderness; **10** Avenue to Kingston; **11** Avenue to Ditton

Bushy Park **12** Lord Halifax's House; **13** Mr Progers's House; **14** New Reservoir and Canal; **15** Old Reservoir and River; **16** Pheasant House; **17** Round Basin; **18** Chestnut Avenue to Twickenham; **19** Avenue to Hampton; **20** Paddock; **21** Green; **22** Offices of the Works

*Based on the inscription on the plan itself

96a Kensington Gardens. View of Round Pond.

96b Kensington Gardens and Hyde Park. View of Serpentine.

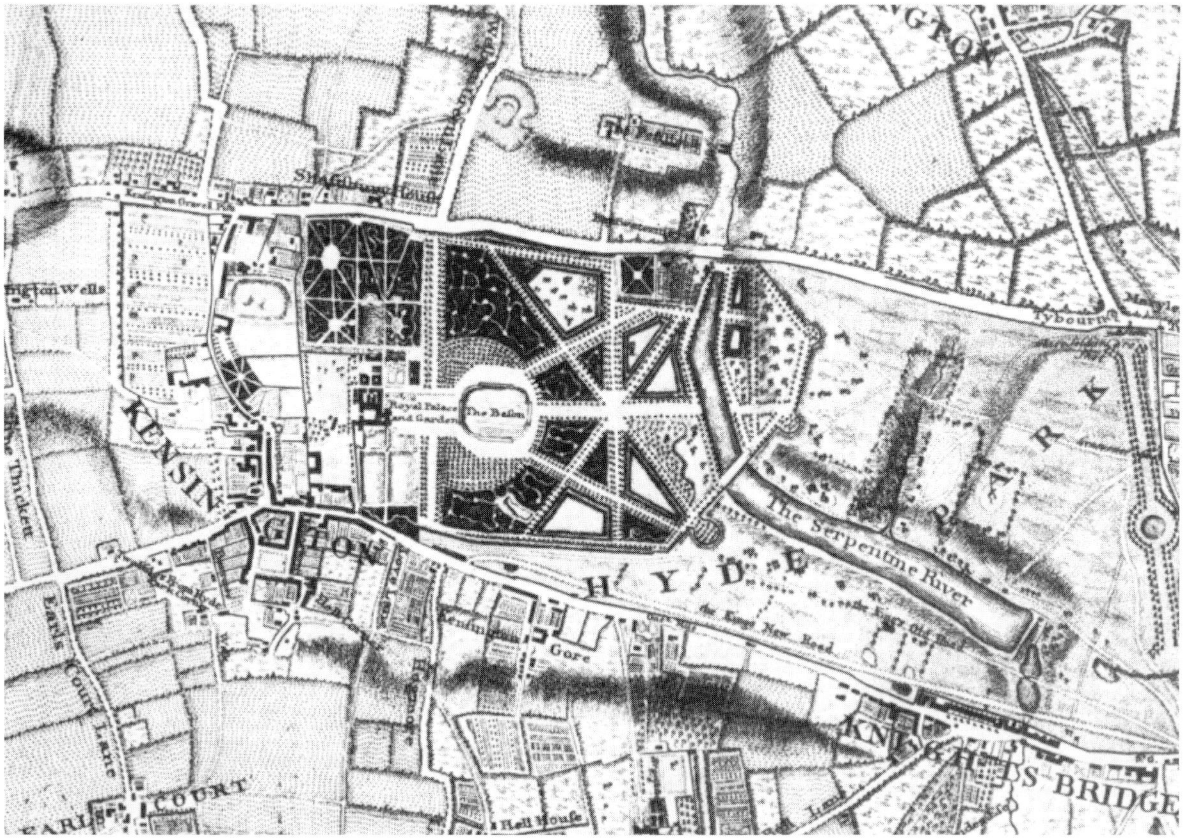

97a Kensington Gardens and Hyde Park. Detail from Rocque, *An Extract Survey of the City's of London, Westminster . . . and the Country Near Ten Miles Round* (1746).

97b Kensington Gardens and Hyde Park. Aerial view 1954.

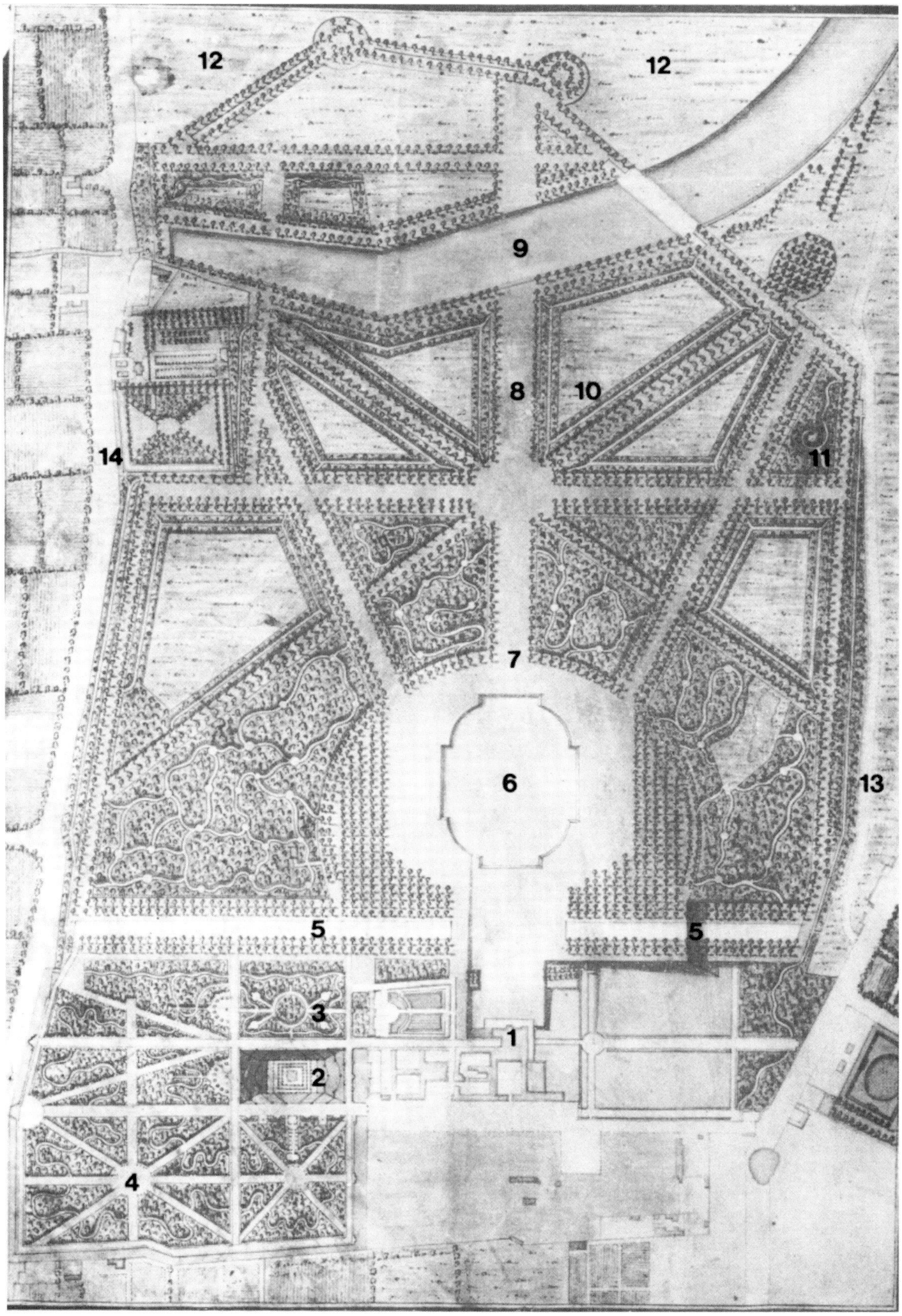

98 Kensington Gardens and Hyde Park. Plan. Drawing by Bridgeman (attrib.). HEH, ST MAP 147.

KEY: **1** Palace; **2** Old Gravel Pit; **3** Old Mount; **4** Wilderness; **5** Broad Walk; **6** Round Pond; **7** Great Bow; **8** Front Walk; **9** Serpentine; **10** Site of Queen's Temple; **11** Mount and Summer House; **12** Hyde Park; **13** King's Old Road (Lamp Road/Rotten Row); **14** Oxford (Bayswater) Road

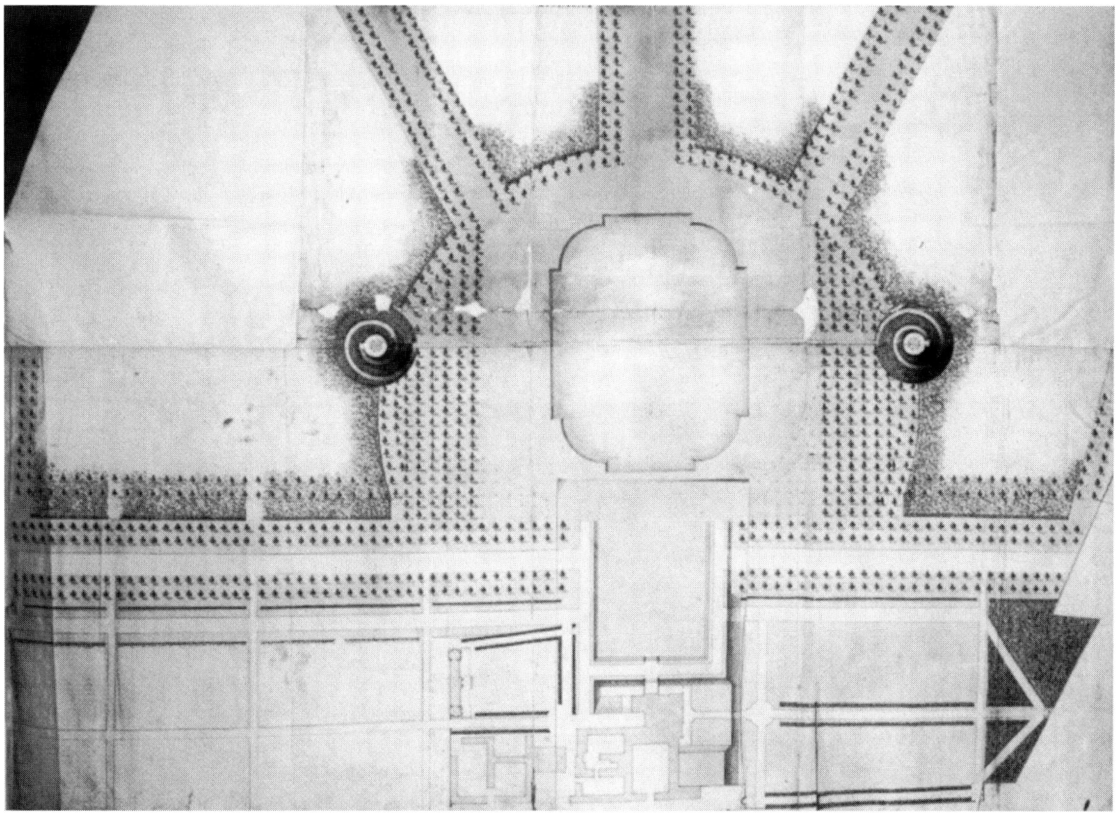

99a Kensington Gardens. Plan of Palace, Broad Walk, Round Pond and Great Bow. Drawing by Bridgeman (attrib.). MSGD a3 * fo.15.

99b Kensington Gardens. View of south-east corner with Mount and Summer House, and King's Old Road (Lamp Road/Rotten Row) by Bernard Lens, the Younger, 1736. Royal Borough of Kensington and Chelsea Central Library, 712.5 KEN/Oa.GC.2251.

100a Kensington Gardens. View from Round Pond towards Palace. Engraving by Rocque and Vivares 1736.

100b Kensington Gardens. View from Serpentine towards Queen's Temple, Round Pond and Palace. Engraving by Highmore and Tinney *c.*1745.

101a St James's Park. View down Mall towards Westminster. Engraving by Maurer and Smith 1741.

101b St James's Park. View from Buckingham House. Engraving by Rigaud and St Torres 1752.

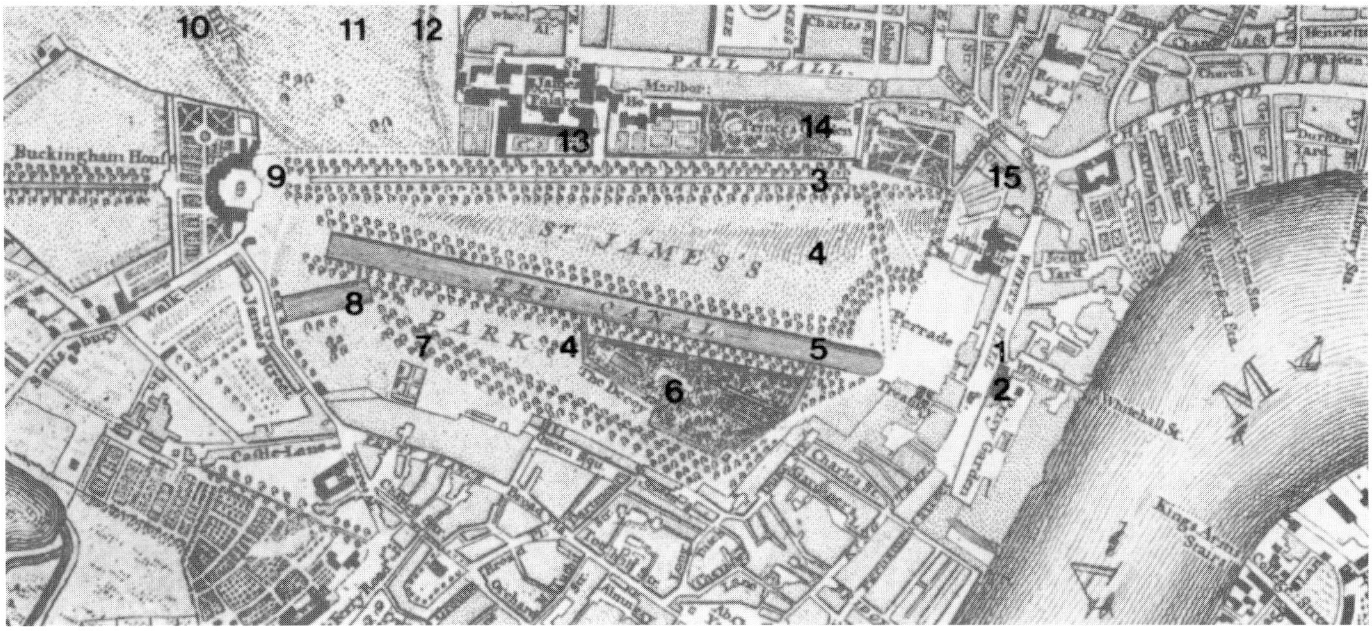

102a St James's Park. Detail from Rocque, *An Exact Survey of the City's of London, Westminster . . . and the Country Near Ten Miles Round* (1746).

KEY: **1** Whitehall; **2** Banqueting House; **3** Mall; **4** St James's Park; **5** Canal; **6** Decoy; **7** Birdcage Walk; **8** Rosamond's Pond; **9** Site of Victoria Memorial; **10** Constitution Hill; **11** Green Park; **12** Queen's Walk; **13** St James's Palace; **14** Carlton House Gardens; **15** Site of Admiralty Arch

102b St James's Park. Aerial view 1949.

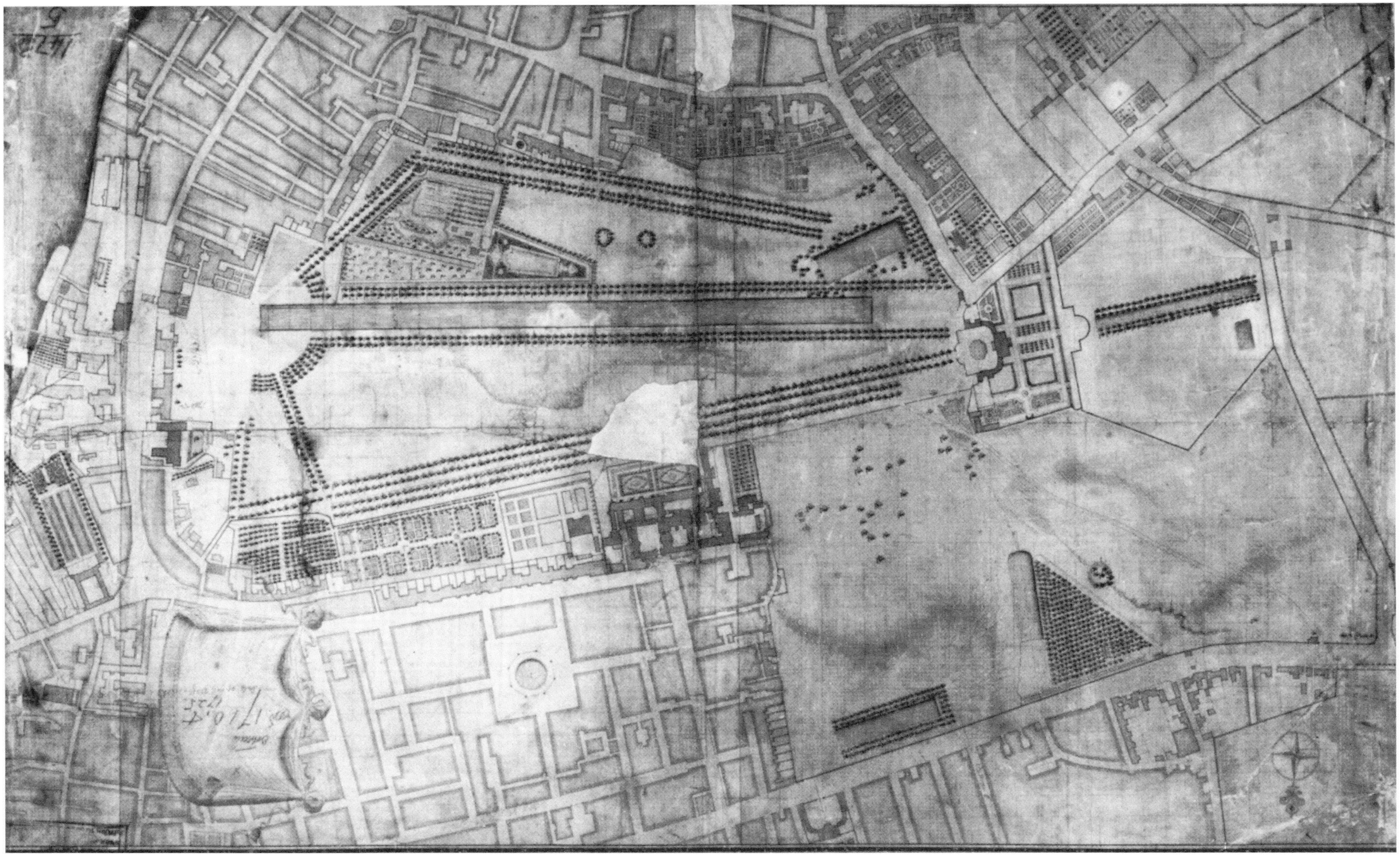

103 St James's Park. Plan. Drawing by Bridgeman (attrib.). PRO, Works 32/70.

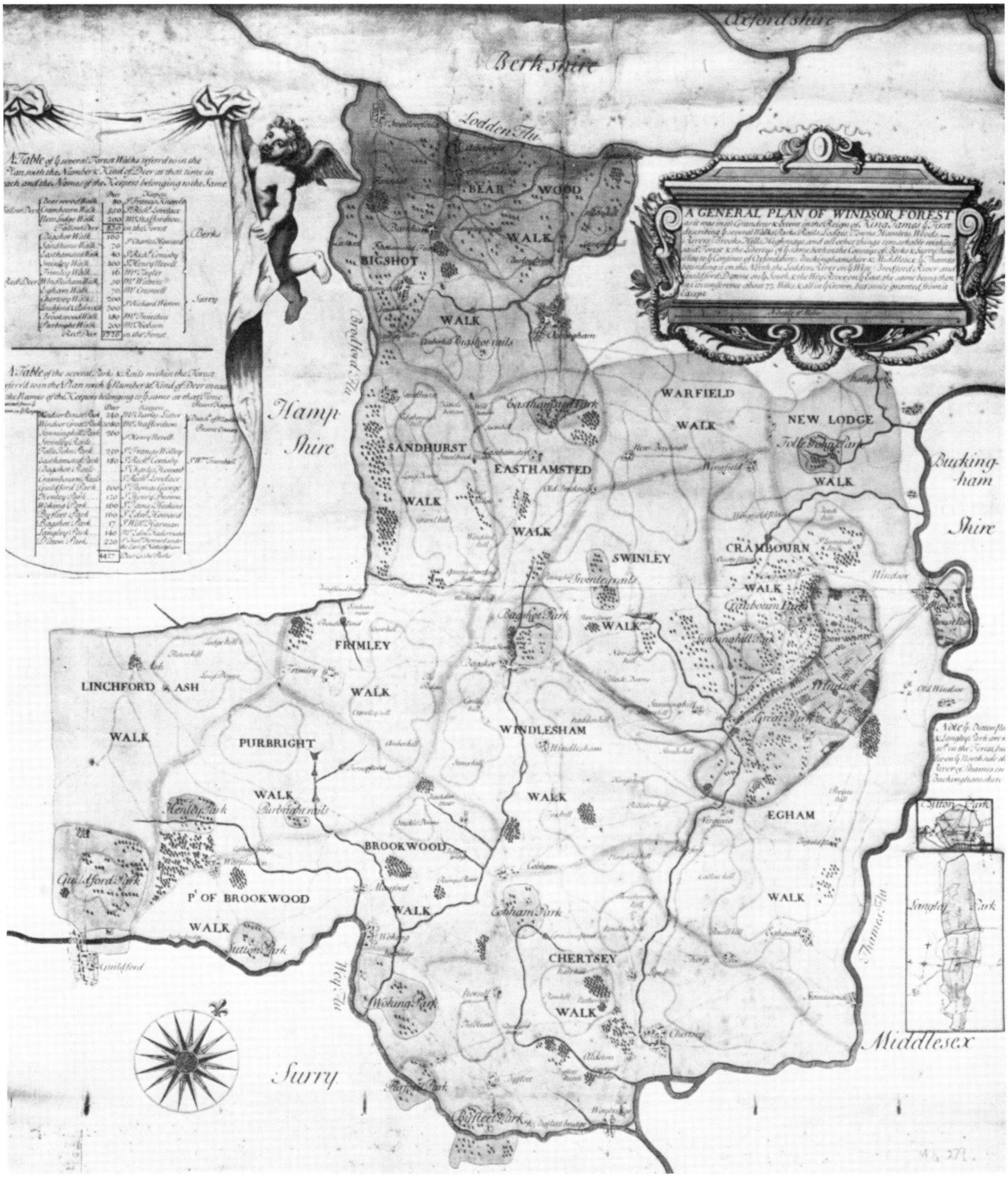

104 Windsor Forest. General Plan of Windsor Forest as it was in the reign of James I. Drawing by Bridgeman signed 'Bridgman Pinxit'. PRO, MR 279 (Cat. No.854).

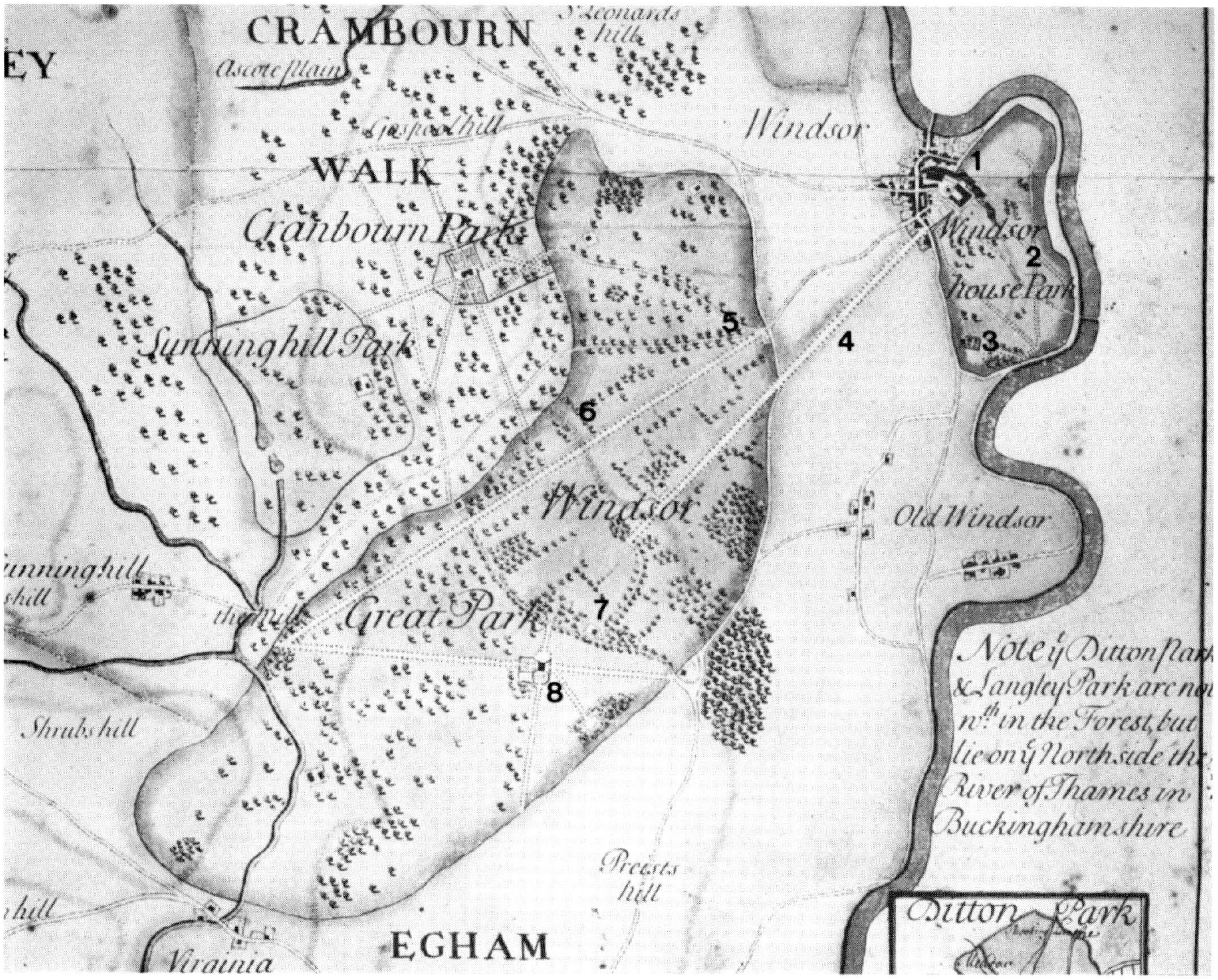

105 Windsor Forest. General Plan. Detail of *Plate 104*.

KEY: **1** Windsor Castle; **2** Home Park; **3** Site of Windsor Lodge (Duke of Marlborough); **4** Long Walk; **5** Queen Anne's Ride; **6** Great Park; **7** Site of Royal Lodge; **8** Cumberland Lodge

106a Windsor Castle. View from north. Drawing by Bernard Lens, the Elder, before 1725. BL, K.VII.40.i.2.

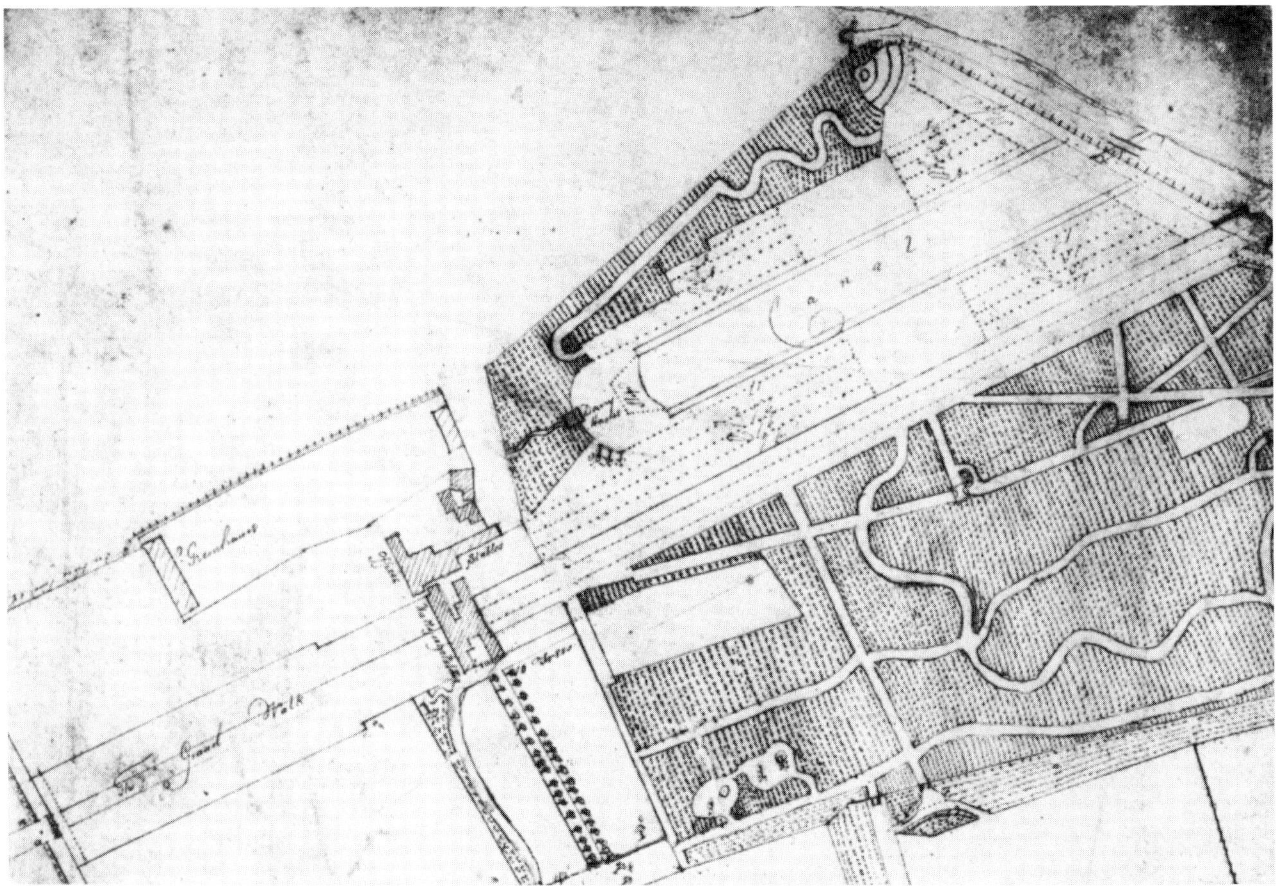

106b Richmond Gardens. Plan of Dairy, Canal and Mount. Detail of drawing by Bridgeman (attrib.). PRO, Works 32/282.

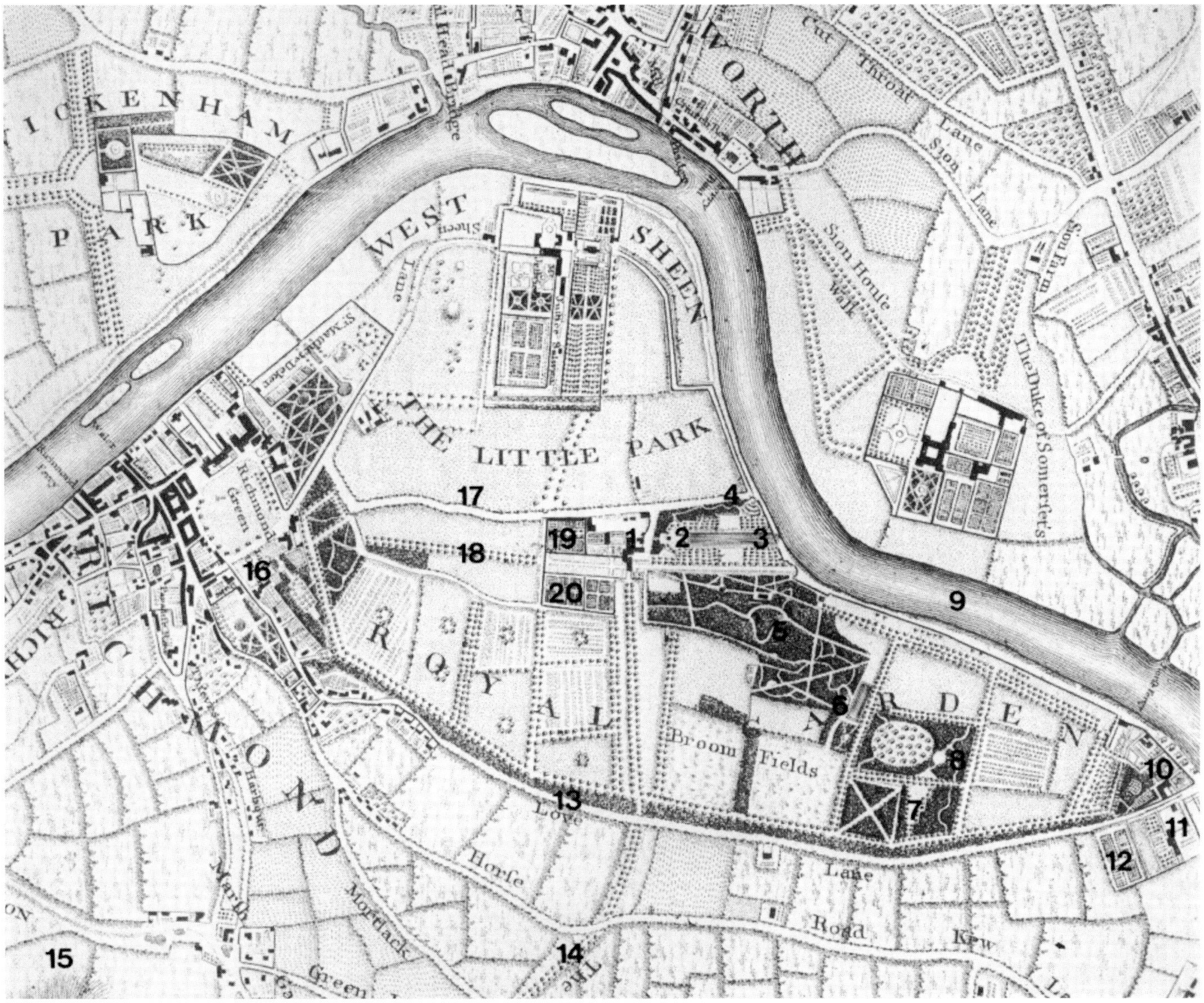

107 Richmond Gardens. Plan. Detail from Rocque, *An Exact Survey of the City's of London, Westminster . . . and the Country Near Ten Miles Round* (1746).

KEY: **1** Richmond Lodge (George II and Caroline); **2** Dairy; **3** Canal; **4** Mount; **5** Richmond Gardens; **6** Merlin's Cave; **7** Amphitheatre; **8** Hermitage; **9** River Thames; **10** Kew Palace (1631); **11** Kew House or White House (Prince Frederick and Princess Augusta); **12** Gardens of Kew House; **13** Love Lane; **14** Queen's Private Road to Richmond Park; **15** Richmond Park; **16** Richmond Little Green; **17** Deer Park; **18** Queen's Walk; **19** Menagerie; **20** Kitchen Garden

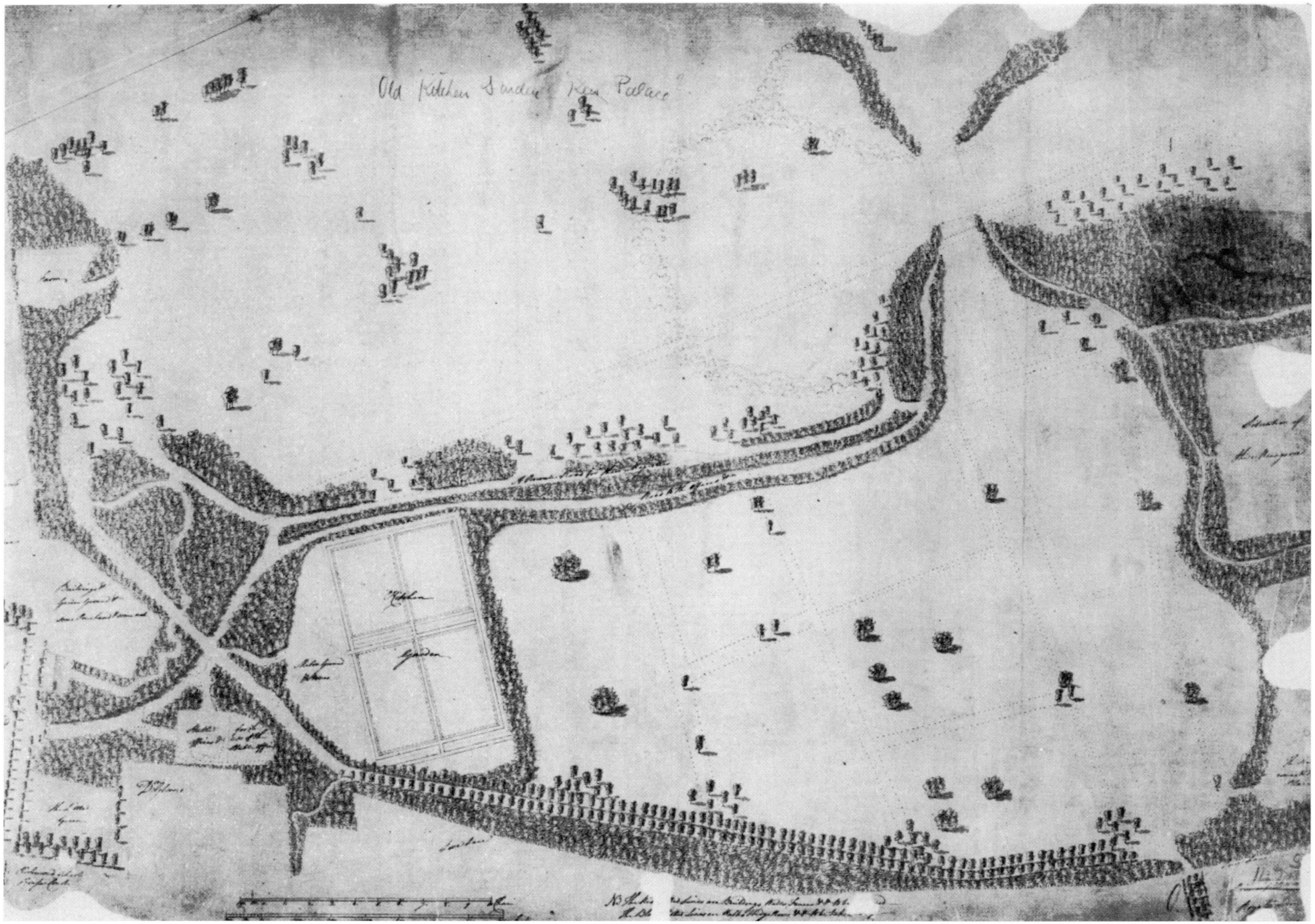

108 Richmond Gardens. Plan. Drawing by Bridgeman (attrib.). PRO, Works 32/96.

109 Richmond Gardens. View of Hermitage. Engraved title-page by Gravelot and Du Bosc 1735.

110a Richmond Gardens. View of Richmond Lodge. Engraving by Chatelain 1736 from *Vitruvius Britannicus IV* (1739), pls 6–7.

110b White Lodge, Richmond Park. Entrance Front. Engraving from *Vitruvius Britannicus IV* (1767), pls 1–2.

111 Stowe. Aerial view from south-east.

112a Richard Temple, 1st Viscount Cobham of Stowe, by Jean-Baptiste Van Loo. Hagley.

112b Stowe. View of South Front *c*.1694. Anonymous drawing. Collection of Hon. R. W. Morgan-Grenville.

113 Stowe. View of South Front.

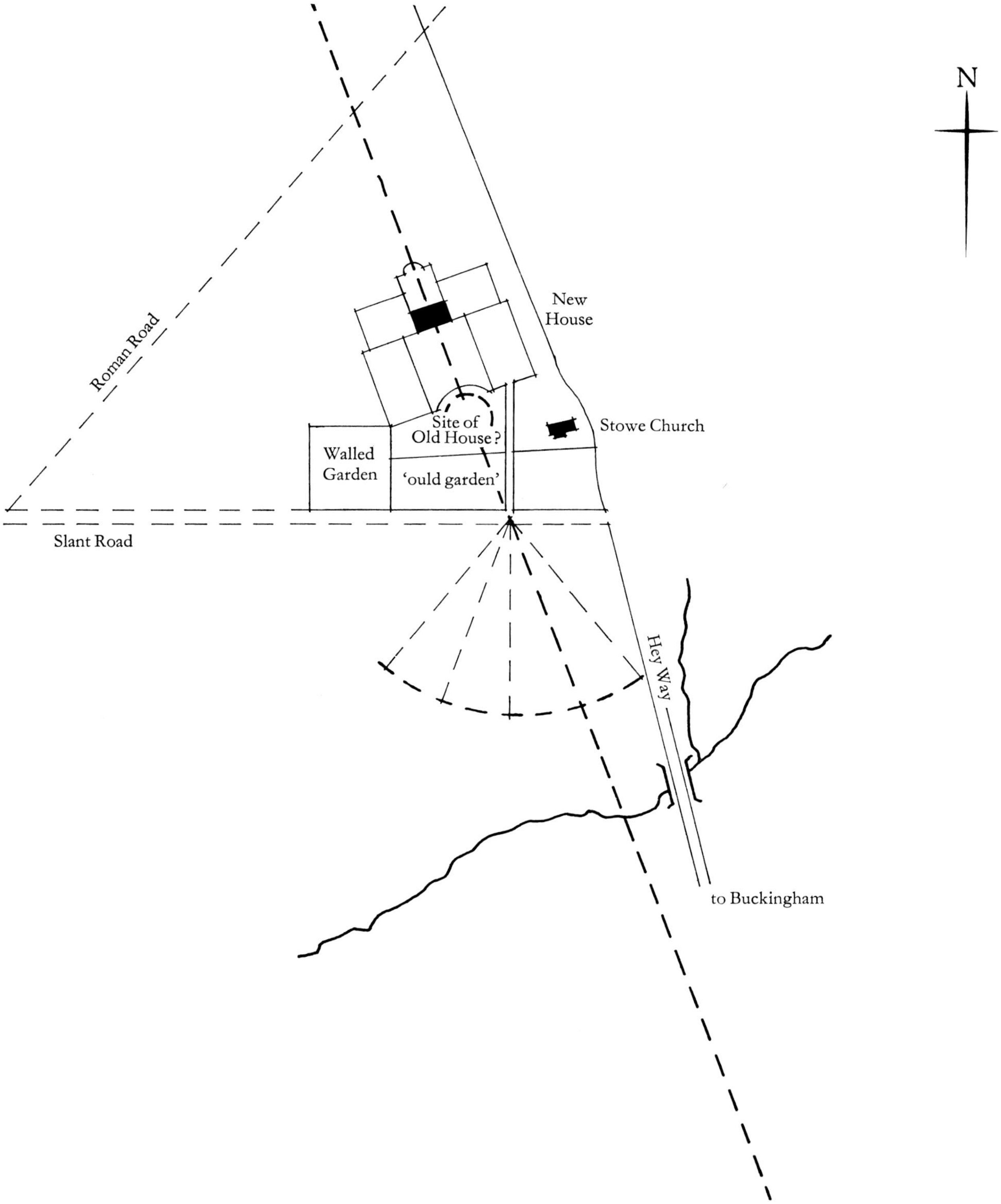

114 Stowe. Layout plan *c.*1680. Reconstruction by George B. Clarke.

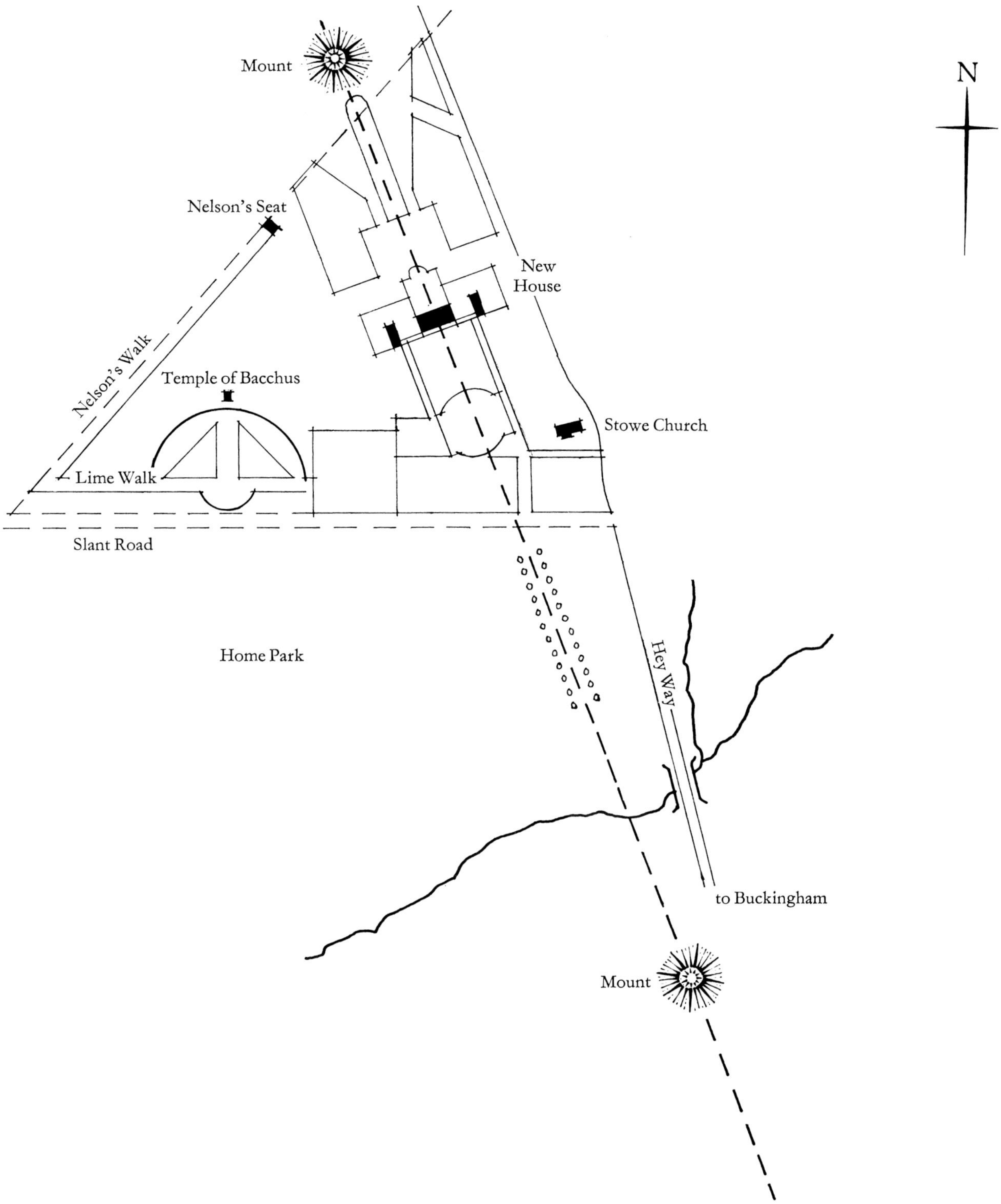

115 Stowe. Layout plan *c*.1719. Reconstruction by George B. Clarke.

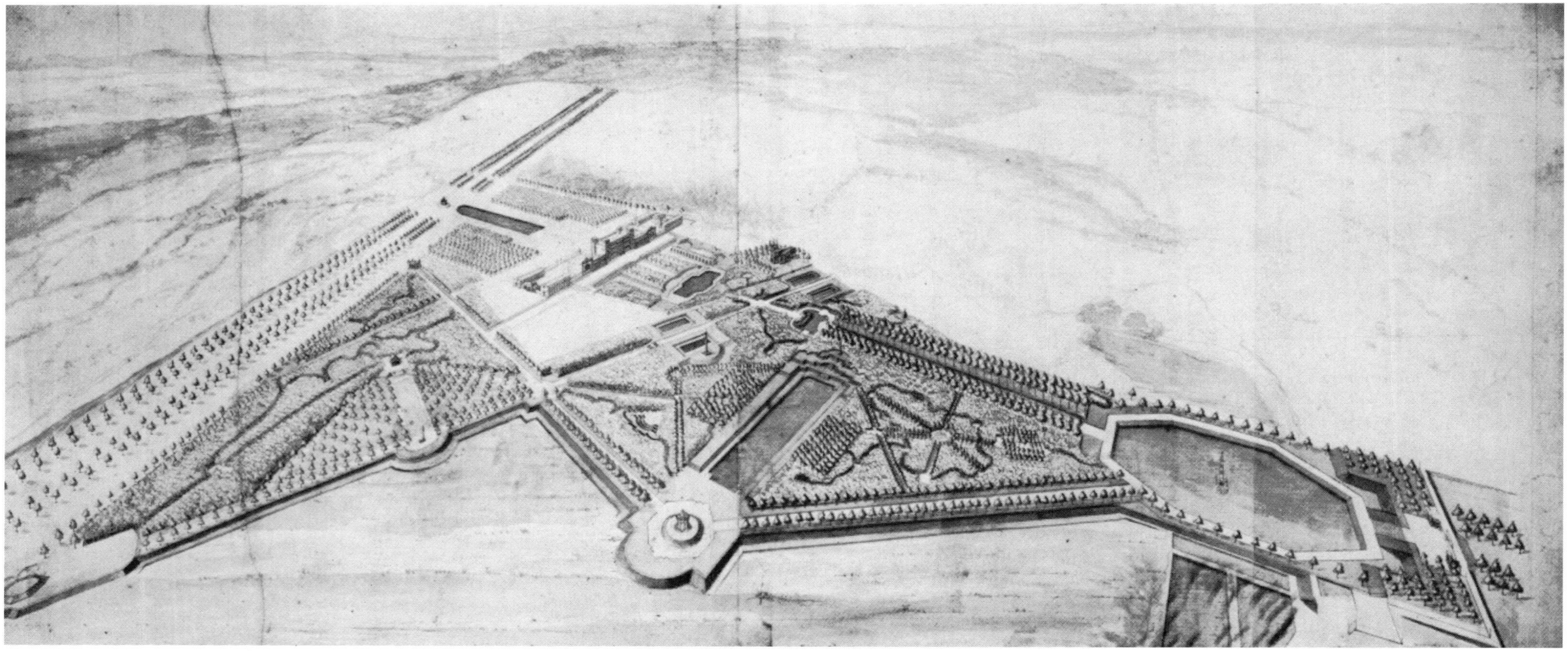

116 Stowe. Bird's-eye view. Drawing by Bridgeman (attrib.). MSGD a4 fo.46.

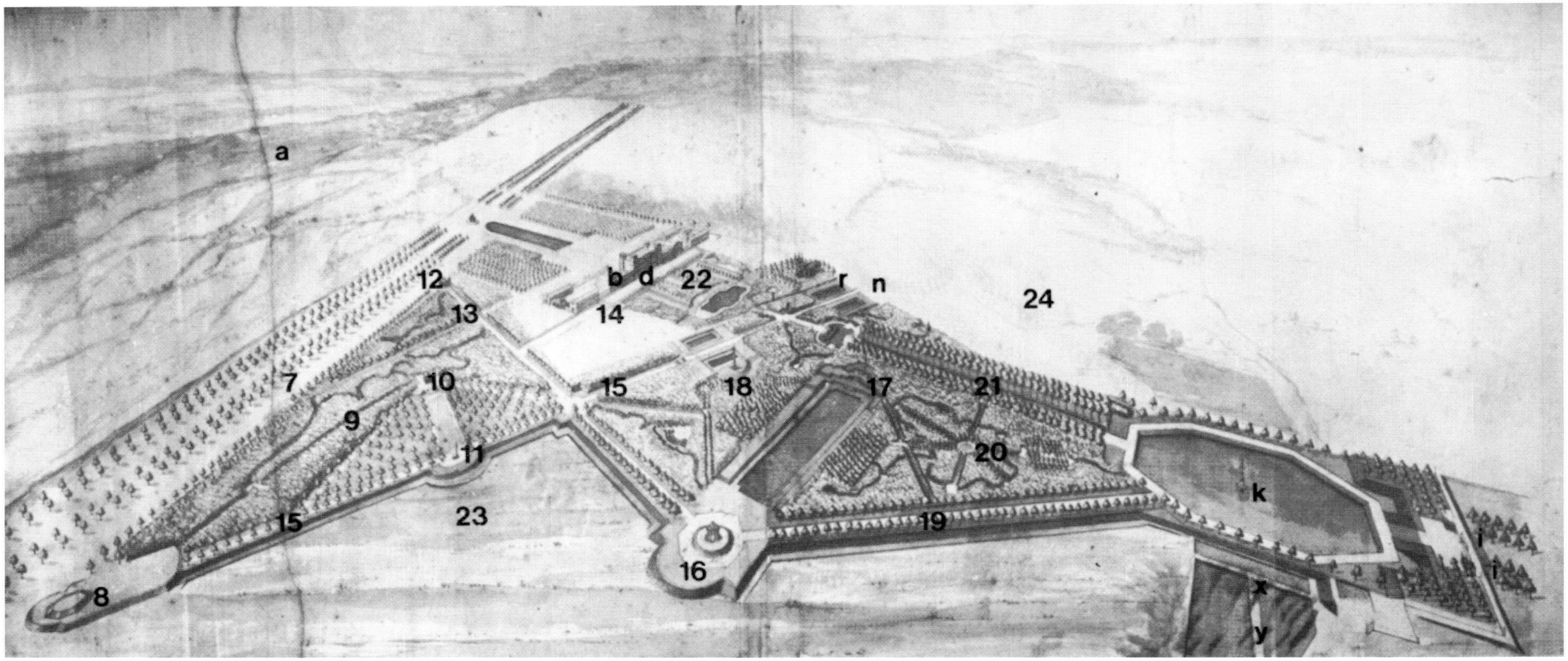

117 Stowe. Bird's-eye view. Drawing by Bridgeman (attrib.). MSGD a4 fo.46.

*KEY: **7** Nelson's Walk; **8** Site of Pyramid? **9** Lady Temple's Spinney; **10** Brick Temple; **11** Coucher's Obelisk; **12** Nelson's Seat; **13** Rogers' Walk; **14** Kitchen Gardens; **15** Great Cross Walk (Limes); **16** Rotunda; **17** Queen Caroline's Monument and Queen's Theatre; **18** King George's Column; **19** Gurnet's Walk; **20** Temple of Sleep; **21** Abele Walk (Poplars); **22** Parterre; **23** Home Park; **24** Hawkwell Hill and Field
a Park and Approach to House, with Equestrian Statue of George I; **b** House and Offices; **d** House Terrace; **i** Lake Pavilions; **k** Octagon Lake and Guglio Fountain; **n** Site of Elysian Fields; **r** Stowe Church; **x** Cascade; **y** Site of Eleven-Acre Lake

*Based on legend to 1739 General Plan reproduced as *Plate 123*

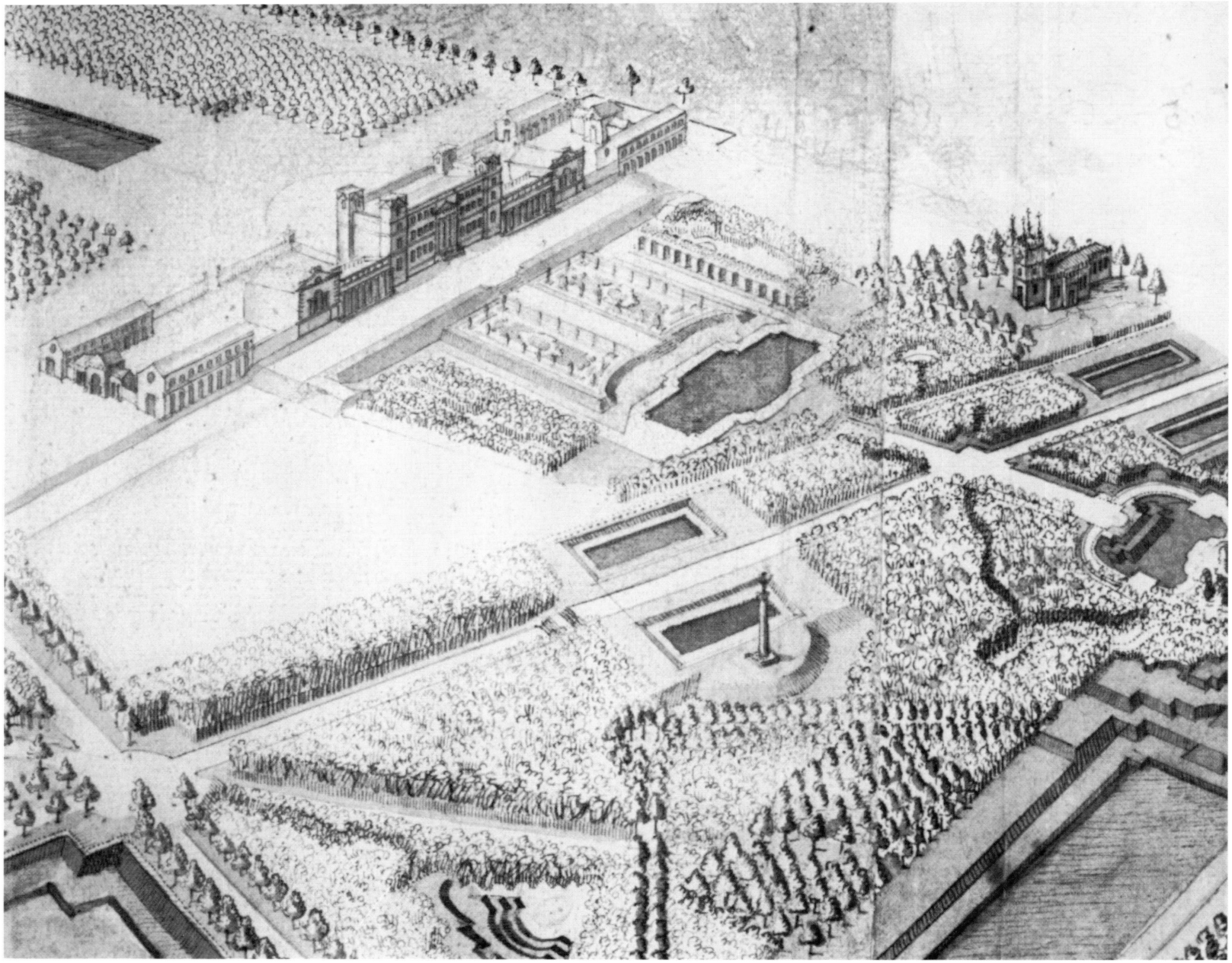

118 Stowe. Detail from *Plate 116* of House, Parterre, Stowe Church, and Great Cross Walk.

119a Stowe. Detail from *Plate 116* of Rotunda facing Home Park and Queen's Theatre.

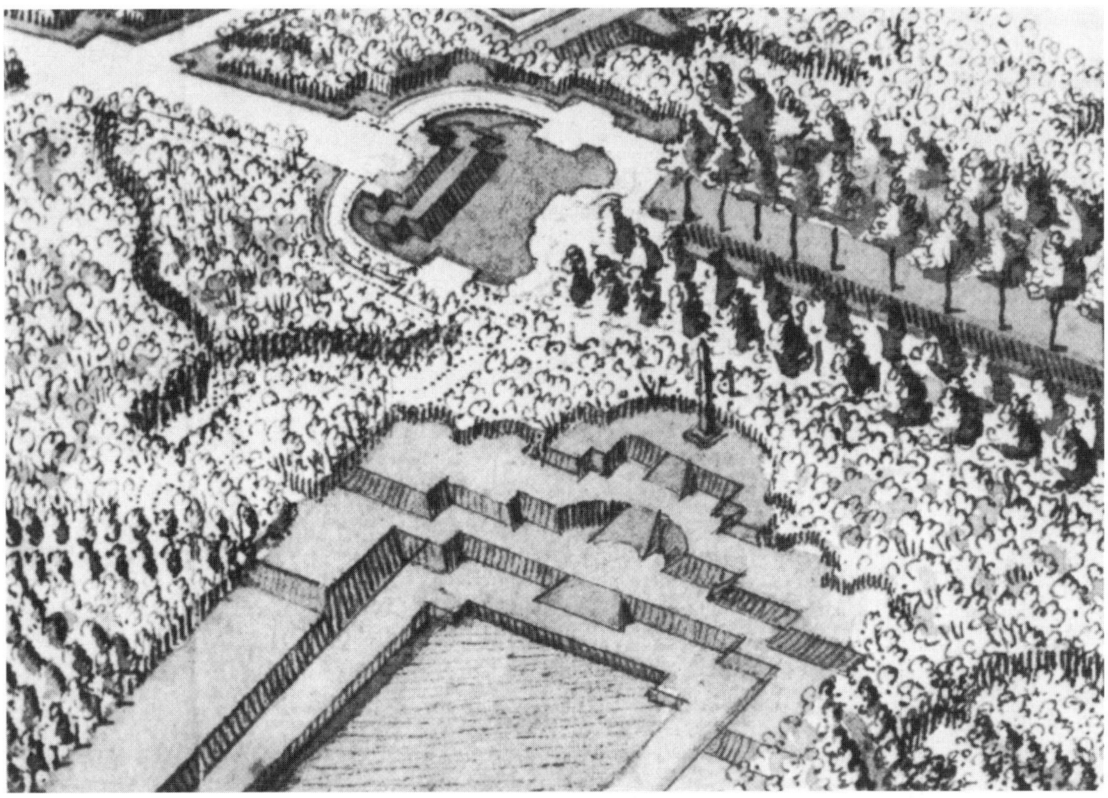

119b Stowe. Detail from *Plate 116* of Queen's Theatre, Queen Caroline's Monument, and Abele Walk.

120a Stowe. Detail from *Plate 116* of Lake Pavilions and Octagon Lake.

120b Stowe. Detail from *Plate 116* of Coucher's Obelisk and Brick Temple set in Lady Temple's Spinney.

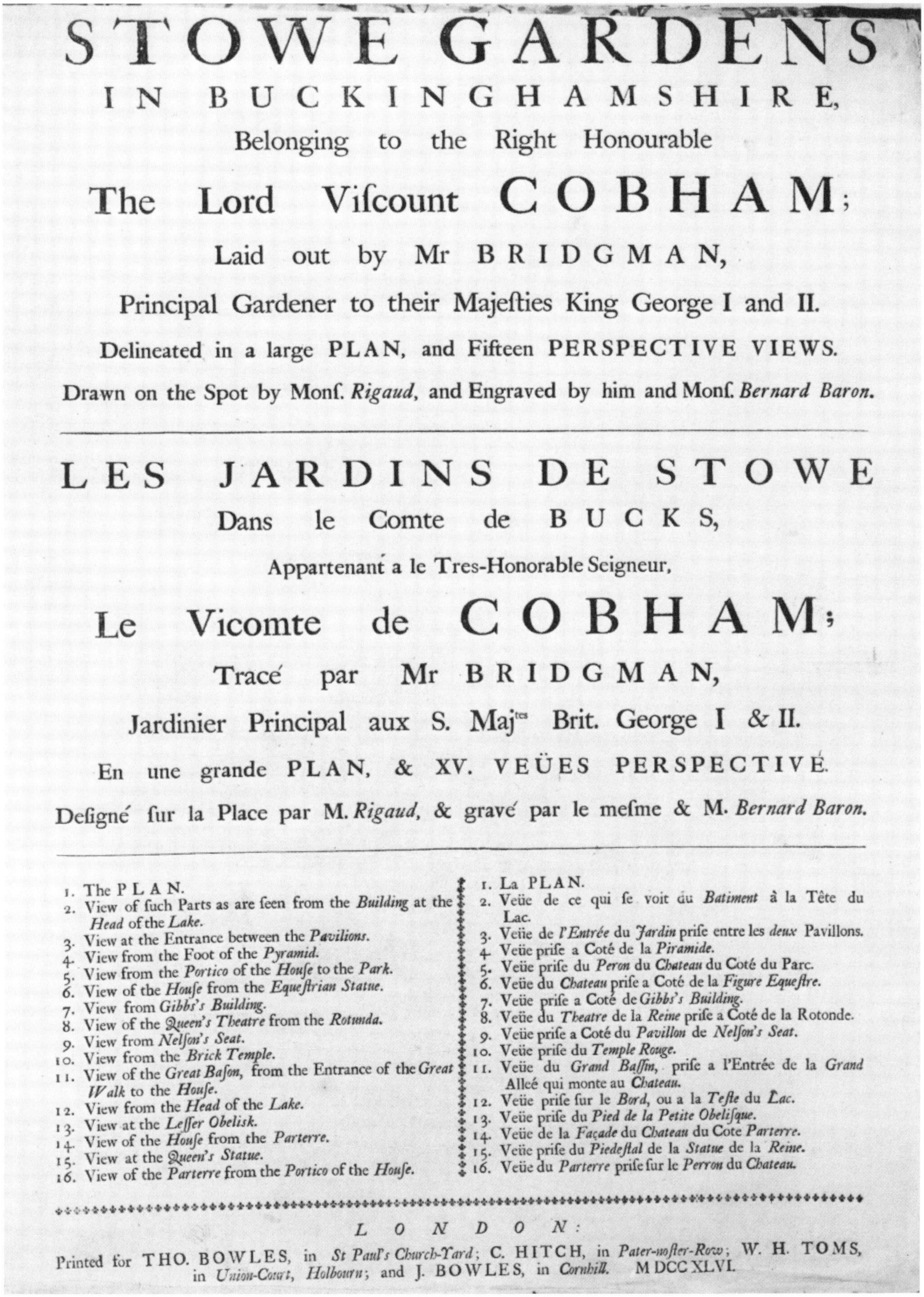

STOWE GARDENS
IN BUCKINGHAMSHIRE,
Belonging to the Right Honourable
The Lord Viſcount COBHAM;
Laid out by Mr BRIDGMAN,

Principal Gardener to their Majeſties King George I and II.

Delineated in a large PLAN, and Fifteen PERSPECTIVE VIEWS.

Drawn on the Spot by Monſ. *Rigaud*, and Engraved by him and Monſ. *Bernard Baron*.

LES JARDINS DE STOWE
Dans le Comte de BUCKS,

Appartenant a le Tres-Honorable Seigneur,
Le Vicomte de COBHAM;
Tracé par Mr BRIDGMAN,

Jardinier Principal aux S. Maj^tes Brit. George I & II.

En une grande PLAN, & XV. VEÜES PERSPECTIVÉ.

Deſigné ſur la Place par M. *Rigaud*, & gravé par le meſme & M. *Bernard Baron*.

---

1. The PLAN.
2. View of ſuch Parts as are ſeen from the *Building* at the *Head* of the *Lake*.
3. View at the Entrance between the *Pavilions*.
4. View from the Foot of the *Pyramid*.
5. View from the *Portico* of the *Houſe* to the *Park*.
6. View of the *Houſe* from the *Equeſtrian Statue*.
7. View from *Gibbs's Building*.
8. View of the *Queen's Theatre* from the *Rotunda*.
9. View from *Nelſon's Seat*.
10. View from the *Brick Temple*.
11. View of the *Great Baſon*, from the Entrance of the *Great Walk* to the *Houſe*.
12. View from the *Head* of the *Lake*.
13. View at the *Leſſer Obelisk*.
14. View of the *Houſe* from the *Parterre*.
15. View at the *Queen's Statue*.
16. View of the *Parterre* from the *Portico* of the *Houſe*.

1. La PLAN.
2. Veüe de ce qui ſe voit du *Batiment* à la Tête du Lac.
3. Veüe de *l'Entrée* du *Jardin* priſe entre les *deux* Pavillons.
4. Veüe priſe a Coté de la *Piramide*.
5. Veüe priſe du *Peron* du *Chateau* du Coté du Parc.
6. Veüe du *Chateau* priſe a Coté de la *Figure Equeſtre*.
7. Veüe priſe a Coté de *Gibbs's Building*.
8. Veüe du *Theatre* de la *Reine* priſe a Coté de la Rotonde.
9. Veüe priſe a Coté du *Pavillon* de *Nelſon's Seat*.
10. Veüe priſe du *Temple Rouge*.
11. Veüe du *Grand Baſſin*, priſe a l'Entrée de la *Grand* Alleé qui monte au *Chateau*.
12. Veüe priſe ſur le *Bord*, ou a la *Teſte* du *Lac*.
13. Veüe priſe du *Pied de la Petite Obeliſque*.
14. Veüe de la *Façade* du Chateau du Cote *Parterre*.
15. Veüe priſe du *Piedeſtal* de la *Statue* de la *Reine*.
16. Veüe du *Parterre* priſe ſur le *Perron* du *Chateau*.

LONDON:

Printed for THO. BOWLES, in *St Paul's Church-Yard*; C. HITCH, in *Pater-noſter-Row*; W. H. TOMS, in *Union-Court*, *Holbourn*; and J. BOWLES, in *Cornhill*. MDCCXLVI.

121 Stowe. Title-page from Thomas Bowles, pub., *Stowe Gardens in Buckinghamshire* (1746).

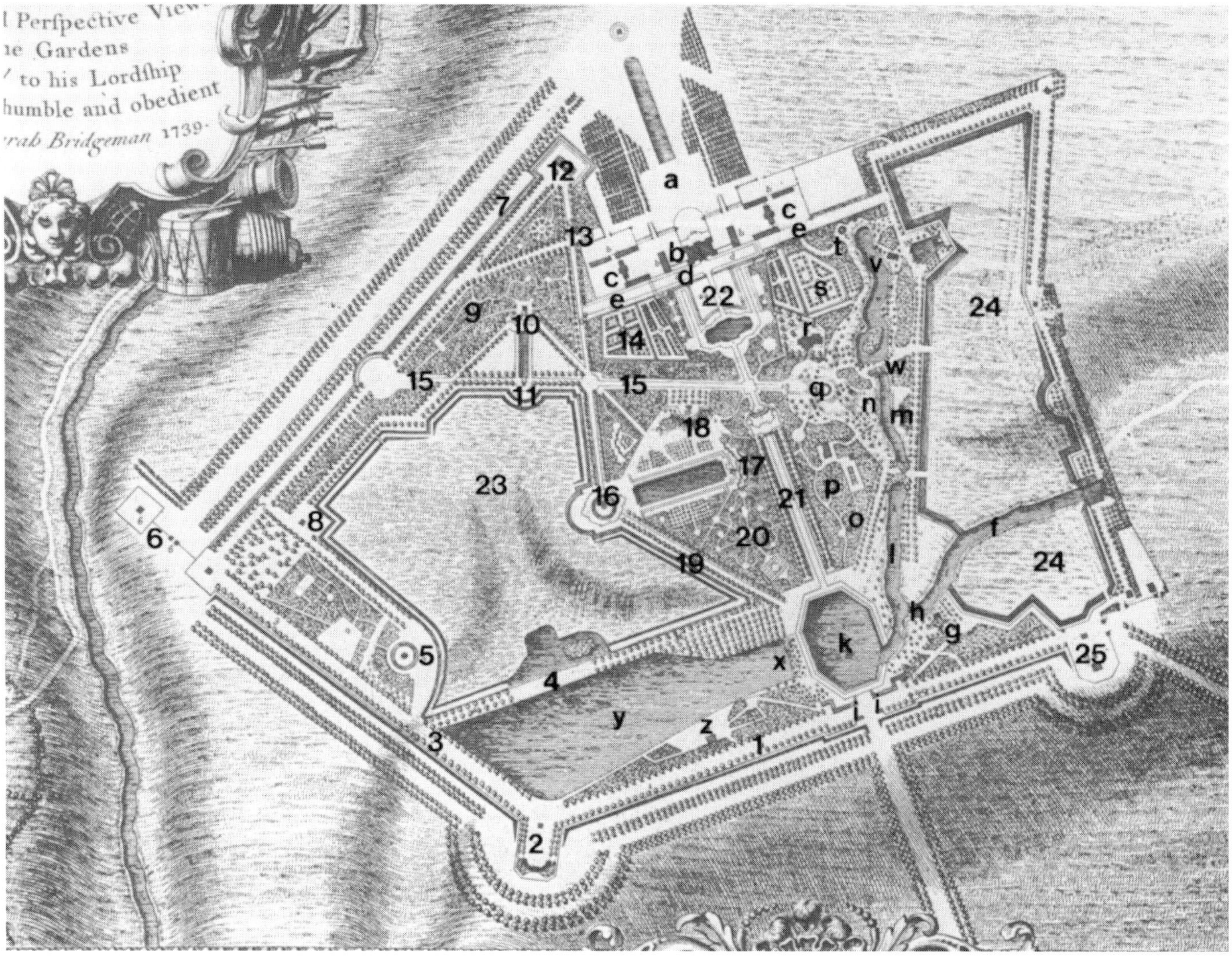

122 Stowe. Detail of main area from *Plate 123*.

KEY: **1** Pegg's Terrace; **2** Temple of Venus; **3** Warden Hill Walk; **4** Lake Walk; **5** Gibbs's Building; **6** Boycott Pavilions; **7** Nelson's Walk; **8** Pyramid; **9** Lady Temple's Spinney; **10** Brick Temple; **11** Coucher's Obelisk; **12** Nelson's Seat; **13** Rogers' Walk; **14** Kitchen Gardens; **15** Great Cross Walk (Limes); **16** Rotunda; **17** Queen Caroline's Monument and Queen's Theatre; **18** King George's Column; **19** Gurnet's Walk; **20** Temple of Sleep; **21** Abele Walk (Poplars); **22** Parterre; **23** Home Park; **24** Hawkwell Hill and Field; **25** Temple of Friendship

a Park and Approach to House, with Equestrian Statue of George I; **b** House and Offices; **c** Two Orangerys; **d** House Terrace; **e** Two Orangery Walks; **f** Upper River; **g** Congreve Monument; **h** Palladian Bridge; **i** Lake Pavilions; **k** Octagon Lake and Guglio Fountain; **l** Lower River; **m** Temple of British Worthies; **n** Elysian Fields; **o** Witch Wood; **p** Witch House; **q** Temple of Ancient Virtue; **r** Stowe Church; **s** Part of Kitchen Garden; **t** Grotto and Shell Temples; **v** Alder River; **w** Shell Bridge; **x** Cascade; **y** Eleven-Acre Lake; **z** Hermitage

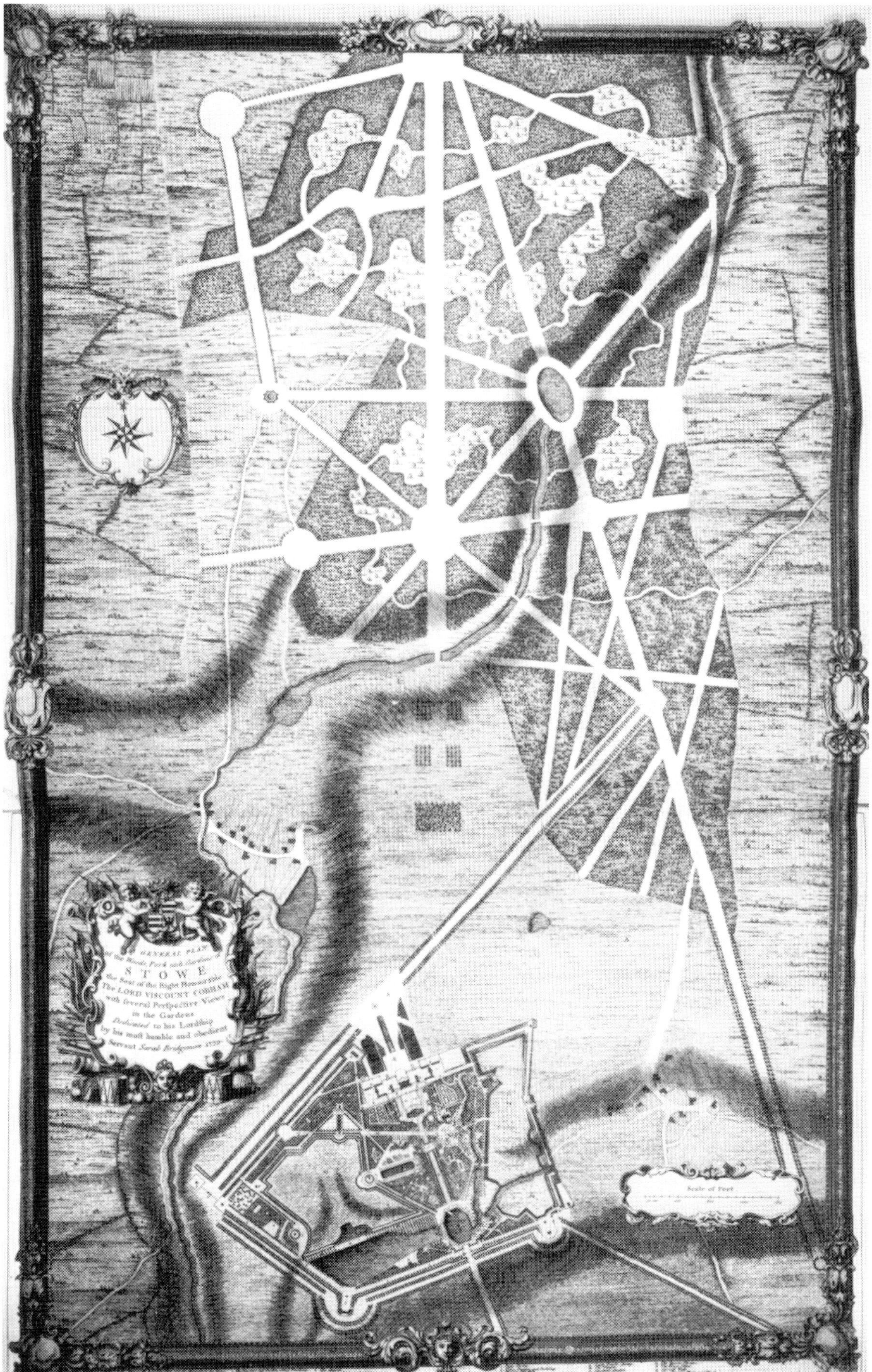

123 Stowe. General Plan. Unsigned engraving from Sarah Bridgeman, pub., *Views of Stowe* (1739).

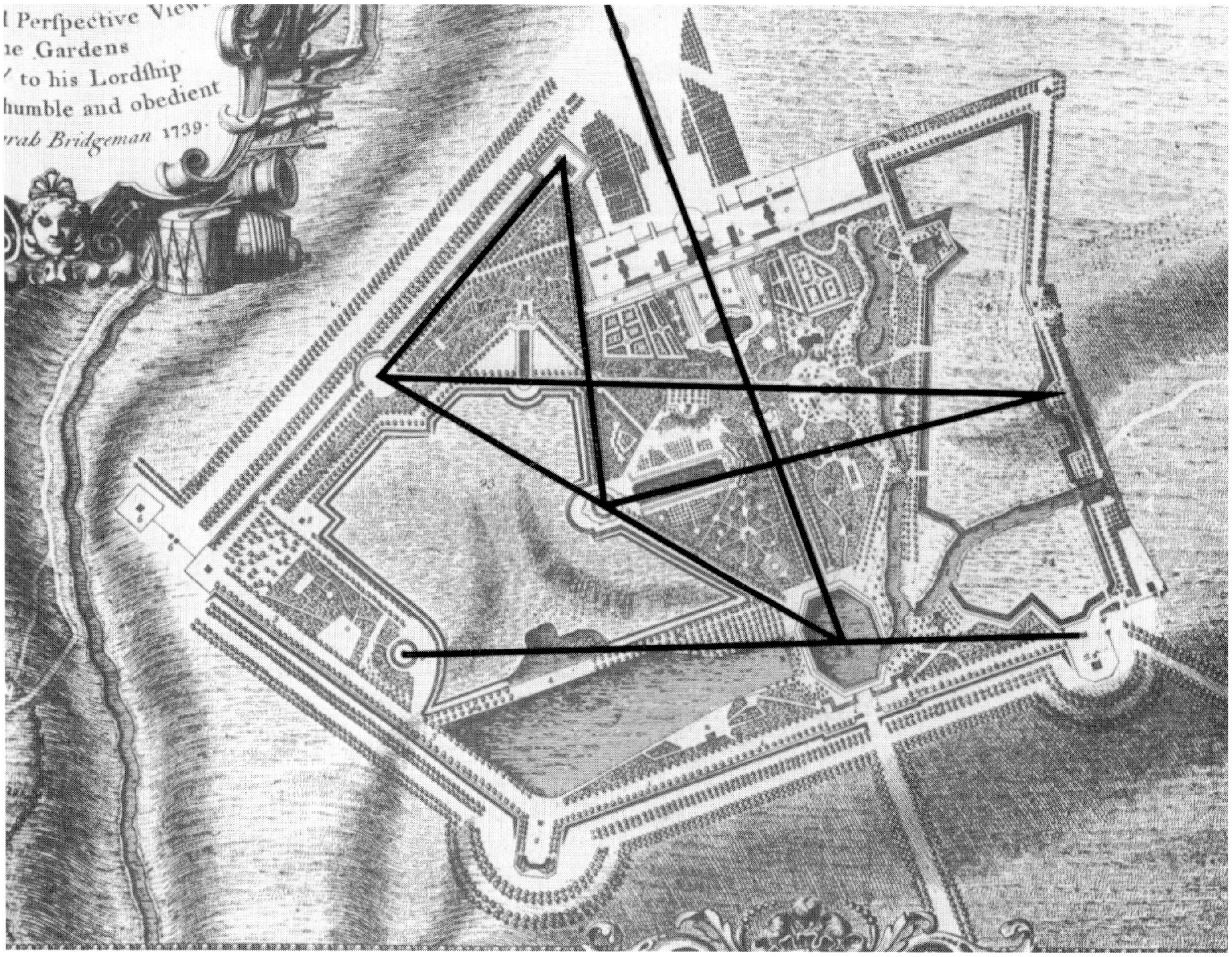

124 Stowe. Detail of main area from *Plate 123* with geometrical pattern superimposed. Based on a drawing by George B. Clarke.

125 Stowe. Vertical detail of main area 1969.

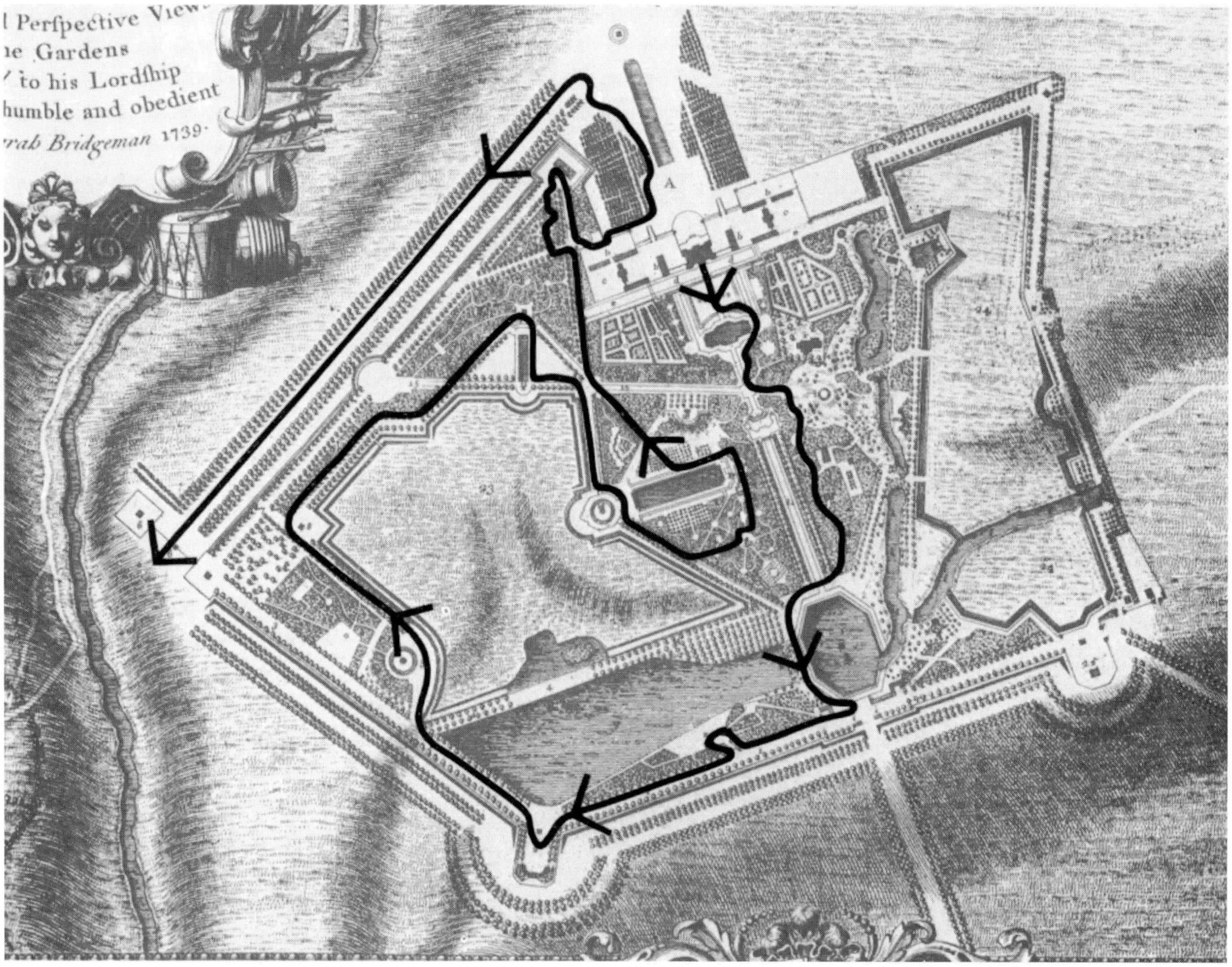

126 Stowe. Detail of main area from *Plate 123* with route of West's walk 1731–32 superimposed. Based on a drawing by Michael J. Gibbon. Although the general route taken by West is clear enough, the details are often vague (for example in his description of the Hermitage and Temple of Venus). Parts of the above diagram therefore must be regarded as speculative.

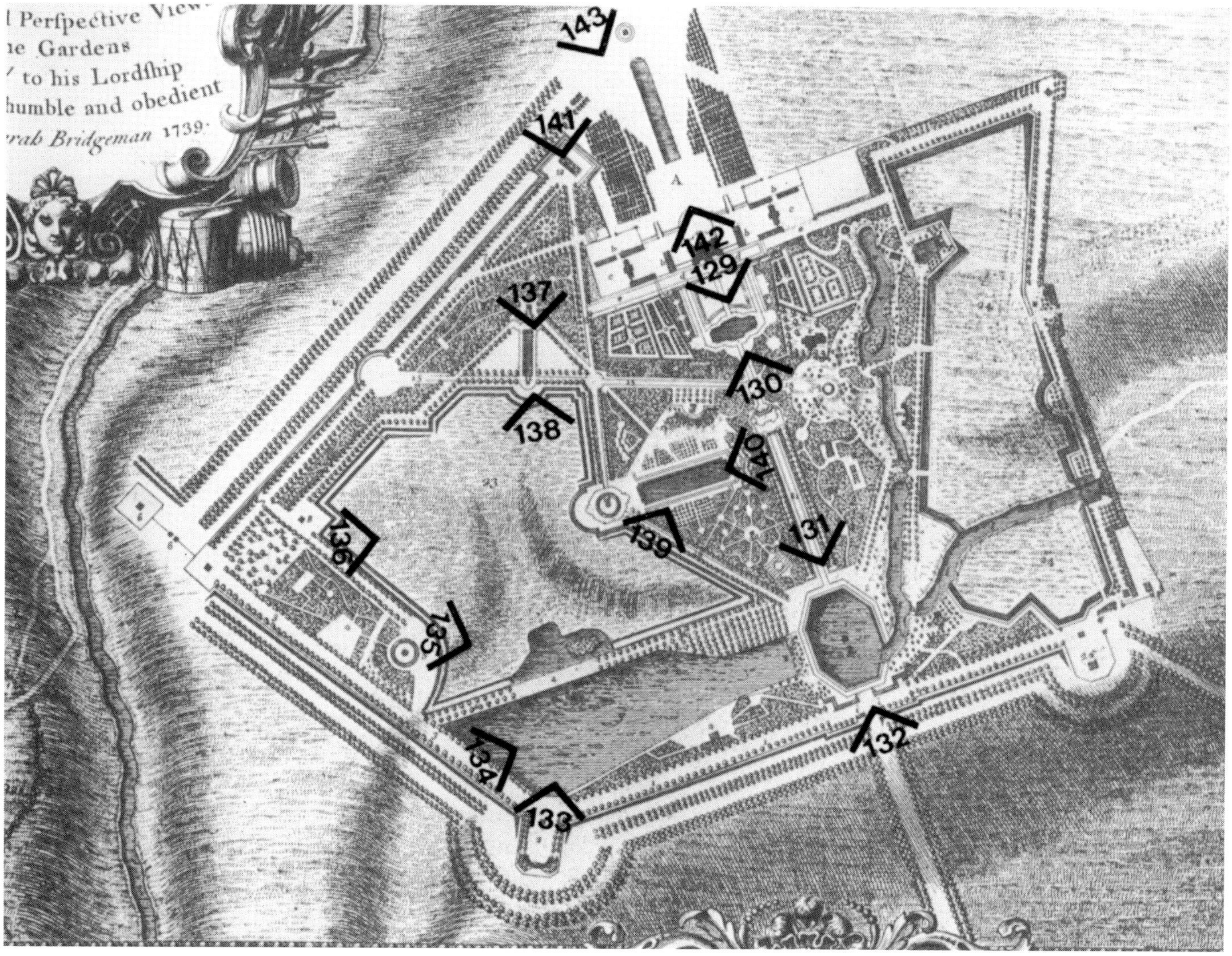

127 Stowe. Detail of main area from *Plate 123* with vantage points of Rigaud's perspectives of 1733–34 superimposed. Arabic numerals indicate the plate numbers of subsequent reproductions of Rigaud's views.

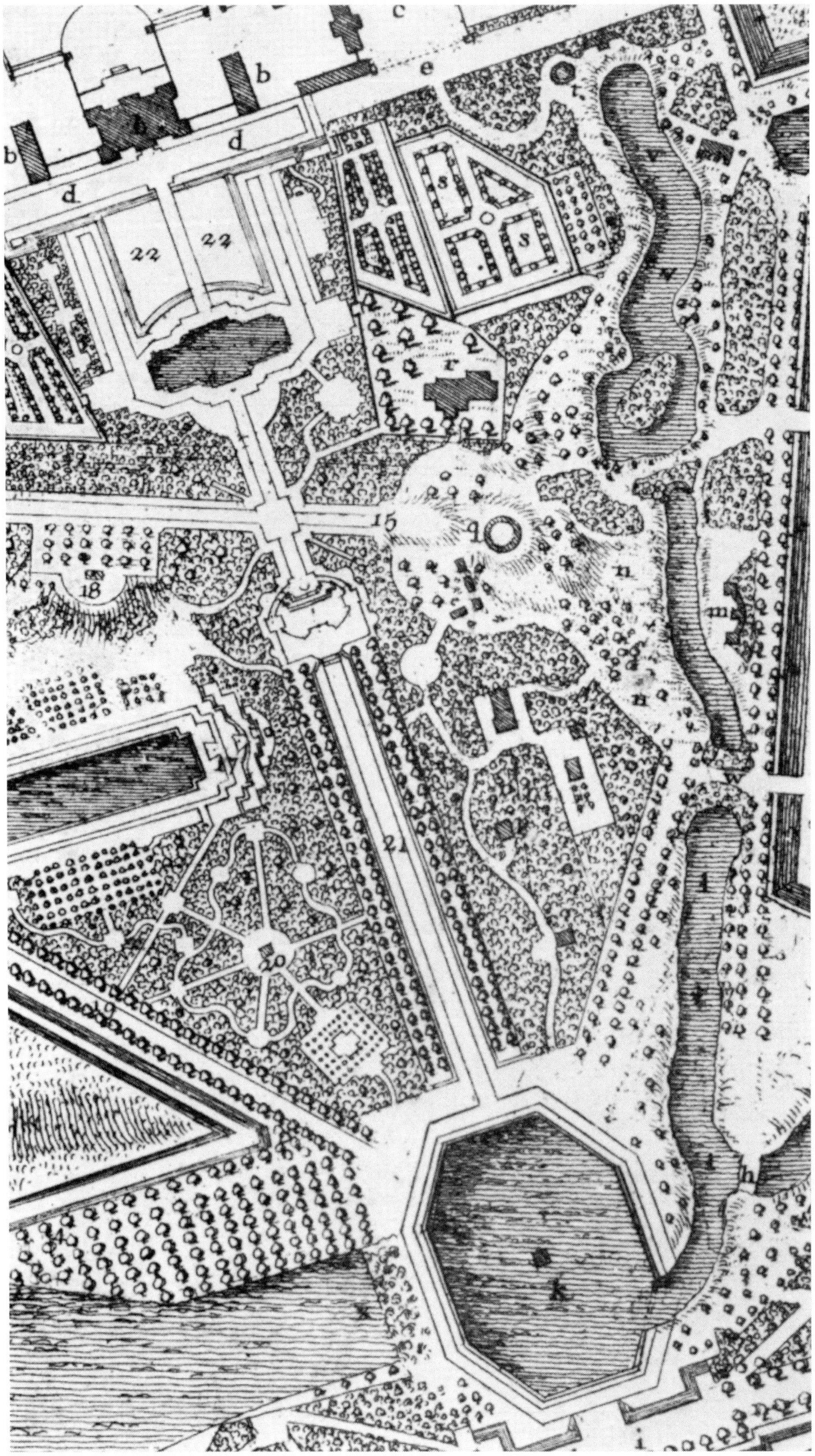

128 Stowe. Detail of Elysian Fields from *Plate 123*.

129 Stowe. Rigaud, 'View of the *Perterre* from the *Portico* of the *House*/Veüe du *Partere* prise sur le *Perron* du *Chateau*'. Ink and wash. 1733–34. MMA (Harris Brisbane Dick Fund, 1942), 42.79 (15).

LEFT TO RIGHT: Stowe Church/Abele Walk/Octagon Lake/Queen Caroline's Monument/King George's Column/Temple of Venus/Rotunda/Gibbs's Building/Home Park

130 Stowe. Rigaud, 'View of the *House* from the *Parterre*/Veüe de la *Façade* du *Château* du Coté du *Partere*'. Ink and wash. 1733–34. MMA (Harris Brisbane Dick Fund, 1942), 42.79(13).

131 Stowe. Rigaud, 'View of the *Great Bason,* from the Entrance of the *Great Walk* to the *House*/Veüe du *Grand Bassin,* prise a l'Entree de la *Grand Alleé* qui monte au *Chateau*'. Ink and wash. 1733–34. MMA (Harris Brisbane Dick Fund, 1942), 42.79 (10).

LEFT TO RIGHT: Lake Pavilions/Octagon Lake/Eleven-Acre Lake/Hermitage

132 Stowe. Rigaud, 'View at the Entrance between the *Pavillions*/Veüe de *l'Entrée* du *Jardin* prise entre les *deux Pavilions*'. Ink and wash. 1733–34. MMA (Harris Brisbane Dick Fund, 1942), 42.79(3).

LEFT TO RIGHT: Gibbs's Building/Pyramid/Home Park/Rotunda/Coucher's Obelisk/Brick Temple/Temple of Sleep/King George's Column/Stowe House/Abele Walk/Octagon Lake/Site of Elysian Fields and Hawkwell Hill and Field

133 Stowe. Rigaud, 'View of such parts as are seen from the *Building* at the *Head* of the *Lake*/Veüe de ce qui se voit du *Batiment* à la *Tête* du *Lac*'. Ink and wash. 1733–34. MMA (Harris Brisbane Dick Fund, 1942), 42.79(2).

LEFT TO RIGHT: Warden Hill Walk/Boycott Pavilions/Pyramid/Gibbs's Building with Statues of British Worthies/Home Park/Coucher's Obelisk/Brick Temple/Rotunda/Gurnet's Walk/King George's Column/Stowe Church/Queen Caroline's Monument/Guglio Fountain/Eleven-Acre Lake/Pegg's Terrace/Hermitage

134 Stowe. Rigaud, 'View from the *Head* of the *Lake*/Veüe prise sur le *Bord,* ou a la *Teste* du *Lac*'. Ink and wash. 1733–34. MMA (Harris Brisbane Dick Fund, 1942), 42.79(11).
LEFT TO RIGHT: Brick Temple/Coucher's Obelisk/Home Park/Rotunda/Stowe House/King George's Column/Stowe Church/Queen Caroline's Monument/Lake Walk/Octagon Lake and Cascade/Hermitage and other buildings/Pegg's Terrace

135 Stowe. Rigaud, 'View from *Gibbs's Building*/Veüe prise a coté de *Gibbs's Building*'. Ink and wash. 1733–34. MMA (Harris Brisbane Dick Fund, 1942), 42.79(6).

LEFT TO RIGHT: King George's Column/Stowe Church/Rotunda/Queen Caroline's Monument/Home Park/Gurnet's Walk/Octagon Lake/Lake Pavilions/Hermitage/Lake Walk/Temple of Venus/Gibbs's Building with Statues of British Worthies

136 Stowe. Rigaud, 'View from the foot of the *Pyramid*/Veüe prise a coté de la *Piramide*'. Ink and wash. 1733–34. MMA (Harris Brisbane Dick Fund, 1942), 42.79(4).

LEFT TO RIGHT: Pyramid/Home Park/Brick Temple/Stowe House/Coucher's Obelisk/Stowe Church/King George's Column/Queen Caroline's Monument/Rotunda/Gurnet's Walk/Octagon Lake/Lake Pavilions/Hermitage/Eleven-Acre Lake/Lake Walk

137 Stowe. Rigaud, 'View from the *Brick Temple*/Veüe prise du *Temple Rouge*'. Ink and wash. 1733–34. MMA (Harris Brisbane Dick Fund, 1942), 42.79(8).
LEFT TO RIGHT: Great Cross Walk/Eleven-Acre Lake/Temple of Venus/Coucher's Obelisk/Home Park

138 Stowe. Rigaud, 'View at the *Lesser Obelisk*/Veüe prise du *Pied de la Petite Obelisque*'. Ink and wash. 1733–34. MMA (Harris Brisbane Dick Fund, 1942), 42.79(12).
LEFT TO RIGHT: Home Park/Great Cross Walk/Lady Temple's Spinney/Obelisk/Brick Temple

139 Stowe. Rigaud, 'View of the *Queen's Theatre* from the *Rotunda*/Veüe du *Theatre* de la *Reine* prise a coté de la *Rotonde*'. Ink and wash. 1733–24. MMA (Harris Brisbane Dick Fund, 1942), 42.79(7).

LEFT TO RIGHT: Nelson's Seat/Rogers' Walk/Rotunda/Stowe House/King George's Column/Queen's Theatre/Queen Caroline's Monument/Gurnet's Walk/Home Park/Octagon Lake

140 Stowe. Rigaud, 'View at the *Queen's Statue*/Veüe prise du *Piedestal* de la *Statue* de la *Reine*'. Ink and wash. 1733–34. MMA (Harris Brisbane Dick Fund, 1942), 42.79(14).
LEFT TO RIGHT: Home Park/Rotunda/Pyramid

141 Stowe. Rigaud, 'View from *Nelson's Seat*/ Veüe prise a Coté du *Pavillon* de *Nelson's Seat*'. Ink and wash. 1733–34. MMA (Harris Brisbane Dick Fund, 1942), 42.79(9).
LEFT TO RIGHT: Rogers' Walk/Rotunda/Lady Temple's Spinney/Nelson's Walk/Boycott Pavilion

142 Stowe. Rigaud, 'View from the *Portico* of the *House* to the *Park*/Veüe prise du *Peron* du *Chateau* du Coté du *Parc*'. Ink and wash. 1733–34. MMA (Harris Brisbane Dick Fund, 1942), 42.79(5).

LEFT TO RIGHT: Gateway/Village of Dadford/Equestrian Statue of George I/Park and Approach to Stowe House/Gateway

143 Stowe. Rigaud and Baron, 'View of the *House* from the *Equestrian Statue*/Veüe du *Chateau* prise a coté de la *Figure Equestre*', from Sarah Bridgeman, pub., *Views of Stowe* (1739), pl.6.

144 Stowe. Ha-ha. Detail of engraving by Rigaud and Baron, 'View of the *Queen's Theatre* from the *Rotunda*/Veüe du *Theatre* de la *Reine* prise a cote de la *Rotunde*', from Sarah Bridgeman, pub., *Views of Stowe* (1739), pl.8.

145 Stowe. Ha-ha. Detail of engraving by Rigaud and Baron, 'View of such parts as are seen from the *Building* at the *Head* of the *Lake*/Veüe de ce qui se voit du *Batiment* à la *Tête* du *Lac*', from Sarah Bridgeman, pub., *Views of Stowe* (1739), pl.2.

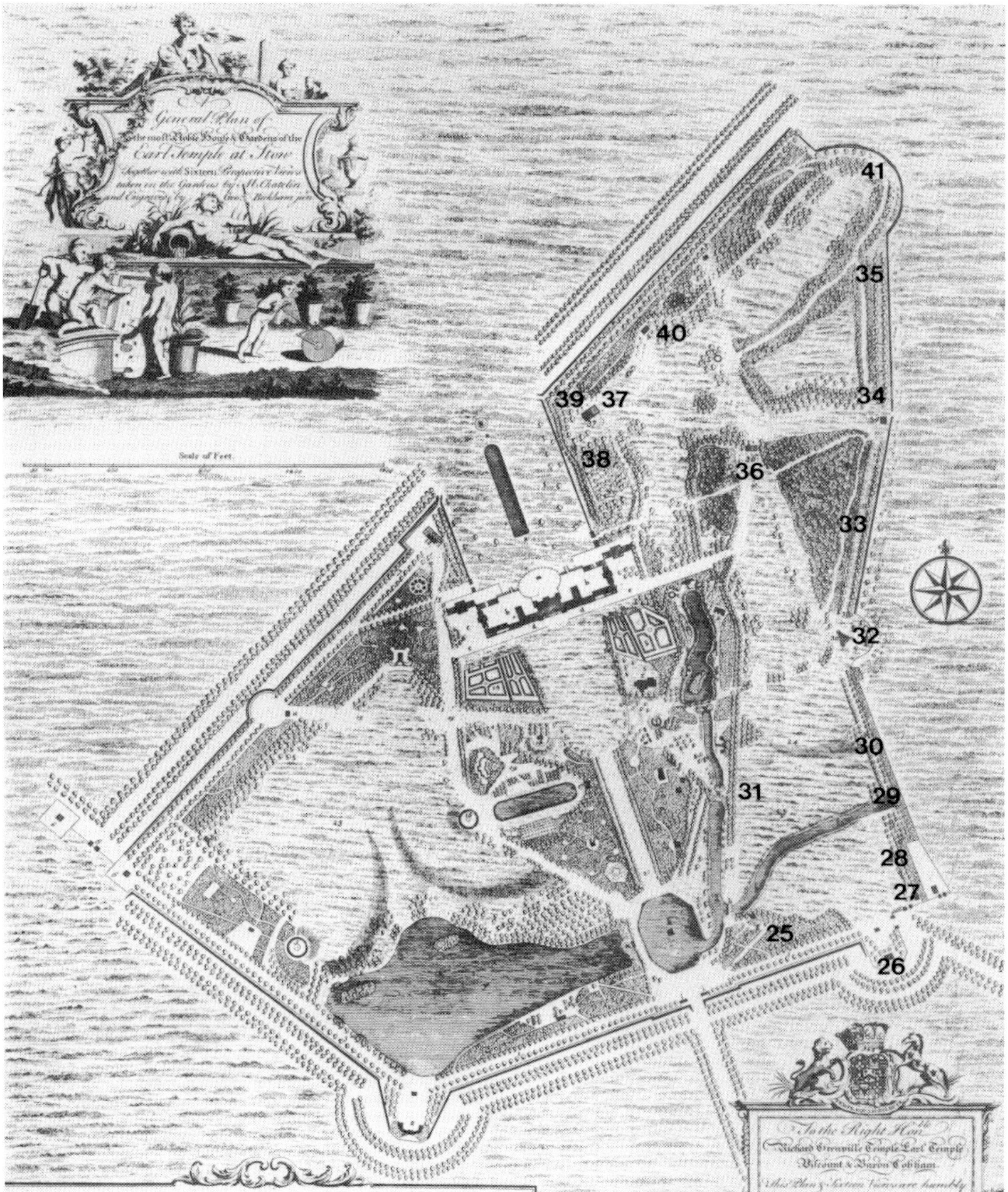

146 Stowe. General Plan. Engraving by Bickham and Chatelain from Bickham, pub., *Views of Stowe* (1753).

147a Stowe. Cascade, Temple of Venus, Egyptian Pyramid, and Fane of Diana. Engraving from Seeley, *Stowe* (1763), pl.2.

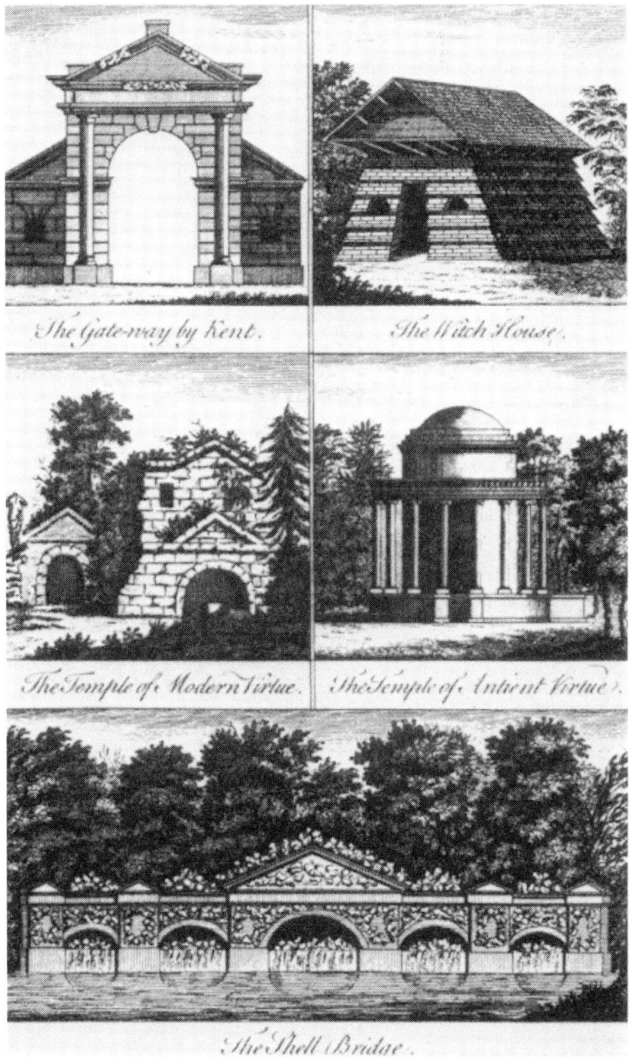

147b Stowe. Gateway (near Boycotts), Witch House, Temple of Modern Virtue, Temple of Ancient Virtue, and Shell Bridge. Engraving from Seeley, *Stowe* (1763), pl.5.

Key to Plate 146 opposite

25 Pebble Alcove and New Garden
26 Temple of Friendship
27 Imperial Closet
28 Hawkwell Mead Walk
29 Palladian Bridge
30 Hawkwell Hill Walk
31 Thanet Walk
32 Gothic Temple
33 Gothic Walk
34 Lord Cobham's Pillar
35 Lord Cobham's Walk
36 Lady's Temple
37 Grecian Temple
38 Grecian Walk
39 Paddock Course Walk
40 Captain Grenville's Monument
41 Triumphal Arch

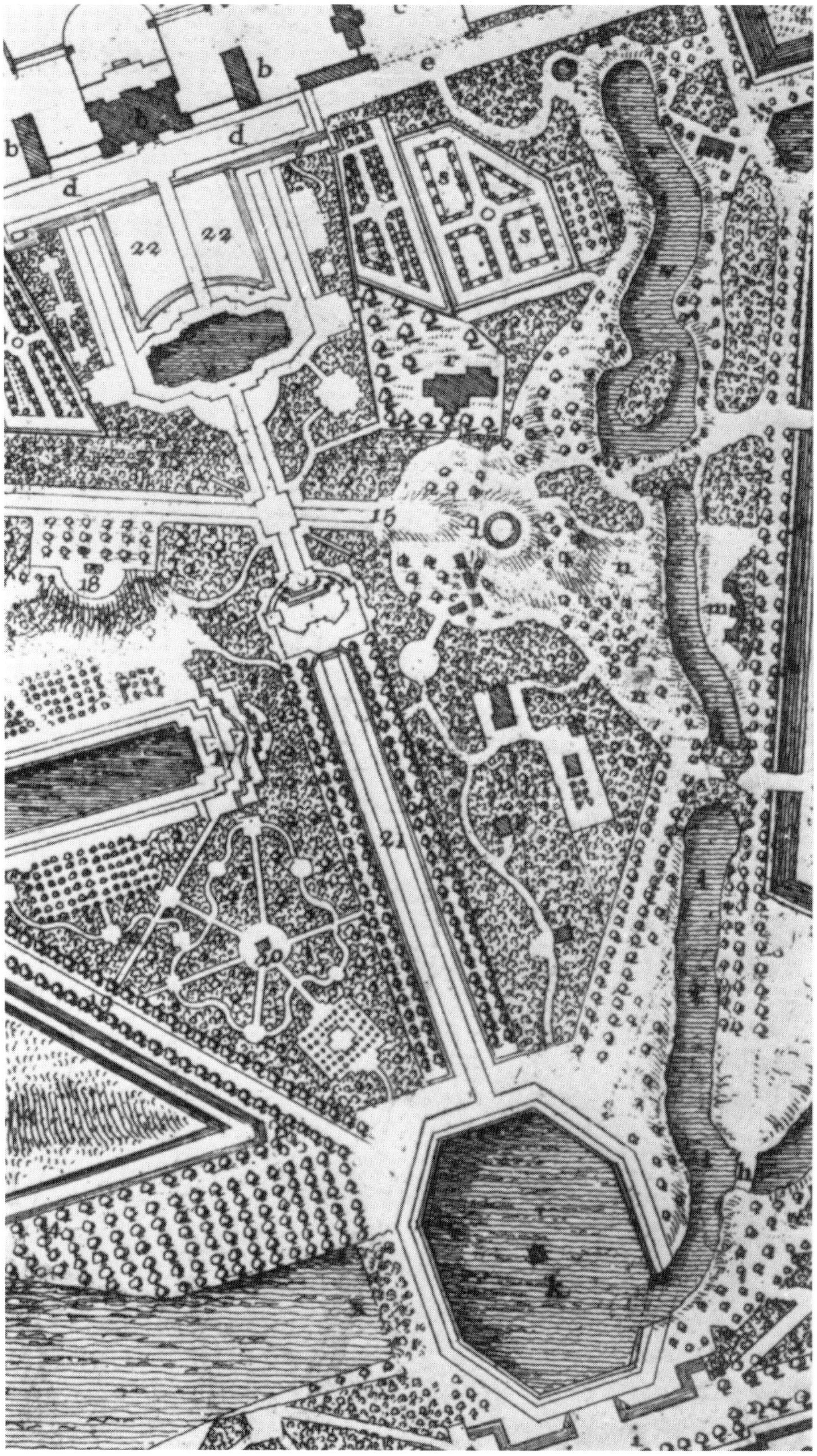

148 Stowe. Detail of Elysian Fields from *Plate 123*.

149 Stowe. Detail of Elysian Fields from *Plate 146*.

150a Stowe. Bickham and Chatelain, 'A View from the Temple of Diana/Le Point de Vüe du Temple de Diane', from Bickham, pub., *Views of Stowe* (1753), pl.d.

LEFT TO RIGHT: King George's Column/Stowe Church/Rotunda/Queen Caroline's Monument/Home Park/Gurnet's Walk/Octagon Lake/Lake Pavilions/Hermitage/Lake Walk/Temple of Venus/Temple of Diana

150b Stowe. Bickham and Chatelain, 'A View of the Queen's Theatre from the Rotundo/Vüe du Theatre de la Reine prise a Cotè de la Rotonde', from Bickham, pub., *Views of Stowe* (1753), pl.g.

LEFT TO RIGHT: Nelson's Seat/Rogers' Walk/Rotunda/King George's Column/Queen's Theatre/Queen Caroline's Monument

151a Stowe. Bickham and Chatelain, 'A View to the Grotto of the Serpentine River in the Alder Grove/Vüe vers la Riviere Serpentine du Bosquet des Auniers prise de la Grotte', from Bickham, pub., *Views of Stowe* (1753), pl.l.

LEFT TO RIGHT: Grotto and Shell Temples/Alder River/Lady's Temple/Cold Bath

151b Stowe. Bickham and Chatelain, 'A View in the Elysian Fields, from the Spring of Helicon/Vüe dans les Champs Elisées, prise de la Fontaine de l'Helicon', from Bickham, pub., *Views of Stowe* (1753), pl.m.

LEFT TO RIGHT: Stowe Castle/Palladian Bridge/Upper River/Hawkwell Hill and Field/Temple of Friendship/Congreve Monument/Lower River/Spring of Helicon, with Apollo and the Nine Muses

152a Stowe. View of Rotunda.

152b Stowe. View of Gothic Temple.

153a Stowe. View of Temple of British Worthies from Temple of Ancient Virtue in Elysian Fields.

153b Stowe. View of Temple of Ancient Virtue from Temple of British Worthies in Elysian Fields.

154a Stowe. View from Palladian Bridge across Octagon Lake to Hawkwell Hill and Field.

154b Stowe. View of Congreve Monument.

155a Stowe. View of Octagon Lake, Lake Pavilions, and Corinthian Arch.

155b Stowe. View of Oxford Bridge and Boycott Pavilions towards Nelson's Walk.

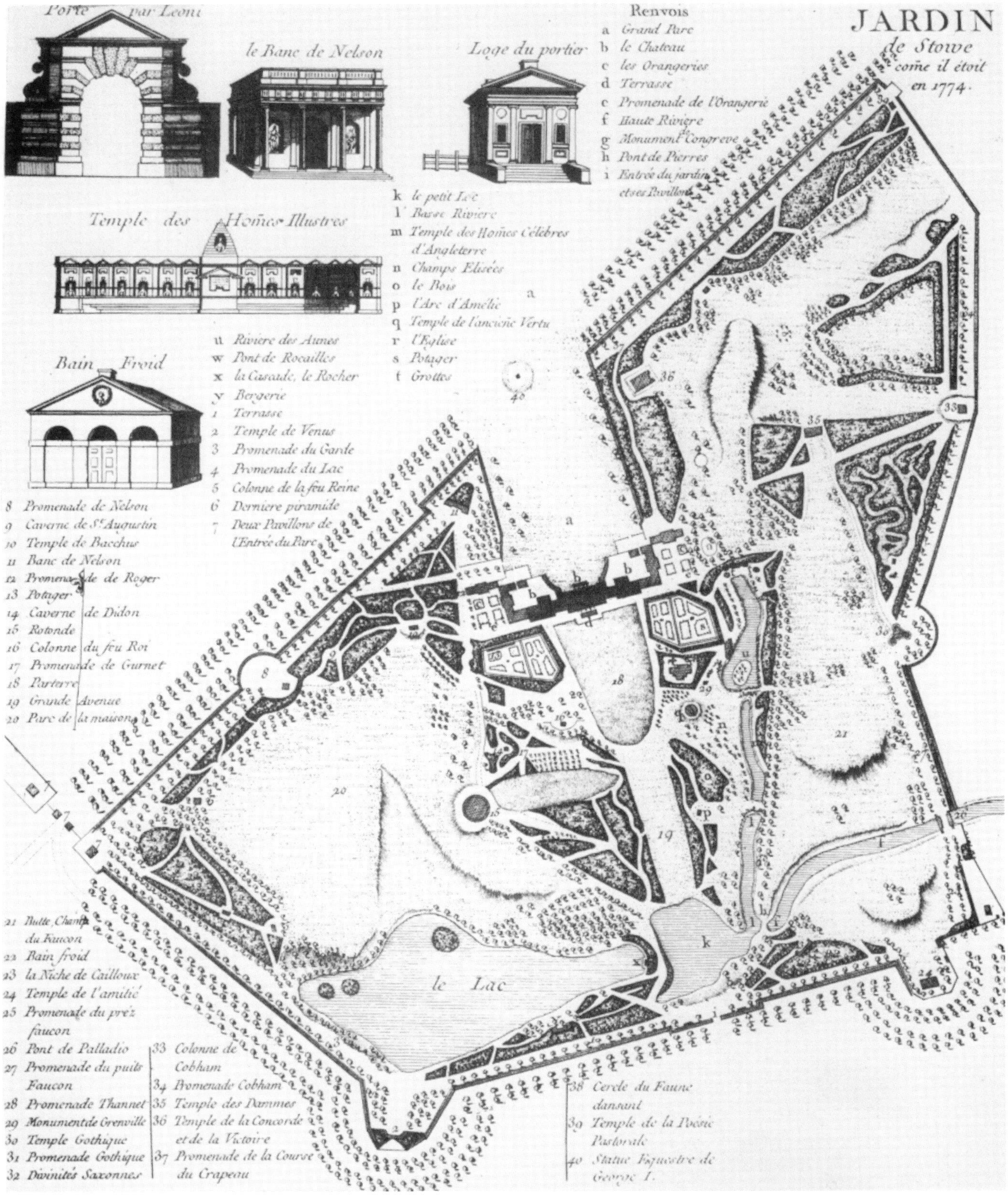

156 Stowe. General Plan in 1774. Engraving from Le Rouge, *Détails des nouveaux iardins à la mode* (1776–88), cahier 4, pl. 18.

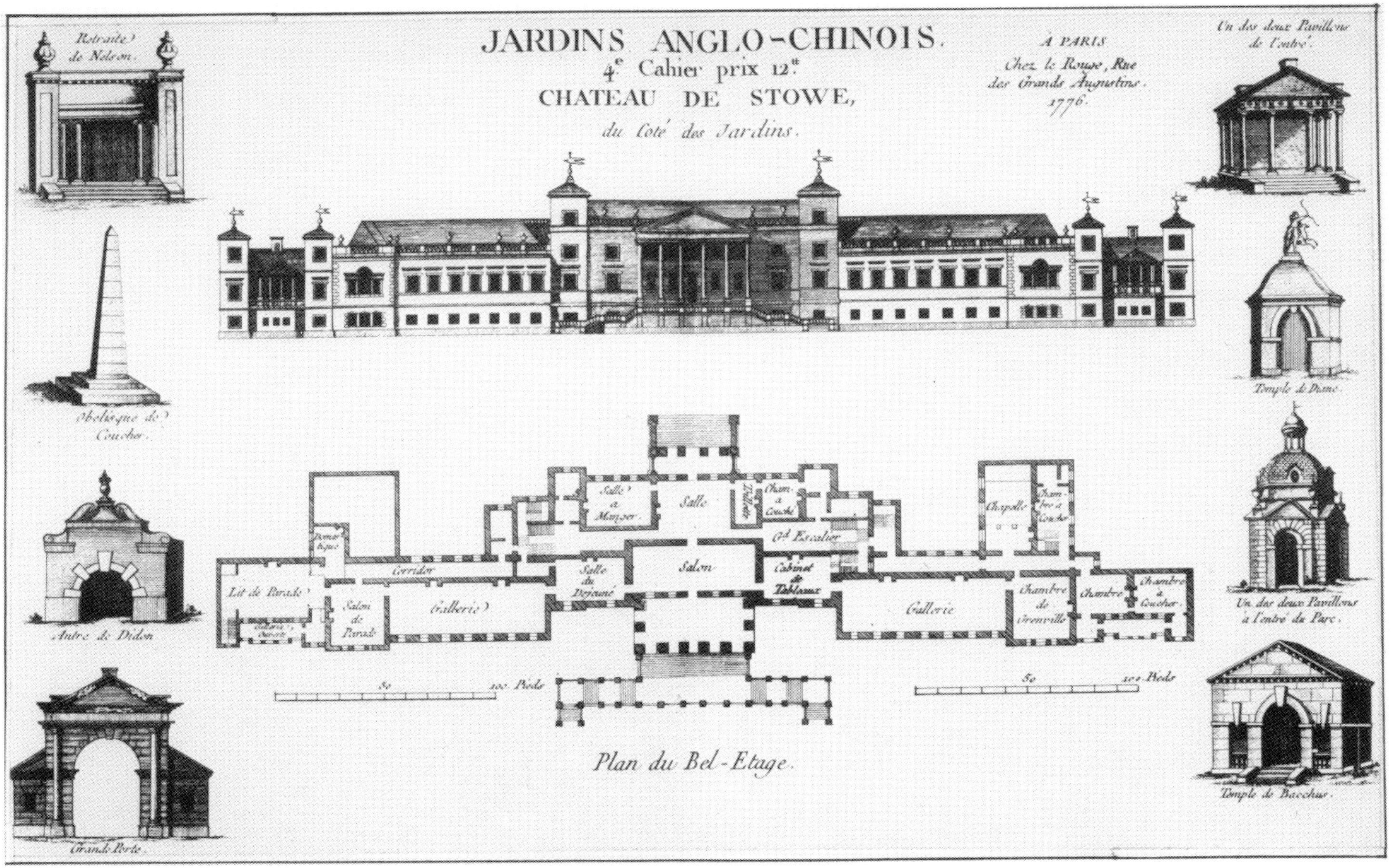

157 Stowe. South (Garden) Front and garden buildings. Engraving from Le Rouge, *Détails des nouveaux jardins à la mode* (1776–88), cahier 4, pl.1.

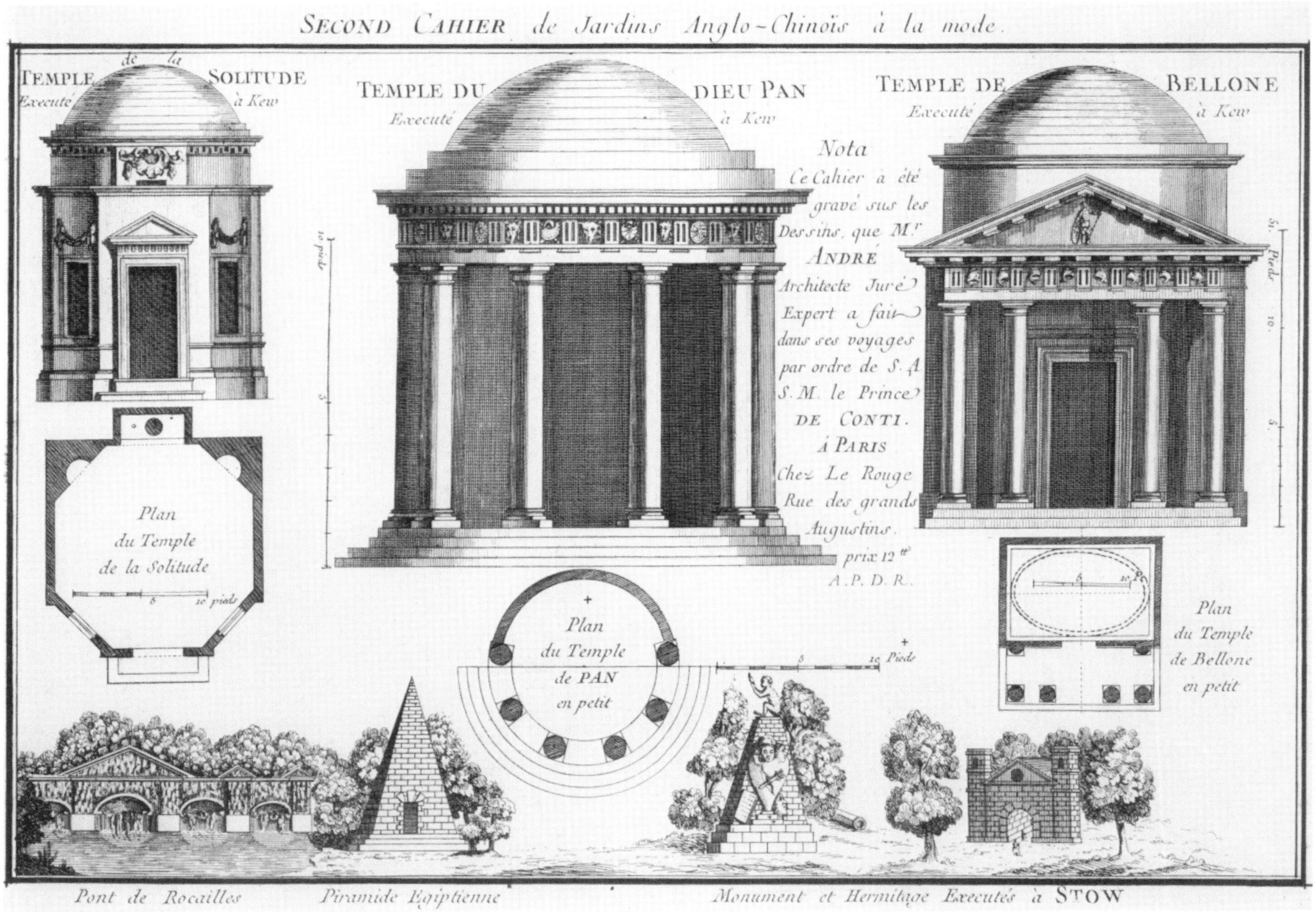

158 Stowe and Kew. Garden buildings. Engraving from Le Rouge, *Détails des nouveaux jardins à la mode* (1776–88), cahier 2, pl.1.

159 *Superbe Jardin Anglais*. Engraving from Le Rouge, *Détails des nouveaux jardins à la mode* (1776–88), cahier 20, pl.4.

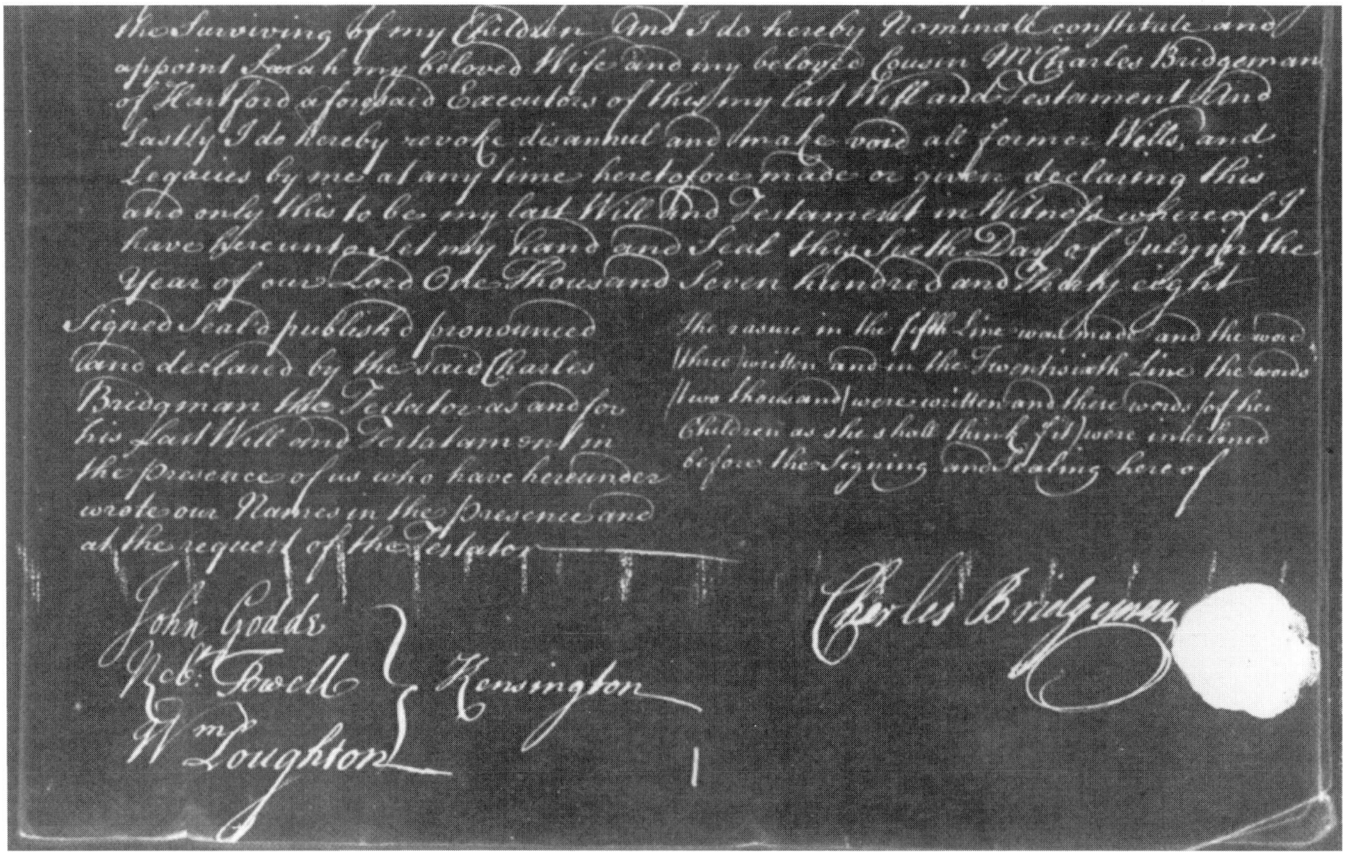
the Surviving of my Children And I do hereby Nominate constitute and appoint Sarah my beloved Wife and my beloved Cousin Mr Charles Bridgeman of Hartford aforesaid Executors of this my last Will and Testament And Lastly I do hereby revoke disannul and make void all former Wills and Legacies by me at any time heretofore made or given declaring this and only this to be my last Will and Testament in Witness whereof I have hereunto set my hand and Seal this Sixth Day of July in the Year of our Lord One Thousand Seven hundred and Thirty eight

Signed Seal'd publish'd pronounced and declared by the said Charles Bridgman the Testator as and for his Last Will and Testament in the presence of us who have hereunder wrote our Names in the presence and at the request of the Testator

John Godde
Robt. Powell
Wm Loughton
Kensington

The rasure in the fifth Line was made and the word Three written and in the Twentysixth Line the words Two thousand were written and these words of her Children as she shall think fit were interlined before the Signing and Sealing hereof

Charles Bridgeman

160a Charles Bridgeman's signature on his will of 6 July 1738. PRO, PROB.11.692 (BRODREPP 1738).

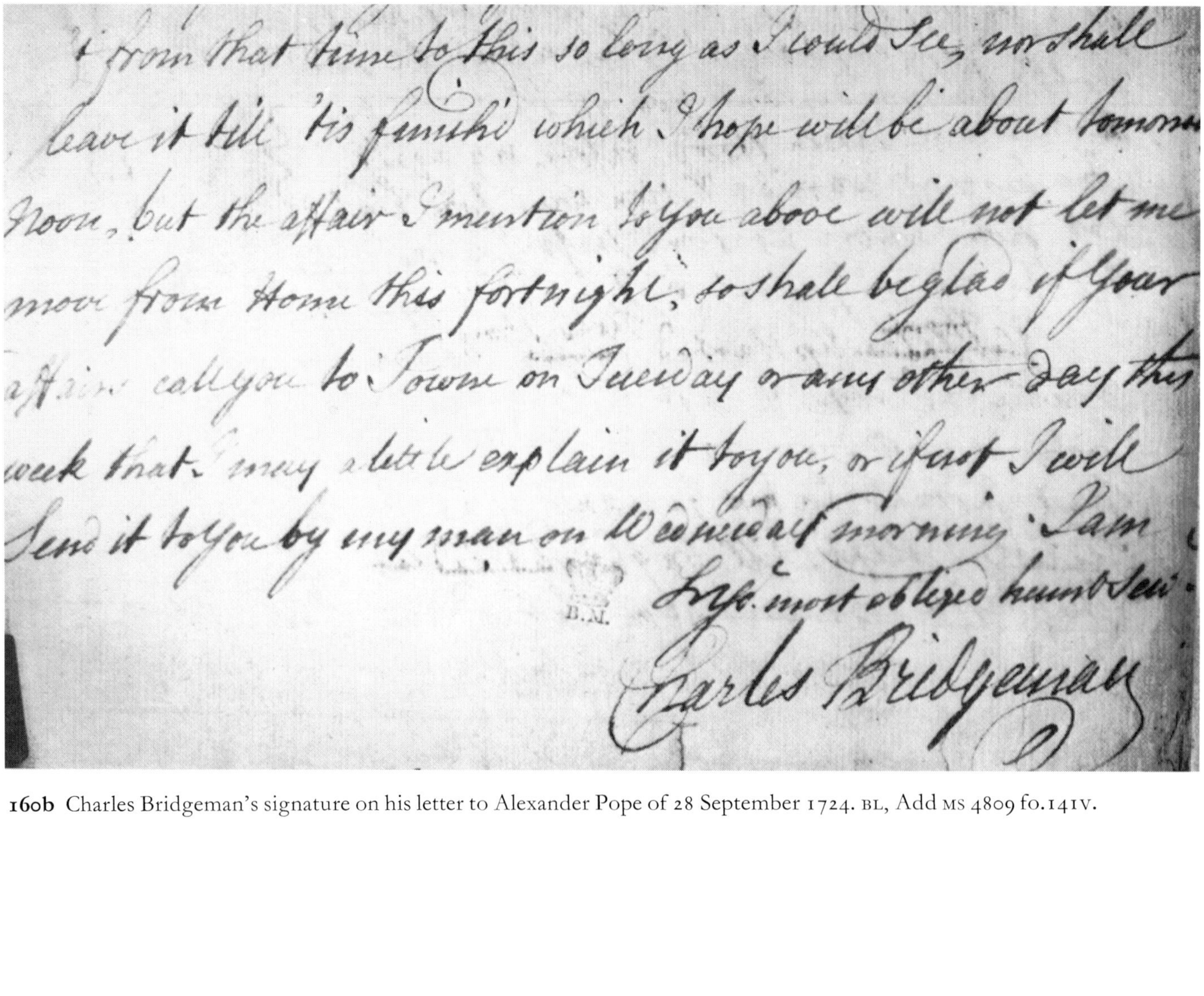
from that time to this so long as I could See, nor shall leave it till 'tis finish'd which I hope will be about tomorrow Noon, but the affair I mention to you above will not let me move from Home this fortnight, so shall be glad if your affairs call you to Towne on Tuesday or any other day this week that I may a little explain it to you, or if not I will Send it to you by my man on Wednesday morning. I am

Yrs. most obliged humb Serv.

Charles Bridgeman

160b Charles Bridgeman's signature on his letter to Alexander Pope of 28 September 1724. BL, Add MS 4809 fo.141v.

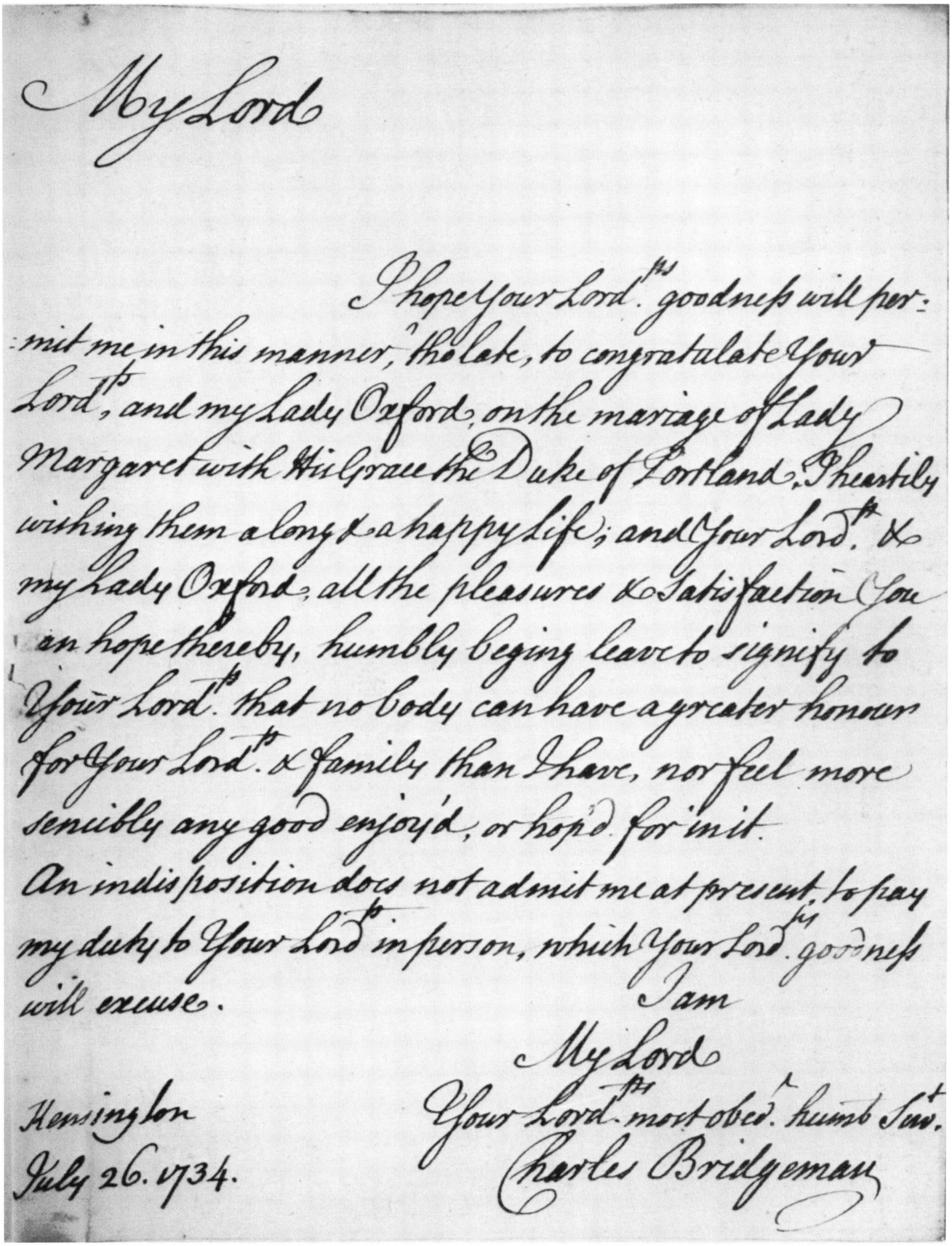

My Lord

I hope Your Lordps. goodness will per:
:mit me in this manner, tho' late, to congratulate Your
Lordp, and my Lady Oxford, on the mariage of Lady
Margaret with His Grace the Duke of Portland; I heartily
wishing them a long & a happy Life; and Your Lordp. &
my Lady Oxford, all the pleasures & Satisfaction You
can hope thereby, humbly beging leave to signify to
Your Lordp. that no body can have a greater honour
for Your Lordp. & family than I have, nor feel more
sencibly any good enjoy'd, or hop'd for in it.
An indisposition does not admit me at present, to pay
my duty to Your Lordp in person, which Your Lordps. goodness
will excuse.

I am
My Lord
Your Lordps. most obedt. humb Servt.
Charles Bridgeman

Kensington
July 26. 1734.

161 Charles Bridgeman's letter to Edward Harley, 2nd Earl of Oxford, 26 July 1734. BL, Loan 29/90 (Portland Papers).

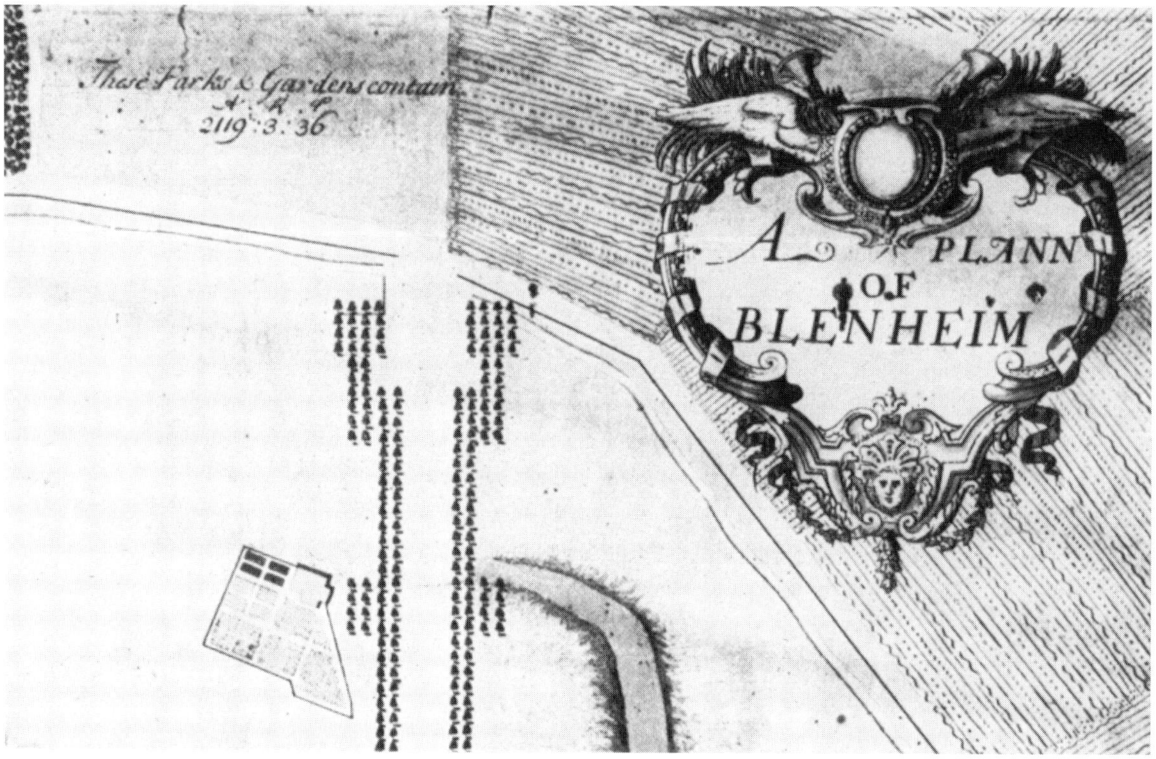

162a Cartouche from Plan of Blenheim. Drawing by Bridgeman signed '1709/Bridgman Discript.' Blenheim.

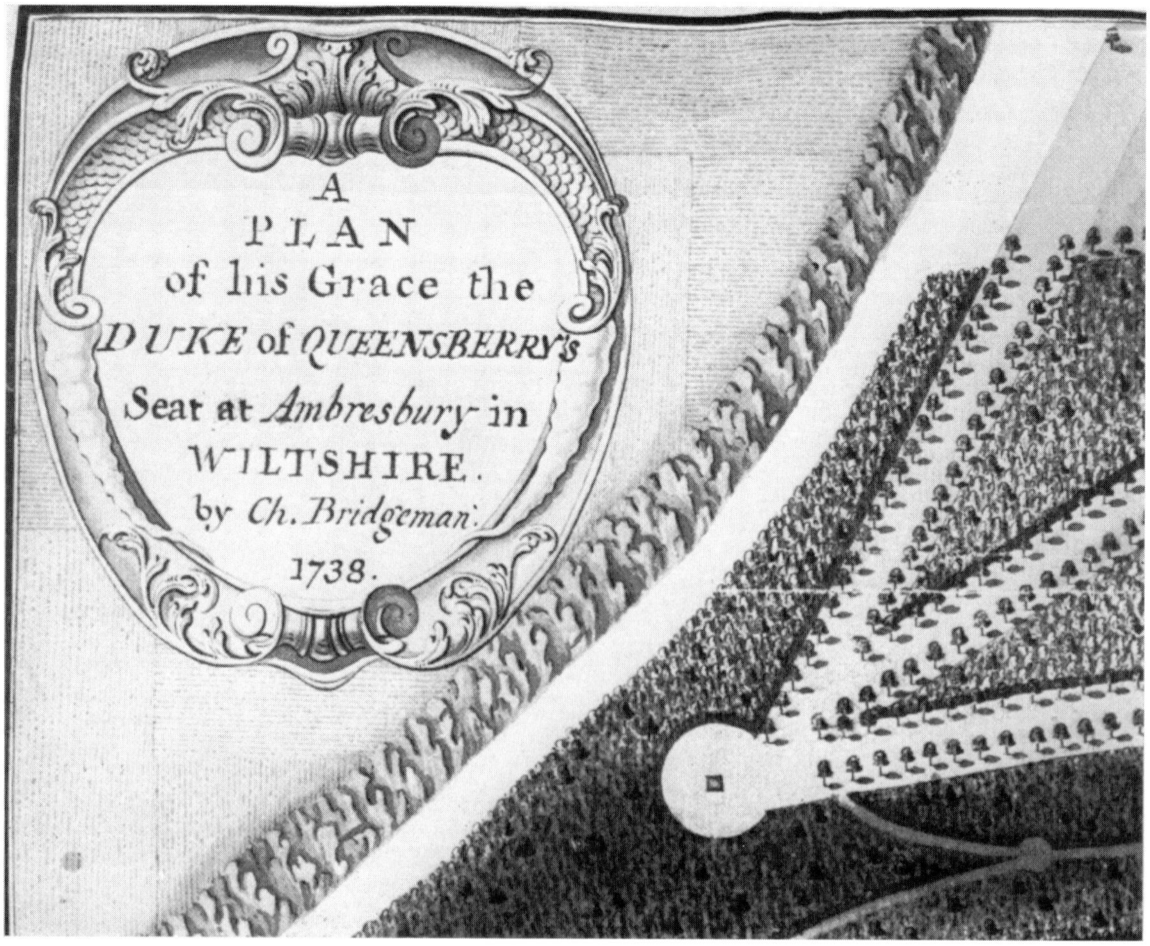

162b Cartouche from Plan of Amesbury. Drawing by Bridgeman signed '*Ch. Bridgeman.*/*1738*.' MSGD a3 fo.32.

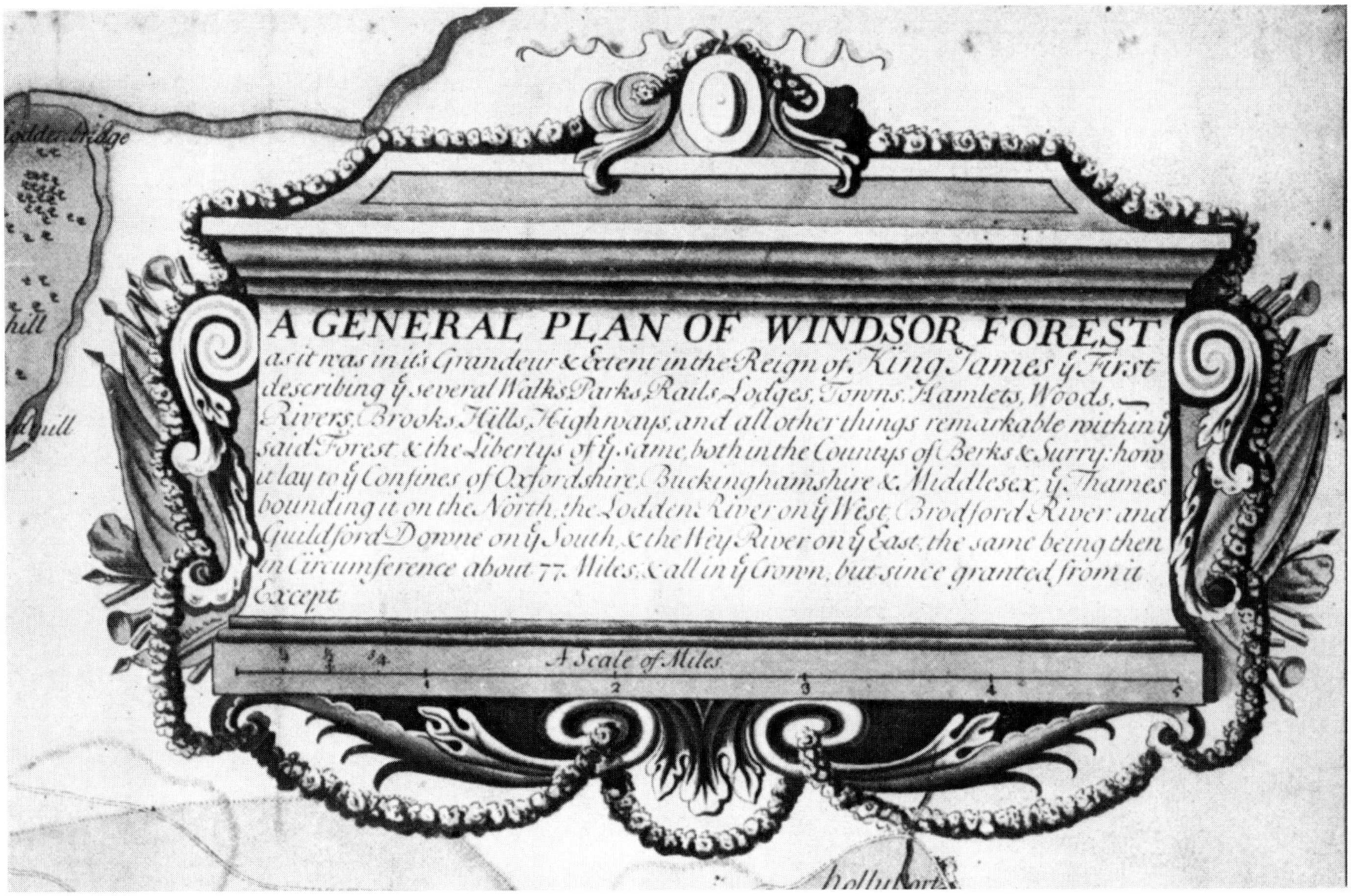

163a Cartouche from General Plan of Windsor Forest as it was in the reign of James I. Drawing by Bridgeman signed 'Bridgman Pinxit'. PRO, MR 279 (Cat.No.854).

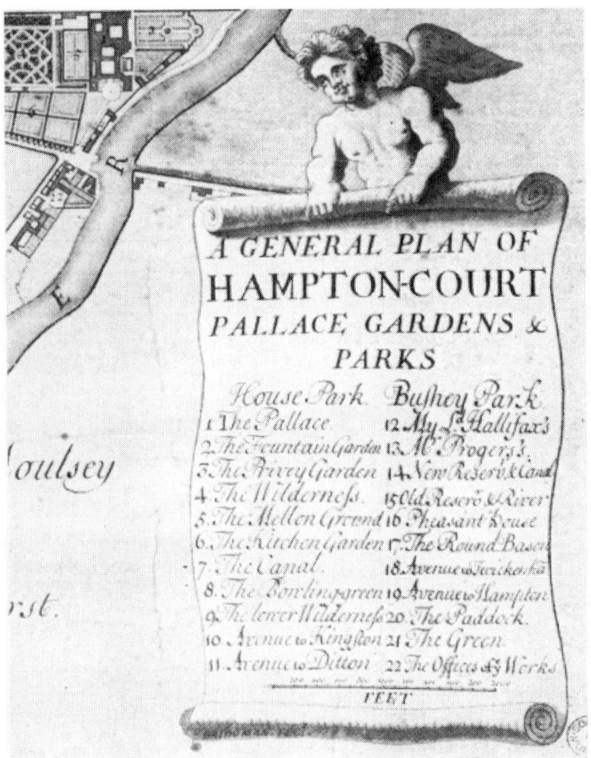

163b Cartouche from Plan of Hampton Court. Drawing by Bridgeman signed 'C.BRIDGMAN FEC^{t}'. Soane, Drawer 36.3.1.

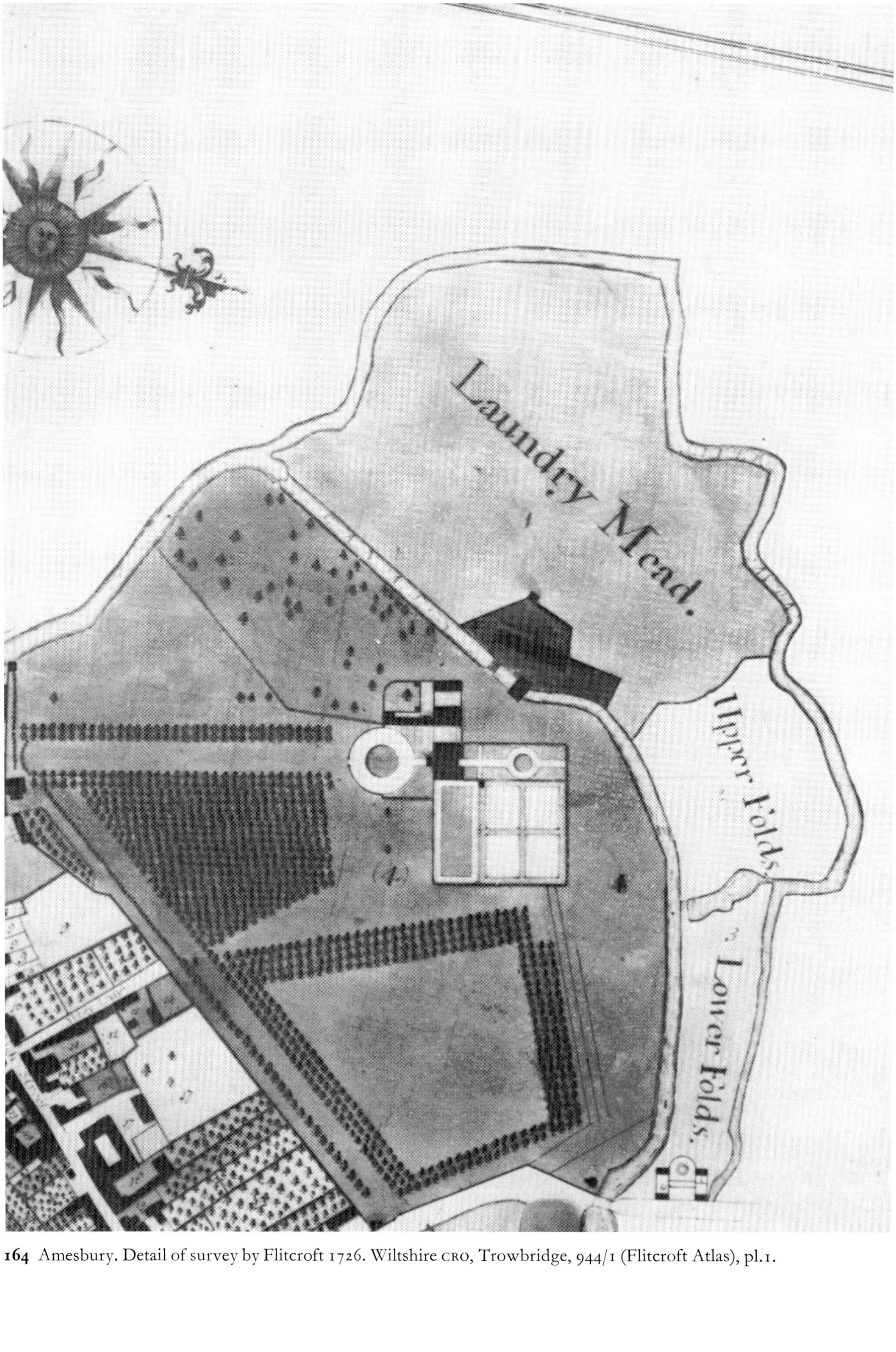

164 Amesbury. Detail of survey by Flitcroft 1726. Wiltshire CRO, Trowbridge, 944/1 (Flitcroft Atlas), pl.1.

165a Claremont. View towards Vanbrugh's Belvedere. Drawing by Kent. BM, 1962. 7.14.51.

165b Claremont. View towards Vanbrugh's Belvedere from Bowling Green. Drawing by Rigaud 1733–34. V&A, D.259–1890 (PD 148).

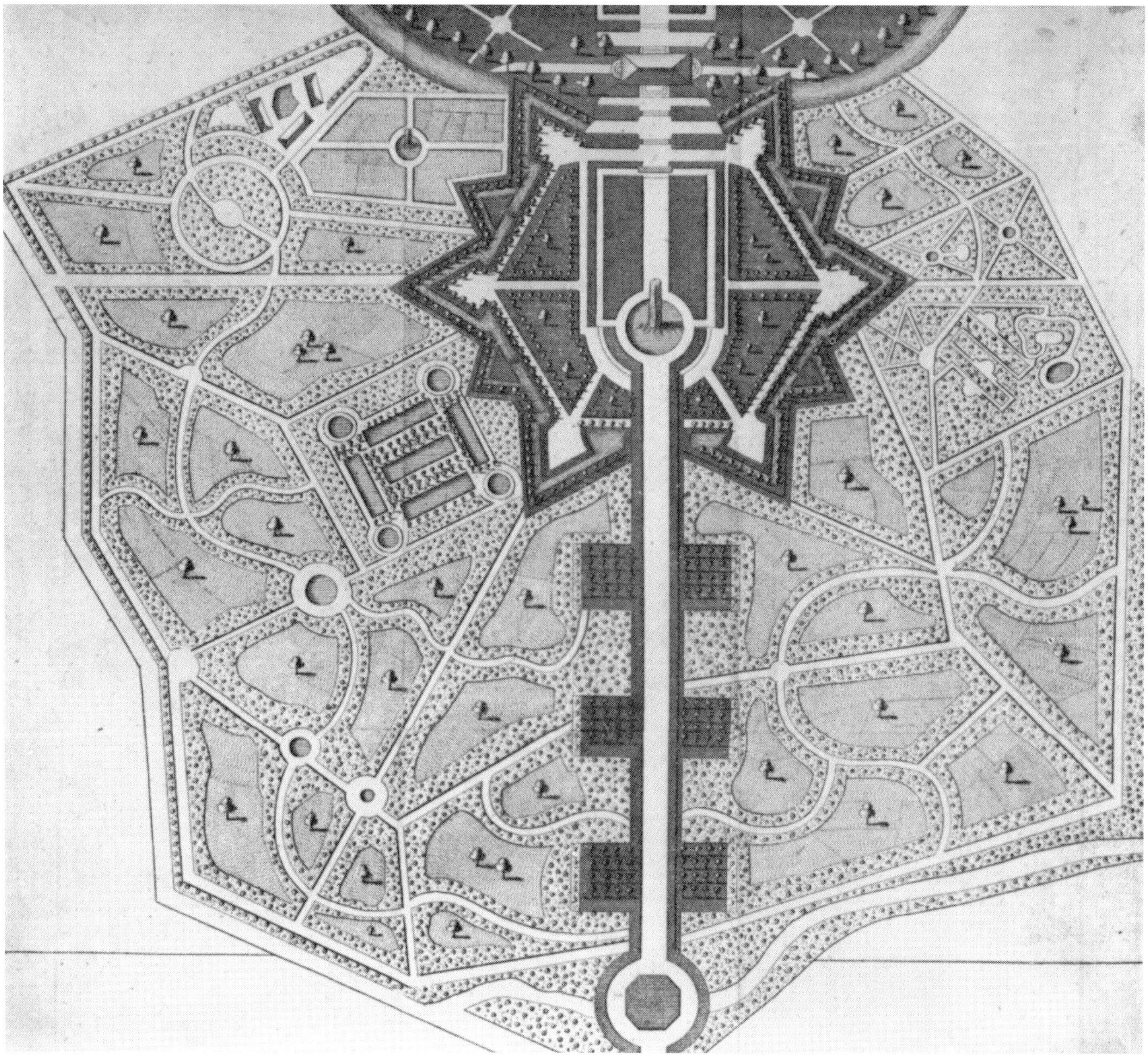

166 'The Manor of Paston divided and planted with Rural Gardens'. Engraving from Switzer, *Ichnographia Rustica* (1718), II, pl. facing p.115.

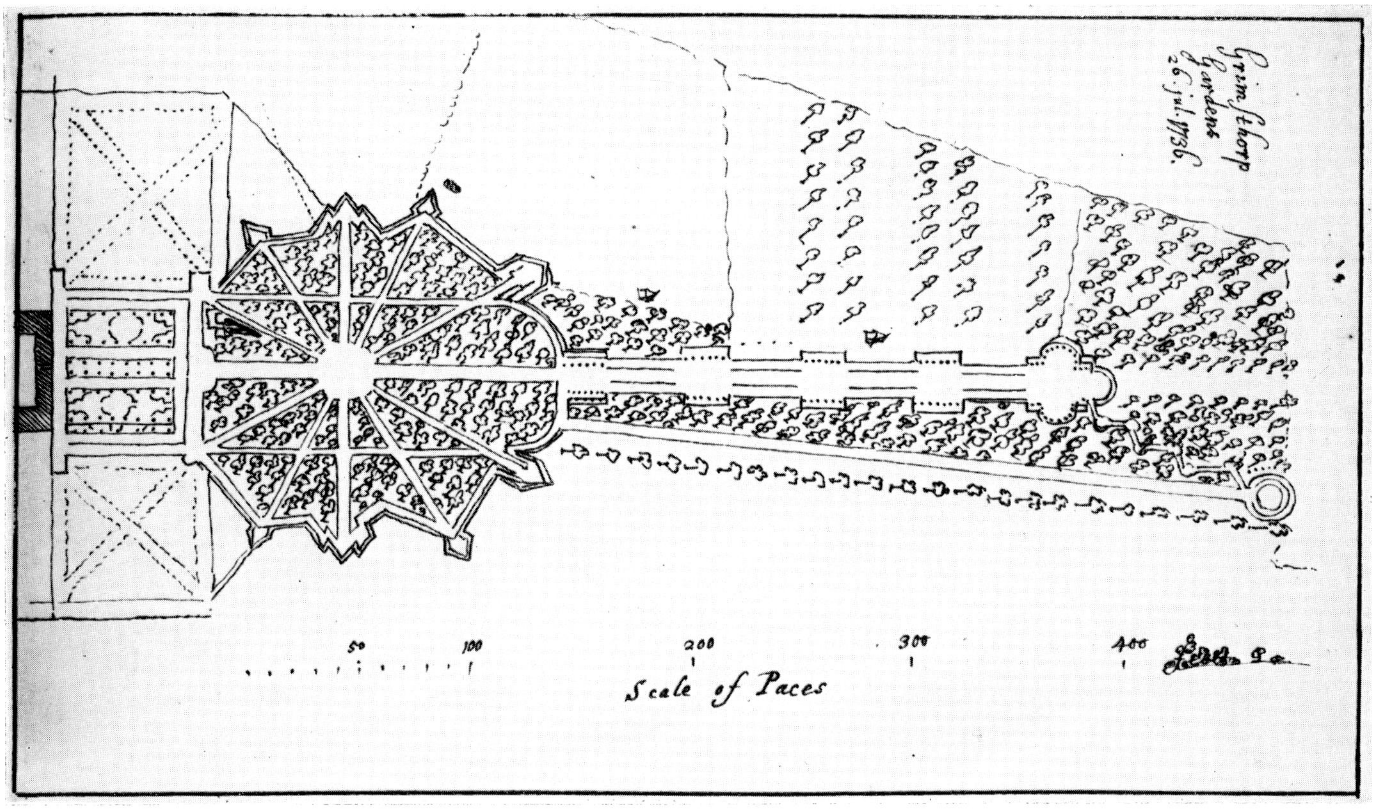

167a Grimsthorpe. Plan. Drawing by Stukeley 1736. Bod.Lib., MS Top.Gen.d.14, fo.36v.

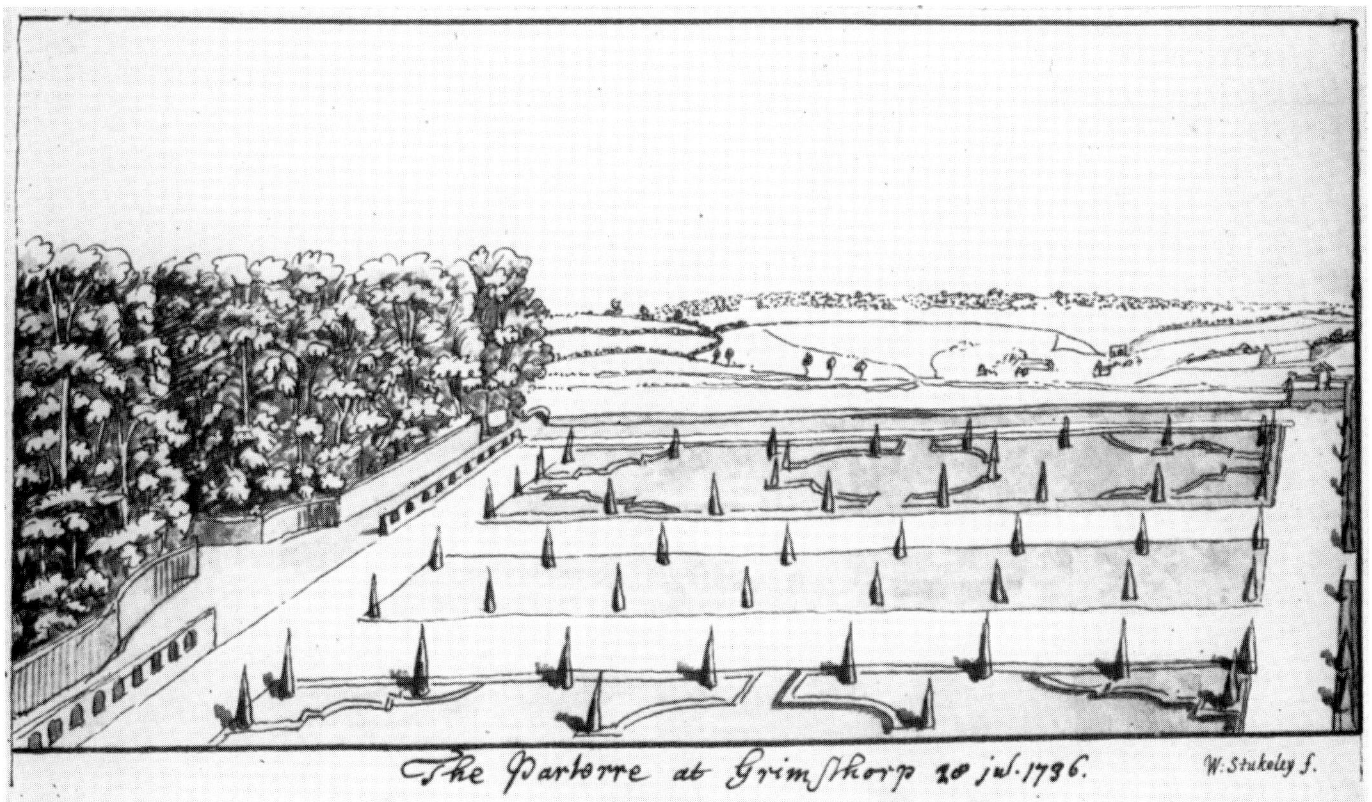

167b Grimsthorpe. Parterre. Drawing by Stukeley 1736. Bod.Lib., MS Top. Gen.d.14, fo.37v.

168a Grimsthorpe. Grime's Walk. Drawing by Stukeley 1736. Bod.Lib., MS Top.Gen.d.14, fo.37r.

168b Grimsthorpe. Duchesses' Bastion. Drawing by Stukeley 1736. Bod.Lib., MS Top.Gen.d.14, fo.38v.

169a Pope, trans., *The Odyssey* (1725–26), title-page (detail). Drawn by Kent and engraved by Foudrinier.

169b Pope, trans., *The Odyssey* (1725–26). Tailpiece to Book IX. Drawn by Kent and engraved by Foudrinier.

170a Gay, *Fables*, I (1727). Headpiece to 'Cupid, Hymen, and Plutus' (Fable XII). Drawn by Kent and engraved by Foudrinier.

170b Gay, *Fables*, I (1727). Headpiece to 'The Butterfly and the Snail' (Fable XXIV). Drawn by Kent and engraved by Foudrinier.

171a Thomson, *The Seasons* (1730). Detail of illustration to 'Spring'. Drawn by Kent and engraved by Tardieu.

171b Spenser, *The Faerie Queene* (1751 ed.). Detail of plate entitled 'Guyon leaves the Palmer & crosses the Idle Lake with Phedria'. Drawing by Kent. V&A, E.885–1928 (I.125a).

172a Temple and Round Pond. Drawing by Kent. Devonshire Collection, Chatsworth.

172b Chatsworth. Temple and Canal. Drawing by Kent. Devonshire Collection, Chatsworth.

173a Woodland Scene. Drawing by Kent. Devonshire Collection, Chatsworth.

173b Woodland Scene by Moonlight. Drawing by Kent. Devonshire Collection, Chatsworth.

174a Chiswick. Detail of drawing by Kent. Devonshire Collection, Chatsworth.

174b Chiswick. Unexecuted Scheme for Lawn and Exedra. Drawing by Kent. Devonshire Collection, Chatsworth.

175a Wooded Theatre. Drawing by Kent. BM, 1962.7.14.48.

175b Wooded Theatre with Urn on Pedestal. Drawing by Kent. Devonshire Collection, Chatsworth.

176a Chatsworth. Canal Basin. Drawing by Kent. Devonshire Collection, Chatsworth.

176b Classical Scene. Drawing by Kent. Devonshire Collection, Chatsworth.

177a Villa Crivelli Sormani-Verri, Castellazzo. Engraving from D. Lucchese, *Delizie della Villa di Castellazzo* (1743).

177b Villa Brenzone, San Vigilio. Busts of Roman Emperors.

178a Woburn Farm, Surrey. View. Engraving by Luke Sullivan 1759.

178b Painshill. View. Engraving by Woollett 1760.

179a The Leasowes. View. Engraving by Jenkins *c.*1779.

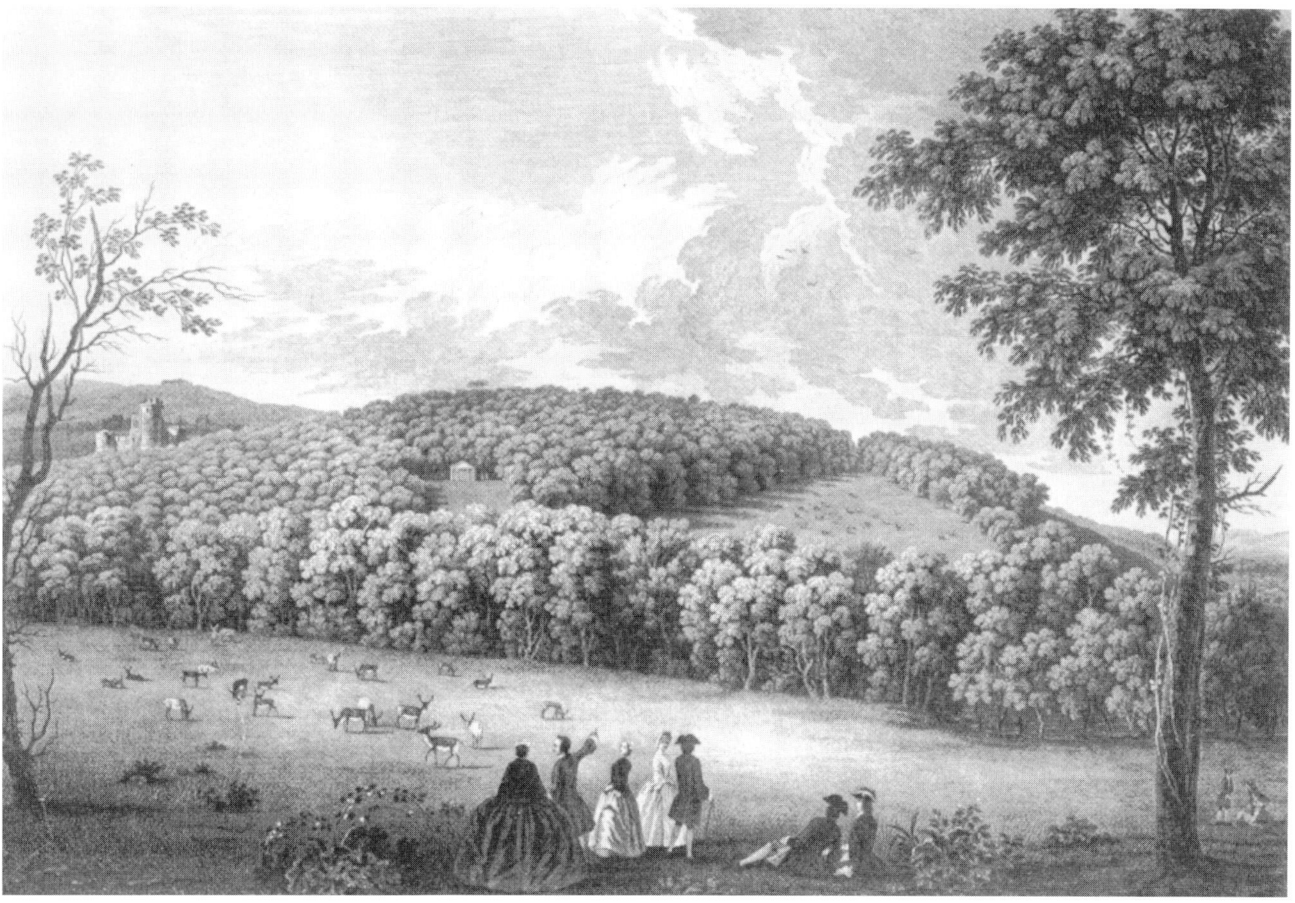

179b Hagley. View. Engraving by Smith and Vivares 1749.

180 Stourhead. View from Hermitage. Drawing by Piper 1779. Nationalmuseum, Stockholm, Låda XI, Pi-e 6 (5).

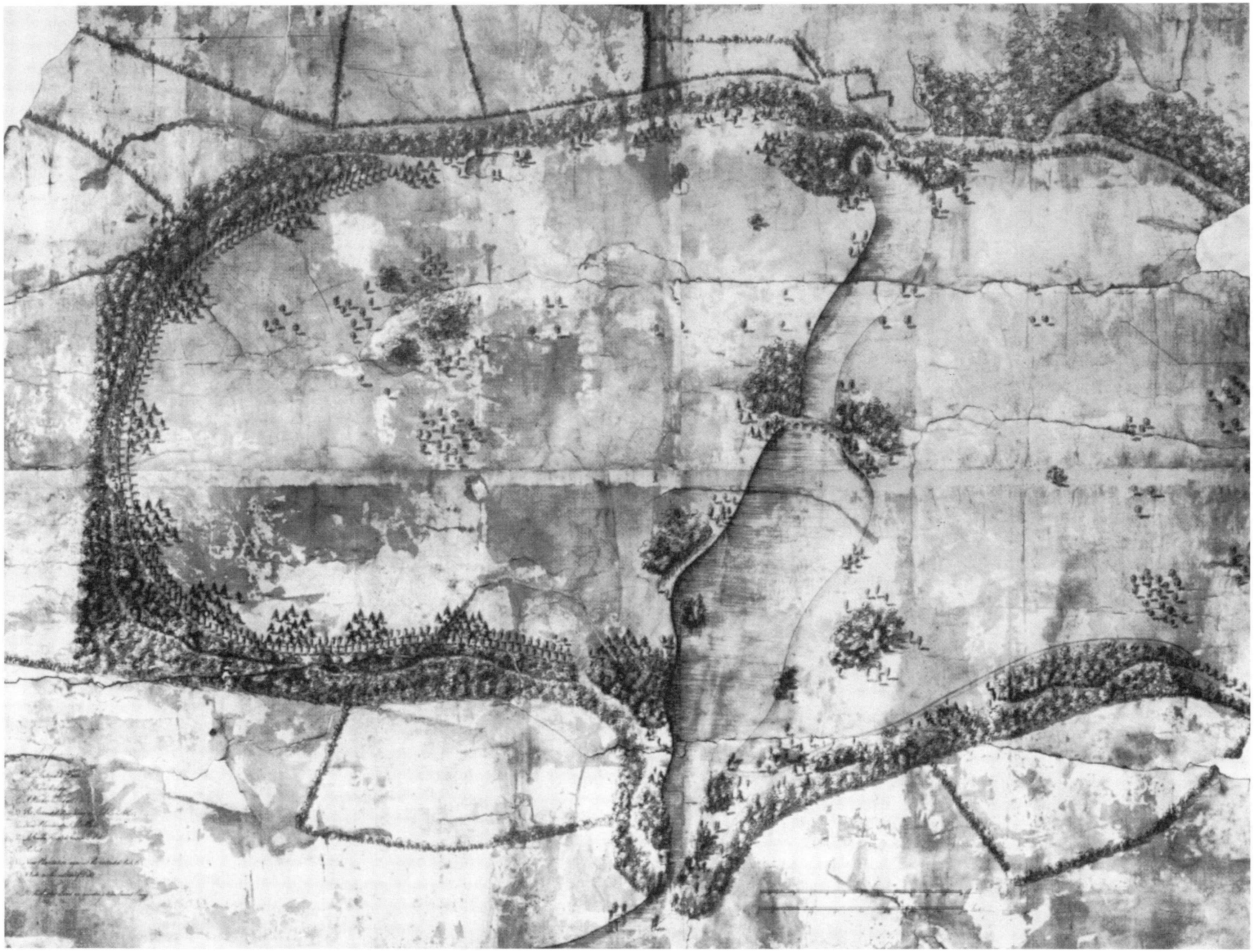

181 Wimpole. Plan. Drawing by Lancelot 'Capability' Brown *c*.1767. Wimpole.

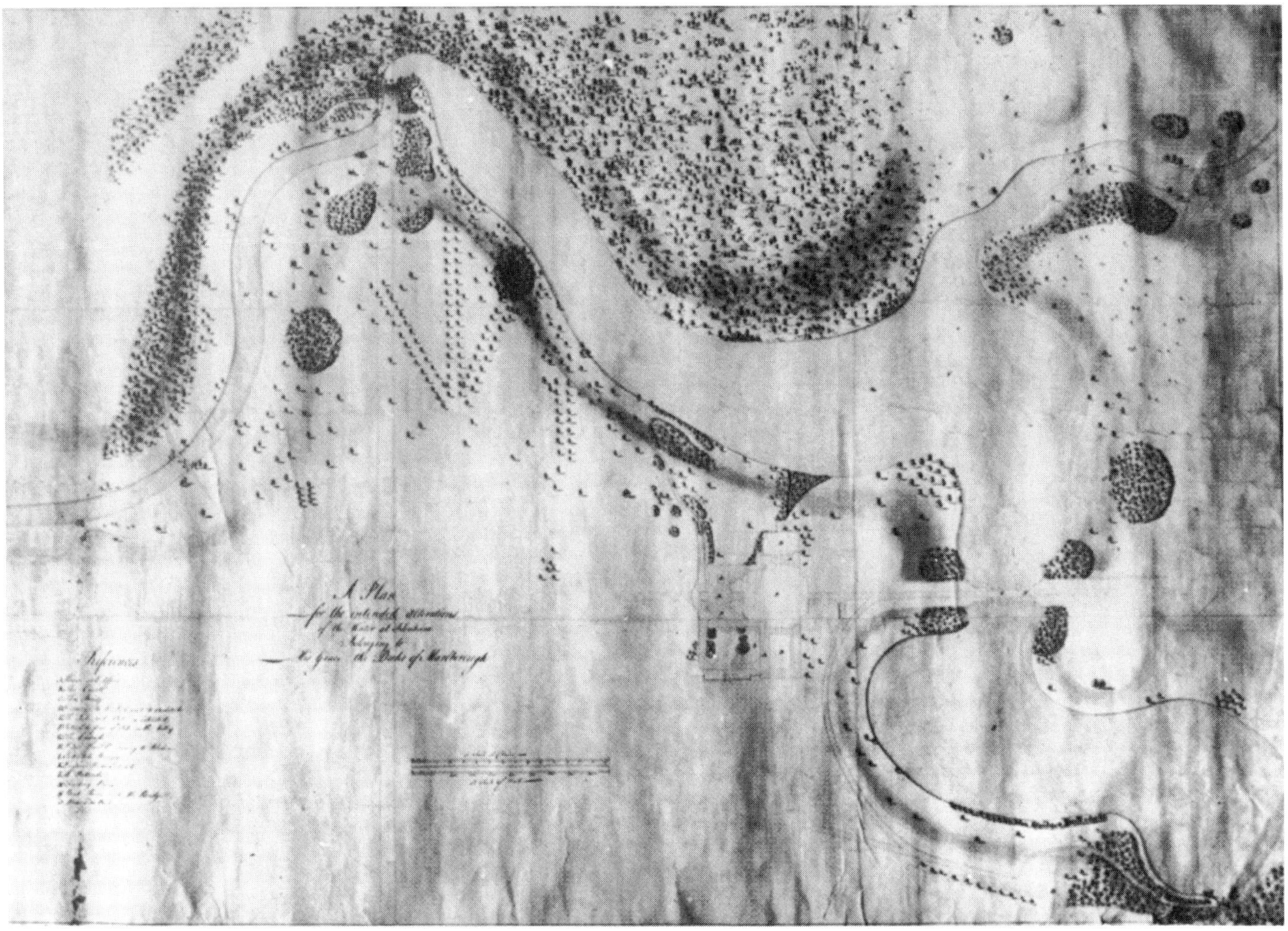

182a Blenheim. Plan. Drawing by Lancelot 'Capability' Brown *c.*1765. Blenheim.

182b Blenheim. View of Palace, Island and Grand Bridge, taken from bottom right-hand corner of *Plate 182a.*

183a Drottningholm. Project for Memorial Temple to Gustav III on Monument Island. Drawing by Piper 1798. Nationalmuseum, Stockholm, Låda VIII, Pi-b 2 (2).

183b Hohenheim. View of ruins of Roman Baths. Aquatint from Heideloff, *Ansichten des Herzoglich-Würtembergischen Landsitzes Hohenheim* (1795).

184 Malmaison. View of Castle from garden. Engraving from Laborde, *Description des nouveaux jardins de la France et de ses anciens châteaux* (1808), pl.4.

185a Bagatelle. View of Chinese Bridge. Engraving by Moreau and Saugrain.

185b Ermenonville. View of Rousseau's Tomb on Island of Poplars, and Temple of Philosophy. Engraving from Laborde, *Description des nouveaux jardins de la France et de ses anciens châteaux* (1808). pl.34.

186a Ermenonville. View of Temple of Philosophy.

186b Ermenonville. Rousseau's Tomb on Island of Poplars. Engraving from Le Rouge, *Détails des nouveaux jardins à la mode* (1776–88), cahier 9, pl.15.

Catalogue of Additional Documents
Drawings and Attributions

Catalogue of Additional Documents, Drawings and Attributions

The following catalogue is arranged alphabetically by place, and indexed on pages 439–441. As in the original edition of *Bridgeman*, the names used for English counties are those which were applicable *before* the reorganization of Local Government in 1974. Similarly, the abbreviations in the catalogue follow the list given under 'Abbreviations' in *Bridgeman*, pages xx–xi.

The largest single collection of Bridgeman drawings remains that in MS Gough Drawings A3 and A4 in the Bodleian Library, Oxford. For a catalogue of them see my 'Charles Bridgeman: Royal Gardener' (unpublished Ph.D. thesis, University of Cambridge, 1962), appendix F(b), pages 396–423. A copy of this appendix is available for consultation in the Department of Special Collections and Western Manuscripts in the Bodleian Library.

The bibliographical references in the catalogue below are limited to those which contain specific material on Bridgeman; they are by no means intended as a comprehensive statement of material published since 1977. Photographs and drawings are reproduced by courtesy of the owners and other sources indicated in the captions to the plates. The seven diagrams of formal elements in Bridgeman's signed plans (*Plates 246* and *247*) were prepared in 1961 for my Ph.D. thesis and are published here for the first time.

AMESBURY Wiltshire

See Bodleian Library, MS Maps, Misc.a.1, which Sir Howard Colvin has suggested may be a plan of Amesbury by Bridgeman, but this is uncertain.

See also *Bridgeman*, pp.50, 53–54, 71n7, 78, 128–28, 130–31, 132, 140, 174, 175–76, 177, and *Plates 36, 37a, 37b, 162b* and *164*

AUDLEY END Essex

See Bodleian Library, MSGD A4 fos 60 and 67, catalogued in *Bridgeman*, p.177, and reproduced below as *Plates 187* and *188.*

See also *Bridgeman*, pp.14n52, 64n107

BADMINTON Gloucestershire

Bridgeman is referred to in four letters written to the 4th Duke of Beaufort (1709–56) when he was Lord Noel Somerset, preserved at Badminton and arranged by him in bundles (FmJ 2/12); each letter is endorsed with the name of the correspondent and date. They are published here by courtesy of His Grace the Duke of Beaufort, and were drawn to my attention by Mrs Margaret Richards and by Professor Andor Gomme, who initially transcribed them.

From the 3rd Duke of Beaufort, 8 February 1733/34

> As to Wootton & Bridgeman I can't tell you what to say for Smith was here yesterday & shakes his Head sadly abt a Pediment [,] the Walls of ye House being very narrow & draw'd in at [the] Top; & likewise queries how it will look in all ye other Fronts since there can be nothing to back it, for it will be much Higher than the Cupillo is now.

From the Duchess of Beaufort, 11 March 1733/34

> The draught Bridgeman sent down for Badminton is one of the Grandest things I have seen, and will I believe answer in the execution as well as it does upon paper. My Ld: seems much please'd with it, and I hope it meets with your favourable opinion, least I shou'd be oblige'd to call my own judgement in question.

From the 3rd Duke of Beaufort, 17 March 1733/34

> I am glad to find the Drawings got safe to Town, and I must beg you to get either Wootton or Bridgeman to draw me out a Plan of ye Foundations of ye Temple & Gateway that I may know ye size of 'em in order to [start] ye setting out [of] ye Ground for levelling it to be ready for planting next Season ... Pray put Bridgeman in mind yt ye Temple is broader than the Plan of ye House he put into ye Design which he left here.

From the 3rd Duke of Beaufort, 30 March 1734 [A postscript]

> pray send ye Plans of ye Ground Plots of ye Houses from Bridgeman as soon as you can for I want 'em sadly.

For the context of these letters see Andor Gomme, 'Badminton Revisited', *Architectural History*, XXVII (1984), 163–82, and his *Smith of Warwick. Francis Smith, Architect and Master-Builder* (Stamford, Lincolnshire: Shaun Tyas, 2000), p.250.

See also *Bridgeman*, pp.71, 84, 88, 118n46, 135, and *Plates 86* and *87*

BLENHEIM Oxfordshire

See Bodleian Library, MS Top Oxon a37*fo.2, catalogued in *Bridgeman*, p.177, and reproduced below as *Plate 189*.

Frances Harris, 'Charles Bridgeman at Blenheim?', *Garden History*, XIII, no.1 (Spring 1985), 1–3, casts doubt on the documentation of Bridgeman's work at Blenheim. Her view is based on the correspondence between Sarah, Duchess of Marlborough, and Mrs Sarah Bridgeman, of ?1739–41, which she believes refers not to Blenheim but to Bridgeman's landscaping at Wimbledon, Surrey. See also Frances Harris, *A Passion for Government. The Life of Sarah, Duchess of Marlborough* (Oxford, 1991), and the catalogue entry below under WIMBLEDON on p.436.

Two of the three letters from the Duchess to Mrs Bridgeman of 6 July, 26 July and 10 September 1741 (published in *Bridgeman*, pp.157–60) are now in BL, Add MS 61478, fos 39–40 (6 July), and 45–46 (10 September). Eight unpublished letters from Mrs Bridgeman to the Duchess of Marlborough, of ?1739–1741, are in BL, Add MS 61478, fos 9–12, 17–18, 31–34, 43–44, 47–48, and 51–52.

See *Bridgeman*, pp.6n12, 14, 15, 23, 31n30, 33, 43, 45–47, 58, 68, 71n7, 98n45, 109, 112, 118n46, 120, 128n1, 129–30, 133, 134, 141, 143, 175–76, 177, and *Plates 23a-25, 162a, 182a* and *182b*

BOUGHTON Northamptonshire

Details of the two Bridgemanic bird's-eye views of Boughton from the west (see *Plates 40, 41a)* are reproduced below as *Plates 191a* and *191b*.

Although the two other plans of Boughton, catalogued in *Bridgeman*, p.177, are no longer ascribed to the Royal Gardener, they are reproduced below as *Plates 190a* and *190b*.

See also *Bridgeman*, pp.50, 54–56, 68, 134n39, and *Plates 41b* and *42b*

BRIGGENS Hertfordshire

See Andrew C. Skelton, 'The Development of the Briggens Estate, Hunsdon, since 1720', *Hertfordshire Archaeology*, XII (1994–1996), 111–28.

See also *Bridgeman*, pp.27, 33n41, 59, 62, 128

BROCKET Hertfordshire

See Bodleian Library, MSGD A3 fo.7 and A4 fo.40, catalogued in *Bridgeman*, pp.177–78, and reproduced below as *Plates 192a* and *192b*.

See also *Bridgeman*, pp.87n107, 177–78

BUCKINGHAM HOUSE London

See Soane, vol.III/42, catalogued in *Bridgeman*, p.178, and reproduced below as *Plate 193a*.

See also *Bridgeman*, p.99

CASTLE HILL Devon

Castle Hill has Bridgemanic features but no firm documentation linking it to the Royal Gardener. See Kenneth Woodbridge, 'Landscaping at Castle Hill', *C. Life*, CLXV (4 January 1979), 18–21; Robin Fausset, 'The Creation of the Gardens at Castle Hill, South Molton, Devon', *Garden History*, XIII, no.2 (Autumn 1985), 102–125; and the correspondence in *Garden History*, XV, no.2 (Autumn 1987), 167–71, which includes a 'reply' by John Harris. A prospect of Castle Hill of 1741 by Jo. Lange (Langs?) is reproduced in Roy Strong, *The Artist and the Garden* (New Haven and London, 2000), plate 251.

See also *Bridgeman*, p.62, and *Plates 54a* and *54b*

CAVENDISH SQUARE London

Bridgeman's work at Cavendish Square is documented in *Bridgeman*, pp.29–30, 32, 60n84, 71, and *Plate 14*. For its context see Todd Longstaffe-Gowan, *The London Town Garden, 1740–1840* (New Haven and London, 2001), especially pp.37, 255n18.

CLAREMONT Surrey

The plan in the Bodleian Library, MSGD A4 fo.81, which was catalogued in *Bridgeman*, p.186, as 'unidentified', has since been proposed by John Harris as being a preliminary design for Claremont. See his article 'The Beginnings of Claremont. Sir John Vanbrugh's Garden at Chargate in Surrey', *Apollo*, CXXXVII (April 1993), 223–226. See below *Plate 193b*. I am grateful to Mr Harris for bringing this to my attention.

The section on Claremont in Strong, *The Artist and the Garden*, pp.232–42, includes an anonymous painting of *c*.1760, reproduced in colour as plate 293, showing the lake and Bridgeman's amphitheatre.

See also *Bridgeman*, pp.36, 48–50, 63, 67, 96, 114n32, 130n14, 131, 132, 133, 135, 138, 140, 142n82, 178, and *Plates 30–32b, 165a* and *165b*

CLIVEDEN Buckinghamshire

Bridgeman's work at Cliveden is referred to in the correspondence of George Hamilton, 1st Earl of Orkney (1666–1737), and his family, in the National Library of Scotland, Edinburgh (Fraser Collection, MS 1033).

On 2 October 1723 Orkney writes to one of his brothers from Cliveden about the landscape there (MS 1033, fo.157), commenting:

> I must doe the best I can but it is a greater work than I thought but I still think it will be much better than was Intended (but the Amphitheatre is quite struck out) wher[e] to get turfe and trees for la grand [*sic*] machine, beside ther[e] is great difficulty to get the slope all that side of the Hill where the precipice was, but Bridgeman mackes difficultys of nothing[.] I told him that if I had thought [it] had been the one Half of what I see it will cost, I believe I never had done it, he says the *begining* is the worst ...

The suggestion here is that Bridgeman may well have designed the amphitheatre at Cliveden, and that 'la grand machine' may have been a hydraulic machine, later abandoned.

For an interpretation of Bridgeman's work at Cliveden see the following three articles by the late Gervase Jackson-Stops: 'The Cliveden Album: Drawings by Archer, Leoni and Gibbs for the 1st Earl of Orkney', *Architectural History*, XIX (1976), 5–16; 'Formal Garden Designs for Cliveden: The Work of Claude Desgots and Others for the 1st Earl of Orkney', *National Trust Yearbook*, 1976–77 (London, [1977]), pp.100–17; 'Cliveden, Buckinghamshire,' *C. Life*, CLXI (24 February, 3 March 1977), 438–41, 498–501.

See also *Bridgeman*, p.127n84

COOPERSALE Essex *or* WELFORD Berkshire

Sir Howard Colvin kindly tells me of a payment of £5.11s. 6d. in 1694 to 'Bridgman the gardener' in volume XLI, 'An Account Book of the Archer Family, Commencing in the Year 1691', in the James Orchard Halliwell-Phillips Collection, Library of Congress, Washington, DC. This possibly relates to either Coopersale (Essex), or Welford (Berkshire), but it is perhaps too early in date to refer to the Royal Gardener. I must thank Charles J. Kelly, Manuscript Reference Librarian at the Library of Congress, for his help with my enquiries.

The possibility that Capability Brown was involved at Coopersale is suggested by a payment to him by John Archer of £36.5s.0d. on 21 April 1774. See Peter Willis, 'Capability Brown's Account with Drummonds Bank, 1753–1783', *Architectural History*, XXVII (1984), 384, otherwise *Design and Practice in British Architecture. Studies in Architectural History Presented to Howard Colvin*

(1984). The complete article appears on pp.382–91, and documents work by Brown on several landscapes with Bridgeman connections.

DALLINGTON Northamptonshire *or* THE ROLLS HOUSE London

Dallington Hall was built or rebuilt about 1726–30 by Francis Smith of Warwick for Sir Joseph Jekyll (1663–1738), the Master of the Rolls, and accounts of Goslings Bank indicate that Jekyll paid Bridgeman £10 on 17 March 1721/22. Jekyll's agent, Professor Andor Gomme believes, was Charles Frewen, and Goslings' records show that he paid Bridgeman £20 on 31 May 1735. See Andor Gomme, *Smith of Warwick*, p.524.

Jekyll was also the client for The Rolls House, Chancery Lane, London (1717–24), designed by Colen Campbell, and the possibility that the earlier payment to Bridgeman refers to this should not be discounted.

DAWLEY Middlesex

For the context of Bridgeman's work at Dawley see B.T. White, *The History of Dawley (Middlesex)* (Uxbridge: Hayes and Harlington Local History Society, 2001).

See also *Bridgeman*, 23n92, 78, 79, 119n48, 132–33, 156, and *Plate 72b*

DOWN HALL Essex

See Bodleian Library, Gough Maps 46 fo.262, catalogued in *Bridgeman*, p.178, and reproduced below as *Plate 196*.

See also *Bridgeman*, pp.27, 72, 73–76, 89, 123n67, 131, 132, 149n6, 176, and *Plates 66a, 67–69*

EASTBURY Dorset

See Bodleian Library, MSGD A3 fo.10 and A4 fo.21, catalogued in *Bridgeman*, p.178, and reproduced below as *Plates 194* and *195*.

See also *Bridgeman*, pp.23, 35, 47–48, 67, 71n7, 80, 108, 120, 129, 130n14, 132, 133, 176, and *Plates 26–29b*

ESHER Surrey

Payment is made to Bridgeman of £52.10s. on 17 March 1734/35 by the Hon. Henry Pelham (1695–1754) in his account at Hoares Bank, London, presumably for Esher Place. Kent worked at Esher from about 1729.

See also *Bridgeman*, pp.48–49, 140

FARLEY Berkshire

The Bridgemanic plans in the Bodleian Library, MSGD A4 fos 24 and 34, wrongly catalogued as Farley in *Bridgeman*, p.178, are in fact of Hackwood. See below under HACKWOOD on p.429, and *Plates 201a* and *201b*.

See also *Bridgeman*, pp.62–63, 67, 102, and *Plate 52*

FULHAM ROAD London

The plan of Fulham Road in PRO, MPE 482 (Cat.No.339), catalogued in *Bridgeman*, p.178, is no longer attributed to the Royal Gardener.

GOBIONS *or* GUBBINS Hertfordshire

Gobions or Gubbins was the seat of Jeremy Sambrooke (*c.*1677–1754), who became a baronet in 1740. There is an undated plan of the estate in the Gloucestershire Record Office, Gloucester (D 1245 FF 75). It is in ink, pencil and water-colour, measures 1555 × 690 mm, and bears the inscription 'Surveyed by Tho: Holmes' in the lower left-hand corner. The drawing, on which Sambrooke's name appears, seems to be the work of several hands, and part of it is in a Bridgemanic style. See below *Plates 197a* and *197b*.

Although they have no plan of Gobions or Gubbins of Bridgeman's date, Hertfordshire Archives and Local Studies, Hertford, possess an anonymous map of the estate (34137) which is catalogued 'as done by Bridgman'. The names 'Holmes' and 'Hunter' appear on it: according to *VCH: Hertfordshire*, II (1908), 247, a Thomas Holmes, who later assumed the name of Hunter, was owner of Gobions or Gubbins (otherwise known as More Hall) from 1802. A suggested date for the map, which I have not seen, is *c.*1815. The former County Archivist, Dr Kathryn M. Thompson, told me of these connections.

See also *Bridgeman*, pp.18, 84, 86–87, 132, and *Plates 83* and *84*

GREENWICH PARK Middlesex

See Bodleian Library, MSGD A4 fo.49, catalogued in *Bridgeman*, p.178, and reproduced below as *Plate 199a.*

The two plans in the National Maritime Museum, Greenwich, Greeenwich Hospital Plans (ART/2), fo.2, and Greenwich Park MSS (ART/6), catalogued in *Bridgeman*, p.179, are reproduced below as *Plates 198* and *199b.*

See also *Bridgeman*, pp.15, 92n15, 114n32

GROSVENOR SQUARE London

Reference is made in *Bridgeman*, p.56n64, to Bridgeman's work on a garden at No.41 (later known as No.46) Grosvenor Square for John Campbell, Lord Glenorchy and 3rd Earl of Breadalbane. For its context see Longstaffe-Gowan, *The London Town Garden*, especially pp.39, 255n23.

HACKWOOD Hampshire

See Bodleian Library, MSGD A3 fo.4, catalogued in *Bridgeman*, p.179, and reproduced below as *Plate 200.*

Martin Wood, currently the owner of part of the Hackwood estate known as Spring Wood, drew my attention to the two Bridgemanic drawings in the Bodleian Library, MSGD A4 fos 21 and 24, mistakenly described in *Bridgeman* as Farley, as being Hackwood. See below *Plates 201a* and *201b*.

Sally Hocking kindly tells me that, although no direct evidence of Bridgeman himself working in Spring Wood has yet come to light, an estate plan of 1725, a detailed survey by John Vardy of 1762, and later evidence such as aerial photographs indicate that Bridgeman's designs for Hackwood itself and Spring Wood were extensively carried out. The scheme for an amphitheatre shown on the Bridgemanic drawing MSGD A4 fo.34 (*Plate 201a*) was not implemented, and a French formal garden was sited in this location instead. However an amphitheatre of a different design, but of Bridgemanic character, was constructed facing the north-eastern corner of Spring Wood.

Switzer includes Hackwood among his list of 'august Designs' in his *Ichnogaphic Rustica* (1718), I, 85, and Gibbs designed a portico and garden buildings there. See Howard Colvin, *A Biographical Dictionary of British Architects, 1600–1840*, 3rd edition (New Haven and London, 1995), p.440. On a more detailed level, the design shown on MSGD A4 fo.34 for the construction of a 'Section of the Tarrasse, Stocade, & fossee ...' is similar to that illustrated in Rigaud's 'View of the Queen's Theatre from the Rotunda' at Stowe.

For advice on Bridgeman's links with Hackwood I am indebted to Martin Wood and Sally Hocking.

See also *Bridgeman*, p88n108, 179

HAMPTON COURT Middlesex

See Bodleian Libary, MSGD A4 fos 62 and 74, catalogued in *Bridgeman*, p.179, and reproduced below as *Plates 202* and *204b*; Hovingham Hall, Yorkshire, MS vol., Architectural Drawings at Hovingham, fo.39, catalogued in *Bridgeman*, p.179, and reproduced below as *Plate 203a*; BL, K.XXIX,14u, catalogued in *Bridgeman*, p.179, and reproduced below as *Plate 204a*; PRO, MPD 23 (3) (Cat.No.1343), catalogued in *Bridgeman*, p.180, and reproduced below as *Plate 203b*.

See also *Bridgeman*, pp.11, 15, 31, 93–94, 114n32, 132, 151–55, 156, 162–64, 165–66, 168, 175–76, and *Plates 93a-95* and *163b*

HARTWELL Buckinghamshire

Sir Roy Strong makes a case for Bridgeman's involvement at Hartwell in *The Artist and the Garden*, pp.224–32, where he suggests that it was 'a garden by Charles Bridgeman with architectural features by Gibbs' (p.230).

Key evidence is the set of eight views of Hartwell by Balthasar Nebot, two of them dated 1738, now in Buckinghamshire County Museum, Aylesbury. They were commissioned by the owner of Hartwell, Sir Thomas Lee, Bt. (1687–1749), a Whig whose friends in Buckinghamshire included the Marquess of Wharton of Upper Winchendon House, and Viscount Cobham of Stowe.

The architect Eric Throssell has prepared a reconstruction of the gardens at Hartwell, based on Nebot's paintings. Mr Throssell informs me that his research points convincingly towards a Gibbs layout, inserted into an earlier Stuart garden, and centred on a previous house not shown by Nebot.

See also 'Nebot's Views of Hartwell House', in Linda Marie Cabe, 'Sets of Painted Views of Gardens, *c.*1726–1740, and the Relationship between Garden Design and Painting in England in the First Half of the Eighteenth Century' (Ph.D. dissertation, Yale University, 1988), I, 180–203.

HOUGHTON Norfolk

For comments on Bridgeman's work at Houghton and other Norfolk landscapes see Anthea Taigel and Tom Williamson, 'Some early geometric gardens in Norfolk', which is a special double issue of the *Journal of Garden History*, XI, nos 1–2 (January-June 1991); and Tom Williamson, *Polite Landscapes. Gardens and Society in Eighteenth-century England* (Thrupp, Glos: Alan Sutton; Baltimore, MD: Johns Hopkins University Press, 1995).

See also *Bridgeman*, pp.35, 61n91, 84, 85–86, 88, 118n46, 120, 132, 180, and *Plates 81a–82*

Horace Walpole's observation in *The History of the Modern Taste in Gardening* (1780) that Houghton was 'laid out by Mr. Eyre, an imitator of Bridgman' is confirmed in four pages of manuscript notes in Horace Walpole's hand, pasted into volume II of Daniel Lysons' *The Environs of London ...* (1795), now at Yale University in the Lewis Walpole Library at Farmington, Connecticut.

Here, Walpole describes Eyre as 'One of the first Improvers of Gardens in the Style of Bridgman before Kent perfected the new & quite natural Taste. Mr Eyre planted for Sr Rob. Walpole the Garden at Houghton, which was in a much greater manner than the ancient formal Gardens in the Dutch Style'.

Walpole's comments refer to Lysons's record on p.61 of his *Environs* that Kingsmill Eyre died in 1743 and that his undated tomb is in the burial ground of the Royal Hospital, Chelsea. Eyre was elected a Fellow of the Royal Society in 1726, and acted as Secretary to the Commissioners of Chelsea College from 1718 until his death on 20th March 1743.

Nowhere in *The History of the Modern Taste in Gardening* or in his correspondence does Walpole give 'Mr Eyre' a first name: he notes the death of 'Mr Eyres of Chelsea' when writing to Sir Horace Mann, 25 March 1743, and the work of 'M. Eyre' at Houghton in a letter to the Duc de Nivernais, 6 January 1785. See *Yale Walpole*, XVIII (1955), 201; XLII (1980), 131.

My visit to Farmington was made possible by Judith Colton, and Catherine Jestis aided my research there.

HYDE PARK ROAD London

See PRO, MPD 164 (Cat.No.338), catalogued in *Bridgeman*, p.180, and reproduced below as *Plate 205a.*

See also *Bridgeman*, pp.92n13, 95, 97–98, 168

KEDLESTON Derbyshire

See the plan of the canal and cascades attributed to Bridgeman (*c.*1725) in the National Trust, Kedleston Hall, Scarsdale Collection. The drawing is in ink, pencil and water-colour, measures 685 × 273 mm, and is reproduced below as *Plate 205b.* See also Leslie Harris, *Robert Adam and Kedleston. The Making of a Classical Masterpiece* (National Trust, 1987), which contains extensive coverage of the Kedleston landscape and illustrates the Bridgemanic plan as plate 52.

Francis Smith of Warwick had built the Kedleston in existence at this time and was back doing alterations between 1724 and 1734. Payment is made to Bridgeman of £51.11s. on 10 November 1722 by Sir John Curzon, 3rd Bt (*c.*1674–1727) in his account at Hoares Bank, London.

See also *Bridgeman*, p.87, for payments to Bridgeman in 1722 and 1726, and other references to Kedleston on pp.33n41, 84, 118n46, 128, 132.

KENSINGTON GARDENS and HYDE PARK London

See BL, K.XXVIII.10.d.1, catalogued in *Bridgeman*, p.180, and reproduced below as *Plate 206b*; Nationalmuseum, Stockholm, CC.2753 (Cronstedt Collection), catalogued in *Bridgeman*, p.180, and reproduced below as *Plate 206a*. I have not seen this second drawing.

The drawing of Kensington Gardens and Hyde Park in the Royal Borough of Kensington and Chelsea Public Library, 712.5 KEN/F, Portfolio 33, catalogued in *Bridgeman*, p.180, is no longer ascribed to Bridgeman.

See also *Bridgeman*, pp.14n52, 15, 31–32, 35, 71n7, 94–97, 118n46, 120, 129, 132, 135, 136, 142n82, 143, 151–54, 162, 164, 168, 176, 180, and *Plates 96a–100b*

LEDSTON Yorkshire

See Bodleian Library, MSGD A3 fo. 19 and A4 fo. 85, catalogued in *Bridgeman*, p.180, and reproduced below as *Plates 207a* and *207b*.

Apparent references to Bridgeman's widow, Sarah, support the possibility that the Royal Gardener worked for Lady Elizabeth (Betty) Hastings at Ledston. Accounts at Hoares Bank, London (Ledger K, fo.304), record two payments from Lady Betty to 'Mrs Bridgeman' of £5.19s.6d. on 27 March 1731, and £21 on 5 April 1731. See also Peter Willis, 'William Kent's letters in the Huntington Library, California', *Architectural History*, XXIX (1986), 158–67.

See also *Bridgeman*, pp.61, 180–81, and *Plate 48b*

LILLINGTON MANOR Warwickshire

See Warwickshire CRO, Warwick, CR.556/197, reproduced below as *Plate 208a*, and the Bridgemanic plan, now low lost, reproduced below as *Plate 208b* from the published version in William Cooper, *The History of Lillington, Leamington Spa* (Long Compton, 1940). Both plans are catalogued in *Bridgeman*, p.181.

A transcript of the descriptive text on the published plan is given in Cooper's book, pp.118–126.

See also *Bridgeman*, p.33n39

LODGE PARK, SHERBORNE Gloucestershire

See Bodleian Library, MSGD A4 fo.68, reproduced below as *Plate 209*. The drawing is in ink and pencil, measures 635 × 622 mm, and has the words 'Esqr Dodintong' on the back. Although inexplicably omitted from *Bridgeman*, this drawing was catalogued in my Ph.D. thesis on pp.421 and 434 where it was wrongly identified as Eastbury. It was correctly identified by Dr David Jacques, who considers Bridgeman's work in 'The Grand Manner: Changing Style in Garden Design, 1660–1735' (Ph.D. thesis, University of London, 1999).

Work by Bridgeman at Lodge Park, Sherborne, for Sir John Dutton, 2nd Bt (1684–1743), is noted in Dutton's will, dated 30 March 1742, published in *Historical and Genealogical Memoirs of the Dutton Family, of Sherborne, in Gloucestershire ...* (1899), compiled by Morgan Blacker, with an introduction by Lord Sherborne.

A transcription of the will is on pp.236–46, and on p.244 we read:

> I strictly enjoin and desire every person in whom my estate shall vest this my will to finish and perfect the plantations I have begun at my new park [ie Lodge Park] and all the other work I entended there pursuant to a plan made by Mr. CHARLES BRIDGEMAN for that purpose which plan I desire may be strictly pursued excepting only in those particulars which I shall direct to be varied from in a paper in my own handwriting which I will leave enclosed in this my will and when the same are finished I desire they may be always kept in good order.

The will itself (with others of Sir John Dutton) is in the Dutton of Sherborne Collection at Gloucestershire Record Office, Gloucester (D678 FAM57).

Sir John Dutton's accounts are also at Gloucester (GRO D678 FAM SETT 148). Katie Fretwell summarises those between 1723 and 1742 in appendix 5 of *Sherborne and Lodge Parks. Park and Garden Survey* (National Trust, 1990), pp.43–53.

We find here that on 22 December 1729 Bridgeman is paid £70 'for his journeys to Shireborn and making a plan for [Sir John's] New Park', which may well be the drawing referred to in the baronet's will. Apart from minor Bridgemanic payments for transport and miscellaneous expenses in 1725, 1729 and 1731, on 24 April 1734 Sir John records payment of two guineas for his 'subscription for Mr Bridgeman's Prints of Ld. Cobham's Gardens' at Stowe.

Kent and Wootton also appear in Sir John's accounts: Kent is paid three guineas on 3 March 1723/4 for a subscription for 'Inigo Jones' works', and thirty guineas on 29 October 1728 for 'his trouble making plans for me at My Lodge & House'; John Wootton thirty guineas on 6 July 1725 for 'a landskip for my Drawing Room Chimney'.

Evidence today of Bridgeman's scheme at Lodge Park is extensive, as shown by Katie Fretwell in 'Lodge Park, Gloucestershire: A Rare Surviving Deer Course and Bridgeman Layout', *Garden History*, XXIII, no.2 (Winter 1995), 133–44.

More than one 'Bridgeman' may have been connected with the landscape at Lodge Park. Briony Blackwell informs me that a gardener William Bridgeman appears in the accounts of the Dutton family of Sherborne of *c.*1693–1710 in Gloucestershire Record Office, D 678 (FAM 55N) and D 678 (FAM SETT 148).

I am grateful to the Gloucestershire County and Diocesan Archivist, Nicholas Kingsley, his predecessor David Smith, and Katie Fretwell, for their assistance with Lodge Park.

LONGFORD CASTLE Wiltshire

Bridgeman's work on the grounds at Longford in about 1737 for Sir Jacob Bouverie, 3rd Bt (?1694–1761), created 1st Viscount Folkestone and Baron Longford in 1747, was noted in *Bridgeman*, pp.58, 88, 118n46.

This is confirmed by Helen Matilda, Countess of Radnor, and William Barclay Squire, *Catalogue of the Pictures in the Collection of the Earl of Radnor*, II (London, 1809), 33, 45. Sir Howard Colvin kindly gave me this reference.

LUMLEY CASTLE County Durham

Two drawings of Lumley Castle, now at Sandbeck Park, Yorkshire, in the collection of the Earl of Scarbrough, may be dated *c.*1721 and attributed to Bridgeman; the better of the two (reproduced below as *Plates 210–212*) is entitled 'Lumley Castle', the other is untitled. Otherwise the drawings are virtually identical. They are in ink, pencil and water-colour, and measure 1205 × 775mm.

These drawings may well have been completed in collaboration with Vanbrugh, who remodelled the south and west ranges for Richard Lumley, 2nd Earl of Scarbrough (*c.*1688–1740) from 1722 onwards. Making at least one if not two visits to Lumley, Vanbrugh wrote in 1721 that he found the castle 'a Noble thing' and that he was able 'to form a general Design for the whole, which consists, in altering the house both for state, Beauty and Convenience; and making the Courts Gardens, and offices suitable to it' (Dobrée and Webb, eds, *Works of Vanbrugh*, IV, 138, 142). Could not Bridgeman have been involved in these proposals?

It is worth noting that Vanbrugh prepared designs for a house for John Hedworth at Chester-le-Street, near Lumley, which Sir Howard Colvin suggests in *A Biographical Dictionary of British Architects, 1600–1840*, 3rd edition, p.211, may have been a rival scheme to one of 1716 by Colen Campbell, 'probably not built'.

Stephen Switzer mentions Lumley Castle in *An Introduction to a General System of Hydrostaticks and Hydraulicks* (1729), I, 274. Switzer worked nearby at Park House, Gateshead, and at Gibside, County Durham. See Margaret Wills, *Gibside and the Bowes Family* (Chichester: Phillimore for The Society of Antiquaries of Newcastle upon Tyne, 1995), pp.15–16.

At Sandbeck there are also drawings of Lumley in Vanbrugh's manner, as well as designs for a gothick fisherman's lodge.

For Bridgeman, Vanbrugh, Switzer and their contemporaries see the essays in Christopher Ridgway and Robert Williams, eds., *Sir John Vanbrugh and Landscape Architecture in Baroque England, 1690–1730*, with an introductory essay by Kerry Downes (Thrupp, Glos: Sutton Publishing in association with the National Trust, 2000).

MARBLE HILL Middlesex

Bridgeman's work at Marble Hill has been confirmed by the deposit in 1992 in Norfolk Record Office, Norwich, of three estate plans forming additions to the Lothian (Blickling) Papers. One of these (MC 184/10/3) is unlikely to be in Bridgeman's hand, but the other two (MC 184/10/1 and 2) may well be, and all three are reproduced below as *Plates 213–215*.

The area of the parterre next to the house (shown in the detail in *Plate 213b*) is characteristic of Bridgeman, and also parallels similar designs by Switzer.

The cartouches on two of the plans (*Plates 213a* and *214a*) indicate that they were drawn for the Countess of Suffolk, that is Mrs Henrietta Howard, mistress of George II, for whom Roger Morris had built the house in 1724–29, with the involvement of Henry Herbert, 9th Earl of Pembroke. See Colvin, *A Biographical Dictionary of British Architects, 1600–1840*, 3rd edition, pp.490, 667. As Mrs Herbert did not become the Countess of Suffolk until 1731, this suggests a date of *c*.1731–38 for the two Bridgemanic drawings, that is after the Morris-Pembroke house was completed.

For help with Marble Hill I acknowledge Jean Kennedy, the former County Archivist at Norfolk Record Office, her successor Dr John Alban, and Jonathan Draper, Jan Hodges, Paul Rutledge, Andrew Wimble, and Terence J. Burchell, who undertook special photography.

See also *Bridgeman*, pp.36, 56, 58, 59, 67, 77, 78, 129, 131, and *Plate 71*

MEREWORTH Kent

See Bodleian Library, MSGD A4 fo. 52, catalogued in *Bridgeman*, p.181, and reproduced below as *Plate 216*.

See also *Bridgeman*, pp.61n91, 117n44

MOR PARK Hertfordshire

See Bodleian Library, MSGD A4 fo. 48, catalogued in *Bridgeman*, p.181, and reproduced below as *Plate 217*.

For Moor Park and other Bridgemanic landscapes in Hertfordshire see The Hertfordshire Gardens Trust and Tom Williamson, *The Parks and Gardens of West Hertfordshire*, edited by Ann Mallinson and Anne Rowe ([Hertford], 2000). Included here is Beechwood House, the subject of research by Lottie Clarke, which has connections with Roger Morris.

See also *Bridgeman*, pp.21n78, 99n50, and *Plate 51a*

RICHMOND PARK and GARDENS Surrey

See PRO, MR 528 (Cat.No.1449) and MR 696 (Cat.No.1437), catalogued in *Bridgeman*, p.182, and reproduced below as *Plates 218* and *219*.

See *Bridgeman*, pp.18, 35, 77, 100, 101–5, 114n32, 118n45, 118n46, 129, 132, 135, 142n48, 143, 166–67, 168, 181–82, and *Plates 70* and *106b–110b*

THE ROLLS HOUSE London *see* DALLINGTON Northamptonshire

SACOMBE Hertfordshire

See Bodleian Library, MSGD A4 fo. 29, catalogued in *Bridgeman*, p.182, and reproduced below as *Plate 220a*.

Payments are made to Bridgeman of £30 on 2 July 1715 and £60 on 16 June 1716 by Edward Rolt (1686–1722) in his account at Hoares Bank, London. These references were given to me by Professor Andor Gomme.

Anne Rowe kindly informs me that significant parts of Bridgeman's gardens still exist in Home Wood, Sacombe. Extensive yew planting remains, as do the raised walk and oval pond, while traces of the outline of Bridgeman's walled garden, canal and basin can be seen on aerial photomaps of 1971.

See also *Bridgeman*, pp.59 60, 118n46, 131, 176, 182, and *Plates 46a* and *46b*

ST JAMES'S PARK London

See Soane, Drawer 62.1.1, catalogued in *Bridgeman*, p.182, and reproduced below as *Plate 220b*.

Andrew Skelton and Miss J. Coburn have drawn my attention to the minutes of the court of directors of Chelsea waterworks, April 1728 – April 1731, in the Corporation of London, London Metropolitan Archives, Acc 2558/CH/1/2–4, which contain references to Bridgeman. Mention is made here of St James's Park and Hyde Park.

See also *Bridgeman*, pp.13, 14, 15, 99–100, 104, 114n32, 129n9, 132, 143, 151–54, 164, 168, 176, and *Plates 101a–103*

ST JAMES'S SQUARE London

See the reference to Bridgeman's work at St James's Square in Longstaffe-Gowan, *The London Town Garden*, pp.195–98, 265, citing the Minutes of the Trustees of St James's Square (1726–1825). Bridgeman was paid £5,630. For the history of the square see Denys Forrest, *St James's Square. People, Houses, Happenings* (London, 1986), especially pp.29–33, 163n2.

See also *Bridgeman*, pp.32–33, and *Plate 16b*

SCAMPSTON Yorkshire

See Bodleian Library, MSGD A4 fos 27 and 66, catalogued in *Bridgeman*, p.182, and reproduced below as *Plates 221a* and *221b*.

The Bridgemanic drawing MSGD A4 fo.37 is no longer believed to be of Scampston, and therefore it appears below as an unidentified estate in *Plate 245*.

See also *Bridgeman*, pp.61, 132, 182, and *Plate 48a*

SHARDELOES Buckinghamshire

Payment is made to Bridgeman of £50 on 27 January 1725/6 by Montagu Garrard Drake (1692–1728) in his account book at Hoares Bank, London. I owe this information to Professor Andor Gomme. Drake's private account book for 1722–27 was donated to Hoares in 1979 and also contains this payment, which endorses Loudon and Felton's ascriptions of the landscape at Shardeloes to Bridgeman noted in *Bridgeman*, p.63n104.

See also *Bridgeman*, pp.63, 79, and *Plate 72a*

SHERBORNE Gloucestershire
***see* LODGE PARK, SHERBORNE Gloucestershire**

SPRING GARDENS London

The attribution to Bridgeman of PRO, MPE 555 (Cat.No.344), catalogued in *Bridgeman*, p.183, has been withdrawn.

See also *Bridgeman*, pp.100n51, 183

SPRING WOOD Hampshire
***see* HACKWOOD Hampshire**

STANDLYNCH Wiltshire
***see* TRAFALGAR Wiltshire**

STILTON, THE BELL INN Huntingdonshire

See Bodleian Libary, MSGD A3 fos 40r, 40v, and A4 fos 3, 51, catalogued in *Bridgeman*, p.183, and reproduced below as *Plates 222–224b*.

After a period of neglect, the architects Saunders Boston completed extensions and upgrading of The Bell in 1990, including the incorporation of the 'Marlborough Suite'. I thank Mr Lian McGivern, former proprietor of The Bell, for showing me these alterations.

See also *Bridgeman*, pp.29, 149, 150n11, 169, and *Plate 16a*

STOWE Buckinghamshire

Publications about Stowe have multiplied since the original edition of *Bridgeman* appeared. For a summary of them see Michael Bevington, 'Select Bibliography: Stowe Landscape Garden', *New Arcadian Journal*, nos 43–44 (1997), 109–21. This issue of the *Journal* (of which 300 copies were printed) bears the title 'The Political Temples of Stowe', and was edited by Patrick Eyre. An expanded version of this bibliography is due to be published as a booklet by the New Arcadian Press, of Leeds, in the year 2002.

Extensive research has been carried out in the Stowe Papers at the Henry E. Huntington Library, San Marino, California, since I first worked on them in 1960 and since the original edition of *Bridgeman* came out in 1977. Publications of Bridgemanic interest citing them include George B. Clarke, 'Where Did All The Trees Come From? An Analysis of Bridgeman's Planting at Stowe', *Journal of Garden History*, 5, no.1 (January-March 1985), pp.72–83. Essays on the landscape and buildings at Stowe by George B. Clarke, Peter Inskip, and Richard Wheeler may be found in *The Huntington Library Quarterly*, LV (1992), 477–532.

Three MS account books kept by the steward at

Stowe, William Jacob, and covering part of Bridgeman's period there, are in the University of Reading Library, Estates of the Dukes of Buckingham and Chandos, BUC 11/1/2–4. Jacob was steward to Viscount Cobham, formerly Sir Richard Temple, 4th Bt, of Stowe (1675–1749). The accounts cover outgoing payments for carpenters, carters, and others, from Michaelmas 1717 to Lady Day 1720.

Jacques Rigaud's views of Stowe were reissued by Ben Weinreb in *Stowe Gardens in Buckinghamshire, laid out by Mr Bridgeman, delineated in a large plan, and fifteen perspective views drawn on the spot by Mons. Rigaud, now reprinted. To which is added an account of the original publication and descriptive notes to each view by George B Clarke* (London: B[en] W[einreb] Publications, 1987).

A painting of the 'View of the Queen's Theatre from the Rotunda' at Stowe was sold by Christie's in London at their sale of 'Important English Pictures', on 22 April 1983, lot 50. It is reproduced as the frontispiece of this book. I am grateful to Edward Elphick of Christie's for providing me with information on this painting.

Richard Quaintance has made a detailed study of the figures in Rigaud's views, in which Bridgeman may be included in those of Stowe. See Richard Quaintance, 'Unnamed celebrities in eighteenth-century gardens. Jacques Rigaud's topographical prints', *Cycnos*, II (1994), 93–131; and 'Who's making the scene? Real people in eighteenth-century topographical prints', in *The Country and the City Revisited. England and the Politics of Culture, 1550–1850*, edited by Gerald MacLean, Donna Landry and Joseph P Ward (Cambridge, 1999), pp.134–59.

A comprehensive coverage of Rigaud's views of Chiswick can be found in John Harris, *The Palladian Revival. Lord Burlington, His Villa and Garden at Chiswick* (New Haven and London, 1994). For the context of Rigaud's views of Chiswick, Stowe and Claremont, see Strong, *The Artist and the Country House,* especially pp.208–10, 217–24, 232–33. This book has Rigaud's '*View of such parts as are seen from the* Building *at the* Head *of the* Lake' at Stowe as endpapers.

For Capability Brown's move from Northumberland to Stowe, and his succession to Bridgeman there, see Peter Willis, 'Capability Brown in Northumberland', *Garden History*, IX, no.2 (Autumn 1981), 157–83, especially pp.166, 181. This article was reprinted as a booklet by the Northumberland and Newcastle Society (of Newcastle upon Tyne) in 1983, to mark the bicentenary of Brown's death in 1783.

See also *Bridgeman*, pp.6–8, 23, 33n41, 39, 48, 66, 67, 81, 86–87, 103, 105 106–27, 128, 129, 131, 132, 134, 138, 140–46, 183, and *Plates 111, 113a–158*

TRAFALGAR *or* STANDLYNCH Wiltshire

See Bodleian Library, MSGD A3 fo.24, catalogued in *Bridgeman*, p.183, and reproduced below as *Plate 225*.

The attribution to Bridgeman of MSGD A3 fos 25 and 36 has been withdrawn.

Possible connections between Bridgeman and John James are explored in Sally Jeffery, 'An architect for Standlynch House', *C. Life*, CLXXI (13 February 1986), 404–6. For James generally see Dr Jeffery's 'English Baroque architecture. The Work of John James' (unpublished Ph.D. thesis, University of London, 1986).

See also *Bridgeman*, p.54n52

TRING Hertfordshire

See Bodleian Library, MSGD A4 fos 25, 32, catalogued in *Bridgeman*, pp.183–84, and reproduced below as *Plates 226a* and *226b*.

See also *Bridgeman*, pp.59, 60, 129, 132, 176, and *Plates 45a* and *45b*

It must be added that Alan Fletcher has recently questioned the identification of MSGD A4 fo.48 (*Plate 45a*) as a plan of Tring. See his article 'Tring Park, Part 1 (1680–1800)', in the Annual Report 1998–1999 of the Hertfordshire Gardens Trust, pp.12–15.

WARWICK PRIORY Warwick

See Warwickshire CRO, Warwick. CR.56, catalogued in *Bridgeman*, p.184, and reproduced below as *Plate 239a*.

See also *Bridgeman*, pp.31n30, 33, 35, 37, 175–76, 184, and *Plate 18*

WARWICK TOWN and PRIORY Warwick

See Warwickshire CRO, Warwick, CR.217, Bundle 1, catalogued in *Bridgeman*, p.184, and reproduced below as *Plate 227*.

See also *Bridgeman, Plate 18*

WELFORD Berkshire *see* COOPERSALE Essex

WIMBLEDON Surrey

Frances Harris, 'Charles Bridgeman at Blenheim?', *Garden History*, XIII, 1 (Spring 1985), 1–3, proposes that correspondence between Sarah, Duchess of Marlborough and Mrs Sarah Bridgeman of ?1739–41 refers to Wimbledon rather than Blenheim, as I had supposed.

Dr Harris informs me that on 1 March [?1748] the Duchess of Marlborough's executors 'Paid Mrs Sarah Bridgeman in full of what was due from her Grace to Charles Bridgeman her late Father deceased at the time of his Death' (BL, Althorp Papers, Add MS 75419, fos 146–147). The sum was £880.17s.0d. which is close to the disputed figure of £897.2s.8½d. mentioned in the Duchess's letter to Mrs Bridgeman of 26 July 1741. See Frances Harris, '"The Best Workmen of All Sorts". The Building of Wimbledon House, 1730–1742', *Georgian Group Journal* (1992), 87–90. As Bridgeman's widow Sarah had died in 1743/44, the Duchess's executors presumably were making payment to the Royal Gardener's daughter Sarah, born in 1720.

See also *Bridgeman*, pp.45, 58–59, 88, 157, 159, 184, and *Plates 43a–44b*, and the catalogue entry above under BLENHEIM on p.426.

WIMPOLE Cambridgeshire

See Bodleian Library, MSGD A4 fos 30, 31 and 35, catalogued in *Bridgeman*, p.184, and reproduced below as *Plates 228, 230a* and *233*; BL, Add MS 36278, M1 (*Plate 230b*); and four Bridgemanic drawings in the Bambridge Collection, Wimpole (National Trust), reproduced below as *Plates 229a, 229b, 231* and *232*.

Other relevant published accounts are Gervase Jackson-Stops, 'Exquisite Contrivances: The Park and Gardens at Wimpole', *C. Life*, CLXVI (6 September 1979), 658–61; Dorothy Stroud, 'The Charms of Natural Landscape: The Park and Gardens at Wimpole', *C. Life*, CLXVI (13 September 1979), 758–62; and Eric Parry, 'Wimpole Hall', *Architects' Journal*, CLXXXIII (26 March 1986), 36–55.

For work at Wimpole by Robert Greening of *c.*1752 see Mark Laird, *The Flowering of the Landscape Garden. English Pleasure Grounds, 1720–1800* (Philadelphia, PA: University of Pennsylvania Press, 1999), pp.115–21, 399–400.

I am obliged to David Adshead of the National Trust for showing me drawings of Wimpole, and facilitating my research at the house.

On p.70 of *Bridgeman* it is assumed that the ballad celebrating an excursion to Wimpole in 1721, entitled 'A Hue and Cry after Four of the King's Liege Subjects who were Lately suppos'd to be seen at Roystone in Hartfordshire', was written by Thornhill, and that the participants were Bridgeman, Wootton, Gibbs, and Thornhill himself.

However, as Professor Pierre du Prey has pointed out to me, this was questioned by William Pinkerton in 'A Journey to Wimpole', *Notes and Queries*, 3rd series, VI (17 December 1864), 490–91, where Wootton is replaced in the identifications by the gem-engraver Charles Christian Reisen (1680–1725), and Bridgeman is given as the author of the ballad. The last two lines of it read:

> Surrounded with Pickax, wth Maddox, and Spade,
> The Ballad is ended, in Wheelbarrow made.

'From the last two lines', writes Pinkerton on p.491, 'we may conclude the piece was written by Bridgeman, who, it will be observed in the original, does not give his own name, but merely "The Gardiner"'. Pinkerton's 'original' is in BL, Lansdowne MS 846, fos 165–166, and is undated.

Two other manuscript versions of the poem, formerly at Welbeck, are now in the Portland literary collection in Nottingham University Library (PwV 416–417). The ascription of authorship to Thornhill is based on Francis Needham's attribution when he published 'A Hue and Cry', in *A Collection of Poems by Several Hands, Never Before*

Published, Welbeck Miscellany, no.2 (1934), 53–56; subsequently this text was adopted by the *Wren Society*, XVII (1940), 11–13.

However the Keeper of Manuscripts and Special Collections at Nottingham, Dr Dorothy B. Johnston, kindly informed me that 'there is no reference to Thornhill on either copy [of the poem]' and that indeed Francis Needham must have realised that the copies were not in Thornhill's hand. This can be seen from the opinion expressed in a letter of 1934 by Robin Flower of the British Museum, which is kept with them in Nottingham University Library.

The Portland (London) Collection in Nottingham University Library contains references to Bridgeman and Wimpole in two files: one group from *c*.1721 consists mainly of references to the Royal Gardener in letters from between John Cossen at Wimpole and Edward Harley (Pl C1/328, 470, 548, 552); the other, in the estates section of the collection, concerns expenditure on the garden and outworks at Wimpole in 1723/4–27 (Pl E3/1/1/11). Again, I owe knowledge of this to Dr Johnston.

See also *Bridgeman*, pp.26, 27, 69–72, 78, 79–80, 88, 89, 129, 132, 141, 142–43, 178, 184–85, and *Plates 73a–75* and *181*

WINDSOR CASTLE Berkshire

See Soane, vol.III/45, catalogued in *Bridgeman*, p.185, and reproduced below as *Plate 234*.

For Bridgeman's work in Windsor Gardens and Parks see Jane Roberts, *Royal Landscape. The Gardens and Parks of Windsor* (New Haven and London, 2000), which includes reproductions of plans by Henry Wise or Bridgeman, or both, as the endpapers and as plates 23, 146, 170, 175, 284, 337, 384 and 404.

See also *Bridgeman*, pp.15, 33, 100–1, 128, 142n82, 151–55, 166, 175–76, 185, and *Plates 104–106a* and *163a*

WOLTERTON Norfolk

See Bodleian Library, MSGD A3 fo. 33, and A4 fos 10, 18, 55, 56, 61, catalogued in *Bridgeman*, p.185, and reproduced below as *Plates 235–238b*.

See also *Bridgeman*, pp.85, 85n94, and *Plate 80b*

WREST Bedfordshire

A plan of Wrest of *c*.1719, by the surveyor Edward Laurence, in Bedfordshire and Luton Archives and Record Service, Bedford. L 33/286 fo.3, possesses Bridgemanic features and is reproduced below as *Plate 239b*. For Bridgeman's possible connection with Wrest see *Bridgeman*, p.51 and *Plate 35b*.

For assistance at Bedford I am grateful to Kevin Ward, County Archivist, and Nigel Lutt.

WROXALL *or* WROXHALL MANOR Warwickshire

Dr Christine Hodgetts has drawn attention to the possibility that the Royal Gardener was involved at Wroxall or Wroxhall Manor. This is based on an illustration in John William Ryland's *Records of Wroxall Abbey and Manor, Warwickshire* (London, 1903), facing p.lxviii, which bears the following caption:

> This plan and survey of the Manor of Wroxhall was made by Mr. Bridgman in the year of our Lord one thousand seven hundred and fourteen: I have known this plan and survey for upwards of sixty-two years when in the possession of my grandfather Christopher Wren, Esqr. Wroxhall February the Eighteenth 1831. Chris Wren.

In 1714, the date of the map, the estate had just been bought by the architect Sir Christopher Wren, though he may never have lived there and it became the home of his son, Christopher Wren, Junior (1675–1747). According to the caption, the original map by Bridgeman measured 6ft. by 2ft. 11in., and Ryland notes on p.xli that it was 'in the possession of J. Broughton Dugdale, Esq.' Its present whereabouts are unknown.

See Colvin, *A Biographical Dictionary of British Architects, 1600–1840*, 3rd edition, p.1087. On p.1092 reference is made to Christopher Wren, Junior, assisting his father at Marlborough House, St James's, for Sarah, Duchess of Marlborough, in 1709–11.

See below *Plates 240a* and *240b*

Warwick had connections with both Bridgeman and Henry Wise, who retired to Warwick when his period as Royal Gardener came to an end in 1728.

See also *Bridgeman*, pp.31n30, 33, 35, 37, 175–76, 184, and *Plate 18*

UNIDENTIFIED DRAWINGS ATTRIBUTED TO BRIDGEMAN

The Bridgemanic plans in the Bodleian Library, MSGD A4 fos 22, 33, 36 and 43, catalogued in *Bridgeman*, pp.185–86, and reproduced below as *Plates 241–244*, are of three unidentified estates.

In addition, the Bridgemanic drawing MSGD A4 fo.37, reproduced below as *Plate 245*, was described wrongly on p.182 of the catalogue in *Bridgeman* as being of Scampston. It remains unidentified.

DIAGRAMS of FORMAL ELEMENTS in BRIDGEMAN'S SIGNED PLANS

No additional drawings signed by Bridgeman have been found since these seven diagrams were made in 1961. See the discussion under 'Catalogue of Bridgeman Drawings', in *Bridgeman*, pp.173–76.

See below *Plates 246* and *247*

Index to Catalogue

References in bold figures are to supplementary plates

Supplementary Plates

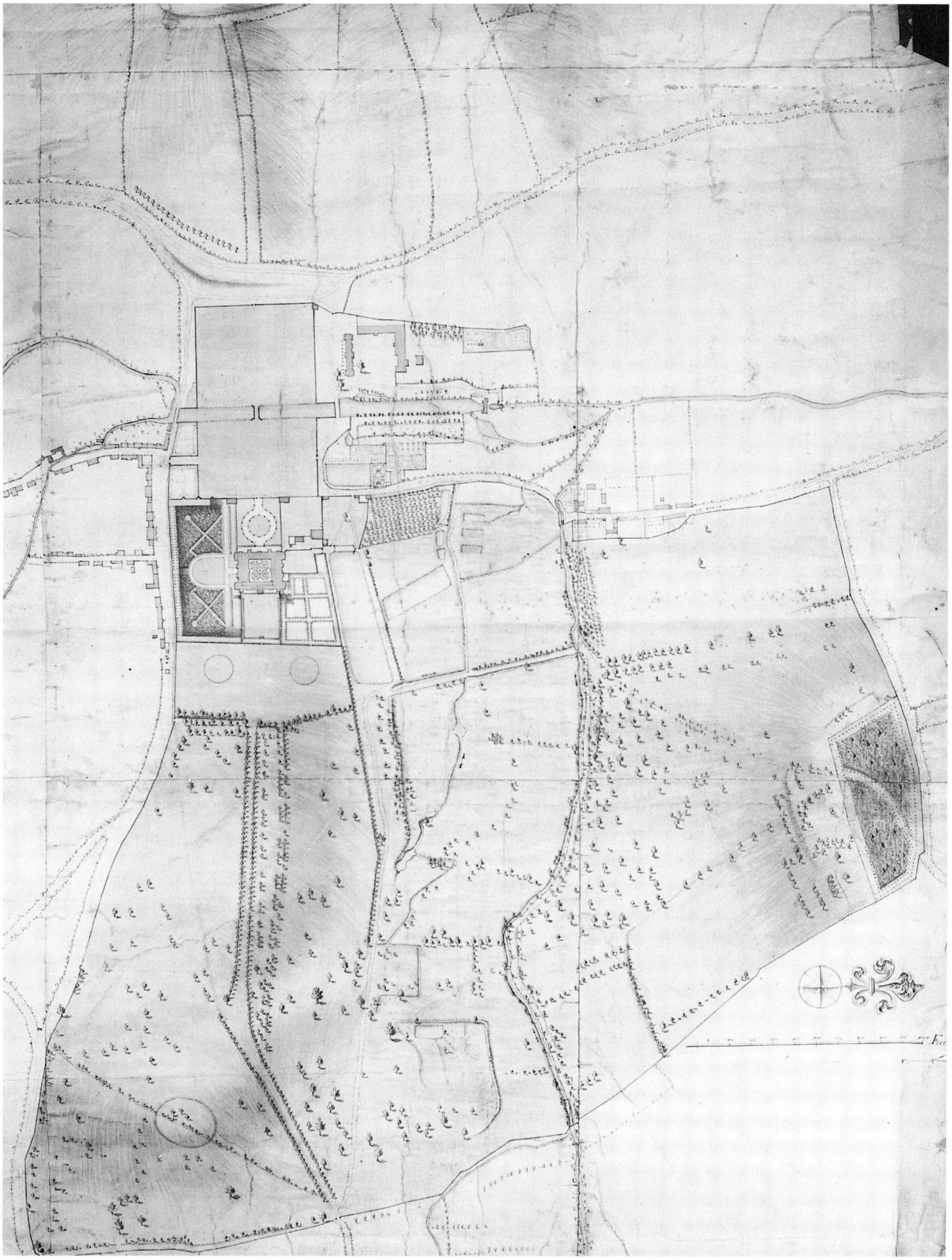

187 Audley End. Plan. Drawing by Bridgeman (attrib.). MSGD A4 fo.67

188 Audley End. Plan. Drawing by Bridgeman (attrib.). MSGD A4 fo.60

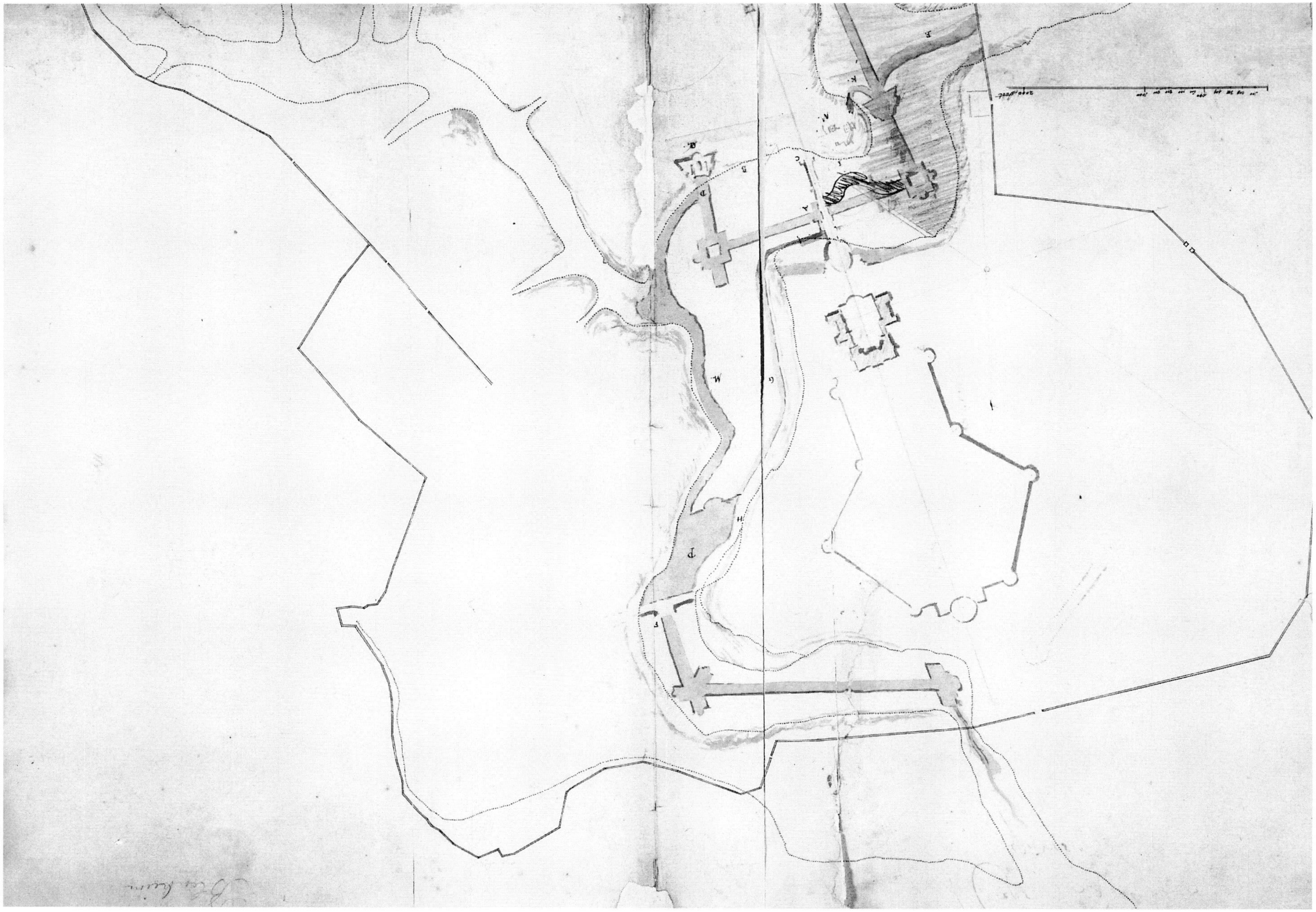

189 Blenheim. Plan. Drawing by Bridgeman (attrib). Bod. Lib., MS Top Oxon a37* fo.2

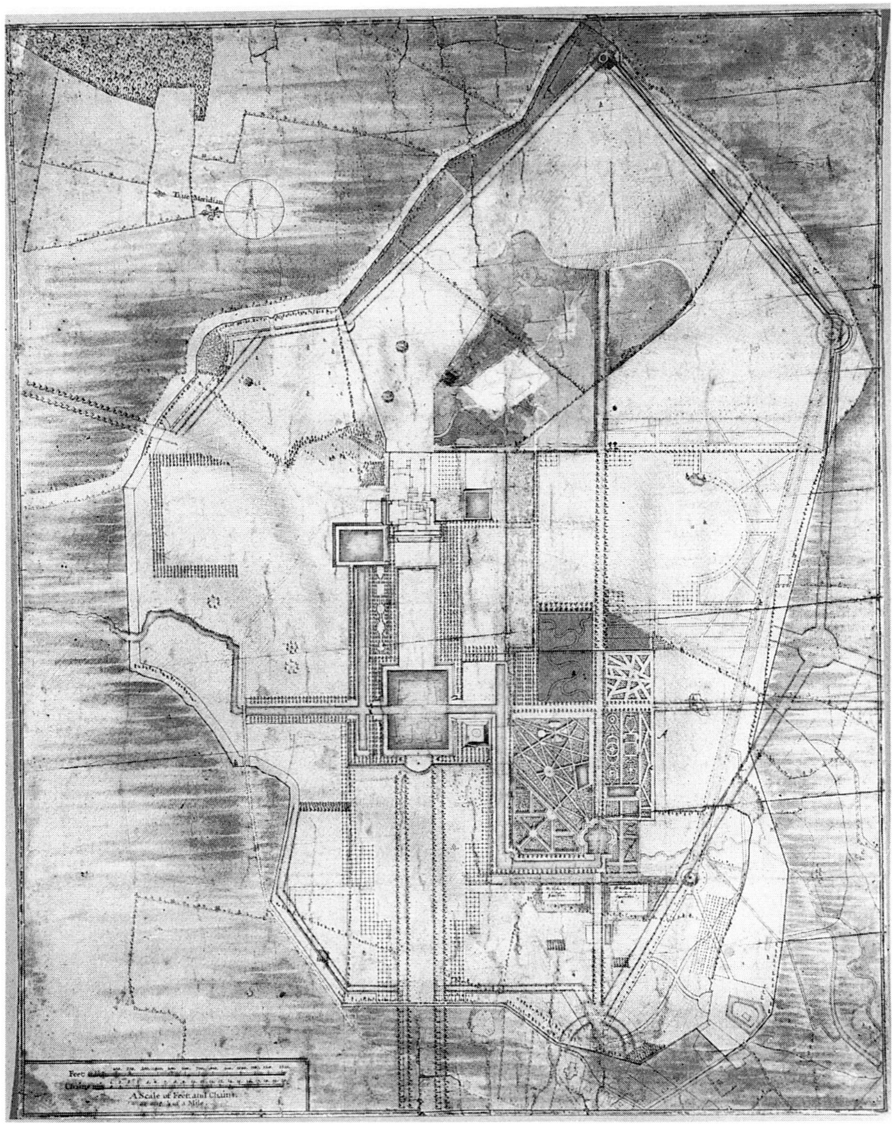

190a Boughton. Plan. Drawing. Boughton House, Northamptonshire (Duke of Buccleuch and Queensberry)

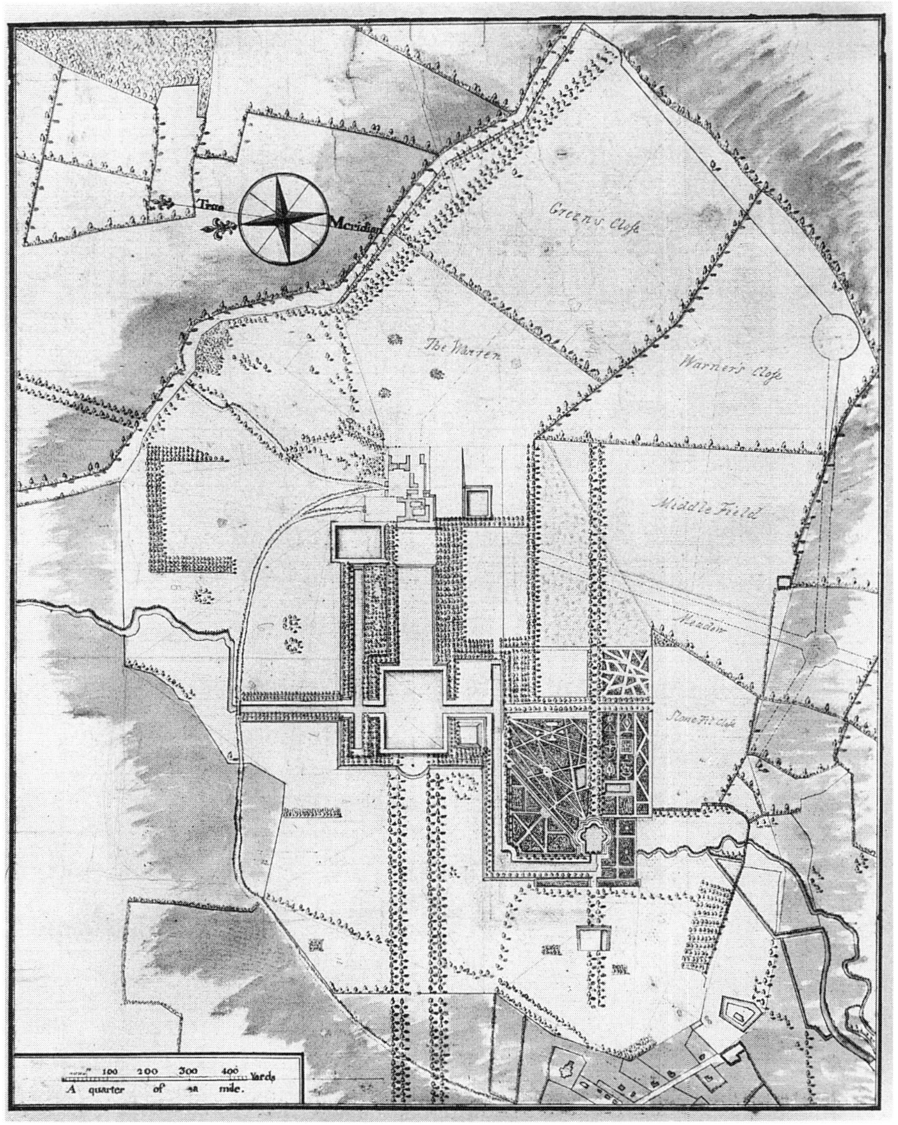

190b Boughton. Plan. Drawing. Boughton House, Northamptonshire (Duke of Buccleuch and Queensberry)

191a Boughton. Detail of bird's-eye view from west *c.*1725 reproduced as *Plate 40*. Drawing by Bridgeman (attrib.). Boughton House, Northamptonshire (Duke of Buccleuch and Queensberry)

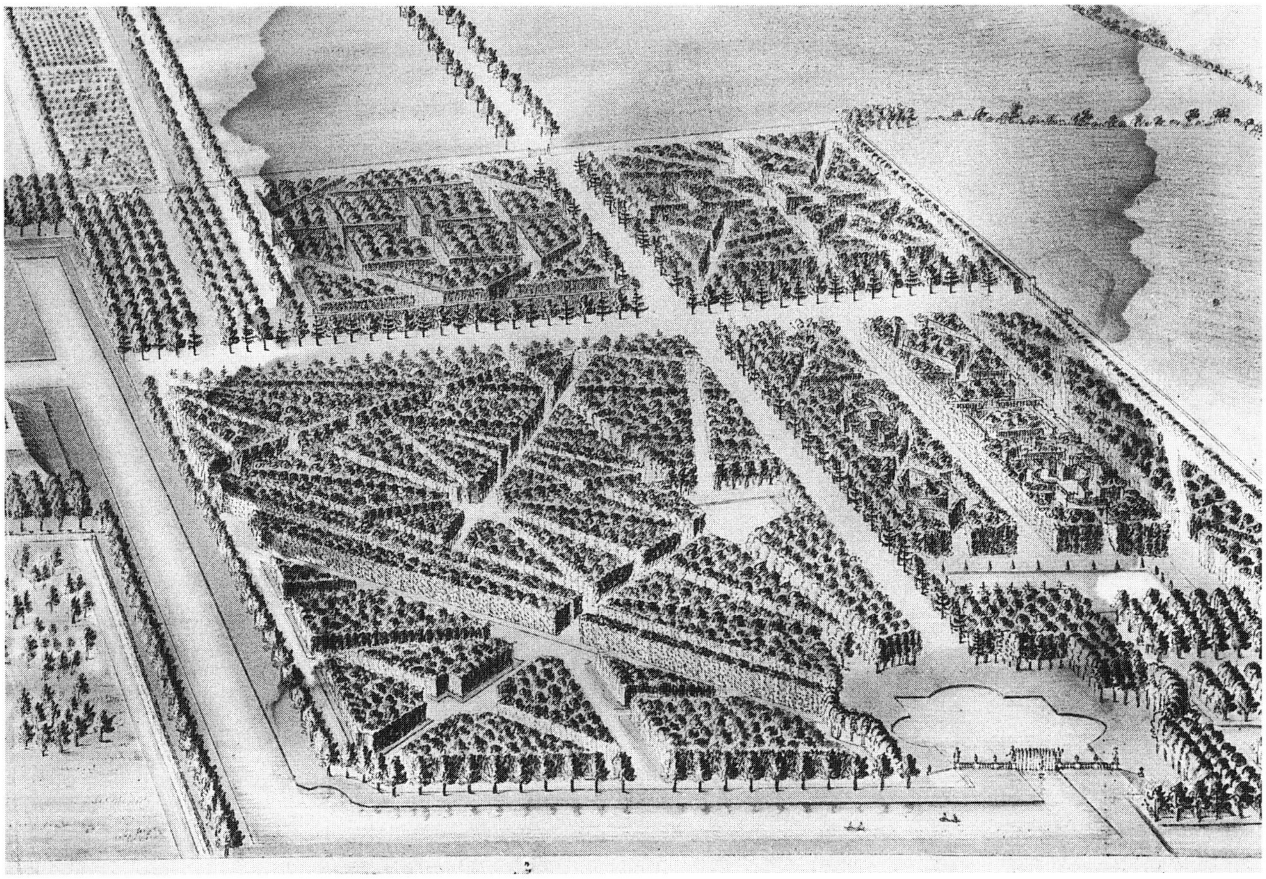

191b Boughton. Detail of bird's-eye view from west *c.*1725 reproduced as *Plate 40*. Drawing by Bridgeman (attrib.). Boughton House, Northamptonshire (Duke of Buccleuch and Queensberry)

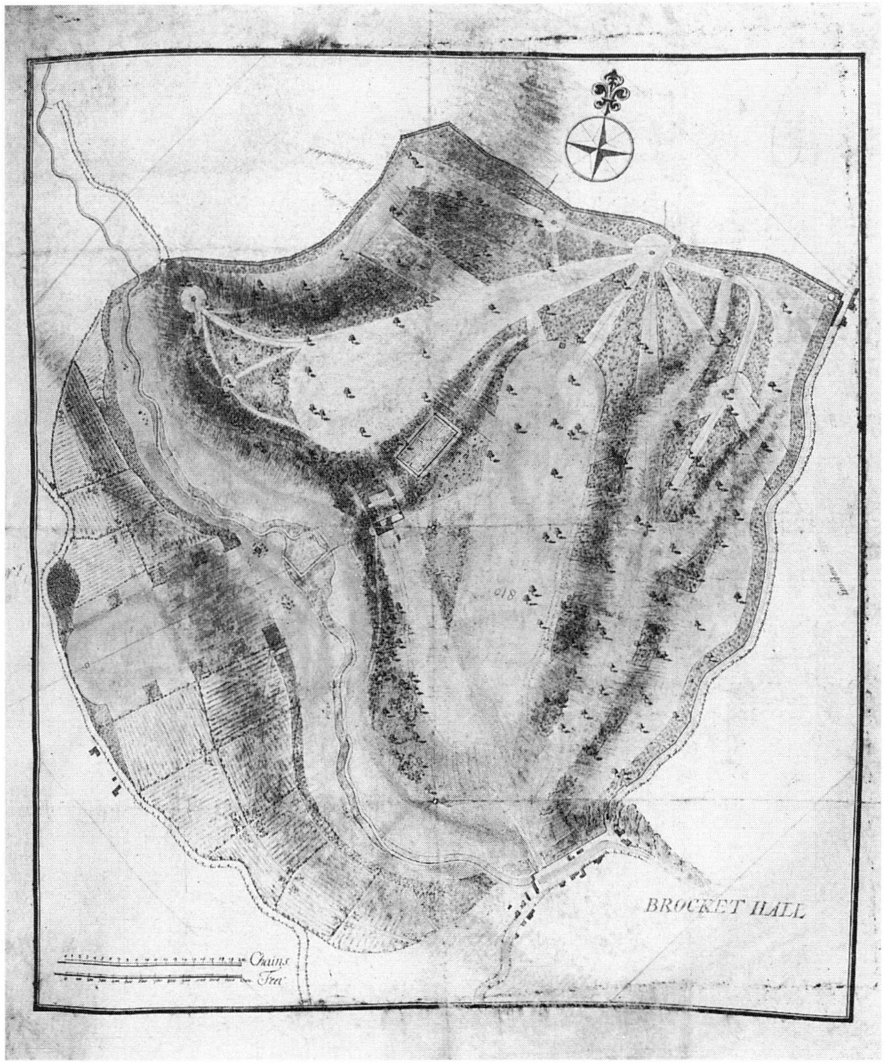

192a Brocket. Plan. Drawing by Bridgeman (attrib.). MSGD A3 fo.7

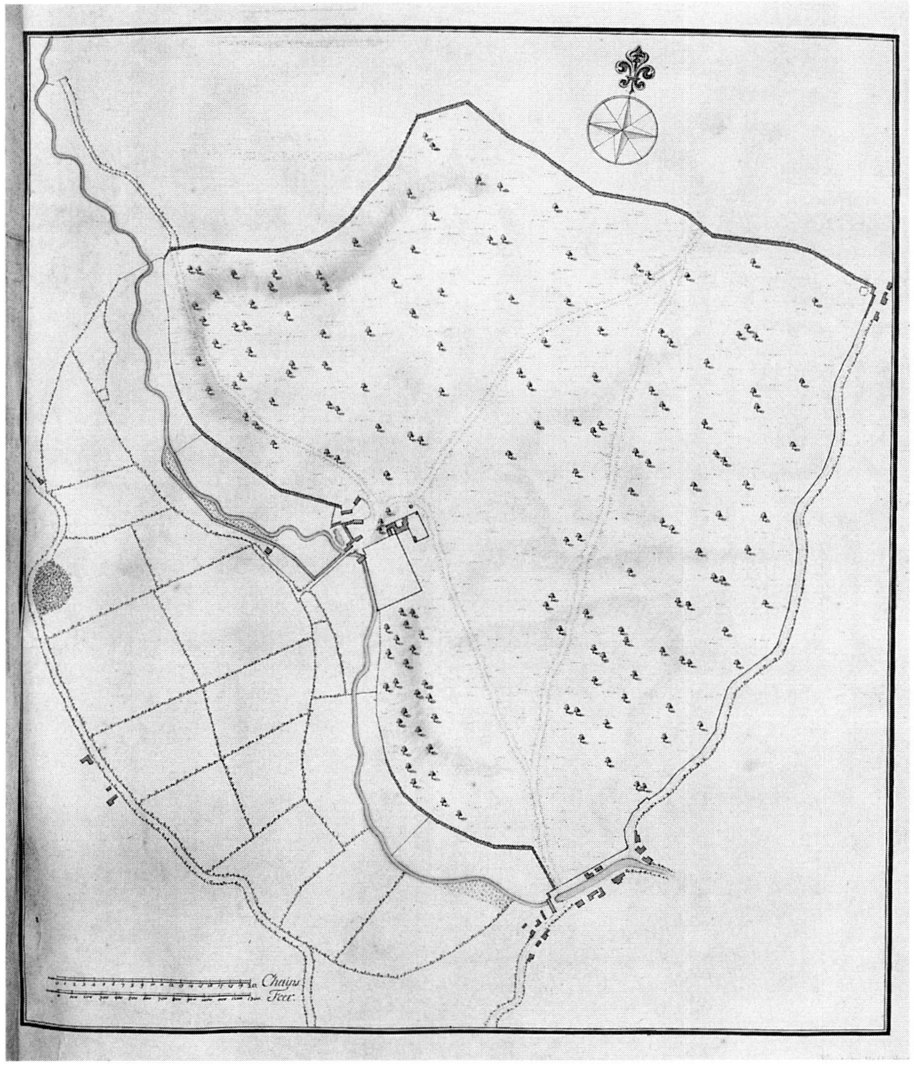

192b Brocket. Plan. Drawing by Bridgeman (attrib.). MSGD A4 fo.40

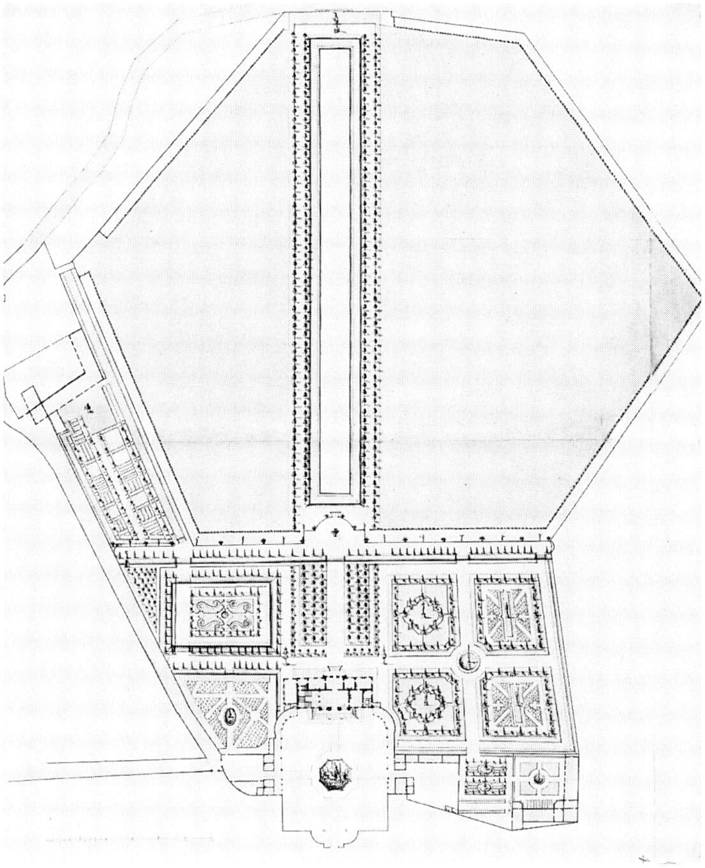

193a Buckingham House, London. Plan. Drawing by Bridgeman (attrib.). Soane, vol.III/42 (Trustees of Sir John Soane's Museum)

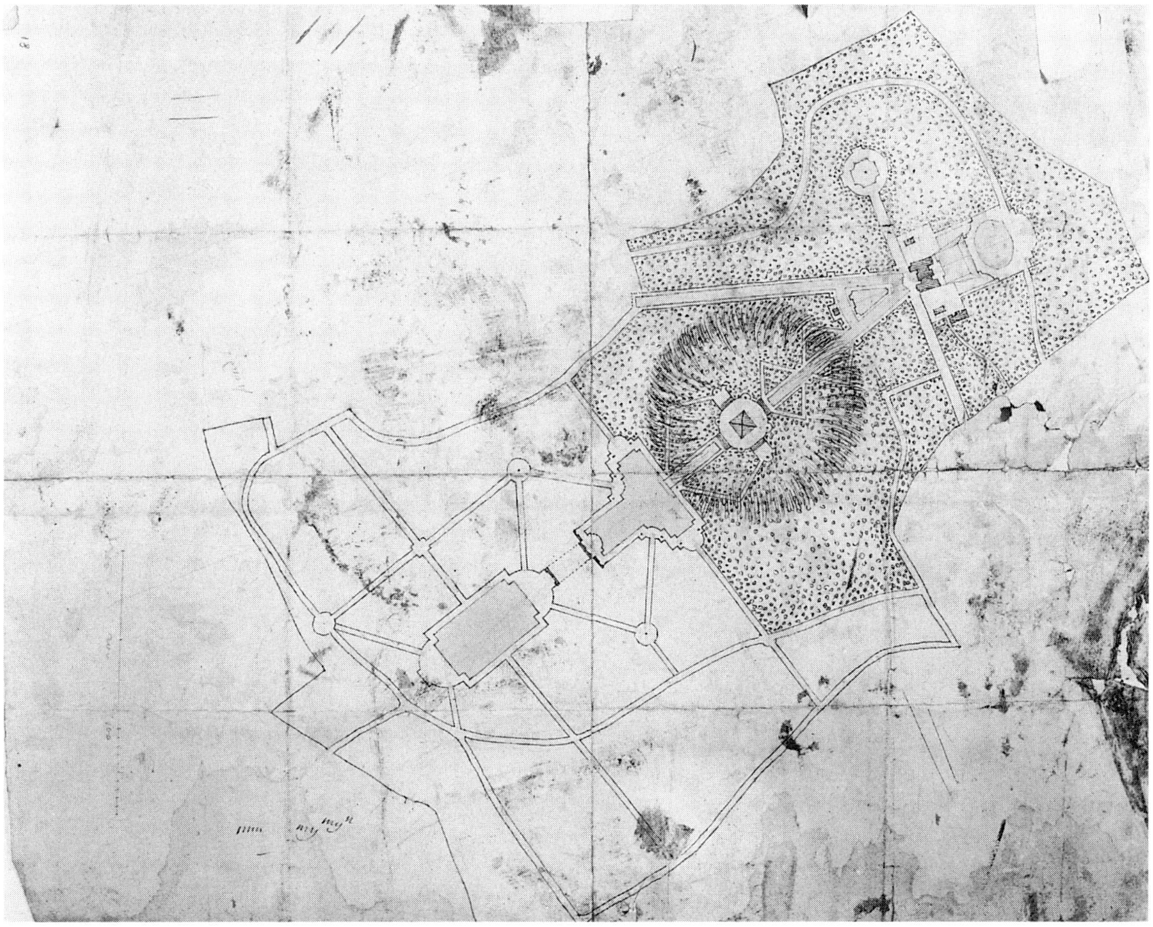

193b Claremont. Plan. Drawing by Bridgeman (attrib.). MSGD A4 fo.81

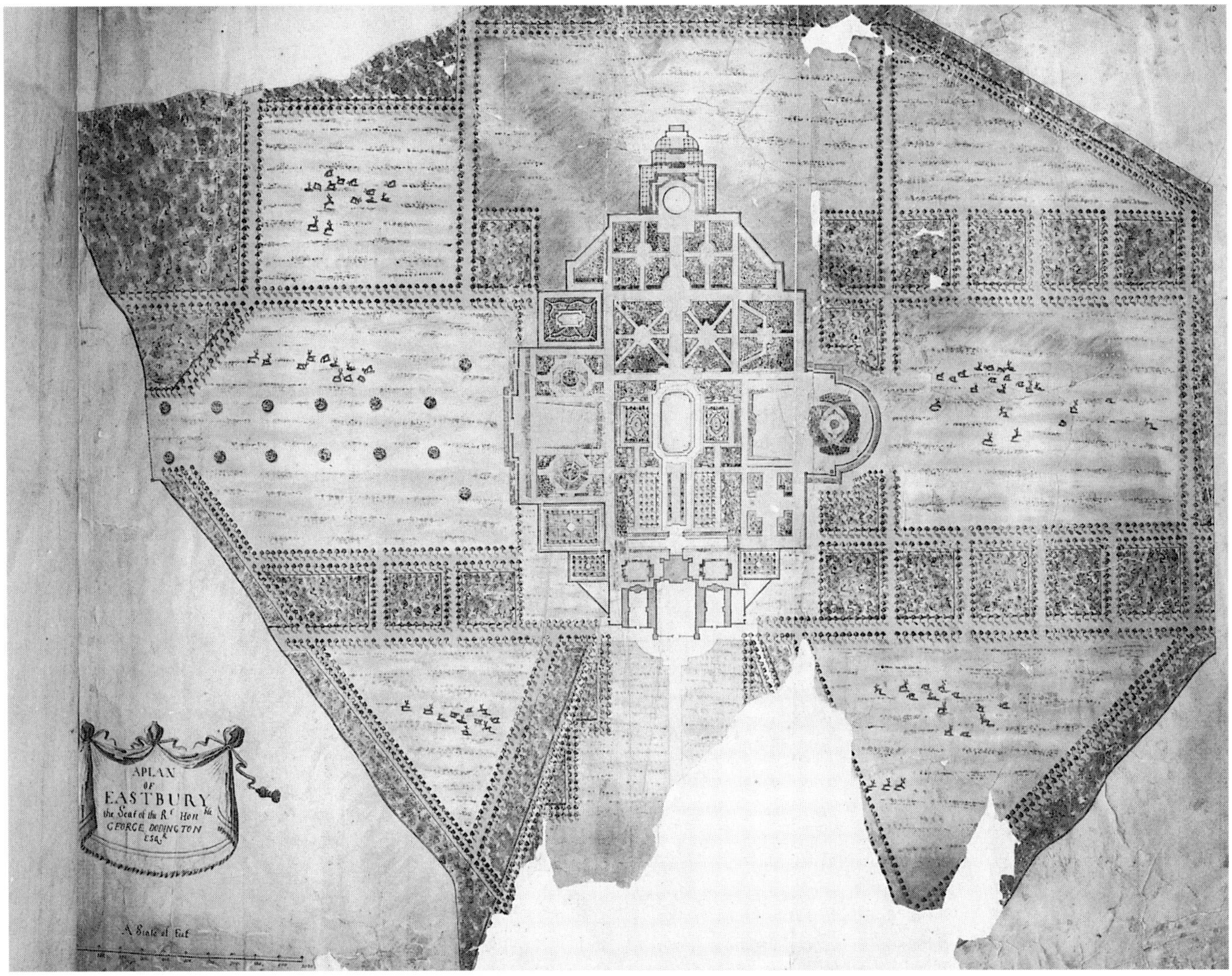

194 Eastbury. Plan. Drawing by Bridgeman (attrib.). MSGD A3 fo.10

opposite
195 Eastbury. Plan. Drawing by Bridgeman (attrib.). MSGD A4 fo.21

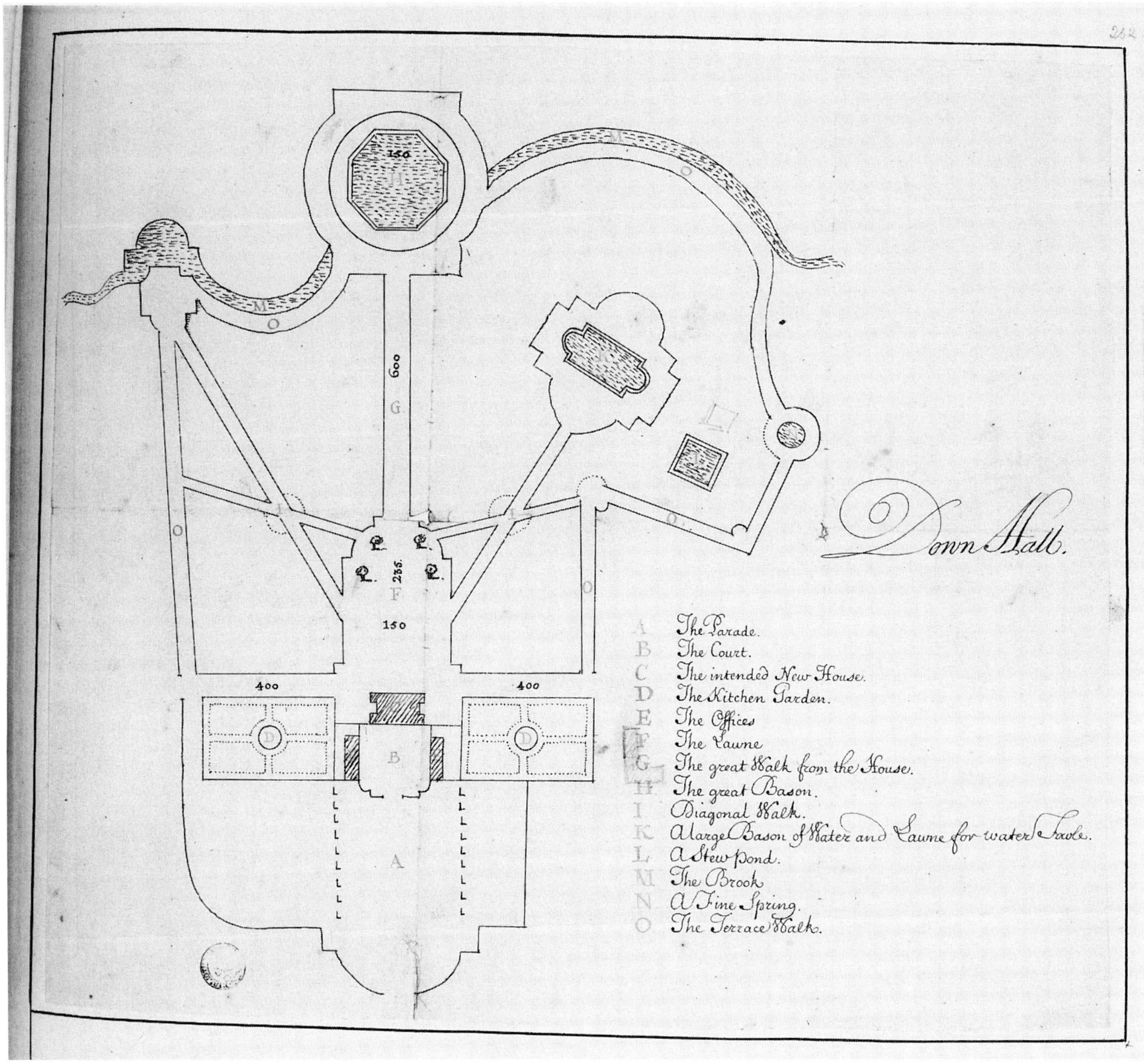

196 Down. Plan. Drawing by Bridgeman (attrib.). Bod.Lib., Gough Maps 46 fo.262

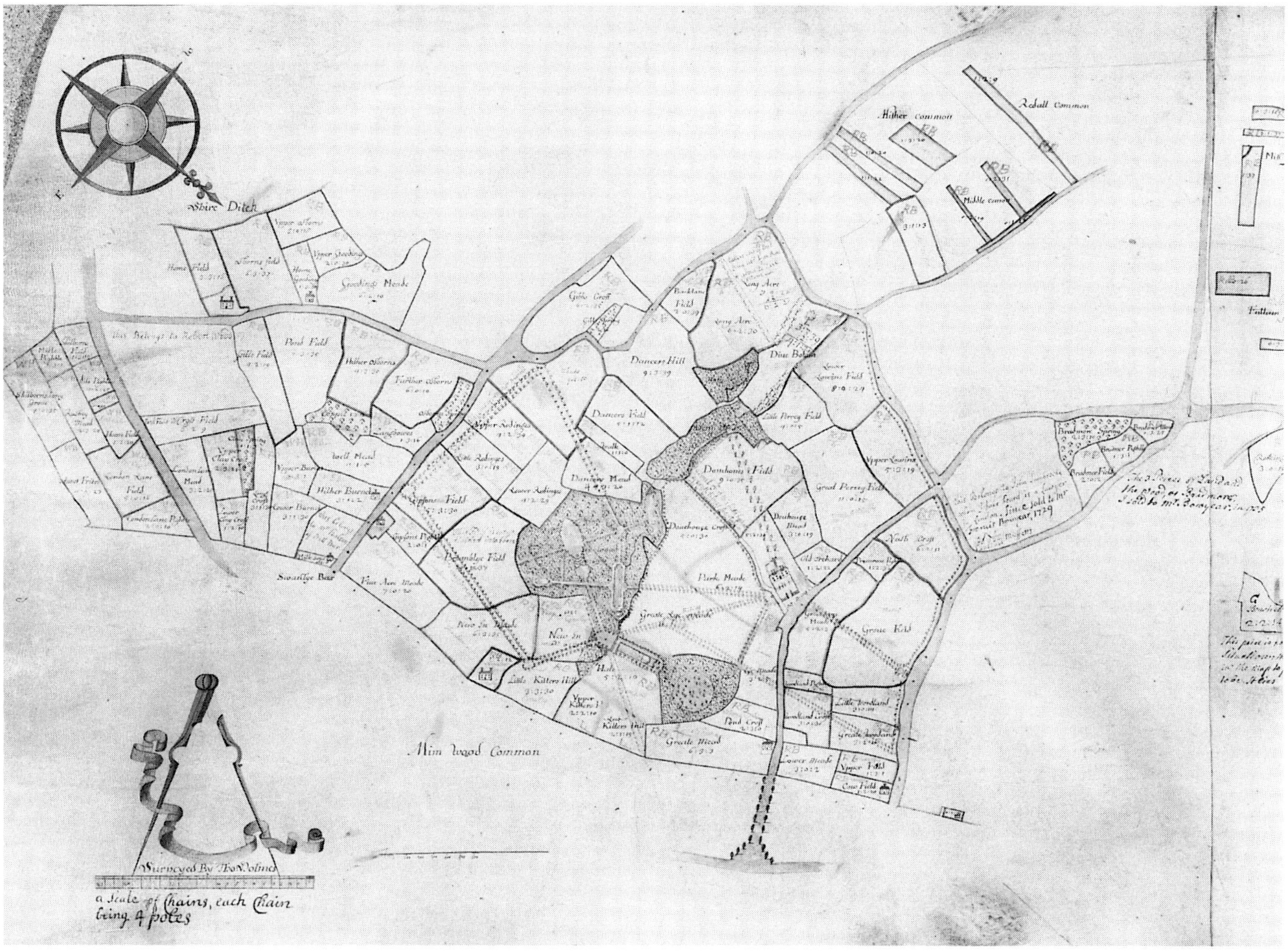

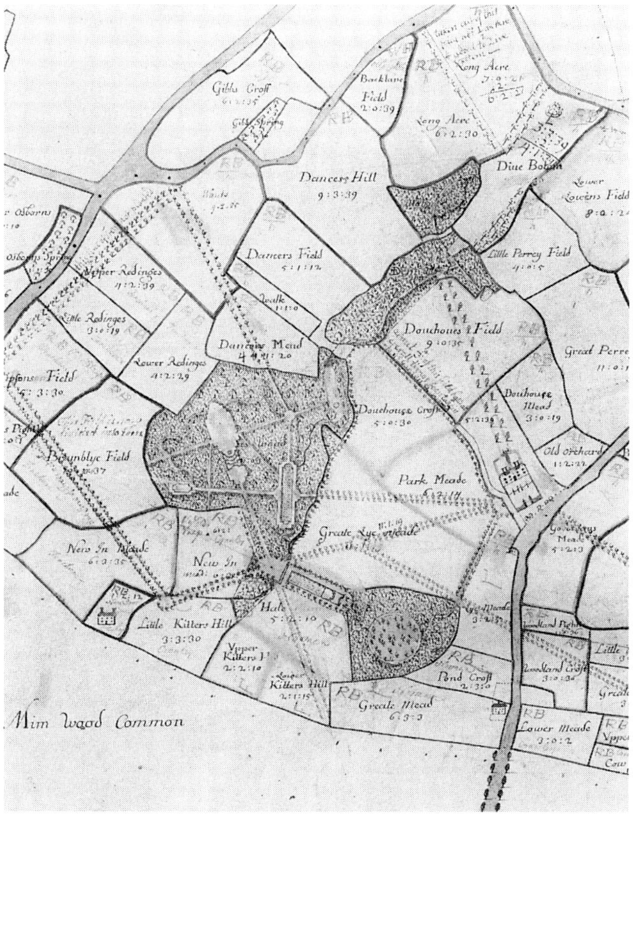

197a Gobions *or* Gubbins. Left half of undated plan by Thomas Holmes and others. Gloucestershire RO, Gloucester, D 1245 FF 75 (Apperley Court Estate)

197b Gobions *or* Gubbins.
Detail attributed to Bridgeman of *Plate 197a*

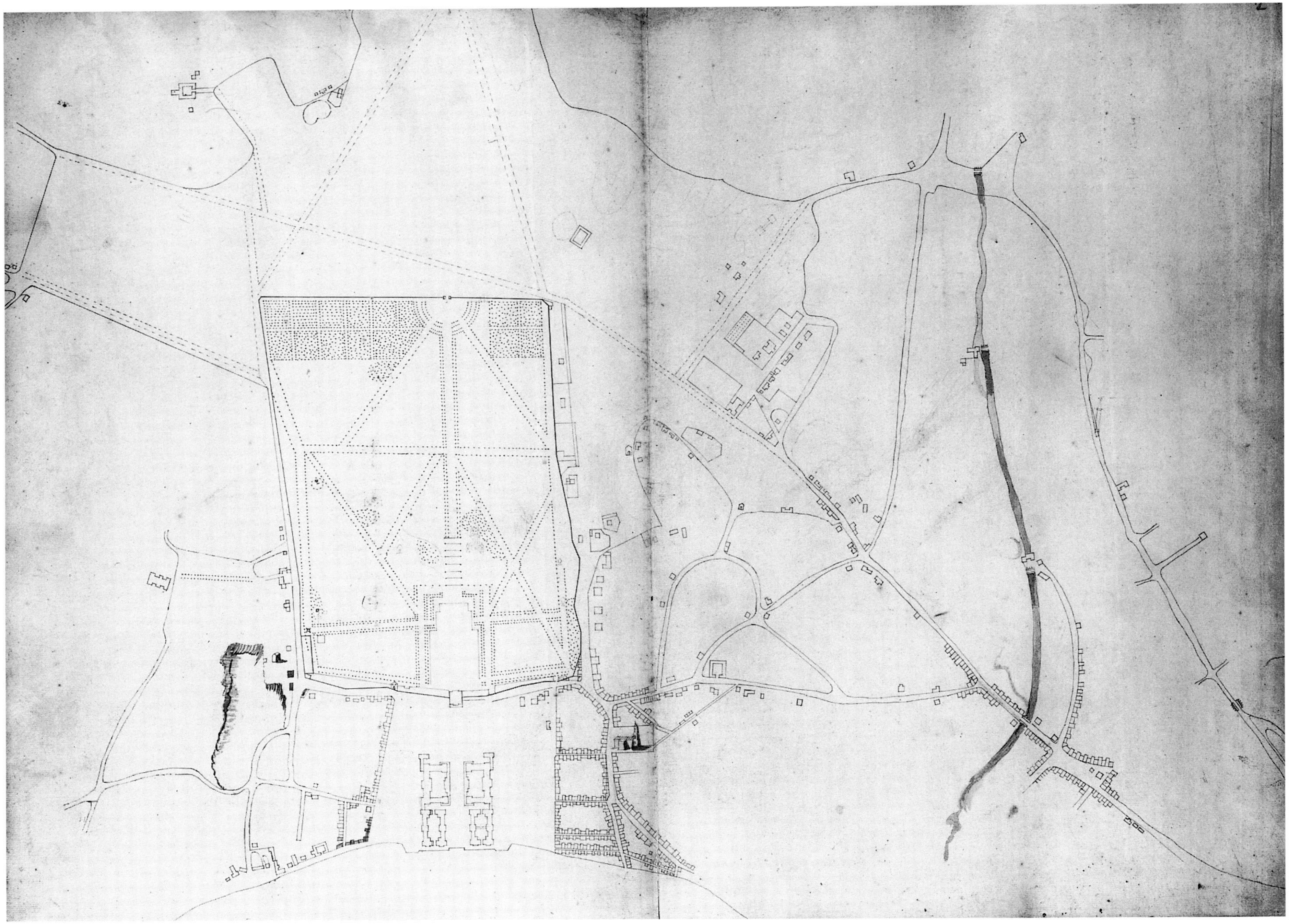

198 Greenwich Park. Plan by Bridgeman (attrib.). National Maritime Museum, Greenwich, Greenwich Hospital Plans (ART/2), fo.2

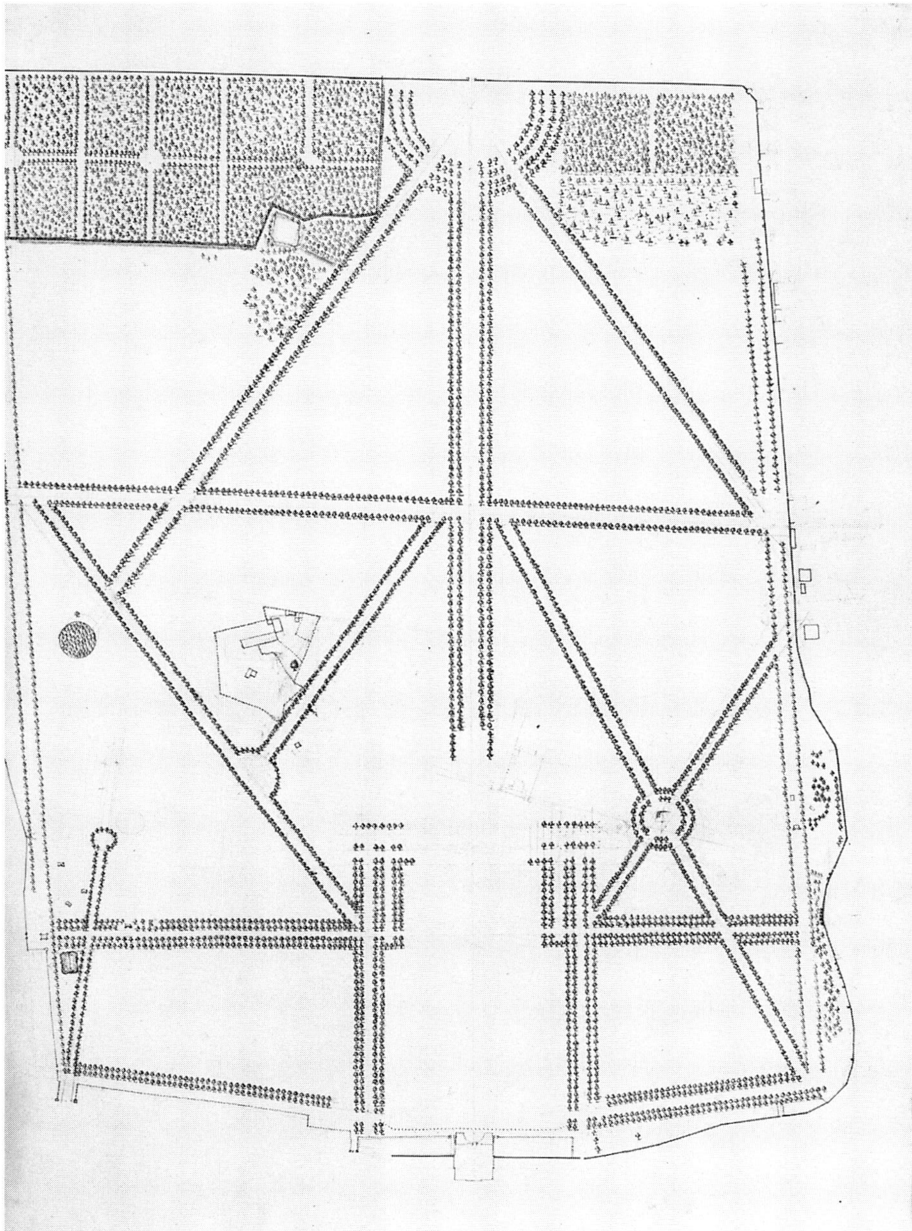

199a Greenwich Park. Plan by Bridgeman (attrib.). MSGD A4 fo.49

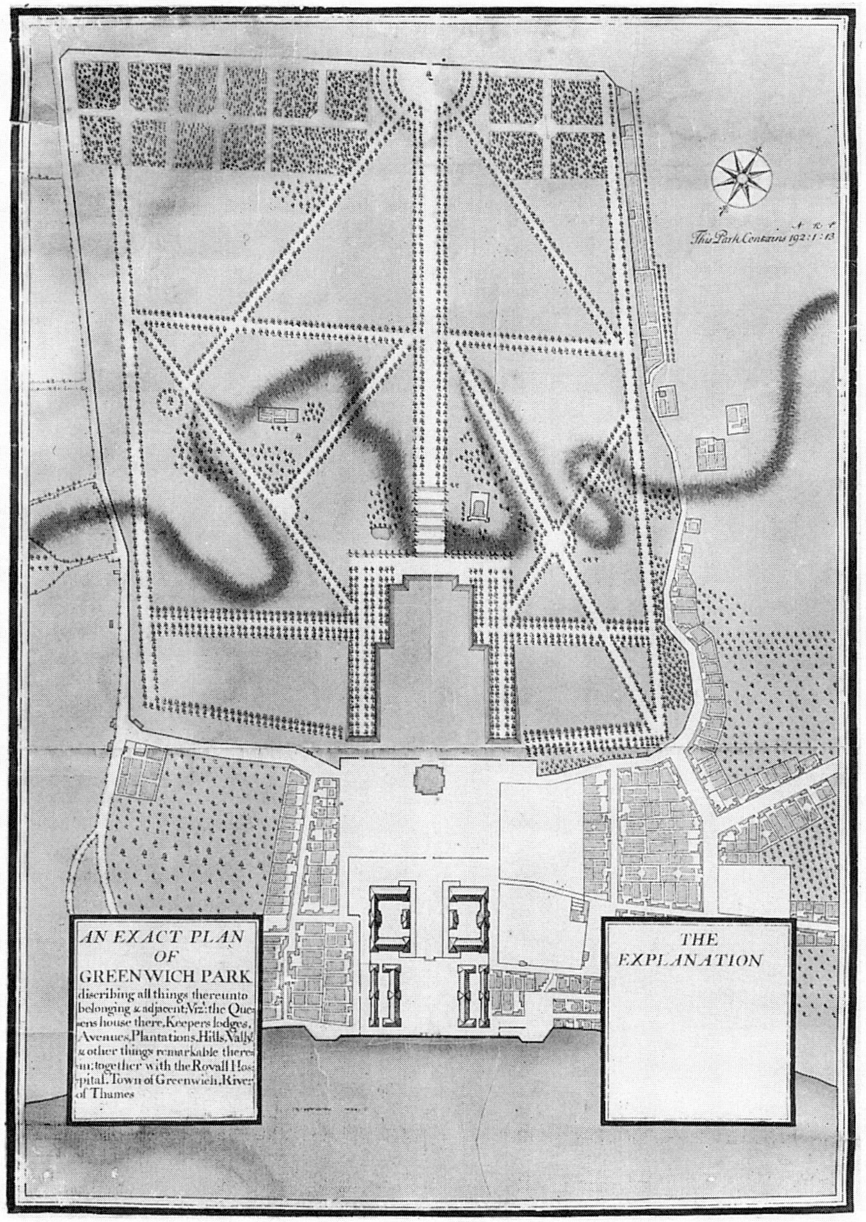

199b Greenwich Park. Plan by Bridgeman (attrib.).
National Maritime Museum, Greenwich, Greenwich Park MSS (ART/6)

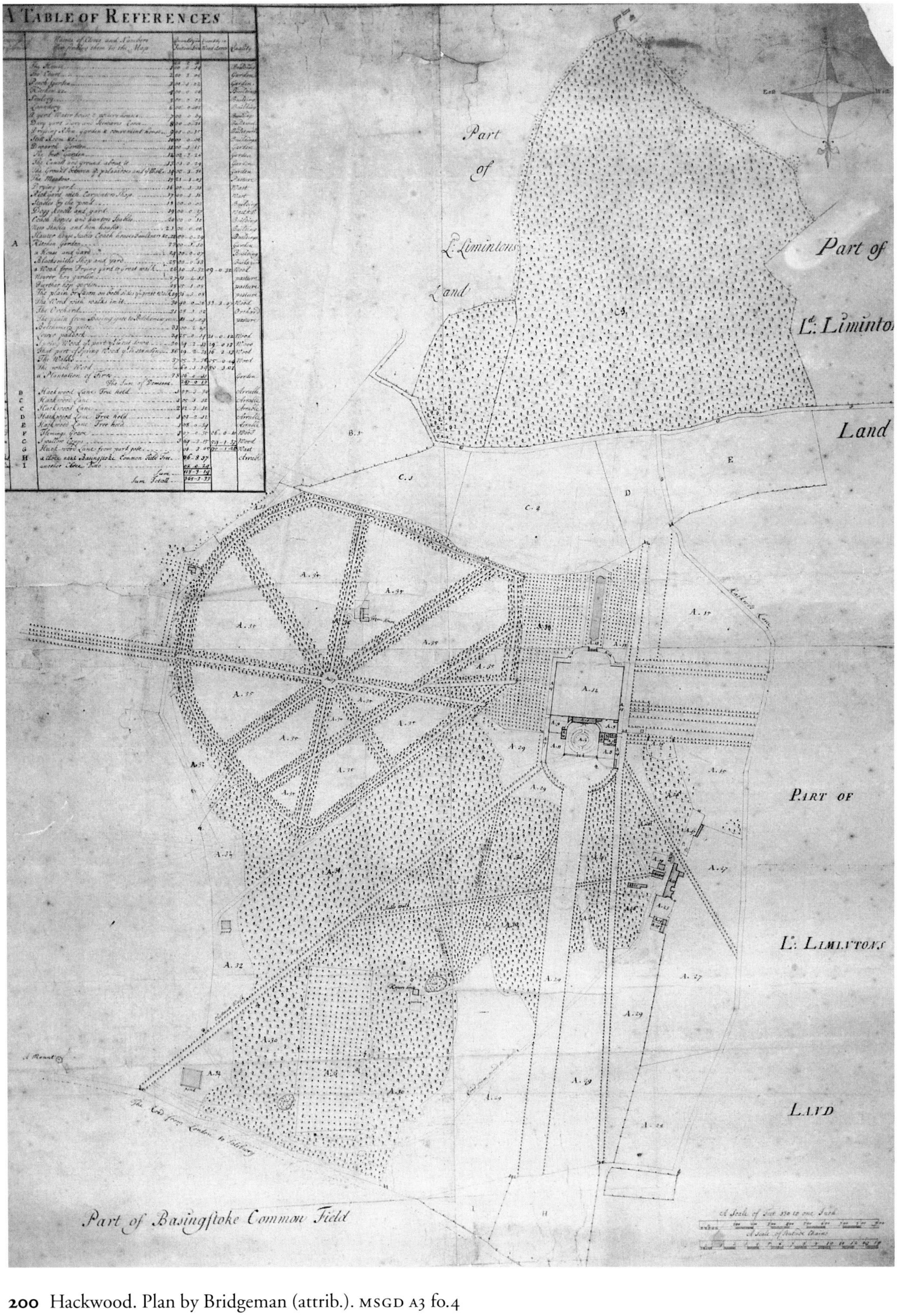

200 Hackwood. Plan by Bridgeman (attrib.). MSGD A3 fo.4

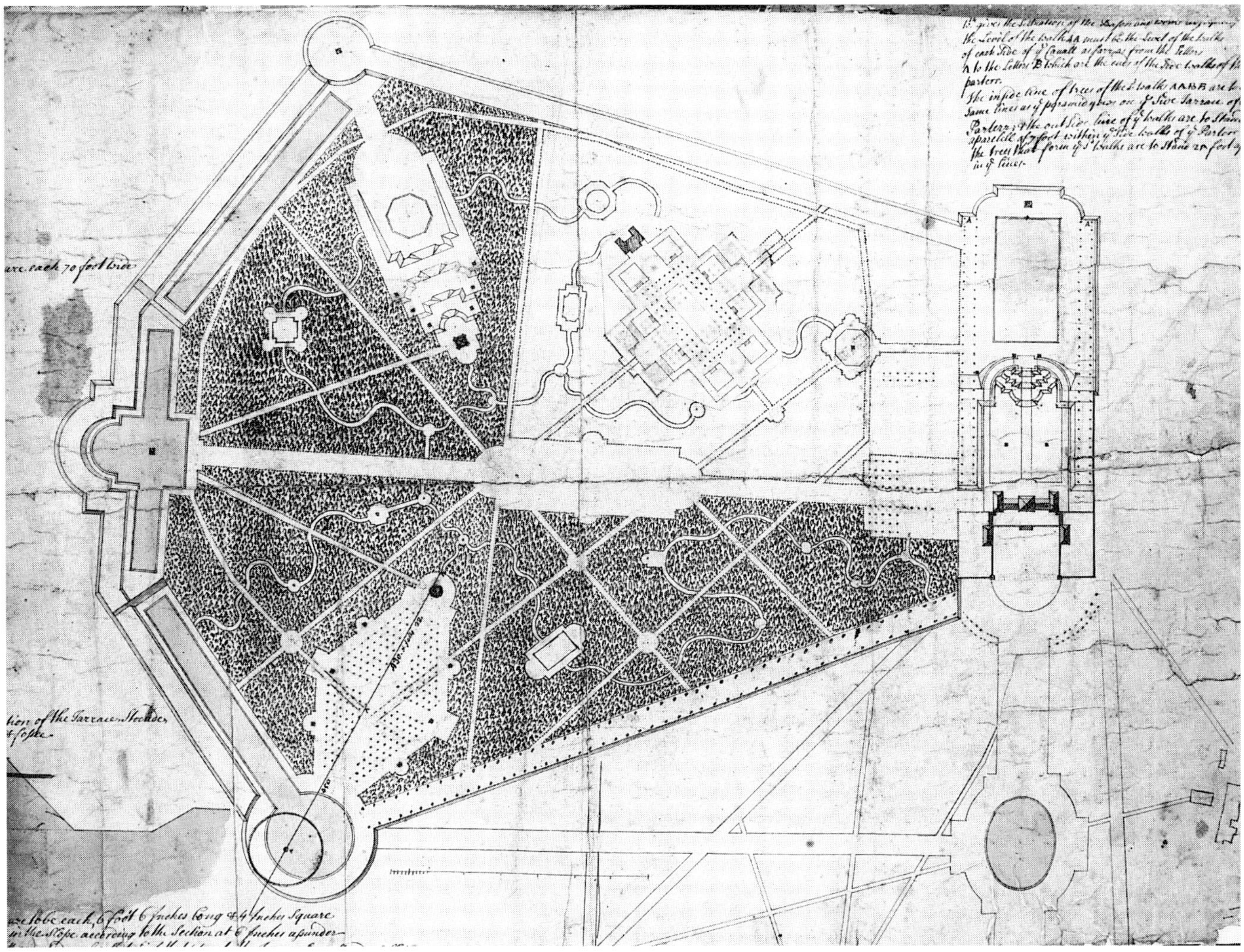

201a Hackwood. Plan by Bridgeman (attrib.).
MSGD A4 fo.34

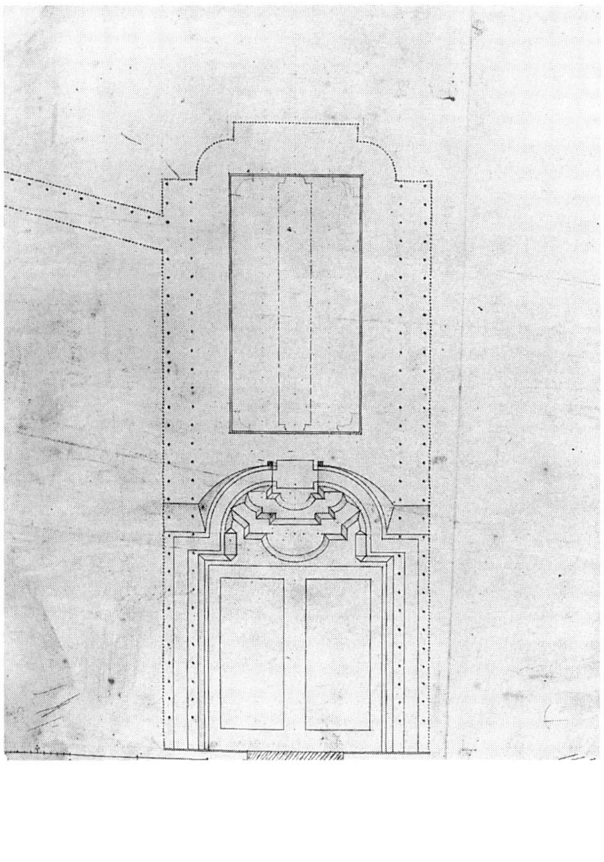

201b Hackwood. Plan by Bridgeman (attrib.).
MSGD A4 fo.24

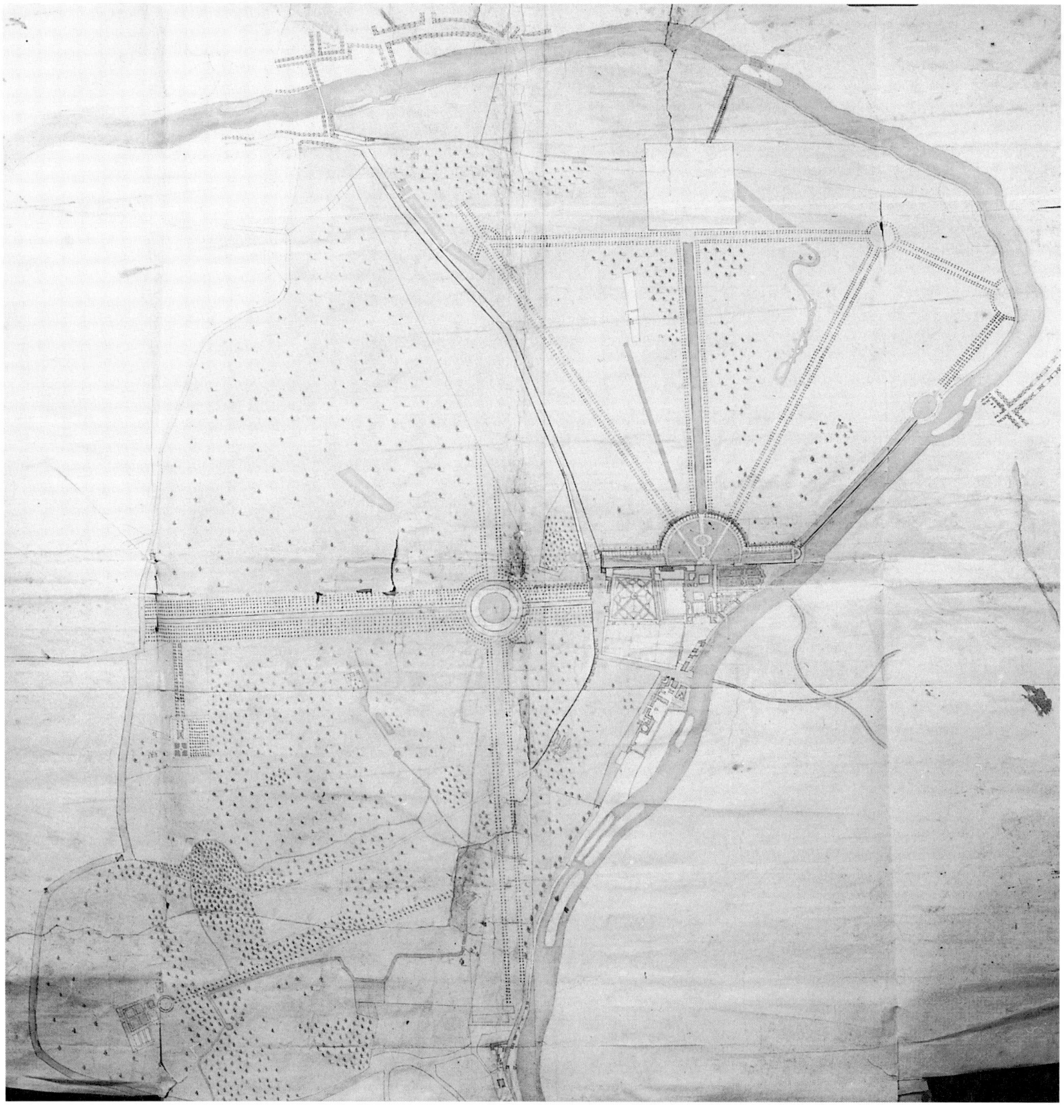

202 Hampton Court. Plan by Bridgeman (attrib.). MSGD A4 fo.62

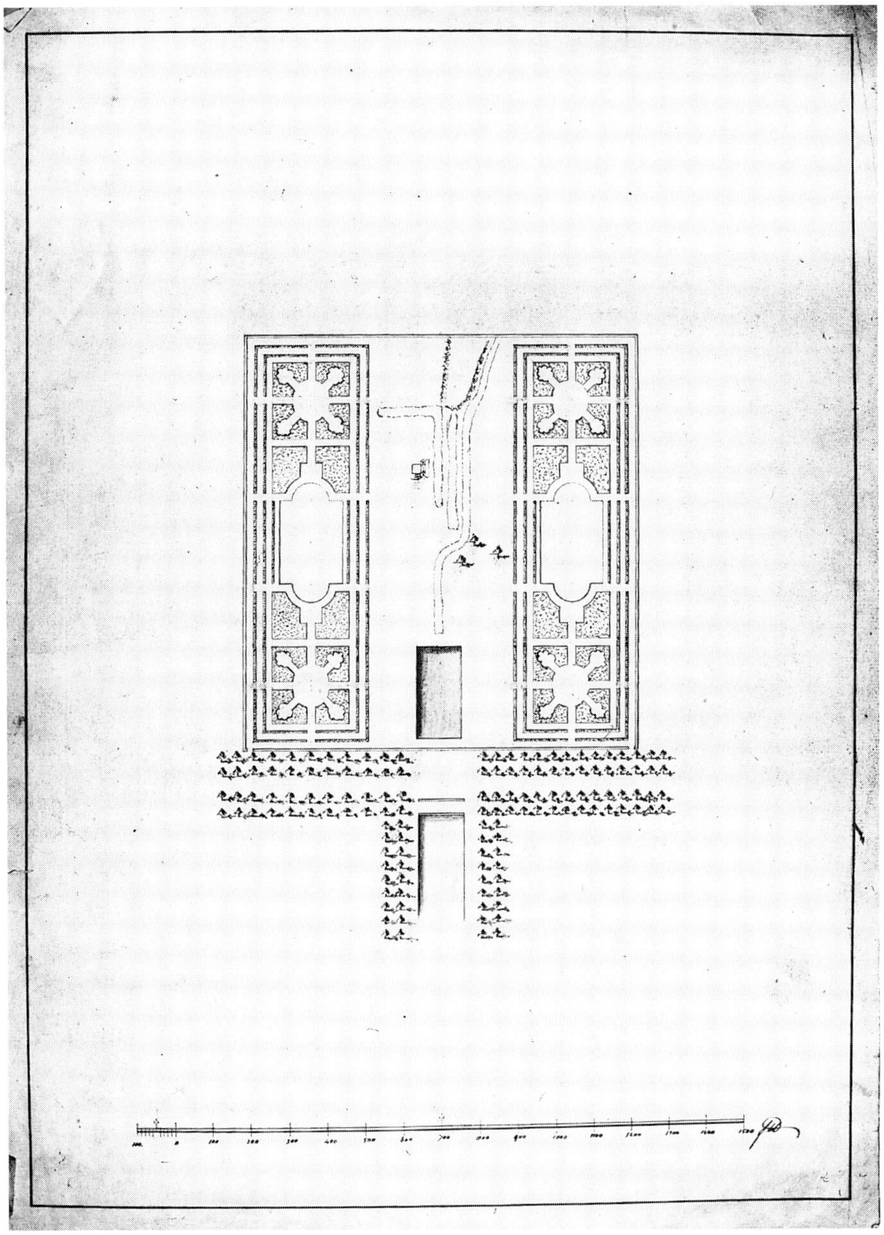

203a Hampton Court.
Plan of Lower Wilderness by Bridgeman (attrib.).
Hovingham Hall, Yorkshire,
MS vol., Architectural Drawings at Hovingham, fo.39
(Sir Marcus Worsley, Bt)

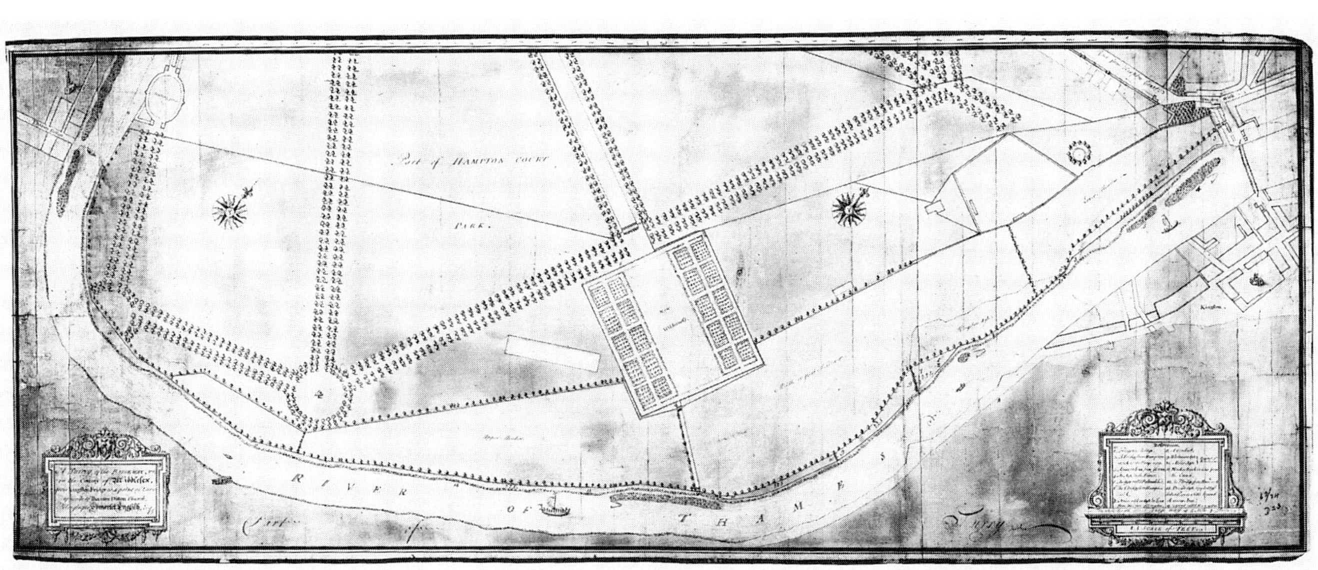

203b Hampton Court. Survey by Bridgeman (attrib.). PRO, MPD 23 (3) (Cat.No.1343)

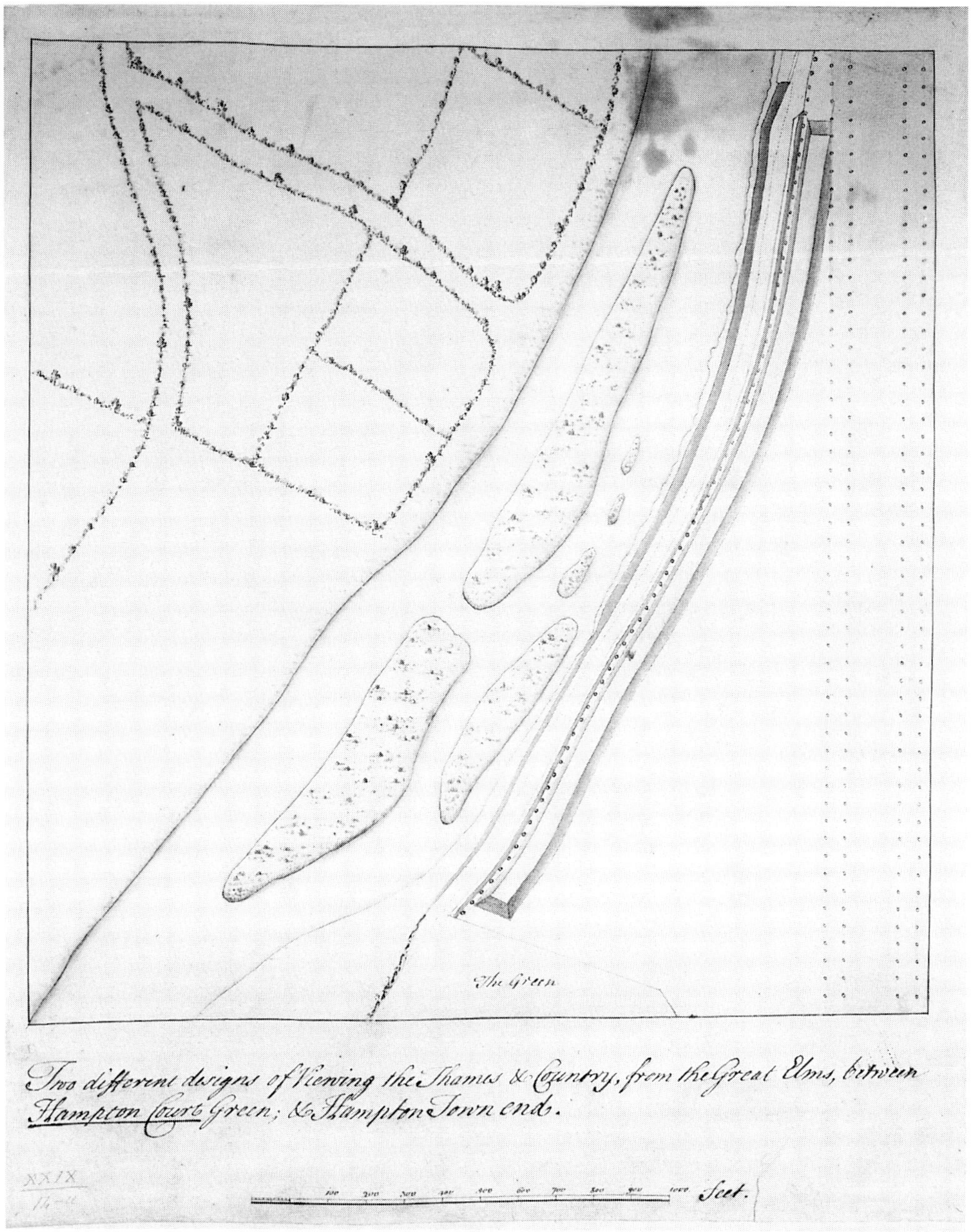

204a Hampton Court. Plan of Islands in River Thames near Hampton Court by Bridgeman (attrib.). BL, K.XXIX, 14U

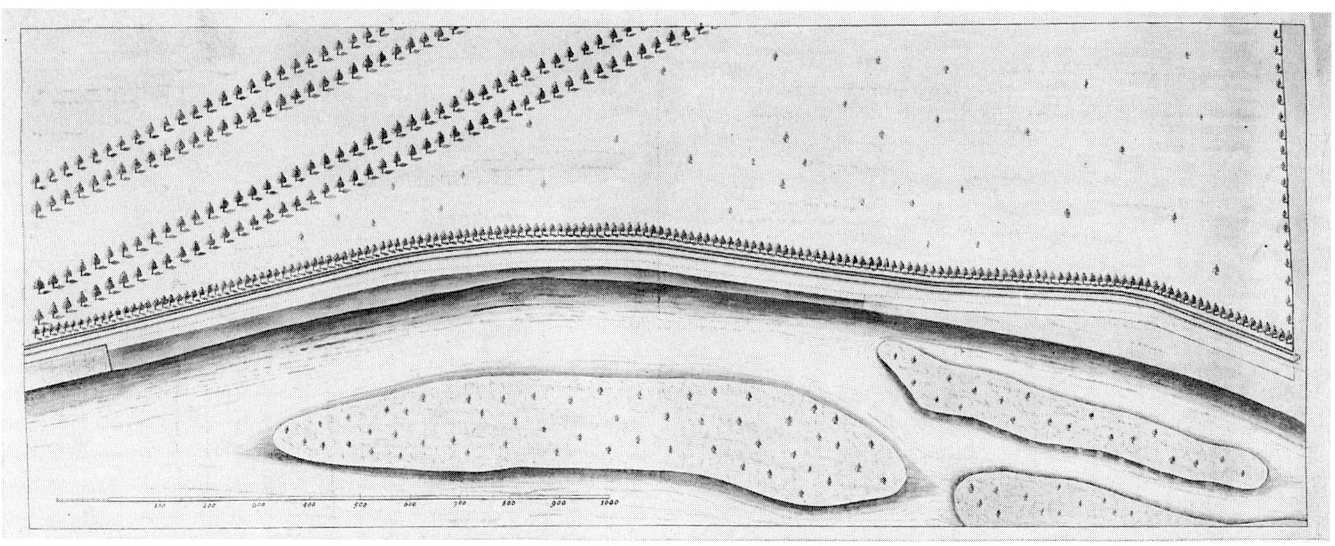

204b Hampton Court. Plan by Bridgeman (attrib.). MSGD A4 fo.74

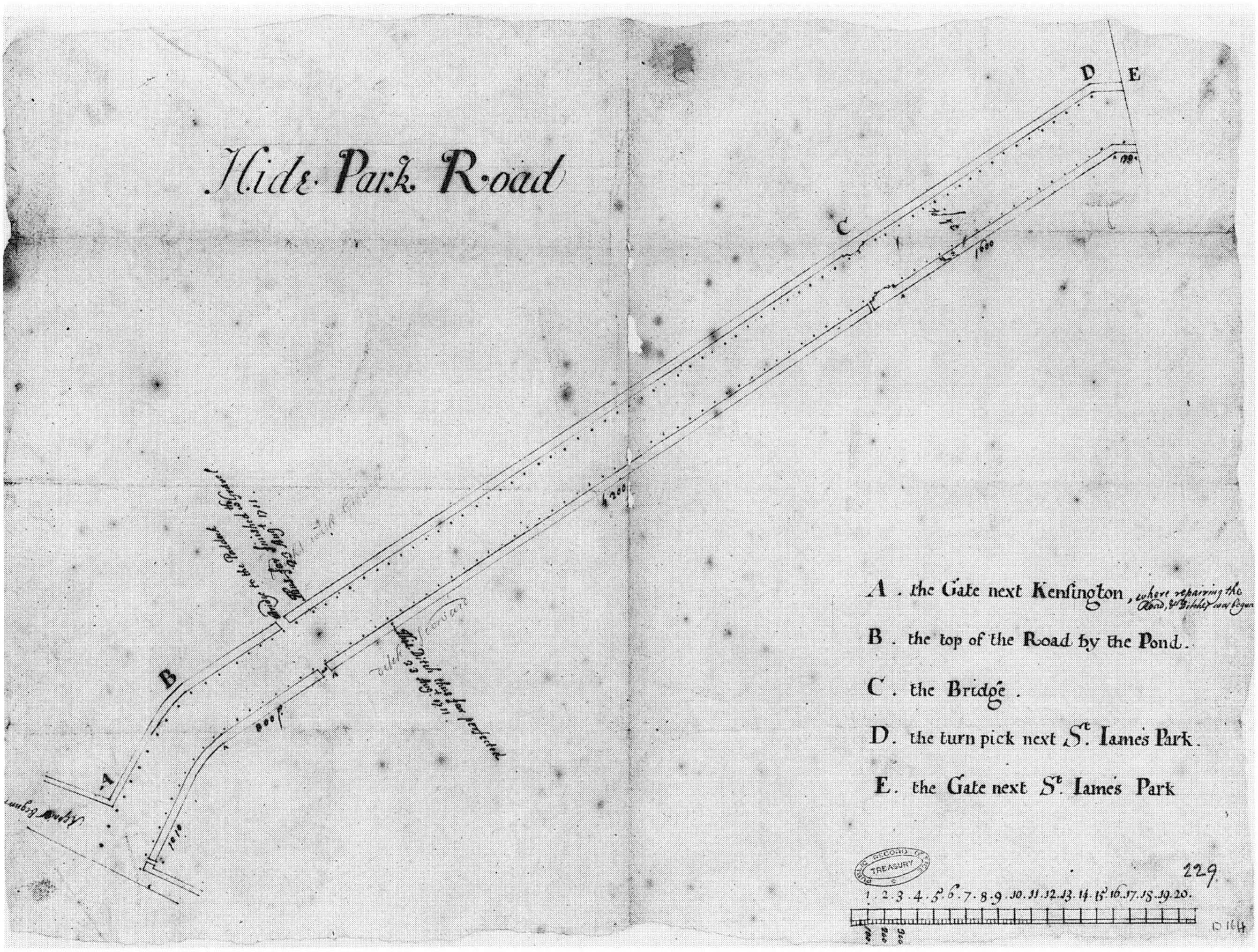

205a Hyde Park Road. Plan by Bridgeman (attrib.). PRO, MPD 164 (Cat.No.338)

205b Kedleston. Plan of Canal and Cascades by Bridgeman (attrib.). National Trust, Kedleston Hall, Scarsdale Collection

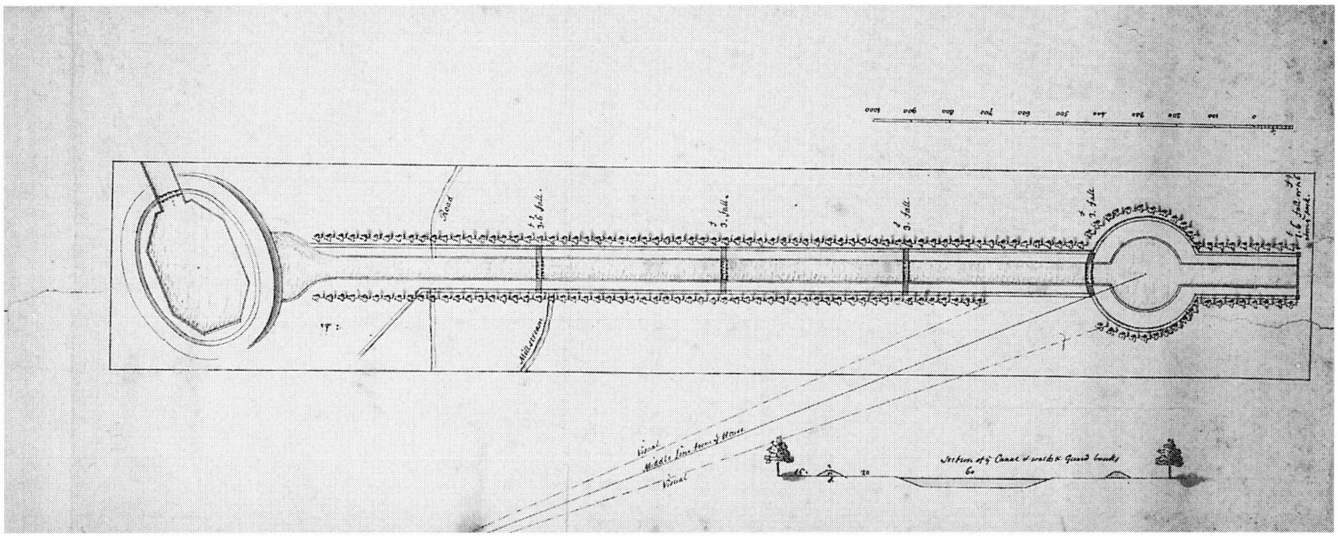

206a Kensington Gardens and Hyde Park. Plan by Bridgeman (attrib.). Nationalmuseum, Stockholm, CC.2753 (Cronstedt Collection)

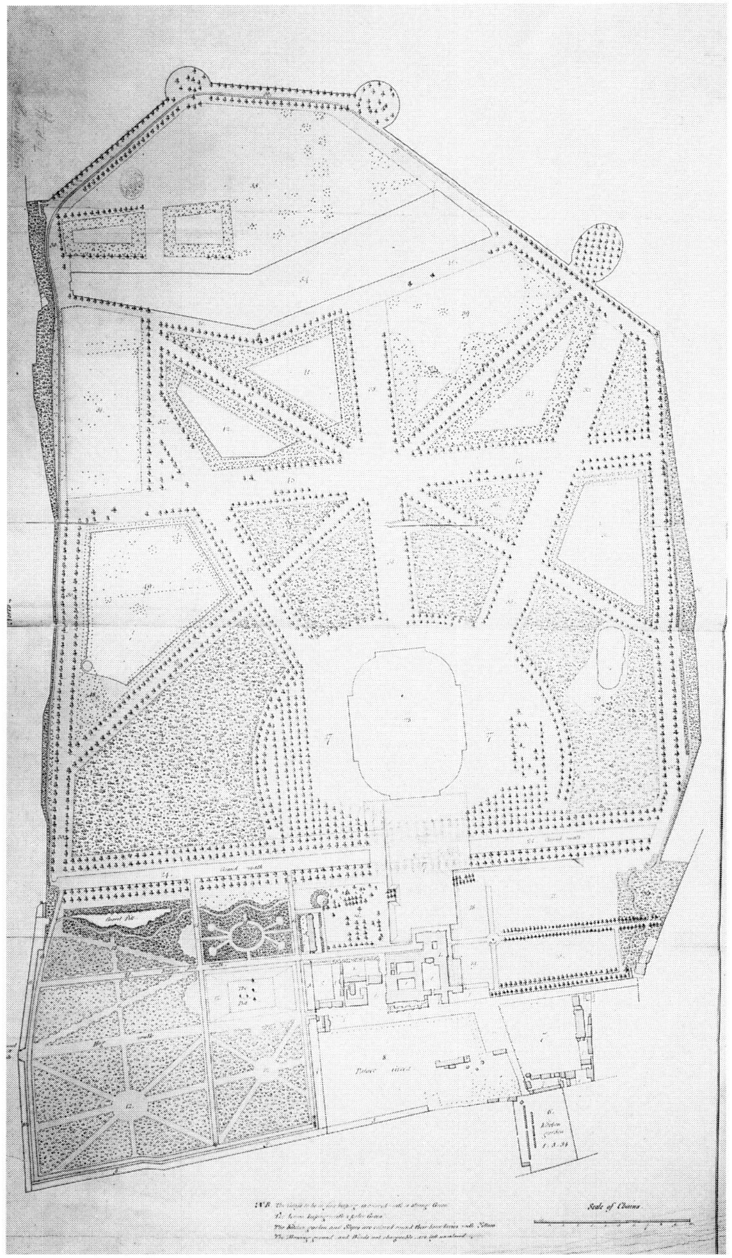

206b Kensington Gardens and Hyde Park. Plan by Bridgeman (attrib.). BL, K.XXVIII.10.d.1

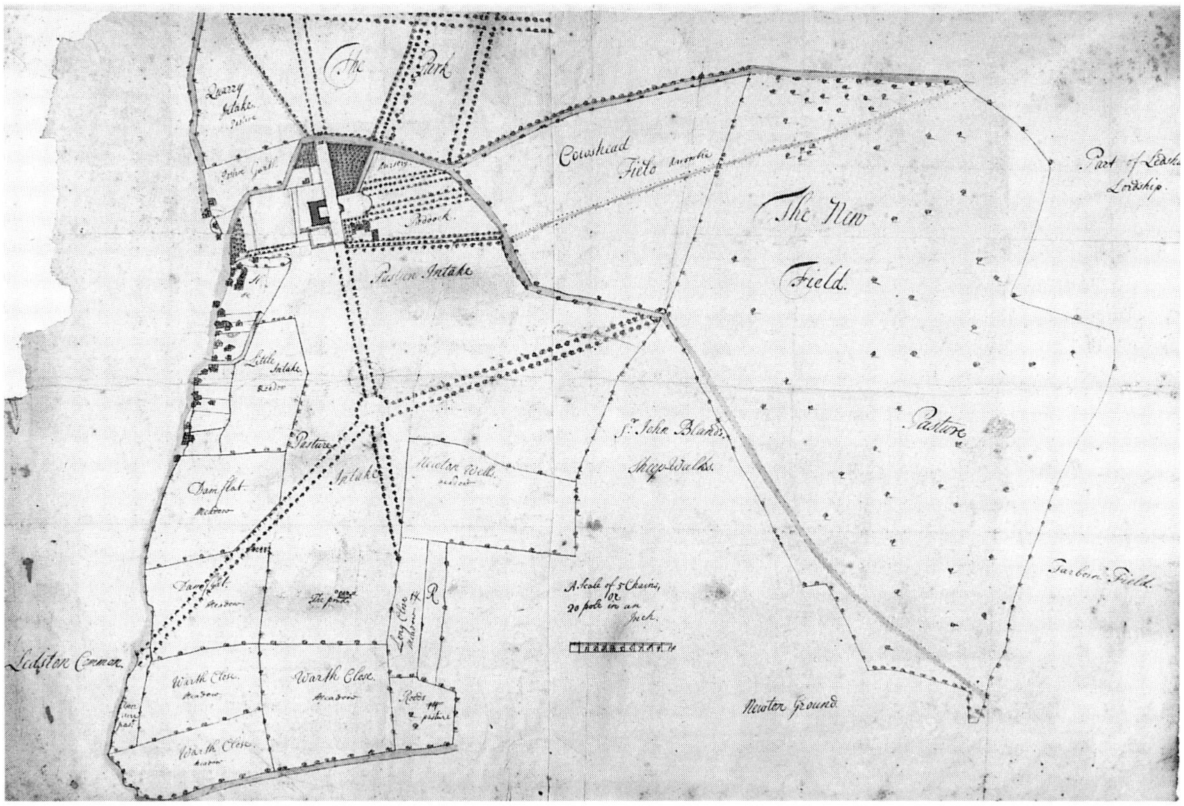

207a Ledston. Plan by Bridgeman (attrib.). MSGD A3 fo.19

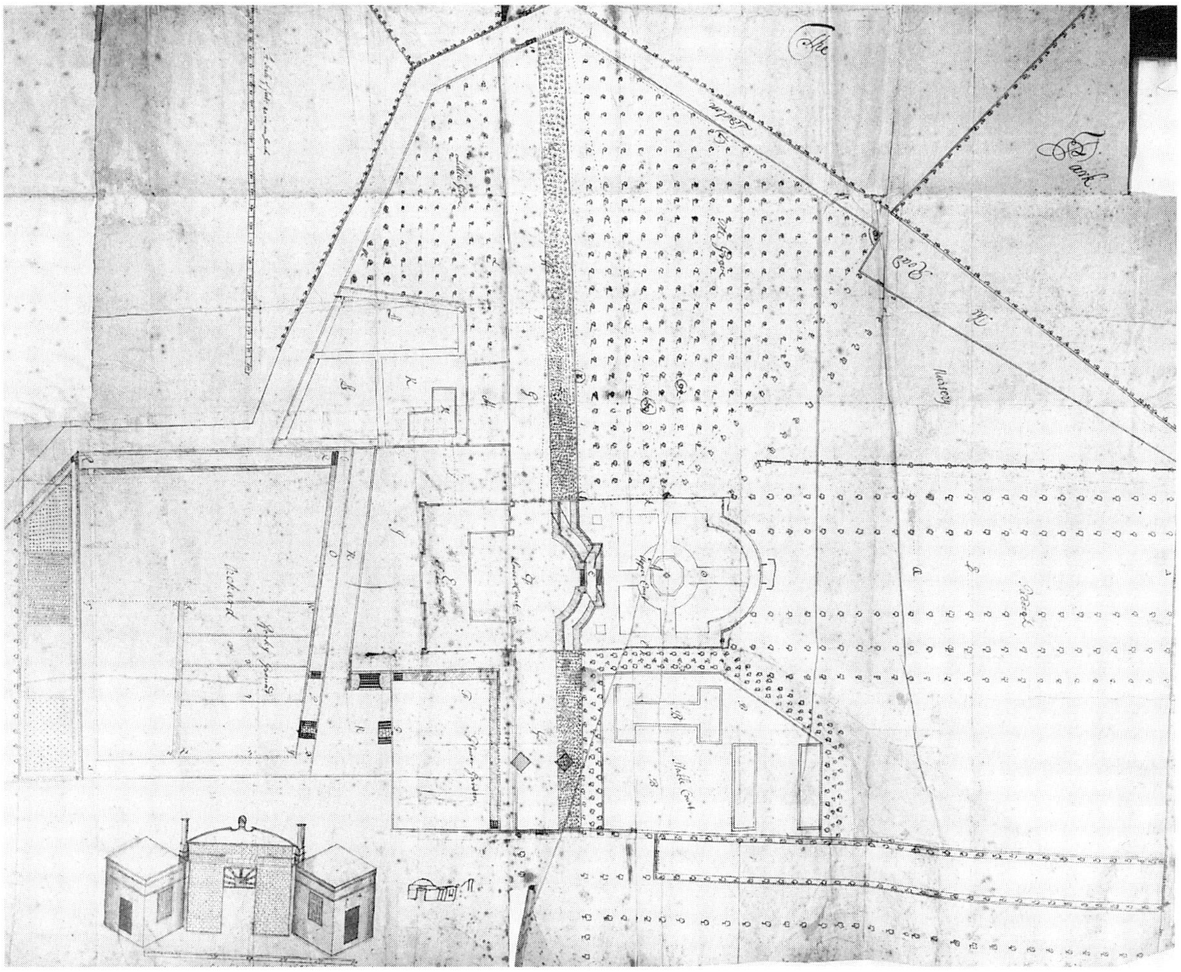

207b Ledston. Plan by Bridgeman (attrib.). MSGD A4 fo.85

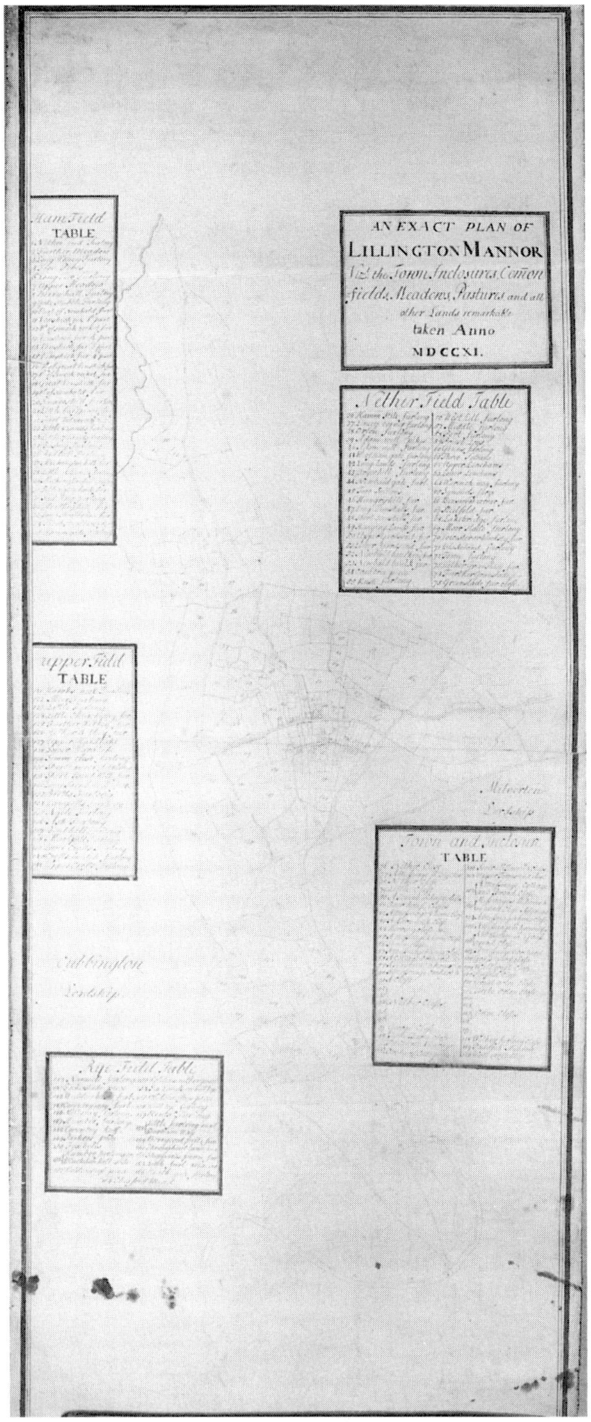

208a Lillington Manor. Plan by Bridgeman (attrib.). Warwickshire CRO, Warwick, CR. 556/197

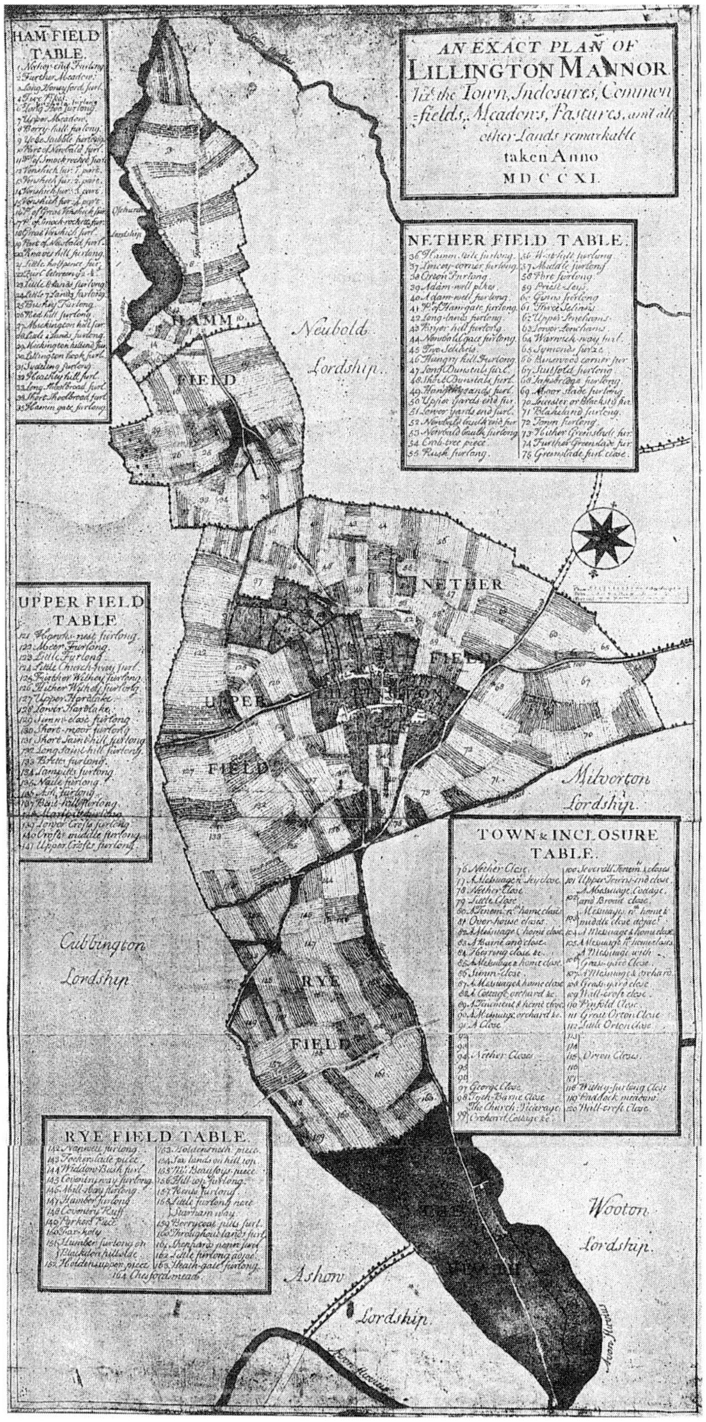

208b Lillington Manor. Plan by Bridgeman (attrib.). Formerly at Lillington Vicarage, now lost, reproduced from William Cooper, *The History of Lillington, Leamington Spa* (Long Compton, 1940), endpaper

209 Lodge Park, Sherborne. Plan by Bridgeman (attrib.). MSGD A4 fo.68

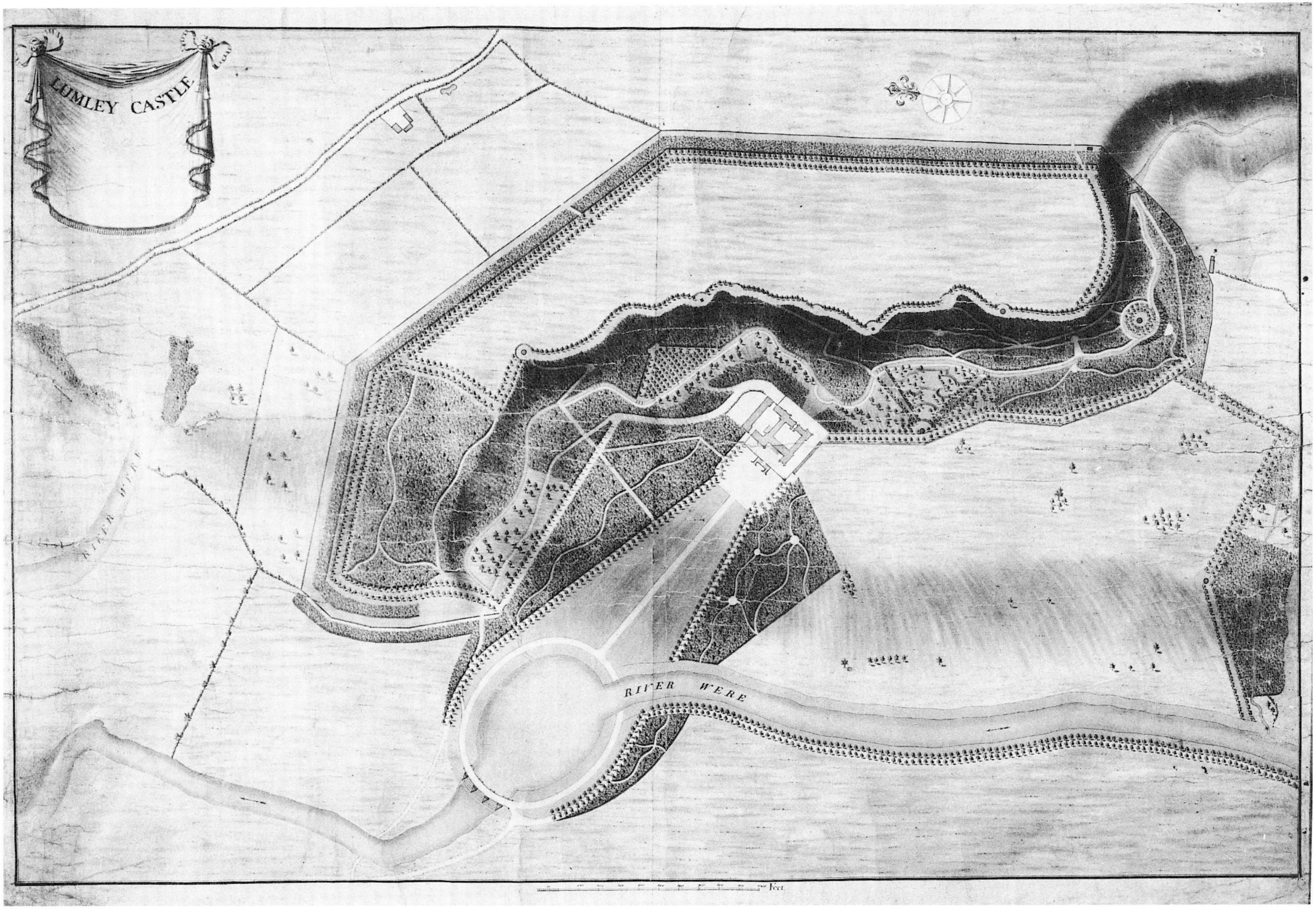

210 Lumley Castle. Plan by Bridgeman (attrib.). Sandbeck Park, Yorkshire (Earl of Scarbrough)

211 Lumley Castle. Detail of plan by Bridgeman (attrib.). Sandbeck Park, Yorkshire (Earl of Scarbrough)

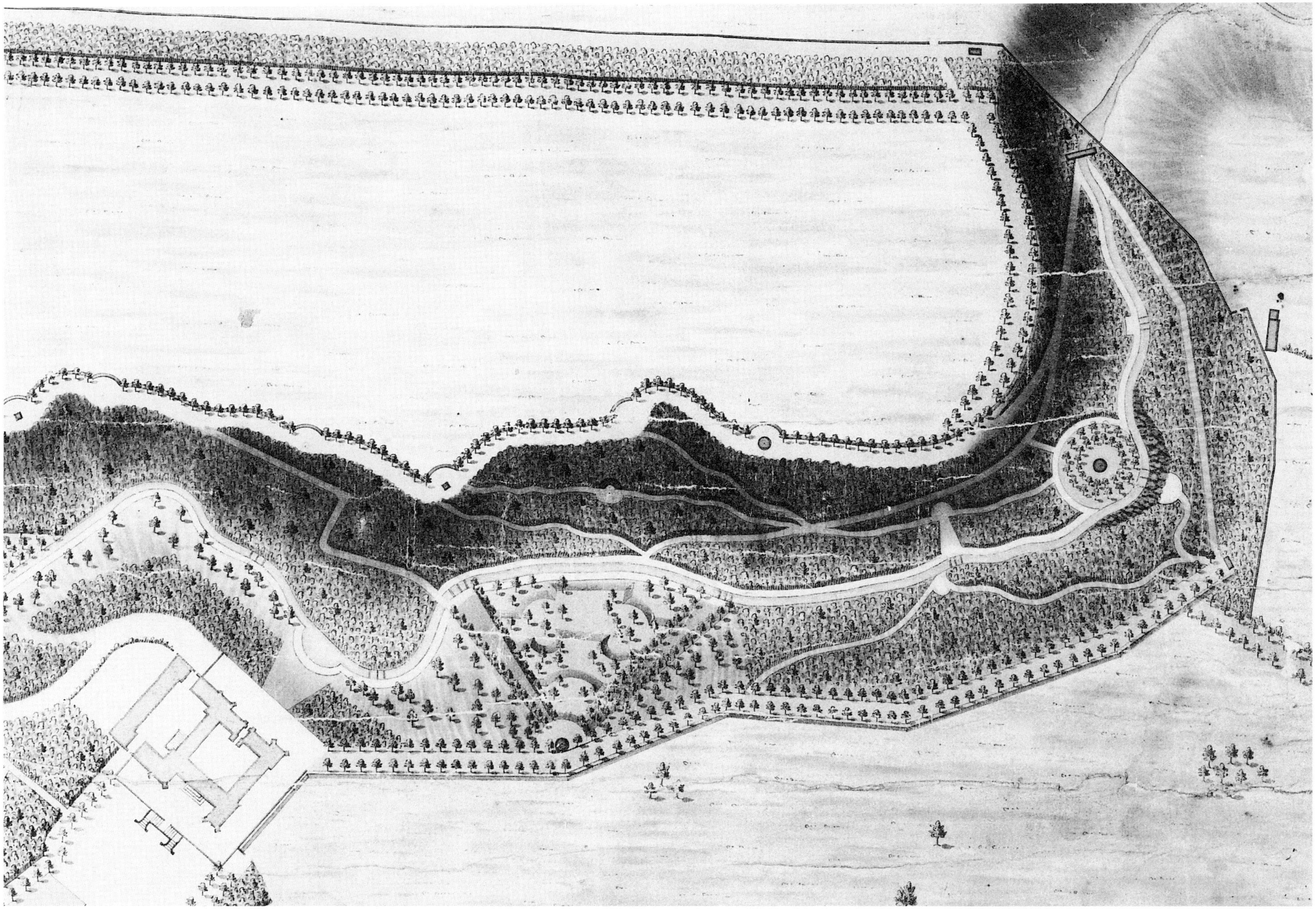

212 Lumley Castle. Detail of plan by Bridgeman (attrib.). Sandbeck Park, Yorkshire (Earl of Scarbrough)

213a Marble Hill. Plan by Bridgeman (attrib.). Norfolk RO, Norwich, MC 184/10/1

213b Marble Hill. Detail of plan by Bridgeman (attrib.) in *Plate 213a*

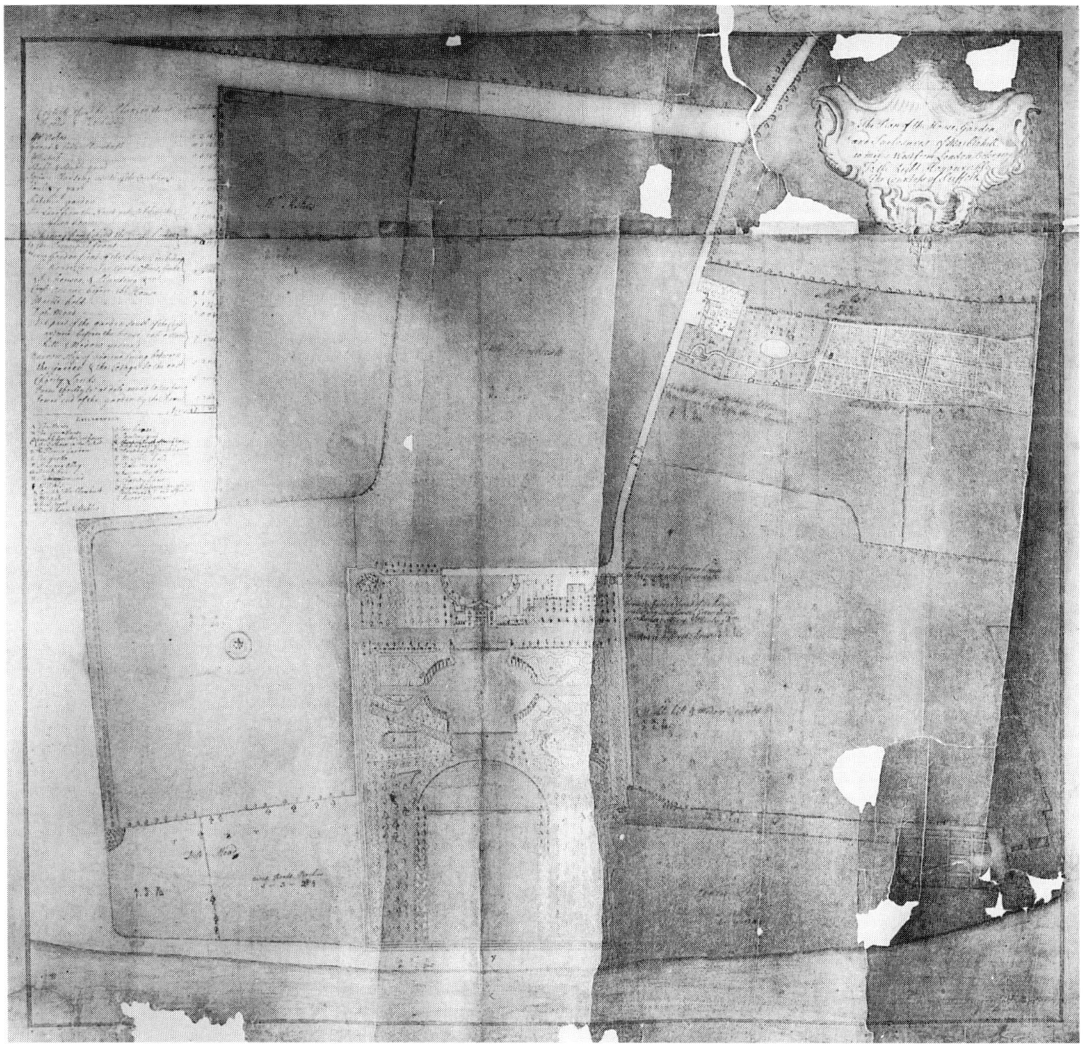

214a Marble Hill. Plan by Bridgeman (attrib.). Norfolk RO, Norwich, MC 184/10/2r

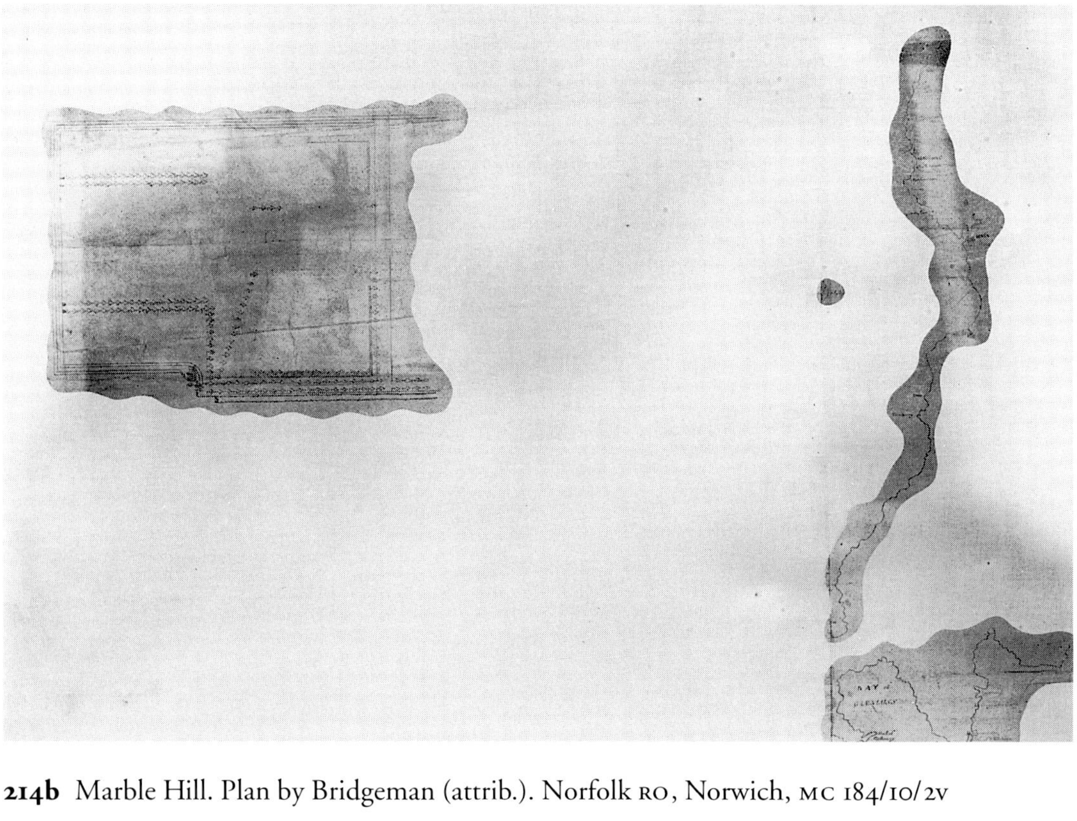

214b Marble Hill. Plan by Bridgeman (attrib.). Norfolk RO, Norwich, MC 184/10/2v

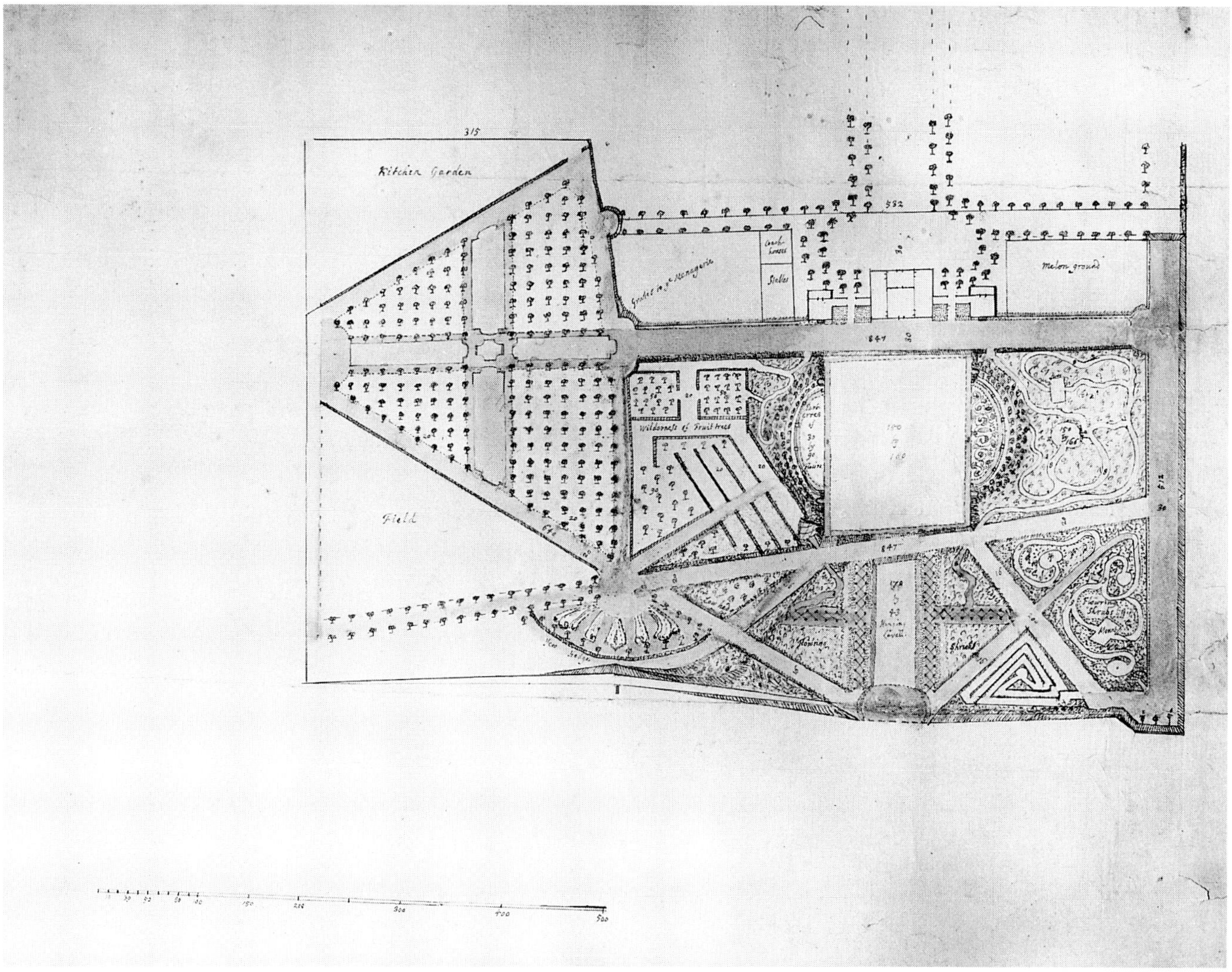

215 Marble Hill. Plan. Norfolk RO. Norwich, MC 184/10/3

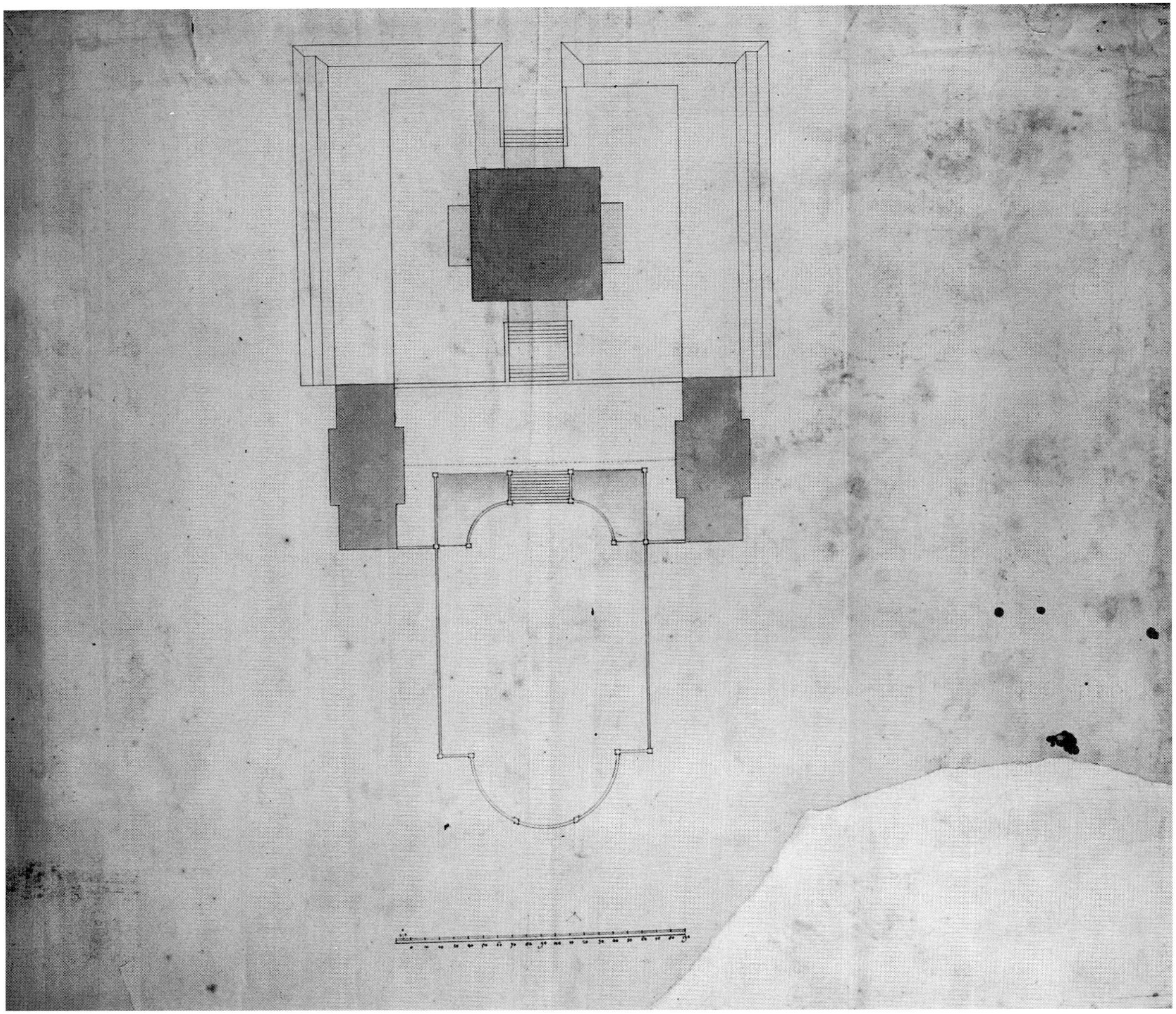

216 Mereworth.
Plan by Bridgeman
(attrib.). MSGD A4 fo.52

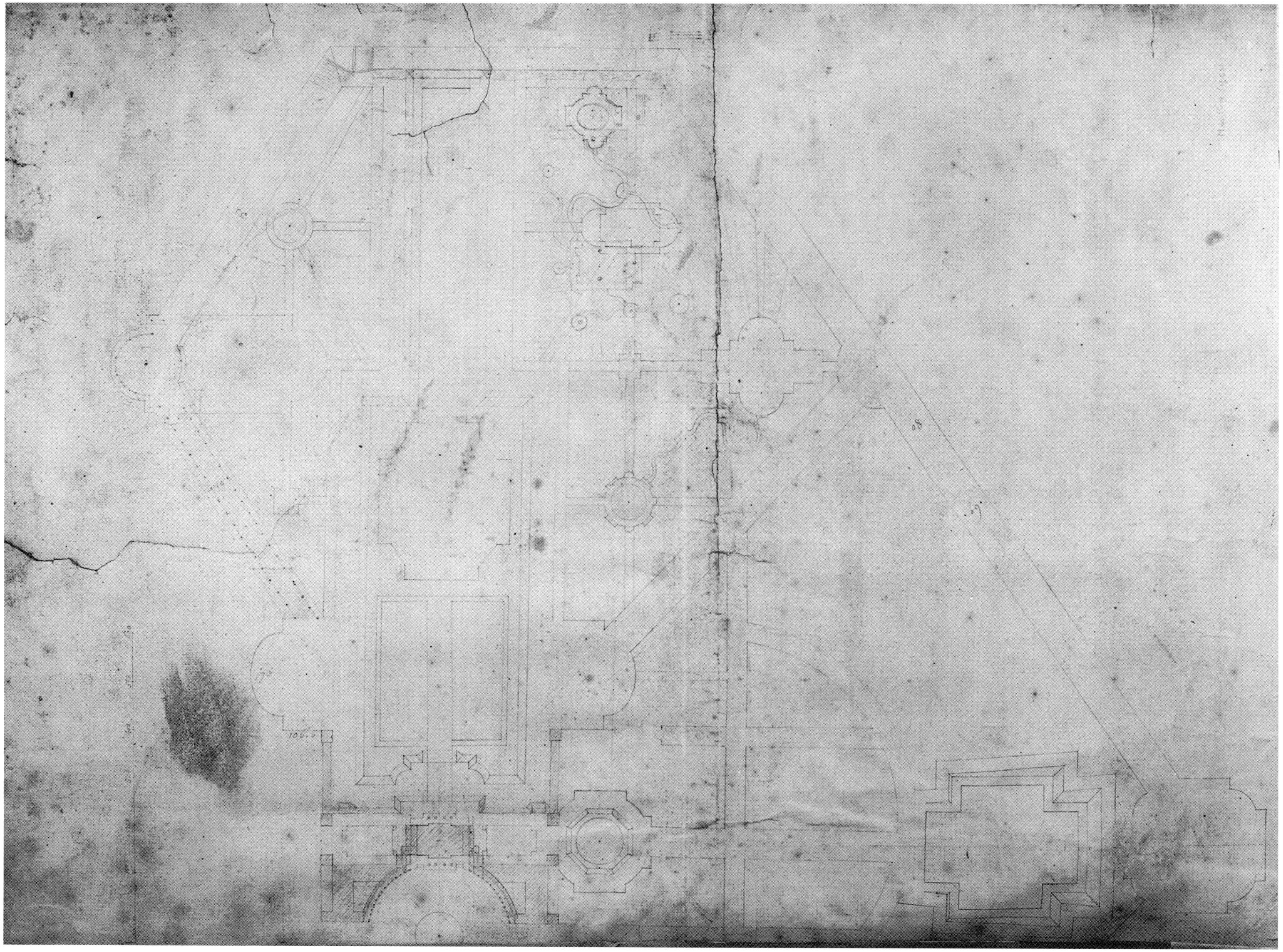

217 Moor Park. Plan by Bridgeman (attrib.). MSGD A4 fo. 48

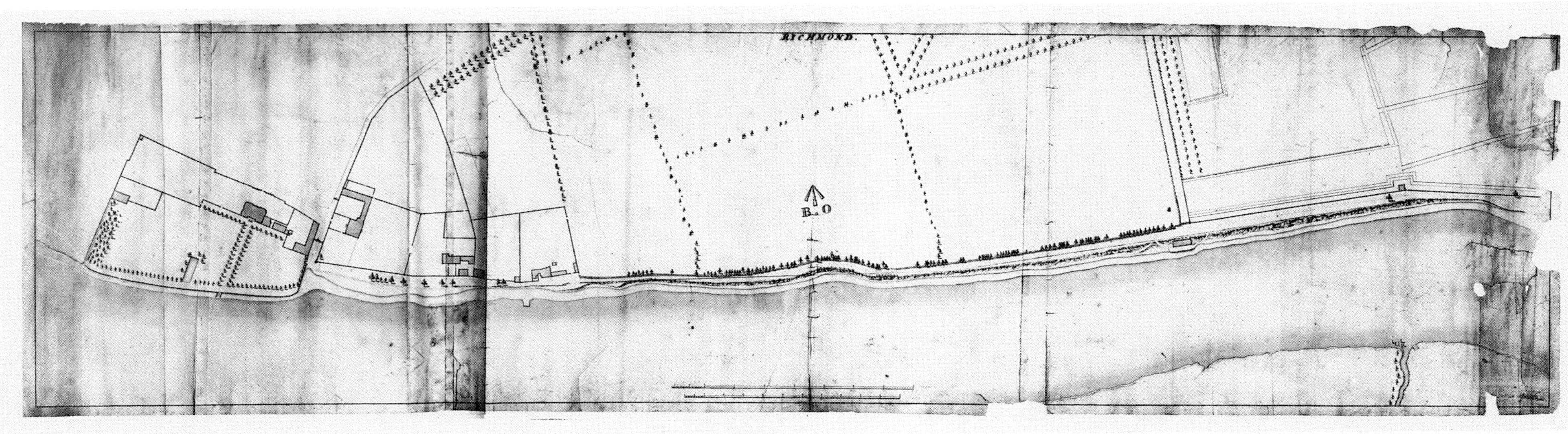

218 Richmond Gardens. Plan by Bridgeman (attrib.). PRO, MR 528 (Cat. No.1449)

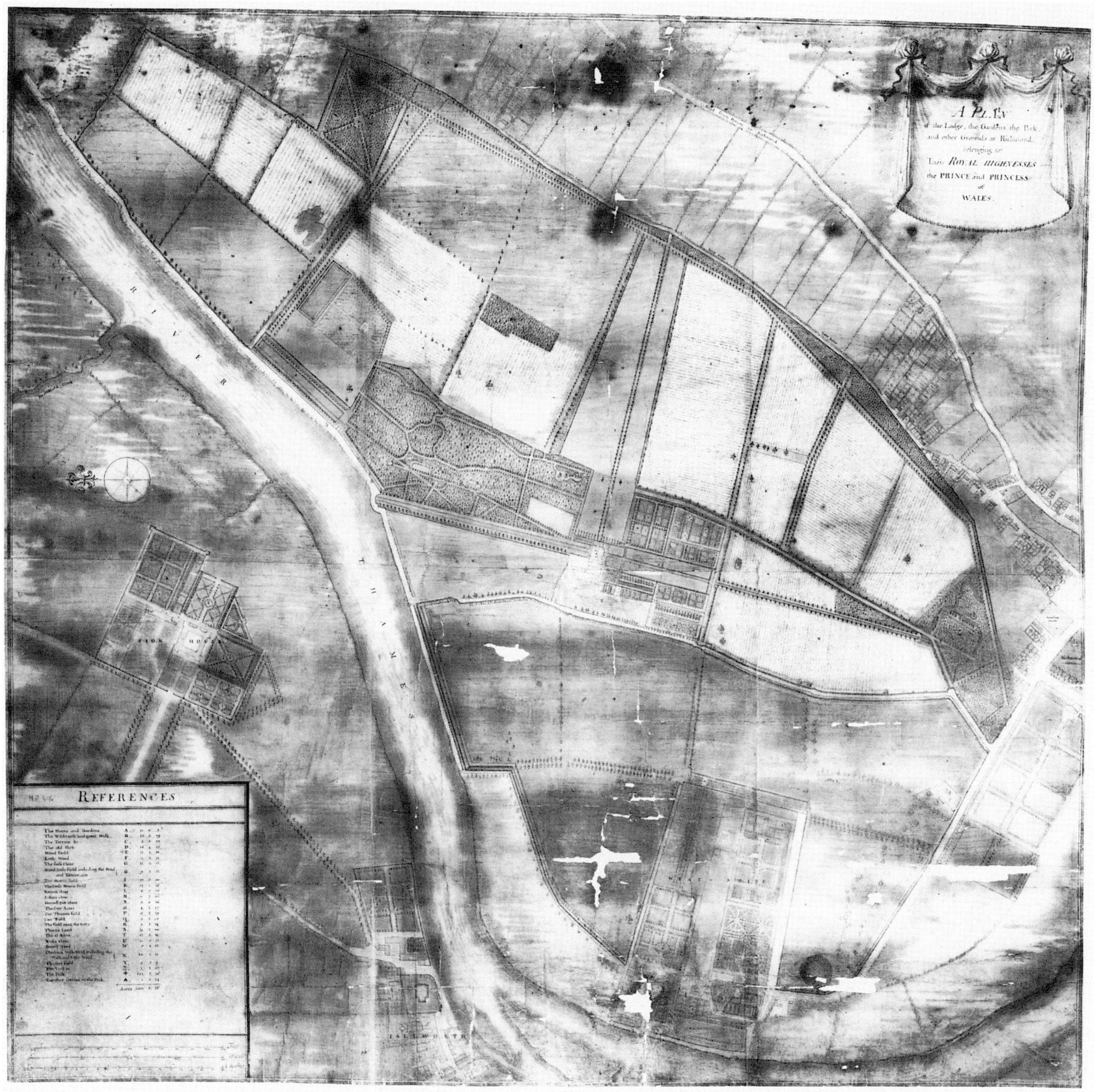

219 Richmond Gardens. Plan by Bridgeman (attrib.). PRO, MR 696 (Cat. No.1437)

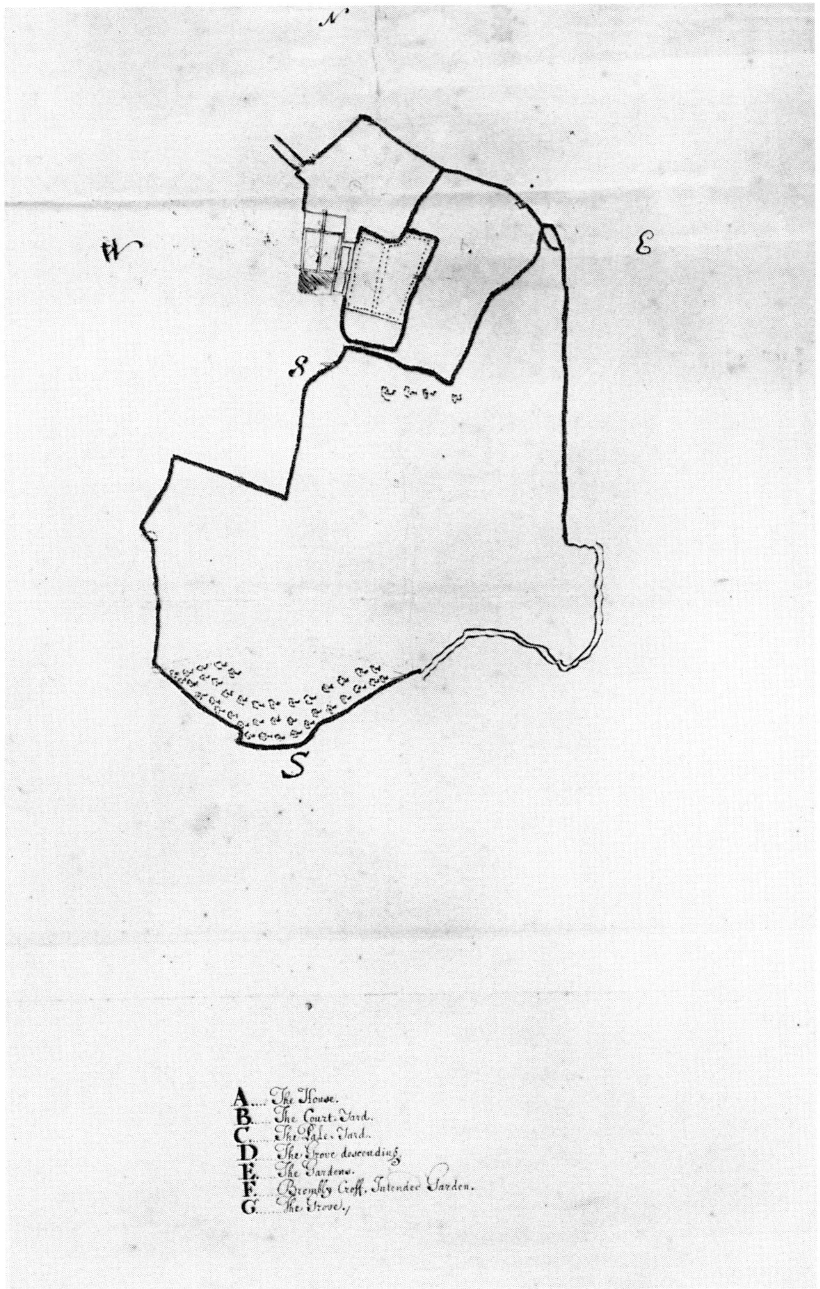

220a Sacombe. Plan by Bridgeman (attrib.). MSGD A4 fo.29

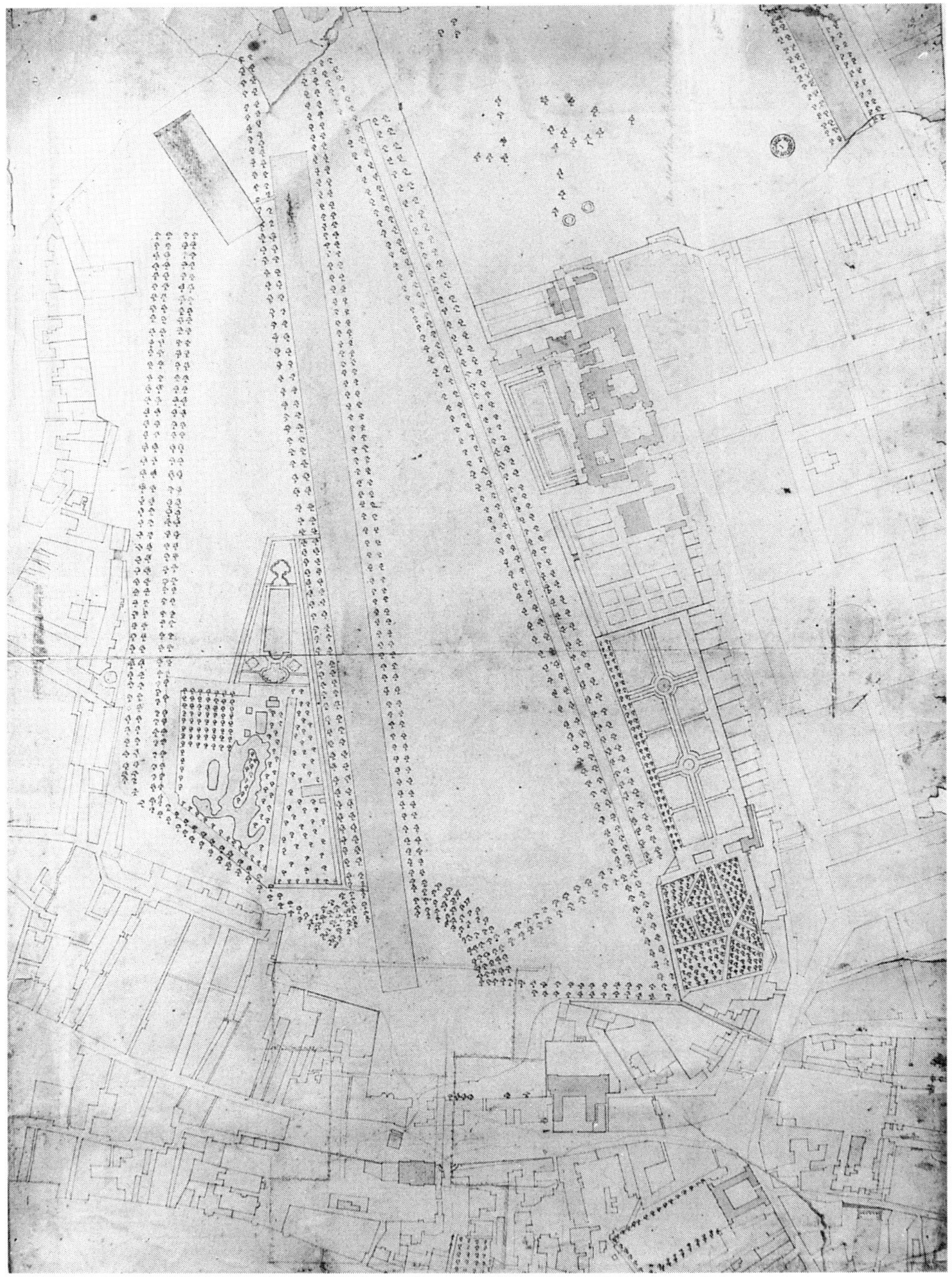

220b St James's Park, London. Plan by Bridgeman (attrib.). Soane, Drawer 62/1/1 (Trustees of Sir John Soane's Museum)

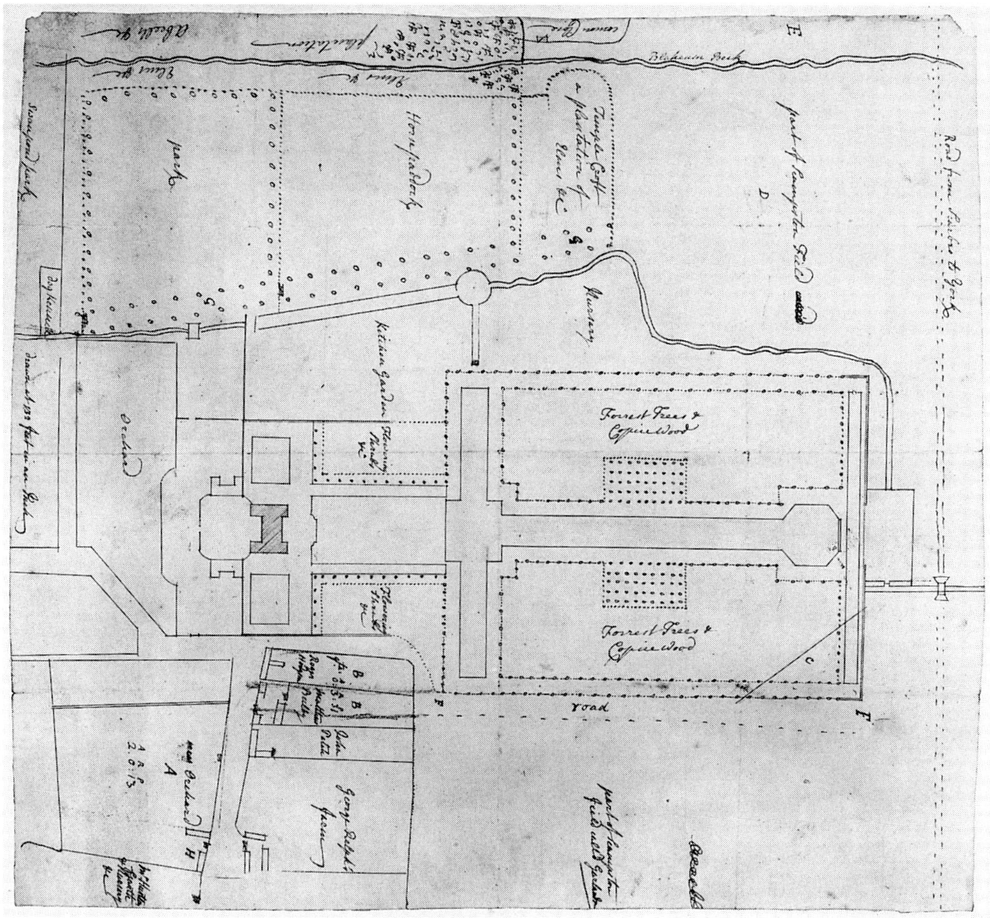

221a Scampston. Plan by Bridgeman (attrib.). MSGD A4 fo.66

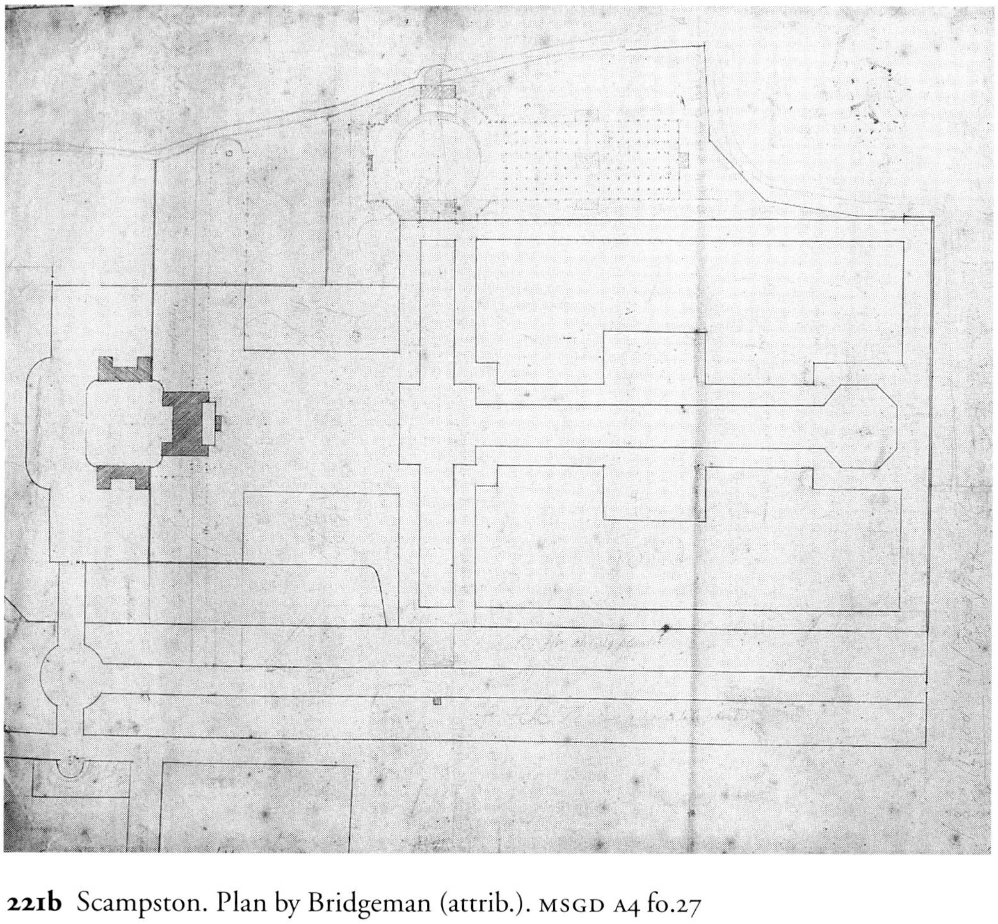

221b Scampston. Plan by Bridgeman (attrib.). MSGD A4 fo.27

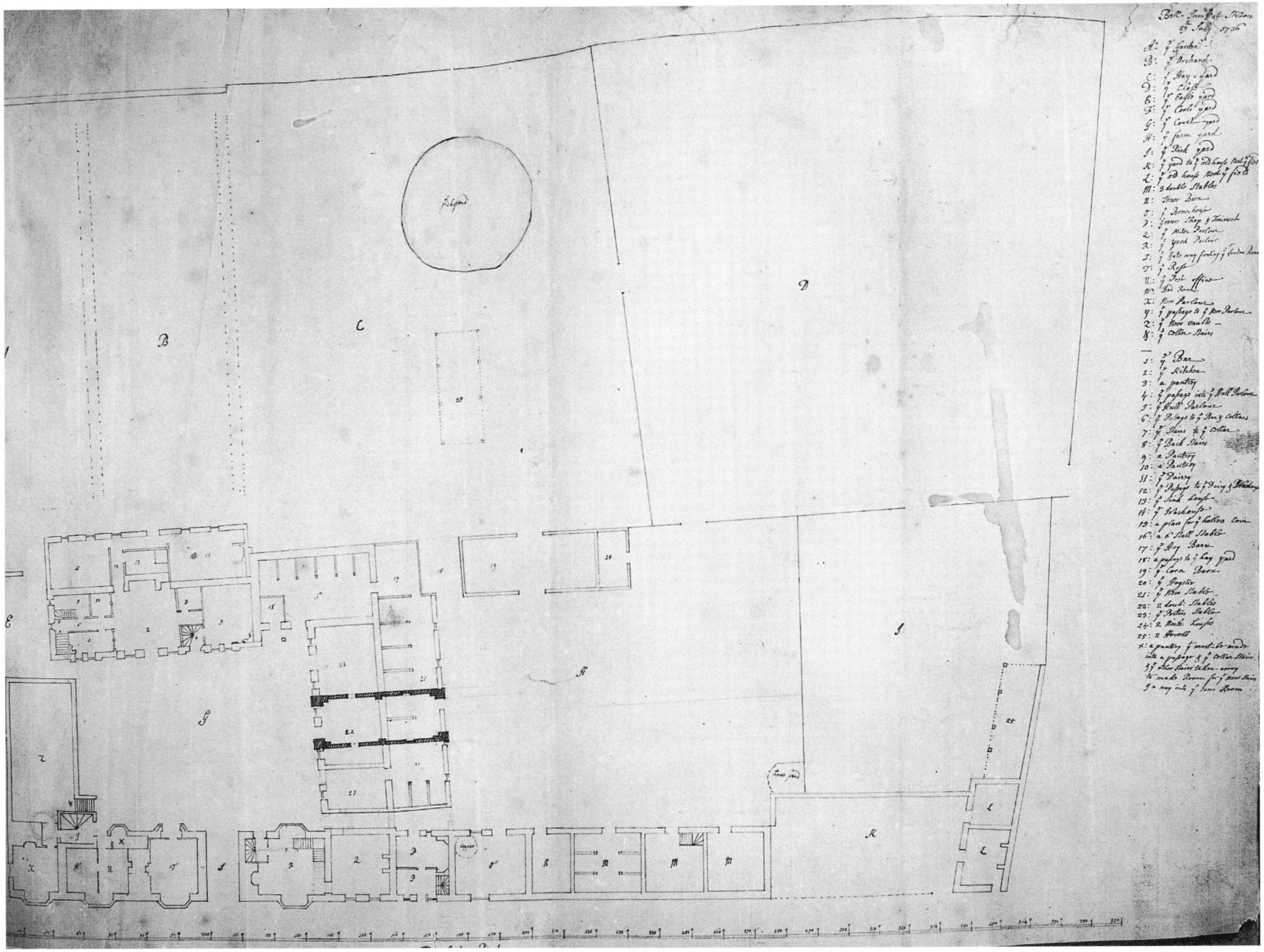

222 The Bell Inn, Stilton. Plan by Bridgeman (attrib.). MSGD A4 fo.51

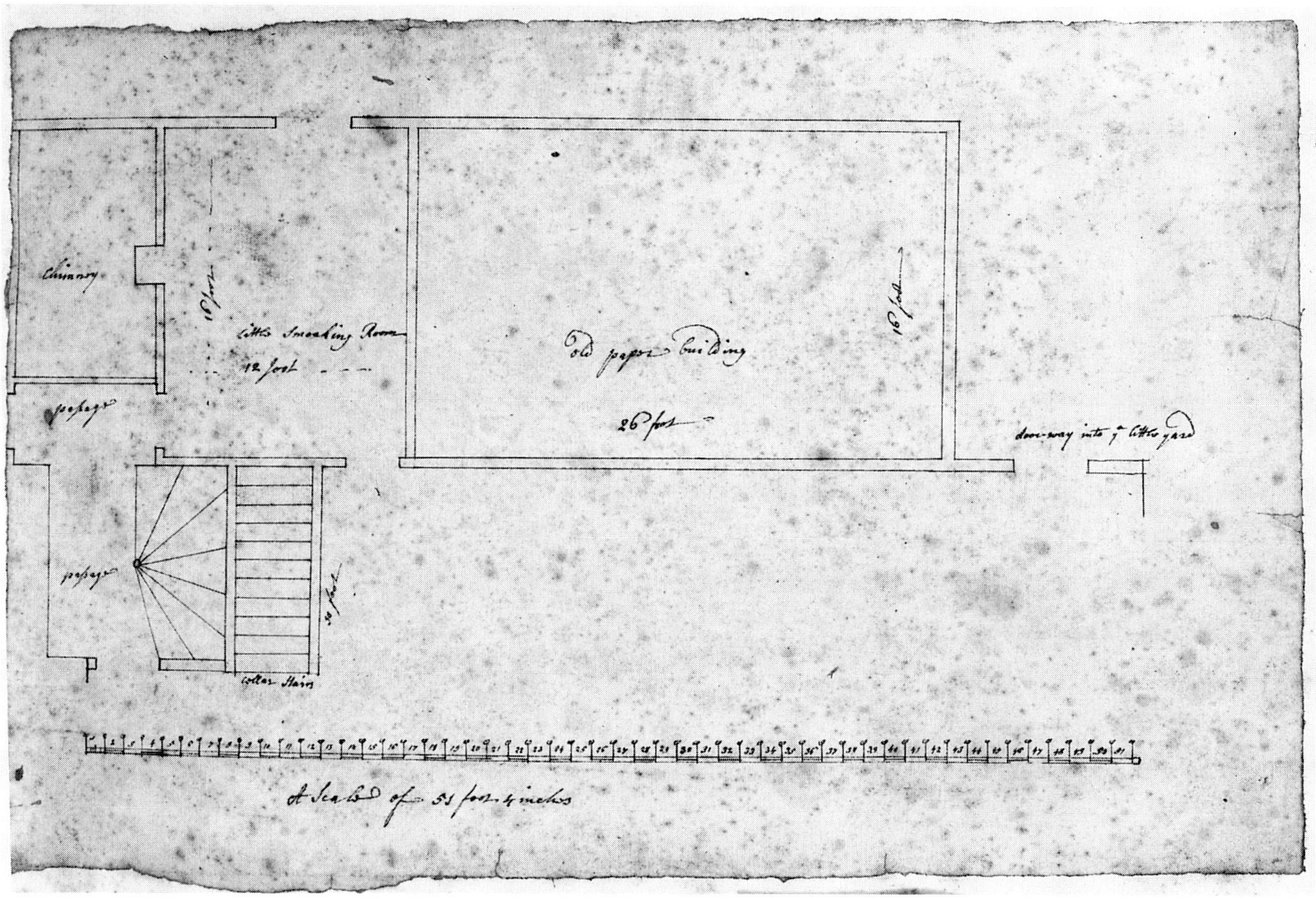

223 The Bell Inn, Stilton. Plan by Bridgeman (attrib.). MSGD A4 fo.3

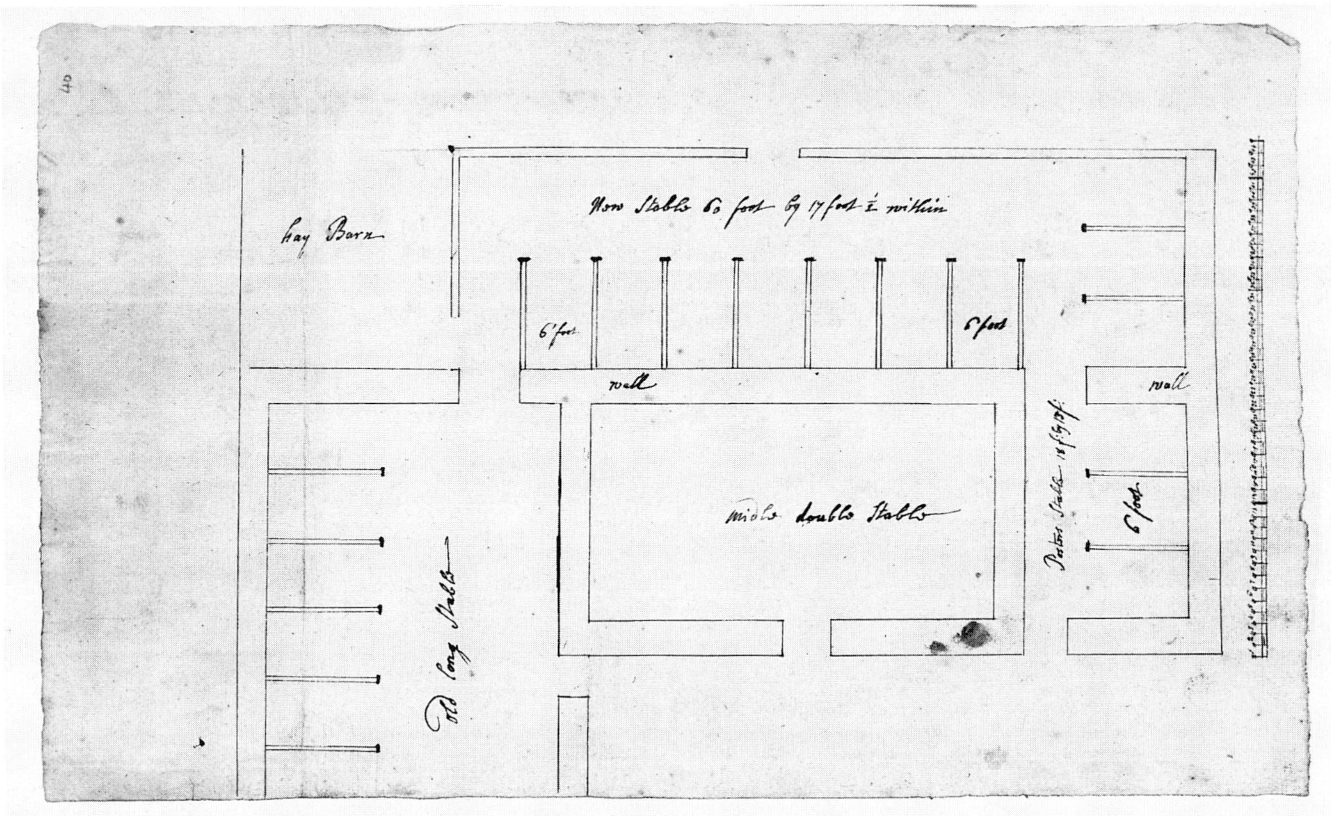

224a The Bell Inn, Stilton. Plan by Bridgeman (attrib.). MSGD A3 fo.40r

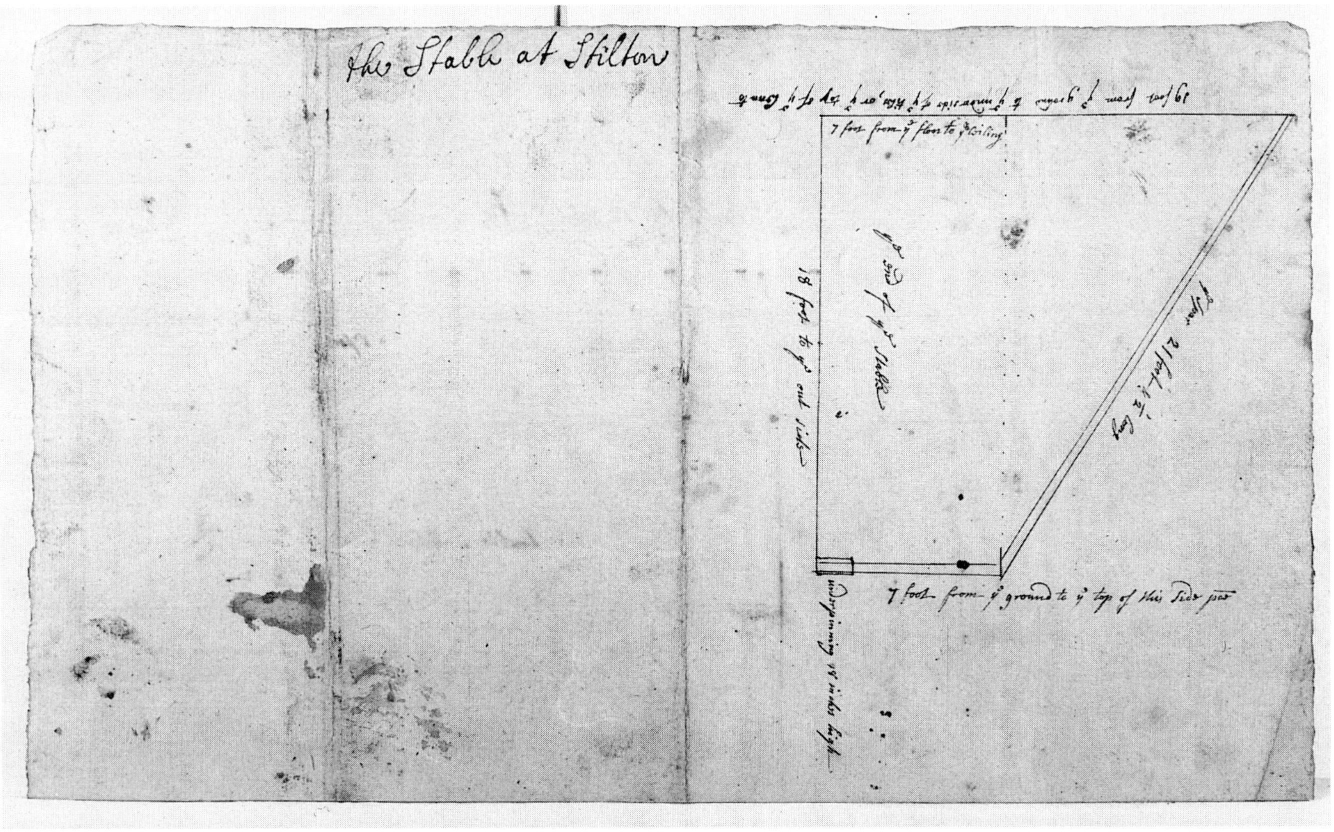

224b The Bell Inn, Stilton. Plan by Bridgeman (attrib.). MSGD A3 fo.40v

225 Trafalgar *or* Standlynch.
Plan by Bridgeman (attrib.). MSGD A3 fo.24

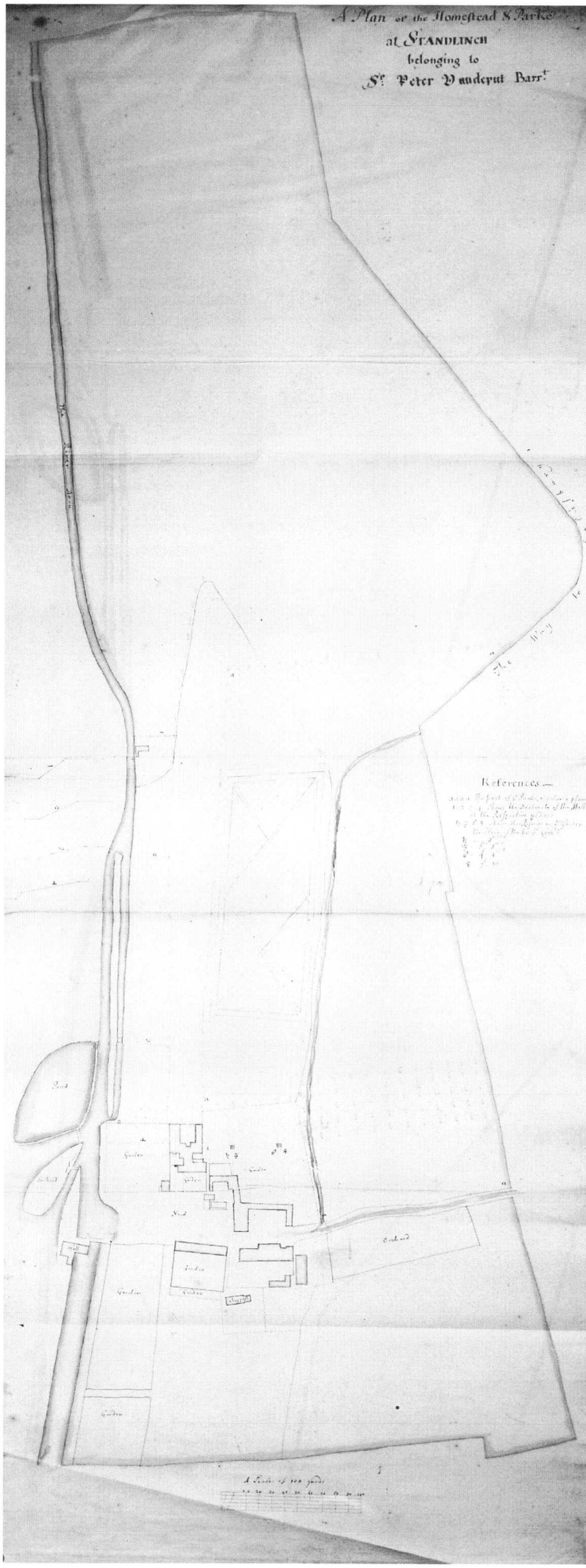

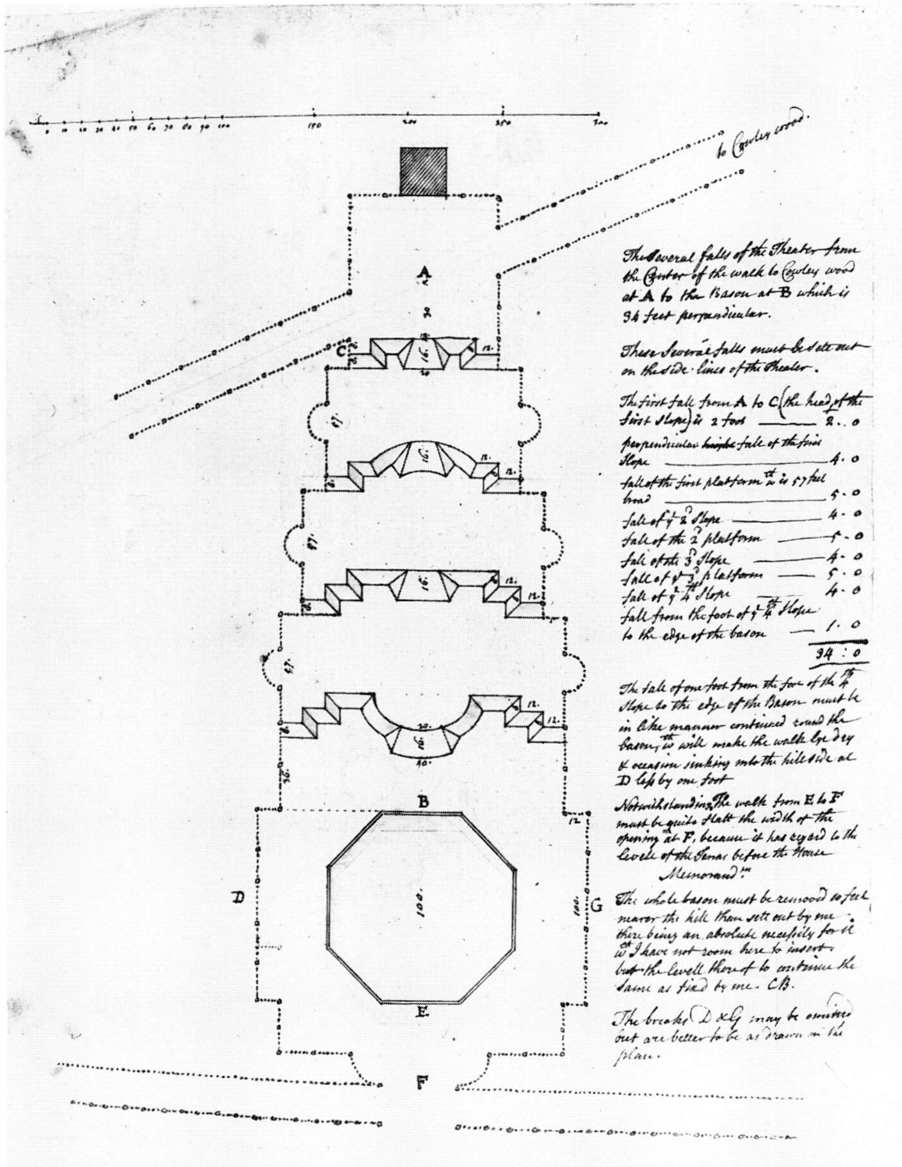

226a Tring. Plan by Bridgeman (attrib.). MSGD A4 fo.25

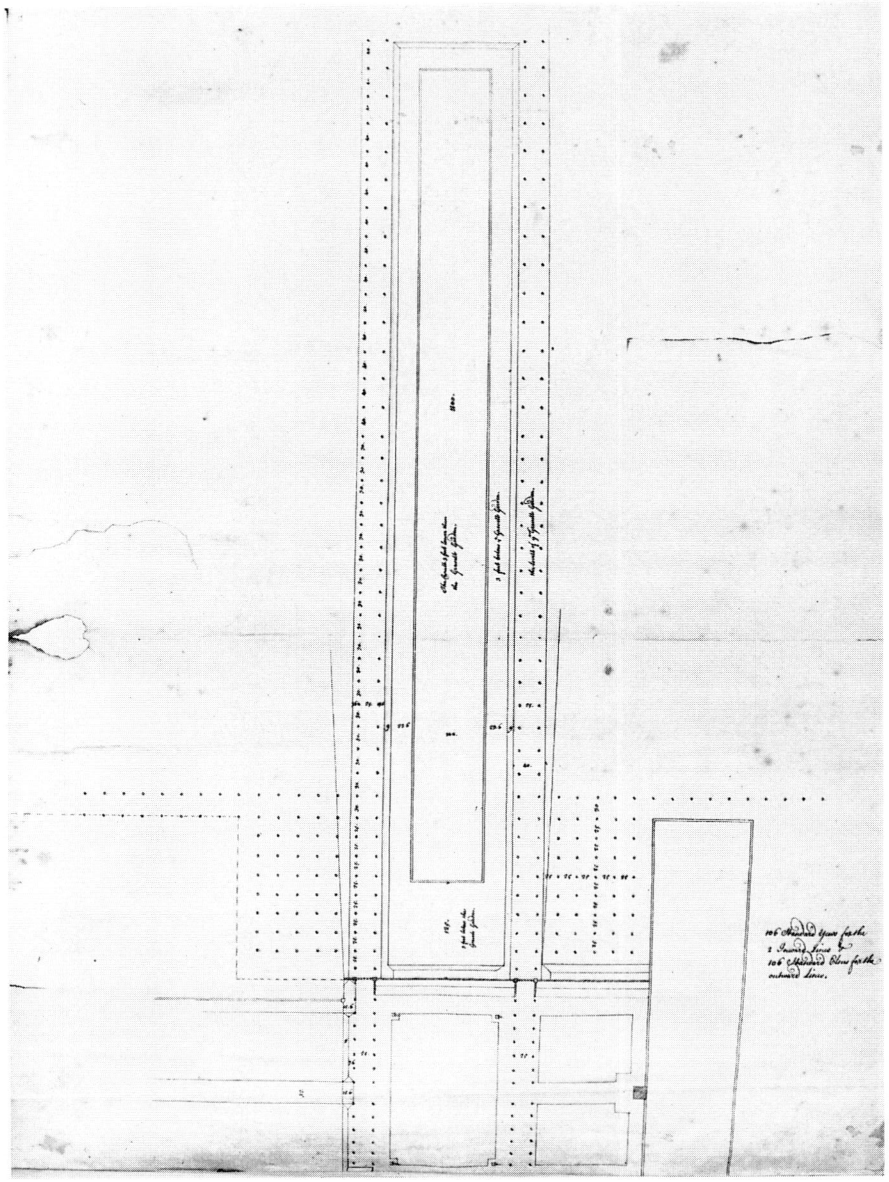

226b Tring. Plan by Bridgeman (attrib.). MSGD A4 fo.32

227 Warwick Town and Priory. Plan by Bridgeman (attrib.). Warwickshire CRO, Warwick, CR. 217, Bundle 1

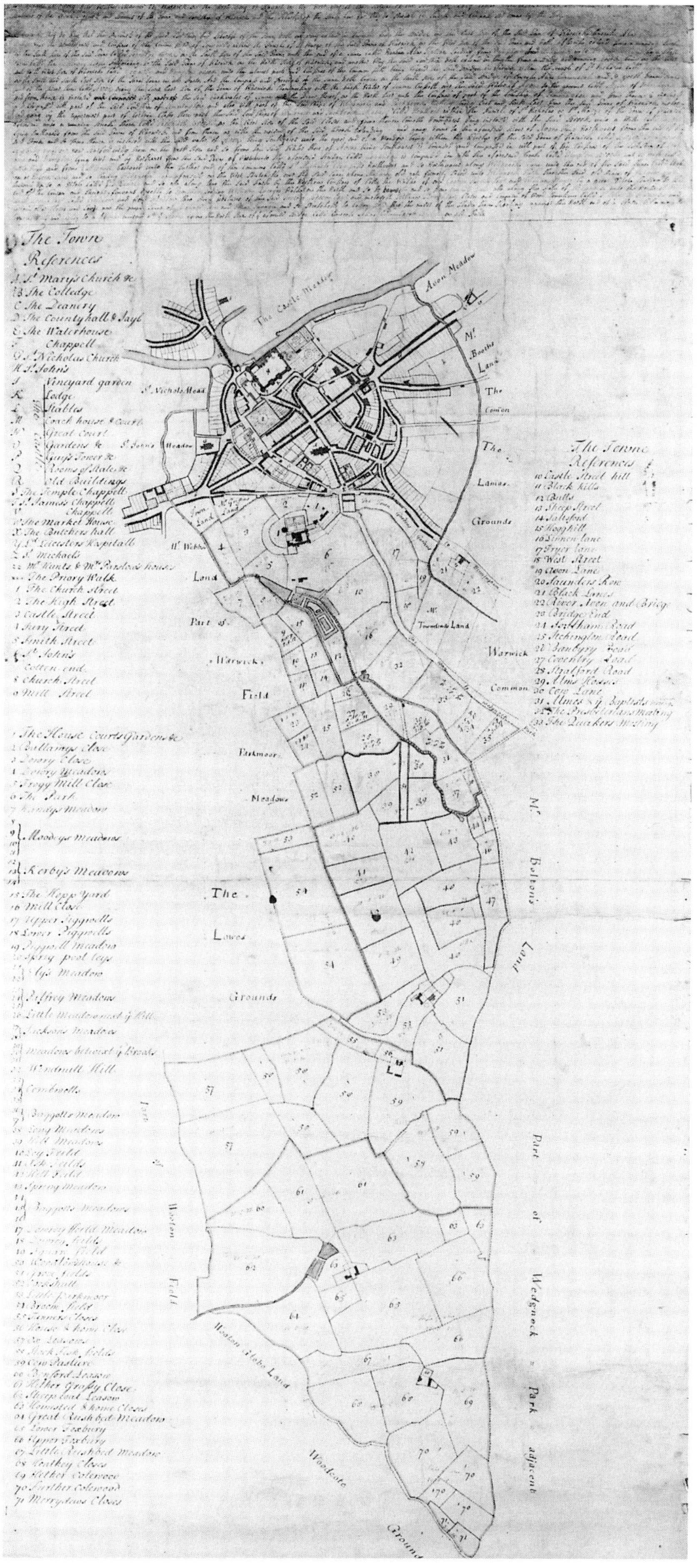

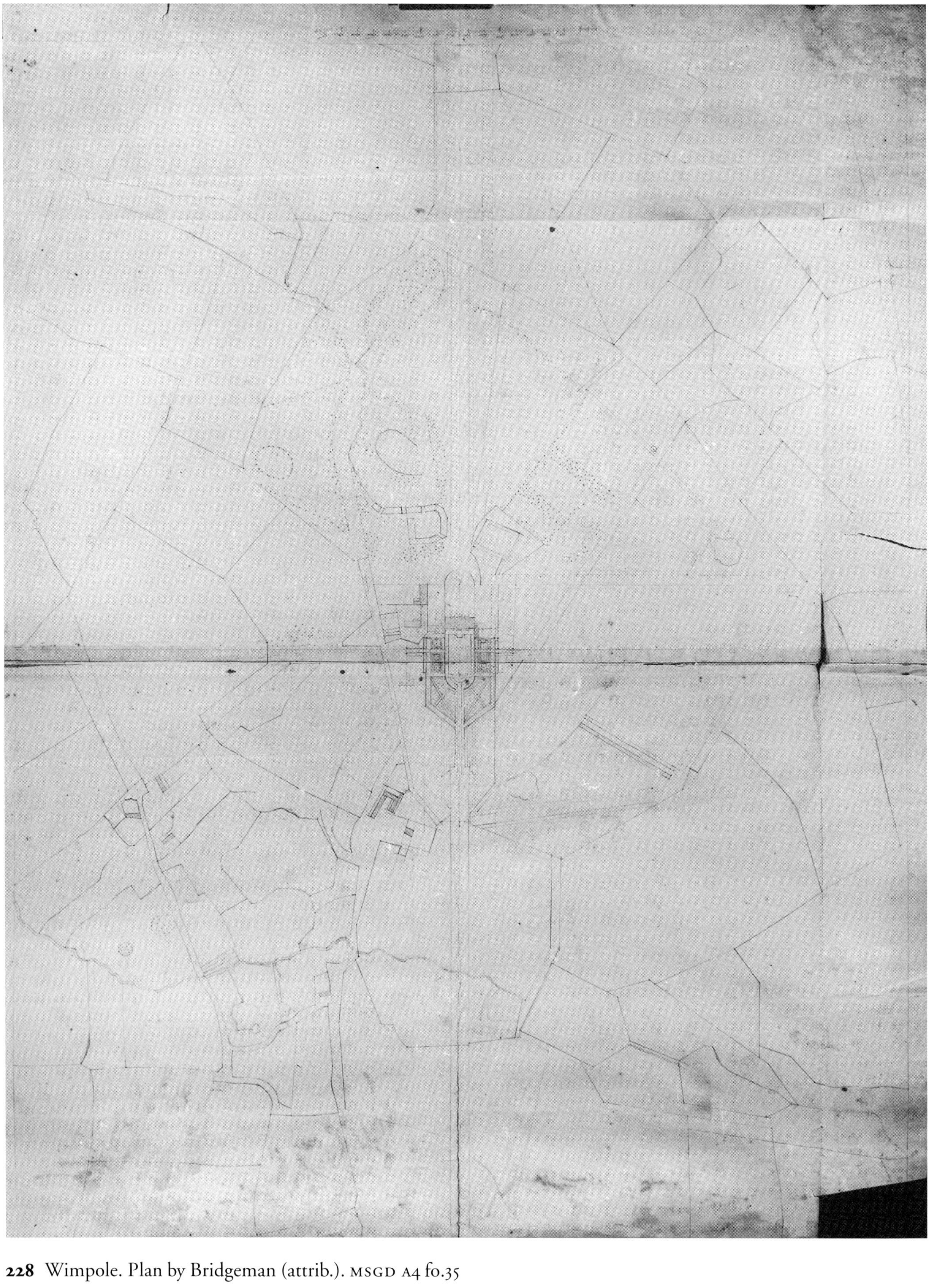

228 Wimpole. Plan by Bridgeman (attrib.). MSGD A4 fo.35

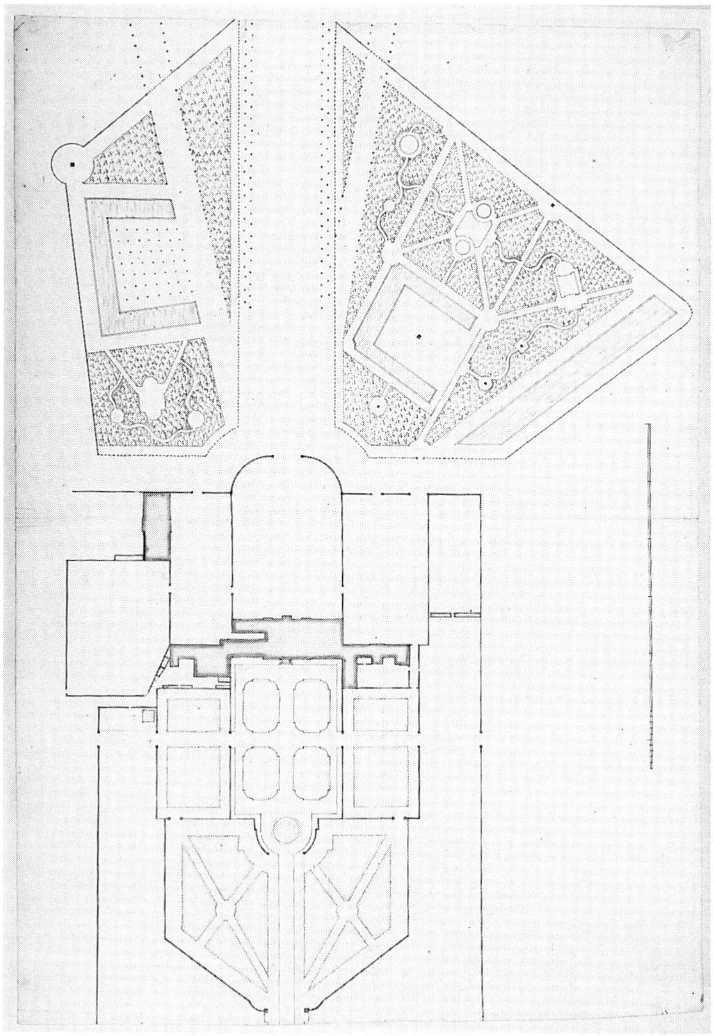

229a Wimpole. Plan by Bridgeman (attrib.). National Trust, Wimpole Hall, Cambridgeshire, Bambridge Collection

229b Wimpole. Plan by Bridgeman (attrib.). National Trust, Wimpole Hall, Cambridgeshire, Bambridge Collection

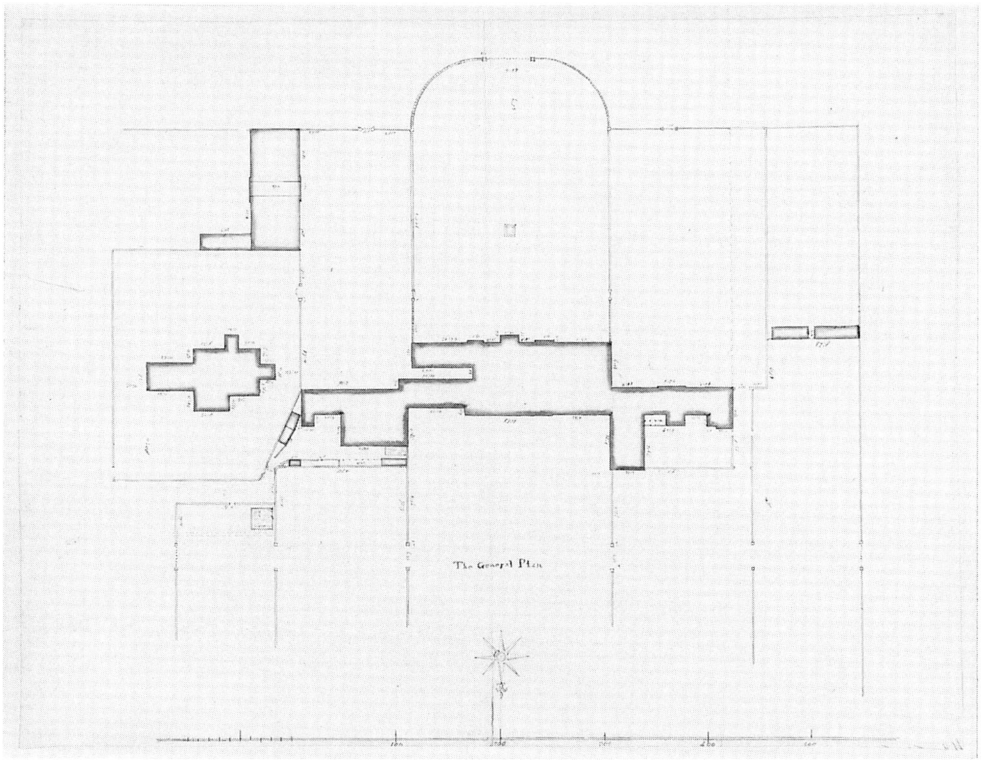

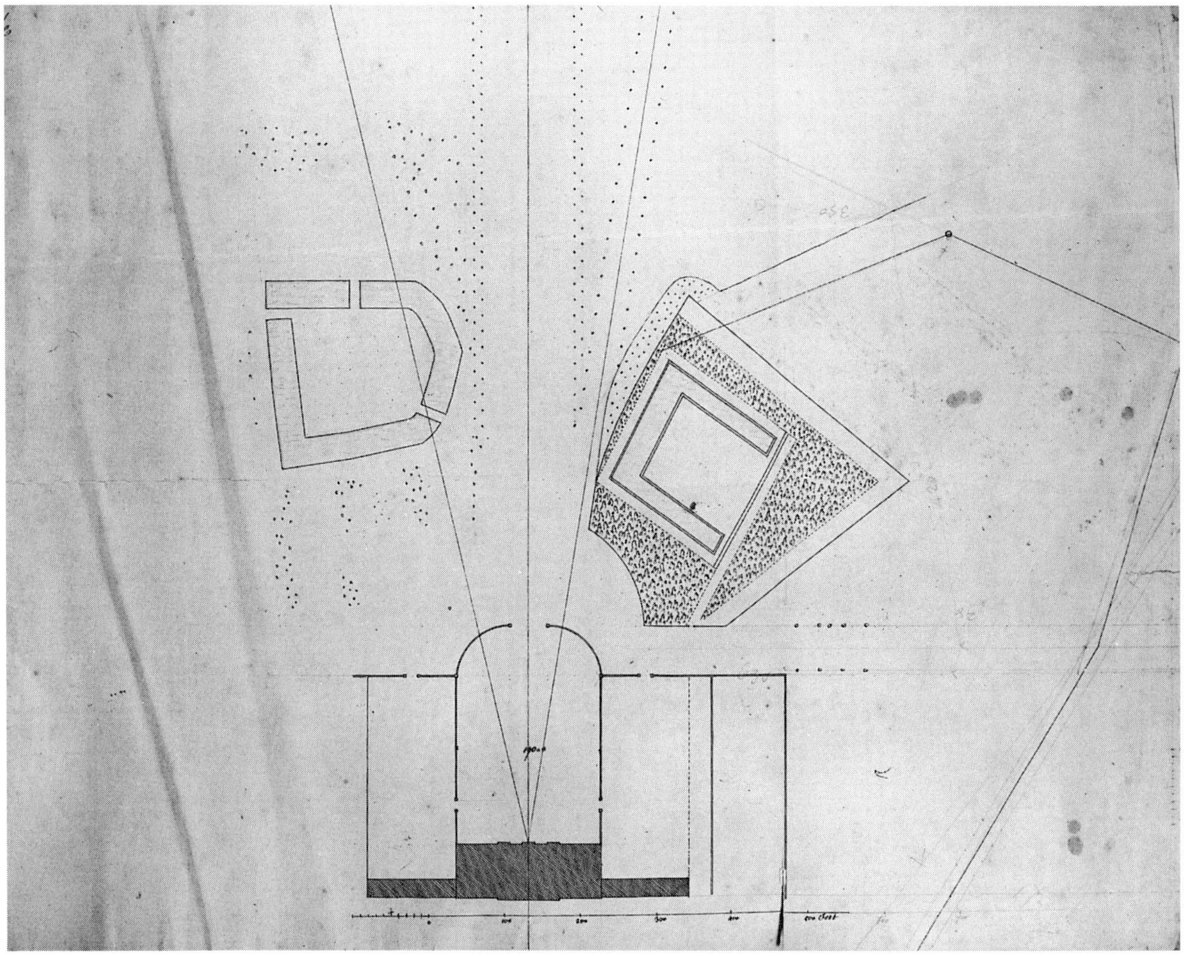

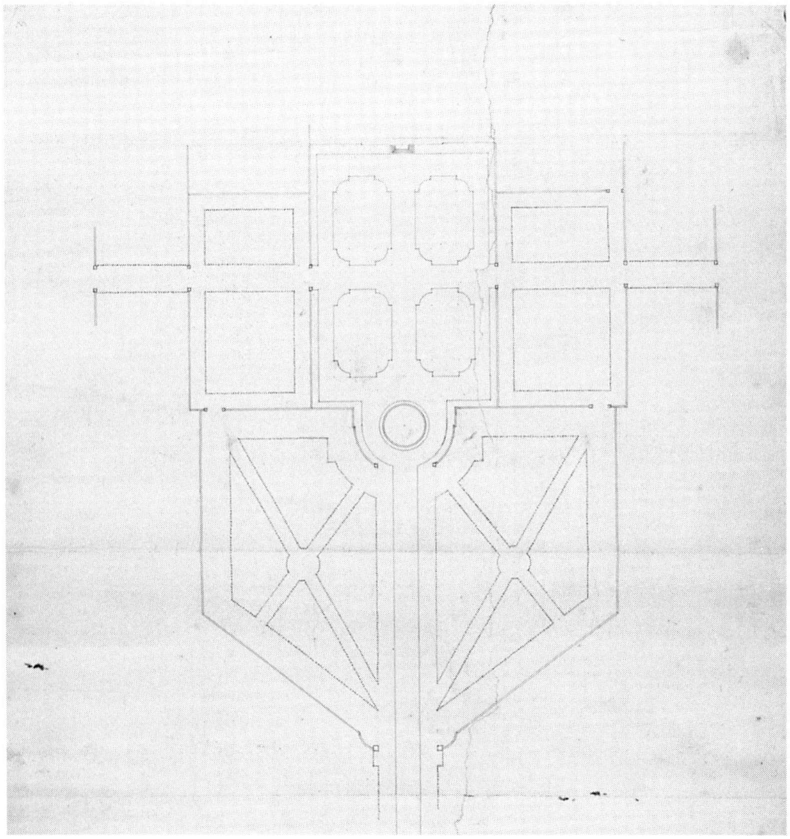

230a Wimpole. Plan by Bridgeman (attrib.). MSGD A4 fo.30

230b Wimpole. Plan by Bridgeman (attrib.). BM, Add MS 36278, M1

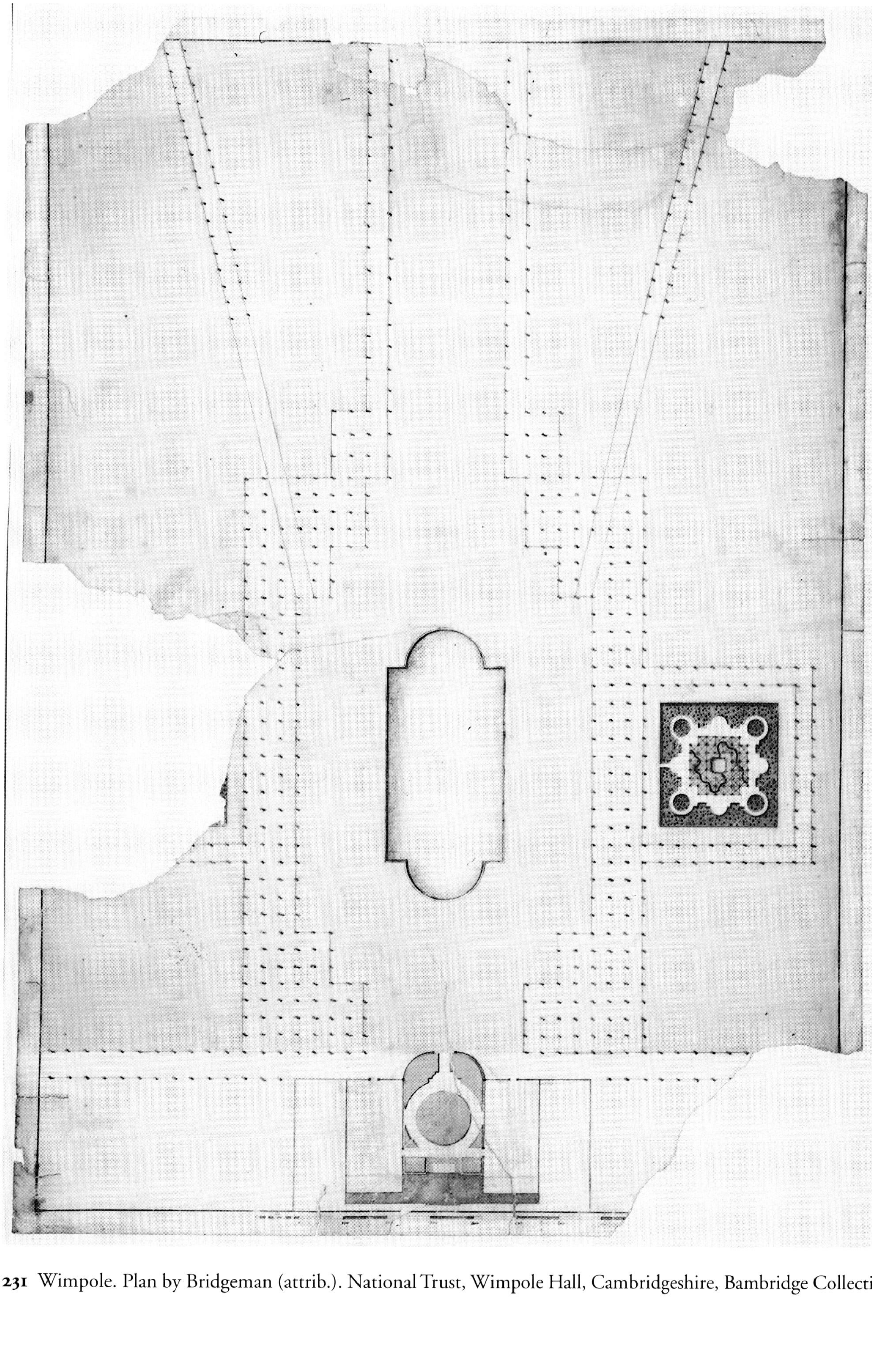

231 Wimpole. Plan by Bridgeman (attrib.). National Trust, Wimpole Hall, Cambridgeshire, Bambridge Collection

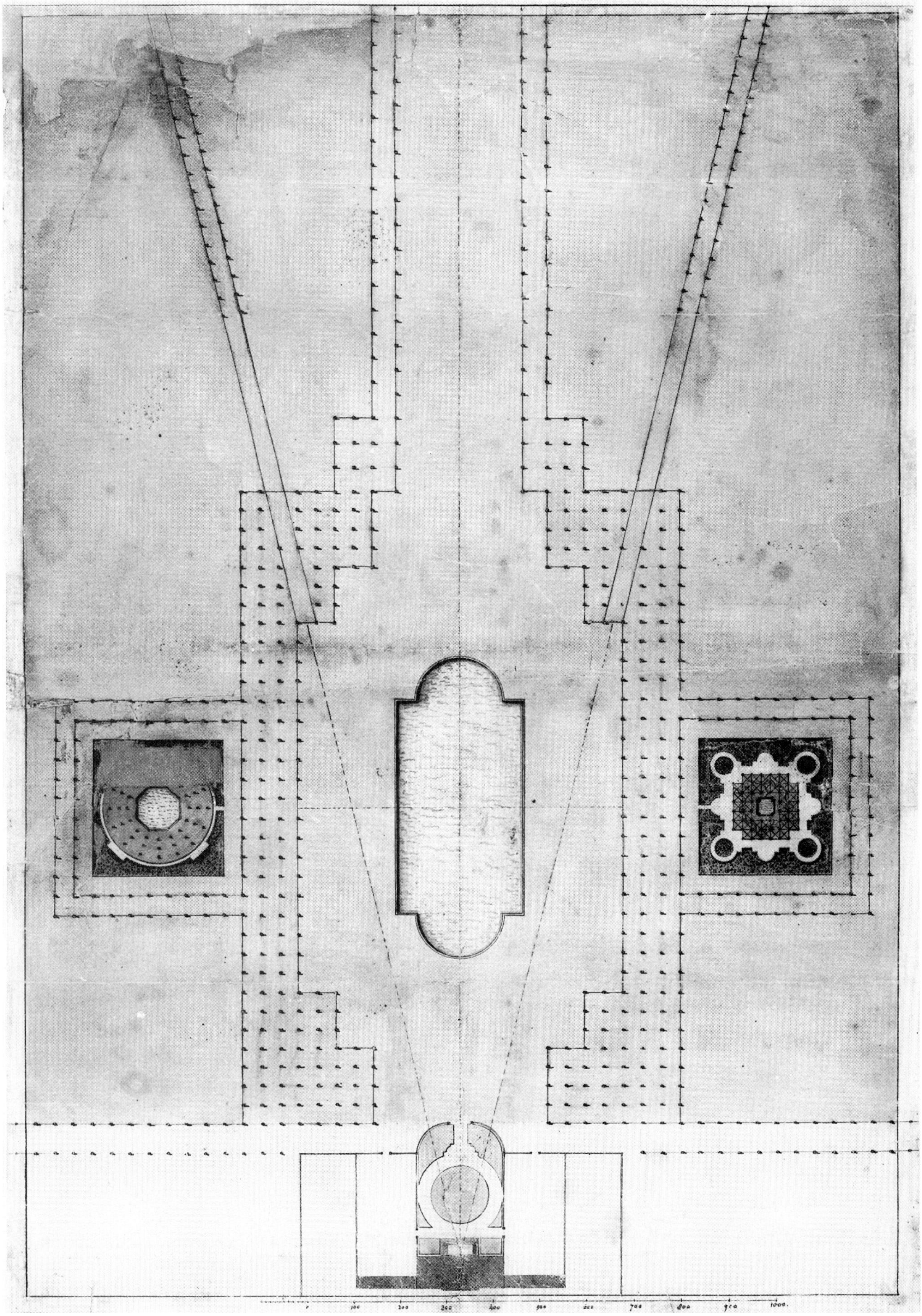
0 100 200 300 400 500 600 700 800 900 1000.

opposite
232 Wimpole. Plan by Bridgeman (attrib.). National Trust, Wimpole Hall, Cambridgeshire, Bambridge Collection

233 Wimpole. Detail of plan by Bridgeman (attrib.). MSGD A4 fo.31

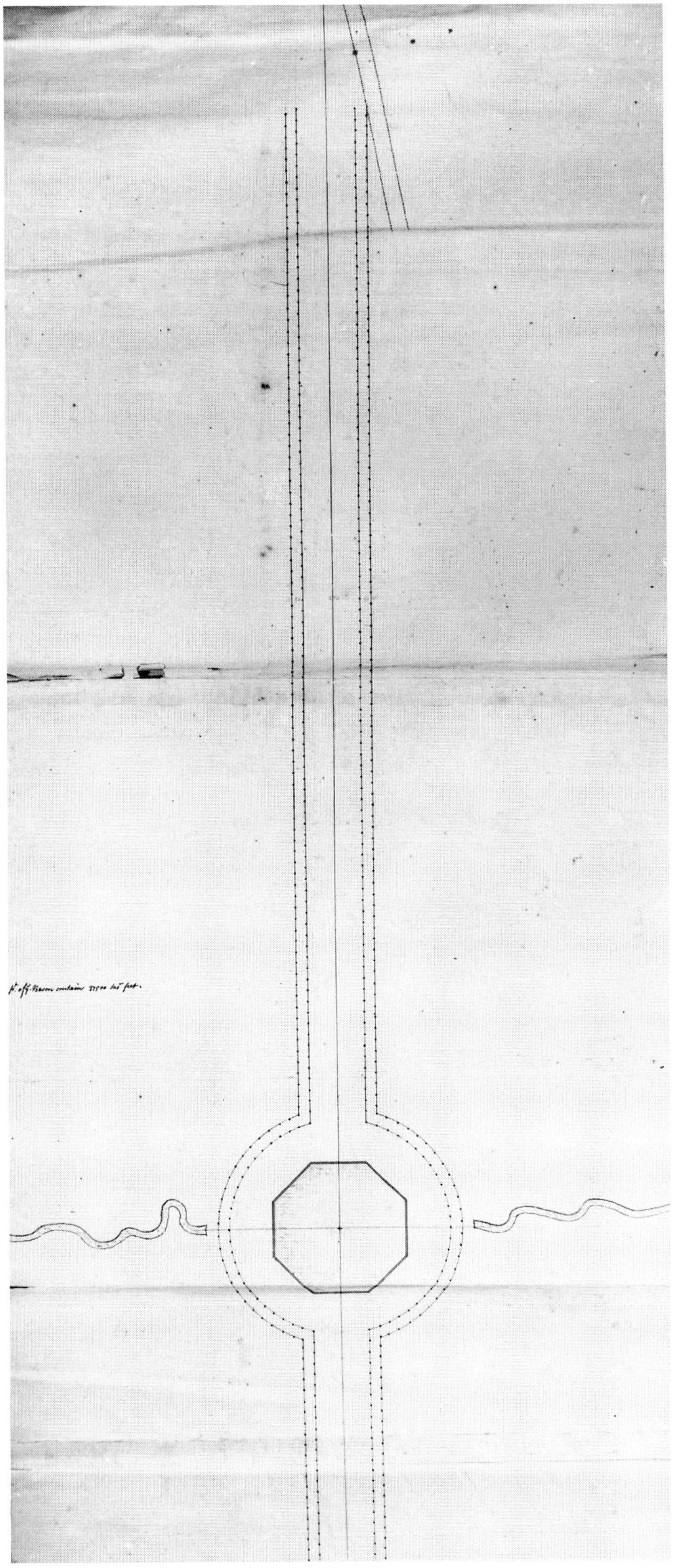

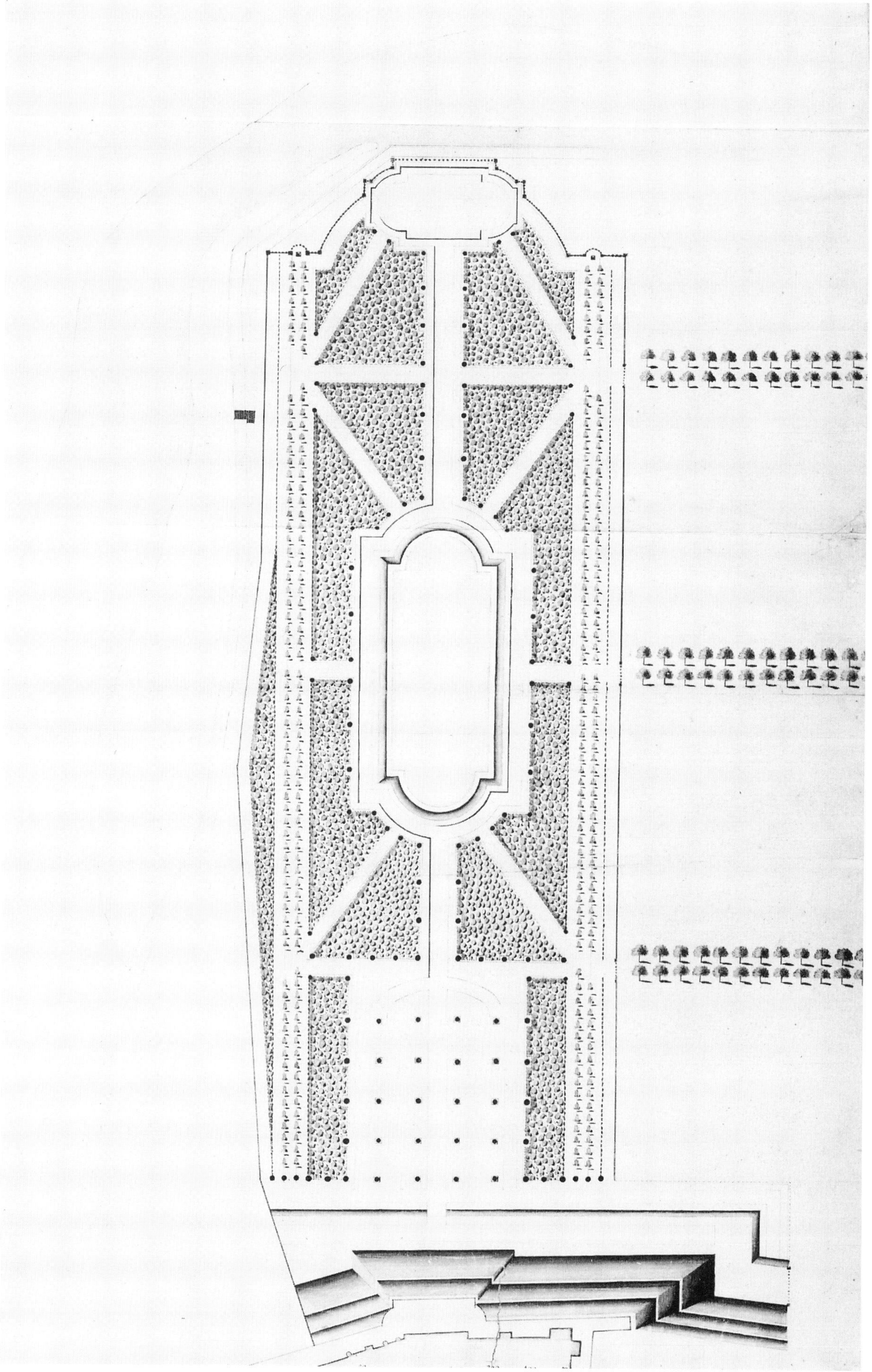

234 Windsor Castle. Plan by Bridgeman (attrib.). Soane, vol.III/45 (Trustees of Sir John Soane's Museum)

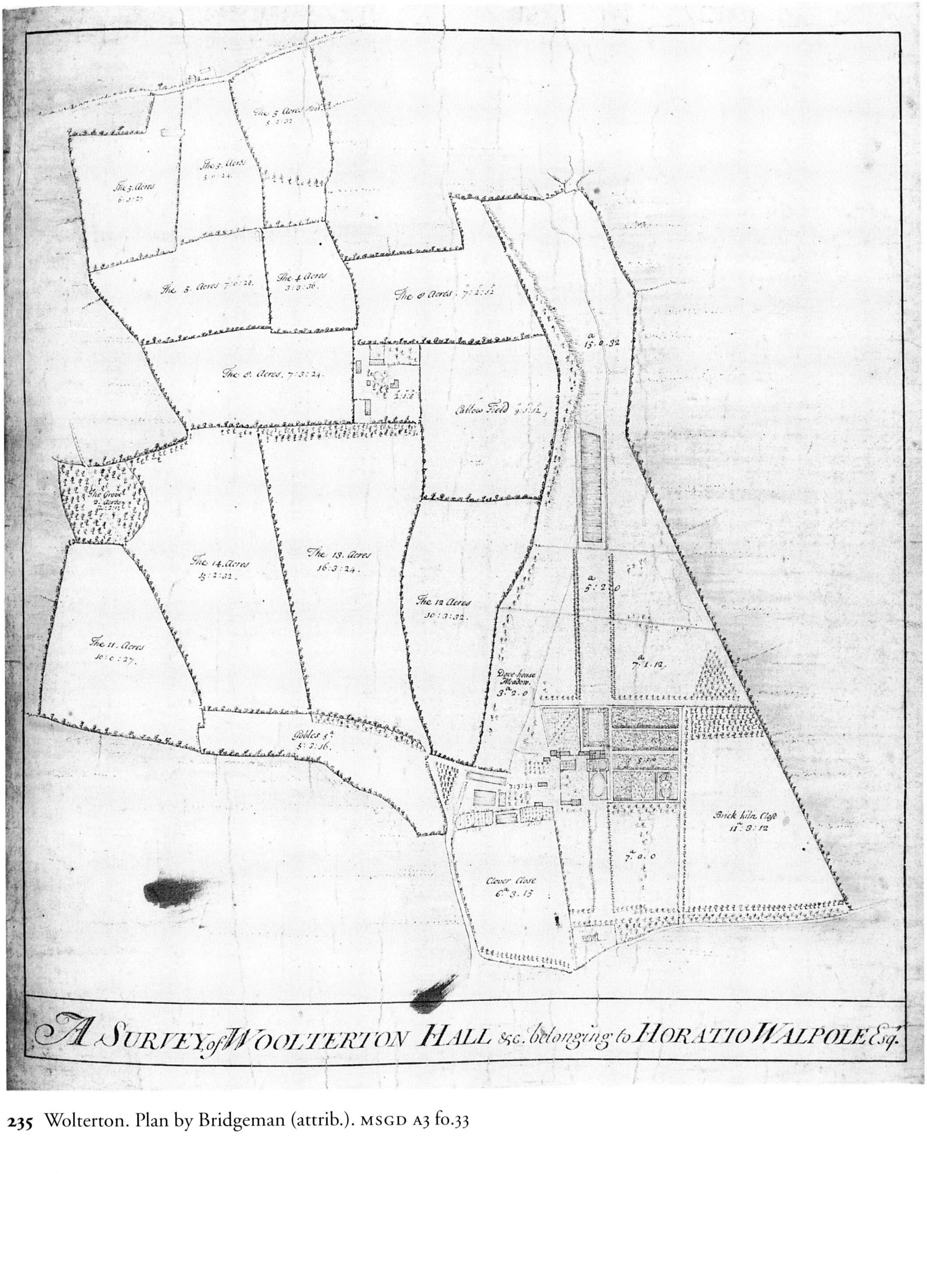

235 Wolterton. Plan by Bridgeman (attrib.). MSGD A3 fo.33

236 Wolterton. Plan by Bridgeman (attrib.). MSGD A4 fo.56

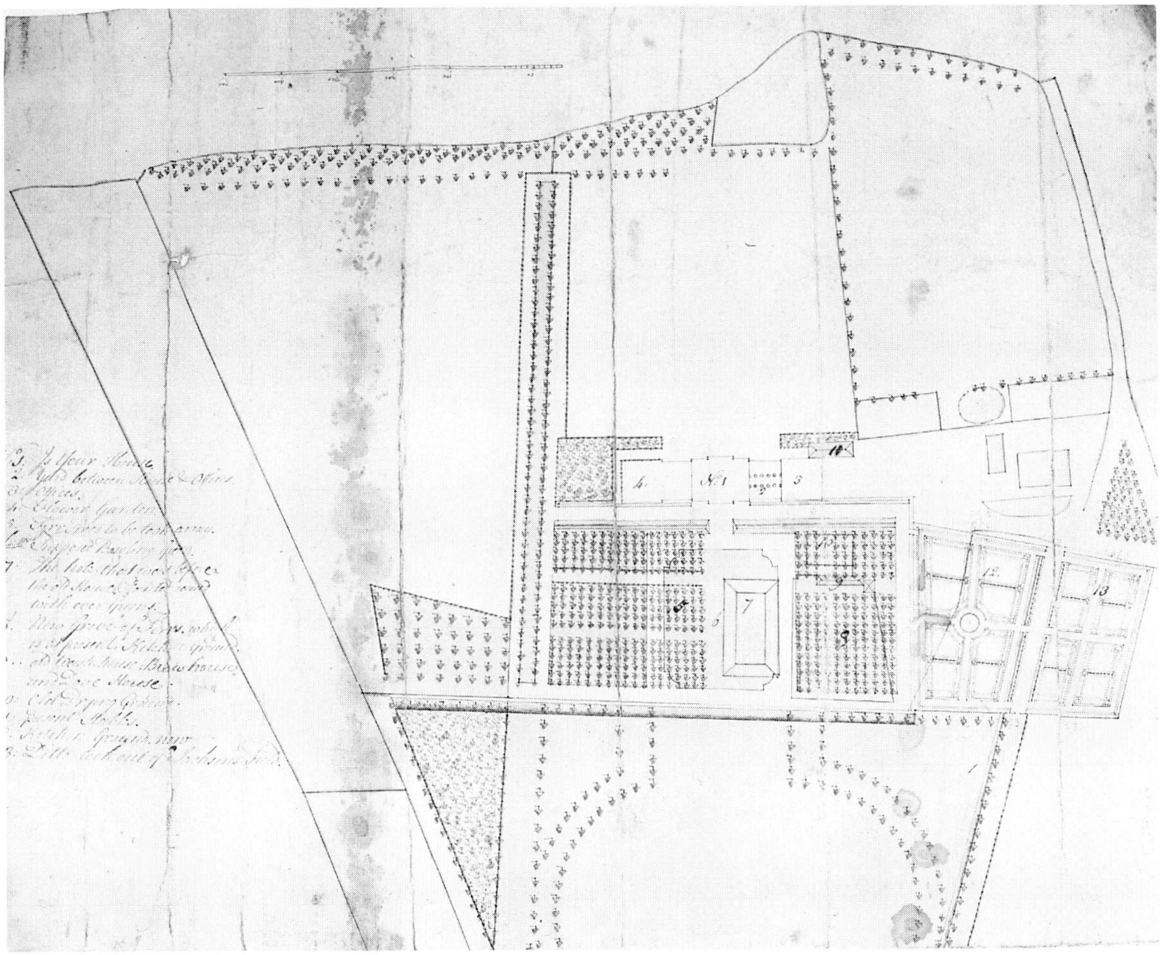

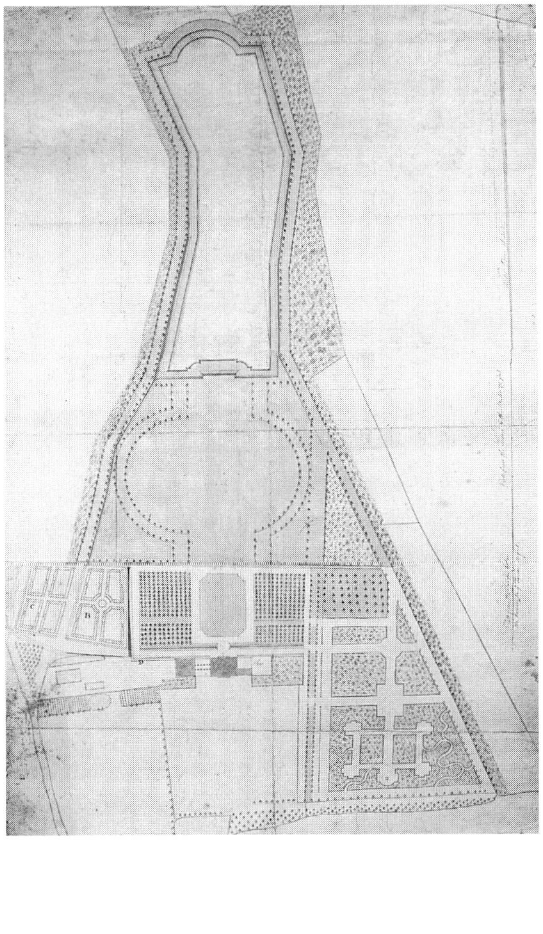

237a Wolterton. Plan by Bridgeman (attrib.).
MSGD A4 fo.18

237b Wolterton. Plan by Bridgeman (attrib.).
MSGD A4 fo.10

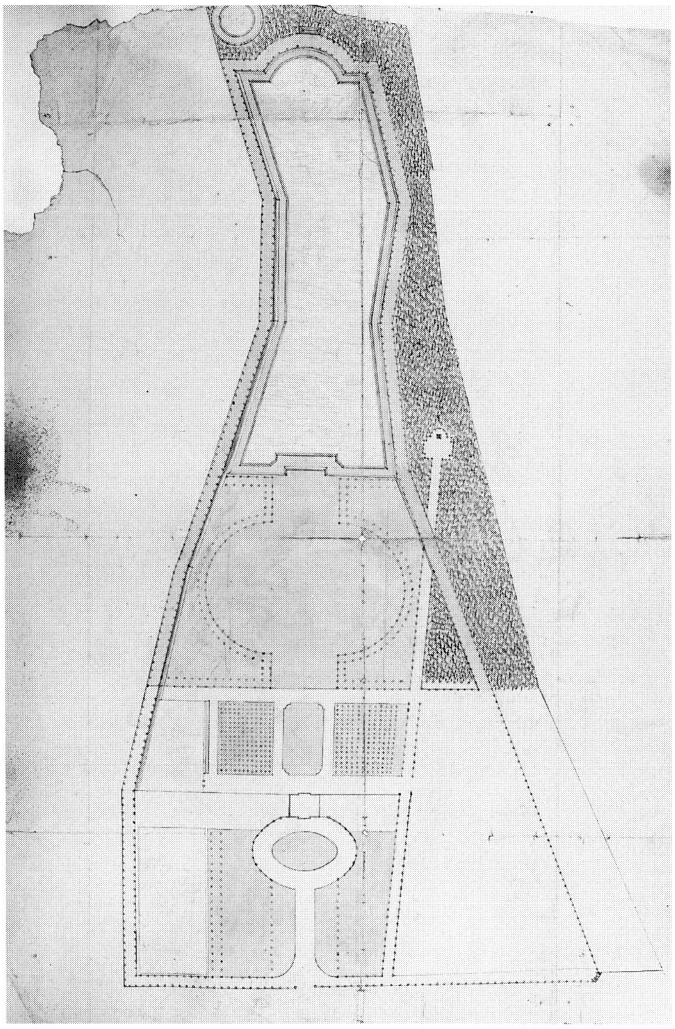

238a Wolterton. Plan by Bridgeman (attrib.). MSGD A4 fo.55

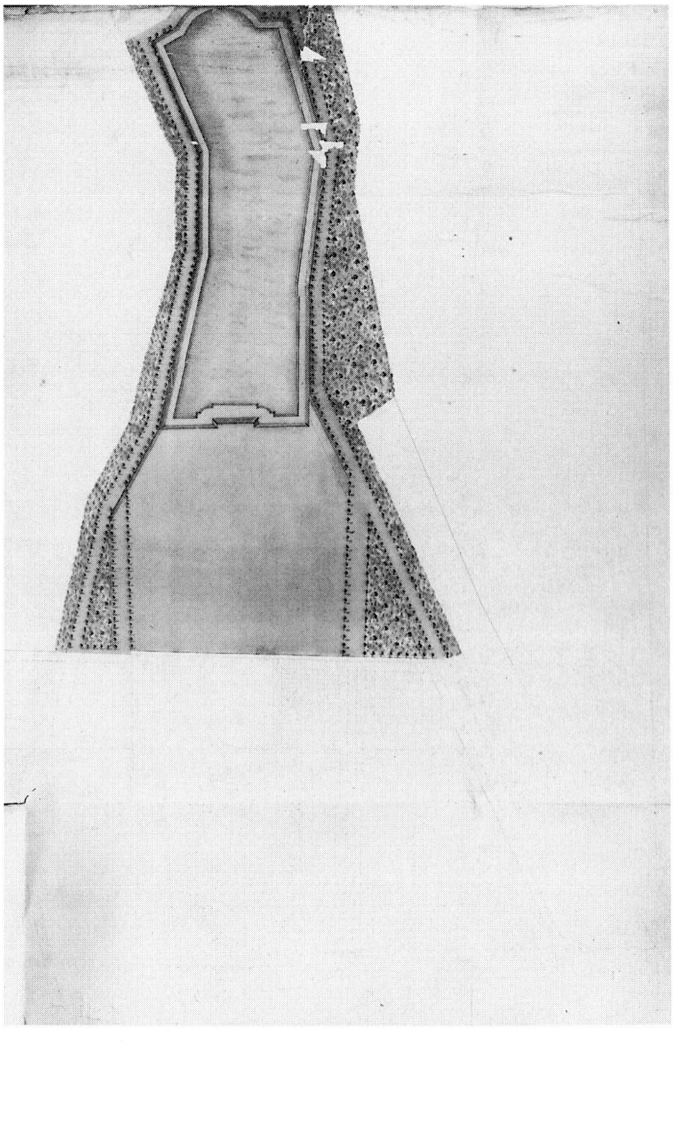

238b Wolterton. Plan by Bridgeman (attrib.). MSGD A4 fo.61

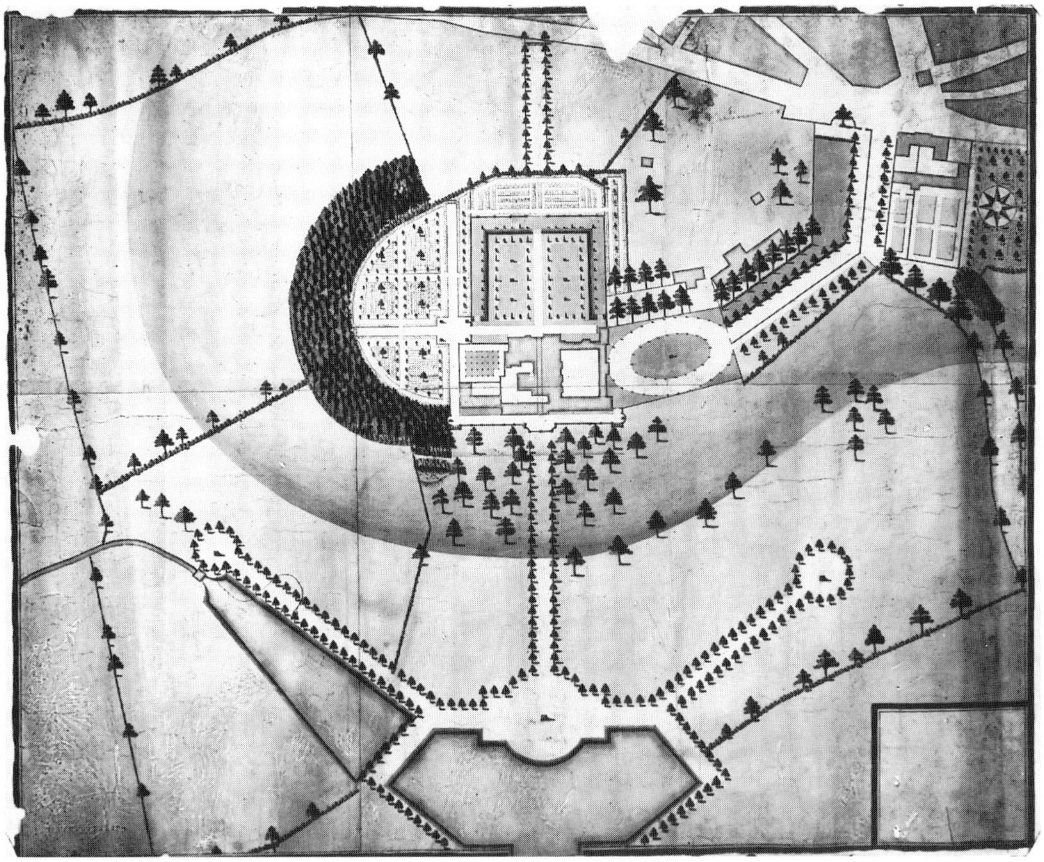

239a Warwick Priory, Plan by Bridgeman (attrib.).
Warwickshire CRO, Warwick, CR.56

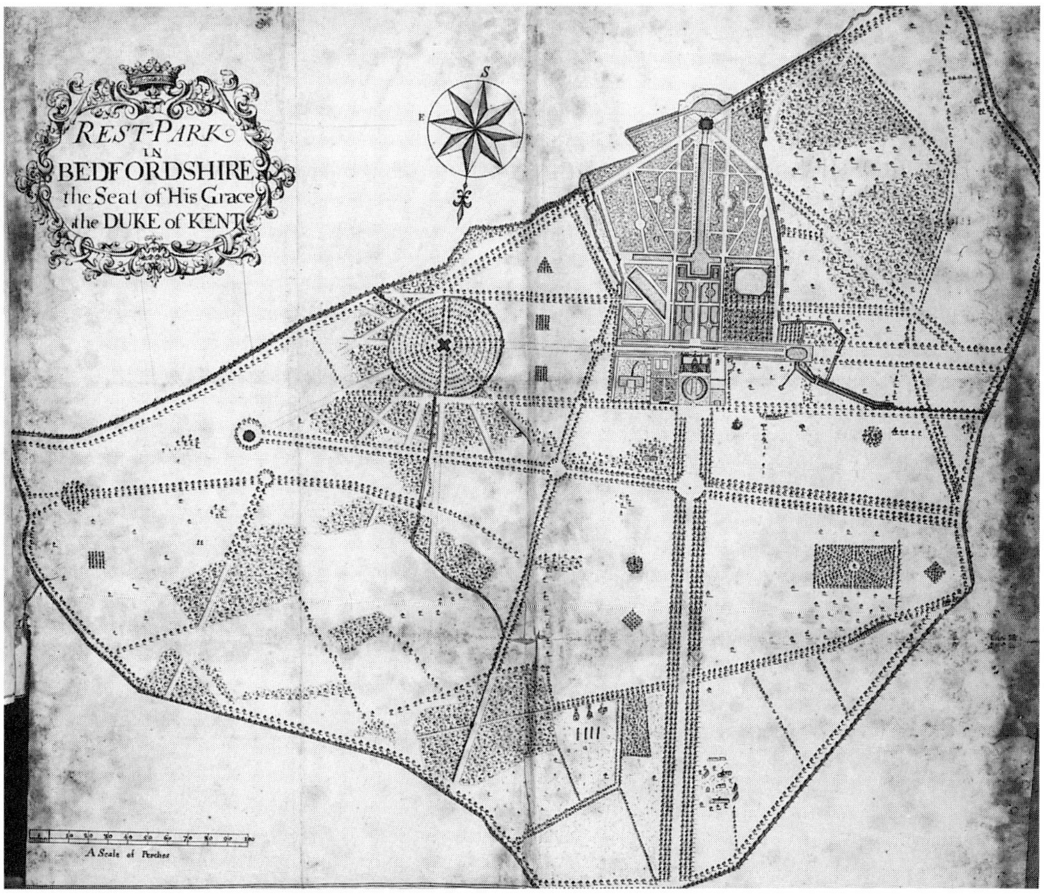

239b Wrest. Plan by Edward Laurence, surveyor, *c*.1719.
Bedfordshire and Luton Archives and Records Service, Bedford, L 33/286 fo.3

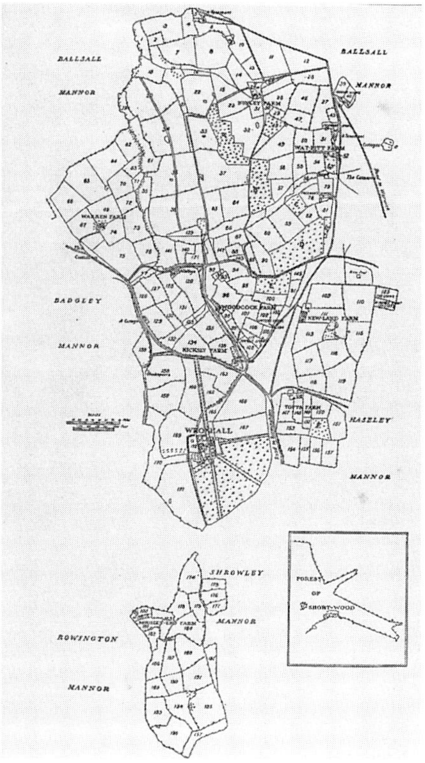

240a Wroxall *or* Wroxhall Manor. Plan and survey by 'Mr. Bridgman' (1714), from John William Ryland, *Records of Wroxall Abbey and Manor, Warwickshire* (London, 1903), facing p.lxviii. Warwickshire CRO, Warwick

240b Wroxall *or* Wroxhall Manor. Detail of plan and survey by 'Mr. Bridgman' (1714) in *Plate 240a*

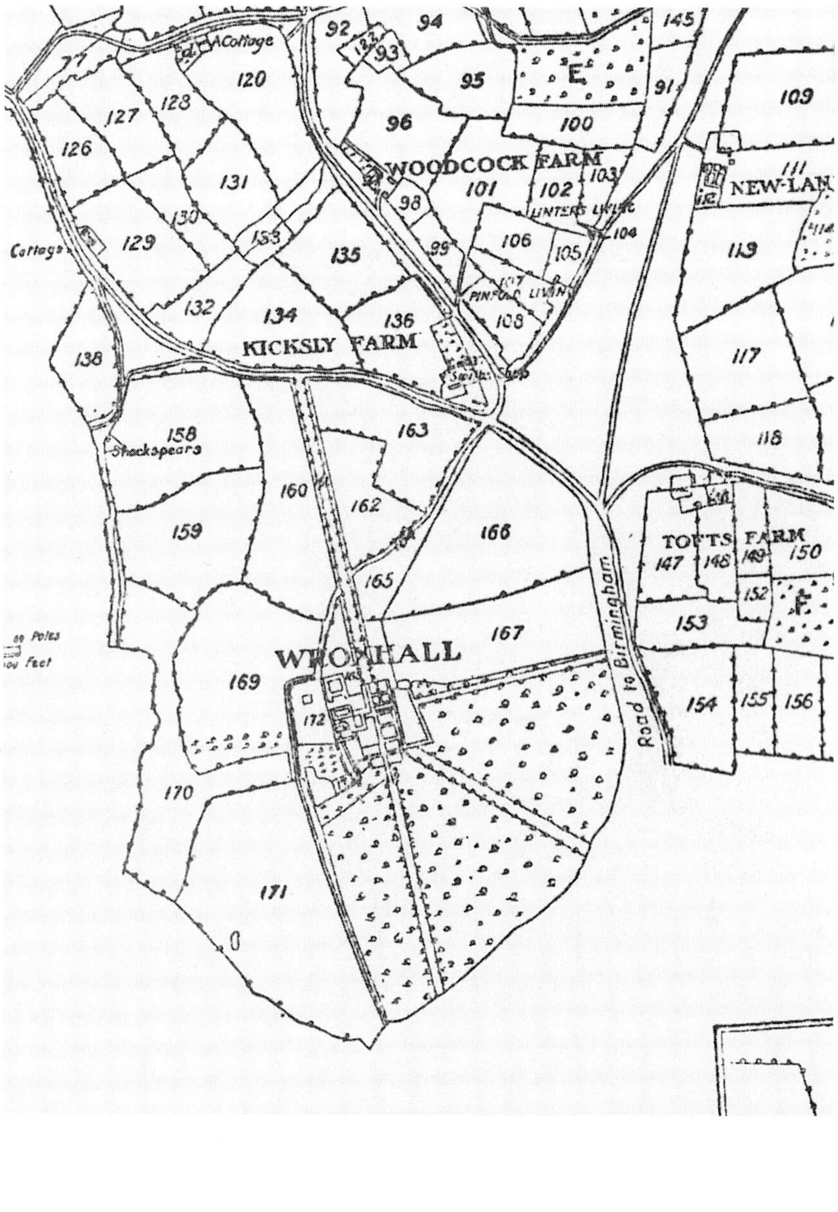

241 Unidentified estate No.1. Plan by Bridgeman (attrib.). MSGD A4 fo.22

242 Unidentified estate No.2. Plan by Bridgeman (attrib.). MSGD A4 fo.33

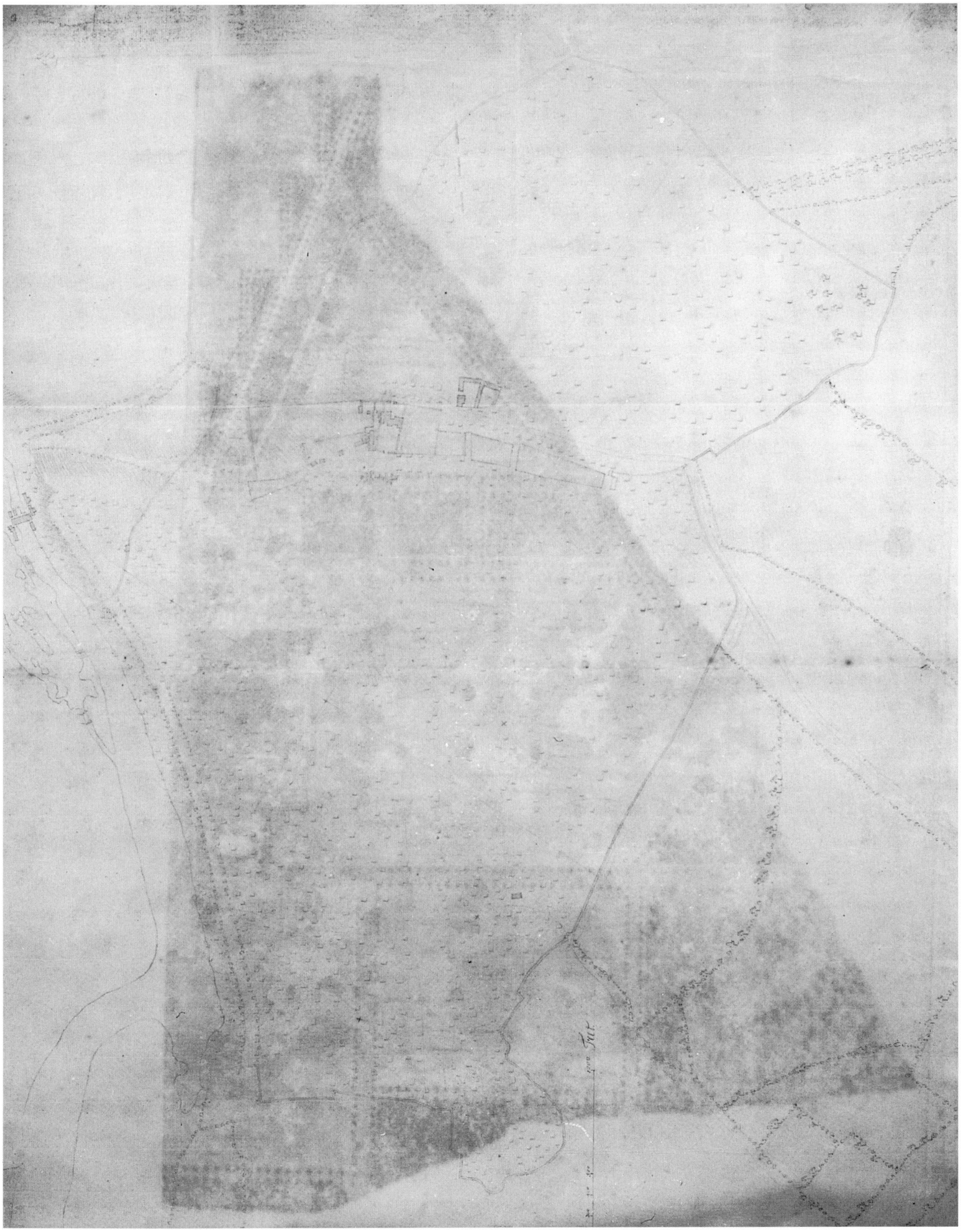

243 Unidentified estate No.2. Plan by Bridgeman (attrib.). MSGD A4 fo.43

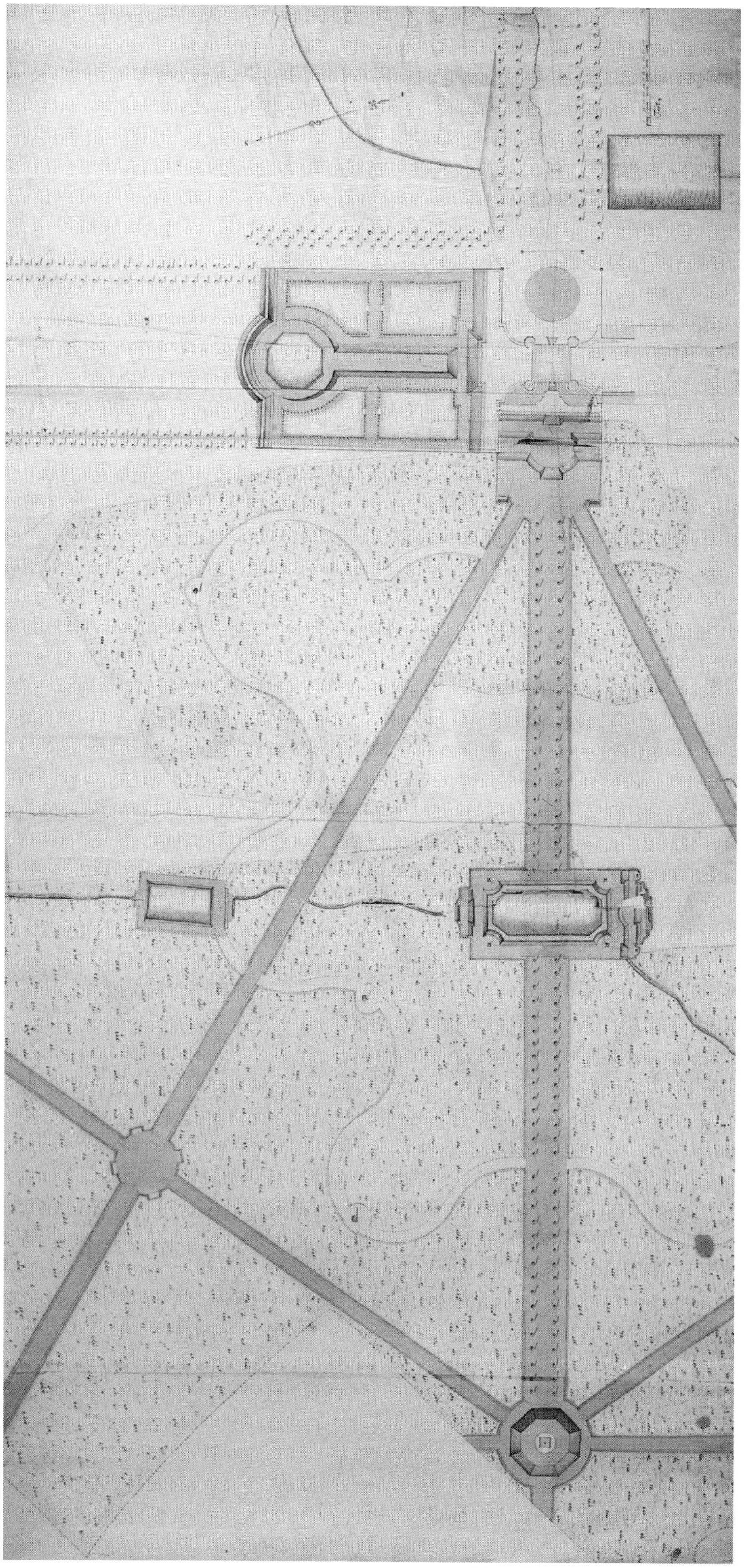

244 Unidentified estate No.3.
Plan by Bridgeman (attrib.).
MSGD A4 fo.36

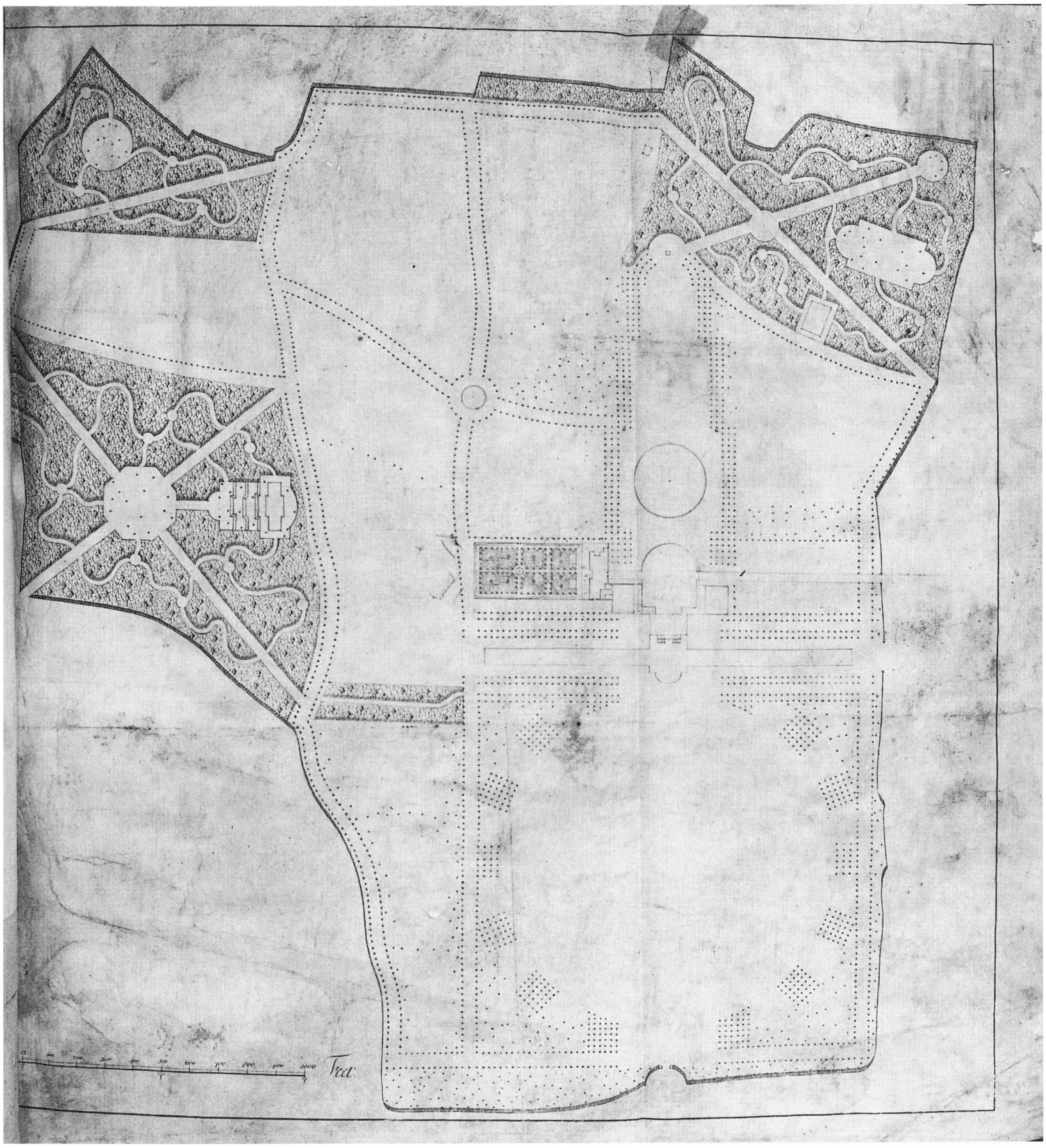

245 Unidentified estate No.4. Plan by Bridgeman (attrib.). MSGD A4 fo.37

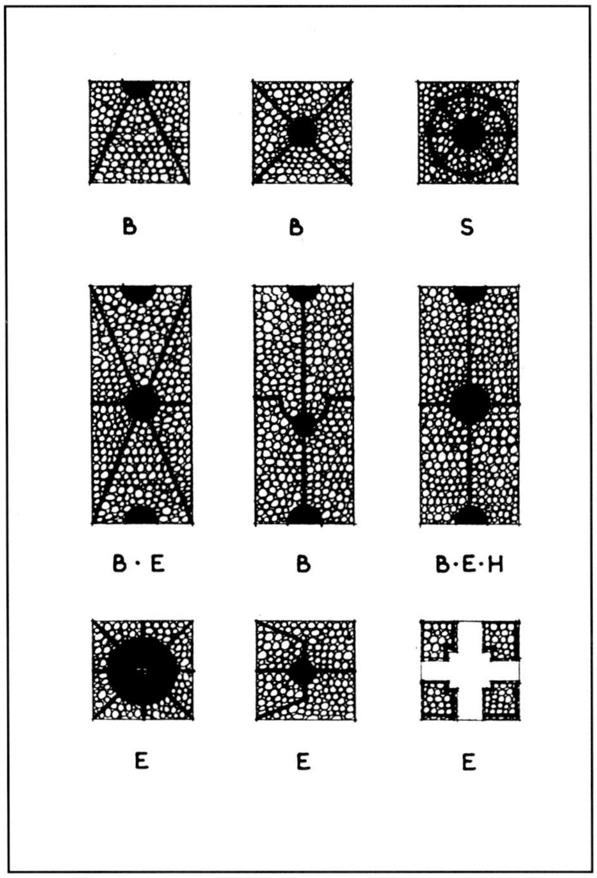

BOSQUETS

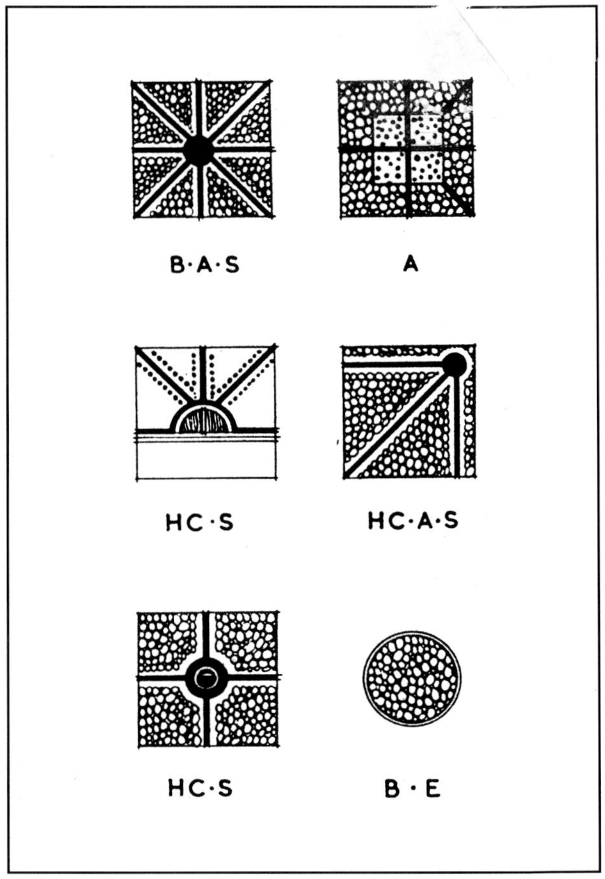

TREES

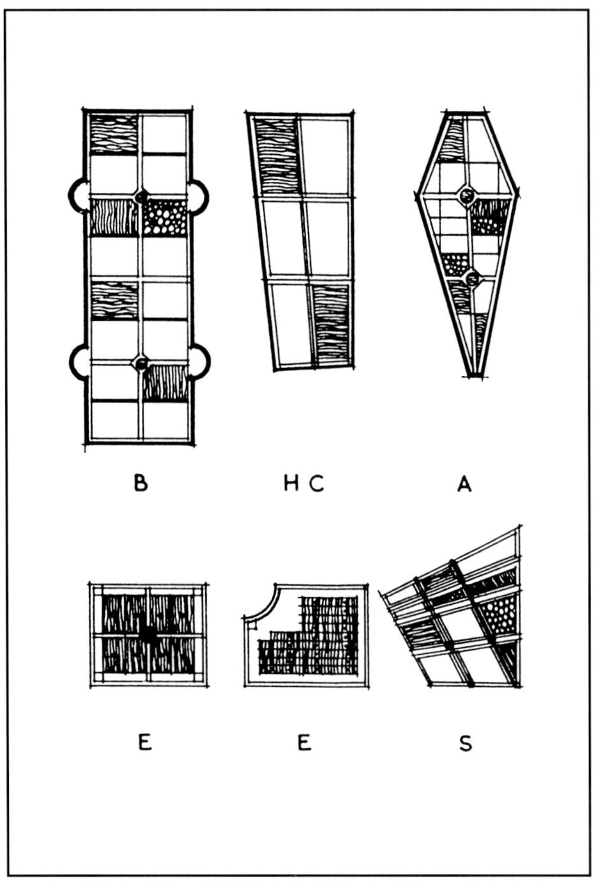

KITCHEN GARDENS

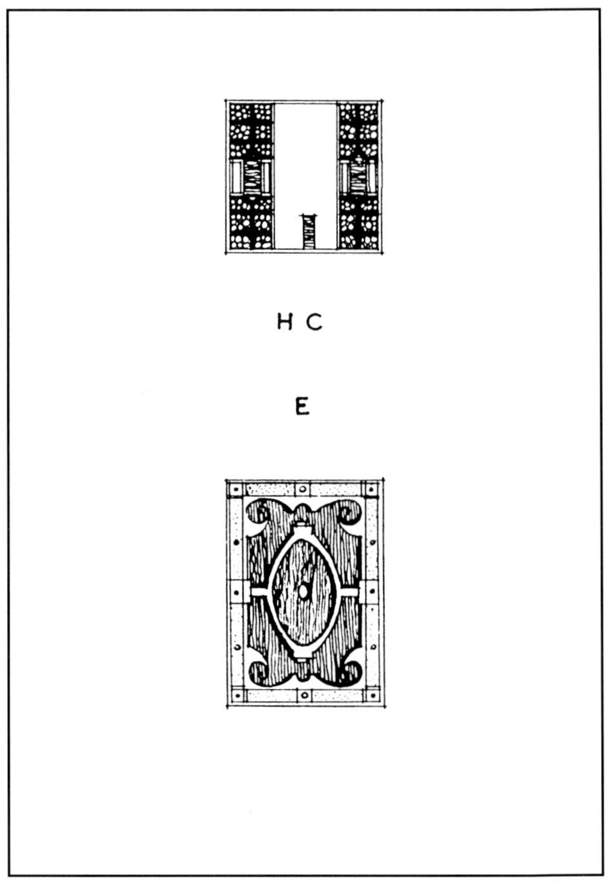

PARTERRES

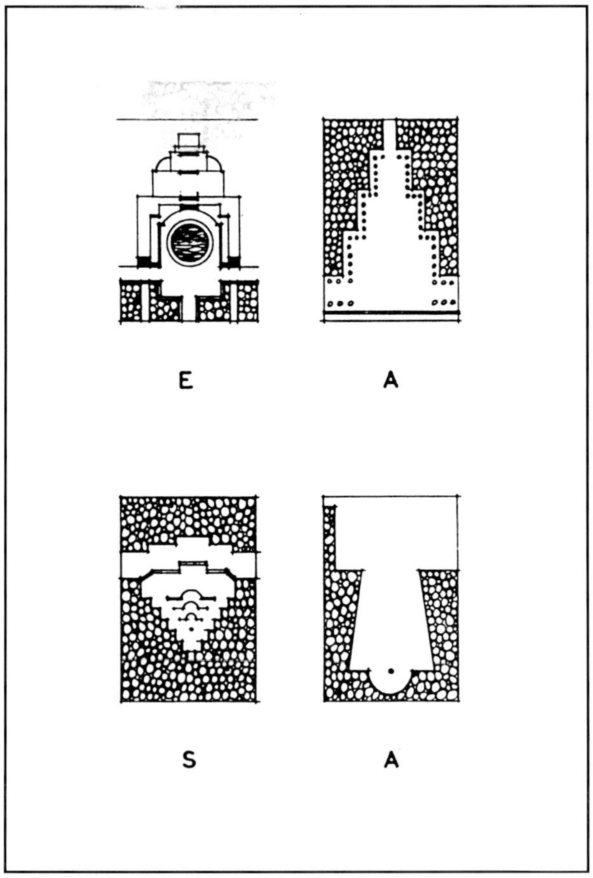

THEATRES

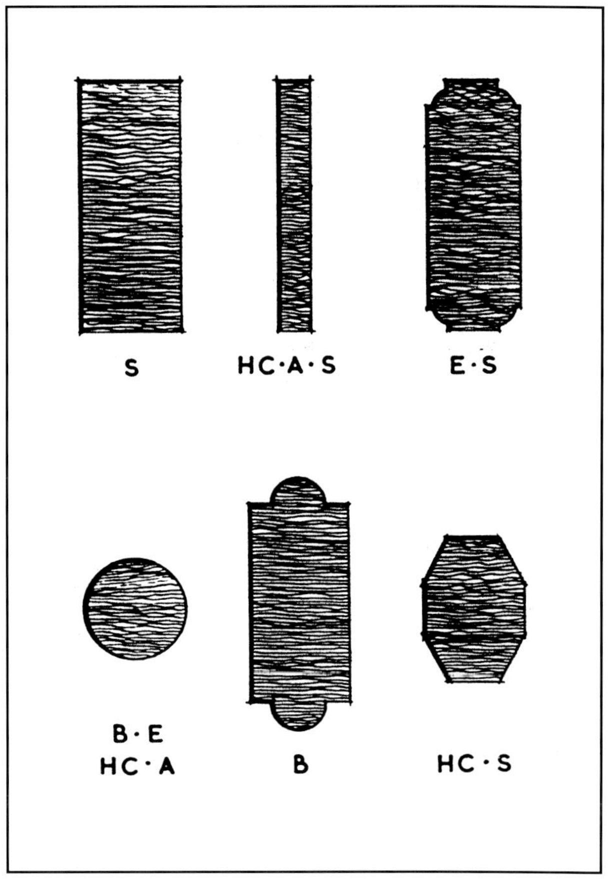

WATER

LAWNS

246 and **247** Diagrams of formal elements in Bridgeman's signed plans. Peter Willis

These diagrams show the formal elements of Bridgeman's signed plans; the informal aspects of his drawings can be seen clearly from other illustrations.

Key to abbreviations

A Amesbury

B Blenheim

E Eastbury

HC Hampton Court

S Stowe

W Warwick Priory